SIX FACES OF
MEXICO

SIX FACES OF

HISTORY   PEOPLE   GEOGRAPHY

MEXICO

GOVERNMENT   ECONOMY   LITERATURE & ART

Editor	RUSSELL C. EWING
Collaborating Authors	EDWARD H. SPICER
	DAVID A. HENDERSON
	PAUL KELSO
	GEORGE F. LEAMING
	WALTER H. DELAPLANE
	RENATO ROSALDO

THE UNIVERSITY OF ARIZONA PRESS

A Word to the Reader —

THE LATE AND DISTINGUISHED ADLAI E. STEVENSON wrote: "A great deal of what North Americans think they know about Central and South America isn't so." The ambassador might have added that many of us are just as poorly informed about the neighbor next door to the United States. The six portrayals in this book have therefore been written in the hope that they will lead the general reader to a better understanding of Mexico.

In SIX FACES OF MEXICO, emphases and new points of view on matters often neglected bring the reader closer to the facts of Mexican life. Those who wish to look further into the Mexican experiences will find useful bibliographies at the end of each section.

Each presentation could stand by itself, but the arrangement of the subjects lends itself to a logical, sequential order. The introductory section sets the background of significant historical trends and epochs. Edward H. Spicer then writes on the fascinating diversity within the unity of the Mexican people: "The longer one knows Mexico, the clearer this unity appears beneath the surfaces . . . " But in both physical environment and society, the nation, unified though it is, remains a land of varieties. David A. Henderson calls this to our attention in the third part, where he analyzes Mexico's physical and cultural geography.

Political institutions, concepts of decision-making, and public policy are critically examined in the fourth section by Paul Kelso. Current trends in the economic life of the republic, and the striking contrasts, are next described and analyzed by George F. Leaming and Walter H. Delaplane. And of the many facets of Mexico, none gives a better understanding of the nation's way of life than its literature and its contributions to the arts. Renato Rosaldo, in the final section, therefore presents the reader with these significant elements in the development of Mexico.

The authors are deeply indebted to many persons who gave unsparingly of their time and resources in seeing this book through to completion. Thanks go especially to Alvin J. Gordon, who expressed the original need for a book of this kind, and urged its development. President Richard A. Harvill of the University of Arizona, a student of Mexican affairs, was ever ready to counsel and encourage the authors and editors through all stages. The Mexican artist, Arístides Mateo "Corín," wielded his brush with great skill in the preparation of a painting for the jacket, and Robert M. Quinn's expertise in Mexican art was used to advantage in the selection of many of the book's illustrations. A considerable number of the photographs were taken especially for this book by Bill Sears.

Among those to whom the project owes a primary debt is Donald M. Powell, assistant librarian of the University of Arizona, who compiled the useful index. The book's physical appeal and the final running flow of copy express the cooperation, patience, and superb craftsmanship of the staff of the University of Arizona Press, under whose imprint *Six Faces of Mexico* now invites your attention as a reader.

RUSSELL C. EWING

About the Authors

RUSSELL C. EWING, editor of *Six Faces of Mexico* and author of the section "Major Historical Themes," is head of the History Department at the University of Arizona. For him, living close to the Mexican border for more than a quarter of a century has not been simply a matter of fact, but of multiple involvement with the common interests of Mexicans and Americans.

Ewing came to the University in 1937, having been a regional historian for the National Park Service. He had previously earned a Ph.D. at the University of California as a student of the historian, Bolton, famed authority on the Spanish borderlands.

The new Arizonan was around just long enough to become thoroughly imbued with the proximity of Mexico and its enticing past, when he was called to three years of service as a Navy officer in World War II.

During the post-war decades, he has served as professor of history, chairman of the department, teacher at the University summer session in Guadalajara, Smith-Mundt fellow in Colombia (1956-57), officer of history organizations, and working author. He also has accepted more than a historian's responsibility for current events, as a member of the District One school board of Tucson in 1956, and again for 1963-65.

EDWARD H. SPICER, who wrote the section "Ways of Life," is professor of anthropology at the University of Arizona. His own "ways of life" varied from shipping out (just after high school) as ordinary seaman on freighters to Germany, Central America, and the Great Lakes, to washing windows and picking oranges in Phoenix; excavating as archaeologist of the National Monument at Tuzigoot, and pithouses near San Francisco Peaks; and spending his honeymoon in the Yaqui Indian village of Pascua on the western edge of Tucson while doing field research for a University of

Chicago doctorate in anthropology in 1939.

During World War II, he served as head of the Community Analysis Section of the War Relocation Authority, which directed the inland movement of the Japanese and Japanese-Americans. He came to the University of Arizona in 1946. Spicer has held two Guggenheim fellowships for field research and writing in Mexico.

In addition to teaching, research, and writing, Spicer spent 1963-64 in Mexico, Peru, and Bolivia, on a National Science Foundation senior post-doctoral fellowship for the study of Indian community development.

DAVID A. HENDERSON, section author of "Land, Man, and Time," is associate professor of geography at the University of Arizona. A National Academy of Science (Office of Naval Research) grant enabled him to study the historical geography of gray whale hunting in Northwest Mexico during a 1965-66 sabbatical, emphasizing his concentration on Mexico.

Although his academic field is Latin America, Henderson describes his interest as "especially Middle America, more especially Mexico, and most especially Northwest Mex-

ico." His interlude with whales is only one of several extended periods of residence and study that the author has spent learning about Mexico's land as it has been modified by man and time.

A native of Colorado, Henderson became a Southwesterner when he came to Tucson and joined the University of Arizona faculty in 1959. He taught previously at San Diego State College and Stanford University, received his B.A. and M.A. from the University of Colorado, followed by his Ph.D. from the University of California at Los Angeles.

PAUL KELSO, author of the section called "A Developing Democracy," is a professor in the Department of Government at the University of Arizona. He joined the faculty at Tucson in 1946, following service in World War II as historical officer for the Caribbean Division of the Air Transport Command.

Two decades of residence, research, and teaching within an hour and a half of the Mexican border have helped to focus Kelso's interest on constitutions, governments, and politics of Latin American countries — Mexico in particular. He has expanded this interest and his fund of firsthand knowledge by frequent and extensive travel in Mexico and several summers of Mexican residence, as well as sessions of teaching in the University of Arizona summer school at Guadalajara.

Kelso received the Bachelor's degree from Ball State University, working thereafter as a newspaper reporter and feature writer. He returned to academic life for a Master's degree from the University of Wisconsin, and a Ph.D. from Ohio State University. Later Kelso continued his teaching career at Ohio State and served as a lecturer at UCLA.

GEORGE F. LEAMING, co-author of the section "An Economy of Contrasts," is a research specialist with the Division of Economic and Business Research at the University of Arizona. For a number of years he has concentrated in particular on trade between Mexico and the United States, including firsthand observations of the rapid development of the Mexican economy.

Leaming's knowledge of the economics of industry and Latin America has not come solely from short visits and academic research. Holder of a degree in mining engineering from Lafayette College, he worked in Chile for three years for the Kennecott Copper Corporation, advancing from mine shift foreman to assistant chief mine engineer. After extensive travel throughout South America and a tour of duty with the U. S. Army, he located in Arizona as a design engineer for the Magma Copper Company.

From their San Manuel mine Leaming came to the University of Arizona where he earned a Master's degree in business administration in 1961. He has combined studies toward a doctorate in economics with teaching courses in business administration, economics, statistics, and research methods.

WALTER H. DELAPLANE, who teamed up for presentation of the section "An Economy of Contrasts," is vice-president for academic affairs at the University of Arizona. Several periods in his busy administrative career have been spent in direct confrontation with Latin American affairs. In 1945-46, he was a visiting professor of economics at the National University of Paraguay; in 1946, lecturer in the Colegio Libre at Buenos Aires, and in 1950, lecturer in the School of Economics at the National University in Mexico City.

Delaplane was professor and head of the department of economics at Texas A. & M., and taught Latin American economics. Later he was dean of the College of Arts and Sciences at Southern Methodist University.

The author's undergraduate work and Master's research were done at Oberlin College. He received his Ph.D. from Duke University where he later joined the faculty of economics, and became assistant to the dean of the graduate school. During World War II years, he served as foreign economics administrator with the Iberian Section of the Foreign Economics Administration's Blockade Division. He became a member of the staff at the University of Arizona in 1962.

RENATO ROSALDO set down the section, "Legacy of Literature and the Arts," in his role as professor of Spanish and head of the Romance Language Department at the University of Arizona. He has applied a lifelong and intensive knowledge of Spanish to building effective relationships on both sides of the international boundary.

As a linguist, he holds the Governor's award for translating from English to Spanish and Spanish to English. He inaugurated a television program over the University's KUAT-TV to teach conversational Spanish. In addition to teaching, he co-directs the University's summer session at Guadalajara, and is a frequent contributor to literary and scholarly Latin American journals. He has served on the executive committee of the Mexico-United States Border Governors' Conference, was coordinator of the executive committee of the Arizona-Mexico West Coast trade, and holds an award from the Mexican state of Jalisco for service to Latin American culture.

Rosaldo came to the University of Arizona in 1955 from the University of Wisconsin, and previously taught at the Universities of Illinois, New Mexico, Minnesota, and California at Los Angeles, following the completion of his Ph.D. at the University of Illinois.

Six Faces of Mexico | CONTENTS

PHOTOGRAPHS

MAPS

CHARTS

TABLES

SIX FACES OF
MEXICO

The hub of activity for Mexico's busy capital is this intersection of the famed Paseo de la Reforma.

— *Courtesy Mexican Government Tourism Department*

Citizens! . . . we celebrate the triumph of
reason over force and the victory of
independence and human dignity over the interests
of ambition and fanaticism.

— *Benito Juárez*
May 17, 1858

Major Historical Themes | RUSSELL C. EWING

THE FOLLOWING NARRATIVE is a summary of some four hundred and fifty years of Mexican history. For more than three hundred of these years Mexico was a Spanish colony. Then during the opening years of the nineteenth century the colony gained its political independence from the mother country; and for a hundred years thereafter Mexico was a land of crises. Dictators came and went; church-state conflicts vexed the nation; foreign intervention exacted its toll; agrarian problems contributed their share to unrest; and out of all this came the Revolution, an upheaval which, since the 1940's, has been labeled the "institutional revolution."

DISCOVERY

Western civilization reached Mexico on a day early in February, 1517, when Spaniards in three ships under the command of Francisco Hernández de Córdoba went ashore at Cape Catoche on the northeastern extremity of the peninsula of Yucatán. Córdoba and his companions were not the first Europeans to reach the peninsula; shipwrecked Spaniards had been cast upon its eastern shores several years earlier, and there is reason to believe that even Columbus had seen the low-lying coast line in 1502 on his fourth voyage. But it was Córdoba's expedition which announced to the world that west of Cuba lay a marvelous country whose inhabitants possessed fabulous riches. Perhaps this was the ever-elusive Cathay (China). Or was it another island like Haiti or Cuba? It took several years of conquest and exploration before the Spaniards learned that they had not found Cathay or another of the Antilles.

But neither Córdoba nor his men were preoccupied with geographical place names. Of more interest, at least for several days, were the ruins of what had once been a great Maya Indian city. Bernal Díaz del Castillo, (companion of Córdoba and later of Cortés who was to write one of the most accurate accounts we have of the conquest) says that this was the largest city the Spaniards had yet seen in the New World. Sufficient reason, then,

for naming it Great Cairo, and for going ashore to see the sights. The soldier historian might have added that Diego Velásquez, governor of Cuba, had instructed the expedition to discover new lands and, perhaps, to enslave Indians.

If it were the intention of Córdoba to capture Mayas for the slave markets of Cuba, he was to be greatly disappointed. The Mayas of Great Cairo were not a peaceful lot and came very near turning the tables on the Spaniards when Córdoba and several of his men were ambushed near the city. "Right after the arrows," writes Bernal Díaz, "they came hand to hand fighting with us and with violent blows with their lances they did us great harm." But of course the Maya was unable to stand up against the superior arms of the white man. Fifteen Indians were killed and two natives were captured and taken aboard Córdoba's ship. Thus was begun a sordid story. Countless thousands of lives, Indian and Caucasian, were to be lost during the next half-century of the conquest of New Spain, a name which was affixed to the country during the colonial period.

Córdoba now up-anchored, set sail and followed the inner coast of the peninsula. At Campeche he found the Mayas friendly and fascinated by the Spaniard's ships; but further on, near Champotón, hordes of natives attacked Córdoba and his soldiers who had gone ashore for food and water. After fifty Spaniards had been killed, Córdoba and his men retreated to their ships. The loss was a serious blow to the Spanish captain; moreover, nearly all of those who had gone ashore were wounded, the captain himself critically. No other choice remained but to return to Cuba by way of Florida!

Who had chosen the long way home? It was Antón de Alaminos, pilot of the expedition, who had served with Christopher Columbus, and it was said that he had accompanied Juan Ponce de León on the latter's famous voyage. Therefore, since the captain and his men were "dying of thirst, for the water we had on board was salt and not fit to drink," and since Alaminos knew that potable water was available in Florida, the two remaining ships (the third had been scuttled, owing to the lack of a crew to man her) crossed the Gulf of Mexico and reached the peninsula and fresh water. One thirsty soldier "drank so much water that he swelled up and died within two days," writes Bernal Díaz. After fighting off hostile Indians, the crew filled the water barrels and trimmed sails for Havana. The island's governor, despite an irascible and suspicious nature, was pleased to learn of the discovery of a new land inhabited by a superior people, a people who might have gold. A second expedition was therefore in order. Captain Córdoba died ten days after returning to Cuba, but other captains were available, and the island was overrun with adventurous Spaniards who would gladly enlist in an enterprise that might be prestigious and financially rewarding. And of course there was always the possibility of finding the land of the Amazons, that storied land of women whom every literate Spaniard knew lived somewhere in the New World.

Authorization for the second expedition was granted by the king's officers at Santo Domingo, the Spanish capital of the New World on the southern shores of the present-day Dominican Republic. Four vessels carrying an army were promptly placed under the command of Juan de Grijalva, a Cuban resident and a man of means. Aboard also were redheaded Pedro de Alvarado and Francisco de Montejo. Alvarado would make his mark as the companion of Cortés and the conqueror of Guatemala, and Montejo was destined to subjugate the Mayas. The ubiquitous Bernal Díaz was also on Grijalva's roster, as were two captured Maya Indians who were to serve as interpreters.

Spanish Possession

On April 8, 1518, after hearing mass, the little fleet weighed anchor at the small settlement of Matanzas, near Havana; eight days later the crews sighted land. But this was not Catoche. They had reached the Island of Cozumel, on the east side of the peninsula south of Cape Catoche. Frightened Indians who had little to offer the Spaniards greeted the soldiers who went ashore. Grijalva promptly read a proclamation stating that the island was now a possession of the Spanish crown, then ordered a resumption of the voyage.

Eight days later the ships put in at Champotón on the west side of the peninsula. But the Mayas here were resting on the laurels they had won a year or so earlier when they had driven Córdoba's army into the sea. The natives had reason to be "very proud and haughty . . . and ready to fall on us when we landed," at least until they discovered that Grijalva and his men were expecting trouble and came well supplied with superior weapons. But even then, the Spanish soldiers spent the greater part of three days with crossbows and swords before the Indians were defeated and took refuge in the nearby swamps. Indian casualties were high, but Grijalva lost only seven men and returned to his ships with sixty wounded. The captain himself had been a target for three arrows, "and had two of his teeth broken."

The expedition continued its course to the base of the peninsula and then turned northward, following the Gulf of Mexico coast to the Pánuco River. Enroute, Grijalva and his men made a cursory survey of the Laguna de Términos, which they named Boca de Términos, "mouth of land's end." (For some time the Spaniards believed that this was a strait between the Gulf of Mexico and the Caribbean.) Farther down the coast they reached a river which they called the Río Grijalva, a name still on the maps of Mexico. The Indians along lower reaches of the river were admonished to accept Emperor Charles as their lord, but the natives, though polite and peaceful, were not in a receptive mood. Their own lord, the Aztec Montezuma, from his capital at Tenochtitlan, had made it quite clear to his subjects that these white intruders should be told to go home. After all, in accordance with a well-known prophecy, Grijalva and his companions were none other than avenging gods now returning after an absence of many years.

Perhaps if properly appeased with rich foods and gold, the gods would forgo their hostile intentions. So Montezuma's Indians, on the banks of the Río Grijalva, prepared them a banquet of roasted fish and fowl. The food was good, as were the gold ornaments which were given to the Spaniards. Then these native ambassadors of good will said that "further on, in the direction of the sunset, there was plenty of gold, and they said 'Colua, Colua, Méjico,' . . . Although the present they brought us was not worth much, we were satisfied, because we thus knew for certain that they possessed gold," wrote Bernal Díaz.

No one could now say that Grijalva's expedition was a wild-goose chase; and above all, Governor Velásquez must hear the good news. Therefore, shortly after the expedition reached the island of San Juan de Ulúa near modern Veracruz, Alvarado was dispatched to Cuba with the good tidings. Meantime the impatient and irascible governor had sent a ship under the command of Cristóbal de Olid in search of Grijalva. Olid seems to have tracked Grijalva as far as Laguna de Términos before his ship was seriously damaged by a storm, compelling him to return to Cuba.

Had Grijalva been supported by his men he no doubt would have explored the greater part of the rim of the gulf and would have established a settlement on its shores. Alaminos, the famous and trusted pilot, advised the captain to turn back, pointing out that one of the ships was leaking badly and that before long the little fleet would be overtaken by storms. Montejo and others, upon learning that Grijalva wished to go ashore and found a town, said it would be impossible to defend themselves against so many hostile Indians; moreover, the captain should know that everyone was exhausted. Valid arguments these were, and somewhere near the entrance to the Pánuco River, Grijalva set the sails for a homeward voyage. Forty-five days later, after retracing the greater part of a course which had been followed for nearly half a year, the ships dropped anchor in the harbor of Santiago de Cuba, "where Diego Velásquez was residing, and he gave us a good reception."

The "good reception" was no doubt occasioned by a display of Indian gold, some of which had been carried to the island in Alvarado's ship. And it may have been the treasures on board which encouraged the governor to send still another expedition to the mainland, for Velásquez had already commissioned young Hernán Cortés to take charge of a voyage to the west.

CONQUEST

Cortés stands high on the list of great names in the history of the conquest of the Americas. And as is so often the case with great men, he has become one of the world's most controversial figures. The official Mexican estimate of him is attested by the absence of bronze figures or stone statues in a land which customarily erects impressive monuments to its heroes. The late Mexican painter, Diego Rivera, portrayed Cortés as a diseased pig. On the other hand, many scholars, such as Salvador de Madariaga, hold that Cortés has been maligned needlessly, that he was no more nor less than a child of the age.

Cortés was born in 1485 in Medellín, Spain, a small town of the Extremadura region which was to be the birthplace of many a conqueror of the New World. His parents were of the lesser nobility and at fourteen sent him to Spain's University of Salamanca, one of Europe's most renowned centers of learning. Latin and grammar were apparently his major intellectual interests, but at the end of two years, despite the protests of his parents, he returned home. Perhaps Cortés decided to sacrifice the scholar's cloister for the active life of world affairs. Then of course the astounding successes of the great Captain Gonzalo de Cordóba in Naples must have aroused the spirit of adventure in the minds of many a Spanish school boy. From the records it is quite clear that Cortés weighed the advantages of joining the armies of the Great Captain against a career in the West Indies. The scale tipped in the westerly direction, when the future conqueror of Mexico learned that Nicolás de Ovando was preparing to depart for Haiti, or, as the island was then called, Española.

Ovando's ships sailed from Sanlúcar in February, 1502, but Cortés was not aboard. *Cherchez la femme!* Cortés was overly fond of women, a trait that contributed in this instance to his serious fall from a roof while attempting to visit his sweetheart. Thus it was that he found himself recuperating when Ovando's ships made their departure; and it was not until two years later, at the age of nineteen, that Cortés was able to sail to Santo Domingo, the principal city in Española and the capital of the Indies.

Sometime near Easter he arrived and presented Ovando with letters of introduction. The governor responded by offering him land, but Cortés rejected it, saying that he had come to the Indies to make a fortune and not to settle down as a farmer. He then struck out on his own. For a time he engaged in mining, and before long he was the possessor of an *encomienda* of Indians, a trusteeship whereby the conquistador as *encomendero* was empowered to collect tribute from the Indians, with the understanding that the Indians must be protected and indoctrinated in the Christian religion. This institution often permitted a Spaniard to enrich himself at the expense of the natives, especially when local authorities of the crown chose to ignore the *encomendero's* abuse of his charges. Cortés may have fallen rather early into this category of *encomenderos,* judging from his desire for power and wealth. In any event, he soon became a man of means and influence. Also, his two years in the university proved to be something more than a status symbol: it prepared him for his position as notary public in one of the towns on the island. Furthermore, and no doubt as a mark of respectibility, he married Catalina Suárez, about whom very little is known.

Meantime, in 1511, Diego Velásquez, who had served under Ovando, was commissioned governor of Cuba and was sent with an army to conquer the natives of the island. Stout Cortés went along as the governor's secretary, but, as was the case with others closely associated with Velásquez, Cortés and he quarreled bitterly. Yet, by 1518, the two were once again on friendly terms, and Cortés held the rather important post of *alcalde mayor* of Santiago, Cuba. The governor's confidence had now risen to the point of entrusting Cortés with the command of an expedition to New Spain.

Why not use an experienced man such as Grijalva for the enterprise? Everyone knew that he was competent and wished to return. But intrigue was afoot and Cortés seems to have urged his well-placed friends to sway the governor. Was not Cortés a wealthy planter who could provide capital for the undertaking? And was it not the king's wish that a venture of this kind must be financed by private funds? To all of this Velásquez agreed, especially in view of the fact that his distrusting nature would not support the wishes of cousin Grijalva. Cortés was the man.

Cortés immediately scoured the island for supplies and ships, and for men who were not only fit to sail ships and bear arms, but who also had a few hundred pesos to invest. Velásquez may have been led astray by exaggerated rumors of Cortés's wealth. And other rumors, spread by the enemies of Cortés, aroused the suspicions of the governor to the point where he ordered Cortés to abandon the project. But Velásquez had misjudged his man. Cortés was not easily dissuaded from a course of action. He chose to disobey the governor at the risk of losing his life.

Other adventurous and prominent souls on the island backed Cortés in his quarrels with the governor, investing in the enterprise and enlisting in Cortés's army. Some, like the pilot Alaminos and the chronicler Díaz del Castilla, were veterans of the expeditions of Córdoba and Grijalva. Some, like Pedro de Alvarado and Francisco de Montejo, had been initiated into the mysteries of Mexico as members of Grijalva's army; and, as in every well-regulated expedition, the names of priests appeared on the roster — Father Juan Díaz and Father Bartolomé de Olmedo.

Sailing West

In mid-February, 1519, Cortés and his army boarded eleven ships and sailed west, despite the governor's insistence that the project be abandoned. In addition to 508 soldiers, 109 seamen and a few supernumeraries aboard the ships, space had been found for sixteen horses, ten brass guns, and four falconets. And somewhere on the flagship must have been the official instructions, dated October 23, 1518, and signed by Velásquez in one of his rare moments of sweetness and light. The burden of the instructions makes it quite clear that Cortés and his men must "treat the Indians well and tell them about the Lord of the Christians and their mighty king." Since the governor wished the expedition to devote most of its energies to trade, all precious objects obtained from the natives "were to be put in a chest with two or three keys, one for the inspector, another for the treasurer, and the other for Cortés." (The crown had a similar arrangement for the royal coffers.) In emergencies, Cortés was to take charge in the same manner that Velásquez himself would if he were present. Moreover, Cortés was directed to take formal possession of all the lands he discovered and to search for the country of the Amazons.

Landfall was at Cozumel, just as might have been expected, with Alaminos as pilot. Some of the men, led by Alvarado, hastened ashore and raided the Indian settlements, an act which Cortés promptly condemned. Actions such as these, at least at this stage of the conquest, would hardly gain the respect of the natives. Then, after some difficulty in placating the fears of the Indians through an interpreter, Cortés "told them we were not going to do them any evil or injury, but only to . . . win them to the knowledge of our Holy Catholic Faith." Above all, they must not worship idols, which, said Cortés, "were not gods, but evil things that would draw their souls down to hell." He therefore ordered the destruction of the Indians' idols and replaced them with an altar, and an image of the Holy Virgin.

In the meantime, he learned that two Spaniards were living as captives of the Mayas on the mainland. They were the survivors of twelve shipwrecked persons who had been cast upon the shores of Yucatán in 1511. All, except these two, Gerónimo de Aguilar and Gonzalo Guerrero, were slain — perhaps sacrificed to native gods — by the Mayas. Miraculously Aguilar and Guerrero had escaped and only a little less miraculously Aguilar, though a slave, was serving the Indians as a military adviser and Guerrero was the contented father of several half-breed children. The two Spaniards were not in accord on matters relating to life among the Mayas, for when they were asked by Cortés to join the expedition, Aguilar hastened to the Spanish camp on Cozumel, while Guerrero chose to remain with his wives and children. Guerrero had "gone native." His Spanish countrymen said he was ashamed to be seen because "he has his nostrils, lips, and ears pierced and his face painted and his hands tattooed." But the "Captain from Castile" had not come to listen to stories of romance and adventure in the jungles of Yucatán. Far more important was the fact that Aguilar was bilingual. Competent interpreters were hard to come by. Little need to waste time with Guerrero while great expectations lay ahead.

The ships moved out and sailed to the west side of the peninsula. The first important stop was at Champotón, where both Córdoba and Grijalva had had serious battles with the inhabitants. Although Indians were still hostile, Cortés fared somewhat better than his predecessors; and it was here, so the story goes, that Cortés first recognized the great importance of the horse in his initial battles with the Indians. To the Indian, the horse — which did not exist at that time in the western hemisphere — was a fearsome and immortal beast. The ever-alert Cortés exploited this for many weeks, until an unnamed Indian in the mountains above Veracruz gave the lie to the superstition by cutting off the head of one of the animals.

Farther down the coast, at Tabasco, the Spaniards again found the Indians ready for battle. But the warlike attitude of the natives did not deter Cortés from hastening ashore and taking formal possession of the country in the name of His Majesty, King Charles, by striking a tree three times with his sword, saying, "if anyone disputes it, he would defend it with his sword and buckler." The king's notary promptly recorded the symbolic act, which was conclusive evidence that the land now belonged to the crown of Spain.

Had it not been for the horses and superior arms of the Spaniards at Tabasco, and the excellent interpreting by Aguilar, the Indians might have destroyed the Spanish captain's army. When the fighting was over, "principal Indians came, saying that . . . the past should be the past, and henceforth they wished to be vassals." As a token of good faith, Cortés was given twenty women, who were baptized by Father Olmedo, and one of whom was thereafter to be known as Doña Marina. Here again, Cortés had met with good fortune, for Doña Marina was to be the Spaniards' loyal friend and interpreter and in that role to save the conquerors from many an embarrassing situation. She could speak Nahuatl, tongue of the Aztecs, and was proficient in Mayan. In the early days of the conquest, before she knew Spanish, she was able to interpret for Cortés by talking with Aguilar, the other bilingual in the group. She was also to bear one of Cortés's sons, Don Martín, a name Cortés gave to his legitimate male offspring as well.

As the expedition approached San Juan de Ulúa, it became clear to everyone that Cortés would stray from the letter of Velásquez's instructions by establishing on the shores of New Spain a permanent colony which would serve as the captain's headquarters for the army he proposed to lead into the mountains against the forces of Montezuma. Simply to go to New Spain to trade, said Cortés, was not the way to extend the Spanish dominions. A town must be founded and the Indians conquered, in appreciation of which King Charles should show "some favours to us, and to the colonists who would come there hereafter." Nor should it be overlooked that the Spaniards were somewhat motivated by the search for gold.

So it was on Good Friday, 1519, that Cortés and his men went ashore and established their headquarters, naming their settlement Villa Rica de la Vera Cruz, which was moved later to the present site of Veracruz. Of course, Velásquez partisans promptly protested the colonization scheme; and the faint-hearted, "who wanted to leave on seeing how large and populous the country was, while the Spaniards were so few," preferred the comforts of home rather than the questionable future of an Indian campaigner. (Estimates on the Indian population of Mexico at the time range from seven to thirty million, speaking no less than fifty different tongues!)

But dissident groups did not know their man. Cortés indeed had ways of dealing with the disloyal and the cowardly — simply to create one's own political and military machines. He promptly established a town council (*cabildo*), assigned his partisans to the judicial and administrative posts, and appointed his most competent and loyal friends to positions of command in his army. Of course, Cortés was elected to the *cabildo,* the first step toward what he called acceptable constitutional procedures. Members of the council then demanded to see the instructions from Velásquez. "He immediately sent for these, and showed them to us and, having been seen and read by us, and well examined to the best of our understanding, it seemed to us that, by those powers and instructions, the said Captain Fernando Cortés, had no longer any authority, and that, they having expired, he could no longer exercise the office of justice, or of captain."

What a surprise! And what a "surprise" it was that the *cabildo* elected Cortés to serve His Majesty as chief justice and captain and "Governor of Your Royal Arms." Judging by Cortés's actions, he was now no longer Velásquez's agent but a loyal and zealous captain directly responsible to King Charles. (According to the distinguished scholar Salvador de Madariaga, Cortés's assumption of authority was in line with acceptable Spanish practices in similar situations. Some historians disagree with de Madariaga on this point.) As proof of sincerity and respect for the crown, "we . . . send you," wrote one of the members of the *cabildo,* "all the gold, and silver, and valuables which we have obtained in this country." Cortés and his men had indeed already obtained a considerable amount of precious loot from the Indians, but it is reasonable to question the *cabildo's* statement that "we keep nothing for ourselves."

In any event, two procurators, Montejo and Puertocarrero, were placed in charge of the king's gold and silver, and sent off to Spain in one of the ships. They also were to plead the cause of Cortés and his men before the king. Montejo deserted at Havana but was soon to return to Mexico to undertake conquest of the Mayas. Puertocarrero reached Spain and was promptly jailed "on a pretended misdemeanor, in carrying away with him to the Indies a woman of Medellín." A jailbird was not likely to gain a sympathetic hearing!

The final step to assure his political and military posture was taken by Cortés when he either scuttled or beached his ships so that the disloyal and timid were deprived of an avenue of escape. (Authorities differ on what actually happened to the ships.) Actions such as these seldom improve the morale of an army, but morale was not Cortés's immediate problem. Far more important was the need of troops — loyal, disloyal, or timid.

An Aztec Welcome

Meanwhile the lord of the Aztecs was busily contriving ways and means for ridding the land of the unwelcome visitors. Shortly after the Spaniards had gone ashore at Veracruz, Montezuma's ambassadors appeared with instructions to urge the "white gods" to return to the country of their origin. For according to Indian legend, Cortés was Quetzalcoatl, an Aztec god who once upon a time had resided in Mexico before leaving the country by sailing east, making it clear that some day he would return. His return now might be that of an angry god. Cortés may or may not have been fully acquainted with the legend as he talked to Montezuma's ambassadors on the beach. In any event, the Spanish captain wished everyone to recognize that he represented a great and friendly king. The native ambassadors replied that they, too, represented a great and friendly emperor, proof of which was in the presents — fowl, maize cakes, articles of gold, cloth of cotton and feathers — which were given to the Spaniards. Cortés reciprocated with glass beads and a handsome armchair for Montezuma, "so that he could be seated in it when he, Cortés, came to see and speak with him." A day or two later, and as further evidence of friendship, the ambassadors gave the Spaniards "a wheel like a sun, as big as a cartwheel . . . of fine gold . . . worth more than ten thousand pesos," together with "another larger wheel of silver, in imitation of the moon." Gold and silver! Unwittingly, the ambassadors had made a grave error. Who now, aside from the partisans of Velásquez, would be so foolish as to abandon Cortés's plan for conquest of the Aztec empire?

Cortés was not one to move unprepared into a new situation. Reconnaissance had already been made of the coast, especially of Cempoala, a settlement of Totonacs north of Veracruz. Cortés had a long talk with Gordo, the town's cacique, or chief. Gordo (The Fat One) had a lot to say. Indians everywhere, from the Valley of Mexico to the Gulf, including the Totonacs on the coast and the Tlaxcalans in the high country, said Gordo, were struggling against the power of the Aztecs. And Cortés learned from his informant that the Totonacs had only recently been forced to pay allegiance to Montezuma and that the Tlaxcalans had long been waging a costly war against the Aztecs in an effort to maintain their independence. What better news could a small army of conquerors have than assurances that all was not well in the camp of the enemy? Cortés immediately pursued the proper tactical course by joining forces with the Totonacs, whereupon Gordo and some of his people were so p.eased that they were willing to tolerate destruction of their idols and places of worship.

On August 16, 1519, and after detailing a handful of men to stand guard at Veracruz, Cortés marched out from Cempoala at the head of an army of four hundred Spaniards, including fathers Olmedo and Díaz and several thousand Indian warriors. Two days later they reached Jalapa. Thirteen days later, on August 31, the army crossed the Tlaxcalan frontier. Here, for the first time since leaving Cempoala, the Indians gave a good account of themselves but were forced to retreat; and perhaps it was here that two of the horses were killed, proof for Indian eyes that the horse was not an immortal.

Finally, after several more battles and with the services of Cortés's interpreters, Doña Marina and Aguilar, the majority of the Indians surrendered, and on September 23 the Spaniards entered the city of Tlaxcala. Contrary to what might have been expected Cortés and his men were received in a most friendly manner. Everywhere, "in the streets and on the roofs, all the Indian men and women with happy faces came out to see us," writes Bernal Díaz; and as a further gesture of friendship, Chief Xicoténcatl housed the Spaniards in his palace and other native buildings. As though this were not enough, gifts of food and women were presented to the soldiers. Of course, the Spaniards were willing recipients of all this; but Cortés did scold the Indians for their initial hostility which had resulted in the death of at least one Spaniard and the wounding of many more. Yet little if anything was said about Indian casualties. More important to Cortés for the moment were live Indians, Tlaxcalans who might join his army for the anticipated conquest of the Aztecs. He knew very well, from both Totonac and Tlaxcalan sources, that Aztec and Tlaxcalan were deadly enemies. It was therefore no surprise when Tlaxcalans allied themselves with the Spaniards, despite the attempts of Montezuma's envoys to convince Cortés that the Tlaxcalans were not to be trusted.

It was now early October, and Cortés was anxious to continue his march to the Aztec capital at Tenochtitlan. But what Indian trails or routes should he follow? North through the high mountains, or northwest by way of Cholula? Some Tlaxcalans advised him to bypass Cholula; Montezuma's envoys said the best way into the Valley of Mexico was through Cholula. Cortés accepted the advice of the Aztecs, not because he trusted them, but because he had learned that Cholula was a large and sacred city of the Aztecs; moreover, according to Bernal Díaz, Cortés wished to talk to the chiefs of Cholula, who had refused to go to Tlaxcala, "for the Tlaxcalans were their enemies and . . . had said many evil things about them and about their Lord Montezuma. . . ."

After a little more than a day's march, Cortés's army, including some five or six thousand Tlaxcalan warriors, reached the outskirts of Cholula. Caciques and priests of the sacred city greeted the captain and his soldiers humbly and apologized for not having extended an earlier welcome. But there were no apologies or welcome for the Tlaxcalans; and above all, said the caciques, the Tlaxcalans should not enter Cholula. To Cortés this was reasonable, and he immediately sent Alvarado and Olid to advise the Tlaxcalans to camp in the fields and to rejoin the Spaniards when they resumed their march. Alvarado and Olid reported that the advice was acceptable; and the Spanish army was then received in a "festive manner" by the Cholulans.

Action at Cholula

Among the many controversial aspects of the career of Cortés, none has generated more heat than his actions at Cholula. For it was here that the Spaniards and their native allies killed not less than 3,000 Indians, among whom were countless women and children. And, of course, as had been the case from the time Cortés landed on Cozumel, native temples and idols were destroyed. It was such deeds as these, together with many a conqueror's lust for gold, that gave rise to the "Black Legend," the myth that all Spanish conquerors were scoundrels.

The facts of the Cholula massacre — and massacre it certainly was — are reasonably clear. Cortés and his men were given quarters by what appeared to be generous hosts. Cortés soon learned, however, that the Cholulans, in league with warriers from Tenochtitlan, were preparing to destroy his army. Cempoala Indians reported that holes in the streets, cleverly concealed under thin coverings of wood and earth, were "full of sharp pointed stakes to kill the horses when they galloped." It was also noted that piles of stones had been placed on the roofs of buildings; "and certainly," writes Bernal Díaz, "this was not done with good intent." Nor was it a good omen to learn that the Cholulans had just sacrificed seven persons to the God of War, for this was a customary victory rite on the eve of battle. Moreover, jars, "with salt, chili and tomatoes," had been prepared for the bodies of the Spaniards! Then some of the Tlaxcalans brought word that several thousand Aztec warriors from Tenochtitlan were ambushed in the nearby ravines and rocky thickets. Finally, and as corroboration of these serious developments, loyal Doña Marina tricked a garrulous old woman of the city into revealing some of the details of the plot.

Only the dullest of men would have attributed all of this to idle gossip of native troublemakers. Alert Cortés hardly fell into this category; to him, counter-strategy called for immediate action. Therefore, when Cholulan priests and warriors were assembled in one of the city's principal plazas, upon a signal from Cortés, the Spanish soldiers attacked, and within minutes the streets ran red with Cholulan blood. That afternoon and the following day hordes of Tlaxcalans ran amok and were the principal instruments of death and destruction. Later, both Cortés and Bernal Díaz said that the fierce enmity between Cholulan and Tlaxcalan made it impossible to stop the slaughter until it had run its natural course.

Impossible? Would it have been impossible for Cortés to have used force to bring peace to the streets of Cholula?

Cortés did summon the Tlaxcalan chiefs to his camp, presumably to arrange a peace; but the summons went out only after the Tlaxcalans had had their feast of violence. The chiefs dutifully appeared before Cortés, who told them to gather together their people

The Temple of the Warriors at Chichén Itzá in eastern Yucatán, one of the first ancient structures to be restored in this hemisphere, is an outstanding example of the blend of Maya and Toltec styles that took place in Yucatán shortly before Spanish conquest. The Mexican feathered serpent motif is dramatically employed in the entrance columns.

and return with them to their own camps in the fields; furthermore, said Cortés, all Cholulan captives were to be freed. As for the Cempoalans, they were to remain with the Spaniards. Cortés now had some strong words for Montezuma's ambassadors. Had it not been for the fact that the Spaniards respected the Aztec emperor and his important vassals, wrote Bernal Díaz, these agents from the Plain of Anáhuac would also have been dealt with rather severely. Cortés then turned to the Cholulan priests and caciques, whom he admonished for having followed false gods, "and he gave them a very clear understanding of the things pertaining to our holy faith." Thus ended a sordid chapter in the history of the conquest. Another was about to be written on the plateau beyond the high peaks of Ixtaccíhuatl and Popocatépetl.

Two months had passed since Cortés had begun the steep climb from the Gulf coast, two hundred miles away. His objective, Tenochtitlan, was now close at hand, about seventy miles as the crow flies — considerably farther by Indian trails. But problems of geography and time were not the captain's immediate concern; he was having trouble with Indian morale. Cempoalans, fearful of the military might of the Aztec, were sure that all invaders of the Plain of Anáhuac would be killed. Even the warlike Tlaxcalans showed some signs of hesitancy as Cortés's army pushed forward, while natives from the nearby town of Huejotzingo warned Cortés of the duplicity and the military prowess of the Aztecs. But conquerors of Cortés's stamp were not easily frightened. He did permit the Cempoalans to return to their homes, but managed to persuade a thousand stout-hearted Tlaxcalans to remain.

As Cortés's army scaled the saddle that lies between Popocatépetl and Ixtaccíhuatl (now known as the Paso de Cortés), Montezuma's ambassadors were lavish in their gifts of gold and cloth, but asked that the Spaniards take the presents and return whence they came. (Shades of the *mordida!*) But Cortés was less susceptible to the temptations of bribery now than at any time since he had left Veracruz, for Tenochtitlan was just a few arquebus shots away. The Spanish captain of course accepted the gifts but rebuked the ambassadors for advising him to follow a trail which would surely have led him into a trap. (The people of Huejotzingo had cautioned him about this.) Moreover, Cortés made it quite clear that he was astonished at the double-tongue of the Aztecs. How could such a great prince as Montezuma send marvelous gifts and honied words while plotting to destroy a friendly people who brought with them the blessings of Christianity and the benevolent authority of King Charles? No need for a satisfactory answer. Conquerors, Spaniard and Indian, moved cautiously along the ambush-free road to the capital of the Aztecs.

The first Europeans to see Tenochtitlan may have been Diego de Ordás and a handful of soldiers who, partly out of curiosity and partly in response to orders from Cortés, climbed the steep slopes of Popocatépetl to examine its active volcanic crater. Bernal Díaz wrote that they reached the brink of the crater and were "delighted and astonished at the sight of Mexico and its cities" lying far below amid the lakes of the Plain of Anáhuac. Cortés mentioned the climb but said the party was turned back by snow and clouds of ashes; he is silent on whether or not Ordás and his companions saw Tenochtitlan, "the place of the prickly pear on the rock." (Legend has it that when the Aztecs chose the site for their city a great eagle was perched on the prickly pear and was eating a snake. The heraldic version of the legend is seen today in the national coat of arms, the eagle signifying strength and justice.)

The confrontation of an apprehensive Montezuma and a somewhat confident Cortés was rapidly approaching. The Aztec monarch had failed to check the onward march of the invaders, a fact which has led many a student of the Conquest to say that Aztec failure was due to a policy of appeasement. Appeasement it surely was, but what other course was open to Montezuma? His vassal states were far from loyal; furthermore, important decisions were not his alone. The political nature of his tribe called for clan approval of group action, which in this new and dangerous situation was predicated on a policy of satisfying the demands of the Spaniards with precious gifts in the hope that they would then leave the country. Failing in this, Montezuma and his advisers turned to the timeworn tactic of ambuscade. This, too, had failed, as had the planned entrapment at Cholula. But the Aztec continued to spin his web: a token resistance to the invaders as they moved from town to town down the steep incline from Paso de Cortés, then an invitation to Cortés to quarter his troops in the heart of Tenochtitlan. What better trap could be devised? One hundred thousand Aztecs — more or less — on their island city would present Cortés with major problems in tactics and strategy.

The Aztec capital, close to the western rim of Lake Texcoco, was joined to the shore by three causeways, one leading south, one west, one north. The south causeway, the longest of the three, ran some four or five miles from the city to the junction of two lesser causeways, one coming in from Ixtapalapa to the east, the other branching off south-westward to Coyoacan. A mile or two beyond the junction were lakes Xochimilco and Chalco, which were separated by still another but shorter causeway.

It was this southern access to Tenochtitlan which Cortés and his army followed, entering the main causeway from the Ixtapalapa branch.

Tenochtitlan

It was now November 8, a red-letter day in the history of Mexico. Vast crowds of Aztecs, on the causeways or close by in canoes, greeted Cortés and his army of four hundred Spaniards and two or three thousand Indian allies. Caciques from nearby towns welcomed the Spaniards "in their language, and as a sign of peace, they touched their hands against the ground, and kissed the ground with the hand;" but greatest of all of the lords of the valley, Montezuma, chose to await the invaders in regal splendor on the outskirts of Tenochtitlan. Some two hundred chieftains were in attendance, and as Cortés's army drew close, Montezuma, assisted by four "richly clothed" chieftains, descended from a litter to welcome the captain from Castile.

The details of this gala occasion are reasonably clear, though one suspects that Cortés, in an effort to impress King Charles, was given to hyperbole. Montezuma, surrounded by his princes, came forward. Cortés then dismounted from his horse to embrace his royal host, a gesture hardly in keeping with Aztec protocol. One was not permitted to touch the royal person: "two lords in attendance prevented me, with their hands, that I might not touch him, and they, and he also, made the ceremony of kissing the ground." Further formalities were now in order, the first of which was words or gestures of welcome from Montezuma and his retainers. "Cortés replied through Doña Marina wishing him very good health," and as a symbol of friendship Cortés placed a necklace of "pearls and glass diamonds" round the neck of his host. Montezuma reciprocated by giving his guest two necklaces, "and from each . . . hung eight golden shrimps executed with great perfection and a span long." Then, in the best tradition of hospitality, Montezuma offered some of the city's apartments to the Spaniards, an offer which was promptly accepted.

In the eyes of the Spaniards, Tenochtitlan was indeed a place of beauty — and a place of revulsion. It was a city of "many wide and handsome streets," of "large and fine houses . . . and . . . exquisite flower gardens," and of beautiful palaces and temples, or *cues,* the largest of which stood on or near the present site of the cathedral; but the *cues,* attended by priests reeking of human blood, offended the Christian sensibilities of Cortés and his men. The so-called great *cue,* a pyramid-like structure dedicated to Huitzilopochtli, or God of War, and drenched in the blood of human sacrifice, was the work of the devil and must therefore be destroyed, so said Cortés. It should be the site for a church, and the idols on the summit of the structure should be replaced immediately by the Altar and the Cross. Fray Olmedo agreed, "but it seemed to him that it was not quite a suitable time to speak about it, for Montezuma did not appear to be inclined to do such a thing." A more propitious opportunity would surely present itself for flushing out the Augean stable.

From the day of his arrival in Tenochtitlan until April, 1520, when Cortés and part of his army were to hasten off to Cempoala and Veracruz to meet a formidable array of Velásquez partisans, the conqueror was not only busy cleaning out the "stables" but was also actively engaged in finding ways and means for the complete subjugation of the Aztecs and their vassals. Significant aspects of these days center on Cortés's success in deposing Montezuma by means of imprisonment, together with a search for precious wealth and for other Indians to conquer. Some of the treasures lay hidden behind a wall in Cortés's apartment; a great deal more lay beyond the rim of the Valley of Mexico.

Students of the Conquest are not in agreement on the wisdom of the imprisonment of Montezuma. Some hold that the act was needless if not reprehensible, while others agree with Cortés, "that it would be conducive to Your Royal Highness, and to our security, that Montezuma should be in my power, and not at his entire liberty, so that he might not relax his intention and disposition to serve Your Highness." True, there was much weeping and wailing on the part of Great Lord's subjects when he was seized and made captive; true also that there were good reasons to believe that the Aztecs were busily preparing to destroy the invaders. An imprisoned monarch could hardly be an effective warlord. But it may have been a belated move, for some Indian warriors had already killed seven Spaniards at Veracruz. Cortés, suspecting the hand of Montezuma in this, promptly seized the Chief of Men and demanded that the leader of the attack be brought to Tenochtitlan. Several days later, Qualpopoca, chieftain of the warriors who had attacked Veracruz, together with his son and "fifteen other persons whom they said had taken part in the murders," were handed over to Cortés. Qualpopoca, upon being interrogated, said that Montezuma had not ordered the attack, "although afterwards," wrote Cortés, "when the sentence, that they should be burned, was carried into execution, all with one voice said it was true that Montezuma had ordered them to do it, and that they had obeyed his command." At this Cortés promptly put Montezuma in chains, which were removed shortly after the burning of the Indians. Bernal Díaz confirmed Cortés's version of Qualpopoca's testimony, but it is reasonable to assume that the Indian shifted the responsibility to Montezuma in a desperate attempt to save his own life.

Meantime, Cortés was preoccupied with the Aztec treasure which lay behind a wall in his apartment. A contemporary described it as "a heap of gold and jewels and precious stones, so high that a man placed on the opposite side could not be seen." Here, indeed, was a bonanza. But where were the sources? Cortés therefore instructed Montezuma "to show me the mines from which he obtained gold." The Chief of Men complied by sending two of his servants to each of the four provinces where the principal mines were to be found; "and" said Cortés, "he asked me to send Spaniards with them, to see how it [gold] was taken out." Thus was begun the first organized Spanish prospecting expedition in the history of Mexico.

Since the Indians in the outlying regions appeared to be reasonably peaceful, no one should have been surprised when Cortés sent a second expedition of Aztecs and Spaniards to the Indian "lords . . . to pray them to assist Your Majesty with some part of what they had. Besides Your Highness' need, this would testify that they began to render service." In other words, Cortés demanded tribute. The demand was answered in the form of one hundred thousand ducats of gold, which, wrote Cortés, was promptly sent to the crown — and more was to come. One fifth of all the wealth in Montezuma's hidden treasure, of which more than six hundred thousand pesos was in gold, was forwarded to King Charles. (The king's share was known as the royal fifth, a legal requirement in such cases.) The remainder was divided among the Spaniards but perhaps not on an equal basis. Some snide remarks rose from the ranks of Cortés's army.

Meantime, Governor Velásquez, fuming and fretting, sent a formidable armada under the command of Pánfilo de Narváez with instructions to apprehend Cortés. In April, 1520, word reached the Valley of Mexico that a fleet of some nineteen ships, carrying a well-provisioned army of about one thousand men, had reached Veracruz. Narváez, so it was said, had come to punish Cortés and his men, "bad men and thieves who had fled from Castile without the permission of our Lord and King." Cortés knew his Cuban adversary. Who would have expected kind words from the partisans of Velásquez? But what really vexed the captain from Castile at this point was the fact that Narváez's words of disparagement were designed for the ears of Montezuma, who, quite naturally, was prone to believe them. Clearly, then, Cortés would have to act promptly and with vigor to demonstrate who was master. Perhaps a little gold and outstretched arms of welcome, buttressed by lance and crossbow, would convince Narváez's soldiers of the error of their ways. Furthermore, and for the record, a formal letter must be sent to Narvárez pointing out that royal tribunals and municipal bodies had already been established in New Spain: Narváez "should not appropriate to himself the said offices without first having received them . . . from Your Majesty."

But, under these circumstances, the pen could not be as mighty as the sword or as persuasive as a few ounces of gold. Friar Olmedo was therefore sent to the coast with an abundance of gold; and an army of some seventy men, under the leadership of Cortés, climbed out of the valley and followed the good friar down the eastern slopes of the sierras. Like every able field commander, Cortés recognized the importance of a reserve force, which in this case was a sizable army of friendly Indians who were ordered to join the Spaniards in the vicinity of Narváez's camp. The Indian warriors obeyed their orders, only to find that their services were not needed. Cortés and his men had already outwitted and outfought the interlopers from Cuba. The battle itself had been little more than a skirmish. Casualties on both sides were light. Cortés himself was unscathed, though Narváez lost an eye in the encounter as well as the loyalty of most of his men. Olmedo's gold, coupled with promises of fabulous wealth for those who would return with Cortés to the Plain of Anáhuac, were good and sufficient reasons for a thousand or more men to desert to Cortés's camp; and the ships which had brought the invaders to the mainland were promptly seized. Narváez himself was held prisoner, but only for a few days. He then departed for Cuba, where his report was a bit upsetting to the Governor.

Meantime, Alvarado, who had taken charge of affairs at Tenochtitlan, found himself in a serious situation. His five hundred men were confronted by thousands of angry Aztecs who could no longer tolerate the white man's determination to destroy the religious practices of the Indians, especially the ritual of human sacrifice. And the time to strike was now, for the annual feast for Huitzilopochtli and Tezcatlipoca had arrived, and the gods must be appeased by human blood. When the Spaniards learned that the Aztecs were assembling to pay homage to the gods, Alvarado promptly sent soldiers to attack the worshippers, an attack which resulted in the death of hundreds of natives. The entire native population now rose in mass and succeeded in driving their attackers to defensible positions behind the walls of the Aztec palace, where Montezuma was still held prisoner. Some say that Alvarado needlessly invited trouble by slaughtering the worshippers. Others maintain that the Aztecs themselves were to blame because the festival was designed to test Cortés's orders against human sacrifice.

Cortés reentered the city at this critical moment; and he may have expressed surprise at not being attacked by the Indians. But divide and conquer was foreign to Mexican Indian battle plans. Had Cortés's march into the Valley of Mexico been checked, there is reason to believe that the Aztec warriors might have destroyed Alvarado's garrison, and Cortés and his command would then have found themselves in dire straits indeed.

Cortés joined forces with Alvarado on San Juan's Day, June 24, 1520, the legendary first day of the rainy season. And rain it did for the better part of a week; but the downpour was chiefly in the form of arrows, lances, and stones. "All the buildings and courts were so full of them we could hardly move about." Finally Cortés sent Montezuma to the fort's roof to plead with the natives to withdraw from their attack; but the Aztecs were not to be turned back. Montezuma's voice was simply an echo of happier days. After a moment, the Indians renewed their attack, in the course of which Montezuma was struck on the head by a stone, "with such force," wrote Cortés, "that within three days he died." These were words for King Charles's ear, for what if Charles were to listen to the Aztecs who said that the Spaniards killed Montezuma? In any event, Aztec authority would soon pass into the hands of courageous Cuauhtémoc, nephew of Montezuma.

Noche Triste

Cortés now chose to flee to the mainland rather than face certain defeat in the city. So, on the dark and misty night of June 30, the Spaniards began their withdrawal down the causeway leading to Tacuba, a retreat that had been planned in secrecy. So much for Cortés's secret; a native woman sounded the alarm when she saw the Spaniards moving down the causeway. Before long thousands of Indians attacked the retreating army of about a thousand Spaniards and three of four thousand Tlaxcalans. Thus began the "sorrowful night" — la noche triste —in which thousands of Indians and over half of Cortés's soldiers lost their lives. Cortés himself received a serious head wound and lost the use of two fingers; and, after reaching the end of the causeway, so the story goes, he wept. Tears there may have been, but perhaps tears of thanks, not of despair. Cortés was not one to lose faith in the Lord. After all, He had spared the lives of a little more than four hundred Spaniards, which was about equal to the number of soldiers who had begun the conquest. What further proof would one want, said Cortés, for being an instrument of God's will? The Spaniards must therefore return to Tenochtitlan.

Return they did, but only after a year of careful preparation. The week following the noche triste was one of constant Aztec harassment of the retreating army's rear and flanks; but a Spanish victory at Otumba enabled Cortés and his men to move rapidly over the mountains to allies in Tlaxcala, where plans were executed for a conquest of the Aztec capital. The few fainthearted were dissuaded from abandoning the rigors of reconquest for a comparatively comfortable life in Veracruz or Cuba. "Fortune is always on the side of the daring," said Cortés, "and . . . God . . . would never permit us to perish." How could anyone disagree with this assertion when some two hundred new Spanish recruits unexpectedly appeared in camp? Some were members of an unsuccessful colonial venture which had been sent to the Pánuco region by the governor of Jamaica; others were from supply ships which arrived belatedly at Veracruz to provision Narváez's army. And who would be so rash as to say that fortune was not on the Spanish side when Cortés succeeded once again in obtaining the support of the Tlaxcalans, who had become somewhat reluctant to follow Cortés back into the valley. They not only agreed to return to Tenochtitlan, but also assisted Cortés's shipwright, Martín López, in the construction of thirteen brigantines, which would be launched on Lake Texcoco for a siege of the city. Meanwhile, in order to protect their lines of supply and their maneuvers, the Spaniards defeated hostile Indians at Tepeaca and founded the town of Segura de la Frontera, a strategic point on the road to Veracruz. Nor was this all. Ships were sent to Española and Jamaica for reinforcements and supplies, especially "horses and horsemen. . . . Foot soldiers armed with shields are of little service, on account of the great number of people and their having so great and such strong cities and ports."

During the opening months of 1521, Cortés launched his attack against the island city. No less than twenty thousand Tlaxcalan warriors, some of whom carried the dismembered brigantines overland to Texcoco, where the boats were assembled, joined forces with approximately one thousand Spaniards. By early spring, after a bloody battle at Xochimilco, most of the countryside was in the hands of the Spaniards; and by the end of April Cortés's ships, each manned by twenty-five or thirty soldiers, were launched on the lake. The siege was to run a bloody course for the greater part of four months, resulting in the utter destruction of the Aztec capital.

The Spread of Conquest

The conquest now spread rapidly over the face of the land. In 1520–21, before the fall of Tenochtitlan, Sandoval had been sent with a handful of soldiers and thirty thousand Indian allies to punish rebellious Indians and to search for gold south of Veracruz. It was a successful expedition, resulting in the founding of two towns, Medellín and Espíritu Santo. The land of the Mixtec and Zapotec, in the modern state of Oaxaca, was invaded in 1521–22 by an army under the command of Orozco. This, too, was a successful venture, for the region was inhabited by advanced Indian cultures and was found to be rich in gold, a report which has been corroborated by archaeologists at Monte Alban and Mitla. In that same year, 1522, Olid carried the conquest westward to lakes Pátzcuaro and Chapala, the land of the Tarascans; and later that year his men established a colony on the seacoast at Zacatula. Then, during the following two years, Olid's lieutenants moved into Colima and Jalisco. In the meantime, Cortés marched northeastward to the Pánuco River, where he defeated an army that had been sent to the region by Francisco de Garay, governor of Jamaica.

Rumors of riches, advanced Indian cultures, and Spanish rivals caused Cortés to send his soldiers southward to Guatemala and Honduras. In 1523–24 fair-haired Alvarado, leading a column of four hundred Spaniards and twenty thousand Indian allies, carried the conquest in Guatemala and San Salvador.

Then Olid, sent to take possession of Honduras, had turned traitor; moreover, the forces of Pedro Arias de Ávila were moving north from Panamá, a threat to Cortés's avowed claim to Honduras. Thus, when a second expedition under the command of Francisco de las Casas showed signs of disaffection, the captain himself set out for Honduras, leading an army of some one hundred and forty Spaniards and three thousand Indians, among them Cuauhtémoc and the loyal Doña Marina.

Cortés's journey to Honduras was one of the most daring feats of the conquest. For the greater part of half a year — from November, 1524, to April, 1525 — Cortés and his army fought their way through the dense forests, vast morasses, and great rivers which lie at the base of the Yucatán peninsula. "The forest," says Cortés, "was such that we could see nothing but the ground where we stood . . . I consulted my compass by which I had often guided myself, though never had we been in such a plight as this. . . ." After days of tiresome struggle through swollen streams and treacherous swamps, the army reached a large marsh, "more than five hundred paces broad, to cross which we sought in vain to find a place . . ." A bridge would have to be built. But who would build it? Exhaustion and grumblings in the ranks were sufficient reason for Cortés to order his men "to take no part in building the bridge, for I would do it with the Indians. . . . " And this they did, with more than a thousand beams fashioned from trees and varying in length from forty to fifty feet! Again, the genius of Cortés enlisted the support of Indians in the cause of their Spanish conquerors, despite the fact there was never a more opportune moment to destroy the white intruders than here in the forests of Yucatán. Cortés and Bernal Díaz say the natives did seize the opportunity. Evidence from other sources, however, supports the contention that at no time on the march to Honduras did the Indians plan to rise up against their Spanish masters. In any event, all sources agree that Cuauhtémoc, accused of conspiring against Cortés, was put to death, together with at least one other chieftain. Was this murder or necessary punishment? The history books in Mexico tend to classify the act as murder.

In April, 1525, some two months after the death of Cuauhtémoc, Cortés and his army completed their trek through the Yucatán wilderness and marched on to Trujillo. Cortés may then have questioned the wisdom of this most hazardous journey, because the traitor Olid had been executed and the forces of Pedro Arias de Ávila were no longer a threat. Furthermore, word had reached Cortés that matters were far from satisfactory on the Plain of Anáhuac. A struggle for power was vexing the inhabitants of Tenochtitlan. Those whom Cortés had charged with administering affairs during his absence were quarreling among themselves and conspiring to unseat the governor general of New Spain, a new and rather impressive title King Charles had conferred on Cortés. Then, when rumors were spread that Cortés was dead, the struggle in the capital became even more bitter.

This was a situation that needed immediate and personal attention. Cortés commissioned his cousin, Hernando Saavedra, captain general of Trujillo, and sent his army back to Mexico City by way of Guatemala. Cortés himself returned by ship in May, 1526. Perhaps the thought of a renewed struggle with forest, stream, and steep mountains, especially at that moment, was a bit discouraging. Or maybe he wished to look into matters at Havana, where he spent a few days before continuing his voyage to the mainland. He was joyously received in both places. In Havana, since Velásquez had been removed by death, Cortés's old cronies gave full vent to their admiration for the conqueror. A similar welcome was extended in New Spain, though his emaciated appearance caused some concern among his friends.

As for Mexico, "The country was on the verge of destruction," wrote Fray Juan de Zumárraga, first bishop and archbishop of Mexico, and "Protector of the Indians." Nothing less than a civil war raged on the Plain of Anáhuac. The partisans of Velásquez were well intrenched, and Cortés's own officers were divided in their loyalties. To make matters worse, Beltrán Nuño de Guzmán appeared in Mexico City to lend his evil genius for avarice and perfidy. He had just come up from Pánuco, where he had displayed a ruthlessness that was shocking even to a ruthless age. In Mexico City, and owing to the support of misguided friends in Spain, he was installed as president of the newly established *audiencia*, a high administrative and judicial body.

In a very real sense, King Charles and his advisors were responsible for the unhappy situation in New Spain. Or perhaps it might be better to say that three thousand miles of ocean made it impossible for Charles to keep abreast of affairs in his distraught colony. Each ship, whether from New Spain or the West Indies, brought conflicting accounts of developments which were already a month or two old by the time they reached his ears. Charles was also Holy Roman Emperor, and was therefore deeply involved in European affairs. How could Cortés and his rivals expect undivided attention from a monarch preoccupied with the spread of the Reformation and two wars against France? Yet, despite the disrupting influence of Martin Luther and the eight years of war against Francis I, Charles did find time to set in motion the machinery for governing his New World colonies.

Cortés's title of captain and governor general was of course impressive, but Charles, for reasons none too clear, was reluctant to invest the conqueror with the powers customarily associated with such positions. So Cristóbal de Tapia was sent to Mexico in 1521 to check on the activities of the Spaniards; but clever Cortés persuaded the royal agent to leave the country with no tangible results. Shortly thereafter the king sent four royal officials to take charge of financial matters. In theory, this may have been a reasonable move; but, as things turned out, the four officers of the crown devoted most of their efforts to stirring up trouble. And double trouble started in 1527 with the establishment of the first *audiencia,* or high court, under the presidency of Guzmán. Just before the judges of this body began their work, a royal visitor, Luis Ponce de León, disembarked at Veracruz to conduct a *residencia* (official investigation) of Cortés. But when this visitor suddenly died, some said that Cortés had made the necessary arrangements for his demise. This may have been little more than vicious gossip. It was Cortés's contention that Ponce de León died from a disease, "almost . . . a plague," which killed many others and was brought into the country by Ponce de León's own ships.

In the light of these developments, together with the fact that enemies were seizing his property, the conqueror decided to present his case, in person, before his Sacred Majesty. Nor was he alone in his decision. Some of his friends, both in Spain and in the New World, had long been advocating such a move. Moreover, the king's Royal Council of the Indies, an agency which had been set up in 1524 to assist in the management of New World affairs, was anxious to talk matters over with Cortés. Therefore, accompanied by a retinue of friends, Spanish and Indian, and well supplied with gold and silver, the "Captain from Castile" sailed for Spain late in 1527.

For the greater part of two years Cortés traveled up and down the peninsula interviewing and being interviewed. He was properly wined and dined, of course, and King Charles and his councilors listened attentively to what the distinguished citizen had to say. Lending an attentive ear was normal procedure. Of more immediate concern than court etiquette, especially from the point of view of Cortés, were rewards for his services. For example, how did the crown stand on his distinguished subject's request "that, if Your Majesty will grant me ten millions of revenue in your realms, and allow me to serve you in Spain, I shall consider it a great favor, even leaving behind all I possess." (It would seem from other evidence that Cortés was seeking a post of colonial minister!) The request was not granted. Very well. Would Charles and his councilors then see to it that Cortés's functions as captain general were strengthened? For the president and judges of the *audiencia* had presented him with an untenable fiat: " 'Under no condition are you to function as captain general without the advice, agreement, and consent of the president and judges.' " Charles may have recognized the serious administration confu-

sion that would arise from such an arrangement, but for reasons best known to himself he chose not to intercede in behalf of Cortés.

Yet, Charles was a grateful monarch. Cortés did receive his reward for winning half an empire for his sovereign: the Marquesado del Valle de Oaxaca, comprising an area of some 25,000 square miles and extending in a somewhat uneven pattern from Veracruz and Mexico City on the north to the Isthmus of Tehuantepec on the south. Twenty-three thousand Indian vassals, living in twenty-two Indian towns scattered over this vast area, were granted to Cortés as serfs; and the income from the lands adjoining the towns, with some restrictions, was given to him and his heirs in perpetuity. Also, he was confirmed in his position of captain general, a title which was little more than honorific. And in response to Cortés's long-standing request, the Marqués del Valle was commissioned to build a fleet for the purpose of making discoveries in the Pacific, or South Sea as it was then called. It was to be understood, however, that Cortés was not to infringe on the territorial rights of Guzmán! Moreover, the Marqués was instructed not to enter Mexico City until a new *audiencia* had been established; and the judges for this body, the second *audiencia,* were soon sent to their post with a long list of instructions. After a short interim they were under the presidency of Bishop Sebastián Ramírez de Fuenleal, who would become one of New Spain's ablest administrators.

In the spring of 1530, accompanied by a new wife, Juana de Zúñiga, daughter of a count and niece of a duke, Cortés and his entourage embarked for New Spain, arriving at Veracruz on July 15. (Catalina Suárez, Cortés's first wife, whom he had married in Cuba on the eve of the conquest of Mexico, died sometime prior to his sojourn in Spain.) The Marqués, despite the honors which had been conferred upon him, soon discovered that his enemies were still active. The judges of the first *audiencia* had not yet been replaced, and Guzmán had just departed with an army to begin a conquest on the west coast, from Michoacán to present-day Sonora, which was to result in the enslavement and murder of countless thousands of Indians. *Encomiendas,* or semifeudal grants, were taken from the partisans of Cortés, and the Indians were forbidden to hold intercourse with Cortés. And the *residencia,* the official but hardly impartial investigation, was still under way. In short, Cortés found himself in much the same position he had been in before his trip to Spain.

Despite this struggle for power on the Plain of Anáhuac, the conquerors found time to lead their armies into the far corners of the land. The Francisco de Montejos, father and son, spent a little more than thirteen years (1527–1541) in subjugating the Mayas of northern Yucatán. Montejo the elder, after serving Cortés for a few years, had struck out on his own. Early in 1527 he was commissioned to establish two cities and two forts on the peninsula, and he was to bear the titles of governor and *adelantado.* (Spanish conquerors everywhere cherished the title of *adelantado,* at least until the middle of the sixteenth century, for it carried special privileges ordinarily denied to governors.) He was also permitted a couple of additional titles and given a handsome grant of land on the peninsula. Of course, he would have to pay the expense of the enterprise, for the crown was not financing projects of this nature. After all, Yucatán was the king's land; therefore, Montejo was the recipient of a gift, a *merced.* In other words, the king and the grantee had entered into a quasi-contractual relationship, whereby Montejo had agreed to establish Spanish institutions on the peninsula in return for the privilege of exploiting a great part of the area. But, as so often was the case with such arrangements, Montejo lost a fortune and the lives of many of his friends in his venture. He finally turned the whole business over to his son, who did manage to subjugate great numbers of the Indians and to found the towns of Mérida and Salamanca.

Meanwhile the conquest spread, by sea and by land, to the southern and western parts of the present United States. In the same year in which Montejo had received his grant, Narváez, the gentlemen who some seven years earlier had lost an eye and the greater part of his army to Cortés, left Sanlúcar, Spain, with six hundred men in five ships "to conquer, occupy, and colonize 'the pro- vinces of Florida'" which then constituted the Gulf of Mexico coastal areas from the tip of the Florida penin- sula to, or a bit beyond, the Río Grande. Like Montejo, Narváez was to conduct his enterprise at his own expense and to be called governor and *adelantado.* Nearly all the members of the expedition perished, but among the sur- vivors was Alvar Núñez Cabeza de Vaca. More about him later.

The Seven Cities

Stories of fabulous people and places, together with the desire for wealth and the wish to spread the Christian faith, pulled soldier, sailor, and priest westward across the Pacific and northward along the Pacific Slope. Some- where to the north, so went one of the stories, was Amazon Island, inhabited entirely by women. Then there was the myth of the lost Seven Cities, a tale of ancient Spanish origin. Rumors now had it that the cities were north of the Plain of Anáhuac. Later when the frontier moved north in the sixteenth and seventeenth centuries, Spaniards crossed the land in all directions in search of people who lived under water, slept in trees, lived solely

The famous Spanish explorers, Marcos de Niza, Cabeza de Vaca, and Coronado and his men, walked or rode horseback for literally thousands of miles across such rugged terrain as this, surrounding the little town of Arizpe, founded in the eighteenth century in a valley of north- western Sonora.

from the odor of food, or had one foot. It was a credulous age, in both the New World and the Old.

South Sea projects, despite the fact that the crown had instructed Cortés to send expeditions across the great western ocean, were, for a time, of minor interest. Yet, as early as 1526, Cortés wrote Charles that he was gathering a fleet at Zacatula which he planned to send to "the Spiceries," so that "Your Majesty may obtain them as your own property." (Portugal was Spain's rival in the East Indies.) Then, in 1527, Cortés, in a first attempt to reach out across the Pacific, sent forth three ships westward, under the command of his cousin, Álvaro de Saavedra Cerón. Two of the vessels were lost. The third, Saavedra's flagship, reached the Moluccas. A year later, in 1529, the commander attempted to return to New Spain but died at sea. The ship then came about and put in at the Moluccas, where the crew was promptly locked in Portuguese prisons. A second project by both Cortés and Alvarado for the Far East never materialized. Northern adventures were more exciting.

During the decade of 1532–42 five major expeditions sought out the mysteries of the north. In 1532 Cortés sent a fleet as far north as the mouth of the Fuerte River. In the following year another expedition discovered Baja California and returned with an abundance of pearls. Here was a bejeweled Lorelei, who was to beckon many a pearl fisher to the peninsula. And perhaps this was the land of the Amazons. If it were, then surely it must be the "California" in *The Exploits of Esplandián,* a popular novel of chivalry. So the name California, or Californias, stuck; and Cortés himself, in 1535, made a voyage to the peninsula to spy out the land, finding pearls but no Amazons. Later Cortés said he heard of the Seven Cities; but was unable to go in search of them because of more pressing matters awaiting him in the capital. A viceroy, Don Antonio de Mendoza, had now taken charge of affairs in New Spain and was inclined to pull in the reins on the conquistadores.

Mendoza, first of a long list of viceroys who were to rule New Spain in the name of the crown for the greater part of three hundred years, was an accomplished diplomat and a staunch absolutist. Charles could not have found a more competent person to bring order out of chaos in New Spain. But the prestigious title of viceroy would not in itself enable Mendoza to do all those things expected of him, such as looking after the welfare of the Indians, managing the king's revenues, supervising trade, commerce, agriculture, mining, and matters relating to war, together with countless other tasks. Mendoza and his successors therefore were not only viceroys but also functioned as governors general and presidents of the *audiencia.* In a word, the viceroy was the Crown's *alter ego,* with some limitations; and of course it took a wise viceroy to know how to perform his duties in the best interests of the state. Mendoza was such a man, as the conquerors were soon to discover; and Guzmán was among the first to feel the iron hand of the viceroy when, in 1537, this scoundrel of New Galicia was sent off to Spain to answer for his crimes.

An important event had occurred near Culiacán about a year before the recall of Guzmán. A band of Spanish slave hunters came upon four survivors of the Narváez expedition: Cabeza de Vaca, Andrés Dorantes, Alonso del Castillo, and the Negro Estevanico, or "little Steve." For the greater part of six years they had been prisoners of coastal Indians in Texas before they were able to seize the opportunity to escape. The westward trek of Cabeza de Vaca and his companions, across the present states of Texas, New Mexico, perhaps southeastern Arizona, and thence down the Sonora Valley, was indeed an Odyssey. And it was certainly a traumatic experience for Guzmán's slavers. "So great was their surprise," writes Cabeza de Vaca, "that they could not find words to ask me anything."

It was also something of a surprise to Mendoza, for it was presumed that all of Narváez's men had perished. The viceroy, of course, was pleased to see the survivors, but he was especially delighted to hear some of the stories Cabeza de Vaca had to tell about the north country, about "permanent houses," "cotton blankets, hides and other things," and "many good turquoises." Could all these things come from the Seven Cities? Was there another Tenochtitlan, another empire as great as that of the Aztec? Perhaps. In any event, it would be a dereliction of duty not to investigate.

Thus was set in motion a wild scramble to reach the Seven Cities. Mendoza, Cortés, Alvarado, and even Hernando de Soto, just setting out on his famous expedition to Florida and the Mississippi, quarreled among themselves for prior rights to the Seven Cities. According to Spanish law, however, the colonies were the crown's personal domain; therefore, royal permission was required for any expedition that was designed to search for the fabulous cities. This, coupled with the hope that great riches would be discovered, led the authorities in Spain to commission the viceroy to fit out an expedition at state expense. The king had spoken. Cortés, Alvarado, and De Soto would have to tend to their own knitting. Cortés did send an expedition into the Gulf of California in 1539 under the command of Juan de Ulloa, but no great cities were found and Cortés returned to Spain in a huff. Mendoza was the undoing of Cortés but the captain did remain loyal to his sovereign. In 1541 Cortés accompanied Charles on a disastrous campaign in Algeria. Six years later, in 1547, the conqueror of Mexico died in Seville at the age of sixty-three, requesting that his body be sent to New Spain. As for Alvarado and De Soto, they had already been removed from the earthly scene. The conqueror of Guatemala had met his death in Jalisco during the Mixtón War, one of the most serious Indian uprisings of the sixteenth century. De Soto, as every schoolboy knows, had been buried in the Mississippi after he and his army had wandered over what is now the southern part of the United States, from Florida to Arkansas.

In the meantime, Mendoza had learned a great deal about the Seven Cities. In 1539 he had sent a reconnaissance expedition up the west coast under the leadership of Fray Marcos de Niza, together with Indian guides and the slave Estevanico, whom Mendoza had bought from the Cabeza de Vaca party. Somewhere north of Culiacán, the Negro was sent ahead with instructions to keep Marcos informed on the importance of the country and its people by sending back wooden crosses of varying size. Crosses soon appeared, one as high as a man. Good news indeed, for such a large cross must signify that Estevanico had reached the Seven Cities of Cíbola as they were soon to be called. It would seem that the slave was reporting on favorable conditions among the Pueblos of the upper Río Grande; yet word would soon pass down the trail that Estevanico had been killed by the Indians.

News of the Negro's death may have been the reason for the Franciscan's hasty retreat to Culiacán and thence to Mexico City; but far more important than the cause for his rapid return was what he had to say. He claimed that he had seen, from a distance, one of the Seven Cities, "larger than the city of Mexico . . . The doorways to the best houses have many decorations of turquoises, of which there is a great abundance." Now although the Indians may have told Marcos remarkable stories about Cíbola, the documents do not bear out his claim that he saw any of the cities. The viceroy, however, chose to accept the word of Marcos, and hastened to send a full-scale expedition to Cíbola under the command of his thirty-year-old friend Francisco Vásquez de Coronado, newly appointed governor of New Galicia.

Coronado, born in Spain, was the son of prosperous, aristocratic parents, but according to the custom of the times his elder brother inherited the entire estate. Francisco Vásquez would therefore have to try his hand in the New World, where many a young fellow had made a fortune. So why wait? Why not book passage with Viceroy Mendoza's fleet, which was about to sail for New Spain? The question was answered by a favorable reply from Mendoza, who not only saw to it that Coronado was aboard when the fleet began its voyage, but was also instrumental in placing his young friend advantageously in the colony. After serving the viceroy in a number of special missions, Coronado was elected to the *cabildo* in Mexico City and in 1538 was appointed governor of New Galicia. Two years later Mendoza commissioned him captain general of a well-provisioned army of about one thousand Spaniards and Indians, all of whom were instructed to march north and take possession of the Seven Cities. The story of the Coronado Expedition has been told and re-told, perhaps with the greatest historical depth and vividness by Herbert E. Bolton in *Coronado: Knight of Pueblo and Plains*. Suffice it to say here that Coronado's army left Compostela, capital of New Galicia, in February, 1540, and for the greater part of two years the captain general and his men were to search for a will-o'-the-wisp. Fray Marcos of course was in the party, for, presumably, he knew the road to Cíbola. But did he? The soldiers suspected that he did not, for somewhere in the San Pedro Valley of Arizona he lost his way. When the army did reach Cíbola, Marcos was probably embar-

rassed, for the Seven Cities turned out to be small Zuñi villages of red earth huts. Some say that a look at the tiny dwellings was good reason for the Franciscan's prompt return to Culiacán. Others maintain that Marcos gave up the venture because he was ill.

But Coronado was not ready to give up, especially when the Indians told him that a marvelous country, called Tusayán, lay northwest of Zuñi. The marvelous country turned out to be Hopi land; but a small detachment of Coronado's army did discover the Grand Canyon. Here, indeed, was a marvel, sans cities, sans houses, sans turquoises. The soldiers were impressed with the great depth of the gorge, but geological surveys were not their forte. Had they not come north to find another Mexico, another Aztec empire?

The quest continued, but in an easterly direction. In the winter of 1540–41 Coronado established headquarters among the Pueblos of the upper Rio Grande; and when spring came he led his men through parts of what are now Texas, Oklahoma, and western Kansas in search of fabulous Quivira, where, said an Indian guide, "the everyday dishes of even the poorest natives . . . were made of gold." But this was nothing more than a tall tale. The Spaniards found Quivira, near Wichita, but no gold. The native guide was promptly garrotted, and a disenchanted army returned to spend another winter with the Pueblos.

Nor were the spirits of the men raised by renewed misfortunes in the Río Grande Valley; and so in the spring of 1542 Coronado broke camp and began his march back down the trail to Culiacán and Mexico City. But all of his men were not present. Some had died, and a few had remained behind, including two friars, Juan de Padilla and Luis de Escalona, both of whom are said to have suffered martyrdom for their zeal. In a sense, Coronado himself became a martyr to a cause. The arduous demands of the enterprise had undermined his health and brought him to the brink of bankruptcy; moreover, he was accused of cruelty and incompetency. Most of the charges against him were dropped, yet some of his contemporaries did believe that he was a failure. In any event, he gave the world a lesson in geography and ethnography.

If Coronado were a failure, then certainly those who went by sea for similar reasons were failures too. Was Hernando de Alarcón's voyage up the Gulf with supplies for Coronado's army, a failure? Alarcón did not find the Seven Cities, nor did he find the army; but he did explore the lower Colorado River, and gave us our first written account of the Yuman tribes. Then, in 1542, under orders from Viceroy Mendoza, Juan Rodríguez Cabrillo sailed up the coast of California in search of the illusive Strait of Anián, which was said to join the Pacific with the Atlantic. This, too, was a fable, partly responsible for having pulled Cortés south on his Honduras expedition. Of course Cabrillo did not find the strait, but he added another chapter to discovery and exploration. Had he not died midway in the voyage, he might have contributed a great deal more to historical geography, for, from his death bed, he instructed Bartolomé Ferrelo to run the ships up the coast. Ferrelo followed instructions but was forced to turn back after reaching a point near the California-Oregon border. On April 14, 1543, after a voyage of 292 days, the ships reentered the home port of Navidad. Thus ended a remarkable twenty-four year epic of European expansion, beginning in April, 1519, when Cortés went ashore at Veracruz. Mendoza could now look at a map of New Spain and see a vice-royalty extending all the way from Guatemala to modern-day Kansas and Oregon. No need, then, to say that the search for the fabulous was fruitless. (Fifty years later, others would renew the search on the northern frontier; and in 1609–10 Juan de Oñate founded Santa Fe, New Mexico, which would be the capital of a vast region and the base for further exploration.)

COLONIAL INSTITUTIONS

These two dozen years will also be remembered as the period when Spaniards, good and bad, built the institutional foundations upon which the civilization of New Spain would stand for three hundred years. The institutions — political, economic, social — were, in the main, familiar ones that the Spaniards brought with them from Spain or from the West Indies. Yet time and environment, handmaidens of history, would remold familiar institutions or bring forth new ones. Old, re-molded, or new, the fact is, Spain's colonial system, for all its faults, was satisfactory for the time. It was Spain, of all the world powers, that was the first to codify its colonial laws: the Recapitulation of the Laws of the Indies not only served the purpose well for sound administration, but also became a pattern for colonial codes of other European nations. And Spain cut out the pattern so well and nailed it down so securely that her colonial rivals succeeded in tearing off only the fringes of her empire.

To govern her New World colonies, Spain established a vast number of agencies, but final authority rested with the crown. The colonies were the king's personal possession, and he created two governing bodies in Spain to assist him in managing the great American empire. One of these, the Council of the Indies, was founded in 1524 and became the supreme legislative and administrative agency for three hundred years, though it did lose some of its power in the eighteenth century. The other agency, the House of Trade, antedated the Council of the Indies and was to have jurisdiction over matters relating to trade, navigation, maritime law, and emigration and immigration. Both of these agencies served their nation well in colonial affairs. The same cannot be said of the rulers of Spain, with the exception of Charles I (1517–1555), Philip II (1555–1598), and Charles III (1759–1788). One might guess that Spain's Golden Age would have been something quite different without the strong hands of the two great Hapsburgs, Charles I and his son Philip II, and the Bourbon, Charles III, who reacted in a positive and reasonably successful manner to the liberal trends of his time. The Enlightenment was a fact, and Charles was prone to face facts.

The Government

The political institutions which Spain erected in the Americas were, in the main, not new. The viceregal system had been employed elsewhere, although not so effectively, and especially in New Spain, where the viceregal office attained fullest development. The incumbent of this high office functioned as captain general, governor, supervisor of the Royal Exchecquer, president of the *audiencia,* and was invested with considerable ecclesiastical power. Fortunately for Spain, during the critical years of the sixteenth century, the two men who exercised these powers were among the ablest of all of the viceroys of New Spain. It was Mendoza (1535–50) and Luis de Velasco (1550–64) who brought some order out of near chaos. Charles and Philip could have done no better had they themselves sat in the viceregal chair. Witness Mendoza's prompt and firm handling of Guzmán and Cortés: Guzmán was sent in disgrace to Spain, and stout Cortés chose to return to the homeland rather than fight a losing battle. Witness also Mendoza's execution of the king's laws. For example, in 1542 the king affixed his signature, "Yo, el Rey," (I, the King) to the New Laws, which, among other things, abolished all *encomiendas* and Indian chattel slavery. A New World priest, Bartolomé de las Casas, and an Old World jurist, Francisco de Victoria, were in a sense, the authors of these laws; but respect for cloth and robe, not to mention higher authorities, had its bounds, especially in the eyes of a feudal oligarchy that could see an end to prestige and wealth if the New Laws were enforced.

Mendoza himself, supported by Bishop Zumárraga, recognized that there were some injustices in the Laws. The viceroy and the bishop argued that the authorities back home had carried humanitarianism a bit too far. King and Council should know that many an *encomendero* was a loyal subject who had helped the crown win an empire. This was not an unfounded assertion, and carried enough weight to cause a reasonable modification of the New Laws, for had there been no concessions to the demands of the *encomenderos,* there might very well have been a civil war. The New Laws, however, were not completely emasculated. The provisions relating to a realistic administration of Indian affairs remained in force, and Mendoza's successor, Velasco, demonstrated that he, too, would see to it that the king's subjects obeyed the laws; so effective was Velasco, that he was called "Father of the Indians."

Of course neither Mendoza and Velasco, nor any of their successors, ruled with a completely free hand. In accordance with Spanish political theory, viceregal power, like that of all colonial officers, was spelled out in detail. Beginning in the seventeenth century, his term of office was limited to three years, a restriction not always observed in practice since the viceroys served at the will of the crown. Nor was the viceroy permitted to marry within his jurisdiction or to hold lands in the colony. He would also have to submit to a *residencia,* or a special investigation, at the end of his term. Then there was always the possibility of a *visitador* being sent from Spain to check on the activities of the viceroy and colonial administration in general. These were only a few of the controls exercised over viceregal power. In other words, it was absolutism at its best.

Of the many agencies of government the *audiencia* was among the more significant, and second only to the viceroy in power, an administrative body as well as a court of law, with authority to correspond directly with the home government. Thus it was another check on vice-regal power, despite the fact that the viceroy was president of the *audiencia* in Mexico City. The crown established two of these bodies in New Spain, one in Mexico City in 1527, the other in Guadalajara in 1548, each with its prescribed jurisdictional area. The judges were usually lawyers from Spain, appointed by the crown which also assigned *fiscales* (king's attorneys) to the *audiencias.* Working closely with these officials and the viceroy were the king's revenue gatherers, the *oficiales reales.* During the first half of the sixteenth century, the title of *adelantado* was also significant, for these individuals were in most respects directly under the authority of the home government.

Cities, towns, and villages, including Indian settlements, were the seats of numerous lesser political officers. Municipal councils, called either *cabildos* or *ayuntamientos,* were composed of *regidores,* or aldermen, who in the earlier period were elected by the townsmen; but in the later colonial period it was not uncommon for the crown to sell the office of *regidor.* Judges or *alcaldes,* police chiefs or *aguaciles,* and a staff of minor officials assisted the municipal councils. The provincial affairs were in the hands of such officers as the governor, the *alcalde mayor,* and the *corregidor.* In the earlier period the governors and *alcaldes mayores* functioned much on the same level. Each was the chief magistrate of an area of considerable size.

In the sixteenth and greater part of the seventeenth centuries the governors' jurisdictions extended over areas known as kingdoms. The Kingdom of New Galicia covered a vast region north and west of modern Colima and San Luis Potosí. In the later part of the sixteenth century, New Galicia was delimited on the north by a boundary which approximates a line drawn from Aco-poneta on the west to Mazapil on the east. The region north of the line then became the Kingdom of Nueva Vizcaya. Shortly thereafter, the Kingdom of Nuevo León was established to the east of the other two and extended to the Gulf of Mexico. During the late seventeenth century and throughout the eighteenth, several provinces, or *gobiernos,* replaced the older kingdoms, and their subdivisions, the *alcaldías mayores.* The chief magistrate continued to be the governor, who was also commander of military forces in his province. Indian villages were under his general supervision, especially on the distant frontiers, but he had to recognize the authority of *corregidores,* or Indian agents, who were responsible for the welfare of the natives everywhere. Yet it was the *corregidor* who often abused his power by exploiting the Indians for his own personal gain.

The pillar of Mexican history until the latter part of the nineteenth century was the Indian; in some respects he still is. During the colonial period he was exploited by his Spanish conquerors, but not so ruthlessly as is commonly believed. Cortés, Alvarado, and Guzmán killed tens of thousands of natives, and it is true that Guzmán was the worst of murderers. It is also true, however, that the Spanish records do not bear out the claims that the best Indian was a dead Indian. The law was very clear that the Indians were wards of the crown and rational human beings, which meant that it would be a serious offense to mistreat them. There were provisions whereby the native could be enslaved for rebellion or apostasy, but aside from this, his person and property were to be respected. If anyone questioned the king's desire to protect the interests of his wards, then let him read the New Laws. There were other laws also, which freed the Indian from the horrors of the Inquisition; and it was well known that the king would enforce the edict forbidding Spaniards to live in Indian villages — unprincipled Spaniards could cause a lot of trouble by quartering themselves among the natives. And if a Spaniard or anyone else, including a native chieftain, got into trouble with the Indians he might very well be hauled before the judges of the General Indian Court in Mexico City.

It would be well at this point to examine two Spanish institutions, the *repartimiento* and the *encomienda,* each created by law to exploit the Indian. The *repartimiento* was a system for allotting Indian workers to the Spaniards for specific jobs, with the provision that the Indian was to be paid for his labor. Such a system, of course, was open to abuse, and abuse there was. Lesley B. Simpson, an authority on both institutions, says that "The excesses committed under the unrestricted *repartimiento* were probably one determinant in the decline of [Indian] population." Nor, according to Simpson, were the Indians any better off with the *encomienda,* a semifeudal institution whereby the conqueror was empowered to collect tribute from the natives while obligated to protect and Christianize them. Here, too, the door was open to grave excesses, so much so that the crown did sign and seal the New Laws, consisting of fifty-four articles, twenty-three of which were in the nature of a bill of rights for the Indian. According to Article 10, the Indians were free persons and vassals of the crown. This was not a problem to anyone, for it was generally understood that the Indians were vassals and free persons. But the other articles, especially 26, 27, 31, and 35, came very near bringing about a civil war because here were laws that no self-respecting *encomendero* could tolerate. Articles 26 and 27 abolished Indian slavery; Article 31 prohibited institutions, public servants, and the clergy from holding *encomiendas;* and Article 35, which aroused the greatest amount of opposition, prohibited the creation of any new *encomiendas* and provided that all *encomiendas* would escheat to the crown upon the death of the *encomenderos.*

The enforcement of such measures would have struck at the very roots of the colonial economy. But fortunately for the *encomendero,* the conquerors could depend on such staunch supporters as Viceroy Mendoza and bishops Fuenleal and Zumárraga. Why not grant "the *encomiendas* in perpetuity. . . . And let the conquerors have preference," Zumárraga asked? "The Spanish vassals are so oppressed," says the bishop, "that they dare not speak. . . . This would not be true if they held the Indians in perpetuity, for they would love them and relieve them of work in order to prevent their running away, and for the sake of preserving [the heritage of] their children." Zumárraga's plea for the rights of the *encomendero,* together with the wise administration of Mendoza, did soften the crown's stand on the strict enforcement of Indian labor laws; but the kings never approved of granting *encomiendas* in perpetuity. Restriction of succession to two lives was as far as the crown would go, a restriction which served to bring about a rift between the descendants of the first families and the latecomers.

The Church

Of the many institutions introduced into the New World by Spain, none was more important than the Catholic Church. It was the crown's right hand, and had been since the late fifteenth and early sixteenth centuries when a series of papal grants established a close church-state relationship, known as the *real patronato,* or right of royal patronage, which, among other things, permitted the monarchs to collect tithes, to present candidates for ecclesiastical offices, to build or supervise the construction of churches and monasteries, and to authorize missionary enterprises. In brief, the crown's rights in church affairs extended to virtually all functions except matters of dogma and doctrine; and these rights were exercised by the crown, the Council of the Indies, and in lesser matters by the high-ranking political officials in the colonies. But these were rights which did not divest the priests of their long-established privileges, or *fueros,* one of the most important of which was that they answered only to the clerical courts for any misdeed.

The Catholic Church began its work in Mexico on the day fathers Olmedo and Díaz went ashore with Cortés on the island of Cozumel. Shortly after the fall of Tenochtitlan, three Flemish Franciscans appeared in New Spain, but it was not until 1523 that twelve Spanish Franciscans, known in Mexican history as the Twelve Apostles, assumed the task of founding the Mexican church. Four years later, in 1527, the oldest Mexican see was established at Tlaxcala and assigned to a Dominican, Julian Garcés. A second bishopric was founded at Mexico City in 1530 and placed under the administration of the Franciscan, Juan de Zumárraga, who was later to become Mexico's first archbishop. By the middle of the sixteenth century, seven bishops administered church affairs in New Spain, and before the end of the colonial period every major city had become the seat of a bishopric.

The regulars, or religious orders — Franciscans, Dominicans, Augustinians, Jesuits, and several others, were among the first of the priesthood to arrive in New Spain, although the Jesuits did not reach Mexico until 1572. The secular or diocesan clergy were on the scene a little later to establish parishes and meet the needs of the more settled areas. Each order abided by its own rules, but all were devoted to the propagation of the faith, either as missionaries or teachers. Some became professors at the University of Mexico, which opened in 1553. Some, like the Franciscans and Jesuits, established schools for the instruction of Indians in the Spanish language and the Christian doctrine, or founded preparatory schools for university studies. Others, like the hospital orders of San Juan de Díos and Nuestra Señora de Belem, administered hospitals, no less than seventy of which were built during the colonial period. Great numbers of convents for nuns were also erected, and there were hundreds of other church edifices, such as monasteries, churches, and missions. No one knows how many thousand priests and nuns lived in these establishments, but it has been estimated that in the eighteenth century there were at least five thousand seculars and perhaps eight thousand regulars in New Spain.

The regulars were not only teachers and administrators of hospitals and other social services, but were also the founders of the mission system that followed the course of empire in the Americas. In New Spain, Franciscans, Jesuits, and Dominicans built hundreds of missions, most of which were on the northern frontiers; and by the closing years of the eighteenth century, great mission chains stretched across Texas, New Mexico, Arizona, and California. The Franciscans were the first of the orders to carry the institution northward, and were to reach the present state of Chihuahua during the 1570's. Two decades later they accompanied the Spanish army to New Mexico; but not until the middle of the eighteenth century were they firmly established in Texas. They were excluded from the northwestern area — modern Baja California, Sinaloa, Sonora, and southern Arizona. This was to be Jesuit land until 1767, when the Jesuits were expelled, not only from New Spain but from all of the Spanish empire. The Franciscans then assumed the missionary enterprise in the northwestern region, though for a time the Dominicans did take charge of several missions in northern Baja California.

Although the first duty of the missionary was to propagate the faith, he was never to overlook the fact that he was also one of the crown's principal economic and political agents. It was the missionary who introduced European crops to the frontier, taught the Indians the most advanced methods of agriculture and animal husbandry, and supplied *presidios,* or garrisons, with products of the mission fields and shops. The missionary often served also as frontier diplomat and ambassador. By processes of acculturation, mission

Indians were brought within the sphere of the Spanish political system, and the archives are full of missionary reports on ways and means of dealing with rival European powers.

Church and state were also partners in the functions of the Inquisition, an institution which dates from the thirteenth century but was not established in Spain until the latter part of the fifteenth century by the Catholic Kings, Isabella and Ferdinand. Its duties were assigned to an inquisitorial tribunal, officially called the Holy Office. It was extended to the New World in 1569 but did not reach Mexico until 1574, prior to which time bishops commonly functioned as inquisitorial officers.

The Inquisition was not created solely for the purpose of rooting out heresy, but also for political purposes. Fifteenth-century Spain was a country of diverse cultural groups; therefore, according to the political philosophy of the Catholic Kings, the Holy Office would be an effective instrument of royal power. A people of one religion would be easier to manage than a nation of "Old" and "New" Christians, Jews, and Moors. With the rise of Protestantism and its threat to the divine right of sovereigns, the Holy Office played an even more important role in the scheme of things. It was a role which occasioned the destruction of vast numbers of lives by the dread *auto de fé,* a procedure of atonement leading to execution, usually by burning under the direction of civil authorities. Yet death was not always the fate of those who ran afoul of the tribunal: one might be forced to atone for his sins by various forms of penance, or the tribunal might settle the case by confiscating the sinner's property. In any event, irrespective of the nature of the charges, all the accused were submitted to secret procedures as well as the horrors of torture. The tribunal's procedures and practices, however, were somewhat limited in severity in the Americas, and the Indians were exempt from the jurisdiction of the Holy Office. Thus, during the two hundred and seventy-seven years of the Inquisition in Mexico, no more than fifty lives were lost at the stake.

Censorship was also within the jurisdiction of the Holy Office. Books by the thousands, especially during the intellectual awakening of the eighteenth century, were prohibited or expurgated because new ideas might jeopardize the very foundations of the empire. Yet a courageous few defied the Holy Office by reading "profane" and "vulgar" books that threatened the absolutism of the crown and the authoritarianism of the church.

The church in Mexico had a powerful role also in economic affairs. In the course of time the church as a corporation came to possess vast estates, and in some cases individual clerics, vicars, and high church officials were the owners of considerable wealth in worldly goods. The mendicant orders — notably the Franciscans — adhered steadfastly to the vow of poverty. On the other hand, the Jesuits, whose rule did not forbid economic activity, "soon had the largest flocks of sheep, the finest sugar plantations, and the best-managed estates." Such situations were not only the rewards of business acumen

but also material witness of grateful Indians and pious parishioners; moreover, the church served as the colony's banker. In a word, the church was a formidable economic institution, and the question has been raised as to whether or not its superior position in this respect was economically sound. By the end of the colonial period half of all landed wealth was in the hands of the church, and under the laws of mortmain it was legally impossible to dispose of the church's property. It would also seem that many of the landed estates of the church were allowed to remain unproductive.

Economic Life

The economic life of New Spain cannot of course be told solely in terms of church history. Spain, like other nations of the day, held mercantilist views: colonies were founded for the benefit of the mother country. A favorable balance of trade was to be maintained, and for purposes of regulation, commerce was restricted to a few ports in Spain and the New World. Until the latter part of the eighteenth century, when Spain embarked on programs of economic and political reform, Veracruz and Acapulco were the only officially recognized ports of trade in New Spain. And, as a further effort to exercise a trade monopoly, intercolonial trade was forbidden, as were any manufactured or agricultural products competing in the marketplace with those of Spain. Added to all this were royal monopolies of tobacco, mercury, playing cards, and a host of other items, together with the crown's claim to one-fifth of all the colonies' precious wealth, such as gold, silver, and gems. Thus both monarch and Iberian merchant profited at the expense of the colonial; but it was always the crown that stood to get the larger share of the wealth, for the tax structure of the mercantilist system was such that no one could evade the revenue gatherer. And, as so often happens, exorbitant taxes led to unrest and revolution. The mercantilist view of economics, with its restrictions and taxes, was to be one of the major causes of the Mexican struggle for independence during the opening years of the nineteenth century.

Trade and travel to and from the New World fell within the jurisdiction of the *Casa de Contratación,* or House of Trade, a royal council residing at Seville. A few lesser agencies, in both Spain and New Spain, assisted the council in its activities, and all legal traffic was carried by fleets, or *flotas.* Two fleets a year, of some forty to seventy ships, sailed from Spain, one destined for Veracruz, the other for a harbor on the Panamanian coast. At a prearranged time, the fleet assembled at Havana for the return voyage.

Acapulco, on the West Coast of New Spain, was also a center of considerable trans-ocean trade. Each year, beginning in 1565 and continuing until 1815, at least one and sometimes two or three galleons made voyages between Acapulco and Manila. The westbound ships were laden with Mexican and Peruvian pesos to purchase silks, spices, and other Oriental goods. Many a man, in Manila and in New Spain, made a fortune from the famous Manila Galleon trade — but it was dangerous business. The long voyage, with all the navigational hazards of the sea, together with piratical raids off the California coast, was indeed a costly enterprise for ship and crew. Costly, too, were the sharp and corrupt practices of not a few who engaged in the trade.

Far more important to the economic life of New Spain than trade were the products of land, mill, and shop. In 1548–49 prospectors discovered great veins of silver at Zacatecas and Guanajuato, whose mines were to pour millions of pesos into the royal coffers and the bank accounts of privileged Spaniards. A few of the native entrepreneurs, including some churchmen, also made fortunes from the mines, but the Indian and *mestizo* miner worked long hours for the rewards of poverty. The mills — textile and sugar — were even less desirable for the worker. Not only were wages exceedingly low, but working conditions were intolerable. Nor was life much better in the fields and on the ranches. The few profited at the expense of the many, and Spanish law prohibited the cultivation of any plant or crop that competed with Spain's products of the soil. For example, colonials were enjoined from growing grapes or cultivating mulberry trees, for this would lead to serious competition in the wine and silk markets; but there were no restrictions on grains or livestock. Maize was everywhere, and to a great extent has remained the life blood of Mexico; and European grains introduced early in the conquest, were grown rather widely. Of course the *hacendado* operated the choice farms and ranches, but tens of thousands of Mexican villagers continued to till their small fields and harvest their native crops as they had been doing long before the arrival of the Spaniards.

Horses and cattle, neither of which existed in the Americas before the arrival of the Spaniards, followed the course of empire, as did other European livestock. Sheep runs and cattle ranches spread far and wide, and as early as the latter part of the sixteenth century it was not uncommon for a cattle baron in the northern regions of New Spain to own 150,000 head. The cowboy, or *vaquero,* with his stolen horse, old saddle, and lance, became a part of the landscape. Three hundred years later "his rodeo, saddle, stirrups (Andalusian in origin), huge spurs, apparel, and even, in all likelihood, character traits" became a part of the landscape of Texas.

The Military Establishment

The soldier, too, was a part of the Mexican landscape, though much is yet to be learned about the military establishment. It was not until the middle of the eighteenth century when England and France posed a threat to Spain's mainland colonies that anything like an organized army appeared in New Spain. Prior to this time, in the sixteenth and seventeenth centuries, Spain's principal defense problems in the New World was how to keep her sea lanes open and her colonial coasts protected against piratical raids. This was a job for her fleets and harbor fortifications. A coast guard was active in the Caribbean, and the Fort of San Juan de Ulúa stood watch over Veracruz while on the west coast, at Acapulco, the guns of Fort San Diego made it quite clear that hostile ships entered at their own risk.

Another military institution of some importance was the presidio, a garrison usually surrounded by walls from which protruded one or two small cannons. The presidio was fundamentally a frontier institution which made its initial appearance in New Spain to protect the silver trains as they made their way from Zacatecas and Guanajuato to Mexico City. The presidio then moved northward with miner, missionary, and rancher, so that by the end of the eighteenth century one chain of garrisons stretched from central Texas to southern Arizona, another from San Francisco to San Diego. The normal complement of a presidio was fifty men under the command of a captain, whose immediate superior was the provincial governor — also a commissioned officer.

Indian depredations engaged the major share of the garrison's attention, but, beginning in the closing years of the seventeenth century and continuing for a hundred years thereafter, the authorities in Spain and Mexico City had reasons to prepare the northern presidios as bastions against the territorial ambitions of France, England and Russia. On the east, the designs of France and England, coupled with the viceroy's plans to protect the frontier against Indian uprisings, led to a reorganization of the cordon of presidios extending from Texas to Arizona. On the west, Russia posed a threat to California which caused Spain, in 1769, to send soldiers and missionaries from Baja California to establish settlements at San Diego and Monterey; and, in 1775–76, Captain Juan Bautista de Anza followed suit by leading a band of colonists from Tubac, Arizona, to San Francisco. Then, to provide adequate machinery to govern the vast northern regions of New Spain, Charles III, in 1776, created a commandancy-general, known as the Interior Provinces and comprising the present border states of the United States and Mexico.

The Social Aspects

It would be well at this point to examine, briefly, the principal elements in the society of New Spain, a society that was feudal in nature. The *peninsular,* or native-born Spaniard, stood at the top of the social ladder and usually held the important offices of state and church. The *criollo,* or creole, was one born in the New World of European parents, and, with rare exceptions, held the lesser offices of state, though he might have been a man of means — landlord, mill owner, cattle baron, mine owner. Below the creole in the social hierarchy was the *mestizo,* an offspring of Spanish and Indian parents. He could expect to make a meager living as a shopkeeper, ranch hand, or soldier. If he were fortunate he might enter one of the religious orders or serve as a secular priest in some small parish. In any event, his life was far better than that of the Negro, who was most likely a slave. And despite the paternal policies of the crown, Indians might pass much of their lives

A strong link in the chain of Jesuit missions was established in the seventeenth century at Caborca, Sonora, by Father Eusebio Kino. Although it was in a state of disrepair until the 1960's, the mission has now been restored by interested citizens working through the Caborca Club de Leones (Lions Club).

as slaves. At any rate, whatever his legal status may have been, it was the Indian who carried labor's burden. From these several cultural and ethnic groups arose numerous admixtures of lower castes — *léperos, pelados, lobos,* and so on.

Life in New Spain was not necessarily a dreary one, as might be expected of a closed society. Spaniards, Indians, and Negroes, then and now, have a remarkable capacity for enjoying the simple pleasures of life. Gambling was perhaps the leading amusement, if not a vice, that caused the government to prohibit the importation of playing cards, but without success. Promiscuity, drinking of alcoholic beverages, and smoking were widespread; and bullfights, cockfights, horsemanship, dancing, singing, and similar activities were common. Of course there was always the *fiesta* for church and civil holidays; and the wealthy displayed their elegance by lavish weddings and balls, where the ladies vied with one another in their bejeweled costumes.

Formal education was for the fortunate few, and the schools at all levels were in the hands of the church. The first school for Indian boys was founded in Mexico City in 1536, and the frontier mission, at times, served as a center of instruction in vocational subjects. Private tutors were often employed by the well-to-do, and it was not uncommon for the rich to send their boys to Europe for higher education. But after 1551, when Charles V decreed the establishment of the Royal University at Mexico City, one could have remained in the colony for his college education, if he were willing to forgo better offerings at the well-established European universities. Or he might prepare himself for higher education at the College of San Nicolás at Valladolid, the beautiful city which now goes by the name of Morelia. If he wished to enter the clergy, he might prepare himself at one or more of these institutions, then complete his studies in a seminary or a college. But formal education, at all levels, was restricted to the male population. A woman might learn to read and write, but her life was circumscribed by the demands of family and church.

Formal education was indeed limited to the few, but it is a misconception to believe that the colonial Mexican cared little about books or literature in general. True, the strict censorship of the press, a function of the church, as mentioned earlier, did make it quite difficult for those with literary appetites. Censors, however, have never been completely successful in their assignments, though they usually create a stultifying intellectual climate. So it was in New Spain. A royal decree of 1531 prohibited the importation of books of romance and profane histories, or in other words, any book which the censors deemed might corrupt the morals of the people — Indian, creole or Spaniard. Yet such books did appear on the shelves of many a private library, especially during the closing years of the colonial period.

The colonials themselves wrote a book now and then, but it usually dealt with a religious subject. The authors in most cases were priests, who sometimes turned from tracts on theology to the writing of grammars and history. And everybody was a poet, but, with

Historically a college town and a center of Mexico's early struggle for independence, Morelia, capital of the state of Michoacán, was earlier known as Valladolid. In the foreground is the University of Michoacán, originally the College of San Nicolás, active today as in colonial times when Father Miguel Hidalgo, early revolutionary leader, was first a student and later the rector. In the background is a church built by the Jesuits in the seventeenth century, now used as the University library.

two notable exceptions, the Mexican bard of the colonial period was not a great writer. The exceptions were Juan Ruiz de Alarcón (ca. 1581–1639) and Sor Juana Inés de la Cruz (1651–1695). Ruiz de Alcarón, perhaps better known as a playwright than a poet, went off to Spain as a young man to study at the University of Salamanca, and since he spent the greater part of his life on the peninsula he is often identified with that remarkble group of writers of the Golden Age. Sor Juana, who spent most of her short life in a convent, is recognized as one of the most accomplished poets in the Spanish language. It is very doubtful, as some have said, that she entered a convent to escape the pangs of unrequited love. But whatever the reason may have been for her choice of the cloistered life, the fact remains that she was the one bright star in the literary firmament of seventeenth-century New Spain. Not until the closing years of the eighteenth century did the mind and spirit of the colony cast off the shrouds of decadence and monotony. The luster of the Enlightenment appeared, both in Europe and America. The colonial period in the New World was drawing to a close. Fifteen politically independent nations would soon replace Spain's American empire. New names would appear on the map: "Mexico" would replace "New Spain."

THE WINNING OF INDEPENDENCE

The causes for the change in political existence arose from the very nature of the Spanish colonial system. An economic and political structure had been founded on the false assumption that what was good for the crown and the oligarchs was good for the empire. Nor had the church kept abreast of history. Archbishops and bishops adhered to medieval concepts of religion and defended the status quo. Corruption was widespread, in both church and state; and the caste system ran counter to man's innate quest for freedom, a quest which had recently established an independent nation in Anglo-America and unleashed forces of violence in France. Creoles listened to the words of Rousseau, Montesquieu, and Danton, and hastened to emulate the founders of the Republic of the United States.

These winds of revolution from the east and the north, swirling with long-standing grievances at home, swept across Spanish America during the second decade of the nineteenth century. And a hurricane blew in from Spain, in 1808, when Napoleon's army unseated the Spanish king and placed Joseph Bonaparte, the emperor's brother, on the throne. All Spain rose in protest. Juntas were hastily formed in Spain and in the colonies to govern until the Spanish king, Ferdinand VII, was restored.

Governing bodies in Mexico City, learning that Joseph demanded loyalty to his regime, were unable to agree on the proper course of action. Viceroy José de Iturrigaray temporized, hoping that a dilatory policy would redound to his advantage. The creoles in the *ayuntamiento,* or town council, proposed loyalty to Ferdinand, but with the understanding that sovereignty should reside in the governing bodies in New Spain. The *audiencia,* composed of peninsulars, said that the town council was presumptuous and revolutionary in its definition of sovereignty.

For the better part of two years the principal agents of government in Mexico City quarreled among themselves, juntas rose and fell, and Iturrigaray was forced out of office by the peninsulars. He was replaced as viceroy by a seventy-nine-year-old general, Pedro de Garibay, who was unable to please anybody. Archbishop Lizana y Beaumont was then placed in the vice-regal seat, and, he too could not govern effectively. Then on September 14, 1810, Francisco Javier Venegas arrived in Mexico City to assume the duties of the high but no longer potent office. Two days later, in the village of Dolores, located some one hundred and fifty miles north of the capital, Father Miguel Hidalgo y Costilla raised the battle cry of independence, the *Grito de Dolores* — "Long live the Virgin of Guadalupe, death to the Gachupines."

Born in the province of Guanajuato in 1753 of creole stock, Hidalgo spent his early youth on a large estate managed by his father. These were the years — so it is said — when the seeds of revolution were planted in his mind, for he was critical of a government that permitted abuses of agricultural workers. This may be true. It may also be true that his student life at the College of San Nicolás, which he entered at the age of fourteen, caused him to question the Spanish colonial system. (The college town itself — modern Morelia — was to be a center of early revolutionary activities.) Further studies as an outstanding scholar at the Royal University in Mexico City, coupled with later experiences as rector of San Nicolás, probably sharpened his critical spirit. Perhaps he was overly critical of the church, especially since he himself was a clergyman. In any event, he was to have his first brush with the Holy Office while serving as rector. His concept of academic freedom was a bit too advanced for the inquisitors, a situation which may have brought about his resignation from the college.

He was now to serve for some twenty years as a priest in small towns, but continued to vex the Holy Office with his unorthodox views. In 1803 he succeeded his brother as curate of Dolores, and for the greater part of the following seven years he devoted his time to the vocational welfare of his parish, which was predominantly Indian. There was also time for reading, especially the works of French authors. Time, too, for exchanging ideas with a restless group of conspirators at nearby San Miguel el Grande and Querétaro. The

most notable of the group were captains Ignacio Allende and Juan Aldama, both of whom contributed their own share of the battle cry raised at Dolores.

The *grito* had been in the making for several months at Querétaro. Hidalgo corresponded with the town's conspirators, and on occasion he attended their meetings. A day in December, 1810, was finally set for the uprising against Spanish rule; but as so often happens to the most closely guarded political secrets, the treasonable plans of the conspirators reached the ears of the authorities. The instrument in this case for revealing the secret was the *alcalde* of Querétaro, Juan Ochoa, whose loyalty to the crown led to the arrest at Querétaro of a few lesser figures among the conspirators. Allende and Aldama escaped the arm of the law, as did the heroine in the story, Josefa, wife of Corregidor Miguel Domínguez. Her sympathies were with the revolutionaries, and upon learning that instructions had been made for the arrests, she promptly informed Aldama at San Miguel about the turn of events at Querétaro. Aldama, Mexico's Paul Revere, then made his famous midnight ride of fifty miles to warn Hidalgo that the Spaniards were coming. There was no other choice but to strike immediately. The bell was rung, the *grito* was sounded, and on the morning of September 16, Hidalgo marched out of Dolores at the head of a poorly equipped army of several thousand Indians. His immediate objective was Guanajuato, a rich mining town and the capital of the province.

Ten Years of War

The Hidalgo revolt was to run its course by January, 1811, but that was time enough to unleash a ten-years war that resulted in the political independence of Mexico. The first major battle was at Guanajuato, which Hidalgo's army reached by September 28. The Spanish commander and his greatly outnumbered army, together with many rich Spanish families, took refuge in the *Alhóndiga de Granaditas,* a large and substantially built granary, which soon fell to the rebels, who massacred the occupants. After virtually destroying the town by looting, the insurgents, fearful of an approaching Spanish brigade, marched south, planning to invade Mexico City. But Viceroy Venegas's troops, under the command of General Torcuato Trujillo, checked the advance of Hidalgo's forces on October 30 at Monte de las Cruces, a point not far from the capital. Had Hidalgo followed the advice of Allende to push on to Mexico City after the battle, a significant victory might have been won. Trujillo's army had retreated in some confusion, and since there was considerable unrest in Mexico City, it is only reasonable to assume that the insurgents might have met with some successes in the Valley of Mexico. But Hidalgo chose to withdraw to Guadalajara, and in the process was harassed by some six thousand loyalist troops under the command of General Félix María Calleja.

Meantime the insurrection had spread to northern and southern Mexico. In the north, guerrilla forces under Rafael Iriarte and Mariano Jiménez — the latter sent northward by Hidalgo — were defeating the *gachupines*. But in the south, the agents of Hidalgo were experiencing varying degrees of success and failure. Insurgents in Oaxaca were roundly defeated, while in the hills above Acapulco, Father José María Morelos was recruiting an army which in a few months would pose a real threat to the king's men.

Hidalgo had established his headquarters in Guadalajara and was flooding the land with endless decrees which liberated slaves, abolished tribute, provided lands for the Indians, and so on. This was all very well, but Hidalgo should have devoted his energies to military matters, at least for the moment, because Calleja's well-trained army was thundering at the gates. Allende was aware of the seriousness of the situation and had come to distrust the priest's cavalier manner of dealing with troops and battle plans, for an unorganized mob of eighty thousand might easily be defeated by Calleja's army of six thousand disciplined professionals. That is precisely what happened when Hidalgo, on January 17, 1811, chose to fight it out close by the bridge of Calderón on the banks of the Lerma, a small river near Guadalajara. The forces of Hidalgo held their position momentarily, but then an ammunition wagon caught fire, causing the insurgent army to flee in great disorder as the flames spread rapidly through the grass.

A small portion of the insurgent forces, including Hidalgo, Allende, and Aldama, then made their way northward, intending to reach the United States; but, on March 21 in the vicinity of Monclova one of their own officers, Ignacio Elizondo, successfully turned his troops against the unsuspecting forces of Hidalgo. Four of the leaders, among them Jiménez, were captured and promptly lodged in jail at Chihuahua City. A military court found them guilty of treason, and on June 26, Aldama, Allende, and Jiménez were executed by a firing squad. On July 30 Hidalgo met a like fate, the delay occasioned by the necessity of bringing the priest before the tribunal of the Holy Office, which found him guilty of the highest of crimes against church doctrine. This he denied: "In all my life I have never parted from the Catholic doctrine, and if I have erred in something it was the result of ignorance." But there was no appeal from the Holy Office's decision. Hidalgo was defrocked and promptly shot. Then, as a gruesome warning to those who dared to dispute the king's authority, the priest's head, along with those of Allende, Aldama, and Jiménez, was sent to Guanajuato, where all heads could be publicly viewed in four cages, one hanging from each of the high corners of the *alhóndiga*.

Hidalgo was dead, but he and his companions were not alone in the struggle against Spanish officialdom, whether in America or in Spain. Word would soon reach New Spain that the mother country itself was in the throes of a rebellion, a rebellion that would bring forth the Constitution of 1812, a charter that "became the beacon of Spanish and southern European liberalism for half a century." For the moment this brought some semblance of peace and order to the colonies,

— *Courtesy Pan American Union*

Miguel Hidalgo y Costilla, a scholarly priest born in 1753, was an early and vigorous protagonist of Mexico's struggle for independence from Spain.

since Spain would now be a constitutional monarchy; moreover, the document guaranteed equal rights to *peninsular* and colonial alike. In recognition of this happy turn of events, the Mexicans changed the name of the Plaza Mayor, or Zócalo, to the Plaza de la Constitución, and replaced the word *"real"* with *"nacional"* on the public buildings. Some now said the fire of rebellion had burned out. True, but embers glowed in the ashes, hot enough to cause a conflagration that, within ten years, would consume the king's authority in New Spain. In 1814, the king himself fanned the embers by repudiating the Constitution of 1812 and restoring absolutism.

Among the several insurgents who vexed the Spanish authorities for the four years following the death of Hidalgo, none was more successful than the *mestizo* priest, José Morelos y Pavón who, some say, was a creole. Like Hidalgo, he had received much of his education at the College of San Nicolás; but unlike the priest of Dolores, Morelos possessed a keen sense of political and social realities. He did not consider himself a defender of the Indians, nor, as some have said of Hidalgo, did he struggle solely for creole autonomy. Morelos was a revolutionary marked by strong overtones of socialism. In January, 1814, he decreed that Mexicans must cease calling themselves "Indian, Mestizo, Mulato, and that they all be known as Americans." He also advocated agrarian reform, and it was he who, in October, 1814, gave Mexico its first charter of liberty, the Constitution of Apatzingán. The document, of course, had little effect beyond the lines of Morelos's army, but it did express the republican aspirations of the majority of the insurgents, and ten years later many of these aspirations would be written into the well-known Constitution of 1824.

The viceroy ordered the destruction of all copies of the Constitution of Apatzingán and redoubled his efforts to defeat the forces of Morelos. Defeated they were, fourteen months after the promulgation of the document. Perhaps the struggle would have continued for a longer period had Morelos not permitted himself to be captured so that his followers could escape. In any event, like Hidalgo, he was condemned by the Inquisition, and on December 22, 1815, he was shot at San Cristóbal, a small village on the outskirts of Mexico City.

Once again the flames of rebellion had been quenched, but the embers still glowed on the high mountains and in the deep canyons in central Mexico. Insurgents such as Vicente Guerrero, Francisco X. Mina, Félix Fernández — more commonly known as Guadalupe Victoria —, Nicolás Bravo, and others led bands of *guerrilleros* who harassed the viceroy's army for the greater part of six years. Guerrero, of mixed Indian, Negro, and Spanish blood, had been a close friend of Morelos, and was to become Mexico's second president. Mina, a native of Spain, where he had been engaged in liberal uprisings against King Ferdinand, appeared in northwestern Mexico in 1817 with a small army of adventurers bent on aiding in the struggle against the mother country. He marched inland, won a few victories, but was captured and shot on November 11, 1817, while Victoria and Bravo continued to roam the countryside and, in time, would become Mexico's first president and vice-president, respectively.

By January, 1818, the revolution had reached low ebb. The new viceroy, Juan Ruiz de Apodaca, reported that he did not need any additional troops, and was confident that peace would reign again. It did, at least for nearly three years. And peace might have settled on the land for an even longer period had it not been for a renewed struggle in Spain for liberalism and the restoration of the Constitution of 1812. Spanish liberalism, aided and abetted by masonic lodges, had strong support in high places in the army; and in January, 1820, Rafael Riego, commanding an Austrian battalion, and Colonel Antonio Quiroga of the Royal Regiment turned their troops against the authority of the crown and proclaimed the restoration of the constitution. Aside from recognizing the serious threat of the Riego-Quiroga rebellion, Ferdinand may also have seen the irony of the affair, for the mutinous troops were on the point of embarking for Buenos Aires, the seat of another revolution which was moving rapidly in the direction of political independence. But it may have been somewhat more than ironical when Ferdinand learned that the leadership of the church in Mexico — and elsewhere — preferred to follow a course of counterrebellion rather than swear allegiance to a liberal government which abolished the Inquisition, dissolved monastic

orders, and rewarded monks who renounced their vows. For the moment the historic union of church and state was severed, a situation that strengthened the position of the New World revolutionaries.

In New Spain, the army of Guerrero was once again on the march in the mountains south of Mexico City, for Guerrero and his men had little reason to believe that the liberal uprising in the mother country would lead to a redress of grievances in New Spain. As the insurrectionists moved closer to the rim of the Valley of Mexico, Viceroy Apodaca sent his troops under the command of the creole Agustín de Iturbide with orders to destroy Guerrero's forces. But the viceroy had placed his confidence in an artful if not traitorous soldier, for Iturbide, although he had fought the insurgents for nine years, would soon join forces with Guerrero. The creole officer could not have found a better time for a change in loyalties, because he had the support of army officers and clergymen who chose separation from Spain rather than submit to the Constitution of 1812.

Shortly before reaching the camp of Guerrero, Iturbide sent a letter to the insurgent leader suggesting that the fighting stop, for "the King of Spain has offered liberal institutions and confirmed the social guarantees of the people." Moreover, "you know that the fortunes of war are mutable, and that the government possesses great resources." Guerrero replied that he did not trust the Spanish constitutionalists any more than he did the royalists, but added that he was willing to place the command of the insurgent army in the hands of Iturbide! Seemingly this was a rather startling proposal to be made by a sincere revolutionary. Was Guerrero himself a traitor? By no means. Iturbide's letter was written for the eyes of the viceroy. The messengers who delivered the letter, or letters, to Guerrero also carried confidential information, the gist of which was that the two protagonists had like interests in an independent Mexico.

The Plan of Iguala

There followed the first meeting between Iturbide and Guerrero, the details of which are none too clear. A few days later, and after many an *abrazo* and the shedding of tears of joy, the two chiefs issued their famous manifesto of February 24, 1821, at the village of Iguala. This document, the Plan of Iguala, was both a declaration of independence and a program for the immediate political future of Mexico. Among other things, it called for a constitutional monarchy; stated that Roman Catholicism would be the only recognized religion; made provisions for a junta to govern until a national legislature was established; guaranteed religion, independence, and union to all the inhabitants of Mexico, commitments to be entrusted to an army that would be known as the Army of the Three Guarantees; and proposed that the Spanish constitution would be the law of the land until an independent government was established in New Spain.

The Plan of Iguala, coupled with unrest among the conservative elements, prepared Mexico at last for its final struggle for independence. Apodaca raised a force of some four or five thousand men in a last desperate attempt to stem the tide of rebellion; but the loyalists were defeated everywhere. The fighting was all but finished when one of the viceroy's own generals, Anastacio Bustamante, cast his lot with the Army of the Three Guarantees. The viceroy was then removed and replaced by General Novella, who, in August, stepped aside for the last of the viceroys, Juan O'Donojú.

Some say that O'Donojú, a freemason of liberal tendencies, was sympathetic to the ambitions of the insurgents. Perhaps. In any event, he did enter into a treaty with Iturbide at Cordoba — about midway between Veracruz and Puebla — on August 24. The treaty virtually incorporated the Plan of Iguala, and even went so far as to guarantee freedom of the press. In other words, the viceroy had committed his government to an untenable position, the recognition of independence. He knew very well that he had no such authority, yet he must have been perceptive enough to see that New Spain had passed into history. Indeed it had, but church-state relationships, militarism, and agrarian problems were to worry the new nation for more than century.

POLITICAL CHAOS AND THE RISE OF SANTA ANNA

On September 27, 1821, Iturbide "The Liberator," and his Army of the Three Guarantees made a triumphal entry into Mexico City amidst hurrahs of welcome. On the following day a governing junta was established in accordance with the Plan of Iguala, and Iturbide, as president of the body, issued a decree proclaiming to the world that Mexico was an independent nation. The junta then created a regency, with both Iturbide and O'Donojú as members, and Iturbide as president. One of the first acts of the regency was to appoint a committee of notables to draft a constitution. But the committee's work was short-lived, mainly because several of the members professed liberal and republican leanings, leanings that were not in Iturbide's dictionary of politics. The committee was promptly deprived of its functions, and some of its members were clapped in jail for their audacity. Iturbide himself then brought together a constituent congress, which proved to be no more satisfactory to his taste than the committee of notables, for it was a congress dominated by a strange league of political bedfellows — bourbonists, who looked to Europe for a prince to sit on a throne in Mexico, and republicans, who quite naturally advocated the presidential form of government. And since neither bourbonist nor republican chose to support Iturbide's political ambitions, the Liberator seized power at the expense of congress, which struck back by reducing the size of the army and by declaring that members of the regency would no longer be permitted to hold positions of command in the army.

Despite Iturbide's high-handed tactics, he was the hero of the hour. On the night of May 18, 1822, Pío Marcha, a relatively unknown sergeant in Mexico City, raised the cry of *"Viva Agustín Primero"* — "Long Live Agustín the First"—, and before long the "vivas" resounded up and down the streets of the capital. This may have been a spontaneous demonstration, but one suspects that Sergeant Pío may have been encouraged by dissident elements in the army and the church. But whatever the reason may have been, the overwhelming popular support for the hero of Iguala was answered by a decree of May 21 proclaiming Iturbide Emperor of Mexico. A month later, in the national cathedral, the Bishop of Guadalajara crowned him Agustín I.

The First Empire

Thus began the short and inglorious history of the First Empire. Bourbonists, masons, and republicans in congress were far from pleased with this turn of events, and Iturbide's congressional opponents plotted to declare the emperor's election unconstitutional. Iturbide promptly arrested the leaders of the plot, a move which served only to create further hostility, even among those who had been somewhat tolerant of the emperor's whims. Iturbide then settled the whole matter — or at least he thought he did—by abolishing the legislature. He may not have known that all was not well in the army either. A handsome, young creole officer stationed at Veracruz — Antonio López de Santa Anna — supported by a goodly share of the army and by Bravo, Guerrero, and Victoria, pronounced against the emperor. A few days later, on February 19, 1832, Iturbide abdicated. A fortnight later he was aboard ship bound for Italy and exile. But he would return a few months later, when he was led to believe that Spain's army was preparing to reconquer the wayward colony. Perhaps he thought his countrymen would welcome him in a crisis of this kind, although he may have been aware of a congressional act which called for his death if he should again set foot on the homeland. In any event, he returned to face a firing squad on July 19, 1824, at Padilla in the State of Tamaulipas. "His execution," says the historian Justo Sierra, "was a political act, not a just act. Iturbide had given his country supreme service. . . . " But others have disagreed with the distinguished Mexican's estimate of Iturbide's place in history.

Upon the fall of the First Empire, a military triumvirate, composed of Bravo, Victoria, and Celestino Negrete, assumed executive power, set up a cabinet, borrowed some sixteen million pesos from England, and waited for congress to present the nation with a constitution. Work on the document began promptly, while a temporary frame of government, known as the Constitutive Act — virtually a copy of the Constitution of the United States — was to serve the nation until a new constitution was adopted. Nine months later, on October 4, 1824, the Federal Constitution of the United Mexican States was promulgated. It, too, in its broader aspects, was patterned after the Constitution of the United States.

Some say it was a weak document because it imposed a federalist system on a nation with little if any experience in self-government, thereby opening the way for military chieftains to have things pretty much their own way. It would have been far more realistic if the nation had launched its republic on a unitary or centralist course, say these critics. Further, would it not have been wiser to extend the president's term for a much longer period than four years? What could a chief magistrate hope to do of a constructive nature, no matter how able he was, in such a short time? And what would happen — and it did happen — if the vice-president chose to disagree with the president on matters of federalism and centralism?

Struggle for Constitution

When the votes for the presidency were counted, it was found that Guadalupe Victoria had the majority, with Nicolas Bravo in second place. Thus, in a manner comparable to the electoral procedure prescribed by the Constitution of the United States until 1804, Victoria assumed the position of chief executive, and Bravo was installed as vice-president. The following four years, 1825–28, were, in the main, years of comparative stability. Not until the closing years of the nineteenth century, with the rise to power of Porfirio Díaz, would Mexico again witness anything like a stable government. But it must not be inferred from this that Victoria's administration solved the problems of the day. Poverty stalked the land, the treasury was empty, the oligarchy in the army and in the church went unchecked, and a bitter struggle between centralist and federalist grew more intense as political rifts developed in the masonic lodges. Leaders of the Yorkrite, or *yorquinos,* advocated the federalistic principle, while the Scottish rite, or *escoceses,* maintained that the republic should be of the unitary or centralist type. Nor were they in agreement on economic and social matters. The *yorquinos* wished to build a new, liberal Mexico by means of radical reforms, while the *escoceses* chose a moderate, conservative course, much like the counterpart in Spain. A Yankee, Joel Poinsett, United States Minister to Mexico, added fuel to the political fire by supporting the aims of the *yorquinos.* His motives no doubt were sincere but somewhat interventionist, so much so that he was forced to pack his bags and go home. Then, too, the winds of social reform in England reached Mexican shores. In 1828, liberals invited Robert Owen to establish a utopian colony in Texas; but the invitation was no more than an intellectual gesture. No such colony was founded.

Victoria's four-year term, successful as it was, ended in a state of confusion and violence. Bravo, the vice-president and staunch supporter of the *escoceses,* quarreled with Victoria, a quarrel which resulted in an abortive revolt. When congress, following the wishes of the *yorquinos,* chose the insurgent hero Guerrero to

Guerrero, nineteenth-century insurgent hero, spent a few days in this Oaxaca cell before facing a firing squad. He had been removed from the presidency by a military dictatorship which plagued the footsteps of reform until the time of Benito Juárez.

succeed Victoria in the office of the presidency, the *escoceses* maintained that they had been cheated, that General Manuel Gómez Pedraza, a conservative of considerable ability, had received the majority votes of the state legislatures and was therefore the constitutional president of the land. There was good reason to believe that the evidence supported the claims of Pedraza, claims that resulted in an uprising which was promptly suppressed.

But the struggle for political stability was by no means ended. Vice-president Anastacio Bustamante, a general with strong leanings towards conservatism, succeeded in unseating Guerrero by force, saying that the president ruled as a dictator. The charge had some basis in fact, for congress gave the president extra-ordinary powers in 1829 to repel a Spanish invasion on the east coast; but these were no more than emergency and temporary powers, and under the circumstances would doubtless have been granted to anyone who occupied the presidential seat. Even though the Spanish invasion was of a minor nature and was therefore turned back, the fact is that liberal Mexican leadership was preoccupied with the fear of a Spanish reconquest. The most important aspect of all this was that it afforded the opportunity for the militarists to seize power and create a highly centralized government with all the evils of dictatorship. Guerrero himself was to be among the first to fall before the firing squad of the new regime, and for the greater part of the following twenty-five years, countless others were cut down by the bullets of the dictators.

The bête noire of the story was the handsome creole, Antonio López de Santa Anna, an army officer who was to be in and out of the office of the presidency on eleven different occasions, from May, 1833, to August, 1855. He entered the political scene by joining Bustamante in a revolt against Guerrero, but it was not long before he led a successful uprising against Bustamante, on the grounds that the latter had taken office unconstitutionally! Then, as a political subterfuge, Santa Anna stepped aside for Gómez Pedraza. The "altruistic" general would have to wait for a more propitious moment for seating himself in the presidential chair.

The year 1833 was the propitious moment when, by devious means, Santa Anna succeeded in getting himself declared president of the Republic; and he was clever enough to permit Dr. Valentín Gómez Farías, a respected liberal reformer, to serve as vice-president. It was a canny move, for the general was soon to test the strength of the reformers by entrusting the affairs of state to his vice-president while the president was enjoying a "well-deserved" vacation on his famous hacienda, Manga de Clavo. Gómez Farías then moved rapidly with his reform program designed to curtail the privileges of the army and the church. But neither army nor church would submit without a struggle. Generals and colonels rose in revolt against the vice-president, and Santa Anna hastened back to Mexico City to "save the nation" from revolution and, of course, to place himself in the saddle of dictator. Gómez Farías hurriedly packed his bags and fled to New Orleans. The military, supported by the church and the *agiotistas,* or money-changers, had won the day.

UNITED STATES-MEXICAN RELATIONS

Meantime, while liberals and conservatives harassed the political life of Mexico, unhappy developments in the distant state of Texas caused further difficulties for the nation, difficulties which arose from a generous colonial policy. Beginning in the twenties, Anglo-Americans, attracted by an abundance of arable land, had obtained colonial grants in Texas from the state government. Authorized by a federal colonization law, these grants were made to *empresarios,* who in turn agreed to distribute the greater part of the grants to the immigrant families who accompanied them to the state. The *empresario* further had to agree to establish one hundred families within his grant, on the condition that all of the grantees would become Mexican citizens. The grantee was also required to pay a nominal fee of thirty dollars for a square league of land. Other inducements were offered the colonial immigrant and the *empresario* — limiting tariff barriers, granting the establishment of private police forces, and permitting the introduction of Negro slavery into the state. Why was Mexico so generous? The system seems to have been designed to solve the long-standing problem of how to colonize the frontier. Also, one might suspect, in view of the threat of "manifest destiny," that the Mexican government envisaged a countercolonization scheme which might check the oncoming tide of Anglo-Americans.

Struggle for Texas

Whatever the reasons may have been for the *empresario* system, the rapid subsequent colonization of Texas led to serious political and social conflicts between Anglo-Americans and Mexicans. One of the early notable conflicts occurred in 1826–27, when the Edwards brothers, who possessed dubious titles to *empresario* grants in eastern Texas, mounted the ramparts and established the Republic of Fredonia! This particular rebellion was promptly put down, partly owing to the fact that such level-headed individuals as Stephen F. Austin let it be known that they doubted the merits of the alleged grievances of the Edwards brothers and that under no condition would they lend themselves to the cause of Fredonia. Austin, pioneer among the *empresarios,* was forever using his influence to bring about harmonious relations between the two cultures. But his was a losing battle, because national laws freed the slaves, revoked the special privileges of the colonists, made Texas and Coahuila one political entity, and nullified the Constitution in 1824. The shadow of states' rights now fell upon the land, and the Anglo-Americans found themselves in the unhappy position of a political minority.

Rebellion was in the wind in spite of the fact that Austin cautioned his friends against extreme measures; and he even went so far as to identify Santa Anna with the liberals! Furthermore Austin made his way to Mexico City in pursuit of peace; but it was a fruitless enterprise. Political anarchy was hardly an environment for the niceties of diplomacy, and the Anglo-Americans in Texas were in no mood to await the day of political stability. The course of history would once again be diverted to the battlefield.

The Texas war for independence lasted from June, 1835, to the middle of May, 1836. In the opening months of 1835, Santa Anna appointed a military commandant for Texas and sent troops to occupy the custom house at Anáhuac. The colonists, under the leadership of William B. Travis, and after an altercation at Anáhuac, responded by successful armed attack upon the town's garrison. Santa Anna meanwhile had suspended civil government in Texas, and had gathered together an army of 3,000 men and marched it into the state. By February, after one or two skirmishes between Texan and Mexican troops, Travis and some 186 other Anglos had taken refuge behind the walls of the Alamo to await the onslaught of Santa Anna's forces. The assault came on February 23. Santa Anna demanded that Travis and his men surrender; but the defenders chose to hold their ground rather than risk their cause and their lives to one who was known for his capricious behavior. The certainties of facing a firing squad were far less inviting than possibly dying for a principle behind the walls of the Alamo. So the Mexicans breached the walls and massacred the defenders, and a month later, on March 27, three hundred Texans met a similar fate at Goliad.

Meanwhile, Austin had been sent to the United States to solicit aid. On March 2 a convention had declared Texas an independent republic, and two days later Sam Houston, a comparative newcomer to the state, was named commander-in-chief of the army. The convention then drafted a constitution modeled upon the federal and state constitutions of the United States. A republic was born, but the future of Texas still remained in the hands of the gods of war. By mid-April, the Mexican army had reached Galveston Bay, and Santa Anna was confident that he would soon triumph over the insurgents. He failed to reckon with the temper of his opponents, and in overconfidence permitted the surprise attack of April 21 on the banks of the San Jacinto. Santa Anna was captured, and on May 14 a treaty was signed pledging the general to secure the Mexican recognition of Texan independence. As might have been suspected, the Mexican Congress rejected the treaty. And as one also might have suspected, the crafty general not only escaped with his life but even succeeded in obtaining free passage on a United States warship which returned him to Mexico!

The political situation in Mexico was running its confused and wretched course. While radical liberals, the *puros,* quarreled with the moderate liberals, or *moderados,* the reactionary generals, supported by the church heirarchy, seized the political prize and established a dictatorial regime. On October 3, 1835, the congress established a centralist government by decree. Congress then assumed the role of a constituent assembly and drafted a centralist constitution known as the Seven Laws, to be proclaimed on December 30, 1836. Aside from restricting the franchise and public offices to the propertied classes, it created the *Poder Conservador,* a strange body of five men authorized to interpret the will of the nation to the extent of deposing presidents, annuling laws, and reversing the decisions of the courts. The document was a curious one indeed. Not even the conservatives could live with it.

As for Santa Anna, he had returned once again to his hacienda. While fighting the Texans, the wily *caudillo* had left someone else to face the brunt of political affairs in Mexico City. In this instance General Miguel Barragán was the victim, but he was soon removed from the scene by a fatal illness, dying the day before the Texans declared their independence. José Justo Corro, a comparative unknown, held the reins of government for a short interlude; then in April, 1837, General Bustamante, returned from exile in France, was elected president. He promised reforms but adopted a reactionary program. Federalist opposition, coupled with a desperate financial situation, came near to unseating Bustamante; and the spirit of separatism swept across the northern states.

Internal conflicts might have reached more serious heights if the nation had not been called upon to defend itself against French arms. Early in 1838, a French fleet of twenty-six ships and an army of four thousand men seized the fortress of San Juan de Ulúa and attacked the city of Veracruz. But why this sudden and hostile action? The answer lies in the fact that for the greater part of ten years of negotiation, the French government had failed to receive satisfaction for claims of six thousand pesos against Mexico. Even though the French claims were somewhat excessive, guns might bring the Mexican government to terms. How a bankrupt nation could hope to come to immediate terms remains unanswered. In any event, Bustamante saw an opportunity to unite the nation: "the voice of the Chief Magistrate is the center of all opinions, of all parties, and without hateful divisions of civil turmoil and calls upon all to defend the dignity, rights and honor of the *patria."* His plea did bring about a momentary cessation of "civil turmoil;" and also provided an opportunity for Santa Anna to come forward in the name of "dignity, rights and honor." Remember, the general's performance in Texas was less than satisfactory. Perhaps his countrymen would at least overlook the Texas disaster if the master of Manga de Clavo drew his sword against the European invaders. And so he did, though his men were somewhat confused about the identity of their attackers: "Down with the Jews! Down with the Saxons!" The general of course was not confused, though he did lose a leg to a French cannon ball. Shortly thereafter, the French forces withdrew, and the question of debt remained for settlement through British mediation.

The generals and their conservative supporters, ignoring economic and social problems, now moved rapidly and ruthlessly in the direction of dictatorial centralism. President Bustamante, too liberal for the conservatives and too conservative for the liberals, was pushed aside by generals Santa Anna, Paredes y Arrillaga, and Gabriel Valencia. They bombarded the capital, and on October 7, 1841, Santa Anna, with all the trappings of a Caesar, entered the city and seated himself in the office of president. But a few months later, when he found his congress leaning in the direction of federalism and liberalism, the "Napoleon of the West" once again sought refuge in the comforts of his hacienda; and, in accordance with his customary practice, others were left to exercise the executive power. In this case, Nicolás Bravo and General Valentín Canalizo were to alternate in the presidency. Bravo, staunch supporter of centralism, dissolved the federalist congress and hand-picked a body of notables who were instructed to draft a centralist constitution.

On June 13, 1843, the Mexican people were given their third constitution, the *Bases Orgánicas de la República Mexicana.* What a splendid document this was for Santa Anna and his military friends! But what a miserable document it was for the welfare of Mexico. Civil liberties were abolished. The franchise was restricted to those who had an income of two hundred pesos, which deprived the vast majority of the privilege of voting. Wide veto power was given to the president, thus making congress a nullity. The president was not only empowered to appoint the governors of the departments, but he could also initiate local laws. Furthermore, he could impose a fine on anyone he pleased, expel any foreigner, and declare war. Perhaps a benevolent dictator might have interpreted the charter in a constructive manner; but Santa Anna and his colleagues were neither benevolent nor constructive.

No one was really surprised to learn that Santa Anna had been elected president under the new constitution. He returned to the capital from his retreat at Manga de Clavo as the man of the hour. A confused populace welcomed him — and shed tears at a special burial ceremony for the general's amputated leg! Yet there was strong opposition to the dictator, so strong that Santa Anna once again withdrew to his hacienda and left General Canalizo to carry on. But, as Santa Anna well knew, Canalizo would not be able to stem the tide of moderation and liberalism; nor would he be able to check the ambitions of other generals who wished to be in the dictator's seat. Fortunately — at least for the moment — a moderate general, José Joaquín de Herrera, stepped in from the wings of this curious political stage, deposed Santa Anna, and assigned new characters to the cast. He proclaimed the restoration of the national congress under constitutional government, and appointed moderates to offices of state. The constitutional government was to operate under the *Bases Orgánicas,* but Herrera apparently was averse to absolute dictatorship. Santa Anna, of course, was of different mind. He raised a private army and marched on Mexico City, only to meet defeat near Puebla and to be locked in jail for a short time before fleeing to Havana as an exile. Some said Herrera was too generous in his treatment of the fallen Napoleon. The Indian humorists suggested that he be boiled in banana leaves, for he would serve the nation better as a tamale than as president. But the humorists were to learn that their tamale would return to lead an army against the forces of the United States.

The Mexican War

The Mexican War, or, as it is often called in Mexico, the War with the United States, had its roots in the 1820's and 1830's, when the westward march of Anglo-Americans reached the fertile plains of Texas. The *empresario* system, as mentioned previously, was bound by its very nature to cause serious friction between two cultures, neither of which was tolerant of the other's historical origins. But to say that cultural conflicts brought on the war between the two nations may be somewhat vague and an over-simplification. Historians have therefore searched for the specific, or the basic, causes of the war, and yet, as is usually the case with problems of causality, historians are not in agreement. Some hold the view that the conflict was the result of a "conspiracy of slavocracy," for, on this view, the slaveholders wished to spread their "peculiar institution" by annexing all or part of Mexico. A few historians refute the charge by saying that the Mexican territory was unsuited to slavery; those who reason thus point out also that Mexican law forbade slavery. Other writers, including some Mexican historians, maintain that an imperialistic trend, in the name of manifest destiny, was a dominant theme in United States history of the period. One recognized authority on the war, Justin H. Smith, chooses to place the responsibility for the struggle on the shoulders of the Mexicans. "Already," he writes, "there were influential and wealthy Mexicans, particularly in the North, who wished or half-wished that the United States would subjugate their country, so that order and prosperity might come. . . . "; and, he continues, "politicians of all parties, fearing to be outdone in the display of patriotism, encouraged . . . Anti-American feeling." Some fifty years ago, the distinguished Mexican historian, Justo Sierra, had taken a similar stand on the causes for the war. His emphasis, however, was not on Mexican chauvinism, but on mismanagement of affairs in Texas, coupled with national disunity, selfish interests of Mexican groups and individuals, and the land-hunger of Anglo-Americans. Then of course there is the "devil theory" which always comes in handy for some of the analysts engaged in seeking the reasons why people go to war. In this instance, President Polk bears the onus, for there are those who say that the United States president deliberately provoked the war by sending troops into the debatable land between the Nueces and the Río Grande. Evidence for such a view is scant indeed. The territorial zone may have been debatable, but even more debatable and lacking in proof is the contention that Polk was hoping for an armed attack upon United States troops so that he could be assured of a declaration of war. Whatever the causes for the conflict may have been, the fact is that war seemed to be the only immediate answer to problems of the moment. The diplomats had failed to maintain an atmosphere of friendship, and the Mexican government had not recognized the independence of Texas; moreover, said the Mexican minister, the annexation of Texas was tantamount to a declaration of war.

Those who dwell on manifest destiny as the cause for the war find strong evidence for their view in the records of diplomacy. Beginning in the late 1820's and continuing until the eve of war, United States ambassadors and special agents had presented the Mexican government with numerous proposals for the purchase of all or parts of the vast region from Texas to San Francisco Bay. The final proposal was made in December, 1845, when John Slidell was sent off to Mexico as minister with instructions to get Mexico to recognize the Río Grande as the boundary between the two nations and to offer twenty-five million dollars for the purchase of California and the region north and west of El Paso. If the Mexican authorities refused to sell that territory, Slidell was to negotiate for the sale of New Mexico, at a price of five million. Mexico, on the verge of bankruptcy, was certainly in the buyer's market; yet, despite financial inducements, ruling cliques in Mexico City recognized political dynamite in the offers from Washington. The sale of nearly one-half of Mexico's domain to the United States would add fuel to the political conflagration in Mexico City.

Slidell arrived in Mexico during the latter days of the regime of the moderate conservative, General Herrera, who extended reasonable courtesies to the minister, but made it quite clear that the Mexican government was not reestablishing diplomatic relations with the United States. Mexico might negotiate on the Texas question, but under no circumstances would the authorities in Mexico City talk about the sale of territory to the *norteamericanos,* who only recently had the temerity to "seize" a great part of their neighbor's domain. And when it became clear that Slidell was not empowered to treat on matters relating to Texas, Herrera's enemies exploited Slidell's mission by making it appear that the president was eager to listen to Slidell's offers and to ignore the Texas issue. Herrera was thus in an embarrassing position, and his rival, the conservative reactionary General Paredes, made political capital out of the matter by telling the people that this was further proof of Herrera's irresponsibility. A month later, on December 31, 1845, Herrera resigned, and on January 2, Paredes took up the reins of government in Mexico City. Slidell stayed on for several more weeks in a futile effort to be received as minister plenipotentiary. He was handed his passport on March 21 and was soon on his way back to the United States.

Events now moved rapidly in the direction of war. During the closing days of March, General Zachary Taylor marched his forces from Corpus Christi to a point opposite Matamoros on the Río Grande. General Pedro Ampudía requested Taylor to withdraw his troops to positions beyond the Nueces. The United States general replied by standing his ground, and on April 25 a company of his dragoons was attacked by Mexican cavalry, resulting in the death of a number of Taylor's men. This overt act of war, but on debatable land, was sufficient reason for Polk to ask congress for a declaration of war. "As war exists . . . by the act of Mexico herself," wrote Polk in his war message, "we are called upon by every consideration of duty and patriotism to vindicate with decision the honor, the rights, and the interests of our country." Two days later, on May 31, the United States was officially at war with Mexico. But the declaration was by no means popular everywhere in the United States. The northern and eastern antislavery sections looked upon all this as a maneuver on the part of the South to extend its "peculiar institution." Nor would it be wise to say that war was popular everywhere in Mexico. Of course the contest at arms provided the political soldiers of Mexico with the opportunity to demonstrate their "love" of country; but a nation of confused, poverty-stricken people, demoralized by the evils of anarchy, was hardly prepared to stand united behind a government whose leaders viewed the country as their patrimony.

After the confrontation near Matamoros, General Mariano Arista sent his troops across the Rio Grande, and for the greater part of two weeks a series of battles occurred at Fort Brown, Resaca de la Palma, and Palo Alto. But Arista's troops were soon to be outfought and outmaneuvered, forcing the Mexican general to retreat to Matamoros, which was captured by Taylor in the wake of a retreating opponent. Taylor's objective now was Monterrey, a key point in his strategy, for he believed that the war could be won by simply defeating the enemy in its northern states. The city was indeed a key point, and it was captured on September 25 after several months of gathering supplies, maneuvering, and fighting disease, and after losing five hundred men to Ampudía's army during a three-day battle. What the Mexican losses were no one really knows, but it is safe to say that Ampudía's casualty lists were long. The rest of the Mexican troops, after a short armistice, were permitted to march out of the fallen city, a concession which was deemed too generous by some of Taylor's critics.

Meantime other armies, from the north and from the south, were moving into the military arena. Colonel Stephen W. Kearny had raised an army of frontiersmen at Fort Leavenworth. In June he began his march to Santa Fé, and on August 16 he entered the town, whose defenders had satisfied their pride with little more than a token resistance. The United States flag was raised, and the colonel took formal possession of New Mexico in the name of his country. The inhabitants, learning that their persons and property would be protected, settled down to peaceful coexistence with their conquerors. Kearny then detached some of his men and placed them under Alexander W. Doniphan's command with orders to proceed to Chihuahua. Kearny himself gathered together a force and led it westward to California by way of the Gila River. By the time Kearny's army arrived in California, the state was virtually conquered. Commodores John D. Sloat and Robert F. Stockton, together with a small detachment of troops under Captain John C. Frémont, had the military situation well in hand. The conquest itself was no great military feat. Upper California, as the state was called at the time, was sparsely settled, and Governor Pío Pico and Commandant José Castro found themselves with a small number of poorly trained militiamen. Furthermore, the state was suffering from divided loyalties to local Mexican factions, and earlier, on July 4, 1846, Anglo-American settlers at Sonoma had proclaimed their independence and had established the "Bear Flag Republic." Six months later, on January 13, 1847, and after a few minor battles, the Capitulations of Cahuenga ended the war for California.

In the meantime Taylor's troops continued to execute a successful campaign south of the Río Grande. In November, 1846, he occupied Saltillo, and three weeks later General John E. Wool, commanding an expedition from San Antonio, entered Parras and then moved southeast a few miles to join forces with Taylor in the vicinity of Buena Vista. This was welcome, for it was known that Santa Anna was approaching from San Luis Potosí with an army of several thousand to replace the defeated army of Ampudía. Taylor might have been even more concerned about the advance of the Mexican army had he known that Santa Anna's scouts had intercepted a message from General Winfield Scott to Taylor stating that the latter must transfer the greater number of his troops to an army which Scott would lead in a planned advance on Mexico City by way of Veracruz. The transfer reduced Taylor's army to 5,000 men who were soon to face 15,000 troops at Buena Vista under the command of Santa Anna. On February 23 Santa Anna launched his main attack. A battle of tactical errors ensued. One division of Taylor's troops retreated when they should have remained in position, while Santa Anna failed to exploit advantages that were open to him. Losses were heavy on both sides, and during the night the "Napoleon of the West" chose to withdraw down the long road to San Luis Potosí. He had learned that his army was no match for the accuracy of Taylor's artillery and the effectiveness of Yankee bayonets. Like Napoleon's army in retreat from Moscow during the fateful Russian winter, Santa Anna's army suffered the exactions of hunger and bitter weather.

By the time the remnants of Santa Anna's troops had reached San Luis Potosí, the war in the northern theater had come to an end. Doniphan had taken Chihuahua City, and in the spring of 1847 he joined forces with Taylor in the vicinity of Buena Vista. The war now shifted to Mexico's lifeline — Veracruz to Mexico City. Both President Polk and Major General Scott, Commanding General of the United States Army, settled on this course of operations, for they disagreed with Taylor's assumption that the war could be won in the north Mexican states.

United States and Mexican forces would face one another in combat for seven months in the heart of Mexico. Scott himself took command in the field, and with an army of some 13,000 men working in close cooperation with the navy, he made an unopposed landing south of Veracruz on March 9, 1847. Ten days later, after a sustained bombardment, the city's garrison surrendered. Meantime, Santa Anna had gathered together a force of approximately 12,000 to challenge the invaders. The challenge came at Cerro Gordo, where, on April 17 and 18, the Mexicans put up a stubborn resistance, only to be outflanked and compelled to retreat to Puebla. The battle was one of the most decisive in the entire war; and had Scott received the necessary supplies and reinforcements, he might very well have marched on rapidly to the Mexican capital. He was instead forced to spend the greater part of three months in Puebla awaiting these sinews of war — time enough for Santa Anna to fortify the approaches to Mexico City and to muster an army of 25,000, a rather impressive number when one considers that Scott, known affectionately as "Old Fuss and Feathers," was in command of a little less than 11,000 when he began his march to Mexico City on August 7.

Of the several battles fought near and in the capital, the most important were at Contreras (August 19-20), Churubusco (August 20) El Molina del Rey (September 8), and Chapultepec (September 13). Scott broke through the outer perimeter of the Mexican defenses at Contreras, a victory which the invaders might not have achieved if General Gabriel Valencia had obeyed Santa Anna's orders. The Mexican troops, falling back rapidly, took up their positions at the fortified bridgehead on the outskirts of Churubusco. The ensuing battle was indeed a bloody one, mainly because the Mexican artillery was manned by deserters from Scott's army who were good marksmen and were known as the San Patricio Battalion; therefore, mercy was not the order of the day, and the bayonet seems to have been used somewhat indiscriminately. It is said that after the defeats at Contreras and Churubusco, Santa Anna had lost no less than a third of his army. The remainder took up defensive positions in the city, while Santa Anna, under the guise of seeking peace, succeeded in obtaining an armistice long enough to permit him to reorganize his forces. After a few days of pointless negotiations, the armistice was lifted, and Scott directed his next attack at El Molina del Rey, mistakenly believing that it was the site of a cannon foundry. The two armies were soon locked in a struggle that lasted for the greater part of two hours before the defenders withdrew to Chapultepec. Chapultepec was to fall five days later to the superior forces of Scott, but not before several gallant young Mexican cadets chose to take their lives rather than surrender.

The war was drawing rapidly to a close, but Santa Anna was reluctant to accept the military facts. He resigned as president; then led a dispirited column of men against a detachment of Scott's troops at Puebla. The battle was little more than a skirmish, after which Santa Anna fled into the mountains with the intention of carrying on the war by guerrilla tactics. But this was just a fantastic scheme. Chaos reigned. Yucatán was in the throes of rebellion, while the northern states appeared to be moving in the direction of secession; and a peace party of *moderados,* together with elements in the church that had always been opposed to the war, were in positions of authority at the capital and were willing to accept peace overtures from the United States. Santa Anna was therefore compelled to lay down his arms, and, after attending a banquet given by United States officers in the best of military traditions, he went to Jamaica as an exile. The war was ended, and during the closing days of July, 1848, the last contingent of Scott's army boarded ship at Veracruz and sailed for home.

The war was over, but a peace treaty was yet to be signed and ratified. Peace negotiations of one kind or another had been under way from almost the moment Scott went ashore at Veracruz. On April 15, 1847, Secretary of State James Buchanan had commissioned Nicholas P. Trist, chief clerk in the Department of State, to proceed to Scott's headquarters as "a confidential agent. . . . Clothed with full powers to conclude a treaty of peace with the Mexican government . . . [and] . . . to take advantage, at the propitious moment, of any favorable circumstances which might dispose that government to peace." These were indeed clear instructions, as was the *projét,* or terms for negotiation, which was also handed to Trist. But the confidential agent would soon discover that "Old Fuss and Feathers," despite Buchanan's lucid use of the language of diplomacy, was unwilling to share his own responsibilities with that of Trist. It was Scott's contention that field commanders should be empowered to negotiate peace treaties under the circumstances in which his army found itself. Without this power, so it would appear from Scott's point of view, the right hand would not know what the left hand was doing; and since both hands were essential for victory, Scott declared that his was both a military and a diplomatic function. A stand such as this, whether reasonable or not, quite naturally led to bitter quarrels between the general and Trist. After considerable prompting from Washington, however, Trist and Scott agreed to cast aside mutual recriminations and to get on with the job.

Diplomatic Contacts

The first diplomatic contacts of any significance between Trist and the Mexican government came in the summer of 1847 while Scott was mobilizing his forces for the attack on Mexico City. Santa Anna had been apprised of Trist's mission, and on July 16 the Mexican president sent a message to congress in which he stated his view on treaty negotiations with the invaders. He made it clear that the nation should not listen to "propositions of any sort which may come from the United States"; furthermore, so he said, Buchanan had affronted the dignity of Mexico by entrusting negotiations to one who "is not invested with any character beyond that of Commissioner." Of course, "the Executive does not wish to do aught but the will of Congress." Of course, too, the will of the Mexican congress was still the will of Santa Anna. But as Scott's army moved victoriously into the Valley of Mexico, the relations between the Mexican president and his congress became strained; and after Santa Anna's defeat at Puebla the *moderados* obtained a majority vote for peace in congress. Manuel de la Peña y Peña, chief justice of the supreme court, assumed the office of president, established the government at Querétaro, and resumed negotiations with Trist.

Trist found himself in a rather awkward position, because Polk had recalled him in October, two months before final negotiations with the Mexican government. Polk's move was doubtless due to political pressures from the Whigs and others who were highly critical of his diplomacy. There is good reason to believe that the political ambitions of some of Polk's generals, notably Taylor, a Whig with presidential aspirations, were not above finding fault with the commander in chief. Nor had Trist been on the best of terms with Scott, also a Whig, who maintained that peace negotiations should be in the hands of the commanding field general. But whatever the reasons may have been for the removal of Trist, Polk's commissioner ignored his recall and chose to carry out his initial instructions. Even Scott had come

to the point of at least tolerating Trist's somewhat arrogant attitude towards Washington.

Negotiations now moved rapidly, and on February 2, 1848, a treaty of "peace, friendship, limits, and settlement between the United States of America and the Mexican republic" was signed at the Mexican village of Guadalupe Hidalgo. The provisions of the document were in general accord with the instruction Secretary Buchanan had handed Trist before the latter's departure from Washington. Perhaps the most significant provision of the treaty, aside from establishing peace between the two nations, was Article V, wherein Mexico ceded more than half of the republic to the United States; and with the cession, gave up its claims to Texas. But the government of the United States, "In consideration of the extension acquired by the boundaries of the United States," agreed to pay Mexico fifteen million dollars. In retrospect, this was a small sum for the vast expanse of territory from the Pacific Coast of California to the western boundaries of Texas. And for the sake of friendly relations between the two powers, it might also be said that the treaty's language which cancelled all claims of United States citizens against Mexico was a wise diplomatic move; but it was clear that "all demands on account of the claims" would be limited to three and one-quarter million dollars.

On February 23, President Polk submitted the treaty to the United States senate. There began a series of heated debates which, aside from reflecting the sectional stand on the institution of slavery, would soon raise further issues with Mexico. Spokesmen for the South maintained that the boundary between the two countries, as established in Article V, was too far north. But northern senators, many of whom had opposed the Mexican war on the grounds that it had been brought about by those who wished to extend slavery into regions which might be acquired from Mexico, held that the South had received the lion's share of the ceded territory. Yet none of the northern senators proposed that the acquisition should be returned to Mexico. The debates continued on this and several other articles, and when the votes were counted it was found that the treaty had been ratified by a narrow margin. Polk promptly signed it, and on July 4, 1848, it was proclaimed in force. And of course it was also the law of the land in Mexico, despite some rather vigorous protests in high places.

Although the treaty was law in both republics, three of its articles soon raised some grave questions. Provisions for an international boundary survey in Article V were not in accord with geographic facts, especially as they related to the site of El Paso. (Framers of the treaty had used a faulty map in the preparation of the article.) Article VI permitted either nation, if it chose, to "construct a road, canal or railway" within one marine mile from either margin of the Gila River. Article XI was a reaffirmation of a responsibility the United States had assumed by a provision in its first treaty with Mexico (1831), requiring the United States to check Indian depredations into Mexico that might originate on United States soil. It was nearly four years before a joint boundary commission was prepared to continue its assignment. By that time railroad engineers had discovered that the Mesilla Valley, west of El Paso and well within Mexican territory, was a natural highway through the mountains which someday would be essential for a transcontinental railroad. Southern railroaders were already dreaming of that day and were soon to press the United States government to purchase the valley, as well as other Mexican land to the west and south of the Gila. Added to this as a reason for renewed negotiations with Mexico was the unenforceable provision in Article XI of the 1848 treaty which called for restricting Indian forays into Mexico. Then, of course, the spirit of manifest destiny continued to assert itself. Perhaps Mexico could be persuaded to renegotiate the problems arising from the treaty and might even consent to satisfy the aims of the expansionists. After all, there was good reason to believe that Mexico would listen; Santa Anna was once again in power and in desperate need of cash. Franklin Pierce, elected president in 1852, may not have been overly concerned with the domestic problems of Mexico, but he was prepared to open negotiations.

The Gadsden Purchase

The man for the job was General James Gadsden, a sixty-seven-year-old soldier turned railroad president. On July 15, 1853, Secretary of State William L. Marcy handed Gadsden his instructions, the most significant items dealing with Article XI and a proposal to adjust the boundary so as to provide a railroad route to the Pacific that would be advantageous to both nations. Gadsden reached Mexico City in August and immediately began negotiations with Foreign Minister Manuel Diez de Bonilla; but it took four months of proposals and counterproposals before a final agreement was reached. And the negotiations would doubtless have run on for a longer period if Gadsden had not been instructed to negotiate on six alternate boundary proposals, one of which extended from a point near Tampico to the southern tip of Lower California. Even Santa Anna could not consider such a proposal, even though he was in dire need of hard cash. Yet he was willing to sell a comparatively small part of Mexican soil south of the Gila and including the Mesilla Valley. The railroaders could hardly object to this, and Gadsden agreed to accept the Mexican offer by affixing his signature to a treaty which, among other things, called for the purchase of some nineteen million acres. Santa Anna's price for the Gadsden Purchase was fifteen million dollars, a figure that was cut to ten million by the United States senate. The Mexican dictator may not have been happy with the five million dollar cut, but there was a revolution brewing at Ayutla. It was now or never. The treaty was therefore ratified by Mexico on May 31, 1854, a month later, on June 29, by the United States, and the following day, ratifications were exchanged at Washington, and Pierce proclaimed the treaty the law of the land.

BENITO JUAREZ AND REFORM

Meantime, Santa Anna's government was riding for a fall, a fall that in part would be brought on by the unpopular nature of Gadsden's treaty. Liberals, radicals and moderate, or *puro* and *moderado,* had been marshalling their forces against "His Serene Highness" long before the treaty was signed. Juan Álvarez, a radical septuagenarian revolutionary and governor of Guerrero, would soon raise an army in the southern mountains that would defeat Santa Anna's troops. Ignacio Comonfort, moderate though he was, was willing to join Álvarez in a common cause against the dictator, at least for the time being, and would operate from his base at Acapulco.

A thousand or more miles away, at New Orleans, radical and moderate exiles had also been planning a final blow at Santa Anna. The life of a Mexican exile in New Orleans was far from pleasant. Benito Juárez, former governor of the state of Oaxaca and a Zapotec Indian, eked out a living in a cigar factory. This was hardly a traumatic experience for Juárez. His had been a life of hard work, one way or another. Born in 1806 in an Indian village high in the mountains above the city of Oaxaca and orphaned at three, he entered the white man's world as a household servant at the age of twelve. To many he appeared stolid, but his close friends never found him dull. One such friend, Dr. Antonio Salanueva, adopted the boy and, for a time, supervised his education, which the doctor hoped would prepare the young Indian for the priesthood. But Juárez, after several years in a seminary, discovered he was not cut out to be a priest. He preferred the law and politics. In 1845 he was elected to the departmental assembly of Oaxaca, and in the following year he won a seat in the national congress. His political views were considered "safe" by the conservatives. Nothing in his early career gave cause for alarm; yet during the closing months of the Mexican war his political philosophy moved in the direction of liberalism. The opportunity to put his philosophy into action came in November 1847, when he was appointed provisional governor of Oaxaca, a post he held until 1852. But his performance as chief executive of the department was that of a moderate liberal. There was nothing revolutionary or radical in his programs for Oaxaca; and his programs were reasonably successful. Santa Anna of course had other views on all this, especially in the light of the fact that a successful Juárez might pose a real threat to the dictator; and there were others who were also somewhat embarrassing to His Highness. All must therefore be hurried off into exile.

Among the several Mexican exiles in New Orleans, none was better informed on Mexican affairs than the forty-year-old creole Melchor Ocampo, ex-governor of Michoacán and heir of vast estates. Unlike most people of his station in life at that time, he had philanthropic tendencies and a deep interest in political philosophy. Perhaps influenced by the *encyclopedists,* Ocampo was a strong advocate of social reform, a social reform he

Benito Juárez, Zapotec Indian president of Mexico and leader of Reform, ordered the execution of the Emperor Maximilian I, and launched the reconstruction of his wartorn country, following intervention by the French.

said that must come to Mexico by widening the base of property ownership for the masses and by dispossessing the church of its privileged position in the economic life of the nation. Mexico's future, then, would no longer be vexed by the senseless struggle between the centralists and federalists and the nation would come to grips with its fundamental economic and social problems. Ocampo's arguments were sound, yet the goals he sought could only be gained by following a course of violent revolution. Juárez, Alvarado, and other men of action were available to follow that course.

While Ocampo, Juárez, and their colleagues were awaiting the day of return to Mexico, Álvarez and Comonfort, supported by a spirited army, rose in rebellion against the *santanista* government on February 24, 1854. On March 1, extremists among the revolutionaries proclaimed the Plan of Ayutla, a manifesto that, among other things, called for the resignation of Santa Anna, establishment of a provisional government, summoning of a constituent congress, and abolition of the poll tax. Álvarez, Bravo, and Tomás Moreno were called upon to lead the revolution. All three were willing to assume the role of liberators, but Álvarez and Moreno were reluctant to endorse the plan publicly; nor was Comonfort eager to subscribe to a document which he believed conveyed the notion that federalism would be imposed on the nation by force. Some minor changes in the manifesto were therefore made, and Álvarez announced that his army would be known as the Army for the Restoration of Liberty, with Moreno second in command. Comonfort's forces would soon join those of Álvarez; but Bravo's day as a revolutionary had run its course. The old insurgent was feeble, and died before the year was out.

Thus was born the Revolution of Ayutla, which, in its inception and for the greater part of a year and a half, was a struggle between the ins and the outs, between the conservatives and the liberals. Local political bosses, or *caciques,* such as Santiago Vidaurri in Nuevo León, Manuel Doblado in Guanajuato, and Santos Degollado in Jalisco, identified themselves with the liberals for personal reasons. A genuine revolution, with all of its social implications, was little more than a preoccupation for political bosses. Even those of higher political persuasion were not in agreement on the proper course of action: the *puros,* like Álvarez and Ocampo, demanded immediate reforms; the *moderados,* like Comonfort, recognized the need for reforms but advocated a program of gradualism.

Of course His Most Serene Highness could not sit and wait for the winds of rebellion to subside in the face of some miraculous turn of events. So, on March 16, against the advice of friends, Santa Anna, at the head of a division of five thousand men, left Mexico City to confront the rebels of the department of Guerrero. The forces of Álvarez retreated and fought a delaying action, and no major engagements occurred until the morning of April 20, when some nine hundred *santanistas* failed in a surprise attack on Acapulco. Santa Anna then turned to bribery in the amount of $100,000; but Comonfort promptly declined to accept any financial inducement to lay down his arms. Somewhat piqued by this refusal, His Highness again attacked Acapulco, but found himself in a dangerous situation. Sickness, desertions, battle casualties, and the approach of the army of Álvarez were sufficient reasons for the dictator to change plans. Perhaps Álvarez would be willing to negotiate; but on the other hand, the old revolutionary was not one to compromise. Santa Anna therefore beat a hasty retreat to the Valley of Mexico, where he announced that he had waged a successful campaign. He then asked the people to go to the ballot boxes to cast their votes either for or against His Highness, with the understanding that voter lists would be published in each town! No one was surprised to learn that Santa Anna had received an "overwhelming" vote of confidence, but a fraudulent election could not block the course of rebellion in a nation which never before had sunk to such depths of political, economic, and social decadency. Nevertheless, and despite the fact that rebels appeared everywhere, Santa Anna remained ensconced in Mexico City until August 9, 1855, when he quietly fled the capital. Several days later, after a formal abdication from office, he sailed from Veracruz into exile. His official career was terminated. He would reappear in the 1860's at the time of the French intervention, but as a common citizen; and he was to die in Mexico City on June 21, 1876.

After Santa Anna's departure, the government at Mexico City rested in the hands of Manuel Carrera, a

conservative. By October, however, Álvarez was the recognized president of the republic and many of the liberal exiles had returned to accept positions of responsibility in the new government. The ministry of relations, the most significant position in Álvarez's cabinet, was given to Ocampo, while the posts of justice, treasury, and war were assigned to Juárez, Guillermo Prieto, and Comonfort, respectively; but Álvarez, under the influence of the moderates, lost the support of Ocampo and Prieto, both of whom resigned within a fortnight. Nor was this to be the end of cabinet crises. Reform legislation and foreign intervention led to countless quarrels and resignations for more than fifteen years.

For seven years, from November, 1855, when Álvarez rode into Mexico City as president of Mexico, until early in 1862 when troops from Spain, England, and France went ashore at Veracruz, Mexico was to experience another critical period in its history, a period known as the Reform. The logic of the Plan of Ayutla could have led to no other conclusion, and the results of the Reform endured through the nineteenth century and into the present. The period itself is quite correctly identified with the Age of Benito Juárez, the incorrupt-

In the southern state of Oaxaca were born two of Mexico's most famous presidents: the dictator, Porfirio Díaz, a *mestizo* from the capital city (shown above), and Benito Juárez, the Zapotec Indian who came from a village high in the mountains to be Mexico's great leader of reform.

ible Indian from Oaxaca. Yet the ideology of the Reform had a positivist as well as a middle-of-the-road direction which was often the work of others. Ponciano Arriaga, Ignacio Ramírez, Francisco Zarco, José María Mata, Miguel Lerdo de Tejada, and, of course, Ocampo and Prieto, were the intellectual leaders whose political, economic, and social philosophies were embodied in reform legislation and in the Constitution of 1857, which, with some amendments, was Mexico's fundamental organic law until 1917. The reform laws and the constitution were the products of young minds that in some instances reflected the lessons of the French Revolution and the socialistic teachings of Pierre Joseph Proudhon. In 1855, Zarco was twenty-six, Mata, thirty-six, Prieto and Ramírez, thirty-seven, Lerdo, thirty-nine, Ocampo, forty-one, Arriaga, forty-four. Even Juárez was only forty-nine. A second generation of revolutionaries had entered the lists. Gómez Farías, seventy-four years old, was to fight on for three more years; but the distinguished group of insurgents who had been at his side for the greater part of half a century were no longer on the scene. Nor was the seventy-five-year-old Álvarez much more than a hero of an earlier day. Factional quarrels within the ranks of the new generation were problems for younger men. Within a month after Álvarez's entry into Mexico City as president, he had resigned, and the government went into the hands of Comonfort the moderate. But the old man would be heard from again as a guerrilla leader in behalf of the Reform.

Ley Juárez and Ley Lerdo

The immediate cause for Álvarez's resignation stemmed from reactions to the first of the famous reforming laws, the *ley juárez,* decreed on November 23, 1855. By limiting the jurisdiction of the military and ecclesiastical courts, it not only raised furor in the army and in the church, but also brought about serious differences among the reformers themselves. Of course, the bishops and the generals maintained that the state went beyond its authority by abolishing the long-established *fueros,* or privileges, of the church and the army; and the hierarchy of the church went even further by announcing that the law was an attack upon religion. But in fact the law had very little if any bearing on matters of theology or dogma. It was designed, as Walter V. Scholes writes, simply as one of the liberal objectives of equality before the law. Soldiers and priests, however, viewed the matter in quite a different light, and raised the battle cry of *"religión y fueros"* — "religion and privileges." on the other hand, *moderados,* prophets of gradualism, were prone to compromise with the enemies of the *ley juárez,* so much so that a serious rift developed between them and the *puros.* Yet both factions, *puros* and *moderados,* were in agreement on requesting Álvarez to resign. Any other course might have jeopardized the liberal program, moderate or radical.

For three years, from December 12, 1855, to January 21, 1858, Comonfort sat in the office of the presidency, and moderate though he was, the *puros,* or radicals, had things pretty much their own way. It could not have been otherwise, for the Plan of Ayutla was the voice of the people demanding immediate reforms; and revolutions seldom follow a moderate course. The Jesuits were expelled, and on June 25, 1856, the *ley lerdo* was passed in an effort to disamortize the vast property holdings of the church. The law was not designed to confiscate but to dispose of church property as well as other corporate property at public auction, the owners to receive the greater part of the income from such sales. In other words, and since about one-half of the valuable lands of Mexico belonged to the church and were not used to their full potential, Lerdo's law was designed to widen the base of private property and to provide the means for greater productivity. And there were more laws of a similar nature to come, despite bitter and sometimes violent opposition from the church and other special-interest groups.

While Juárez, Lerdo, and others were laying the legislative foundations for the Reform, a constituent assembly, in accord with the Plan of Ayutla, was drafting a new constitution, which appeared in its final form on February 5, 1857. It, too, struck at the privileged classes. It called for the "reestablishment" of representative, republican government under a federalist system of thirty-three states and one territory. Freedom of speech, press, and religion were among the more important items in the document, as was the separation of church and state. Special tribunals, retroactive laws, slavery, and titles of nobility were prohibited. Education was to be free, and every man had a right to embrace any profession or any industry. But the constitution was not so clear on questions of religion. A constitutional mandate for religious toleration, said the moderates, would only lead to further opposition from the church. The time was not ripe for a fiat of this nature. *Puros,* somewhat reluctantly, agreed to compromise by casting their votes for Article 123, which clearly stated the superiority of the civil government over church officialdom. Thus, in a way, toleration came in the back door, but the church hierarchy scarcely viewed the outcome as a compromise. Nor did other conservatives look with favor on the new constitution. Even though the document contained a clause announcing the sacredness of property, the landed aristocracy, supported by the militarists and the church hierarchy, resorted to violence in the name of a common cause. No one was therefore surprised to learn that General Félix Zuloaga, on December 7, 1857, had issued the Plan of Tacubaya, which called for the election of a new constituent assembly and conferred dictatorial powers on Comonfort, who supported the plan in the belief that his middle-of-the-road policies would thwart the ambitions of the extremists, on both the right and the left. But he was in error. Neither group was of a mind to follow the high road of peaceful compromise.

Comonfort's dictatorship lasted less than a month. On January 11, Zuloaga issued a second *pronunciamiento.* Comonfort must resign. The dictator's policies, said the general, were tainted with liberalism and must therefore be revised by the conservatives. What better instrument for this than the army? Policies would be made by the sword.

The nation was now confronted with the Three Years War, or War of the Reform. For the better part of ten days, the troops of Comonfort waged an unsuccessful battle against Zuloaga's forces in Mexico City. On January 21, Comonfort left the capital, and was soon to go into exile in the United States. Juárez, who had been jailed by Zuloaga but released by Comonfort, made his way to Guadalajara as the new president, an office he assumed in accordance with the constitutional provision that the first in line of succession to the presidency was the minister of justice, a post held by Juárez in Comonfort's cabinet. But the conservative atmosphere at Guadalajara was not conducive to liberal reform; nor was the city the best strategic location for a contest with Zuloaga's government. Therefore, after narrowly escaping assassination, Juárez removed his temporary capital to Veracruz in the spring of 1858.

The War of the Reform ran its course until December, 1860, when Juárez was to reenter Mexico City in triumph. During the early stages of the struggle, the liberals were scattered and disorganized, a situation that enabled Zuloaga and his principal subordinates, such as the Indian Tomás Mejía, Leonardo Márquez, and Miguel Miramón, to win the battles. But as the year 1858 unfolded, the hopes of the reformers rose, for there was a falling out in the ranks of the conservatives which brought about the resignation of Zuloaga and the ascendancy of Miramón. Yet a similar, though less serious rift, appeared in the camp of Juárez. Degollado, Ocampo, Vidaurri, and Lerdo were not always of one accord on matters of state. Ocampo, desperately seeking funds for a bankrupt treasury, negotiated a treaty with the United States which, had it received the approval of the American senate and the dissident elements of the Mexican liberals, might very well have alienated Mexican sovereignty over a considerable amount of territory for the sum of four million dollars. Of course, the Miramón government exploited this, the McLane-Ocampo Treaty, to its own advantage. What further proof was needed to support the conservative charge that Juárez and his radicals were not above selling out to the *norteamericános?* The reformers might have asked a similar question: Was Miramón concerned with the best interests of Mexico when he negotiated a loan of $600,000 in return for $15,000,000 in Mexican government bonds? Was Miramón selling out to Jecker, the Swiss banker who made the loan to the conservative government? Time was not far distant when Juárez himself would be compelled to examine the constitutionality of the loans, and then make a decision which would bring to Mexico another tragic era.

Laws of Reform

Meantime, while conservative and liberal armies ravaged the land, and while each of the two governments sought financial aid, a series of laws, known as the Laws of Reform, were being conceived by Lerdo, Ocampo, and Manuel Ruíz, a newcomer to the Juárez cabinet. When the laws were promulgated in July, 1859, at Veracruz, the council chambers of the church resounded with storms of protest. For this was legislation which not only disestablished the church but delivered severe blows at the very foundations of clerical power. The wealth of the clergy was nationalized; exclaustration of the regulars was ordered; regulations for acquiring ownership of nationalized property were drawn up; and the civil registration of marriages, births, and deaths were to be compulsory.

The church hierarchy and the military oligarchy in Mexico City redoubled their efforts to rid the nation of

Juárez and his revolutionary government; but the spirit of reform had captivated the minds of the hungry and the dispossessed, too numerous to be turned back by the armies of Miramón. In the summer of 1860 his forces met telling defeats. By December, the liberal general, González Ortega, supported by *guerrilleros,* were pounding on the gates of Mexico City; and on the twenty-second of the month Ortega defeated the last of the conservative armies. Miramón and his associates hastily packed their bags and fled to Jalapa. A short while later Miramón boarded a French vessel that carried him to Europe. Meanwhile, on January 1, 1861, Ortega marched triumphantly into Mexico City. Ten days later Juárez, dressed in black and seated humbly in a black carriage, entered the capital — a strange sight for a city used to drums and trumpets on such occasions. For the first time a civilian had come to town to rule the nation.

The civil war had virtually ended. The compelling problem now, aside from the urgency of needs for economic and political reconstruction, was to carry forward with the Laws of Reform, "which," stated Juárez, "are an essential part of our institutions." Perhaps they were; and perhaps the majority of the Mexicans supported them. But, even though Juárez had banished several of the more hostile bishops, the clergy and their allies would not concede defeat, and they actively embarrassed the government in its attempts to enforce the laws. Then, shortly after Juárez was reelected to the presidency in June, the president's liberal associates quarreled with one another and were rarely in agreement on the proper course of action. Juárez therefore found himself in a difficult position, a position which might have been corrected, at least for the moment, had the president chosen the path of the dictator. But Juárez, in 1861, viewed his office in the light of the constitution, a legalistic stand that permitted conservatives and dissident liberals alike to exercise a freedom that was hardly conducive to the objectives of the Reform. Nor was the cause of the Reform served, when, in June, Ocampo and Degollado were killed by the conservatives. And a cloud was moving in from across the Atlantic which, for the greater part of a decade, would cast a shadow over all programs of reform.

FRENCH INTERVENTION AND MAXIMILIAN

Foreign intervention, of one sort or another, had vexed the life of Mexico, and would continue to do so until well into the twentieth century. The storm that was blowing in from the Atlantic had its origins in twenty years of scheming and plotting by conservative Mexicans residing in Europe who preached the doctrine of monarchy for their homeland. Arch-conservative and wealthy Gutiérrez de Estrada published a pamphlet as early as 1840 in which he advocated a European monarch for a throne in Mexico, and then went off to Europe in the hope that he could gain support for his monarchical ideas. Believing that he could arouse official interest in his plans, he charged the United States with expansionist designs; moreover, he wished the crowned heads to accept his conviction that the United States was a dangerous threat to the European political system. And to those who defined international relations in terms of economic theory, Gutiérrez would have protested that the United States planned to monopolize the trade of the Western Hemisphere.

No one of political stature took Gutiérrez seriously until events in Europe in the late 1850's created an atmosphere tending to promote his aims and those of other Mexican advocates of monarchy. Napoleon III was now on the French throne and had visions of building a colonial empire; prominent Spanish officials dreamed of a reconquest of Mexico and went so far as to draft a constitution for the former colony. England was cool to the idea of political intervention, but was willing to take a firm stand on matters relating to claims.

The opportunity for intervention and policies of firmness came in 1861. On April 15, Lincoln declared that an "insurrection" existed in the United States. Very little effective opposition to the European powers in their designs for Mexico could be expected from a nation engaged in civil war. Three months later, on July 17, the Mexican congress, following the recommendation of Juárez, declared a two-year moratorium on all foreign debts, $15,000,000 of which were Jecker claims.

Widely regarded as an ill-advised step, this provided France, England, and Spain with a pretext for armed intervention; and no one was seeking a pretext so avidly as Napoleon III. He had taken Jecker under his wing, had inclined a very attentive ear to the pleas of the Mexican monarchists, and was finding tangible support in the Spanish and British foreign offices. In September, Carl Schurz, United States ambassador to Spain, informed the Spanish government that the United States would not oppose Spain's intervention in Mexico, if intervention did not result in subversion of the republican form of government or in acquisition of Mexican territory. A month later, on October 31, England, Spain, and France signed the London Convention, an agreement for joint intervention in Mexico. The document itself was little more than a nod in the direction of international law; it is better known for its escape clauses.

In January, 1862, the troops of Spain, England, and France went ashore at Veracruz, presumably for the sole purpose of collecting the debts from the receipts of the custom houses. It would appear that England and Spain did view their missions in this light; but Napoleon III had other designs on Mexico. Encouraged by his Spanish-born wife, Eugénie, he was prepared to send his troops on to Mexico City. An action of this sort was hardly in accord with the spirit of the London Convention. Spain and England therefore promptly withdrew their forces. Other means would have to be found for satisfying their claims.

Visions of Empire

The Emperor of France had visions of establishing an empire in America, not only to serve as a buffer against the United States, but also to provide a source of raw materials; and these were visions which Mexican conservatives and clericals exploited. In particular, Jóse Manuel Hidalgo, a wealthy Mexican exile and friend of Eugénie, believed the time was now ripe for placing a European prince on a throne in Mexico City. The ideal man for the job, so said Hidalgo and his conservative Mexican friends, was the young Archduke Ferdinand Maximilian Joseph, a brother of the Austrian Emperor Franz Joseph, of the house of the Hapsburgs. Maximilian, a naive idealist, agreed to accept the crown of Mexico on the condition that the Mexicans really wanted him as their emperor. He was soon told that a plebiscite had been held in Mexico which clearly demonstrated his great popularity. He was not told that the plebiscite was rigged, that decisions from the Mexican capital rested on French bayonets, and that the majority of the Mexicans followed the leadership of Juárez. Had he not been such a naive young man, he might have suspected that something was "rotten in Denmark," for knowledgeable European statesmen warned him of the dangers of a throne in Mexico. And why did he fail to listen to what some of the wise rulers had to say about the enterprise? Queen Victoria made it quite clear that the British would not become involved. True, her brother Leopold, King of the Belgians and the archduke's father-in-law, was sympathetic to his daughter's desire to be queen of Mexico. But it is also true that Leopold cautioned Maximilian against accepting the word of the French Emperor. Indeed, Maximilian should have doubted the wisdom of the whole business when he was told that he would have to renounce any claim to the Hapsburg throne if he chose to wear the Mexican crown. He renounced his claim to the Hapsburg dynasty, but with considerable reluctance, and then went off to his magnificent palace at Miramar near Trieste, where on April 10, 1864, and in the presence of Mexican monarchists, he ascended the Mexican throne as Maximilian I. Four days later he and Charlotte boarded a frigate which would carry them to their New World capital. Their immediate objective, however, was Rome, where they hoped to receive the Pope's blessing. Pius IX extended the papal blessing to his royal visitors, but was quick to admonish Max "that, though the rights of nations are great and must be satisfied, those of the church are even greater and holier." The new emperor was known to be somewhat liberal in religious matters, which no doubt led the Pope to sound out his visitor on one of Mexico's most serious problems. But Max did not rise to the bait, except to say, in effect, that he would have to protect the rights of the state. Of course, no one could quarrel with the emperor's statement of this fundamental point of political theory. But had the young idealist been realistic and well informed on Mexican history, he would have desired to enter into a frank appraisal of church-state relationships in Mexico. Certainly nothing was more fundamental to the future of his empire. Certainly, too, nothing was more fundamental to his coronation than the partisans of the Mexican church. And so it was that Maximilian I made his first great error as emperor by not entering into an honest and open discussion with Pius IX on Mexico's basic problem.

Meantime Napoleon's army, together with a few Belgian troops, had fought its way from Veracruz to Mexico City and was fanning out to more distant points. But the invaders had discovered that their campaigns were somewhat more difficult than had been anticipated. On May 2, 1862, a Mexican army commanded by Ignacio Zaragoza had defeated the Count of Lorencez and his French troops on the outskirts of Puebla. Lorencez promptly withdrew to Veracruz, saying that he would not have been defeated had he not been misled by faulty intelligence from both the French Ambassador, Dubois de Saligny, and General Juan Nepomuceno Almonte, Napoleon's puppet ruler of Mexico. But the Emperor of France was not in a mood to look kindly upon the misfortunes of the count. Lorencez was therefore relieved of his command and replaced by one of France's most distinguished soldiers, Major General Elias Frédéric Forey, who landed at Veracruz in September with reinforcements and a letter of instructions making it very clear that whoever might come to sit on the Mexican throne would have to respect the wishes of France. But it was not until June 10, 1863, that Forey rode into Mexico City, after flooding the country with proclamations expressing the good intentions of the French, and after organizing an army that could win the battles. And Almonte was soon dismissed from office for "reasons of state."

The armies of Juárez were now in retreat. In May, the Mexican president, his cabinet, and a few thousand troops had left Mexico City for San Luis Potosí. By March, 1864, General François-Achille Bazaine, who had replaced Forey, had forced the Juárez government to take its stand on the far northern frontiers of the republic. It was indeed a perilous stand, for Zaragoza and Comonfort were dead, Doblado and Ortega were asking Juárez to resign, and Vidaurri would soon go off to Mexico City to join the ranks of the invaders. But *juaristas* were still putting up a good fight in the south: Juan Álvarez had things pretty much his own way in Guerrero, and a young officer, Porfirio Díaz, was master of affairs in Oaxaca.

On May 28, 1864, Emperor Maximilian I landed at Veracruz. A fortnight later, on June 12, the conservatives handed him the reins of government in Mexico City. But the ceremony was little more than a formality. Mexico's new emperor would not rule the land. Bazaine, Napoleon's agent, gave the orders and guided the course of the Mexican imperial government, while Archbishop Labastida let it be known that the church looked with jaundiced eyes on Maximilian's refusal to restore church property; nor was the archbishop tolerant of the emperor's general view of ecclesiastical affairs. And when Maximilian seated a few liberals in his council of ministers, conservatives reproached him.

But the emperor experienced little opposition from the masses, especially from those behind the French lines. The Mexicans were exhausted by endless conflicts, and were willing to behave as long as there was a semblance of peace and order. Yet Max seems not to have understood that this was a peace of exhaustion, especially by the time of his tour of pomp and ceremony to Querétaro and Guanajuato in the summer of 1865, a tour that had been staged by the monarchists, and during which he was falsely told that Juárez had abandoned Mexican soil. His conscience therefore permitted the issuance of the infamous decree of October 3, 1865, which ordered the death of *juaristas* without trial! After all, to bear arms against the state was treason. This was precisely what Juárez believed; and the Mexican president was not now adverse to responding to the decree by permitting his own officers to forgo courtroom formalities in cases of treason.

The October 3 decree was not an act of terror for terror's sake alone. It was something of a desperate move on the part of the French in the belief that an action of this sort would hasten the end of hostilities. For the greater part of three years the invaders had crossed and recrossed the land, and in February of 1865, Bazaine had even forced Díaz to surrender; but the *juaristas* had not thrown in the sponge, nor were they likely to do so. Furthermore time was running out for the Emperor of France, and the United States was no longer preoccupied with a civil war. On February 12, 1866, Secretary Seward demanded the withdrawal of the French troops. Since everyone knew that the *norteamericanos* had strongly opposed the imperial enterprise in Mexico from its very inception, Seward's note was no surprise. And would Seward implement his note with well-seasoned troops? This was only one horn of Napoleon's dilemma. The other was in Europe. Bismarck and his Prussian army were preparing for a showdown with the French. French troops had better come home. Bazaine was therefore instructed to gather together his men, and on February 5, 1867, the French general and several contingents of his army packed their gear and began their homeward journey. By the middle of March French troops were no longer on Mexican soil.

Napoleon may have thought that Maximilian would would also recognize the facts of life and return to Europe. But the "archdupe," as the Mexican Emperor was commonly called by his British and American opponents, chose to stay at his post, even though he found himself without an effective army. His naïveté had led him to believe that Bazaine would succeed in creating an imperial Mexican army in accordance with French promises. But quarrels between and among both native and foreign commanders presented Bazaine with problems which he either chose to ignore or to consider insoluble. Maximilian was therefore in command of little more than a token force when the French army was recalled. Yet the artless young emperor continued

lace his trust in Napoleon, a trust that led him to
ept, although with some hesitation, his wife's sug-
ion that she go to Europe in the summer of 1866
seek support for her consort's empire. Napoleon
Eugénie shed tears in the presence of Charlotte,
their royal majesties found neither money nor men
an overseas empire on the brink of destruction.
e policies rested on realism, not on lacrymose feel-
for the misfortunes of friends. Nor was Charlotte
to turn to her father, for the King of the Belgians
been dead for seven months. Perhaps the Pope
ld counsel a successful course of action. Charlotte
efore hastened off to Rome, only to arrive at her
ination with strong symptoms of insanity. She was
ly convinced that there was a plot afoot to murder
There was no such plot; but her mind had been
royed by frustration and fear. She never again
ined her sanity, and was to die in Belgium in 1927.

fly the palace of an emperor, Chapúltepec Castle in
ico City is now a museum. A portrait of the ill-fated
imilian I is among the visible reminders of European
ats to Mexico's political independence.

Collapse of Empire

The withdrawal of French troops from Mexican
soil hastened the collapse of Max's empire, a collapse
that might have come sooner had Generals Miramón,
Tomás Mejía, and Márquez not remained loyal to the
end. But loyalties alone do not win battles or build
empires; and sometimes the most loyal are little more
than sycophants, such as Father Agustin Fischer, a self-
appointed authority on affairs of state who created false
images of success in the mind of the Mexican monarch.
So when Maximilian marched forth from Mexico City
in February, 1867, to enter once more into battle with
the *juaristas* at Querétaro, his regime was rapidly drawing to a close. His army was small and poorly equipped,
and the rank and file had lost its zeal to die for a losing
cause. And once the French troops had withdrawn, the
majority of Mexicans everywhere openly cast their lot
with Juárez.

For the greater part of four months, from March
to the middle of June, Maximilian and his army managed to ride out the storm at Querétaro. Juárez and
his cabinet, still quarreling, had now established temporary headquarters at San Luis; and Díaz, on April 4,
entered Puebla and was soon to besiege Mexico City.

By May it was clear to Juárez that Díaz had the situation well in hand at the south. A final blow must now be directed at Querétaro, which was little more than a pocket of imperialists held down by the forces of Juárez. Mariano Escobedo, a juarist general, offered Maximilian an opportunity to escape from this indefensible position, but the emperor, as any courageous Hapsburg might have done, would not desert his friends. Then, early in the morning of May 15, one of Maximilian's "friends," Miguel López, turned traitor by permitting the *juaristas* to enter the town without a struggle. Again, the emperor had the opportunity to escape; but again, too, he chose to remain, even though he was now aware that he might have to face a firing squad. And so he did, on June 19, together with Miramón and Mejía on the Hill of Bells at Querétaro. Of course the kings of Europe were somewhat disturbed by all of this, and many a royal plea for clemency reached Juárez. But the kings did not know their Mexican, nor did they know their Mexican history. A grant of clemency for Maximilian would have been tantamount to an admission that the Reform was not important and that foreign intervention should be looked upon lightly. "Maximilian of Hapsburg," writes Juárez, "only knew the geography of our country," nothing more; and the monarchy was "the crime of Maximilian against Mexico."

RECONSTRUCTION AND THE RISE OF PORFIRIO DIAZ

A few days after the deaths on the Hill of Bells, Mexico City fell to the army of Díaz, and on July 15 Juárez himself made his second triumphal entrance into the capital in the famous black suit and black carriage. Two days later he issued a manifesto justifying his actions at Querétaro, and he soon began the difficult task of reconstructing a war-torn nation. And it would be a task without the experienced assistance of Álvarez, Ocampo, Doblado, Comonfort, Degollado, or Miguel Lerdo de Tejada, for all of them were dead, as was Vidaurri, shot for having turned traitor. Moreover, Juárez would discover that the congress was not in accord with his plans for economic and political stability. Nor did the opposition look kindly upon the United States, even though Seward would himself make a trip to Mexico City late in 1869 with messages of good will and friendship. Yet messages of these kinds are seldom free from history's bright light, especially when the light's rays are manipulated by those who may profit from a little distortion of facts. Should the Mexicans, for example, assign the Mexican War to limbo? And what about Seward's record of expansionism? Juárez's opposition found a sympathetic audience for these and other themes of Manifest Destiny; and the themes were good copy for a British press that chose to speak with authority on the allegedly evil ambitions of the United States. And the conservative opposition had an ally: latent, divisive tendencies were in the president's own camp. Yet the bulk of a nation of some eight or nine million, hungry and illiterate, stood patiently in the wings while their leaders disagreed on the proper courses of action.

Call to Election

The immediate course of action, said Juárez, must follow the lines of his *convocatoria,* or proclamation, which was released on August 14, 1867. It called for a national election, but more importantly proposed five constitutional amendments aimed at making significant changes in the organization of congress and that body's relations with the office of president, together with proposals for extending the franchise and limiting the powers of the states. Juárez no doubt believed that his proposals were sound, as did Sebastián Lerdo de Tejada, brother of the dead Miguel and member of Juárez's cabinet. But the opposition in congress maintained, with a measure of truth, that the *convocatoria* would give exceptional if not dictatorial powers to the president. Moreover, since the proclamation called for a referendum, the proposed amendments would probably receive a vote in the affirmative, simply because Juárez was the hero of the hour.

Juárez was indeed popular, but his reelection in October was not a mandate for the congress to follow the president's leadership as expressed in the *convocatoria;* and some of his liberal friends were piqued when the president refused to take their advice on cabinet appointments. Cabinet members did resign after congress confirmed Juárez's election, but the president was not of a mind to bring many new faces into the executive department; therefore, nominations for cabinet posts were, in the main, a roster of the chief magistrate's loyal veterans. The opposition did its best to reject the nominations, but a majority of the chamber's votes were cast for Juárez's nominees: Lerdo, Ignacio Mejía, Blas Balcárcel, Martínez del Castro, José Iglesias. This did not mean, however, that the cabinet question was settled, any more than it had been during the critical days of the Intervention. Even Francisco Zarco, the respected editor of the newspaper *Siglo XIX,* soon cast his lot with the opponents of the government. He preached the doctrine of capitalism, and had little patience with those who advocated antichurch measures; yet no one doubted his loyalty to the principles of liberalism. But it was a liberalism that said the old guard, and most especially Lerdo, must go; and astute politicians could not afford to ignore Zarco. Nor could Juárez overlook the criticisms of Manuel María de Zamacona, who had at one time served as minister of relations, only to be put on the shelf during the latter days of the Intervention. He was now telling the nation that the *convocatoria* was designed to extend dictatorial powers to Juárez. The president did not deny that he was requesting extraordinary powers of the congress, but maintained that the powers would only be temporary. After all, there was rebellion in the states of Yucatán, Puebla, Guerrero, Jalisco, and Sinaloa; assassins, thieves, and kidnapers were everywhere. A chief

In June, 1867, Emperor Maximilian and the generals, Mejía and Miramón, were executed on the Hill of Bells at Querétaro, capital of the modern state by the same name. A chapel called Shrine of the Bells now marks one of the important occasions on which imperialism was rejected.

executive, so said Juárez, could hardly be expected to meet these problems with any degree of success without a grant of exceptional powers. Yet he did consent to bow to some of the demands of the opposition by appointing Ignacio L. Vallarta to the post of *gobernación,* a ministerial office of major political authority. Vallarta, a jurist and strict constructionist of the constitution, might now be a counterweight to radical policies of Lerdo; but six months after the appointment Juárez accepted Vallarta's resignation. Lerdo was to remain in the cabinet, but would become one of Juárez's rivals in the presidential election of 1871.

The campaign for the presidency in 1871, in one form or another, had been a major theme since the election of 1867. Lerdo had been preparing the nation for his candidacy by subtle means, while General Porfirio Díaz, one of the heroes of the famous battle at Puebla on May 5, 1862, and a staunch supporter of Juárez during the entire period of the Intervention, had now turned against his chief, on the grounds that the president ruled without regard for the constitution.

The year 1871 was a critical one in the history of the Mexican presidency. It was a national election year, and the opposition, supported by Díaz and Lerdo, made a desperate effort to unseat Juárez. The politically ambitious Díaz said the time had come to remove a president who ignored the constitution and virtually ruled the nation as a military dictator. The general's observations were not profound, for everyone knew that Juárez would use his office to the fullest extent in an effort to restore peace and to travel once again on the road to reform. But did the means justify the ends? The means at the moment were for Juárez to control the balloting, and he had the power to do so, despite the fact that even some of the *puros* had defected to Díaz. Lerdo, too, questioned the means, though his program differed little from that of the *juaristas*; but unlike Díaz, he was free from any charge of personal hostility to Juárez. The Lerdist party simply believed that its candidate could do a better job by working more closely with the intelligentsia, the capitalists, and the lawyers.

When the ballots for president were counted, neither Juárez, Lerdo, nor Díaz was in the absolute majority column, Juárez having received 5,837 electoral votes, Díaz 3,555, and Lerdo 2,874. It was now congress's constitutional duty to choose one of the three for the high office, and on October 12 that body declared that Juárez had been reelected. Of course no one was surprised by the decision; and as further proof of Juárez's strength, the nation's voters had increased the numbers of *juarista* congressional deputies by twenty. Lerdo accepted the political verdict and remained in Juárez's government, while Díaz chose to redress his grievances by force.

The Plan of La Noria

On November 13, the general incited the nation to revolt by publishing his Plan of La Noria, prefacing the document with the statement that the chief executive was a dictator and should therefore be removed from office. Free elections must be returned to the nation, so states the plan, and the Constitution of 1857 must be recognized as the supreme law of the land. The plan then went on at some length about the establishment of trial by jury, the abolition of the sales tax, the revision of the tariff laws, and the extension of freedom to local governments. Clearly, all of this was an appeal to arms, a military pronouncement designed to place Díaz at the helm; but the appeal was not widely accepted. The general found very little effective support for his plan in Mexico City, though his partisans in Oaxaca and especially on the northern frontier did lend ear and rifle to the cause of Porfirio. The government troops managed, however, to bring the Oaxaca rebels to terms rather promptly, but it was a year or more before the *porfiristas* in the north laid down their arms.

But Díaz and Lerdo had an ally — death. On the morning of July 19, 1872, Juárez was cut down by a heart attack. Lerdo, president of the supreme court, was then raised to the office of president in accordance with the constitution, and one of the first acts of the new president was to grant amnesty to the rebels. Neither Díaz nor his followers were in a mood for compromise, but for the moment they found it the better part of wisdom to submit to Lerdo's amnesty decree.

Lerdo continued the policies of Juárez, and in 1874 the Laws of Reform were incorporated into the constitution. In the following year, Lerdo was elected to the presidency for a four-year term. Then when he announced that he would run for reelection in 1876, the *porfiristas* came forward in January of the same year with a pronouncement known as the Plan of Tuxtepec, which called for "effective suffrage" and no "reelection" and proclaimed Díaz head of a revolution against the government. And it was a revolutionary movement which obtained some tacit support north of the international border, for Díaz had journeyed to the United States for money and volunteers without protest from Washington. Some say it was an official silence occasioned by the alleged charge that Lerdo had refused to grant American railroaders special privileges in Mexico.

After a defeat of his revolutionaries at Matamoros, Díaz recrossed the international border, regrouped his forces and, disguised as a Cuban doctor, succeeded in reaching Veracruz by ship and then made his way to Oaxaca. Meantime, Lerdo had declared himself reelected, only to discover that José Iglesias, president of the supreme court, held the election invalid and that he, Iglesias, was the constitutional president. Then in October the *lerdistas* were decisively defeated at the battle of Tecocac, and on November 21 Lerdo fled to the United States. If Iglesias expected Díaz to recognize the president of the supreme court as president of the republic, he was greatly mistaken. On November 23, 1876, Díaz rode triumphantly into Mexico City. A month later Iglesias was forced into exile. The Age of Díaz was in the making.

THE AGE OF PORFIRIO DIAZ

Díaz, like Juárez, was a native of Oaxaca. Born to mestizo parents in that state's capital on September 15, 1830, he spent the greater part of his youth at odd jobs to support a widowed mother and a half-dozen brothers and sisters. Though these were years of hardship for Porfirio, he did manage to find some time for formal education; and by the late 1850's he had risen to a position of distinction in the army and was a loyal follower of Juárez. Then came the political chaos of the 1870's, a chaos which Díaz and his army friends were quick to exploit; thus, for the greater part of thirty-five years, from the winter of 1876 to the spring of 1911, Díaz would rule Mexico with an iron hand. He would be elected to the presidential office for seven terms, and there might have been an eighth had he chosen to seek the office in 1880. His role as dictator, from revolutionary president to "grand mogul," as one Mexican puts it, would have its staunch defenders and its bitter critics. Land barons, foreign and domestic, coupled with the power of the foreign investor, would be his principal supporters. A disciplined army, an effective police force known as the *rurales,* and a policy of not enforcing the Laws of Reform would bring peace to the nation. And economic policies would place Mexico in a most favored nation position in the world's financial capitals. It would indeed be a land of peace and prosperity, a peace and prosperity that rested on the insecure foundations of rural mass poverty and dictatorship; but "Díaz-potism" would not check the mainstream of Mexican history for all time. The ideals of the Plan of Ayutla and the Laws of Reform were far from running their course; nor would the small farmer, or *campesino,* view with complacency the alienation of his lands by the *hacendado*.

The "Indispensable Man"

The opening years of the Age of Díaz, from 1876 to 1884, witnessed the foundations of a dictatorship that would hold Mexico in its grip until 1911. In February, 1877, Díaz was addressed as "interim president." In May of the same year he took office as constitutional president, and several foreign powers, with the exception of the United States, promptly recognized the new government. Díaz of course was a bit concerned about Washington's reluctance to extend recognition, even though it was clear why the United States took this position. For example, would Díaz honor a claims agreement signed in 1868? Then, too, would the new government take adequate steps to stop cattle rustlers and bandits from crossing the border? And what disposition would Mexico make of the troublesome Free Zone? (In 1851 Mexico created a "Free Zone" in Tamaulipas and adjacent to Texas for the purpose of encouraging settlement by permitting the importation of duty-free foreign goods, a policy that enabled Texas merchants to obtain goods through the channels of contraband. Eastern manufacturers and suppliers in the United States quite naturally asked for a suppression of the zone.) These were questions which were satisfactorily answered by Ignacio Luis Vallarta, one of Mexico's most successful secretaries of foreign relations; and in May, 1878, the United States extended full recognition to the Díaz government. Thus was laid a most important foundation in foreign affairs upon which was to be erected an impressive economic structure for "Díaz-potism." Also, Díaz was strengthening his domestic political posture by posing as a sincere constitutional magistrate when in 1878 he approved an amendment to the constitution prohibiting immediate reelection; and he "gracefully" stepped aside in the presidential election of 1880 by permitting a friend, General Manuel González, to assume the office of chief magistrate. Some say that González was an honest and able man and that his scandalous administration was the product of Díaz's intrigues. In any event, Díaz became the "indispensable" man in 1884 and was returned to the office of president for a second term. Three years later, in 1887, he saw to it that the law permitted a single reelection, and in 1890 a constitutional amendment permitted indefinite reelections. He also created a mounted police force (the *rurales*), demanded absolute obedience from his army, reorganized the civil service, and soon succeeded in placing the nation on a sound financial base. To the superficial observer, Mexico had at last found a chief executive who would bring peace and prosperity to a long-suffering nation. Other observers would soon discover that peace and prosperity, without liberty and justice, would create an atmosphere for a successful revolution. The firing squad was a handy instrument for the moment but hardly a solution for ignorance, poverty, and social injustice.

Those who look upon the Díaz epoch as a highly successful period are impressed with Mexican financial and business statistics. In 1900, the nation's revenues were about 74,000,000 pesos; in 1910, about 110,000,000. Exports and imports amounted to a little more than 154,000,000 pesos in 1893; in 1910, to something like 499,000,000. There was a favorable balance of trade, and the national debt was insignificant. Foreign investments amounted to about three billion pesos, the greater part of which was United States capital; and few nations could boast of a better banking system. Factories multiplied by the hundreds. Gold, silver, and copper were mined in fabulous amounts. In 1880, approximately 31,000,000 pesos of gold and silver were mined; in 1910, 124,000,000, and Mexico was the world's second greatest copper producer. The petroleum industry was also pushing ahead rapidly, especially during the closing decade of the Díaz regime; the output of crude oil averaged about 10,000 barrels daily by 1910. Large sums were spent in public works, and railroads were built at a rapid pace. In 1876, there were only 691 kilometers of railways in the republic, but by 1910 the figure was about 25,000 kilometers. Thus, from all of this and other impressive statistics, one might say that *porfirismo* was

— Courtesy Pan American Union

Porfirio Díaz, military hero during the struggle against French intervention, became the dictatorial president of Mexico for more than thirty years. His regime was finally swept away in 1911, by the forces of the Revolution.

good for Mexico, or, as Frank Brandenburg writes, "Mexico really began its economic progress under the aegis of the old autocrat." But, as Brandenburg and other authorities on Mexico quickly point out, the Díaz regime either ignored or deliberately turned its back on Mexican history: economic, political, and social reforms for the welfare of the majority. The Age of Juárez would not die in vain. In other words, to use Cosío Villegas' figure, the hands on the clock of the Mexican revolution were already approaching high noon when Díaz first entered the office of the presidency. Díaz stopped the clock for the greater part of thirty years but failed to destroy its mechanism. He not only failed to destroy its mechanism, but adopted policies that served only to oil and rewind the mainspring that would force the clock to begin its revolutionary time-keeping once again.

Demand for Agrarian Reform

Of the many significant elements in this mainspring, none was more important than the demands for agrarian reform. Despite the fact that Mexico was predominately a land of *campesinos,* or peasants — their very way of life rooted in the soil — Díaz's land policies were feudalistic, thereby depriving the peasant of his *milpa,* or small plot of ground, and establishing a system of peonage. Vast haciendas were created, and Díaz gave "colonization" companies grants of public land in return for surveys and ridiculously small payments; and it was usually the foreigner who was the proprietor of millions of acres of land acquired under the colonization laws. Though no one knows exactly how much of the lands of Mexico — agricultural, grazing, forest, mineral — were managed as colonial grants and haciendas, the records make it clear that only the few were the proprietors of most of the nation's natural resources. And it is also clear that the peon, the most numerous of Mexico's citizens, existed at the whim of the *hacendado.*

The land systems of Mexico had their roots in the pre-colonial and colonial periods, and in some respects still do. Long before the arrival of Cortés at Veracruz, the Indians were familiar with feudal tenure, as well as with communal landholding. Each of these systems, with some basic differences, had its historical counterpart in Spain, and each was introduced into the New World. The Indian was therefore no stranger to the functions of the *encomienda* and the Spanish *ejido,* or village common land. There is no need here to dwell on the *encomienda,* for a summary of the institution was made earlier in this narrative. But just a word on the *ejido.* A similar institution existed in the Aztec empire, and as early as 1567 the Spanish crown granted *ejidos* to Indian villages. And of the several Mexican land systems, none has been more fundamental in the agrarian history of Mexico. The village farmer wanted his small plot of land, and was willing to die for it. The *hacendado,* who built his domain at the expense of the peon or *campesino,* was considered by the village farmer to be his worst enemy.

Although the hacienda did not spring in all its aspects from the *encomienda,* the *hacendado* had his counterpart in the *encomendero,* for each managed his vast estate as a feudal lord. The hacienda itself was the product of the acquisitions of land by clever and questionable means rather than by outright grants from the state, as was the case with the *encomienda*; and the term "hacienda" was in common usage by the eighteenth century. During the latter part of the nineteenth century it came to be the major form of land tenure in the nation. During the Díaz epoch it was not only the major form of land tenure but also a powerful political instrument of the state. What better way could be devised for compelling the peon to behave than by special legislation for the *hacendado?* And the *rurales,* or national police force, were always available in case the peon got out of hand.

Some have argued that the hacienda system was a sounder economic institution than the *ejido,* an argument based on the assumption that lands worked in common will not produce a surplus for the needs of the nation. Moreover, so the argument runs, the *ejido* by its very nature would neither provide the incentive nor the capital for economic growth. In the main, arguments of these kinds were valid, as has been clearly demonstrated by the history of the *ejido;* yet they were a weak defense of the hacienda system during the régime of Díaz. Great tracts of arable hacienda lands lay fallow year on end, and few *hacendados* kept abreast of developments in either farming or livestock raising;

nor were *hacendados* overly conscious of marketing techniques. They were far more interested in living abroad — in London, Paris or Rome — than in remaining in their great homes on the haciendas to give more immediate attention to their estates. It was therefore the manager's duty to see to it that things back home were run sufficiently well to provide the absentee landlord with funds for the luxuries of Europe; and profits, of course, must not be dissipated on such things as wages and better living conditions for the peon. The peon's wages were the same as they had been for a hundred years, even though the prices of corn, beans, and other necessities had increased by as much as 300 per cent. The peon was compelled to buy at the *tienda de raya,* or hacienda store, to which he was constantly in debt; and his family lived in one of the one-room adobe shacks located half a mile or more from the main buildings of the hacienda — no running water, no bathrooms, no comfortable furniture, no flower gardens here. But the manager's home nearby was modestly furnished and had a kitchen, one or two bedrooms, and perhaps running water and a bathroom. Of course the *hacendado's* mansion lacked none of the necessities of the good life, the good life of conspicuous consumption. The big house, standing on an acre or more of land and approached by tree-lined driveways and surrounded by well-tended gardens, was often an impressive establishment of thirty or forty oversize rooms extravagantly furnished. And no self-respecting *hacendado* was without a stable of the finest horses and lavish caparisons. With all this and other symbols of affluence, the *hacendado* occupied a singularly significant position in the social structure of Mexico. But in a nation of mass poverty and social injustice, coupled with a rising tide of fear and hatred of foreigners, the day of the *hacendado* was drawing rapidly to a close. A revolution was in the making, a violent revolution that would unseat the militarist and the clergy as well as the landlord in his great house.

THE REVOLUTION

The Mexican Revolution — always with a capital "R" — was no different from other national revolutions in one major aspect: intellectuals and idealists provided the inspiration and the theoretical principles. One such intellectual, Justo Sierra, held the post of secretary of education in Díaz's ministry, and was the founder of the National University. He questioned the positivism of the *científicos,* the name applied to a group of lawyers, bankers, and businessmen, some of whom held cabinet posts in Díaz's cabinet. The minister of finance, José Ives Limantour, was leader of the group and subscribed to the theory that "liberty . . . constituted a privilege of the select; the weak would have to yield" to the superior man. Although Sierra was in general agreement with the *científicos'* concept of history, he would not accept the view that liberty must be restricted to the few. History, he said, is a progressive movement in the quest for liberty, an ideal that must be sought by all the Mexican people. His students were attentive; two of them, José Vasconcelos and Antonio Caso, founded the *Ateneo de la Juventud,* or Youthful Athenaeum, in 1908, a small but active body that dared to discuss revolutionary ideas. (The time would come, late in the Revolution, when Vasconcelos would come near a full circle in his philosophy. Caso would stand fast and remain a revolutionary throughout his life.) But others came forward with ideas more extreme than those of either Caso or Vasconcelos.

Rise of the Liberal Party

Among the noteworthy of this group were the Flores Magón brothers, Ricardo, Enrique, and Jesús. Ricardo, born in Oaxaca in 1873 and influenced by his admiration of Juárez, became an active opponent of Díaz as early as 1892. It was the year of the third reelection of the dictator, and Ricardo, together with a number of student-led demonstrators, made it quite clear that Díaz had very little respect for the Constitution of 1857 or for the Laws of Reform. This demonstration did not change the course of "Díaz-potism," but Ricardo and some of his like-minded associates continued their opposition to the dictator, demanding a return to constitutional government and insisting upon the enforcement of the Laws of Reform. In 1900 Ricardo and Eugenio L. Arnoux created a medium for their revolutionary ideas by the publication of *La Regeneración,* an anti-*porfirista* journal which was to vex the dictator for several years. And by 1900 Ricardo had joined forces with Camilo Arriaga, another bitter opponent of Díaz and the founder of the *Club Liberal Ponciano Arriaga,* which became the model for fifty such "Liberal Clubs"; but Ricardo's brand of liberalism would be tainted with Kropotkin anarchism.

Díaz, for a time, tolerated the liberal clubs, but he moved quickly against the Magón brothers and some of their more extremist companions. Ricardo soon found himself in and out of the infamous Belén prison, and in 1903 he and his brother Enrique, together with Juan Sarabia, an intellectual with revolutionary leanings, took refuge in the United States, and in 1905 established their headquarters in St. Louis. The *Regeneración* continued to be the *magonista's* principal revolutionary organ; and a young idealist in Coahuila, Francisco I. Madero, is said to have saved the cause of the St. Louis liberals by sending them a considerable amount of money. A year or so later, Madero withdrew his support, both financial and ideological, simply because he did not believe that a genuine revolution would be patriotic. Of course, Díaz was in agreement with Madero, so much so that he succeeded in bringing charges of libel against the *magonistas* in a United States court, with the result that Ricardo, Enrique, and Juan Sarabia were arrested.

But revolutionaries are seldom discouraged by arrests and imprisonments. By February, 1906, the *Regeneración* was once again in print, and the *mago-*

nistas, supported for a time by Arriaga, had established a junta to draft a program for a liberal Mexican party. On July 1, the group published its famous *Programa del Partido Liberal* in St. Louis. The reader of the document was informed that "The Liberal Party fights against the despotism reigning in our country today" and that "The points in this program are nothing more than basic general principles for the establishment of a truly democratic government." The basic principles consisted of fifty-two points, but the greater number were more socialistic than democratic. The items dealing with revisions for the constitution and the enforcement of the Laws of Reform were not very startling; but this was not the case with the sections on capital, labor, lands, and the church. The church for example must no longer dominate the educational systems of Mexico. Education must be laical and compulsory to the age of fourteen, and the state should provide ways and means for educating the poor. The state must also regulate hours and wages for labor, establish a labor code, forbid child labor, and so on. And some strong statements appeared in the program about the redistribution of arable lands. For example, landowners would be required to give their unused but productive lands to the state for distribution to any citizen who sought such lands for agrarian purposes. The authors of the program then wrote some two thousand words of high rhetoric, adding a phrase or two about the "pirate Maximilian"; and everyone should know that "we are proud of our compatriots, Juárez and Lerdo de Tejada." Everyone should know, too, that the Liberal Party was the party of "Reform, Liberty and Justice."

While the junta was formulating its program, some of its members, by one means or another, encouraged labor unrest in Mexico. Late in the spring of 1906 the *magonista* liberal club at Cananea, Sonora, helped direct the course of a strike at the American-owned Green Consolidated Copper Company. The strike was promptly quelled by Mexican troops and armed Americans, but in a manner which created further hostility to the Díaz government. Liberals and other discontented elements in Mexico could now ask the question, Was this not clear proof that Díaz was not only anti-labor but pro-American as well? Then in September, members of the Liberal Party were active in an armed attack on Jiménez, Chihuahua, and in an abortive insurrection at Acayucan, Veracruz; and violence occurred elsewhere, the most serious of which was in January, 1907, at the Río Blanco textile mill near Orizaba. It was perhaps the most bloody of the several strikes and insurrections of the time, and there is good reason to believe that the *magonistas* played an active role here as they had at other places in the nation; yet the troops of Díaz remained in control of the labor situation, and would continue to do so for four more years. It would also be four and more years of division in the ranks of the liberals; and *magonistas* who resided in the United States would run afoul of the law and be harassed by Díaz's agents. Ricardo Flores Magón would soon lose his influence over Mexican labor, but he

— Courtesy Pan American Union

Francisco I. Madero, a precursor of the Revolution, became president of Mexico in 1911; he was assassinated in February, 1913.

would continue his revolutionary activities, one way or another, until his death on November 21, 1922, in Leavenworth Penitentiary while serving a twenty-year term for a violation of the United States Espionage Act.

The old dictator had succeeded in holding the *magonistas* at bay, but the forces of revolution were to gain momentum with the approach of the presidential election of 1910. For instance, porfirian prosperity, such as it was, suffered a serious setback after the 1907 recession in the United States. Then two years later, in 1909, crop failures caused great suffering in the rural communities. Hungry and starving peasants were in a mood for rebellion.

Díaz himself unwittingly prepared the way for the rebellion by welcoming an interview with James Creelman, an American reporter who published the results of the interview in *Pearson's Magazine* in 1908. The article stated that Díaz would not stand for reelection in 1910 and would welcome political opposition in the coming election. There is good reason to believe that the eighty-year-old president had permitted this, the "Creelman Interview," for foreign consumption and not for the Mexican press. In any event, Creelman's article appeared in the Mexico City *El Imparcial,* which created quite a stir; and so did *The Presidential Succession of 1910,* a book that appeared on the newsstands and elsewhere in 1909.

The author of the book, Francisco I. Madero, was the son of a well-to-do *hacendado.* Born on October 30, 1873, on his father's hacienda in Coahuila, he was

reared in a family of fifteen children. He was a sickly child and physically small. Two ladies at Parras taught him to read and write, and at the age of twelve he was sent to the Jesuit College of San Juan in Saltillo. In 1887, he went to France to continue his formal education and to travel during vacation periods. Four years later, in 1891, he read several issues of the *Revue Spirite,* a journal founded by Allán Kardec, a well-known writer on spiritism. What the *Revue* had to say about mediumistic phenomena and about Kardec caused Madero to hasten off to the offices of the publication in search of Kardec's works. He found them. "I did not read them," he says, "but devoured them, because their doctrines, so rational, so beautiful, so new, captivated me, and since then I consider myself a spiritist." Then for a time, and doubtless owing to the influence of the spiritualists, Madero turned to the study of Oriental religions. In 1892 he returned to his father's hacienda for a short visit. He then accompanied his father, two sisters, and two brothers to California, where he enrolled at the university at Berkeley. Late in 1893 Francisco was once again on his family's hacienda, with the responsibility of assisting his father in the management of the Madero estate. The young man soon demonstrated considerable competence as an administrator of his father's property; and like the sons of many wealthy Mexican families of the day Francisco became somewhat unrestrained in his personal habits. He tells us, however, that these were habits he abandoned as a result of the great emotional distress arising from the illness of his mother. Then, in 1903, he married Sara Pérez, the daughter of a well-to-do Mexican landowner. She appears to have encouraged Francisco to follow the paths of a serious and righteous life; and it was a life which would now be dedicated to politics.

Guidelines for Action

Madero's book, *The Presidential Succession in 1910,* establishes guidelines for political action. The book itself, divided into three parts, is not a masterpiece of historiography or political theory, nor is it a literary gem. The first part is a summary of Mexican history, dwelling on the evils of militarism. The second section, a superficial analysis of absolute political power, is a restrained attack on the Díaz regime. But it is the third and final section of the book that is the most important one. Mexico, he says, is ready for democracy. Neither Vice-President Ramón Corral nor General Bernardo Reyes, the popular governor of Nuevo León, should be elected in 1910 to the vice-presidential office, for this would simply mean that one or the other of these *porfiristas* would ultimately succeed to the presidency and thereby prolong the age of despotism. And how would the nation rid itself of despotism? The answer, according to Madero, would come from the formation of an anti-reelection party, a party that would give the nation effective suffrage and would stand on the principle of no reelection. But suppose the candidates of the opposition were defeated, even though the election may or may not have been free? Madero replies by stating that defeat at the polls would not be the critical issue; the important point would rest on the fact that the nation would be preparing itself for future electoral freedom. In any event, the people must not resort to revolution. A revolution, he says, would only aggravate Mexico's problems.

Was Madero deeply concerned with Mexico's basic problems, such as economic and social reform? He skirts these subjects in his book; nor would he face them squarely even after he reached a position of political power. He therefore has his critics; but no one can deny that his little book did contribute to awakening a nation to its immediate political problems. Economic and social reforms would soon follow in the wake of effective suffrage and no reelection.

But Madero and the Magón brothers were not alone in their attacks on the dictatorship. In the northern frontiers of the nation a movement had been under way for some years to support the *mestizo* governor of Nuevo León, General Bernardo Reyes, as Díaz's successor. Though Reyes was a *porfirista,* he had governed well. Under his administration Nuevo León had not only become the most prosperous state in the republic but was also the first Mexican state to have a workmen's compensation law. The general was therefore popular, but there is little reason to believe that he was a staunch advocate of freedom, despite the fact that his son Rodolfo believed that his father would give Mexico a democratic government. Rodolfo had little difficulty in convincing others that the general should replace Díaz, and a *reyista* party soon appeared.

The general may or may not have been the instigator of the Reyist boom, but in any event the *cientificos* down in Mexico City were a bit concerned. They feared and detested Reyes. They wanted their own leader, Limantour, in the presidency. Then for a moment it looked as though the old dictator himself would please both the *reyistas* and the *cientificos.* He brought Reyes into the cabinet as secretary of war, and word soon got around that Limantour was being groomed for the presidency and that Reyes would serve as Limantour's chief advisor. But this was little more than a rumor. The crafty old man sent Reyes back to Nuevo León, and someone discovered that the law prohibited the son of a foreign citizen to sit in the office of the presidency. Limantour was therefore disqualified, for his father had been a French citizen. Meanwhile Díaz arranged to have the presidential term extended to six years and also established the office of vice-president. But, of course, his choice for the newly created position would not fall to either Limantour or Reyes when the election of 1904 came around. Ramón Corral was his man, a *cientifico* who had governed Sonora with an iron hand and had an unenviable reputation, mainly because of the manner in which he had mistreated the Yaqui Indians. But Díaz was not searching for a popular man for the vice-presidency. Who would want to assassinate Díaz if the dictator's succes-

sor would be Corral? Then as a further move by Porfirio to shore up his position, he resorted to his well-known technique of divide and rule, in this instance by supporting a group of avowed reformers, among whom was his own secretary of justice, Joaquín Baranda. But Baranda was not deceived for long. He handed in his resignation shortly after the election of Díaz and Corral in 1904.

The young intellectuals, such as Vasconcelos, Luis Cabrera, and Andrés Molina Enríquez, were now busily engaged in searching for an answer to the dictatorship, of which none was more critical than Molina Enríquez, who soon published his *Los grandes problemas nacionales,* a sound, analytical study of Mexico's unfortunate agrarian situation. The book caused quite a stir, as did a reappearance of the *reyistas,* who were now willing to settle for the vice-presidency in the coming election. After all, the eighty-year old president could not rule forever. Díaz promptly settled this matter by sending Reyes on a special mission to Europe.

Reyes was gone, but Madero was still in the country and building a formidable political machine, which counted among its numbers a sizable group of *reyistas.* He carried his word of "effective election" from one end of the land to the other. Almost everywhere he was welcomed by vast crowds, and in April, 1910, an anti-re-electionist convention nominated him for the presidency, and the Díaz family physician, Francisco Vásquez Gómez, for the vice-presidency. Díaz soon had to admit that the mild-mannered man from Coahuila was posing a serious threat to the dictatorship. It was therefore no great surprise to learn that Madero had been jailed at San Luis Potosí, on the charge of inciting rebellion against the government. A month later, in July, the elections were held, and, quite naturally, Díaz and Corral were reelected. But the Madero family still had influential friends among the *cientificos,* who managed to arrange bail for Francisco. He promptly made his way to San Antonio, Texas, and issued a revolutionary manifesto, dated October 6, 1910, and known as the Plan of San Luis Potosí. It called for the nullification of the July elections and the installation of Madero as president, promised free elections and other reforms, and instructed the Mexicans to rise up in arms against the dictator on November 20. He then sent his brother Gustavo and Vásquez Gómez to Washington and New York for financial and any other assistance they might receive for Madero's cause. At long last Madero had enlisted in the ranks of the revolutionaries.

Díaz now had a real revolution on his hands. Rebellion broke out everywhere. In Chihuahua a storekeeper, Pasqual Orozco, together with a bandit chieftain, Pancho Villa, raised an army which soon had the federal troops on the run. In Morelos, Emilano Zapata and his peasants were leveling haciendas, and *querrilleros* everywhere were making life uncomfortable for *porfiristas.* Nor was this all that Díaz had to face. There had been a cooling off in Washington toward the dictator, owing mainly to the fact that Díaz had invited trouble by being a bit too friendly to British oil interests to please their counterparts in the United States. Furthermore, Washington was sending troops to the border, a move which Díaz thought might lead to armed intervention. Díaz did manage, however, to persuade the United States to prevent revolutionaries from shuttling across the border; but Madero had already returned to Mexico.

By May, 1911, the armies of Madero, Orozco, and Villa were having things pretty much their own way. The federal troops were losing in the north, and on the eleventh of the month Ciudad Juárez was captured by the *maderistas*. On the following day, Zapata captured Cuautla in the south. On May 21, Díaz's command at Ciudad Juárez signed a treaty with Madero which provided for the resignation of Díaz and Corral and the establishment of a provisional government. Limantour had been recalled from Europe in February, in the faint hope that he might use his genius to put out the fires of revolution that were sweeping across the nation. But neither Limantour nor anyone else could stop the powerful forces of revolution that had been in the making for a decade or more. Díaz would have to resign; and resign he did, on the night of May 24. A few days later he was aboard ship on his way to exile in Europe, shortly to be followed by Limantour. Two years later, on July 2, 1915, Díaz died in Paris.

Madero entered Mexico City on June 7, 1911, a conquering hero, the "Apostle of the Revolution." Nineteen months later he would be dead from a murderer's bullet; yet he might have lived a great deal longer had he not permitted himself to fall into a series of critical errors that not only brought rifts between him and other precursors of the revolution, but also permitted *porfiristas* to spring the trap that ended Francisco's career. His first error was to allow Francisco León de la Barra, Díaz's foreign minister, to serve as provisional president from May 26 to November 6. Only three members of De la Barra's cabinet were true revolutionaries, and Madero seems not to have raised any objection to this rather strange situation. Nor did Madero see the dangers of appointing members of his family to important posts. Nepotism was certainly a questionable policy for winning friends. Then when Madero chose José María Pino Suárez as his running mate in the November elections, many a revolutionary raised a storm of protest. Of course, Madero was elected president, but there were others more competent than Vice-President Pino Suárez, an ineffectual little man from Yucatán. And what was Madero doing about agrarian reform? Very little. True, he had not considered the agrarian problem a vital issue, but he had said that something must be done for the landless. Agrarianism may not have been a vital issue in Madero's thinking, but it certainly was a matter of major concern to Zapata and to thousands like him. It was also a major concern of the congress, the famous Twenty-Sixth Legislature, famous for its great debates and independence; yet Madero failed to see the signs of the times. Zapata would now issue his *pronunciamento,* the Plan of Ayala. Madero, it said, had betrayed

the Revolution and was therefore no longer the president of Mexico. Shouting "Land and Liberty," the *zapatistas* leveled the haciendas and seized the land; and in February, 1912, Orozco pronounced against Madero. In the meantime, Reyes, who had returned to Mexico, joined Félix Díaz, Porfirio's nephew, in an armed revolt; but neither Reyes nor Félix Díaz were casting their lot with Zapata. Madero sent an army under General Victoriano Huerta against the forces of Orozco. Huerta succeeded in defeating Orozco's rebels, but Orozco managed to take refuge in Arizona. The rebellion of Reyes and Díaz was also suppressed; and the two were arrested and jailed, finally, in Mexico City. But Madero's troops failed to defeat the hordes of *zapatistas,* who continued to harass the haciendas and to tell the peons that Madero was an "autocrat, destroyer of the Plan of San Luis Potosí. . . . Forward! The light of liberty now shines brightly on the horizon!" Even Dr. Vásquez Gómez had turned against Madero, while the president's "loyal" general, Huerta, stood in the wings preparing to seize the government.

A Doomed Regime

Madero's regime was obviously doomed — obvious to everyone but the chief magistrate himself. By February, 1913, the forces of reaction were in the ascendancy in Mexico City. Army officers freed Reyes and Díaz from their prison cells, and on the morning of the ninth, under the command of Reyes, an army of counterrevolutionaries trained their guns on the National Palace. For ten days *(la decena trágica),* the central plaza and the streets of Mexico City were bathed in blood; among the dead was Reyes himself. By the eighteenth, it was clear that Madero's government would fall; and no one in the capital was more desirous of this than Henry Lane Wilson. He arranged a secret meeting with the army leadership, from which he obtained an agreement that Huerta should become provisional president of the republic, but that Díaz would succeed him when the next elections were held. Madero and Pino Suárez were promptly seized and held under house arrest. Wilson then revealed, in the United States Embassy, and in the presence of foreign diplomats, the agreement that had been made with the army. The agreement was signed by the diplomats, an agreement that was to be known as the Pact of the Embassy. Wilson then informed Washington that the "despotism had fallen" and that Huerta's government should be recognized. But Washington refused to honor its ambassador's recommendation. No doubt a *de facto* government did exist in Mexico, but a new administration was about to take office in Washington, the administration of Woodrow Wilson — and Woodrow was never one to look with favor on governments that rested on the sword. And the Mexican sword was already bloody. On the evening of February 22, Madero and Suárez were removed from the palace and were assassinated on their way to the penitentiary. Naturally, Huerta was "shocked." The death of the two men, according to the official report, had been an accident! The apostle was dead, but not the Revolution.

For seventeen months, Huerta would set his course in the direction of the "good old days," the days of *porfiriato*. It would be a ruthless course, one of death to the agrarians and anti-re-electionists, or to anyone else who was a threat to Huerta's counterrevolution; yet — at least during the early months of his rule — Great Britain and other European powers recognized his government, as did China and Japan. English bankers were also happy with the new developments in Mexico; and an English bond issue of 7 million pesos went to Huerta's treasury. After all, this might not have been an undue risk for creating a favorable atmosphere for English mining and oil interests in Mexico. A few *norteamericanos* may have had similar intentions, but President Wilson was not prepared to curry favor with Huerta through loans or any other method that might support the dictator. Henry Lane Wilson was recalled, and the American president sent an agent to Mexico with instructions to ask Huerta to resign and to hold elections for a new president. Loans might then be forthcoming from the United States. Huerta responded by seeing to it that his congress demanded his retention in office. By February, 1914, President Wilson raised the embargo on arms, arms that soon reached the armies of Huerta's opponents.

The Fall of Huerta

It was now Huerta's turn to fall. Zapata's army in the south continued to pillage, burn and kill. In the northwest, Álvaro Obregón, a soldier-farmer, was raising an army to fight the forces of Huerta. Pancho Villa commanded an army in the north, and Pablo González was the leader of anti-*huertistas* in the northeast. The Army of the Constitution was in the making, an army whose supreme leader was Venustiano Carranza, who called himself the "First Chief." Though Carranza had made a fortune as a national senator during the Díaz regime, he chose to identify his interests with those of Madero during the closing days of the *porfiriato*. And of the many controversial figures in Mexican history, none is more so than Carranza. Was he a staunch revolutionary, or was he mainly an opportunist? He certainly was not one who believed in a social revolution. In any event, his Army of the Constitution, together with the policies from Washington, would bring the collapse of the Huerta government.

Woodrow Wilson's lifting of the arms embargo enabled the revolutionaries to control the greater part of northern Mexico by April, 1914; and the American president had gone even further in his will to force Huerta out of office. The steps in this stage of developments began at Tampico, when some American sailors were arrested by the Federals. The men were released, but the United States admiral then demanded a twenty-one-gun salute to the American flag, a salute that was not forthcoming. A few days later, on April 21, and after learning that the German ship *Ypiranga* was about to deliver munitions to Huerta, American troops seized the city of Veracruz. Some two hundred Mexicans lost their lives in defense of this strategic port on Mexico's eastern coast. Even Carranza, who had been hoping that the United States would recognize the legitimacy of the Army of the Constitution, was quick to denounce the American action; and the captain of the *Ypiranga* managed to put the munitions ashore. Then, too, since the occupation of Veracruz was a clear action of intervention, to which Latin Americans have always been sensitive, Huerta exploited the situation by posing as Mexico's defender against the "colossus of the North." His new role, however, did not turn aside the Army of the Constitution. Villa's Army of the North, Obregón's Army of the Northwest, and González's Army of the Northeast were moving rapidly on the capital. It was little more than a mad race to Mexico City. Villa, however, had had a falling out with Carranza, and requested Obregón to work closely with the commander of the Army of the North. But Obregón ignored the request, and pushed on. On August 15, 1914, Obregón and Carranza entered Mexico City, but Huerta had saved his scalp by making a hasty departure for Europe. By 1916 he was in the United States, where, in Texas, he was plotting an attack upon the Mexican rulers, a plot that ended in his arrest; and shortly thereafter he died.

The triumph of Obregón and Carranza, writes Howard Cline, "was a prelude to even further anarchy." Indeed it was. The First Chief did issue decrees which seemed to embody the spirit of the Revolution. For example, he abolished peonage, provided for the distribution of lands, legalized divorce, and so on; but neither Zapata nor Villa was duly impressed with Carranza's supposedly deep interest in a genuine revolution. Villa had already withdrawn his support of Carranza, and Zapata and his peons were unimpressed with official documents—"Land and Liberty" now. For the moment, all three—Carranza, Zapata, Villa—agreed to settle their differences through the deliberations of a convention. The convention was assembled — the famous Convention of Aguascalientes. But it was hardly a gathering of friends. Compromises were not welcome, and, since the meeting was in *villista* territory, Villa's army dominated the proceedings. Finally, it was agreed that General Eulalio Gutiérrez, a man who merited considerable respect, should serve as provisional president.

Guitérrez accepted the nomination, but discovered that Mexico's most competent general, Obregón, would not associate himself with the *villistas*. Carranza, said Obregón, was more dependable than Villa. Guitérrez, perhaps somewhat reluctantly, appointed Villa general of the provisional government.

Guitérrez's conventionalist government was short-lived. The armies of Villa and Zapata rode in and out of Mexico City for a time, and at will; but Obregón's superior generalship finally succeeded in expelling the *villistas* and *zapatistas* from the great valley. Guitérrez, by January, 1914, had been forced to concede defeat to the *carrancistas,* and took refuge in the United States.

Sitting confidently behind the shield of Obregón's army, Carranza came forth with more decrees of a revolutionary nature, decrees designed to win popular support for his cause; and none of the edicts was more important for both his search for popularity and the further course of the Revolution than the decree of January 6, 1915. "Considering that the most general . . . discontent of the farming population . . . has been the seizure of their common lands . . . I have ordered the following. . . ." In twelve succinct articles Carranza ordered the return of lands illegally taken, and, if additional lands were necessary, the holdings of the *hacendados* were to be given to those in need of lands. A national agrarian commission was to be created, and local military authorities were to enforce the decree. Carranza had thus put himself on record as an agrarian reformer, but his performance in this role was not satisfactory, at least to Villa and Zapata. The civil war continued; but in April of the same year Obregón all but destroyed Villa's army in the famous battle of Celaya. Villa beat a hasty retreat northward, never again to be a serious threat to the *carrancistas,* other than to stir up trouble with the United States.

The administration at Washington recognized Carranza's government in October, 1915. Villa now turned his wrath against the *norteamericanos.* In January of the following year the *villistas* murdered sixteen American engineers at Santa Ysabel, Chihuahua. Two months later Villa's men crossed the international border and killed a score or more of inhabitants of Columbus, New Mexico; and similar raids vexed other American towns. President Wilson, unable to get assurances from Carranza that the raids would stop, sent General John J. Pershing on a punitive expedition; but the clever Villa eluded the general, and the expedition did little more than stir up further hostility to the United States. Pershing was called home, and would soon be sent to Europe to command American troops in World War I. Then, in an attempt to exploit the Mexican-American rift, Germany undertook to lure Mexico to the cause of the Central Powers. But the forces of the Revolution would not be turned aside by European quarrels, and a new constitution was already in the making.

In December, 1916, a constitutional convention had assembled at Querétaro to draft the charter. A little more than a year later, on February 5, 1917, a decree informed the world that Mexico was now living under a new constitution. Not only was it new; it was a true revolutionary document. Carranza was not overly pleased with it, even though the delegates to the convention had more or less been chosen because they were *carrancistas.* As the work of the convention proceeded, and owing in great part to the influence of Obregón, Molina Enríquez, and Francisco Múgica, Carranza's conservative constitutional views received very little support. The First Chief was wise enough, however, to see that his own political future would be short-lived unless he accepted the document.

The Constitution of 1917, in its broad outlines, was fashioned after French and American theories of republican government: division of executive, legislative, and judicial functions; respect for personal and property rights; special rights for state and local governments. These were all more or less in the classic tradition; but far more important were the revolutionary, socialistic articles of the instrument.

None of the items in the document were more revolutionary than articles 27, 123, and 130. Article 27 stated that "Ownership of the lands and waters . . . is vested originally in the nation, which . . . has the right to transmit title thereof to private persons. . . . The Nation shall at all times have the right to impose on private property such limitations as the public interest may demand." Moreover, "In the Nation is vested the direct ownership . . . of all minerals or substances, which . . . form deposits of a nature distinct from the components of the earth itself. . . ." This doctrine of property rights was not startling, so far as its historical origins were concerned, for during the colonial period title to all lands was vested in the crown. Article 123 extended vast rights and privileges to labor. The workday was to be eight hours; women and children were not to engage in unhealthy work; persons between twelve and sixteen were not to work for more than six hours in any one day; minimum wages would be established; strikes and lockouts were recognized; together with a long array of other rights and privileges. Article 130 was the work of the convention's anticlericals. The congress was not to enact any law "establishing or prohibiting any religion"; marriage was to be a civil contract; "ministers of any denominations may never . . . criticize the fundamental laws of the nations"; to practice the ministry one would have to be a Mexican by birth; the church was forbidden to participate in public education; and the places of worship were to be state property. In effect, Article 130 was little more than an extension of the Laws of Reform.

Quite naturally, the church, *hacendados,* and foreign landholders were upset. The Mexican government, they said, was "socialistic and anti-Christ." American oil companies were angry at the turn of events, and especially so when Carranza decreed that Article 27 was retroactive. But neither *hacendado,* clergyman, nor foreigner could stop the revoluntionary clock. The constitution was a record of the Revolution; and the Revolution itself would continue to evolve along the guidelines written at Querétaro.

But Carranza did not follow the guidelines with any degree of sincerity. Labor, following the leadership of Luis Morones, turned away from the First Chief, who was now the president of the republic; and the agrarians had lost all of their confidence in the government at Mexico City. In retaliation, Carranza offered a reward for the head of Zapata; and, on April 10, 1919, this great agrarian revolutionary was assassinated. Even Obregón, who had returned to his farms in Sonora, threatened the rule of Carranza. The president failed to find an army that would stand up against the Sonoran. Carranza, aware that he was in a most insecure position, packed his bags and boarded a train for Vera-

¡DALE, SEÑOR, TU ETERNO DESCANSO; Y QUE LUZCA PARA EL LA ETERNA LUZ!

COMO VIVIO ASI MURIO, EN LA PAZ Y EN EL OSCULO DE CRISTO, DE QUIEN FUE VICARIO FIDELISIMO AQUI EN LA TIERRA.

El Arzobispo de Guadalajara, CARDENAL JOSE GARIBI RIVERA, y el V. CABILDO METROPOLITANO, uniéndose al duelo universal y a los sufragios del pueblo católico de todo el mundo, ofrecerá en la Santa Iglesia Catedral Basilica Metropolitana, a las 10 de la mañana del próximo lunes 10, SOLEMNISIMAS HONRAS FUNEBRES PONTIFICALES, por el eterno descanso de nuestro Santisimo Padre el Papa JUAN XXIII, en el séptimo dia después de su fallecimiento. La Oración Fúnebre estará a cargo del M. I. Sr. Maestrescuelas Dr. Don José Ruiz Medrano. Se invita a todo el pueblo de Guadalajara a asistir, uniendo sus oraciones con el celebrante en este luctuoso HOMENAJE POSTUMO.

Guadalajara, Junio de 1963

Secular society though it may be, Mexico's bond to both the church and the traditions of European culture is often in evidence. This poster was issued by the Archbishop of Guadalajara to announce funeral solemnities on the seventh day following the death of Pope John XXIII.

cruz, hoping to take a ship that would carry him into exile. He never reached his destination. His train was attacked, and while fleeing his pursuers he was murdered on the night of May 21, 1920, in the Puebla Mountains.

Period of Reconstruction

The following fourteen years, from 1920, when Obregón rode into Mexico City with forty thousand troops, until December, 1934, when Lázaro Cárdenas was inaugurated into the presidency, would be a period of constitutional reconstruction. A great deal would be said about democracy and reform, and all the official documents would be carefully stamped with the slogans *sufragio efectivo; no reelección,* and everywhere one would hear the shout, *viva la Revolución.* But, with rare exceptions, elections would seldom be free, and the constitution's Magna Charta for labor and the agrarian reformer would be honored more in the breach than in the observance.

The period began, however, with a great deal of hope for the future. Obregón was elected president in 1920. Like Carranza, he did not give his full support to the constitution; and like Díaz he ruled with an iron hand. But unlike either Carranza or Díaz, Obregón recognized that Mexico would not turn its back on the

Revolution. Obregón therefore geared his policies to the facts of political life. He wooed the army by giving the generals special considerations. He then gained the support of organized labor by making concessions to Luis Morones, who guided the destinies of the CROM *(confederación regional obrera mexicana),* which claimed to have no less than 1,200,000 members by 1924; but no more than token support was given to agrarian reformers, who now looked to the intellectual Antonio Díaz Soto y Gama as their leader. The ministry of education went to José Vasconcelos. Backed by substantial financial support, he established no less than a thousand schools in the republic, and his emphasis was on rural education and the Indian heritage of Mexico.

Though Obregón was giving direction to the Revolution, discontented elements at home and abroad plagued his administration. Leadership in the church defied the anticlerical articles in the constitution, a defiance that arose mainly from the fact that some generals, agrarians, and laborites insisted on a prompt and literal interpretation of Article 130. Obregón himself was not hostile to the church, but when the hierarchy of the church flaunted its authority in January, 1923, during the dedication of a monument to "Christ, King of Mexico" at Guanajuato, Obregón felt compelled to go so far as to expel the apostolic delegate. The faithful everywhere responded with a *Viva Cristo Rey,* and for the moment it appeared as though there would be a violent struggle between church and state. Fortunately this did not occur.

The church-state quarrel in Mexico reached the headlines of the American press, and one or two publishers advocated armed intervention to save the Mexicans from "attack upon religion." Even a few congressmen and other high-placed officials said the time had come to send in the troops, not only to restore Christianity to Mexico, but also to protect the property rights of Americans; and it was the question of property rights that was of major concern to oil companies, especially if such rights were in danger of being confiscated under the provisions of Article 27. The Harding administration then withheld its recognition of Obregón's government until it was assured that Article 27 would not be applied retroactively. Obregón was a bit reluctant to override Carranza's earlier decree on the matter; but, as a price for recognition, the Mexican president informed Washington that American claims to Mexican property acquired before 1917 would not be jeopardized by Article 27. Still, Washington hesitated to take the word of Obregón. Secretary of State Charles Evans Hughes then sent commissioners to Mexico City to confer with the Mexican president. Recognition was now close at hand. The American commissioners, together with their Mexican counterparts, signed what has since been known as the Bucareli Agreements. Washington was satisfied, not only because the agreements implied that Article 27 would not be applied retroactively, but also because provisions were made for future claims commissions. In August, 1923, the United States extended full recognition to Mexico.

Meantime, Obregón was grooming Plutarco Elías Calles for the presidency in the coming election of 1924. Calles was a two-fisted revolutionary of forty-seven from the state of Sonora, and during his early life he had experienced the evils of poverty. He had served in Carranza's army and cabinet, and was now Obregón's secretary of government; and, at least for the moment, he was known as a spokesman for both the laborites and the agrarians. It would therefore seem that Obregón had chosen the logical man for the presidency. But Adolfo De la Huerta, also a native of Sonora and Obregón's minister of finance, was not at all impressed with the logic of the matter, nor were the conservatives. Anti-Calles factions — moderate, liberal, conservative — declared for De la Huerta, and in December, 1923, a short-lived *cuartelazo,* or barracks-revolt, attempted to seat De la Huerta in the presidency. The shooting and killing continued for three months, and might have run an even longer course had Obregón not obtained arms from the United States which contributed to the defeat of De la Huerta, who fled to Los Angeles. Peace had been restored, and Alberto Pani, who had succeeded De la Huerta as minister of finance, had brought some financial stability to the country. But would peace and money in the treasury, coupled with Calle's promises to worker and peasant, bring to Mexico effective elections, prosperity, land for the landless, and liberty for the masses?

For a decade, from 1924 to 1934, Calles would rule Mexico, first as its constitutional president until 1928, then as chief counselor to his successors, Emilio Portes Gil, (1928–29), Pasqual Ortiz Rubio (1929–32), and Abelardo Rodríguez (1932–34). Labor and agriculture also came under Calles's watchful eye. Luis Morones entered his cabinet as secretary of labor and industry; and by 1927, CROM, which was protected by the state, had increased its membership to 2,250,000. Morones grew wealthy and politically powerful. Businessmen and industry were at his mercy, while the workers, as their wages rose and their social security benefits became something of a reality, followed their leader, even though he was corrupt. But Calles was not shocked by the questionable practices of Morones — a labor force of more than two million, under state control, was a machine of some significance to the *jefe maximo de la Revolución* (principal chief of the Revolution), as Calles chose to call himself. And in the meantime, to demonstrate his good faith to the peasants, Calles had appointed a young friend, Luis León, as minister of agriculture. León, like Morones, was soon riding in expensive cars and living in plush apartments; yet Calles and his secretary did expropriate a few haciendas and allot them to villages to be worked under the *ejido* system. Also, agricultural credit banks were established, irrigation projects were begun, and seeds, tools, and fertilizers were given to farmers. But the *jefe máximo's* heart was not in a land reform program that centered on the distribution of lands to the villages. It was the small farmer outside the village who often received as much support, if not more, then the *ejida-*

tario; and it was the kind of support that created a great number of loyal *callistas.* It was also the kind of support or policy that did little to please the vast number of villagers.

The Church-State Crisis

Meantime, while laborites and agrarians were receiving some of the fruits of the Revolution, Mexico was once again confronted with a crisis in church-state relations. In January, 1926, the Catholic hierachy issued a statement, which, in effect, instructed the faithful to cast aside all loyalty they may have had to those articles and sections of the constitution which were "transgressions against religious liberty and the rights of the Catholic Church." To Calles this was little less than treason. He promptly closed convents and Catholic schools, deported foreign priests, and demanded that priests register with the state. By July the quarrel was moving rapidly in the direction of violence. Catholic laymen went on a buyer's strike in an attempt to embarrass the national economy. On July 31, the priests themselves went out on strike by refusing to offer any public mass. Non-believers and hoodlums, including a few generals, looted, burned, and confiscated the property of the churches and seized the homes and lands of the faithful. The faithful, especially in the states of Michoacán and Jalisco, under the name of *cristeros,* retaliated by destroying public property and by murdering school teachers and anyone else identified with the Calles regime. *Callistas,* too, were not averse to murder. Many priests and *cristeros* were either shot or hanged. For the greater part of three years, until the spring of 1929, the religious war, with all the horrors of violence, vexed the republic.

The Vatican, of course, protested against this course of events, as did many a citizen in the United States, including several senators, congressmen, editors, and Secretary of State Frank B. Kellogg. But it was not only Mexico's religious problems that disturbed these gentlemen; they and oil companies were vitally concerned about what they claimed were Calles's confiscatory policies. Throughout 1925, 1926, and well down into 1927, spokesmen for the oil companies and editors of the Hearst press accused Calles of not keeping his promise to recognize the property rights of American interests in Mexico. Then, when Kellogg declared that "The Mexican Government is on trial before the world," relations between the two nations worsened. Calles — and quite correctly so — replied by saying that all nations are always on trial before the world. Kellogg may not have been duly impressed with Calles's reply, and late in 1926 the secretary of state was convinced that there was a Bolshevik conspiracy afoot in Mexico. This was going too far. Even conservative editors of American newspapers pointed out that Kellogg was ill-informed on Mexican history.

During the closing weeks of 1926, it was rumored that a break in diplomatic relations between the two republics would soon occur. Fortunately, however,

Calles opened the door for an amicable settlement of differences by suggesting that the issues at stake be submitted to the Hague Court. Business interests were quick to react by advocating arbitration. Although the issues at stake were neither submitted to the Hague Court nor to arbitration, relations between the two powers moved in a friendly direction when, late in 1927, President Coolidge sent Dwight W. Morrow to replace Ambassador James R. Sheffield. Morrow, unlike his predecessor, gained confidence and respect in both low and high places in Mexico. He made a sincere effort to understand Mexico's problems, and Calles himself acted positively upon some of the counsel given to him by the American ambassador, especially on matters relating to land reform. Morrow said that he believed the distribution of lands was going at too fast a pace. Calles responded by ordering a slowdown in handing over the large estates to the little farmers. It was a move that was well received in the United States; and the threat of intervention passed.

Meantime, Calles was making preparations for the coming presidential election of 1928, and his choice was none other than Obregón. But, in order to reinstate Obregón, the constitution would have to be amended, a feat that was not too difficult for the *jefe máximo*. Not only was the constitution amended to permit the reelection of a former president, but the presidential term was extended to six years. Of course, Obregón was elected, only to be assassinated by a religious fanatic. Congress was then called into session, and, at the bidding of Calles, named the former governor of Tamaulipas, Emilio Portes Gil, to serve as president for one year.

Birth of the PNR

Portes Gil served out his term, but was careful to follow instructions from Calles. Brakes on the agrarian reform program were released, and labor laws were enforced with considerable rigor; Morones and his CROM, however, were no longer in the good graces of Calles. Labor itself was divided, and a young intellectual of Marxist leanings, Vicente Lombardo Toledano, was gathering together a sizable following of workers. And tension between the government and the church was eased in June, 1929, when the clergy was assured that in spiritual matters it was supreme. Then, before stepping down from office, and under the direction of Calles, a party was born — the PNR *(partido nacional revolucionario)*.

In 1929 an election was held to choose a man to serve out the remainder of Obregón's five-year term. Again, the *jefe máximo* saw to it that the people chose the "right" man, Pascual Ortiz Rubio, who was something of a political unknown. José Vasconcelos, who was the opposing candidate in the election, shouted fraud and corruption and went off in a huff to the United States. Indeed, the rule of Calles had become corrupt; and agrarian reformers were pushed aside, and labor unions, including the CROM, were stripped of

— Courtesy Pan American Union

Lázaro Cárdenas, president of Mexico from 1934 to 1940, ushered in an era of increased economic independence, and gave identification to the PRM as Mexico's major political party.

power. And ugly differences between church and state again arose. Then, in September, 1932, Calles announced that Ortiz Rubio would soon resign. Resign he did — and he took a "hard-earned holiday" in the United States. (It would seem that Ortiz Rubio had forgotten, on one or two occasions, to consult the *jefe máximo*.) The title of president now fell to Abelardo Rodríguez, another of Calle's cohorts and one who built a fortune by questionable means. In any event, Rodríguez, recognizing the political necessity to bow in the direction of the Revolution, did give some support to both labor and the agrarian reformers.

In 1934, on the eve of the next presidential election, the National Revolutionary Party adopted a Six-Year Plan and nominated Lázaro Cárdenas for the presidency. The plan was, in a sense, a campaign document. It promised the people that within six years the nation, under the leadership of the party, would achieve its goals in agrarian reform, labor legislation, education, industrialization, and so on. And Cárdenas was Calles's choice for the job of implementing the plan.

Cárdenas, a son of the state of Michoacán and a general, was known for his honesty and devotion to the Revolution. "But unlike the elders of the Revolution," says Hubert Herring, "Cárdenas had never forgotten the village where he was born — its rutted roads; its adobe houses with thatched roofs and dirt floors, its lack of a school and a physician." Indeed he had not forgotten, and shortly after his election to the presidency he set about implementing the Six-Year Plan by action, especially in those matters relating to agrarian reform.

Calles presumably liked reform, provided it bore his stamp of approval. Therefore, when Cárdenas chose to guide the destinies of the republic without following the advice of Calles, a rift developed between them.

The nation's politicians and jobholders now found themselves in an unhappy position: they would have to come forward as *callistas* or demonstrate loyalty to the new president. Those who chose to remain in the Calles camp soon discovered that they had terminated their political future. They had not reckoned with Cárdenas's popularity, nor had they predicted that this thirty-nine-year-old general would demonstrate such a clear knowledge of the techniques of Mexican politics. But there was a new twist to the techniques: those who failed in their loyalties to the new administration were seldom eliminated by violence, for Cárdenas's support from the masses and the ranks of a younger group of revolutionaries gave him sufficient power to clear the land of stubborn *callistas* without benefit of bullets and bayonets. Thus, one day in 1935, a messenger told Calles that he was about to board a plane for the United States — and so he did. Others of the old guard soon followed Calles into exile, or found themselves without positions of responsibility in the government.

A Friend of the People

Much of Cárdenas's popularity rested on the new president's ability to meet the demands of labor. Working closely with Lombardo Toledano's new CTM *(confederación de trabajadores mexicanos)* — Cárdenas encouraged the workers to strike for higher wages and other benefits. Conservatives and anti-labor groups, both at home and abroad, were of course a bit disturbed with this trend in organized Mexican labor. Some said the CTM was communist inspired. There is no doubt that Lombardo Toledano leaned to the left, but there is little evidence supporting the contention that the CTM was a tool of Moscow. In any event, there is considerable evidence to demonstrate that the workingman's wages did rise; yet the cost of living rose nearly as rapidly as the increase in wages.

Cárdenas was indeed a friend of labor, but the greater part of his zeal for the welfare of the masses found its expression in his agrarian program. *Ejidos* soon blossomed all over the land, and on many an occasion he himself took a personal hand in the restitution of lands to the village farmers. It was no rare event for the *presidente* to appear suddenly in some distant hamlet and take prompt action on petitions for lands, or upon any other problem confronting the inhabitants of the community. By the end of his administration, he had distributed no less than 45 million acres to the villages, more than double the amount that had been given to the peasants prior to his election. But the peasant was to discover that it took more than a grant of land to make farming profitable. Where were the seeds, the livestock, the machinery? How did one obtain credit; and what did "credit" mean? Then, if credit, seeds, and so on were found, there was still the

matter of experience and skill in being a successful farmer. But, despite the unfortunate economic problems involved in Cárdenas's agrarian program, it is pretty clear that the peasant, as a rule, was far better off than he had been down to 1936.

It was programs such as these — labor and agrarian — that renewed the fears of foreign investors and landholders. It was therefore no great surprise when, on March 18, 1938, Cárdenas issued his famous decree which expropriated the holdings of seventeen oil companies owned by British and American interests. The companies and their respective governments quickly lodged strong protests with the Mexican government. The companies may have predicted that some such action was certain to come from Mexico City, since the companies had by one means or another failed to honor the decisions of the Mexican Labor Board which upheld the demands of oil workers for higher wages, better living conditions, vacations with pay, and a host of special benefits. By March, 1938, the demands were not granted; and the oil workers had been out on strike since May, 1937. Then came the decree. Then came, too, the debate on the legality of Cárdenas's action.

It was a bitter debate. Again, the oil companies took the stand that the Mexican government went beyond the law in claiming ownership of all the subsoil; moreover, they questioned Cárdenas's wisdom in breaking Obregón's promise in 1923 and a Mexican Supreme Court decision in 1927 which upheld the claims of the oil companies. Cárdenas replied by pointing out that the ownership of the Mexican subsoil was as old as colonial history. The oil companies were not overly impressed with this kind of argument, nor with such things as the sovereign rights of the Mexican nation and the social function of property. The oil companies, both in England and in the United States, carried their complaints to their respective governments. The American State Department and the British Foreign Office reacted promptly by sending strong notes of protest to the Mexican government in defense of company claims. Cárdenas remained firm, and answered by saying that, after all, the companies would be reimbursed for the loss of their property, in an amount based on the records of tax receipts. But were the records accurate? The debate started all over again, with Cárdenas winning most of the arguments. Perhaps he would not have been so successful had there not been a world war under way, and had not Franklin D. Roosevelt been working so hard at his Good Neighbor Policy. Finally, in April, 1942, a joint Mexican-American commission reached a settlement of some twenty-four million dollars; a few years later the British companies settled for a little more than twenty-one million dollars. Neither the American nor the British companies were overly pleased with the settlements, for they had deemed their investments to be four or five hundred million above those honored by the Mexican government. But of course the Mexican people were quite happy with their victory over "imperialism"; and as Howard Cline writes, "Mexicans hail this event as the beginning of their real economic independence."

Cárdenas was the most highly esteemed man in Mexico by the close of his administration. He had not only demonstrated that he was a son of the Revolution in his policies of agrarian reform and in his successful nationalizing of the oil industry, but that he was also a realist in dealing with the church. Unlike Calles, he was sensitive to the deep-seated Roman Catholic heritage of the nation. Priests were no longer submitted to official outrages, and anti-clerical laws were rescinded. And in 1938 he had renamed the official party. It would now be called the PRM *(partido de la revolución mexicana)*. In brief, it was indeed an impressive record that Cárdenas passed on to his successor in 1940.

The PRM presidential candidate for that year was Cárdenas's secretary of defense, General Ávila Camacho, a man who was hardly known beyond military circles. His political philosophy had been somewhat conservative, and he had made it quite clear that he was a Roman Catholic. He had not been a strong advocate of Cárdenas's land reform policies, nor was he known to be a supporter of the demands of labor. It is therefore somewhat difficult to understand the PRM endorsement of the general. He won the election, though it was a hotly contested one. Dissident groups had put forward the candidacy of General Juan Almazán, who had gathered in a fortune from public works contracts. His political views were conservative if not outright reactionary; and there was good reason to believe that he had Fascistic tendencies. When the votes were in, after a bloody day at the polls, Almazán cried fraud and corruption. From the evidence it would seem he was reciting facts; yet it would also seem that Ávila Camacho had the support of the majority of the voters who took the trouble to register their choice.

"REVOLUTION TO EVOLUTION"

In December, 1940, Ávila Camacho was inaugurated, and for the following six years his administration followed a course to the economic and political right. It was a course that was due in great measure to the failures of agrarian reform. The *ejidos* had not fulfilled the many economic and social demands of the peasant. Perhaps Cárdenas had overlooked the difficulties in plans designed to bring rural Mexico suddenly into a twentieth-century environment. Indian and *mestizo* peasants were not prepared to grasp even the essentials of modern farming, with all of its ramifications in technology, marketing, science, credit, and so on; yet no one could truthfully say that agrarian reform, together with a positive recognition of the rights of labor, had not given the masses a new lease on life. No longer was peonage the rule of the land. No longer was the worker sold to the lowest bidder. Nor would Ávila Camacho's middle-of-the-road or conservative policies turn back the agrarian and labor clocks; they stopped for awhile but would run again on dials marked "Revolution to Evolution," to borrow the title of Howard Cline's well-known book.

Industrialism has been the key word in this new trend in Mexican life since 1940, and it is an industrialization that stems in great measure from the influence of World War II. Shortly after the Japanese attack on Pearl Harbor, Mexico pledged support of the United States, and in May, 1942, Ávila Camacho's government declared war on the Axis powers. An agreement was soon signed by the United States and Mexico which provided for 200,000 migrant Mexican workers, or *braceros,* to be sent to the United States; and some 300 Mexican fliers were sent to Formosa and the Philippines. Of course all of this resulted in important economic developments. Mexican copper, steel, mercury, and other critical materials were produced at a rapid rate, and new Mexican businesses began to appear. Also, normal Mexican imports were no longer available; the nation therefore produced an increasing amount of steel, cement, textiles, and other items for home consumption. Then, since the *ejidos* could hardly supply the needed foodstuffs for a war economy, new lands were opened and developed with modern farming machinery and techniques. Arising out of all this economic growth were new fortunes and conspicuous consumption.

But there were other facets of Mexican life during the war years which were not so pleasant. Inflation and speculation stalked the land, and fanatical *sinarquistas* condemned the "godless" Revolution and became easy preys of Axis agents. God, home, and country, said the *sinarquistas,* were being destroyed by the ruling groups in Mexico in alliance with the *norteamericanos.* A million or so villagers may have associated themselves with *sinarquismo,* which in some of its aspects was reminiscent of the earlier *cristero* movement; yet the church hierarchy was critical of the means employed by the *sinarquistas* to reach their objectives. This new fanatical reactionary group did vex the administration of Ávila Camacho, and it is a movement which continues to raise its head but with considerable less support than formerly.

By 1946 Ávila Camacho could review his six years in office with a sense of accomplishment. Inflation there was, and many a person had grown wealthy by questionable practices; yet the nation as a whole had moved ahead. The ever-present agrarian problem was still unsolved, but the masses were given a Social Security Institute, which provided the machinery for meeting the needs of the unemployed, the sick, and the aged. And the year 1946 witnessed a change in the name of the official party. It would now be the *partido revolucionario institucional,* or the PRI, the revolutionary institutional party whose presidential candidate was Miguel Alemán, Ávila Camacho's minister of the interior and onetime governor of Veracruz. The choice was a reasonable one, but there were those who had hoped the party would put forward the name of Ezequiel Padilla, former minister of foreign affairs and a staunch supporter of western hemisphere policies as announced by the United States. But the majority of the Mexicans were not pleased with Padilla's avowed friendship with

"...Industrialization has been the key word in the new trend in Mexican life since 1940."

Mexico's northern neighbor. It was in effect a friendship that no doubt helped to eliminate Padilla as the official party's candidate.

A Civilian President

Quite naturally, the party's choice was the people's choice; and quite naturally, too, Alemán viewed the United States as a good neighbor. For example, President Truman flew off to Mexico City, where he was cordially welcomed, and Alemán returned the visit to be greeted in Washington and elsewhere in the United States with an impressive display of honors of state. The friendly relationships of the two nations continued throughout Alemán's administration. The Export-Import Bank made extensive loans, as did other United States agencies, to assist Mexico in its industrial and agricultural projects; and of the many projects, none was more impressive than either of what has become known as Mexico's TVA's, one of which lies in the Papaloapan basin on the eastern coast, the other which lies in the Tepalcatepec basin on the western coast. American capital, public and private, was also of considerable assistance to Mexico in its effort to control hoof-and-mouth disease, to rehabilitate railroads, and to develop hybrid corn.

But despite the fact that the overall economic level of the nation was in a comparatively healthy state, Alemán's domestic policies or programs invited opposition. Agrarian reformers questioned his emphasis on private farms, many of which were said to have fallen into the hands of the president's friends. And there were those who disagreed with his definition of "small" stock-raising property as consisting of enough land to raise five hundred head of stock. No doubt the criticisms were valid from the point of view of the revolutionary; yet Alemán's agrarian policies, not the least of which were his large-scale irrigation enterprises, did bring Mexico a little closer to providing its citizens with an adequate supply of food. And nowhere are the results of these policies more obvious than in Sinaloa and Sonora, where farming communities are providing the nation with a great amount of its food.

Urban labor also came forward at times to announce that the president was neglecting the workingman. It is true that Alemán's labor policies were not geared to all the mandates of the constitution; yet it is also true that labor was busily engaged in building a great number of steel, cement, sugar, cotton, electrical, oil and other industrial establishments. Of these many enterprises, none was more impressive than PEMEX *(petroleos mexicana),* the national petroleum monopoly, which was now under the competent direction of Antonio Bermúdez. Many a workingman also found employment in the modernization of Veracruz and Acapulco, and in the building of hospitals, clinics, and playgrounds. The cost of all of this was quite substantial; but funds were made available by the National Lottery, the Social Security Institute, and the Nacional Financiera, an institution similar to Herbert Hoover's famous Reconstruction Finance Corporation. And Alemán even found some $25 million to build an impressive University City on the outskirts of the capital.

Alemán, Mexico's first civilian president since Madero, had served his country well. He had indeed, if one discounts the corruption that followed in the wake of easy money and fat contracts for special friends. But powerful factions within the official party were not prone to forgive and forget; nor were the masses pleased with inflation and the conduct of some of Alemán's companions. There was even some talk of removing Alemán from the presidency. The factions, however, did manage to reach a *modus vivendi,* and all agreed to support Adolfo Ruiz Cortines as the PRI candidate in the coming election of 1952.

Ruiz Cortines had spent the greater part of his political life as a career civil servant. In 1943, owing to the influence of Alemán, he was elected governor of Veracruz, and in 1948 he entered the office of secretary of the interior in Alemán's cabinet. The new secretary, who was sixty-one in 1952, was respected for having served the nation for so many years without yielding to the temptation of enriching himself at the expense of the state. It was a reputation which no doubt contributed to his election, but it was an election that found the PRI's opposition unusually strong. Miners and villagers tended to cast their ballots for General Henríquez Guzmán, while the so-called traditional conservatives voted for Efrain González Luna, and the leftist for Lombardo Toledano. Of all the votes

cast, perhaps as many as one-fourth were marked for Ruiz Cortines's opponents. The PRI could no longer say that the people's choice was overwhelmingly in favor of the official party's candidate.

Many no doubt expected a mediocre administration under the guidance of an honest, colorless little man from Veracruz. They would soon discover, however, that their new president's honesty and long experience with the facts of Mexican life would be put to good use. His appointments to cabinet posts demonstrated that he knew the right man for the right job; and his selection of officers for other responsible positions was further proof of Ruiz Cortines's recognition of competency.

His administrative team moved quickly and effectively in the direction of economic matters. Alemán's public works projects were carried forward, and government-owned enterprises, such as railroads, petroleum, steel, and so on, were modernized and, where possible, consolidated. The nation's food supply was also of major concern to the president, who chose to think in terms of "agricultural reforms" rather than in an atmosphere of the revolutionary concept of "agrarian reforms." What the farmer needed, so he argued, was not more land but better means of production and freer access to credit. It was not long before many an *ejidatorio* was using improved seeds, more fertilizers, and farm machinery for the first time; and for the first time many a peasant had access to irrigation waters. Also, the resources of agricultural credit banks were readily available for the villager. But Ruiz Cortines's policy of a balanced economy did not permit the supply of capital to be channeled entirely in the direction of the farmer. Industry and small businesses found that they too were encouraged to share in the nation's economic growth.

Economics was no doubt the key word in Ruiz Cortines's administration; yet the president realized that economic policies, or any other policies, would mean very little without PRI support. By 1954 he not only had the support but was also a figure that had to be recognized by official party's machine. A year or two later he informed the several factions in the party that his young secretary of labor, Adolfo López Mateos, would be the PRI's presidential candidate in 1958. Furthermore, on the eve of the election, Ruiz Cortines even gained support of opposition parties for his candidate. When the ballots were all in, it was discovered that 90 per cent of the voters had registered their approval of López Mateos; and it was the first presidential election in which women were permitted to vote — another achievement of Ruiz Cortines. He had not by any means won all the battles. He had been forced to devaluate the peso from 8.60 to the dollar to 12.49, and widespread poverty continued to take its toll of human dignity. Nevertheless, his record was highly commendable, and when he left office he was still the honest, uncorruptible Ruiz Cortines.

The forty-eight-year-old López Mateos had reached his high office after nearly thirty years as a working and faithful member of the official party. He was the son of a village dentist, who died while Adolfo was a child, an event that forced his mother and her five children to move to Mexico City in search of work to support her family. The boy himself accepted a share of this responsibility, and by means of part-time work, scholarships, and teaching, he succeeded in obtaining a degree in law. His interest in politics developed rather early, and by the age of twenty he was already an active member of the PNR machine. Cárdenas's attention was soon attracted by the young man's concern for social reform, a concern that was rewarded by employment in several government agencies. In 1946 he entered the national senate, and in 1952 he became Ruiz Cortines's campaign manager. Again he was rewarded: Ruiz Cortines brought him into the cabinet as secretary of labor; and few secretaries of labor had succeeded so well as López Mateos in settling labor disputes without losing organized labor's respect. In a word, López Mateos was well qualified for the presidential office.

On December 1, 1958, López Mateos entered the high position of chief magistrate; six years later he would end his term with an impressive record. Like his predecessor, he took into his administration competent men, among the more notable of whom were Jaime Torres Bodet, secretary of education, Gustavo Díaz Ordaz, secretary of government, Manuel Tello, secretary of foreign affairs, and Julian Rodríguez Adame, secretary of agriculture. No significant changes were made in the management of the nation's financial and industrial institutions; even the appointment of a new director of PEMEX, Pascual Guitérrez Roldán, caused no great amount of excitement. Petroleum policies would continue to follow the course established by Antonio J. Bermúdez. Foreign companies would still be granted contracts to explore for new oil fields, and more than a hundred wells would be opened before López Mateos reached the mid-point in his encumbancy. By the end of his term not only would the production of petroleum reach an unusually high point, but new refineries would be completed and quantities of specialized products would be placed on the market. And much of all of this was initiated under the direction of Bermúdez.

PRI Moves Forward

López Mateos had reached maturity during the violent and doctrinaire periods of the Revolution; but his sense of history seems, in great measure, to account for his so-called middle-of-the-road, Mexicanism policies. Since the one "law" of history is change, it is reasonable to assume that these were policies that reflected López Mateo's refusal to stand fast with the doctrinaires. This did not mean, however, that he turned the revolutionary clock back; instead, he chose to move the nation ahead under the rules of the institutional revolution without ignoring the goals set forth in the constitution.

— *Courtesy Excelsior, Mexico, D. F.*

Early in the 1960's Mexico's participating role in the affairs of Western hemisphere nations was demonstrated by such meetings as this one in Mexico City of President López Mateos, U. S. President John F. Kennedy, and Mrs. Kennedy.

There were times when neither labor, farmer, nor businessman clearly understood or approved the middle-of-the-road policies of the president. The private business sector had some fear of a leftist trend; but when López Mateos succeeded in putting down a railroad strike in 1959 that was supported by communists — many of whom were promptly sent to jail — the private business community breathed a bit more comfortably. On the other hand, but only for a moment, López Mateo's reputation as a friend of labor was questioned. Two years later, wages had increased by about 15 per cent; and labor was to learn, so long as it operated within the bounds of the law, that the workingman's rights were not only respected but enforced. And those who insisted on an agrarian policy that would place a major emphasis on the communal *ejido* were critical of the president's land program; yet López Mateos has been credited with redistributing nearly as much land as was disposed of by Cárdenas. True, López Mateos did not turn his agricultural policies on an *ejido* axis, mainly because very little arable land was now available in the republic; moreover, the president, as was the case with several of his predecessors, viewed the *ejido* as being somewhat unsound in its economic aspects. Therefore the small private farm engaged a major part of his attention. He also carried forward the official party's nationalization policies, notably in the fields of the electric power and motion picture industries.

López Mateos also demonstrated considerable competence in his relations with foreign powers. He made it quite clear that his government would not accept any ideological dictation from Moscow. The longstanding Chamizal boundary dispute with the United States was settled, and he reached an accommodation with his northern neighbor on the distribution of the waters of the Colorado River. He refused, however, to stand with the United States on its anti-Castro policies. Non-intervention had been and would continue to be a sacred tradition of Mexican foreign policy; yet the friendship of the two nations was not seriously threatened by differences of opinion on Cuban policies. And few American presidents had received as warm a welcome as President John F. Kennedy during his visit to the Mexican capital. López Mateos also strengthened Mexico's ties with its Latin American sisters, notably in his effort to gain Mexico's participation in the Latin American Free Trade Area.

Upon the approach of the 1964 election, López Mateos selected his secretary of government, Díaz Ordaz, as the PRI presidential candidate. No strong objections to the selection were made by the significant members of the official party, and on December 1, 1964, Díaz Ordaz became president of the republic. By spring of the following year little evidence supported the charge that the conservative tendencies of the new president would very likely provide a new direction to the institutional revolution. Nevertheless the business community became uneasy with the policies of Octaviano Campos Salas, secretary of industry and com-

— *Courtesy Mexican Government Tourism Department*

President Díaz Ordaz, elected in 1964, appeared to be following the moderate course of economic and political development which his predecessors had charted in the 1940's.

merce — uneasy because Campos Salas represented the "revolutionary left" of the PRI. But the cabinet was weighted with conservatives, a situation which no doubt led the president to bring Campos Salas into the machinery in an attempt to achieve a balance between factions of the left and right in the official party. In effect, Díaz Ordaz's appointment followed the tradition of his immediate predecessors, who carefully maintained a reasonable ideological balance in the ministry; and the policies of Díaz Ordaz have shown evidence of following the paths of "evolution" that began in the 1940's.

SUGGESTED READING

The following list is by no means an exhaustive bibliography. Rather it has been designed for those who might wish to look a little deeper into the history of Mexico; and the present essay itself rests in great measure on many of the items.

ALBA, VICTOR. *Las ideas sociales contemporáneas en México*. Mexico: Fondo de Cultura Económica, 1960.

ALEXANDER, ROBERT. *Communism in Latin America*. New Brunswick, N. J.: Rutgers University Press, 1957.

ALESSIO ROBLES, MIGUEL. *Historia política de la Revolución*. Mexico: Ediciones Bota, 1938. (1946, ed.).

BANNON, JOHN FRANCIS, ed. *Bolton and the Spanish Borderlands*. Norman: University of Oklahoma Press, 1964.

BEALS, CARLETON. *Porfirio Díaz, Dictator of Mexico*. Philadelphia: J. P. Lippincott Company, 1932.

BETETA, RAMON. *The Mexican Revolution, A Defense,* 1937.

BOLTON, HERBERT EUGENE. *Outpost of Empire: The Story of the Founding of San Francisco.* New York: Alfred A. Knopf, 1939.

————. *Rim of Christendom: A Biography of Eusebio Francisco Kino, Pacific Coast Pioneer.* New York: Macmillan Company, 1936.

BOURNE, EDWARD GAYLORD. *Spain in America, 1450–1850.* New York: Barnes and Noble, Inc., 1962.

BRANDENBURG, FRANK. *The Making of Modern Mexico.* Englewood Cliffs, N. J.: Prentice-Hall, Inc., 1964.

BRENNER, ANITA. *The Wind that Swept Mexico: the History of the Mexican Revolution, 1910–1942,* [including] *184 historical photographs assembled by George R. Leighton.* New York, 1943.

CALDERON DE LA BARCA, FRANCES. (Frances Inglis). *Life in Mexico.* New York: E. P. Dutton and Co., Inc., 1954. (Everyman's Library.)

CALL, TOMME C. *The Mexican Venture.* New York: Oxford University Press, 1953.

CALLCOTT, WILFRED H. *Church and State in Mexico, 1822–1857.* Durham, N. C.: Duke University Press, 1926.

————. *Liberalism in Mexico, 1857–1929.* Stanford: Stanford University Press, 1931.

————. *Santa Anna: The Story of an Enigma Who Once Was Mexico.* Norman: University of Oklahoma Press, 1936.

CHEVALIER, FRANCOIS. *Land and Society in Colonial Mexico: The Great Hacienda.* Translated by Alvin Eustis. Edited by Lesley Byrd Simpson. Berkeley: University of California Press, 1963.

CLENDENEN, CLARENCE C. *The United States and Pancho Villa: A Study in Unconventional Diplomacy.* Ithaca: Cornell University Press, 1961.

CLINE, HOWARD. *Mexico, Revolution to Evolution, 1940–1960.* New York: Oxford University Press, 1962.

————. *United States and Mexico.* Cambridge: Harvard University Press, 1963.

CORTES, HERNANDO. *Hernando Cortés Five Letters, 1519–1526.* Translated by J. Bayard Morris. New York: W. W. Norton and Company, 1962.

CORTI, EGON CAESAR. *Maximilian and Charlotte of Mexico.* 2 vols. Translated by Catherine Alison Phillips. New York and London: A. A. Knopf, 1929.

COSIO VILLEGAS, DANIEL, ed. *Historia Moderna de México.* 7 vols. Mexico: Editorial Hermes, 1955–.

————. *The United States Versus Porfirio Díaz.* Translated by Nettie Lee Benson. Lincoln: University of Nebraska Press, 1963.

CRONON, DAVID E. *Josephus Daniels in Mexico.* Madison: University of Wisconsin Press, 1960.

CUMBERLAND, CHARLES C. *The Mexican Revolution: Genesis Under Madero.* Austin: University of Texas Press, 1952.

DABBS, JACK AUTREY. *The French Army in Mexico: A Study in Military Government.* The Hague: Mouton and Company, 1963.

DIAZ DEL CASTILLO, BERNAL. *The True History of the Conquest of Mexico.* Translated by A. P. Maudslay. New York: Farrar, Strans, and Cudahy, 1956.

DULLES, JOHN W. F. *Yesterday in Mexico: A Chronicle of the Revolution, 1919–1936.* Austin: University of Texas Press, 1961.

DUSENBERRY, WILLIAM H. *The Mexican Mesta: The Administration of Ranching in Colonial Mexico.* Urbana: University of Illinois Press, 1963.

FERGUSSON, ERNA. *Fiesta in Mexico.* New York: A. A. Knopf, 1934.

FLORES MAGON, RICARDO. *Epistolario revolucionario íntimo.* 3 vols. Mexico: Grupo Cultural "Ricardo Flores Magón," 1924–25.

GIBSON, CHARLES. *The Aztecs Under Spanish Rule: A History of the Indians of the Valley of Mexico, 1519–1810.* Stanford: Stanford University Press, 1964.

GOMARA, FRANCISCO LOPEZ DE. *Cortés: The life of the Conqueror by His Secretary.* Translated and edited by Lesley Byrd Simpson. Berkeley: University of California Press, 1964.

GRUENING, ERNEST H. *Mexico and Its Heritage.* New York and London: The Century Co., 1928.

HARING, CLARENCE H. *The Spanish Empire in America.* 2d ed. New York: Oxford University Press, 1947. Rev. ed. 1952.

KUBLER, GEORGE. *Mexican Architecture in the Sixteenth Century.* 2 vols. New Haven: Yale University Press, 1948.

LANNING, JOHN TATE. *Academic Culture in the Spanish Colonies.* New York and London: Oxford University Press, 1946.

LIEUWEN, EDWIN. *Arms and Politics in Latin America.* New York: Council on Foreign Relations, 1960.

McBRIDE, GEORGE M. *The Land Systems of Mexico.* New York: American Geographical Society, 1923.

MADARIAGA, SALVADOR DE. *Hernán Cortés: Conqueror of Mexico.* Chicago: Regnery Co., 1956.

MORLEY, SYLVANUS G. *The Ancient Maya.* Stanford: Stanford University Press, 1946.

MOLINA ENRIQUEZ, ANDRES. *Los grandes problemas nacionales.* Imprienta de A. Carranza e hijos, 1909.

MOSK, SANFORD A. *Industrial Revolution in Mexico.* Berkeley: University of California Press, 1950.

MOTOLINIA, TORIBIO DE. *History of the Indians of New Spain.* Translated by Elizabeth Andros Foster. Berkeley: Cortés Society, 1950.

OBREGON, ALVARO. *Ocho mil kilómetros en campaña.* Mexico: Fondo de Cultura Económica, 1959–60.

O'GORMAN, EDMUNDO. *Seis estudios históricos de tema mexicano.* Xalapa and Mexico: Universidad Veracruzana, 1960.

PARKES, HENRY BAMFORD. *A History of Mexico.* 3rd ed. Boston: Houghton-Mifflin Co., 1960.

PINCHON, EDGCUMB. *Zapata the Unconquerable.* New York: Doubleday, Doran and Co., Inc., 1941.

POWELL, J. RICHARD. *The Mexican Petroleum Industry, 1938–1950.* Berkeley and Los Angeles: University of California Bureau of Business and Economic Research, 1956.

POWELL, PHILIP WAYNE. *Soldiers, Indians and Silver; The Northward Advance of New Spain, 1550–1600.* Berkeley and Los Angeles: University of California Press, 1952.

PRESCOTT, WILLIAM H. *The Conquest of Mexico.* 2 vols. New York: E. P. Dutton and Co., Inc. (Everyman's Library).

PREWETT, VIRGINIA. *Reportage on Mexico*. New York: E. P. Dutton and Co., Inc., 1941.

QUIRK, ROBERT W. *The Mexican Revolution, 1914–1915; the Convention of Aguascalientes*. Bloomington: Indiana University Press, 1960.

REED, NELSON. *The Caste War of Yucatán*. Stanford: Stanford University Press, 1964.

RIVERA, DIEGO, AND WOLFE, BERTRAM. *Portrait of Mexico*. New York: Covici, Friede, 1937.

ROEDER, RALPH. *Juárez and his Mexico. A Biographical History*. 2 vols. New York: Viking Press, 1947.

ROSS, STANLEY R. *Francisco I. Madero: Apostle of Mexican Democracy*. New York: Columbia University Press, 1955.

RUIZ, RAMON EDUARDO, ed. *The Mexican War: Was It Manifest Destiny?* New York: Holt, Rinehart and Winston, 1963.

SAENZ, AARON. *La política internacional de la Revolución: estudios y documentos*. Mexico: Fondo de Cultura Economica, 1961.

SAHAGUN, BERNADINO DE. *A History of Ancient Mexico*. Translated by Fanny R. Bandelier. Nashville: Fisk University Press, 1932.

SCHURZ, WILLIAM LYTLE. *The Manila Galleon*. New York: E. P. Dutton and Co., Inc., 1959.

SIERRA, JUSTO. *Evolución política del pueblo mexicano*. Edited and annotated by Edmundo O'Gorman. Mexico: Universidad Nacional Autónoma de México, 1957.

SIMPSON, EYLER N. *The Ejido, Mexico's Way Out*. Chapel Hill: University of North Carolina Press, 1937.

SIMPSON, LESLEY BYRD. *The Encomienda in New Spain: The Beginning of Spanish Mexico*. Berkeley: University of California Press, 1950.

————. *Many Mexicos*. 3rd. ed. Berkeley and Los Angeles: University of California Press, 1959.

SINGLETARY, OTIS A. *The Mexican War*. Chicago: University of Chicago Press, 1960.

SMART, CHARLES ALLEN. *Viva Juárez! A Biography*. Philadelphia: J. B. Lippincott Company, 1963.

STEPHENSON, NATHANIEL W. *Texas and the Mexican War; A Chronicle of the Winning of the Southwest*. New York: Yale University Press, 1921.

TANNENBAUM, FRANK. *Mexico: The Struggle for Peace and Bread*. New York: A. A. Knopf, 1950.

————. *Ten Keys to Latin America*. New York: Alfred A. Knopf, 1962.

THOMPSON, F. ERIC. *Mexico Before Cortez*. New York, 1933.

————. ed. *Thomas Gage's Travels in the New World*. Norman: University of Oklahoma Press, 1958.

TISCHENDORF, ALFRED. *Great Britain and Mexico in the Era of Porfirio Díaz*. Durham: Duke University Press, 1961.

TOWNSEND, W. CAMERON. *Lázaro Cárdenas, Mexican Democrat*. Ann Arbor: University of Michigan Press, 1952.

VAILLANT, GEORGE C. *Aztecs of Mexico*. Garden City, N.Y.: Doubleday, Doran and Co., Inc., 1944.

VASCONCELOS, JOSE. *A Mexican Ulysses: An Autobiography*. Translated and abridged by W. Rex Crawford. Bloomington: Indiana University Press, 1963.

WEYL, NATHANIEL AND SYLVIA. *The Reconquest of Mexico: The Years of Lázaro Cárdenas*. London: Oxford University Press, 1939.

WHETTEN, NATHAN I. *Rural Mexico*. Chicago: University of Chicago Press, 1948.

There are, then, the two sides of the picture:
Mexico heterogeneous, unassociated; and a unified Mexico,
a Mexico with a strong personal profile.

— *Moisés Sáenz*

It is necessary, then, that we become accustomed
to understanding all national unity, not as an internal
co-existence, but as a dynamic system.

— *José Ortega y Gasset*

Ways of Life | EDWARD H. SPICER

ONE OF THE GREAT WONDERS of Mexico is the variety of her people. For this most of us are prepared by travel brochures and guidebooks, so that we expect a kaleidoscope of colorful costumes and bright fiestas from Chihuahua to Chiapas. We are not so well prepared for the other great wonder of Mexico, namely, her unity. The longer one knows Mexico, the clearer this unity appears beneath the surfaces, like the warp threads of a many colored serape.

The diversity was there before the Spaniards came. The twelve or fifteen kinds of women's dresses that we see on the streets of Oaxaca and the twenty different men's outfits in the villages of highland Chiapas are curious and insistent reminders of the 10,000 years of successive migrations of stone age people from the north. The twenty major languages and ninety or more dialects of southern Mexico also reflect today the thousands of years of self-sufficiency in the narrow valleys and mountain basins of a rugged land over which fast travel even now can only be by air. The ancient people who came to Mexico did not find broad connecting valleys, river systems like the Hwang Ho or the Mississippi, where people as well as streams could flow together, mingle, and become one. The "empires" which the Indians built before the coming of the Spaniards hung together loosely; the great Maya, Zapotec, Toltec-Aztec, Mixtec, and Tarascan civilizations set up hierarchies for tribute payment and created wider circles for trade, but seem barely to have spread religious beliefs and language beyond the bounds of the language group among whom they originated. The differences

among modern Mexicans are therefore deep-rooted — like those that stem from diverse tribe and shifting empire in central Europe and southeastern Asia.

When the Spaniards came they wrought a slow miracle. They began a remarkable welding together of the diverse Middle American peoples. They did this not by inspiring the Indians everywhere to a new common loyalty to the King of Spain — far from it, nor did they produce any real sense of common identity between Indians and transplanted Spaniards. It was rather that by dint of hard-working and inspired missionaries, by means of the whipping post and the uprooting of thousands for forced labor, by the imposition of a master class with common aims, they introduced, from one end of New Spain to the other, fundamental ideas and ways of doing things. Within one hundred and fifty years after Cortés burned his ships behind him, in the far northern desert thousands of Yaquis (who nevertheless fought off every expedition sent against them) and hundreds of thousands of Mayas in the bush of Yucatán were reciting prayers in Spanish and honoring the Virgin Mary. And in between, millions of other Indians were doing the same. Thus, long before the Spaniards' own civilization began to crumble in the 1700's, foundations were well laid for a new economy with the revolutionary feature of domestic animals; for a new social structure of family, class, and town government; and for a new religion oriented toward mankind rather than toward the tribe. This foundation was cemented from the start with the common language of Castilian Spanish amid the medley of Indian tongues. It was to require centuries before a common sense of nationality as Mexicans would begin to emerge, but the seeds of a common identity were planted with an amazingly effective hand by the invading Spaniards. Under the surface everywhere in Mexico today one finds a fabric of common custom and belief that makes the country one. It is a unity in diversity which is still, however, very much in the process of growing.

The *Voladores,* high-flying dancers of the Totonac Indians, perform on Corpus Christi day, but represent birds as their ancestors did in pre-Christian times. Their spectacular rites are presented in front of the pyramid of El Tajín, prehistoric ceremonial center in Veracruz, dating from before 500 A. D.   — *Courtesy Mexican Government Tourism Department*

[65]

In pleasant lake villages to the South, the Mexican people of Tarascan heritage combine crafts and customs from the pre-Spanish past with a religious life based on the calendar of the Catholic saints, and pursued in the guardian shadow of the village church. The modern town of Tzintzuntzán stands below the ruins of the great capital of the Tarascans.

INDIAN MEXICO

THOSE ASPECTS OF MEXICAN LIFE which are Indian exist and continue to develop on three different levels. There are what might be called the inner margins — those communities of Indians which have been isolated from the center and hence from contacts with other people. Here life is closest to the pre-Spanish Indian; the Indian language is in use in the home and in other activities. The way of looking at life and the beliefs about man's reason for existence are Indian, and the viewpoint is markedly different from that which dominates the town dwellers. There are communities of this sort in all the geographic regions of Mexico, although some are very small as are those in Baja California and Coahuila. Some are isolated largely as a result of geographic conditions, in mountain valleys difficult to get into, as in Chiapas where live the highland Maya peoples, or in the rugged mountains of Oaxaca among the Zapotecs, or in the Sierra Madres of Chihuahua where live the Tarahumaras. Others have been isolated more as a result of attitudes fostered by their relations with Spaniards and Mexicans, like the Yaquis of Sonora in their easily accessible delta lands, or the Valley Zapotecs of the Isthmus of Tehuantepec. These "inner margins" of Mexican life are not communities which have merely passively preserved an ancient past; most have borrowed much from Spaniards and all have lost, through the centuries, a great deal of their native culture. These peripheries of modern Mexico are rather places where, for a variety of reasons, a sense of identity as Indians is strong and where the Indian languages function as the important vehicle of common experience.

The inner margins are the foci of Mexican diversity, and they are unmistakably Indian. It is true nevertheless that a great deal of the common culture of modern Mexicans is also Indian. It is partly Indian in origin, like the combination of Spanish techniques of construction with the Indian form of houses, or the blending of the Aztec with the Spanish vocabulary in the Mexican language, or the weaving of wool introduced by the Spaniards on the native belt looms. Everywhere, in the worship of the gods, in the processes of village government, in the dances and other arts there has been and still continues a fusion of Indian and European. These mixed ways in rural life and in a large part of city life — these blends of cultural traditions — are the essential Mexico. It is often hard to tell which tradition is dominant, if either. The important point is that here, too, in the villages which are not isolated, as well as those that are, if one looks for it, one may find Indian Mexico. It is not a self-conscious Indian Mexico, and the Indian traits sometimes are apparent only to the historian of culture. Nevertheless it is important in understanding the people of Mexico to realize that they have for four hundred years not merely resisted or accepted European civilization, or merely discarded or clung to a "barbarian" way of life, but that they are engaged in a much more creative process, namely, the adaptation of two different sets of values and ways of life. The living center of Mexican life is not a simple European transplantation, it is rather an ever new, because ever growing, fusion of cultures.

There is a third "level" of Indian Mexico, which must be mentioned to avoid being misled by much that is written by Mexicans themselves about their Indian heritage. This is the use of Indian culture as a symbol of the distinctiveness of Mexico among modern nations. Mexican intellectuals have wished to separate themselves from a purely Spanish identification; they have tried to find an identity distinct from any Europeans. In doing so they have sought to give Indian culture and Indians a special significance in the general heritage of Mexicans. But their writings and their utilization of Indian elements in the arts have not necessarily had anything to do with present-day Indian life in the communities of the inner margins or in the ongoing fusional processes. Thus Cuauhtémoc, as the Aztec prince who resisted the Spaniards, has been elevated to the position of a hero in Mexican history — as a symbol of Mexican independence from Spain. Aztec motifs, even though they are actually esoteric and unintelligible to the average university student, are used in the architecture of the national university. Such symbols involving Indian forms are very important in the growth of a self-conscious Mexican nationalism in the modern international arena, but they have little relation to the lives of people who call themselves Indian. The local prejudices against Indian ways of life, as in the mountains of Chihuahua with respect to the Tarahumaras, are not at all affected by the employment of Aztec symbols in the schoolbooks or even by the presentation of Tarahumara dances by folk dance groups among students of the National University in Mexico City.

The Indian Languages

Wherever the sense of being Indian is strong and definite, there the Indian languages are the languages of home life. There are today in Mexico at least 3,000,000 people who speak Indian languages.[1] This number is small as compared with the 35,000,000 total population. Moreover the general population has been increasing over the past forty years at a rate much faster than has the Indian-speaking population. Nevertheless the number of speakers of Indian languages is as large as the whole population of the modern nation of Uruguay and almost as large as Guatemala. It also might be pointed out that the population of the United States in 1776 was about 3,000,000.

What characterizes the Indian speaking population of Mexico as a very different kind of entity from the population of the United States in 1776 is its great diversity. When Cortés landed in 1519 there were possibly 25,000,000 people in the region that now constitutes Mexico[2] and, of course, all spoke Indian languages. No one knows with certainty just how many Indian languages were in use. There were many; one widely accepted estimate puts the figure at at least 180 distinct languages,[3] most of which had anywhere from four or five to a dozen different dialects. Today there are still one-fourth that number of languages, while the number of dialects has probably greatly decreased. Some of these surviving languages of modern Mexico are spoken by mere handfuls of people — such as Seri on the coast of Sonora which is used by barely 250

persons or Lacandon in the jungles of Chiapas used by 150.

Those languages which today have the most speakers are precisely the ones which had the most in the days of Cortés. The languages and dialects of the language family (Uto-Aztecan) to which Aztec belonged are spoken today by approximately 1,000,000 people.[4] If as some scholars believe there were nearly 5,000,000 who spoke these languages in 1520, then the moderns constitute 20 per cent of the ancient population. No other Indian language group in Mexico is so large. There are nevertheless nearly a half million persons who speak Mayan languages and Mayan is and was the second most important language family in Mexico. It has, however, declined proportionately more than Aztec, for there were probably 3,000,000 Mayan-speaking people at the time of the Spanish conquest.[5] These two families together are now, as then, the dominant groups and today constitute one-half of all Indian language speakers in Mexico. Only two other language families rival them in numbers, Zapotec and Mixtec, which were also probably next in importance to Aztec and Maya when the Spaniards arrived. Those who speak these languages today number together less than half a million, almost equally divided between the two.[6] These four persistently dominant language families through the centuries — Aztec, Maya, Zapotec, and Mixtec — are very different and must have contributed to different views of the world by their speakers. They by no means represent the range of language types in Mexico, but we shall limit ourselves to a description of only three of these as suggestive of what the Indian languages are like.

AZTEC

The language of the Aztecs belongs to the most far-flung of North American Indian language families — Uto-Aztecan. Closely related, like the Romance languages of Mediterranean Europe, Uto-Aztecan languages at the beginning of the Spanish conquest were spoken from what is now Idaho to Nicaragua. Languages related to that spoken by the Ute Indians of Utah and Colorado marked the northern border of the family, and languages like that of the Aztecs marked the southern border. No other language family in North America extended so widely as this 4000-mile spread. The language of the Aztecs whom Cortés conquered was just one among six or seven closely related languages in the vicinity of the Valley of Mexico — that of the Aztec capital, Tenochtitlan, and its immediate satellite communities around the Lake of Texcoco. In addition there were distinct but very similar languages spoken at the cities of Texcoco, Atzcapazalco, Tlaxcala, and others within a radius of perhaps eighty miles of Tenochtitlan. Today these languages are still spoken by the rural people within the same area in the states of Mexico, Puebla, Morelos, Hidalgo, and Querétaro. There are more distantly related languages of this general group spoken in Jalisco, Guerrero, and in tiny enclaves southward as far as Nicaragua. These last

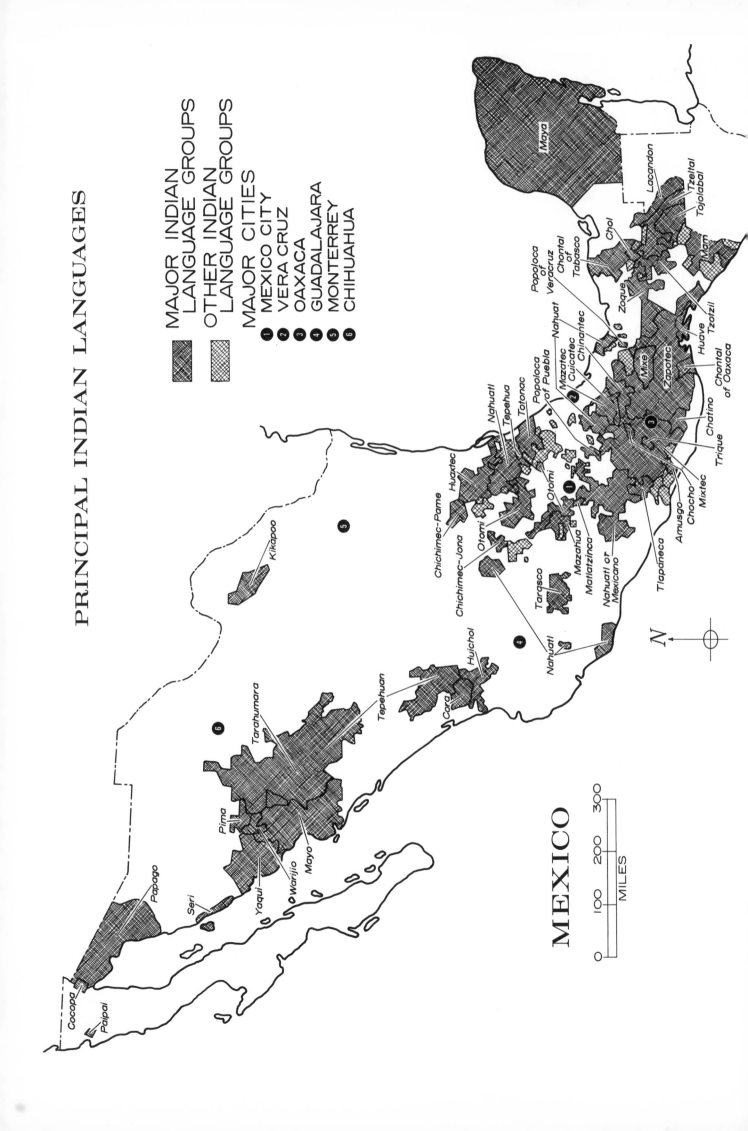

PRINCIPAL INDIAN LANGUAGES

MAJOR INDIAN
LANGUAGE GROUPS

OTHER INDIAN
LANGUAGE GROUPS

MAJOR CITIES
1 MEXICO CITY
2 VERA CRUZ
3 OAXACA
4 GUADALAJARA
5 MONTERREY
6 CHIHUAHUA

MEXICO

MILES
0   100   200   300

N

Maya

Lacandon
Tzeltal
Tojolabal
Chol
Mam
Zoque
Tzotzil
Popoloca
of
Veracruz
Chontal
of Tabasco
Nahuat
Chinantec
Mazatec
Cuicatec
Mixe
Huave
Zapotec
Chatino
Chontal
of Oaxaca
Trique
Mixtec
Chocho
Amusgo
Tlapaneca
Nahuatl
Tepehua
Totonac
Popoloca
of Puebla
Otomi
Mazahua
Matlatzinca
Nahuatl or
Mexicano
Huaxtec
Chichimec-Pame
Chichimec-Jona
Otomi
Tarasco
Huichol
Cora
Tepehuan
Kikapoo
Tarahumara
Pima
Warijio
Mayo
Yaqui
Seri
Papago
Cocopa
Paipai

are surviving results of the extension of the Aztec political power southward.

In the immediate vicinity of modern Mexico City, that is, within eighty miles of the prehispanic location, there are possibly a dozen different dialects still in use. Closest to Mexico City where the so-called Milpa Alta dialect is spoken, the people call their language Masewalkopa (which means literally "in Indian fashion").[7] Fifty miles to the south a somewhat different dialect is spoken which the people call Masiewalli.[8] In both these terms one may see the word which is and was generally applied by speakers of these languages to themselves, that is, *masewal* or as one often sees it in Spanish documents, *macegual*. The people of Tenochtitlan did not call themselves Aztec; they used the term macegual. But they believed that they had come from a place in the northwest which they called Lake Aztlán and from this mythological place name was derived the term which the Spaniards adopted, namely Aztec. We shall use this in our discussion of the language, because it has come into such wide use in all the historical and popular writing. Most students of the language now call it Nahuatl, or at least apply this term to the immediate group of Uto-Aztecan languages of which Aztec was one; they also distinguish the Nahuatl languages of the vicinity of modern Mexico City from what they call the Nahuat languages farther south into Nicaragua. It has become common among modern Mexicans to speak of the Aztecs as the "Mexicans" and their language as Mexicano. Mexico was an alternative name for the Aztec capital of Tenochtitlan.[9]

There is another dialect of this group of languages which is called Classical Nahuatl. This is a form based on the language of Tenochtitlan and reduced to writing very shortly after the conquest by the Franciscan missionaries. Classical Nahuatl and the Milpa Alta dialect are thus both derived from a common ancestral language. Classical Nahuatl has been studied and taught by scholars through the centuries and is at present a well-established subject in courses at the National University. There are abundant works of literature in it, and scholars have begun to translate these and study their content with care. An example of their influence in modern Mexico is to be found in the careful study of the literature and philosophy of the Aztecs based on perusal of such texts by Ángel María Garibay[10] and Miguel León-Portilla.[11] Classical Nahuatl is not the same as the language in actual use in the villages near Mexico City, for it has been kept alive mainly by scholars who are influenced by Latin and other Indo-European languages, but it is obviously very similar. It is characteristic of Mexico, as a reflection of the class structure, that these two dialects of the Aztec language have developed quite separately. The scholars sometimes send a student into an Indian village to listen to the folk speech, but this has no influence on Classical Nahuatl which is a "dead" language.

Aztec, which we use to include the various present-day dialects, is always described by students as simple (in the sense that its sounds are not difficult for Europeans to hear and reproduce) and as "sonorous," "euphonious," "liquid," and generally pleasant to listen to. It employs fewer sounds than English, twenty-two or twenty-four, and lacks the sounds of b, d, g, and f. It is the absence of the voiced stops together with the rarity of consonant clusters which causes Europeans to call the language liquid in sound. A French student has likened the sound flow to that of Japanese. He was calling attention to the characteristic alternation of consonant and vowel with few consonant clusters, a trait in which Japanese and Aztec do resemble one another. An example of this characteristic which gives the "liquid" sound to Aztec is "mepam po powa," (he) "weeds agave rows" or "wa ininonka sowatl laliwis chipawak," "this woman here is very white" (referring to the snow-covered volcano Ixtaccíhuatl).[12] The consonant cluster *nk* in the latter example is one of the few common consonant clusters, others being *lp, mp,* and *kt*. The *tl* in the word "sowatl" (woman) is not a cluster of consonants, but rather stands for the distinctive voiceless "l" sound which is of very frequent occurrence in Aztec. It is the sign of a noun and occurs so often that it adds a whispering effect to the flow of "singing" syllables resulting from the alternation of vowel and consonant. Since syllables are not heavily stressed, the total effect of Aztec on the ears of speakers of European languages is of softness and lack of either the staccato of spoken Mexican Spanish or the constantly interrupted emphatic periods of English.

Aztec was a language capable of richness and variety of expression. A literature of poetry and philosophy as well as history was developing in the Aztec language at the time the Spaniards interrupted its growth and imposed Spanish as the dominant language for literary expression. Today except for the somewhat rootless classical Nahuatl of the universities, Aztec remains a folk language. Its potential for growth, however, remains as great as ever. Its expressive possibilities have been made clear, both by the students of the living folk language and the scholars who study the fragments and texts written in Aztec shortly after the conquest by Franciscan missionaries and sons of Aztec chiefs.

One of the outstanding characteristics of the language is its capacity for what the linguist Benjamin Whorf calls "derivation."[13] That is, a considerable series of words can be derived from a root-word, as in English we derive from a noun "care" the adjective "careful" and then from that a noun again "carefulness," as well as an adverb "carefully." In Aztec, according to Whorf, the possible derivations are almost "limitless." It was also true that the formation of new words by compounding was frequent and easy in Aztec, that is, the putting together of root-words to form new ones, as in modern German. These two characteristics made Aztec a flexible language, capable of growth and elaboration of ideas. It is evident from the recent studies of Garibay and León-Portilla that abstract terms had been well developed by the time of the Spanish conquest, and hence, that Aztec was a language in which philosophic thought could find ready expression.

Specifically, Aztec is quite different in structure from any European language, and as would be expected, shares many characteristics with other North American Indian languages. A sentence, if it contains a verb, is likely to have the verb first, with subject and predicate following in no set order. The verb is not merely a simple root-word, but is more highly inflected than a Latin verb. The Aztec verb expresses tenses, that is, past, present, and future, by means of endings after the manner of Latin, but goes far beyond Latin in the shades and variety of meaning which can be expressed through such suffixes. Relatively little interested in time in our sense, the Aztecs were very much interested, as a result of the nature of their language, in whether or not an action was repetitive, whether statements were hearsay or not, and many other "aspects" or "modes" of doing. These were expressed in distinct verbal affixes of which there were twenty or more and some of which could be inserted within the verb stem, as infixes rather than suffixes. These together with the personal pronouns as subjects and objects which were affixed in front of the verb stems make the Aztec verb a complex and highly expressive form.

An historical accident has led to the extreme separation of literary and folk forms of the Aztec language. The Aztec taught in the universities of Mexico is something of a dead language and a symbol of esoteric learning, as ancient Greek and Latin are. The living Aztec language of the Indian villages goes a separate way — its speakers until now, at least, quite out of touch with classical Aztec. Whether the folk language will be affected and will develop, as young Indians in increasing numbers attend the university, remains to be seen. Meanwhile the two forms of Aztec, classical and everyday, stand as a reflection of the class structure of Mexico, with its two ways of life — that of the wealthy educated inheritors of European culture and that of the poor people rooted in the Indian traditions and until now insulated from the effects of European culture.

The Aztec language has left its permanent mark on the map of Mexico. Wherever one sees place names ending in *tlan* or *tla* or *la* or *tan,* one may be sure that Aztec influence has extended there in some way. Thus on the coast of Sinaloa on the Gulf of California one finds the port of Mazatlán, and this marks the northern extent of Aztec influence. The suffix *tlan* means "near" and one finds it in many places, from Mazatlán southward to the Isthmus of Tehuantepec, along with names ending in *tla* like Mitla in Oaxaca, or in *tan* like Juchitán on the Isthmus. These represent the farthest northern and southern extensions of Aztec military power or trade influence. One finds in the vicinity of Mexico City hundreds of such Aztec place names, but looks in vain in Chiapas and Campeche or in Sonora and Chihuahua for these signs of Aztec influence.

MAYA

Next to the Uto-Aztecan languages, the most widely spoken when the Spaniards arrived were the languages of the Mayan family, and it is still true that Mayan languages are spoken by more people in Mexico than are any other Indian language except Aztec. Today more than 500,000 speakers of Mayan languages and dialects are to be found in Mexico, and another 500,000 live in neighboring Guatemala.[14] The area of Mayan-speaking people is and was much more compact than that of the Uto-Aztecans; all live contiguously in Chiapas, Yucatán, and Guatemala, except for small outlying linguistic islands to the north. In northern Veracruz and in San Luis Potosí there are several thousand speakers of Totonac and Huaxtec, both languages related to Maya and considered to be members of the Mayan family.

Throughout the lowland of the peninsula of Yucatán a single dialect was in use at the time of the arrival of the Spaniards. This was the prevailing language of the Maya "Empires," and it is believed that the hieroglyphics of the prehistoric monuments and temples were developed by speakers of this dialect in whatever form it had 2000 years ago.[15] If phonetic keys are ever worked out for interpreting the glyphs, therefore, it will probably be in the language of the lowland Maya. This is still spoken by 200,000 people in the state of Yucatán alone and by thousands more in Quintana Roo, Campeche, and Tabasco, where it shades into other major dialects of the Mayan family. While it has not until recently had the kind of attention which Nahuatl has as a "classical" form taught in the universities, it nevertheless achieved closer integration with Spanish and the cultivated world. The great majority of persons in Yucatán since the conquest have been speakers of Maya; many mestizos in the peninsula since Spanish arrival have spoken only Maya. Spanish-speaking people have been forced to learn the Maya language in a way that they have had to learn no other regional language of Mexico. Maya has been, in short, a dominant language in its region — at least until recently. It has never ceased to be a written language, although it has changed alphabets. But it is steadily being eclipsed, as public schools place Spanish in an increasingly dominant position.

Maya is a very different language from Aztec, even though some modern linguists believe that evidence will ultimately be established linking the two great language families of Uto-Aztecan and Mayan to a common ancestor.[16] While Aztec has been described as "liquid," Maya has never impressed students in this way. Compared with Aztec it has been described as "harsh." This is because of a number of common sounds which do not occur in Aztec — for example, a consonant like a *k* but stopped at the back of the mouth; and a whole series of stops which are followed by glottalization, or that is to say, by closure of the vocal chords.[17] Thus *t, p, ch,* and *ts* are all glottalized. Their occurrence gives a so-called "gutteral" sound to Maya speech which strikes Spanish- or English-trained ears as somewhat "harsh." Moreover the "singing" quality of Aztec, resulting from alternation of consonant, vowel, consonant, vowel, is absent. The usual pattern of a Maya word is consonant-vowel-consonant or vowel-consonant. In other words, phrases and words often end in a consonant, and stems of words tend to be monosyllables, so that the flow of sound is broken by stops rather than flowing with vowels. There exists also one voiced stop *b* in contrast with the absence of voiced stops in Aztec. Thus Maya sounds differently from Aztec.

The number of recognized sounds is greater in Maya than in Aztec—namely, twenty-nine. As in Aztec, long, or really doubled, vowels are important. Persons unaccustomed to these "twinned" vowels must listen closely in order not to confuse meanings. Thus the word for "snake" is *kan,* while the word for sky is *kaan.* The word for "bone" is *bak* and the word for 400 is *baak,* for road *be,* for an exclamation of pain *bee.*

The ways of building words and elaborating meanings in Maya and Aztec differ widely in that while the same general procedures are followed as for all languages, there is a very different emphasis. While Aztec uses compounding extensively, Maya uses it very little. While Aztec makes great use of both prefixing and suffixing in developing meanings of both nouns and verbs, Maya relies almost wholly on suffixing. Pronouns, for instance, are placed after, rather than in front of, verb stems, in contrast with Aztec.

The Maya language, like Aztec and most of the other Indian languages of Mexico, has left a permanent mark on the land in the form of place names and also of family surnames. Thus place names in Yucatán and other southeastern states which end in or contain the syllable *tun* such as Ebtún, Uaxactún, etc. are Maya in origin, the *tun* meaning stone and being part of a landmark type of place name. Other syllables which are Mayan and which appear repeatedly in southeastern Mexico, as well as in Guatemala are *kab* (meaning earth), *-mul* (meaning hill), *-chen* (meaning cenote or natural well) and as a prefix *tik* or *tek* meaning "place of." And there are others such as *-al, -na, -lub,* and *-ab.*

The Maya dialects shade into one another as one moves from the lowland up into the highlands and from the jungles of the Petén on southeastward into Guatemala. The languages usually distinguished, such as the very widespread Maya Yucatecan of the lowlands, Tzotzil-Tzeltal of Chiapas, and Chol and Mam of Guatemala differ from one another far less than do the languages of the Uto-Aztecan family. While Mam at the far southeast of Mayan territory differs greatly from Yucatecan Maya, it is true nevertheless that the languages shade into one another and that Mam speakers, for example, are understood by their immediate neighbors the Cakchiquel, and so on across the whole span. This suggests much more stability of location during the recent history of Maya dialects than for the Uto-Aztecans, and much less shifting of territory in the centuries before the arrival of Spaniards.

ZAPOTEC

A third major group of languages in Mexico is the Zapotec. These are spoken by nearly a quarter of a million people in an area much more concentrated

and smaller in size than the territory over which Mayan languages are spoken. They are confined to the single state of Oaxaca, where at least six languages with dialects are spoken.[18] The Zapotec languages of the southern mountains of Oaxaca, those of the northern mountains, those of the valley in which the city of Oaxaca lies, and those of the Isthmus of Tehuantepec are the major varieties. Swadesh (1949) has commented on the great number of dialects in this family and on the great linguistic variety generally of the Southern Highland region of Mexico in which these dialects occur. Their great degree of differentiation suggests a history of mutual isolation through centuries; and yet it is perfectly clear that people of many Zapotec-speaking communities which maintain distinctive dialects are, and have been through centuries, in constant contact with one another through the widely extended market systems that characterize the whole Zapotec region.

The Zapotec languages are sharply different from either Aztec or Maya, for unlike either, they employ tone; that is, the pitch at which vowel sounds are spoken has significance. In the mountain dialects four tones are common — high, low, rising, and falling; the word for beans in one of these is *da* (spoken with a falling pitch), while the word for grease is *da* (spoken with a rising tone). Also in contrast with Aztec and Maya, Zapotec uses a full series of voiced stops — *b, d,* and *g.* And to make the contrast more complete, the vowels do not vary in meaning according to their length. Thus the Zapotec languages present a strikingly different sound from the other two major languages of Indian Mexico. The structure of words and sentences also makes use of quite different principles. One may turn to Miguel Covarrubias's lively account of the Zapotec spoken by the people of the Isthmus of Tehuantepec for an understanding of this language and its peculiarities.[19]

The Future of Indian Languages

Besides the three languages which we have picked from the many of modern Mexico for brief characterization, it must be remembered that there are some forty more. The number of persons speaking Indian languages in Mexico in the 1960 census was reported as 3,030,254. Of these 1,104,955 were monolingual, that is spoke only an Indian language, while 1,925,299 spoke both an Indian language and Spanish. The changes in the numbers, according to census figures, of Indians who spoke only Indian languages from 1940 to 1960 are shown in Table I (next page).

The figures must be taken only as roughly indicative. In the first place it must be recognized that they give only the numbers of persons over five years of age and hence only a part (though a large part) of the persons living in communities in which only an Indian language is used. The variations between decades cannot be taken as significant. They represent most probably variations in census procedures, rather than significant variations in numbers of any of the groups. Probably the safest interpretation is simply that the number of persons in Mexico speaking Indian languages and with no knowledge of Spanish has remained somewhat more than 1,000,000 over the last 20 years. If we consider the 1930 census figure for monolinguals, we may extend this figure another ten years backwards. The 1930 figure was 1,185,162. Thus there seems to have been a stabilization of the number of monolinguals over the past generation, despite increase in literacy program activity and the extension of federal rural schools.

We shall not present all the figures regarding speakers of Indian languages who also speak Spanish, but will compress them as shown below in Table II.

Table I
Number of Persons (Five years of age and over) Speaking Only Indian Languages

Language Spoken	No. of Persons 1940[20]	1950[21]	1960[22]
Nahuatl (Uto-Aztecan)	360,071	212,813	297,285
Mixtec (Mixtecan)	124,994	76,946	106,545
Maya (Mayan)	114,011	50,912	81,013
Zapotec (Zapotecan)	104,661	60,680	78,763
Otomí	87,404	57,559	57,721
Totonac (Mayan)	59,242	54,333	63,794
Mazatec	55,743	47,167	73,416
Tzotzil (Mayan)	49,194	44,103	57,235
Mazahua	39,587	16,254	15,759
Tzeltal (Mayan)	34,502	31,856	55,951
Mixe	27,238	21,005	34,587
Huastec (Mayan)	25,628	17,276	18,724
Chinantec	20,387	15,702	23,066
Tarascan	19,637	9,796	12,432
Chol (Mayan)	19,499	18,898	32,815
Tlapanec	14,411	12,234	23,997
Tarahumara (Uto-Aztecan)	11,717	8,166	10,478
Chatino (Zapotecan)	8,586	8,259	10,231
Amuzgo (Mixtecan)	7,540	5,839	11,066
Tojolobal	6,882	–	3,779
Mayo (Uto-Aztecan)	6,667	2,509	1,837
Zoque	6,581	4,804	7,683
Popoloca	6,298	1,564	3,053
Chontal	5,624	1,539	–
Cuicatec (Mixtecan)	4,261	–	2,553
Mam (Mayan)	2,555	–	–
Cora (Uto-Aztecan)	1,724	228	3,731
Tepehuan (Uto-Aztecan)	1,520	1,583	1,766
Chichimec	940	–	–
Huichol (Uto-Aztecan)	795	1,035	3,932
Tepehua	733	–	–
Yaqui (Uto-Aztecan)	307	199	545
Matlatzinca	123	–	–
Papago (Uto-Aztecan)	91	–	–
Others (16 in 1940)	7,865	–	8,226
	1,237,018	795,069	1,104,955

Table II
Number of Speakers of Indian Languages (Bilinguals and Monolinguals) in Mexico[23]

1930	1940	1950	1960
2,251,086	2,490,909	2,447,609	3,030,254

These figures suggest an increase of more than half a million over the 30 year period, but it would seem (as in the case of the figures on monolinguals) that the census counts are probably not consistent enough to permit any acceptable inferences. Thus we may believe that there are somewhere between two and a half and three million speakers of Indian languages in Mexico, but the trend in regard to increase or decrease will remain doubtful at least until another census is taken.

It has been estimated that at the rate of disappearance indicated by census figures for 1940 and 1950 there will be no more Indian language speakers by the year 2007.[24] Like all such predictions based purely on census figures, this is wholly unreliable, as indicated by the 1960 census. There is nothing constant about the conditions which accelerated the decrease in number of speakers of Indian languages from the 1500's to 1890 in Mexico. Conditions have changed sharply twice since 1890, in 1910 and also in 1936, and there are new conditions now, for example, the reduction to writing of all the surviving Indian languages of Mexico by the Summer Institute of Linguistics workers, whose interest is religious but whose effects are broadly social. A great deal depends also on the policy of the National Indian Institute as it moves more and more into the field of formal schooling. At present its members are split over the desirability of teaching Indian languages. As always there are the self-styled practical ones who believe that the quicker Spanish is learned, the better off the people will be economically. But there are also those who stress the Indian languages as a basis of self-esteem and sound progress. Policy based on the latter view may grow stronger. This could have a profound effect, especially in areas where there are hundreds of thousands of Indians as among the highland Mayas who are being encouraged to maintain a community solidarity.

The future of the Indian languages in Mexico is a fascinating adventure of possibilities, and one may look at it from more than one point of view.

The Indian People

The Indians of Mexico do not have territorial boundaries which contribute to keeping them separate from other Mexicans — in the way that Indian tribes on reservations do in the United States. There are only two special land arrangements for Indians in Mexico — for the Yaquis of Sonora and for a handful of Yuman-speaking Indians in extreme northern Baja California. None of the others have had special land arrangements of this kind. Except in these instances there are not any sharp geographical boundaries between the people who call themselves Indians and those who do not.

Nevertheless, feelings of separate identity are strong through the republic from north to south, and where a visitor may casually see no difference in dress and manner or hear very little in speech which indicates the presence of an Indian people, there still may be strong cleavage between Indian and non-Indian. The surrounded — and penetrated — Indian enclaves of the north sometimes have sharper boundaries, largely because the surrounding *mestizos* are less influenced in language and cultural ways by Indians than are the *mestizos* and *ladinos* of the south. Indian and non-Indian populations in the south merge with one another along very indistinct cultural boundaries. The *ladinos* of the south often are bilingual in their Indian-dominated areas.

YAQUIS AND OTHERS OF THE NORTHWEST

There are eleven Indian enclaves in the northwest. Three of these are groups of some size — 50,000 Tarahumaras in Chihuahua, 30,000 Mayos in Sinaloa and Sonora, and possibly 20,000 Yaquis in Sonora — who occupy economically important land and resources. The other eight are much smaller, and have maintained themselves in areas of geographical isolation in which Spaniards and Mexicans have had little economic interest. These are the 600 Paipai and Kiliwa of northern Baja California, the 250 Seris of Tiburón Island and the Sonoran coast, the 1200 Warihios of western Chihuahua, the 300 Papagos of northern Sonora, the 1000 Lower Pimas of southeastern Sonora, the 2000 Tepehuanes of the Western Sierra Madre Mountains chiefly in Durango, the 4000 Huicholes of Jalisco and Nayarit, and the 4000 Coras of Nayarit. These 123,000 Indians of the northwest have maintained their separate identity through more than 400 years of Spanish and Mexican control. Most are willing today to call themselves Mexicans; but they do insist that they are primarily Yaqui, or Tarahumara, or Huichol, or Seri, and refuse to let go of that sense of separate historical experience. Modern programs of the Mexican government, like those of the Spanish colonial government, seek to implant a new sense of nationality — often with some

success — but the sense of being an Indian people remains as strong as ever; perhaps intensified in many cases.

Of the northwestern aboriginal peoples, the Yaquis are unquestionably the most famous. There is a popular idea that they maintained a savage life and resisted the civilization of the Spaniards throughout the three hundred years of contact and then suddenly joined the Revolution of 1910 as soldiers under General Obregón, throwing their savage fighting ability to the advantage of the Revolution. This is a myth of the revolution. Nothing could be further from the truth. The 25,000 Yaquis of what is now southern Sonora accepted Jesuit missionaries with unusual readiness in 1617 when Jesuits first appeared among them. For seven years previously they had been asking for missionaries (always in short supply in this period in northwestern New Spain), and were pleased when they finally arrived. Almost as a unit the whole tribe was converted and immediately built churches and grouped themselves into new and larger towns under missionary direction. For a hundred and twenty-five years the Yaquis were peaceful and, as the Jesuits reported, unusually avid to follow their missionary teachings.[25] This century of peace had a profound effect on the Yaquis and turned them into town-dwellers and Christians, conditions from which they never reverted despite later events which turned them against Spaniards and after that against Mexicans. Today they regard themselves as purer Christians than the Mexicans who surround them and are inclined to look on themselves as more civilized than other Indians such as the Papagos who are rural in way of life.

Nevertheless the Yaquis had resisted military domination from the very first contact with Spaniards. They defended their river — the modern Río Yaqui — against the slave-raider Diego de Guzmán and then

In the midst of an urban thoroughfare, like an island in the stream of modern change, a young man hires a professional letter-writer to put his thoughts on paper, pointing up the inevitable lag between a fast-growing population and a relatively new educational system.

fought an amazingly successful campaign of resistance against the highly capable and, up to that point, successful Captain Hurdaide who was paving the way northward for the establishment of Jesuit missions. In 1610, the Yaquis drove Hurdaide southward and then, as victors, made a treaty and asked for missionaries. But, having kept the military Spaniards out of their territory, the Yaquis welcomed the missionaries, and thus began their century and a quarter of intensive learning of town life and Christian ways. This continued until 1740 — when conflict with Spaniards crystallized in a bloody war. Later during the nineteenth century they fought for possession of their land, often with great success. It is these successes in battles against Mexicans that have resulted in their reputation as warlike people.

The Yaquis live today in small towns along the lower part of what used to be the Yaqui River in southern Sonora. There is now no water in the riverbed because it is taken out for irrigation at the northern margin of the Yaqui country. Large canals lead to the south of the old channel where non-Yaquis have carved out of the traditional tribal territory a vast and fertile acreage. Since 1956, canals have made the north bank, where Yaquis still live, also of great agricultural potential. Some 10,000 Yaquis live along the north bank in a small portion of their former homeland, where they are undergoing an extensive government program of economic development. Most Yaquis live here in the homeland area in seven or eight settlements bounded on the north by the mountains where they used to maintain guerrilla fighters for their independence. President Lázaro Cárdenas set aside for exclusive Yaqui ownership this remnant of the tribal land. This was done in the same manner as in the United States — as a protection against the steady land encroachment which had been going on for two centuries. It is the only important Indian reserve in Mexico, but it is not managed like a U. S. reservation.

The streets of Yaqui villages are wide; the houses are of woven cane (carrizo) or of cane-and-mud wattle with roofs of earth piled on top of cane mats which rest on crotched posts of mesquite. Typically, the houses are surrounded by fences also of woven cane. The effect generally is of spaciousness, in contrast with the crowded contiguous adobe houses of so many Mexican small settlements. The modern town sites — Potam, Vicam, Torim, Rahum — along the old river course, are, in the Yaqui view, on sacred ground. The eight towns into which the Jesuit missionaries grouped Yaquis around the newly built churches between 1617 and 1626 became sacred and inviolable, along with the whole tribal territory, during the long struggles to maintain their independence and full control of their land after the Mexican war for independence. There grew up in Yaqui religion a mythology of the sacred "Eight Towns" which is a fundamental tenet of the modern conservative view and for which Yaquis have died by the hundreds. In each sacred pueblo there is still a town organization in which church and civil functions

are tightly interwoven. Yaqui music and dancers, especially the pascolas with bearded masks and the deer dancer, have become well known in the northwest, where the deer dancer appears on the seal of the state of Sonora, and even nationally, as the deer songs and dance have been incorporated into the National Ballet.

Among the most interesting groups of Indians in all Mexico are the Kunkaak, who live in Tiburón Island and along the Infiernillo straits of the west coast of Sonora. Mexicans call them the Seris. There are only some two hundred and fifty of them left, dwindled from possibly ten times that many in the 1600's when Spaniards first encountered them as nomadic fishers and hunters in the Sonoran desert. All efforts at forcibly changing their way of life have failed during three hundred and fifty years. To be sure they have changed; they have adopted iron for making their detachable harpoon heads with which they hunt sea turtles; they use manufactured fishhooks and dynamite and plank boats like the Mexican fishermen of the coast; they drink sugar-sweetened coffee; they use wheat flour to make fried bread and they buy cloth for clothes and even rent outboard motors for their fishing and turtle-hunting expeditions. But the fact remains that they have never all been permanently converted to Christianity, and they have resisted efforts to make farmers and town-dwellers out of them. They have refused to move inland and stay there; they have stuck to their desert coastal strip, and in the last forty years they have begun to increase just a little in numbers despite a continuous decline in population for a hundred years before. They live now in their own chosen way, well aware that it is different from that of other Mexicans, well aware that they are regarded as poor and as the object of charity by Americans and Mexicans who have read about them in the newspapers and magazines.

The Jesuit missionaries who were phenomenally successful in reducing the Indians of Sonora to town life tried to re-make the lives of the Seris in the early 1700's. They succeeded in persuading a few hundred to move inland along the San Miguel River above Hermosillo and set them to farming. More might have come, but we shall never know because the forcible appropriation of their newly acquired land by soldiers from the nearby presidio of Pitic caused the Seris to abandon mission life and attempt to destroy the Spanish settlements nearby. This led in 1749 to retaliation by the army commander who captured and deported to Guatemala all the wives of the rebellious Seris.[26] Thirty years of warfare between Seris and Spaniards followed; the Jesuits' program of conversion and reduction had completely failed. Seris raided the growing Spanish population of Sonora, maintained an impregnable headquarters in the mountains of southern Sonora, and continued to carry on their traditional seacoast hunting and fishing. Eventually starved out, however, many Seris were persuaded to settle down to a proposed farming life again near Hermosillo at what was called Villa Seris. This time Franciscan missionaries attempted to convert them. The whole venture failed and for another hundred years the Seris kept the westward-venturing Spaniards terrorized.

They became known as ferocious, although there is no evidence that they were any more ferocious, if as much so, as the Spaniards and Mexicans who one-sidedly reported the mutual raiding. It is clear that the Mexicans did not restrain themselves from shooting defenseless women and children or from breaking up families and deporting children to live apart from their parents. Hatred was mutual, and hence atrocity stories were told by both sides. The Seris were regarded as cannibals, and as their condition of life worsened under pressure from the superior weapons of the Mexicans, they gained a reputation for all the worst and most inhuman vices that their enemies could imagine.

In the 1880's again, efforts were made to "tame" the Seris by forcible roundup and establishment at Villa Seris. This time the effort ended as a result of an attempt by Mexicans to poison the Seris through contaminated food. The Seris gradually dispersed again, only to fall afoul of Mexican cattlemen who were moving into the Seri lands for grazing country, now that they were able to tap the water supply through the use of windmills. Still a third major attempt to convert the Seris through training two of their youths to become priests failed in the 1880's. A series of attacks and counterattacks between the Seris and the encroaching cattlemen, which came to be known as the Encinas Wars, steadily decimated the Seris and forced the members of the various bands to come together into a single group.

Barely surviving the onslaught of the cattlemen, the Seris, settling at Kino Bay, began to sell fish to Mexican traders. Here further unfortunate experiences led to government interest in their plight and various efforts at schooling and economic aid were attempted, mediated by Roberto Thompson of Hermosillo. Gradually, during the 1940's and 50's, Seris began to increase in number, as trade in fish and sea turtle developed and stabilized their economy, but kept it focused on the sea where it had been traditionally. A 25 per cent increase in their number between 1950 and 1960 suggested that they were perhaps once more stabilized in their old habitat. Many new influences had begun to affect them strongly. One of these was a school; another was an evangelistic religious sect. There was no indication that any of these influences, if they conflicted with the seminomadic fishing life, would succeed any more than similar efforts had in the past.

The Seris lived in colorful fashion on the Sonoran gulf coast, devoted to the sea, but they also hunted deer insofar as deer were not being killed off on Tiburón Island. Their life was in transition in the 1960's from the freer wandering to a more settled way. They still painted their faces for a variety of reasons in traditional elaborate butterfly wing and other designs — a fact which attracted the attention of tourists whose women also painted their faces, somewhat less elaborately. Well acquainted with modern medicine as a result of various efforts to help them in measles and other epidemics, they still employed traditional curing techniques utilizing the native leaves of the elephant tree and the old curing songs. They maintained puberty dances for girls and their traditional system of bride payments. While they had gone through a phase of Protestantization in which they were baptized in the sea and some of their numbers became preachers (a process involving temporary abandonment of face painting) they still maintained their own set of beliefs about the supernaturals, including those in the sacred caves of the island and coast. They were very much dependent on the economic system of modern Mexico, although living in their own way outside of, rather than dominated by, that system. Predictions of their disappearance continued to be made as they had for the previous hundred years.

The Yaquis and Seris are only two of the enclaved Indian groups of northwestern Mexico. All are strikingly different from one another, each maintaining something of the aboriginal tribal character which they possessed when the Spaniards entered this rugged desert and mountain region. None had been subjected to any political domination. All lived in separate independent villages and towns or roamed as free bands. Not all have survived to the present, but all fought for their independence and for survival. A few tribes died out; some were culturally assimilated to the Mexican way of life, like the Opatas of central Sonora. The remaining large groups, apart from the Yaquis and Mayos and the Seris, lie in the mountain valleys of the great Sierra Madre range, which extends southward from the United States into the central heartland of Mexico.

KICKAPOOS

The Indian population of the northeast was so sparse and culturally so undeveloped that none of its communities survived the Spanish Conquest. All were absorbed into the advancing front of the Spanish settlers, providing they were not killed off at first contact. Only in Coahuila is to be found any Indian group — the Kickapoos — and these are immigrants from far to the north. They once lived in the Great Lakes region, along with the Sauk and Fox and other Algonkin-speaking Indians well known in United States history. They were pushed west and south by the advancing Anglo-American settlers, and eventually a portion of the Kickapoos sought independence in Mexico, where they agreed to help Mexicans fight Comanches in return for freedom on a grant of land in northern Coahuila. They live there today, a little enclave of three hundred people speaking their ancient Algonkin language and practicing the medicine-bundle religion which they brought with them and in which their distinctive sense of Kickapoo identity resides.[27]

TARASCANS

Western Mexico, the scene of the Tarascan empire at the time of the arrival of the Spaniards, suffered probably the most devastating military conquest of any region of New Spain. This resulted simply from the fact that an unscrupulous Spaniard was placed in charge of "pacifying" the region without adequate restraints. His name was Nuño de Guzmán, and he stands in Mexican history as the most ruthless and needlessly destructive of all the conquistadores. Possibly Pedro de Alvarado was of the same stripe, but he never had quite so free a hand for so long a time. Other, smaller fry were also vicious, but none had the scope of Guzmán. Yet, strangely, he is not a figure in Indian mythology of the region. Rather their mythology has placed tremendous emphasis on one of the most dedicated and constructive of all the figures of the conquest — Vasco de Quiroga, or "Tata Vasco."

The area which is now Michoacán, Guanajuato, and Jalisco, including the great productive Bajío and the plains of Celaya, was occupied by the Purépecha people in the early 1500's. These were the people later called Tarascans by the Spaniards, the name by which they generally go today. The Tarascans had developed a civilization somewhat like that which had grown up in the Valley of Mexico. There were city states and many of these paid tribute to a strong dynasty which maintained its palaces and governing center at Tzintzunztán on Lake Pátzcuaro. The king or head of this dynasty at the time of Cortés's onslaught on Tenochtitlán was named Zuangua.[28] He received the news of the Spaniards in somewhat the same way as did Moctezuma, that is, with hesitation, with uncertainty as to whether he was confronting supernaturals or vanquishable human beings. As in the case of the Aztecs, the hesitations of the ruler were fatal. The contingent of Spaniards ultimately sent on to Tzintzunztán destroyed the Tarascan power, which had successfully withstood Aztec efforts of conquest for centuries, and took over the political and military control of the area of Tarascan influence. The man who assumed power was Nuño de Guzmán, who was as thirsty for gold as any conquistador had ever been. He tortured and killed nobles and commoners in efforts to get them to tell where gold supplies existed. He destroyed villages and was utterly ruthless when he encountered the slightest resistance. The needless destruction led to his recall and to a terrible decline in the prosperity and welfare of the region.

Toward the north in Jalisco, Indians had fled before and behind him to the hills, where there was a last stand of those finally irreconcilable to Spanish rule. This last-ditch effort to fend off Spaniards became known as the Mixton Wars and resulted in the ravaging of most of what is now the state of Jalisco. Of the Indians, there seem only to have been left in that area some colonies of the Nahuatl-speaking peoples in the vicinity of modern Guadalajara, a city founded by Guzmán. Others fled permanently or were killed off in the Mixton and preceding wars. The greater part of the region was thus left open for settlement by Spaniards, who proceeded to flock in and to take over the very rich Bajío lands of eastern Jalisco and Guanajuato and the extensive good pasture and sometimes orchard lands of the rest of Jalisco, so that this became rapidly a non-Indian area, a stronghold of rural *mestizo* life from then till now.

Meanwhile farther south in Michoacán, where the ravages had been similar but where, as Guzmán moved on, he left some Indian communities broken in the valleys but reunited and reenforced in the mountains of Michoacán, a program of rehabilitation was inaugurated. A man who had come over to serve on the *audiencia,* but who became devoted to direct social service, became the dominant influence for years. This was Vasco de Quiroga, a Dominican who eventually became Bishop of Michoacán. For years he worked intensively all through the area. He had been inspired by some of the European Utopian ideas of the era and particularly, as had some other missionaries, with the ideas and ideals for social life of Sir Thomas More set forth in the "Utopia." Tata Vasco, as the Indians came to call him, began to apply these. He set up "Hospitals" which were community centers where he sought to minister to the sick and to organize or reorganize productive craft activities, such as pottery, weaving, woodwork, and metal work.

Perhaps most significant of all, he developed an organization which had as its focus veneration of the Virgin, but which became a sort of overall community organization — which now developed to fill the gap left by the disintegration of the Tarascan political structure. Generally in the lowlands the efforts of Vasco de Quiroga resulted in the rebuilding of communities; here there was a real loss of native ways and a substitution of the new Utopia-inspired community life of the hospitals. Today this traditional sixteenth-century organization is the focus of conflict, as factions of agrarians, *cristeros,* and conservatives have grown up. In Tzintzunztán are remnants of the old tightly integrated system of obligations for putting on expensive fiestas year after year in honor of the saints of the Catholic calendar. Today the church itself is opposed to these, but their hold is strong.[29]

In the mountains that rise to cool latitudes, with their cover of lovely pines which extend westward from Lake Pátzcuaro, there are villages of Tarascans where to some extent the destructive force of the conquest was escaped. Here the special type of community organization fostered by Quiroga did not become important. Here, in the shadow of the new volcano, Paricutín, something of Indian Mexico remains. The federal government has made efforts in this area to reduce the Tarascan language to a written form; for here the language is vigorous, in contrast with the lowlands where, even though people think of themselves as Indians, they have frequently ceased to make any use of the Tarascan language. Here in the mountain villages the Purépecha language is used; and during the 1940's, village bulletin boards were established where current news was posted in the Tarascan language, as teams of community workers established schools where there had been none before, and where, after a great deal of careful study, a written form of Tarascan was introduced.

Rimming the calm and lovely surface of Lake Pátzcuaro in the highlands of Michoacán is a slow-changing community of Tarascan people who still identify strongly with Indian Mexico; their subsistence, transportation, and daily society revolving around the setting of the jewel-like lake.

These villages in the pleasant mountain setting of Michoacán are among the areas of continuation of Indian life and culture. They do not present the appearance of the enclaves of the north, yet they are more like them than are the Indian communities farther south. The boundaries are not so sharp between Indian and *mestizo* as they are in the north; the deculturated Tarascans of the valleys and lakes are linked by marriage and family with the mountain Tarascans. A common sense of identity has survived despite, or perhaps because of, intense village rivalries such as those which developed in the 1600's between Pátzcuaro and Tzintzunztán. In the mountain villages and some of the others there are, moreover, flourishing crafts which are distinctive of various villages and groups of villages.

The handmoulded pottery of these villages, the red glaze, the cream-colored pottery of Tzintzunztán with its green, rudely sketched life-figures that one may buy now all over Mexico and the United States — these are fusions of Indian and Spanish techniques. The same is true of the carved wood and of the copper work of Santa Cruz for which now the "raw" materials are gleaned from the streets and rubbish cans of Mexico City. Here near Uruapan is a craft island in the modern world, with variety, geographical specialization, with color and originality, and it continues to grow and change.

Other folk arts of the Tarascan country, shared by Indians and *mestizos,* are dances, drama, and music. The Little Old Men, the Shepherds' Plays, and a host of musical mimes and *sones* are characteristically Michoacán, if not Indian. They are fusions of the two traditions. And we find fusion in the marriage customs where there survives a symbolic form of bride capture, but the dominant character of the religious life is set in terms of the cult of the Catholic saints.

In the Tarascan country, former President Lázaro Cárdenas was born and brought up, and probably there is Tarascan blood in his ancestry. It was he who in recent times paid more attention than any other president of Mexico to the special and particular problems of Indians. He may not have been wise in all his attempts to solve them, but he was active, as in his attempt to protect Yaqui lands by presidential decree. Similarly Cárdenas's recognition of special Indian problems not identical with the other rural problems of Mexico resulted in his encouraging the United Nations to set up the training center of CREFAL to work with such problems and to train young people from all over Latin America. Cárdenas gave his house at Pátzcuaro for a study and teaching center, and since 1947, the Tarascan villages in the vicinity of Pátzcuaro have been the focus of community development work, so there is now a sort of renascence of the spirit of Tata Vasco.

THE NAHUATL-SPEAKING PEOPLE

In the area where speakers of the Nahuatl languages were dominant before the coming of the Spaniards, one does not find tribal enclaves as in the north, or even strong tribal identity, as in the west where the Tarascans somehow still present, in the face of steadily accelerating assimilation to the general Mexican culture, some tribal kind of consciousness. One may go to Tepoztlán, where tourists have been going since 1930, directed by the books of Robert Redfield[30] and Stuart Chase,[31] and hear one of the Nahuatl languages spoken. One may go to the group of villages around Milpa Alta, closer to Mexico City, within thirty miles of the Zocalo, and hear what is probably the most direct descendant of the tongues spoken by the Aztecs at Tenochtitlan. One may go elsewhere in Puebla or Hidalgo or Veracruz or in the fastness of Guerrero where Nahuatl languages are spoken, and sweathouses *(temazcales)* are used, and one has no question about being in Indian country. But one does not find the sense of a bounded entity of Indian people. One finds greater or less sense of unity in different towns and villages, more or less organization, and more or less devotion to progress, but one searches in vain for the kind of consciousness of themselves as "we, the tribe" which is immediately apparent among the smaller northern groups, be it Tarahumara or Yaqui or Huichol.

Most writers are really talking about the history and conditions of the Nahuatl-speaking peoples of the central Plateau when they talk about the Indians of Mexico. It is their history and their "idols behind altars" which have become identified with the Mexican background. It is Tepoztlán in Morelos which has become the type of the "Mexican Village" as a result of Robert Redfield's brilliant characterization of it in 1930 as a "folk community," Stuart Chase's somewhat idealized view of the "machineless men" of Tepoztlán, and the recent "re-study" of the village by Oscar Lewis[32] which paints a very different picture. Then there is the still more recent study of Tecospa lying within the Federal District called the *Virgin's Children*.[33] These few and various pictures do not quite hang together and raise more questions than they settle about the nature of modern descendants of the Aztecs.

The nearly one million Aztec and culturally related people are everywhere peasants, not to be thought of as tribal people like the Yaquis still in the process of being brought into the national state. They have been a part of one state or another for centuries, perhaps for nearer a millennium. They are people of villages and towns, not tribes. The villages are not, and have not been through the years, sure of one another. They tend to be hostile to, or at least suspicious of, not only outlanders but of each other. There is a fear of exploitation and often, in crowded areas, of competition for land. Pervading daily life is a fatalistic spirit, clearly a product of the long history of oppression and disorganizing interferences emanating from the capital.

Even the Nahuatl-speaking Tlaxcalans who had been allies of Cortés in his attack on Tenochtitlan and

who had a measure of self-rule for fifty years or more after the Aztecs were conquered did not escape the heel of the conquerors. They were merged quickly enough, in the view of the Spaniards, with the other Indians. With all the others, they suffered population decline as a result of measles, smallpox, and probably tuberculosis. Towns of ten thousand people became suddenly, in a matter of a year or less, villages of 3000 or 4000. As this decline in the numbers of the people continued, the Spanish system of *encomienda* and *repartimiento* laid the foundations for a society divided against itself. In those areas where a powerful line of conquistadores became established, Aztec feudalism was transformed into a similar but more ruthless European type of feudalism. An example would be those large areas established by Cortés and his son, areas including Nahuatl-speaking people in what are now Mexico, Morelos, and Puebla.

The Spanish lords sought tractable Indian men and set them up as "caciques," or chiefs, putting them over the people as labor overseers and collectors of tribute. The power of these men became great, and they were the ones who worked with the missionaries and the later secular clergy, requiring the Indians to build thousands of churches and seeing to it that the Indians attended them. The workers were shifted about whenever necessary in the interest of more productive mining or agriculture as dictated by the Spanish overlords.

Tepoztlán in Morelos may be taken as an example. It was an important Indian town at the time of the conquest and has remained what is called a free village to the present. The son of Cortés became the *encomendero* or overlord of the town immediately upon its subjection. He required that the Indians produce so much corn as tribute and he also recruited laborers from the town to work, often some distance away, in mines or on haciendas set up elsewhere. The population steadily declined, perhaps by as much as one-half between 1540 and 1590. Herds of goats and cattle were introduced, and idle land was worked under the forced labor system by Indians employed by the Spaniards.

Meanwhile, on a grand scale, intermixture took place between the Spanish men in charge and the Indian women. A new breed of men and women was steadily created — the *mestizo*.[34] Often the *mestizos* in this phase were brought more under the influence of the Spanish fathers than the Indian mothers. A non-Indian way of life developed, and there were now in the village two kinds of people — Indians and non-Indians. The *mestizos* were similar to, but by no means identical with, the top Spanish social stratum in their way of life. They were too poor for that, but they were oriented away from the Indian life-values. The Indian culture was looked down on by Spanish missionary and Spanish foreman alike, and moreover the Indian communities, even the free villages like Tepoztlán, were either disrupted and hence offered little, or were reorganizing along lines dictated by the power-holding Spaniards. Thus, while everywhere most of the substance of daily life — food, housing, sickness and curing, even religious belief — was basically Indian for both *mestizos* and Indians, a new framework for the whole was developing which was derived in large measure from Spanish culture. It was this which gave orientation to the emerging *mestizo* segment of society. It did not embrace a majority in the Nahuatl-speaking areas until perhaps the end of the seventeenth century. From then on, the framework became increasingly important.

Intermingled as the Indian- and Spanish-oriented people were on haciendas and in free villages during the nineteenth century, the differences between them became fewer and fewer. Illiterate and with a sense of desperation about continuing to hold what land was left to them, the people of Tepoztlán managed somehow to maintain their free village status and were not absorbed by any of the expanding haciendas around them. They were, however, reduced to a life of poverty and dependency on the large landholders of the area.

Nevertheless, a school teacher, Mariano Rojas, who made his residence in the village during the last half of the nineteenth century, became a founder of a society for the teaching and learning of Classical Nahuatl. His activities in the village in the 1880's and 90's were part of a growing interest among Mexican intellectuals in the "Indian heritage" of Mexico. Rojas and others associated with him contributed to this interest among intellectuals in Mexico City, fifty miles away.

As numerous Tepoztecos found it impossible to live well in the village, they moved to Mexico City and there established a "colony" of transplanted villagers who maintained an interest in Tepoztlán and sought to aid in its "improvement." This tie with the metropolis was maintained through the revolution and to the present, playing an important part in the life of the village, contributing perhaps to its modernizing more rapidly than other similar villages.

Like most villages of Morelos during the 1910 Revolution, Tepoztlán experienced invasions and counterinvasions. During most of the period from 1912 to 1918, the village was evacuated and those men who were not in the army fighting with or against Emiliano Zapata lived scattered widely in less accessible parts of Morelos. There was strong support among the rank and file for Zapata and his program of breaking up the haciendas and redistributing the land to the peons who had worked it. But there was characteristically no unity discernible in the relationship of the Tepoztecos to the issues of the Revolution. It would appear that they fought on both sides, that there was no overwhelming conviction about any issue, and that the Revolution as a social movement swept the Tepoztecos this way and that.

The fact is that within the village there was a sharp two-class split which had been generated by the economic forces of the hacienda period. On the one hand there were the sons of *caciques*, that is, the men who had served as foremen or assistants in some way to *hacendados* during the Díaz period. These people

had therefore been better off economically than others and had identified their interests with the Porfirian status quo. On the other hand there were the rank and file villagers. After the fighting of the Revolution ended, schisms occurred in the 1920's and 1930's, and power shifted from one clique to another over issues such as whether or not the forests of the village should be unrestrainedly used for charcoal or whether they should be used in accordance with governmental conservation measures. In general the "sons of caciques" were in favor of unregulated use of resources, the common people in favor of regulation and acceptance of governmental plans in the use of forest resources and in the management of the lands as *ejidos*. These locally important issues have shaped the village politics.

Steadily the Nahuatl language has become less important and with it most features of distinctive Indian culture and consciousness of Indian heritage. In a sense there is a reverse trend here as compared with the intellectual movement to which Tepoztecos contributed in Mexico City. As the latter has emphasized Indian heritage, the village has become progressively less interested in this heritage. While 95 per cent spoke Nahuatl in the 1920's when Redfield studied the village, 50 per cent spoke it some thirty-five years later.[35] This reflects the influence of a federal school and a generally intensified contact and communication with the urban world of Mexico through the busline and other communications with Cuernavaca and Mexico City. However, no one knows whether this is the trend in villages generally of the Nahuatl-speaking area.

The people of Tepoztlán are not an isolated triblet like the remnant Seris. They are not a recently powerful tribe like the Yaquis with memories of military strength and triumphs against the Mexicans. They are not an infiltrated and disintegrated group culturally like the Tarascans. They are probably to be understood best as a slowly rebuilding conquered group whose heritage of suspicion and of disintegrated community life is undergoing a new synthesis. The elements of this synthesis are primarily the metropolitan culture of the Western world relayed through the capital, with the small-town, de-tribalized, *mestizo*-Indian peasant-like culture. No one has sufficiently studied this process to know how it works. What we know of Mexican cultural history suggests that it is not a simple replacement of "Indian" culture by "modern" culture, whatever that may be. It is a process of new growth, somewhat like the new synthesis which took place in the *barrios* of the colonial period, where Catholic and Aztec world views fused into something new.

Now it would seem that the threshold of change is the village school where teachers recruited from all over Mexico and trained in the city are in residence. In fact, this new form of cultural center is represented quite simply and symbolically wherever one goes in central Mexico. The old church (for example at the village of Texcotzinco near Texcoco across the now-dry lake from Mexico City in Nahuatl-speaking country) stands in its sombre wrought-stone glory as it did in

The synthesis of cultural elements in modern Mexico is effectively symbolized by the frequency of church and school buildings standing next to each other; the one institution working to preserve historical patterns of thought and behavior; the other focused on growth and change as appropriate to youth.

colonial times, representing still that great crystallization of human energy guided by the Catholic missionaries and the new hope of the Indians who cut and laid the stones. It stands with its surrounding wall and its enclosed *Campo Santo* — its accumulation of the dead of the village collected around the enduring church. But alongside, a small building asserts itself in a wholly different style, low with only three rooms, built obviously in the spirit of function and economy, not prodigal, not ornate. It consists of simple rooms; there is no kind of decoration inside or out except for the name of a local distinguished schoolteacher in bold black letters across the whole front. The focus is on busy children, so the rooms have light to work by, and the court surrounding has swings and a basketball court. The new building is within the very churchyard; the church is regularly attended. All who go to church must see the school and the name of the revolutionary

leader emblazoned on it. It is obvious that the school is here beside the church because it has an important place in the lives of the villagers.

The modern way of bringing about synthesis is plainly different from that practiced by the Catholic missionaries. They tore down temples which had been the shrines of public life among the Aztecs for centuries, then built new temples with new images on the same spot or very close by — as witness the Basilica of the Virgin of Guadalupe just below the hilltop where rose the ancient shrine of Tonantzin, Aztec goddess of growth. In the current process, the old focus of community life and devotion is not torn down. The church still stands, and community life still has a focus there. But alongside, well-manned, and active five days weekly, not merely a day or two a week, is the modern link between the rural life and the metropolitan vision of the future. As in the case of the colonial churches, the teachings are decided upon at a place far away. The dominant political party has made a strong effort through the years since 1917 to shape teaching in the rural school. It is a new synthesis, not built on ruins as was the earlier, but evidently involving recognition that significant revolution in human lives must depend on a process of growth and the competition of alternatives. Paradoxically the new process of cultural change is evolutionary in terms of the church-and-school symbol, while the old church-directed process was revolutionary.

This symbol — rural school in churchyard — is perhaps the best of all summaries of what is happening today in Mexico. To understand it one must know something of the background of the church and its amazingly successful penetration and reorientation of Indian life toward a universal religion. One must realize that this reorientation was never complete, that there was a decline in level of integration after the colonial period when churches so often reverted to the status of shrines of a small region, often becoming refocused on almost a neighborhood basis, but remaining active centers of community life and organization. One should understand too the story of the rural school in Mexico, of how it filled a vacuum. Between the *calpulli* in which Tepoztecans, for example, were educated in Aztec times, and the school of Mariano Rojas, formal schooling beyond the catechism generally did not exist for rural Mexicans.

The rural school today is one fruit of a real national movement and remains a centrally controlled system. Everywhere, not only in the Nahuatl country, one sees this workshop of the present synthesis. In a context of ideas about the geologic ages, space travel, state dominance in economic life as well as government, and the irrelevance of supernatural belief to important matters, regularly presented in the textbooks, still stands the church with its intricately ornamented representation of heaven and the angels and the saints; it stands as a center of devotion and often of vigorous community organization.

Back in the village of Tepoztlán, life is still divided between hoe and ox-plow tilling of the *milpas,* between that is, the Aztec-founded methods of cultivating maize and the methods introduced by the Spaniards. Some houses are of wattle still, but most are of adobe brick and roof-tile as introduced by the Spaniards. Tortillas and chile and beans are still basic, but always of course with coffee and sugar and Coca Cola. And the ceremonial life is directed toward the Virgin and the saints and guided by the Catholic calendar, since the old Aztec calendar is forgotten, but El Tepozteco is still important and inspires visions. Here the *comparsas* organized to dance on church occasions present the jumping Chinelos at the Carnival (Mardi Gras) in a fusion of native dance and mimicry with Christian occasion.

Two interpretations of the spirit of the Nahuatl villages are usually regarded as opposing.[36] Redfield emphasized a wholeness of life which he caught glimpses of in the fiesta cycle and the rhythms of daily activities. One emerges from his book with a sense of villagers living full lives. On the other hand Lewis, using projective tests and intensive observation of families of all kinds, emphasized repression and constriction in personal relations and gives us a picture of not very happy, suspicious people in a small town. Which is true? One may as well ask which is the true United States small-town life — that described by Sherwood Anderson, Sinclair Lewis, James West, or the Lynds? None is the whole truth, but all give insights.

It is certainly true that among these Nahuatl-speaking people, there is not much creative expressive activity. The native crafts have died out or are dying; the ceremonial life is characterized by a certain sameness of dance and music. It is not in this region that the distinctive arts of the Mexican folk community are vigorous. But elsewhere the Nahuatl-speaking people carry on some of the finest of Mexican popular arts. Tepoztlán represents only one trend in modern Nahuatl life.

INDIANS OF OAXACA

To travel from Mexico City to the city of Oaxaca is to gain great respect for Aztec troops and traders who made the journey on foot. There were no broad valleys to follow for any distance at all. There were no flat plateaus; there were not even continuous ridges where a tortuous road might be made. The only way to go was up and down, up and down, league after league. The country is rugged and difficult every foot of the way. Yet the Aztecs had opened up trade routes for their *pochtecas,* or travelling traders, through to the isthmus at the time the Spaniards landed. They had been doing so for some time, and two dominant people. in this region to the south of the Aztecs — the Mixtecs and the Zapotecs — were affected by the Aztec maneuvers.

The Zapotecs were a people widespread in the area of what is now the state of Oaxaca, occupying most of the central and eastern part. They had been expanding for several hundred years toward the east, pushing smaller tribes eastward or absorbing them. But they were in turn being pushed from the west by the Mixtecs, an expanding group native apparently to the Puebla highlands. As the Spaniards came on the scene, the Zapotecs were in control of the Valley of Oaxaca in the central part of the modern state and of the highlands to the north, south, and east of the valley as well as the southern and western part of the Isthmus of Tehuantepec. For an unknown number of centuries, Zapotec "kings" had made their headquarters in the cities now called Teotitlán del Valle, Záachila, Zimatlán, and Mitla. They had built the great center of Monte Albán, but it was abandoned by 1500 as the Mixtecs pressed from the west. They called themselves "ben'zaa," which means "cloud people."

Like the Aztecs and the Tarascans, and unlike the Mixtecs who were less able to achieve a general political unity, the Zapotecs were an "empire" during the

1400's and 1500's and probably earlier. They had traditions of kings, for example Záachila I, II and III and Cocijoesa, who was "king" when the Spaniards came. Apparently better versed in statecraft than the Tarascan and Aztec kings, Cocijoesa somewhat successfully manipulated Aztecs against Mixtecs, but in the end suffered a similar fate to that of Moctezuma as his power was usurped by the ruthless Cortés and Alvarado. The Zapotecs were remarkable architects and built elaborate mounds and tombs; they were still building the complex cruciform tombs of Mitla when the Spaniards interrupted their independent development.

The Zapotecs did not offer serious resistance to the Spaniards. Once, however, in 1660, the headmen of the Oaxaca valley cities revolted, unable to put up with the vicious administration imposed by the descendants of Cortés, who inherited the Valley of Oaxaca from the conquistador, and the rigid program of the Dominicans. They were quickly put down, and those who had dared to lead, asking for moderation in tribute and a few other reasonable requests, were beheaded. Their heads, posted on the highways entering the city of Oaxaca, afforded the usual demonstration of Spanish power and ruthlessness.[37]

Probably the valley Zapotecs suffered as much disruption from the *encomienda* system as the Nahuatl-speaking people. Since the conquest they have not shown much tendency to political unity with the rest of the country or with each other. The Zapotecs have been and still are characterized by bitter local rivalries. The rivalry between the two towns in the Isthmus Zapotec country — Juchitán and Tehuantepec — is legendary. It led to wars in the nineteenth century and to division within the state of Oaxaca during the 1910 revolution. During the epoch of Porfirio Díaz, the political boss of the state was an Isthmus woman, Doña Juana Cata Romero, longtime friend of Díaz. She made headquarters in Tehuantepec and gave that town dominance in the late nineteenth century, no doubt stimulating the rival Juchitán to a secessionist tendency during the epoch of revolution following.

It must be recorded, however, that perhaps the most unifying hero of Mexico, the symbol of greatest personal integrity, of respect for the law, of constitutional democracy, was the Zapotec Indian Benito Juárez. He was a mountain Zapotec brought up in earliest childhood in the beautiful Guelatao country in what is now called the Sierra de Juárez, north of the city of Oaxaca. Benito herded goats around a beautiful mountain lake where now there has been established a horticultural experiment station in his honor. He early entered the orbit of metropolitan life in the city of Oaxaca where he studied law and adopted the *mestizo* way of life. Nevertheless, as a symbol of the Indian foundations of the nation, he is of major importance in the ideology of modern Mexico.

The state of Oaxaca is still a very loosely united congeries of village groups often at war with one another over land boundaries, speaking different dialects though only a few miles apart, and frequently forcing federal troops to come up into the mountains to settle their longstanding feuds so that basic law and order may be maintained. The Zapotecs are no more a unified tribe in feeling today than are the Aztecs, and in custom they exhibit a greater diversity. This probably reflects the fact that their pre-Spanish empire was more a collection of city states than a unified political structure.

Today there survive many handicrafts of importance — the modified crafts, combining the ancient with the Spanish-introduced techniques. The green-glazed pottery of the village of Atzompa on the Mixtec-Zapotec border, the unique polished black ware of Coyotepec, and the orange ware of Ocotlán, decorated in fugitive white, are abundant not only in Oaxaca markets but also elsewhere in Mexico. The weaving center of Teotitlán del Valle and the cast metalwork of the city of Oaxaca are important in this center of the modern popular arts of Mexico.[38] Also here the arts of dance and dance drama exist in vigorous fashion — in the form of the feather dance in Zapotec towns such as Teotitlán del Valle, Zimatlán, and elsewhere. With spectacular large feather headdresses, the famous performance is much more than a dance. It is one of those characteristic fusions of Spanish and Indian folk art, a remarkable drama of the conquest, with characters costumed as Moctezuma, as Cortés, as Spanish and Aztec soldiers, and as Malinche. The dance drama, characterized by great leaping dance steps and by much intricate action and pantomime to strings and drums, lasts for four days and is justly famous throughout Mexico. Of the many distinctive ceremonies, we may mention the *calendas* with elaborate flower-headdresses, and trading fiestas where men, women, and children construct the rancho or the mescal plantation of their dreams as they sit beside a Mitla shrine during New Year's eve and then sell this dream place to the highest bidder for worthless paper "money." It seems to be characteristic of the Zapotecs that trade is built into their religious life. They are known, particularly the market women of Tehuantepec, as traders and as lovers of the marketplace. Here in the city of Oaxaca there are to be seen colorful fiestas hardly equaled anywhere else — the end of the year *buñuelos* and the breaking of dishes in the streets, which recalls the old Aztec ceremony, and the recently stimulated fiesta of the radishes which like so much else combines the old and new. The fiesta regime is rich and constant, but these festivals, stemming out of the colonial cultural fusion, are only part of the modern scene. They share the interest of the people with the modern fiestas of the labor unions, in which the Virgin of Guadalupe serves as patroness of labor. In these, on May 1, taxi drivers and bus drivers drive for hours, as secretaries, typists, and other white-collar workers and groups of farmers march through the streets of Oaxaca, behind their modern symbols — the anarchist martyrs of Chicago, the striking laborers of Cananea, and others. And a general strike, such as the one in the summer of 1954, brings out as many people in as deep a mood of serious purpose as do the saints' fiestas. Thus Oaxaca, rooted in its Zapotec traditions, moves in the stream of history, as ancient traditions and new myths and experience intertwine. Despite their local feuds, the Zapotecs seem perhaps more vigorous as a people than any others we have considered thus far.

MODERN MAYAS

The Maya Indians are an important entity in modern Mexican life, but they are not a unit. There is wide variation among them. They are not a disintegrating people, marginal to the present currents of development, like the Tarascans; they have not lost as much of the colonial fusion of cultures as have the Aztecs, nor have they suffered so long in such solitary misery the peonage which deculturized the Aztecs; they are more like the modern Zapotecs in their cultural variety, and in the vigorous continuing growth of the fusion of traditions; but they are very different also from the Zapotecs. For one thing, the Zapotecs show more marks of domination and today are not culturally dominant in their region to the extent that the Mayas are. For another, Zapotecs have obviously been more completely cut off from their great past than the Mayas; Zapotecs generally do not have quite so strong a sense of history. But the Zapotecs of "Indian Mexico" are certainly more like the Mayas than these two are like any Indian peoples farther north.

It is clear that there are at least two quite different cultural worlds among the Mayas — that of the highland and that of the lowland people. The highland Maya culture of Mexico centers in the state of Chiapas where Indians speak languages belonging to the Tzotzil and Tzeltal groups.[39] In Chiapas today there exist the most obvious scars and current symbols of ethnic conflict to be found anywhere in the republic of Mexico. There are similar marks of Indian-*mestizo* conflict elsewhere as in the Chihuahua Tarahumara country, but there they are confined to a small area. In Chiapas the whole region, including the streets and marketplaces of San Cristóbal de las Casas, the second largest city of the state, exhibits these marks of complex and conflict-ridden group relations.

Here also are to be found the most colorful outward manifestations of cultural diversity in all Mexico. Here not only the women, as in Oaxaca and Yucatán, but also the men, wear clothing which proclaims village origin and disclaims the acceptance of either the white *calzones* of the Porfirian epoch or the modern denim pants. The men follow a general style of poncho-like shirt, short pants, broad, beribboned, and carefully woven hat, diminutive cloak; and heavy leather sandals that echo ancient Maya footgear. But every village has its different colors and different shapes, so that amid a common participation in a tradition of colorful clothing, distinctive local individuality is vigorously maintained. In contrast with other areas of Mexico, like the Tarahumara, it is apparent that such clothing is not in the category of the barely surviving or dying custom. It is worn unabashedly as the right and proper way.

Everywhere the Indians are in the majority, but as elsewhere they do not hold the power. They are well aware that the economic and political life of the state is in other hands. They are aware of a history of exploitation during colonial times and feel a solidarity against the non-Indians who are called here, not *mestizos,* but *Ladinos,* as they are in Guatemala. Dominant in the city and some towns, the *Ladinos* display an an attitude of superiority which is symptomatic of prevailing bad group relations. It is a misnomer, however, to call these "race" relations. It is clear that skin color has nothing to do with anyone's being considered either *Ladino* or Indian. The basis for distinction is cultural, that is, the language one speaks, the kind of house one lives in, the kind of clothes one wears, and to some extent the kind of food one eats. Beneath these there are the attitudes and value orientations of which the people on both sides of the cultural line are very conscious and which lead to classification in one of the two categories of *Ladino* or Indian. A real interest in farming, for example, is Indian; a real interest in making money, on the other hand, and being relieved of farming the land, is *Ladino*. A fatalism about men's fate is Indian; a faith in some kind of progress through political action is *Ladino*. Around these values have developed a passivity characteristic of Indians as a whole and an activism characteristic of the *Ladinos* which leads to local as well as state dominance in many villages.

Meanwhile the Indian communities go on in a very old tradition, as always employing a fusion of Spanish and ancient Mayan political forms, oriented inward or centripetally. Villages such as Chamula and Zinacantán and Larrainzar among the Tzotzils have been in about the same locations since before the Spanish conquest. They are organized for local government in a hierarchy which derives its offices from sixteenth-century Spain and pre-Spanish Mayan tradition. Every man goes through the levels of the hierarchy in the course of his life, serving his village until he becomes an elder — a *principal* — and joins the old men who make the decisions which the hierarchy executes.

One characteristic of the region is the existence of "vacant villages." For example, Chamula, not far from the state capital of San Cristóbal, is inhabited most of the year only by a few religious functionaries. The people of the municipality of Chamula live in smaller communities, called *parajes,* where their farms and herds are centered. The big colonial period church is located at Chamula, and in thatch houses near the church live the only year-round residents, the ceremonial officials of the community. Here at Easter and on the occasion of other important ceremonies of the Tzotzil calendar, come the Indians from their *parajes*. Here they hang Judas in effigy from the church during Holy Week and here they hold barter markets in the church grounds. Since 1954 they also come to seek aid from the doctors in the fresh new clinic built, with the permission of the elders, not far from the church, by the National Indian Institute.

In the highland Maya Country before the coming of the Spaniards, the Indian communities were independent entities, outside the tribute-paying network of the expanding empires of the lowland Mayas. The way of life was generally similar, in basic social organization, in supernatural belief and mythology, and in material culture, but the highland Mayas were "underdeveloped," in relation to the empire-building Mayas. The autonomous groups of villages, which persist today as tightly integrated social units, existed then and were the boundaries of the social life. When the Spaniards came, the integration of these village clusters was if anything intensified. The great Dominican missionary Las Casas, in honor of whom was named San Cristóbal Las Casas, worked among the highland Mayas. The missionaries brought about the usual fusion of native and Spanish Catholic ways of life. The effects of the *encomienda* system penetrated here sufficiently strongly to lay a foundation of deep hostility and distrust between Indian and Spaniard, but not sufficiently to disintegrate the villages, as among the Aztecs or even the valley Zapotecs. The net effect was probably a tightening of the locally oriented communities.

At times when the Indians felt the pressure strongly from the Spaniards and later from the Mexicans there were vigorous movements to oust the non-Indians and bring the Indians into controlling positions. These took the form of nativistic movements and were most characteristic of the nineteenth century. But the recent important movements are descendants of an early one which took place in 1711–13. The focus was among the Tzeltal-speaking people at Cancuc where a young girl, after a series of miraculous appearances of the Virgin, began to speak with the voice of the Virgin. She advocated the elimination of all white men from Maya country. A century and a half later the desire to manage their own religious life apart from Mexicans resulted in the crucifixion of a Maya youth as the Tzotzils' own Christ. This led to a revolt against *Ladino* controls in 1869 and ultimate forcible subjection of the rebellious Tzotzils by the *Ladinos*. Among the highland Mayas, cults of crosses with special supernatural power are important in religious life today. Also vigorous are the conception of animal-counterpart souls for each person and the belief that an individual's fate and general health are determined by the behavior of this counterpart in its abode on a sacred mountain in the vicinity.

The highland Maya villages are in the throes of a change as drastic as that inaugurated by the coming of the Spaniards. They are undergoing a new program designed to change them from locally oriented communities to ones incorporated into the Mexican national state. The government of Chiapas has long advocated the change but employed techniques which only stimulated withdrawal or conflict. Recently the National Indian Institute has moved in with a program specifically designed to bring about the national integration. The clinic at Chamula mentioned above is one of many clinics and medical centers introduced in the last twelve

years into the highland Maya villages. And the medical program is only part of a broad program of education, road-building, resource development, and agricultural improvement which has been administered during this time from San Cristóbal. The modern methods are different, but the changes sought are as great as those which the Spaniards attempted.

The lowland Mayas present a very different picture.[40] By lowland Mayas we mean those who live on the peninsula in the states of Yucatán and Quintana Roo and in fewer numbers in Campeche. Here there are 300,000 people who speak the Maya language, more than half of whom also speak Spanish. They live under a wide variety of conditions. Many live in Mérida, a city of nearly 150,000, and one hears the Maya language spoken as one walks in the plaza or in any city crowd. There are Mayas employed in the factories of the city and there are Mayas in the professional and business life. Also on all the plantations of the state of Yucatán are Mayan agricultural laborers. In the small rural villages everywhere in the peninsula, in the bush or on the highways there are Indians, well aware and proud of their Indian background. The difference in race relations from the highland area is apparent in many ways and is symbolized in the terminology employed. Here, strangely enough, the Indians, or Maya-speakers, are generally called *"mestizos"* and the people who are "non-Indian" in the sense that one is *Ladino* in Chiapas are called *"catrines."* The open group hostility of the Chiapas highlands is rare or absent here.

There is even a kind of Maya cultural dominance. The Mayas are conscious of a glorious background which moreover is apparent to everyone in the reconstructed ruins such as Uxmal and Chichén Itzá. One of the most notable contrasts between highland and lowland is the wide similarity of Indian culture in the lowlands. The language is uniform. That is, the lowland dialect of Maya which was probably also the language of the stone glyphs of the ancient cities, varies hardly at all from Campeche to Quintana Roo. Although the Indian population is three times as large as in the highlands there are few cultural variations of much importance from village to village. From the Quintana Roo villages to Mérida the "ipil" (as the Yucatecos call it), or woman's dress, is basically the same. The only variation is in the many-colored embroidery which borders the neck opening. In contrast with the elaborate belted skirts and blouses of the highlands the lowland woman's dress is a simple white shift-type garment hanging loosely to the mid-calves, short sleeved and usually square-necked. Women wear it over an undergarment with no belt, no adornment except the narrow neck border, with not the slightest effort to fit the figure. Everywhere urbanite and rural Maya woman wears the same "ipil."

Also the shape of the native house, if not the materials, is almost without variation. An oval ground plan and a high-peaked thatch roof are the characteristic elements. This form one sees in the city of Mérida, as well as in the villages. The walls may be of masonry; there may be concrete or tiled benches facing each other beside the front door. Or the walls may be of vertical poles and the floor of dirt. Whatever the materials, the house is a Maya house of distinctive form, and one feels that it will long persist. This minor variation around a basic formal type in language, dress, and housing is indicative of the fundamentally similar cultural pattern of all lowland Maya life. There are nevertheless variations of some importance — which may be best understood in the light of history.

The Mayas in the peninsula of Yucatán when the Spaniards arrived were not a powerful and organized people. They had, by 1527 when the Spaniards attempted their first landings, disintegrated as an empire. The dynasties which ruled Chichén Itzá and Uxmal and built those and so many other remarkable cultural centers had lost cohesion. No great architectural efforts were in progress. The great Maya cities were already in ruins. Scattered over the peninsula were sporadically-warring family groups. The Mayapán League had attempted during the 1400's to forge a peace, but with little success. There was no organization to which any Mayas subscribed except their feuding family-focused groups. There was no possibility of sustained defense against the Spaniards, although the first to attempt conquest were turned back. The Spaniards

returned and established themselves. But the land was not productive of anything in which the Spaniards were interested. Although some *encomiendas* were set up and given to the conquistadores of Yucatán, there was no influx of Spanish population and no great effort to make the holdings productive. Later Cortés came with a party to extend the conquest into Guatemala and passed through the Maya region. However, the link with the mainland of Mexico was tenuous throughout the colonial period.

While missionaries succeeded in implanting many beliefs and practices in the Maya region as elsewhere in New Spain, this did not involve to as great an extent the transformation of native customs. Rather the dominant process was a sort of splicing together rather than a fusion. Thus the Maya pantheon of deities continued to have meaning for the people in very much the same form which it had always had. The gods of sky and winds and clouds — the Yuntzilob — were not transformed into Christian saints, but kept their Maya form and most of their old powers. Yet the Christian saints, the novenas, the cross, and other forms were by no means rejected. On the contrary they were accepted as elsewhere, but not so much intertwined and dominant in the fusion as side by side. The Maya part of the religious heritage has maintained its own identity much more clearly.

The Yucatecan house type is distinctively Mayan. The oval ground plan and high-peaked thatch roof are constants, but the house is fitted into many different kinds of village plans, material and ornamentation varying with the environment.

On the peninsula the colonial period was one of less intense domination of Indian by Spaniard, of less destruction of native life than characterized the period in central Mexico. This may have had something to do with the intense conflict which broke out some twenty-five years after the Mexican War for Independence. This War of the Castes, as it was called, raged through the middle of the nineteenth century, beginning in the decade of the 1840's. The "War of the Castes" was not a single war. It consisted of many skirmishes during which some Mayas were occasionally organized behind the battle cry of "Death to the Whites." Indians who had worked as peons on the plantations escaped into the bush of Quintana Roo. Others formed new villages and stayed away from the labor recruiters for the rising henequen producers. Sporadic hostilities continued into the early twentieth century.

The immediate results were several: the continued growth of big plantations, many of them forced to use imported slave labor such as Yaquis; the deculturation of thousands of Indians along lines similar to the deculturation carried on in Morelos and other central Mexico regions of intensive hacienda development; retirement of thousands of Mayas to bush areas of Yucatán and Quintana Roo where they could be isolated from the plantations; and ultimately (as it occurred elsewhere in Mexico, for example in Western Tarahumara country) the formation of nuclei of Indian groups implacably hostile to Mexican-Spanish culture. Groups of implacables took up residence in the least accessible bush country of Quintana Roo. Here they separated themselves as completely as possible from contact with Mexicans and set up their own village organization as military units. In their re-isolation, they developed nativistic cults like that of St. John of the Talking Cross, with a new fusion of Christian and older Maya elements.[41] In the twentieth century it became possible for these re-made Indian communities to increase their income by working as collectors of chicle for the chewing gum industry of the Americas.

The Nature of the Inner Margins

It should be clear that from the northwestern desert corner of the republic of Mexico to the southeastern tip of the republic in the jungles of Quintana Roo, there are Indian groups with a sense of their own historical identity. Few if any of these are dying and disintegrated peoples to be viewed as merely anomalous curiosities. They are people in groups of from tens to hundreds of thousands who have a common history, who have adapted in their own differing ways to the succession of conquests and political incorporations through the centuries. They have languages of their own in which their common experience and traditions are embodied and which are the means for expression of the uniqueness they feel as a people. They vary in the degree of pride which they feel and in the intensity of their common feeling. Some are uncertain of their place in modern Mexico, while others, like the Mayas,

are moving dynamically into their regional society. They vary in the extent to which their distinctive character is nurtured by or tied in with the currently developing economic patterns. Some find roles in the modern economy through traditional crafts or through sale of fish or other products. Some do not, having only their labor to sell in the growing industrialized world. The Indian cultures of Mexico are actively adapting to new circumstances, just as they always have.

Yet obviously the people who follow Indian ways constitute only a small part of the nation as a whole. By the most generous estimates, there are only 3 million speakers of Indian languages. To this, if we wish to speak in terms of maximums, we might add another million who identify themselves as Indian, even though not speaking an Indian language. But if we do so, we probably should subtract nearly a million from the bilingual speakers of Indian languages whose orientation is not in that direction. In whatever way we make our estimate, there are fewer than three million who can be called Indians by any criteria, that is, less than one-tenth of the nation. Whether the number of Indians has been declining or increasing over the past fifty years no one can really say. The number of speakers of Indian languages seems not to have declined in this period, but the figures are very uncertain. No figures exist regarding identification as Indians. Whatever these trends, we may look forward to an increasing awareness of and sympathy with Indian aims on the part of the intellectuals in Mexico. In this sense the importance of Indians as a national influence is increasing, especially among those who control the political and administrative power of the country.

It is very important to recognize in this connection that the reality of Indian Mexico is not a unity. It consists of many separate and distinct Indian identities. It is difficult to find in the various Indian cultures a common set of characteristics.[42] If there were common elements of basic importance, we could reckon with an important national force. There is, however, at present no real communication between Yaquis, Zapotecs, and Mayas, however strong their sense of self-identity may be. The objectives of traditional Yaquis regarding independence on their land may in a very general way coincide with the objectives of many bush-dwelling Mayas in Quintana Roo, but there is little more in common here than there is with rural Mexican agrarians throughout the nation. What is most distinctive in the ideology of each of the Indian peoples is not shared with the others. And communication is not intensifying among the Indian groups; rather what is growing is communication between Indian groups and the non-Indians, through the rural school system and the periodicals and other mass media in the nation.

It is a little misleading therefore to emphasize, as we did above, that the number of Indians in Mexico is as large as the population of the USA in 1790 with all that such an emphasis would imply regarding a people with potentialities for political and economic development. It is also misleading, though perhaps less so, to point out that the population of Switzerland is little larger than the Indian population of Mexico and that there are as many Indians in Mexico as there are Norwegians in Norway. The point is that the Indians of Mexico are not a single entity of that order of magnitude. They are many entities, entities which are real enough, but which have great significance in only two ways for the nation. One of these ways is as cultural forces in their regions. The Mayas have influenced and will continue to affect the style of life in Yucatán and the peninsula in important ways. This will be intensified as the university continues to teach the Maya language as an academic subject, and as pride in a unique history connecting the living with the builders of the great ancient cities increases with each new reconstruction. There will be increasing influences of this sort regionally throughout Mexico. This is, moreover, encouraged in interesting ways by national policy in the program for the popular arts.[43] Regionalism is one important way in which Indian identity and custom influence the life of the nation.

The other is in connection with the national sense of identity — the point of view about themselves which Mexicans in general hold. Such national self-conceptions are always influenced by the self-conscious intellectuals of an era, who try to define the distinctive features of a given "national culture." Drawing continually now on the rapidly expanding knowledge of the existing Indian entities in Mexico, not only anthropologists but more importantly the writers of history and geography textbooks and special studies, the literary men and women, the government officials in "cultural" bureaus, the reporters for the national periodicals are continually engaged in an effort, sometimes quite consciously, sometimes not, to incorporate and synthesize the Indian heritages with the general Mexican. Diego Rivera and other painters laid some foundations, but they had only a most general view of the Indian. It is probably true now that what is being done effectively along this line rests on detailed and technical knowledge of the varied Indian groups as gathered by Yurchenko in music, by Pozas in biography, and by many others encouraged by the National Indian Institute.

The National Indian Institute

Mexicans have looked at Indian Mexico in three major ways. On the one hand they have developed in common with other Americans north and south what they call *Indigenismo*. This is the intellectualized effort to define the relationship of Indians and Indian cultures to the developing nations of the various Latin American countries. It is an effort founded on sympathy, or let us say more precisely on sentiments ranging from sympathy and fair dealing to romanticizing and idealization. The range of thought, if not of action, is broad; the effort has been continuous since Bartolomé de las Casas. *Indigenismo* is an important part of Mexican culture. It is not our place here to trace

its influence and trends; we are concerned rather with its object matter — the Indians of Mexico.

Another approach to the Indians in Mexico has been characterized by different sentiments ranging from very negative valuation of Indian culture to the feeling that however remarkable Indian culture may have been, it has no future. It follows that Indians therefore should be pulled into the important mainstream of development as rapidly, efficiently, and painlessly as possible. This is the viewpoint which underlies the establishment of the program of boarding schools in Indian areas for bringing Indian children together to be educated to take their places in the towns and cities of Mexico. Such *internados,* as they are called, are in operation in many parts of Mexico under the direction of the federal Department of Education. They are attempting to level cultural differences and aim their programs at eliminating, or at least not emphasizing, the sense of Indian consciousness which we have discussed. This approach is generally coupled with a refusal to pay any attention to the Indian languages, to act as though they did not exist. To many Mexicans this ignoring of Indian cultures and identities seems eminently practical.

The approach is allied to that of the 1940 national census, which attempted to describe the "Colonial Indian Culture" of Mexico by means of an index which identified Indian ways with bare feet, sleeping on mats, and the wearing of *calzones*. This resulted in a calculation that approximately 50 per cent of the people of Mexico were "colonial Indian" in way of life. A hopeless confusion of terms was involved. As an indicator of what was generally disapproved and regarded as in need of change by government officials, the index was unassailable, but it must be recognized that its category of "Indian" lumped together the poor people of Mexico and those who spoke Indian languages. The assumption that all poor people were Indian is not justified and is indicative of a viewpoint that Indian cultural characteristics ought to be eliminated. When the figures for barefooted people and mat-sleepers were added to those for speakers of Indian languages, we had a remarkable example of the adding of oranges and apples to give a sum total of lemons.

A third approach to Indian life in Mexico has developed very recently in the program of the National Indian Institute. This has stemmed from *Indigenismo,* and supporters of the Institute at its founding in 1948 were prominent Indianists — Manuel Gamio and Alfonso Caso. But the program has developed action programs for bringing Indians in touch with the rest of the population in a way which is new for Indianists.

The program of the National Indian Institute, called INI in Mexico, deals with Indians as real people, not as symbols of cultural background.[44] We may expect, however, that acquaintance with real Indians on the part of the staff of the Institute will have increasing influence on the ideas about Indian culture which are current among Mexicans generally.

The INI has been responsible more than any other agency for reliable determinations of the numbers of

Indians. Its work has been set up in eleven different areas of concentration of speakers of Indian languages. On this basis, centers for reaching the Indians with modern medicine, literacy programs, crop improvement, etc., have been established among Mayas (two centers), Mixtecs (two centers), Mazatecs (two centers to handle Indian relocation required by Papaloapan regional development), Nahuatls and others (one center in Guerrero), Cora-Huichols (one), Tarascans (one), Yaquis (one), and Tarahumares (one). It will be noted that Zapotecs and Otomís, despite relatively large numbers, have not been provided with coordinating centers; in the case of Otomís, this is because other government efforts have been in operation for some time: namely, the Patrimonio Indígena del Valle de Mezquital at Ixmiquilpan in Hidalgo.

The objectives of the INI are very clearly stated. The aim is to integrate the Indian communities into the national political and economic life. The emphasis is on the community and hence there is a contrast with Indian programs in the United States which have focused on the individual. INI attempts to develop every means of modern communication in the Indian areas; roads are built where there were no roads; the Spanish language as well as the Indian is taught in the centers and in the schools; modern doctors are brought in and clinics are established. INI expects and promotes change. In other words, INI's program is an effort to plan the integration of Indians into the national life of Mexico. But a basic principle is that Indians themselves must participate in this planning. Also Indians must provide materials and labor for improvements. And Indians are trained as "promoters," that is, to do the teaching and to serve as informal extension agents in their home communities. Care is taken that the selection is done in part by the Indian community and not wholly by INI personnel. The objective is to strengthen the integration of the Indian community at the same time that wider ties are encouraged in local municipalities. INI encourages the formation of co-operatives to produce and market the local products. The basic principle of INI is that the Indian community is quite capable of self-government and of guiding its own destiny in the modern world — given some intelligent outside assistance.

The INI program is indicative of a new role for Indians in modern Mexico. The INI leadership works with respect for Indian culture, but also recognizes the need for continuing change. Members of the INI staff are active in presenting their information about Indians and also about Indian viewpoints to the reading public. Through INI's work and its communication, a new process of integration of Indian life with that of the nation as a whole has begun to take place.

MESTIZO MEXICO

We hear of conquerors being culturally assimilated by the people they conquered, the Manchus by the Chinese for example. In Mexico the Spanish conquest did not quite have this result, but nevertheless it is very clear that the conquering Spaniards did not turn Mexico into a new Spain. There has been no simple process of absorption of natives by conquerors or of conquerors by natives, either racially or culturally. On the contrary, race, language, and culture have intermingled in contrasting and usually complex ways.

The rapid decline of the Indian population in the early years of conquest, together with the large-scale interbreeding of the small number of Spaniards with Indian women, resulted in laying the foundations for a steady growth of mixed-blood population. Today the predominating genes in the gene-pool of Mexico are obviously Indian, yet the Spanish or European contribution is also heavy.[45] The proportion of mixed-bloods has been accelerating very rapidly for three centuries. This steadily increasing numerical dominance of a mixed population is probably one of the factors accounting for the lack of importance in Mexico of racial prejudice, where attitudes of superiority focus on cultural, not biological, differences, in contrast with the United States. The overwhelming majority of people in Mexico are composed biologically of this Spanish-Indian mixture, with Indian greatly predominating. A widely quoted figure for the total emigration of Spaniards to Mexico during the whole three hundred years of the colonial period is only 300,000, and Whetten estimates that Spaniards and their Mexican-born children together, that is, creoles, never amounted to as much as 10 per cent of the population at any time during the period.[46] After the War for Independence in the early 1800's and most especially since the 1910 revolution, the rate of increase of this new Indian-Spanish biological variety has tremendously accelerated. In the region of the Isthmus of Tehuantepec and along the Pacific coast in the states of Guerrero and Oaxaca, there is a population with some Negro admixture, resulting from the importation of Negro slaves during the colonial period. Estimates regarding the number of persons of Negro-Indian-White ancestry range as high as 300,000, for the most part confined to southern Mexico.[47] There is no doubt that in these mixtures, again, the Indian genes greatly predominate. Hence the population of Mexico is biologically basically Indian, but the White and Negro admixture, the former especially, has been sufficient to bring about the formation of a new variety of the Indian.

The name for this variety of man in Mexico is *mestizo*. The term should probably be confined to the biological sub-race, but it has not been — either by Mexicans or by commentators on Mexico.[48] We also use it, as the only handy word so far widely employed, to apply to the characteristics of those people in Mexico who do not identify themselves as Indians. Our emphasis, however, is on customs, beliefs, and ways of looking at life — or in other words cultural traits. In such instances it would be much better to employ some technical word invented for the purpose, which would not perpetuate the confusion between race and culture. People of mixed blood frequently, as among Yaquis and Mayas and probably every other people of Mexico, identify themselves as Indians and follow Indian ways. On the other hand, there are certainly hundreds of thousands of people in Mexico who happen to have only Indian ancestry but who identify themselves as non-Indians. Thus racial characteristics in themselves do not distinguish Indians and non-Indians in Mexico, and the terms in which we make our distinctions ought to be purged of racial connotations. However, unsatisfactory as it is, we will follow custom and employ the word *mestizo*. When we say "mestizo," we do not necessarily imply that persons of mixed genes are involved. It is true nevertheless that the overwhelming majority of those who are characterized by non-Indian cultural traits are of mixed ancestry.

Mestizo Mexico, then, is that cultural world of Mexico which contrasts in important ways with Indian Mexico. In most regions, it cannot be said to have distinct territorial boundaries. In fact, rarely does it have clear boundaries. *Mestizos* penetrate in some way or other into almost every Indian community in Mexico, sometimes as permanent residents, sometimes as traveling traders or temporary residents of some other kind. *Mestizo* Mexico is made up of people who use the Spanish language, most usually as monolinguals, for although the great majority of Mexicans are strongly Indian biologically, the overwhelming majority are Spanish linguistically. The linguistic contrast between Indian and *mestizo* is fundamental. No Indian can move into the world of the *mestizo* without knowledge of the Spanish language. This is the hallmark of the non-Indian cultural world.

Dialect Areas of Mestizo Mexico

The Spanish spoken in Mexico is far from uniform over the nation. There is at least as much variation as one finds in the forms of American English spoken in Massachusetts, in Indiana, and in Mississippi. In the vocabulary employed, in the speed of speaking, and in the characteristic local idioms, Mexican Spanish differs from region to region. Enough study of these dialect variations has been made, so that we may confidently list at least three major dialects: (1) Mexican Spanish proper which is that spoken in central Mexico where the heaviest population occurs at the southern end of the Central Plateau; (2) Yucateco which is the form of Spanish heard in the peninsula of Yucatán and especially in the state of Yucatán; (3) Norteño which is spoken in the band of northern states including Nuevo León, Coahuila, San Luis Potosí, Zacatecas, Chihuahua, Sinaloa, Sonora, and Baja California. None of these, except possibly Yucateco, is wholly uniform within itself, but we can nevertheless consider language variation in Mexico in these general categories. In doing so, we ignore the fascinatingly varied language worlds of the transitional Indian-Spanish dialects such as those spoken by many Yaquis and Mayos of the north; the backwoods speech of long-isolated descendants of early settlers in groups of mountain villages in every major region; and other forms such as the speech of Tabasco and of the Gulf Coast which perhaps merit rank as major, more-or-less stabilized dialects of Mexico.

The dialect of Spanish spoken by the people of central Mexico, especially in and around the cities of Mexico, Guadalajara, and Puebla is certainly derivative from sixteenth-century Castilian which was brought as the standard language to New Spain by the first soldiers and administrators. In this northern part of New Spain there was a sprinkling of Spaniards from most parts of the homeland, so that no one of the provincial varieties of the language prevailed and the standard Castilian was free to be adopted and to develop. Already, however, almost as soon as introduced, certain features were lost. Thus the lisped *c* sound which was fashionable in the sixteenth century did not take (which suggests a lack of polish in the introducers) and the double *l* sound soon became a simple *y*. These characteristics of American Spanish have long been identified and they give Latin American a common base vis-à-vis European Castilian. A number of other differences have been pointed out, especially the trends toward a few features of word order that differ. Much in the manner of American English, there have been gradual drifts in phonetics and in syntax, which have resulted in many differences, but perhaps the vocabulary additions from Aztec are among the most striking developments. It has been calculated that more than four hundred words in frequent everyday use in Mexico have been borrowed from Nahuatl.[49] This is to be expected when one considers the numerous borrowings which the Spaniards made from the Aztec food and household customs and which have continued through the centuries to be important in Mexican life. Some examples of this borrowing of basic cultural elements accompanied by the incorporation of the words for these elements in the language of the conquerors are the following:

FOODS OF THE CORN COMPLEX

tamales	the fiesta food of steamed cornmeal enclosing meat and chile
tortilla	the toasted cornmeal cake
atole	the cornmeal gruel often served with chocolate
pozole	the hominy-like corn food
pinole	meal of toasted corn

and scores of other words for varieties of Aztec foods and drinks, including *chile* and *mezcal*, the drink made from the century plant;

HOUSEHOLD UTENSILS

comal	the clay dish for toasting tortillas
metate	the stone hand-mill for grinding corn
mecate	rope
petate	mat for sleeping or other purposes
petaca	covered container like a trunk

and many others;

MISCELLANEOUS

copal	the resin widely used as incense for religious processions
huipil	woman's square-cut shirt-waist
jacal	house of wattle-and-daub or other simple construction
cuate	twin

and *coyote.*

This is merely a very short list to indicate the nature of the borrowing from Aztec. The central dialect of Mexican Spanish has also borrowed words from other Indian languages, such as the very generally used term for sandal, namely, *huarache,* borrowed from Tarascan. Such borrowed words are strange to the ears of modern Spaniards. They have been usually labelled "barbarisms" by the grammarians, but they are secure and distinctive parts of modern Mexican Spanish. As compared with the other major dialects of Mexican Spanish, the central variety may be characterized with respect to speed and rhythm of speech as very rapid and staccato.

It is this dialect which has become the standard language of Mexico, dominant in the schools, in the national literature, and in the language of government. It is therefore at present impossible to assign it any modern geographical boundaries, for it penetrates everywhere in the nation, as schoolteachers from central Mexico, trained in the capital, open federal rural schools in the most remote mountain villages.

In Yucatán, as Victor M. Suárez has pointed out in his study of "Spanish as it Is Spoken in Yucatán,"[50] there are many differences. In general, speech is slower and the stress in many words is shifted forward a syllable. The sound of *b* preceding t becomes that of *p.* Suárez lists a number of other differences from central Mexican such as the contraction of the final syllables of words ending in -*ado* to -*ao,* as in *soldado* (soldier) becoming *soldao,* but this and others seem to be widespread in Mexico among rural speakers, or perhaps those who have little or no schooling. It does seem to be true that many of the words borrowed from Aztec which are common in central Mexican Spanish are not employed in the Spanish spoken in Yucatán. There are on the other hand several hundred words borrowed from Maya which are of frequent occurrence. Some of these are

bob	for	club or heavy stick
chich	for	grandmother
holoch	for	cornhusk
op	for	tortilla
pibinal	for	roasting ear (of corn)
chan	for	small
cenote	for	natural well in the limestone
batab	for	Indian cacique, or, that is, as now in English "chief."

There are scores of others borrowed or adapted from Maya having to do with the native plants and animals and with the foods that are commonly eaten by everyone in Yucatán.

The dialect of the Norteños is the variety of Spanish which developed in the northern ranching country, the area where there were more holders of land suitable for cattle rather than farms than anywhere else in Mexico. It was in the broad reaches of the Chihuahua and Nuevo León plains and the intermontane valleys of Sonora that this dialect developed. One hears it in places as widely separated as northern Sinaloa and San Luis Potosí, but perhaps the Sonorense version is the most distinctive of all. Here the contraction of final syllables and the marked slowness of speech leads to a different effect from the rapidly spoken central dialect. One thinks sometimes of the slow Papago or other northern Indian languages when listening to Sonoran Spanish, but it is unlikely that there has been any appreciable effect from Indian languages. For here the Indians were the fewest in numbers and here no single Indian language was dominant in the work groups impressed by the Spaniards. The large scale hacienda recruitment included *mestizos* as well as the great variety of Indians, so that Indian language influence was the exception rather than the rule. Thus the Indian words in Norteño are primarily the same Nahuatl ones as in the south, and there is no important regional distinctiveness in vocabulary derived from Indian sources.

More recently, however, there has been important borrowing in the Norteño dialect. But this has been from the American English of the border, not from Indian languages. In the 1880's the English-speaking people borrowed nearly the whole vocabulary of the cattle ranch as well as the ways of raising cattle from the Norteño Mexicans. Gradually as more and more English-speaking people poured into the region during the twentieth century, the borrowing began to shift the other way, until at present there is a large vocabulary of what Mexicans call *"pochismos,"* which is to say, words borrowed from English or ideas from English translated directly into Spanish. These are almost as numerous as the Nahuatl borrowing of the central dialect. Some examples are the following:

lonche	lunch
parquear	to park a car
jonrón	home run
rallador	radiator of a car

A full list of such borrowings indicates that there are certain special areas of culture from which they come, just as the borrowing by the English-speaking people in the 1800's involved the special areas of cattle-raising and mining. Now it is sports and machinery primarily. The use of such words as those quoted in Spanish language newspapers and by radio broadcasters of the border towns is frequently decried by the arbiters of the language farther south. *Pochismos* are indeed spoken of as barbarisms just as the borrowed Nahuatl words have been through history. But the influence goes on and we may expect that there will be shifts again when the balance of trade in words responds to the growth of vigorous cultural interests on one side or the other of the international boundary.

The dialects of Mexican Spanish have not yet left their marks on the land as have the Indian languages, but it should be noted that there have been three phases of place-naming by the Spaniards. The first followed the plan of naming places either for cities in Spain or for Christian saints, the new name often attached to a native place name. The second phase in place naming was marked by a reaction against the Spanish names and often a substitution of the name of a hero of the War for Independence, as in the case of Valladolid in Michoacán which became, after the War for Independence, Morelia, named for Morelos, the framer of the 1824 constitution. Thus also what had been Antequera (named for a town in Spain) became Oaxaca (a corruption by the Spaniards of a Zapotec place name). The third phase has been marked by the attachment of the names of revolutionary heroes or distinguished Indians or Indianists to existing place names, such as Oaxaca de Juárez, San Cristóbal de las Casas, or Cuauhtémoc.

There are thus three major dialectical divisions of modern Mexico. Within each there are variant rural forms. These three language areas correspond roughly to modern cultural areas, but only roughly. It would seem, however, that there are somewhat different current tendencies in the north, the center, and the south.

The Spanish-Derived Culture of Mestizo Mexico

Mestizo Mexico has no clear geographical boundaries, not only because individuals who have the *mestizo,* non-Indian outlook have penetrated everywhere in the republic, but also because the very institutions by which they live constitute a continuum linked with Indian communities. That is, important features of *mestizo* life, such as the saint's day fiesta and godparent-godchild relationships, are also important in the lives of the various Indian groups. It is not that Indians and *mestizos* share only one or two of these institutions, but rather that a whole series of them in all the most significant areas of living link the Indian and the *mestizo* societies. The forms of these institutions are well known to both; the meanings vary greatly as do the details of elaboration. But the forms do provide a bridge between and a common substance to life in *mestizo* and Indian communities.

It may have been that the 1940 census-takers were thinking of these institutions when they formulated the Colonial Indian Cultural Index. What their terminology does not indicate is awareness of the fact that hundreds of thousands of non-Indians over the nation participate in these social institutions which were formed during the colonial period and constituted the framework of village life everywhere. Today where they are under attack both from devotees of the ideology of the 1910 revolution and from the Catholic Church, the

resulting factions in village life do not consist of Indians vs. *mestizos*. There are Indians and *mestizos* on both sides.

The customs and beliefs to which we refer derive the greater part of their form from institutions introduced by missionaries and colonial administrators during the sixteenth and seventeenth centuries. These adepts in the transformation of the Indian cultures did not, of course, present the whole complex civilization of the Spaniards. This would have been impossible. They were relatively few. They came from all the different provinces of Spain, not only from Andalusia and Estremadura as has been believed,[51] and they came from other countries as well. What these varied Europeans introduced were selections from European culture, which the framework of Spanish policy and particular circumstances required. Not the whole range of religious ceremony as known even in any one part of Spain, not the whole complement of agricultural tools employed by Spaniards, not the range of variations of village plans and organizations characteristic of rural Spain — but rather a very limited selection, that which the officials in charge regarded as important, was introduced.[52] These selected traits were presented to the Indian population with that amazing effectiveness which characterized the Spanish program from one end of New Spain to the other. As the Indian communities reorganized their life around them, the *mestizos* everywhere found their lives focused in the same institutions. Through the centuries it is this "Culture of the Conquest" which has become the common ground of Indian and *mestizo* in Mexico. A new selection of traits is now being presented in the federal rural schools and through other government units, which will, it is hoped by directors of the programs, replace elements of the Spanish-Indian synthesis, but meanwhile the *mestizo* culture of the villages and towns still finds its orientation in the older ways.

Besides the strongly rooted food complex of the host of maize dishes, beans, and chiles, which derives, of course, directly from the Indian cultures, *mestizo* culture may be said to have as its framework the following European-derived elements: the cult of the saints which is at once a religious, social, and economic institution; the democratic system of local government characteristic of the rural villages and towns; the godparent and *compadre* network of social relationships which extends the family system in important ways; a set of concepts about disease and curing and witchcraft which is closely related to the beliefs of folk Catholicism; and a traditional music of voice and instrument, principally the guitar. The general frame of *mestizo* culture can be outlined in a description of just these elements; the full content of the rich *mestizo* culture would require far more extended consideration. We shall limit our discussion to these fundamental elements and attempt finally to give this institutional outline some life by a consideration of the values and motives which actuate *mestizos* in contrast with Indians, in their day-to-day life with the supernaturals and with one another.

Papier-maché figures and masks of saints and devils in the farm fields often symbolize the failures and successes of rural agriculture. Villagers expend much time and energy in preparing such pageantry in which even the farm animals have their part.

THE CULT OF THE SAINTS

It is conceivable that the saint's day fiesta in Mexico is on its way out. For some years there have been campaigns against fireworks as dangerous and unnecessary causes of blindness and other injuries in children. The extreme elaboration of such fiestas in various parts of the country to the point where they become a serious obstacle to the accumulation of wealth or the raising of the standard of living has led the Catholic Church, as well as advocates of agrarian and other economic reforms, to oppose them. This has resulted in some modification of methods of sponsoring fiestas. Yet it would seem that although modification in various directions will continue, the saint's day fiesta is built into too many aspects of Mexican life for it to disappear in any predictable future. It is not simply an expensive luxury; it is a social and religious institution which has many important functions in *mestizo,* as well as Indian, life.

The fiesta is only one manifestation, although perhaps the most important, of a deep-rooted set of beliefs about men and higher powers. The fiesta with its deeply serious focus and its light-hearted peripheries has been a major expression of Mexican life, able to take into itself and let go of minor elements from both Indian and European culture. The fiesta is an annual culmination of a community's feelings about the higher powers in whose care it believes itself to be. These sentiments, beliefs, and ritual acts are what we mean by the cult of the saints.

The term cult probably does not do the institution justice. It is not uniform over the nation, it does not rest on formalized doctrine, it has a thousand varied expressions. The object of interest, for example, varies

from a battered stone image newly uncovered by a plow in a Tarascan field to the Virgin of Guadalupe herself with the full official sanction of the Catholic Church. The saints, or *"santos,"* are a strange variety, to the non-believer, of different objects or representations, but they have many essential features in common. The *santo* is a supernatural being which resides in a particular place and ministers to human beings only in that place. The *santo* has miraculous powers, especially for curing, but also for bringing various kinds of good fortune. The *santo* is on good terms with, if he is not actually one of, the Christian pantheon. The *santo* will respond to human actions and enjoys being honored by men. Every village in Mexico, whether Indian or *mestizo,* has its own saint, the patron, or patroness, of the community. The people of the village seem to think of the saint as theirs, or possibly it is a sentiment that they are the saint's. At any rate there is a strong sense of mutual obligation, which receives its annual expression in the elaborate saint's day fiesta designed to honor the saint in a manner enjoyable to him or her and to everyone else. It requires great fireworks, *castillos,* or castles, and other kinds of whirling and fire-spouting devices. It may require a mock bullfight, or a real one. It requires processions in which everyone can participate, walking with a candle and showing one's faith and pride in the local supernatural being. It requires prayers by the people, whether there is a priest present or not, and the singing of *alabanzas,* the sacred songs. It requires incensing and special devotions peculiar only to that *santo.*

The celebration of the fiesta costs money — for candles, incense, perhaps new clothes for the *santo,* fireworks, and food. There are many ways in Mexico for raising the funds. A plot of land in the village may be set aside for the saint and someone chosen each year or two to work that land and give the proceeds for the maintenance of the saint, or all the men of the village may join in. There may be a sort of head tax, as in many villages in central Mexico, including those of the Nahuatl-speaking peoples, levied each year to cover expenses, which every bona fide resident of the community must pay publicly. An individual and his wife may make a sacred vow to carry out the arrangements and foot the bills and such a couple may be assisted by all their official friends, that is, *compadres,* and their relatives so that it is not wholly an individual burden. There may be groups of four or more couples who make the sacred vow jointly to carry out the fiesta. There are many different arrangements which vary from region to region. Most seem to stem from the Spanish Christian introduction of the *cofradía,* an organization of lay people to assist in the church ceremonies, and the vow, often as a penitence, to serve. But there probably existed some similar type of Indian religious service of the supernaturals which fitted well with this European introduction.

Often in the central part of Mexico a saint is the patron of a single *barrio,* a subdivision of a village or town, and his powers are not highly regarded outside that small area. Again the saint may have a reputation throughout a wide region for miraculous powers, such as San Esquipulas whose reputation extends from Guatemala as far north as Oaxaca. A regionally important saint becomes the object of pilgrimages and gives rise to local cults focused around images over the whole region where his powers are known. The Child of Atoche has a widespread reputation in northern Mexico. These local and regional systems of worship have a life of their own apart from the Catholic Church, and perhaps represent surviving cults of similar character in pre-Spanish days, but now very much re-interpreted in Christian terms and rituals. They are indeed in this respect bridges between Indian and *mestizo* cultures. One finds *mestizo* villages devoted to saints which appear to be, in name only, Saint Anthony, Saint John, Saint Joseph, or Saint Michael. The greatest of all the saints in Mexico is, of course, the Virgin of Guadalupe, the dark-skinned Madonna of the ancient Aztec hill of Tepeyac and of the modern third largest basilica in the Catholic world. As patroness of the whole nation of Mexico, her cult, which is intensive among Indians and *mestizos* alike, is at present one of the strongest unifying powers in the country.

LOCAL GOVERNMENT

The saint-oriented village was one of the great creations of the sixteenth- and seventeenth-century missionaries. The missionaries also had a hand in reorganizing the government of the villages along the lines prescribed by the Spanish king, but they shared in this program of change with the governors appointed by the crown. A great effort was made by the colonial administrators to establish Indians in a type of community which followed the plan of organization of rural communities in Spain, or at least the plan of one ideal form. Indians were brought together in *"congregaciones,"* that is, concentrated into larger units than those in which they had been living. These new settlements were set up as free villages, with an annually elected set of officers who had responsibility for law and order, for public works, and at least indirectly for church management.[53] The same type of community government was established for non-Indian settlements. It constituted a basically democratic and representative form of local government, although inevitably, as part of the Spanish royal system, it was subject to arbitrary decree and interference from above.

Locally elected judges *(alcaldes),* governors, mayors, sheriffs *(alguaciles),* church governors *(fiscales),* captains, and a host of other officers became common throughout Mexico. The roster of officers was not uniform, but depended in different regions on a variety of circumstances, and in most features of the organization there was variation, but a basic pattern was established which as Simpson points out[54] remains essentially the form of local government today, despite even the phase of almost complete usurpation of power by the federal government during the administration of Porfirio Díaz in the late nineteenth century.

This local community had both a physical and a political form which has become the dominant type in Mexico, even in most of the heavily Indian areas. Physically it is composed of a central plaza, in or facing which is the church, and surrounded by commercial and governmental buildings built flush with the street. Around the plaza as a center, the community is divided into squares by a system of streets in grid pattern. This town plan, which was not actually a common pattern at all in Spain, was an ideal creation of the Spanish colonial planners. Now one finds it as the basic plan of large cities, small towns, and even tiny villages. The annually elected officers are chosen from the villagers at large by a sort of acclamation, and they take office on the Day of the Kings, January 5. In many parts of central and southern Mexico, especially in the more Indian communities, all the men of the community expect, in the course of their lives, to move through a succession of offices whence they ultimately emerge as elders. It is then the body of elders, those men who are not currently serving in the prescribed offices, who constitute the decision-making power of the community. The ladder-like progression in village offices appears to have been a New World adaptation of the Spanish system.

Upset by the *encomienda* and later the Porfirian-supported hacienda system of government-by-landlords, but still surviving through the 1910 revolution, many of the features of the old representative system are being newly formalized, under different names, in the municipal and *ejido* government of the current era. The plaza-oriented grid pattern, democratic small town is one of the most characteristic institutions of *mestizo* Mexico, and yet like the cult of the saints, it is shared

Strolling bands of musicians are all over Mexico, from the border centers of entertainment to the historically patterned fiestas of the interior. Such groups as this one in Michoacán, a state of the Western Highlands, often accompany a procession on the highway from village to village.

with the Indian communities at least in its broad outlines. It rests on two foundations — the Spanish-planned colonial settlement and the Indian village.

GODPARENTS AND COMPADRES

A third introduction of the Spaniards which spread to the most remote Indian communities and yet has remained a foundation of *mestizo* life is the godparent system. This is at once an institution which reinforces a family economically and links that family in an indissoluble bond with the church organization. It does, however, more than that, for it also establishes a network of relationships which crisscross every Mexican community and through which effective cooperation in all activities is maintained. It accomplishes this because every godparent functions as a co-parent, or as it is said in Spanish, a *compadre,* with the biological parents of the child he sponsors. Godparenthood is thus a complex and an important social institution as we find it in operation in modern Mexico.

The missionaries laid great stress on having godparents for the baptism of Indian converts. They often took with them into new areas previously converted Indians for the express purpose of having them serve as godparents for the newly baptized. In doing this they were introducing an ancient Christian custom which had long been strongly emphasized in Spain and elsewhere in southern Europe.[55] It was a set of customs very similar to various forms of ceremonial sponsorship among the Indians, in which a family selected a friend or neighbor or kinsman to serve as "ceremonial father" perhaps in some important religious activity. As ultimately implanted in New Spain, the godparent system took a host of different forms. The Yaquis of the north elaborated it in a most extensive manner, so that a Yaqui may have as many as sixteen godfathers and the same number of godmothers. Among other

peoples in Mexico it is usually important, but ordinarily not so elaborate.

The essentials of the system are simply these. The parents of a child invite a man and a woman, often husband and wife, to serve as sponsors for some important crisis rite in the life of their child. The rite may be baptism, confirmation in the church, marriage, ritual curing, entrance into a religious organization, or any of a dozen other rituals that are important in that particular community or region. In serving as a sponsor, the godparent assumes a permanent obligation to the child which usually involves economic assistance in time of need and may involve many other duties of a ceremonial sort or in connection with illness. The obligation is mutual between godparent and godchild and a very high degree of respect is enjoined for the child in his relations with the godfather or godmother. The relations are unbreakable once inaugurated, so that a lifetime obligation goes into effect. Also the godfather or godmother is immediately obligated, and this too is mutual, to the parents of the child as the co-parent or *compadre.* This similarly calls for help in economic and other crises. Ordinarily the sponsoring rite becomes the basis for a continuous series of gifts between the families involved. Many children mean many godparent relationships and many *compadres.* Thus the system of kinship obligations in any community is extended very widely through this form of ritual kinship and tendencies to friendship and cooperation may be reinforced.

While in Indian communities the ceremonial sponsoring system tends to be purely a reinforcing mechanism for all the other relationships based on the family and kinship, in *mestizo* communities there is often a great tendency to use the system as a means of linking the poor with the wealthy for both the material and the prestige benefits which may result. There is some reason to believe that extensive employment of the *compadre* relationships in Mexico is an adaptation to the break-up of family life attendant on the *encomienda* system and the periodic community disruption in Mexican life down to recent times.

CURING PRACTICES

Another common element in Indian and *mestizo* culture is the set of beliefs about health and disease. Every rural community in Mexico (and in the world) has its local curers, its traditionally trained practitioners who treat diseases by means of herbal remedies. In addition, in Mexico there are curers, either men or women, who claim to understand and to know how to treat through magical practices a number of diseases which have different causes from those diseases which yield to the herbal medicines. These have been described as folk diseases. They include what seem to be disturbances of the personality as well as what are obviously some sort of physiological conditions. One such disease is called *"susto,"* or shock, in the north and *"espanto"* elsewhere; it is believed to be caused by the unexpected seeing of a supernatural being or by any other sudden, unexpected situation which the person does not take as part of the ordinary course of daily life. Persons may waste away with this complaint and may be cured by a variety of magical rituals. Another of this type of disease is *"muina,"* the causes of which are believed to be the feeling of violent anger, humiliation or insult, or perhaps any sort of serious frustration. If a person is afflicted with *muina* he loses appetite, may lose weight, and, it is believed, may die unless special attention is paid to diet. This involves another aspect of

this set of beliefs, namely, the concepts of hot and cold foods and associated phenomena. The idea of hot and cold in connection with health and illness seems to have been brought by highly educated persons such as missionaries among the Spaniards and other Europeans. They derived it from knowledge of sixteenth-century European medicine and diffused the ideas among the inhabitants of New Spain, including, of course, the Indians. The ideas, it is interesting to note, are not part of the general rural conceptions of disease in Spain. Just what is classified as hot or cold and therefore is appropriate for this or that illness in Mexico varies greatly from one area to another. In central Mexico there is an elaborate classification which recognizes the following categories: hot, very hot, cold, very cold, fresh, very fresh, and temperate. Water and some of its derivatives are cold, although frozen forms are hot. Animals that spend time in water are also cold. The sun and phenomena connected in various ways with the sun are classified as hot. Some foods change from fresh to temperate in the process of cooking. The classifications become very complex in the hands of different *curanderos*. The importance of the hot and cold concepts in connection with disease is the effect on body temperature. An emotional state can change the temperature. Treatment involves the special knowledge necessary for diagnosis and for selection of foods or other substances for their effect on body temperature.

Another of these widespread aspects of belief about disease is the highly elaborated concept of *mal ojo* (or illness caused by the glance of an evil eye) in all of its ramifications. This is related to witchcraft, or the practice of black magic, which again has a great variety

Beyond the border towns and the international boundary between the United States and Mexico, the roadside shrine becomes a frequent sight. The shady interiors are decorated, and the candles lighted by rural families such as this one, accompanying a woman with an injured leg to the shrine.

of beliefs and practices connected with it. These are knit into *mestizo* life not only as a more or less self-consistent system of concepts about health, but also as they are related to the cult of the saints and other aspects of relations with the Christian-derived supernaturals. For frequently the cures for *mal ojo* or for *espanto* or the other folk diseases include ritual appeals of various kinds to the Virgin or to any of the saints. There appears here, as in the other institutions we have discussed, a great deal of blending of sixteenth- and seventeenth-century European belief and curing practice with a wide variety of Indian ones. Here as elsewhere there is a fusion of the two, and it is not by any means clear that any one of the regional varieties of health and curing system is derived any more from the European than from the Indian traditions.

MUSIC

The music of *mestizo* Mexico is most distinctive and derives almost wholly from European sources. The missionaries played an extremely important part in the diffusion of musical instruments throughout New Spain. The Indians had developed only simple whistle-type wind instruments and drums (both of the hide-headed and the vibrating wooden-tongue types). They had invented only the simplest sort of one-stringed instrument. When the missionaries came, they taught Indians to make violins, harps, and other stringed instruments, and very early trained choirs in the European singing of the period. These introductions spread as widely as any other elements of European culture. On this base has grown the distinctive Mexican music of the *corrido,* the string band *(mariachis),* and all the regional types of music and dance that today characterize the *mestizo* society.

LANGUAGE

It is easy enough to see how the Spanish language in its diffusion to the remote corners of Mexico provides a common ground for the growth of a Mexican culture. Along with the Spanish language we must recognize that the institutions we have mentioned also provide at many points in the cultures of Indian and *mestizo* a common basis for development. We have moreover selected only a few of the most important of these common elements. There are others.

FAMILY LIFE

At the same time there are certain institutions characteristic of the *mestizo* way of life which are at odds with basic features of Indian culture. These, equally with the ones described, have their origin in Spanish culture. The most important of these institutions, and the one to which we shall confine our attention, is the family and its associated aspects, such as the relations of the sexes. There is a marked contrast between *mestizo* and Indian families. In general the family among *mestizos* is organized on the basis of placement of authority in the oldest male.[57] A father, or grandfather if the family consists of three genera-

tions, is the authoritative head to whom all defer. A grown son who is married but living in the same household with his father pays deep respect and defers always to the authority of his father. Women and younger members of the family are even more deferential. No family matter is approached on a basis of equality between man and woman; the man always takes the initiative and executes the family policy, even though it has been formulated in some kind of conference. However, the usual mode of decision is not through conference so much as through individual and authoritarian action of the male household head.

This patriarchal family pattern is characterized also by other fairly consistent features. Child-rearing is dominated by the father who employs authoritarian methods, especially after an initial period of very early childhood when more permissive techniques are common. Daughters are subject to special shielding, especially when the courtship period begins, and are regarded as unable to withstand male advances generally. Consistently with this males are generally encouraged to develop unrestrained sexual activities, and high value is placed on virile male sexuality. Each of the patterns mentioned contrasts considerably with corresponding Indian patterns.

THE MESTIZO WORLD VIEW

While *mestizos* and Indians share a number of highly important formal patterns of culture, certain fundamental ones differ, such as the patterns of family organization and male-female interpersonal relationships. The shared patterns also, as we have indicated, do not have the same qualities in *mestizo* and Indian culture. Village government, for example, may, despite its forms, be carried out in a *mestizo* village very much in terms of the *caudillo* pattern, that is, as an adjunct to the dominance of a personal clique in the local community. In short, while parts of the structural framework of custom are very similar, the goals and the motivations which seem to actuate Indian and *mestizo* exhibit sharp contrasts.

Some very full records have been made of the world views of Indians, of how they regard the universe and the role of men in it, of the ideals regarding men's relations to one another, of what has been the past of mankind and where men are now headed. These important matters have been discussed at length by anthropologists with Indians in different parts of Mexico, and some effort made to determine to what extent the views of the world presented are characteristic of whole groups, like the lowland and highland Mayas or others. The best of these have been done for the Mayas. Redfield became intimately acquainted with a village leader, Eustaquio Ceme, among the lowland Mayas, a man who wanted his village to progress. Ceme's view of life is presented in two books.[58] A fascinating account of the personal philosophy of a highland Maya which reflects the traditional view of things in the village of Chenalhó is also available.[59] Against these we may see only some general statements by John Gillin[60] and others, since we have as yet no adequate autobiographical records for *mestizos* comparable to the Indian ones. What we shall present is based largely on study of *mestizos,* or *Ladinos* as they are called there, in southeastern Mexico and Guatemala. The elements of *Ladino* viewpoint which we shall select for presentation seem to characterize *mestizos* widely through Mexico and Guatemala.

One of the most marked qualities of the *Ladinos* among whom Gillin lived was a view of the natural world as something which could be mastered and turned to men's account. There was an important contrast between *Ladinos* and Indians in this respect. Where an Indian tended quite consistently to be fatalistic about existing conditions, to accept them, and not to strive to change them, a *Ladino* tended with equal consistency to see almost any condition as alterable. This gave rise to a constant striving, a restlessness, and vigorous unwillingness to let things take their course without some kind of human interference. Viewed by an outsider, *Ladino* life seemed to be characterized by a persistent lack of harmony between men and the universe, in contrast with the Indian ideal and apparent realization of an ongoing harmony. The urge to mastery and change is apparent not only in the *mestizo* view of men's relation to the natural universe, but also to the social world. Commands, the give-and-take of words, bickering, and more or less continuous efforts to influence one another's behavior in the family and in public meetings are highly characteristic of *mestizos.* A constant verbalized concern with the behavior of others is an accepted part of *mestizo* daily life, in contrast again with an apparent indifference, or at least not verbalized interest in others' activities among Indians, even when such persons may be members of one's own family. Often, as Indians see *mestizo* behavior, it appears to be "angry" activity, like the buzzing of a bee at a person, or perhaps equally often the *mestizo* seems domineering.

Gillin and others have also commented on the way in which *mestizos* generally view men's relationship to the land and to time. In contrast with Indians, who generally have feelings of being deeply in the land, as being in an almost mystical way linked with it, the typical *mestizo* view is that land may be an instrument for improving oneself and therefore desirable as a thing to be owned, but the relationship hardly goes beyond such mechanical connection. Land is to be bought and sold and passed around in any way that individuals may find advantage in the transfers. The *mestizo* himself does not look forward to being involved in working the land; true enough, he frequently is so involved, but this, he hopes, is a step to better things. Along with this view of the land goes an attitude towards labor with the hands that is extremely negative. *Mestizos* see themselves as ideally free from hard manual work, and especially the work of preparing and planting and harvesting on the land. While Indians characteristically focus on maintaining a stable location, the traditional location of the village, and tend to see the center of the world in their own comunity, *mestizos* tend to be city-oriented. They see a rural location where they are currently situated as a part of a larger whole, if not the whole nation, at least a city-focused region of some sort. Thus they are not enwrapped in a local world to the extent that Indians tend to be, and their orientation

This public laundry represents a simple form of "modernization," in Hermosillo, Sonora, where freeways, modern buildings, current fashions, and mechanized agricultural industry co-exist with fragments of the past.

"... the *mestizo* world is future-oriented, toward new and better times."

is consistently outward toward an expanding system of local communities whose life is geared to a larger community.

With regard to time, the *mestizo* world is future-oriented, toward new and better times. There is built into it an expectation of better conditions somewhere, perhaps right where they are if they can command the means for improvement. If not there, then they keep themselves aware of opportunity to move. An interest in heaven as a better place is also present, but seems to be far more integrated into the lives of women than of men, who accept belief in heaven as a future better place, but maintain their basic interest in improving the material world about them. Here the contrast with Indian time orientations is most clear. An Indian community seems intent on continuing to realize an order of man in the universe which was defined in the past. Hence ceremonial and political activities are strongly focused in an effort to maintain this past-defined harmony and balance in the world. The *mestizo* view is based in no such conception of an ideal and ordered past; he strives to bring about change toward a better life.

In this future-oriented world based on efforts to change and control men and nature, the *mestizo* is strongly individualistic in contrast with the community-oriented Indian. An individual and his own distinctive personality or spirit is a sacred entity. It is not expected that individuals will conform unless they are effectively commanded to by another who is able to give them an advantage. A sense of obligation, deep and abiding, to the collective unit of the village such as characterizes Indians, seems almost absent in *mestizo* communities. Here the organization of the community rests on the strong man who agressively controls and commands. He is the leader, the *caudillo*. At the same time, each individual, or at least each individual man, having such a distinctive and important spirit, must be sure at all times that he is being appreciated, or perhaps better said, given the highest respect. This makes for a great degree of sensitivity to insult, a constant being on guard to be sure that due respect is accorded by every other male in the community. Such conception of an individual as being susceptible to slurs, or capable of such independent and masterful action, seems foreign to Indian viewpoints.

These are suggestive of the kinds of values and orientations distinctive of the *mestizo* cultural world. They make of the institutions which are common to them and to Indians quite different elements of culture

THE MEXICANS:
AN EMERGING PEOPLE

In most commentary on Mexico today, the Indian segment of the population is dismissed as having no influence, not even latent,[61] for example, or at best as an "elusive"[62] element of the population. Indians are by no means elusive, one learns if one visits communities in Mexico and has some conception of history and of the cultural elements in terms of which Indians identify themselves. Indians are tangible enough, if one takes the trouble to get acquainted with them, as Guiteras-Holmes and others have. They are elusive in census tables perhaps, because the censuses have not always been based on the realities of social life. Perhaps also the persisting influence of Indian cultures in Mexico is elusive in the sense that it is hard to measure and evaluate. This will be less difficult to assess as more study of the *mestizo* component of Mexican culture is carried out and our knowledge here begins to match the relatively abundant knowledge which we have regarding Indian life.

There are certain profound differences between Indian and *mestizo* approaches to life, as we have indicated. It is entirely possible that the *mestizo* approach will become completely dominant and that what we know as Indian cultures today will disappear. The aggressive character of *mestizo* society would seem to indicate this as a very strong possibility. If this were to happen, however, it would be well to remember that one of the major influences on *mestizo* culture has been and is at present an Indian influence. *Mestizo* culture is not distinctively Mexican only because of its geographical location and its own peculiar history; part of its distinctiveness arises from the Indian components in the religious, political, and social institutions which we have sketched. This influence did not by any means work itself out during the colonial period when the processes of cultural fusion were bringing about the synthesis of Indian and European cultures. It is built into the religious and social framework of modern Mexico and will continue to affect the course of adaptation of rural people to the newer programs of change which emanate from the metropolis.

In addition, however, there is another recent development which should restrain us from an over-simple view of Mexican culture as a result of increasing dominance of the *mestizo*. In the first place, the basic *mestizo* culture is by no means identical with the selection of cultural institutions which are being promulgated currently by the federal government in its various programs of education, agricultural improvement, etc. It is a deeper, richer entity than that, just as the Indian cultures were, in relation to the selections from Europe which constituted the "Culture of the Conquest." Further, one of the programs of the federal government itself, namely, that of the National Indian Institute, is profoundly altering one set of conditions which had seemed until recently rather well-stabilized. The INI program seeks to rouse Indian communities to awareness of the possibility of choosing elements from the dominant peoples and incorporating them without disintegrating their own community life. This certainly means that extensive changes will take place in rapid succession in coming years everywhere that Indians exist. One may raise the question: what influence will Indians, increasingly aware of the modern world and not taught to despise their own, have on the course of development of Mexican culture?

NOTES

1. León-Portilla 1962: p. 65

2. Borah and Cook 1963: p. 88

3. Mason 1940: p. 58

4. León-Portilla 1962: p. 83; León-Portilla 1959: pp. 64-65. This figure is an estimate for 1960 based on the proportion between monolinguals and bilinguals as indicated in the figures on Nahuatl-speaking persons for 1950. See León-Portilla 1959.

5. Thompson 1954: p. 29

6. León-Portilla 1959: p. 65. These figures are for 1950, and the total number of monolingual and bilingual speakers of Zapotec and Mixtec languages is not given in León-Portilla 1962. Hence we are here relying on the assumption that there has been no decrease between 1950 and 1960, a very safe assumption in view of the generally low figures given in the 1950 census.

7. Whorf 1946: p. 368

8. Pittman 1954: p. 5

9. Whorf 1946: p. 368

10. Garibay K. 1953

11. León-Portilla 1956

12. Pittman 1954: p. 59

13. Whorf 1946: pp. 368-9

14. Arriola and Valverde 1962

15. Thompson 1954: p. 82

16. Swadesh 1949

17. Tozzer 1921. The account of the Maya language given here is based almost exclusively on Tozzer's grammar of Maya.

18. Swadesh 1949

19. Covarrubias 1946: pp. 304-310

20. Whetten 1948: p. 56

21. León-Portilla 1962: p. 83

22. *ibid:* p. 83

23. The 1930 and 1950 figures are from León-Portilla 1959: p. 65; those for 1940 from Whetten 1948: p. 55; and those for 1960 from León-Portilla 1962: p. 65.

24. Lewis 1958: p. 241

25. Spicer (ed.) 1961: pp. 7-93

26. Spicer 1962

27. Ritzenthaler 1956

28. Foster 1948

29. Carrasco 1952

30. Redfield 1930

31. Chase 1931

32. Lewis 1951

33. Madsen 1960

34. Comisión de Historia 1961

35. Lewis 1960: p. 6

36. Redfield 1930 and Lewis 1951

37. Covarrubias 1946

38. Sayles 1955

39. Guiteras-Holmes 1961 and Pozas 1962 for highland Maya life.

40. Redfield 1941 and 1950

41. Villa Rojas 1945

42. I believe, however, that more intensive comparative study will reveal some general common values, just as detailed knowledge of Indian cultures in the United States has done.

43. Caso 1950, see the Prologue.

44. Caso 1958

45. No adequate study has been made of the racial composition of the Mexican nation.

46. Whetten 1948: p. 50

47. Aguirre-Beltrán 1957

48. See, e.g., Gillin 1949.

49. Alcocer 1936

50. Suárez 1945

51. Foster 1960: p. 31

52. Foster 1960: pp. 227-234

53. Simpson 1959: p. 82-93

54. *ibid:* p. 91

55. Mintz and Wolf 1950

56. Madsen 1960: p. 161

57. Bermúdez 1955: pp. 67-82

58. Redfield 1962; pp. 212-230; Redfield 1950: p. 171-178

59. Guiteras-Holmes 1961

60. Gillin in Tax 1952: pp. 195-212

61. Scott 1959: p. 65

62. Cline 1962: pp. 91-100

SUGGESTED READING LIST

Eric R. Wolf — *Sons of the Shaking Earth.* (Chicago: 1959)

A general book, written in a vigorous style, which considers in more detail most of the materials presented in this chapter.

Oscar Lewis — *Life in a Mexican Village.* (Urbana: 1951)

This is a detailed and fascinating account of every aspect of life in Tepoztlán, Morelos, where thirty-five years ago almost every person spoke Nahuatl and where today only a fraction use the language.

Robert Redfield — *A Village that Chose Progress.* (Chicago: 1950)

The story of a Maya village which has succeeded over a thirty-year period in rising to be the head village of its municipality, told with a view to what is happening under the label of "modernization."

C. Guiteras-Holmes — *Perils of the Soul, The World View of a Tzotzil Indian.* (Glencoe: 1961)

A highland Maya man tells his life story to a sympathetic recorder who relates what he says to the culture which has formed this world view.

BIBLIOGRAPHY

AGUIRRE BELTRAN, GONZALO

1957 *Cuijla. Un pueblo negro.* Fondo de Cultura Económica: Mexico, D. F.

ALCOCER, DR. IGNACIO

1936 El español que se habla en México. *Instituto Panamericano de Geografía e Historia, Publicación No. 20.* Tacubaya, D. F.

ARRIOLA, J. L. AND V. M. VALVERDE

1962 "Guatemala" pp. 57-63, in Indians in the Hemisphere Today. *Indianist Yearbook, Inter-American Indian Institute.* Vol. XXII, Mexico.

BERMUDEZ, MARIA ELVIRA

1955 *La vida familiar del mexicano.* Antigua Librería Robredo: Mexico.

BORAH, WOODROW AND SHERBURNE F. COOK

1963 The Aboriginal Population of Central Mexico on the Eve of the Spanish Conquest. Ibero-Americana: 45. Berkeley and Los Angeles, California

CARRASCO, PEDRO

1952 Tarascan Folk Religion. An Analysis of Economic, Social, and Religious Interactions. *Middle American Research Institute, Publication 17,* pp. 1-64. New Orleans: Tulane University.

CASO, ALFONSO

1958 *Indigenismo.* Instituto Nacional Indigenista, Mexico, D. F.

1950 "Prólogo" in "Bibliografía de las Artes Populares Plásticas de México." *Memorias del Instituto Nacional Indigenista,* Vol. 1, No. 2, Mexico, D. F.

CHASE, STUART

1931 *Mexico, A Study of Two Americas.* The Macmillan Co.: New York.

CLINE, HOWARD F.

1962 *Mexico, Revolution to Evolution, 1940–1960.* Oxford University Press: New York.

COMISION DE HISTORIA

1961 *El mestizaje en la historia de Ibero-America.* Instituto Panamericano de Geografía e Historia, Mexico, D. F.

COVARRUBIAS, MIGUEL

1946 *Mexico South.* New York.

FOSTER, GEORGE M.

1948 Empire's Children, The People of Tzintzuntzán. *Smithsonian Institution, Institute of Social Anthropology, Publication No. 6.* Washington, D. C.

1960 Culture and Conquest: America's Spanish Heritage. *Viking Fund Publications in Anthropology,* Number Twenty-Seven. Wenner-Gren Foundation for Anthropological Research, New York.

GARIBAY, K., ANGEL MARIA

1953 *Historia de la Literatura Náhuatl.* Mexico, D. F.

GILLIN, JOHN

1949 Mestizo America in *Most of the World, The Peoples of Africa, Latin America, and the East Today.* Columbia University Press: New York.

1952 "Ethos and Cultural Aspects of Personality." Sol Tax (editor), in *Heritage of Conquest.* Glencoe, Illinois.

GUITERAS-HOLMES, C.

1961 *Perils of the Soul: The World View of a Tzotzil Indian.* The Free Press: Glencoe, Illinois.

LEON-PORTILLA, MIGUEL

1956 *La Filosofía Náhuatl.* Mexico, D. F.

1959 Panorama de La Población Indígena de Mexico. *America Indígena,* Vol. XIX, No. 1, January. pp. 43-73.

1962 "Mexico" in Indians in the Hemisphere Today — Guide to the Indian Population. *Indianist Yearbook, Inter-American Indian Institute,* Vol. XXII, Mexico, D. F.

LEWIS, OSCAR

1951 *Life in a Mexican Village: Tepoztlán Restudied.* University of Illinois Press: Urbana.

1958 México desde 1940. *Investigación Económica,* Organo de la Escuela Nacional de Economía. Vol. XVIII, No. 70. Universidad Nacional Autónoma de México. Mexico, D. F.

1960 *Tepoztlán: Village in Mexico.* Henry Holt and Co.: New York.

MADSEN, WILLIAM

1960 *The Virgin's Children, Life in an Aztec Village Today.* University of Texas Press: Austin.

MASON, J. ALDEN.

1940 The Native Languages of Middle America in *The Maya and Their Neighbors,* pp. 52-114. New York.

MINTZ, SIDNEY W. AND ERIC R. WOLF

1950 An Analysis of Ritual Co-Parenthood (Compadrazgo). *Southwestern Journal of Anthropology,* Vol. 6, No. 4. pp. 341-368.

PITTMAN, RICHARD SAUNDERS

1954 A Grammar of Tetelcingo (Morelos) Nahuatl. Supplement, Language Dissertation No. 50. *Language: Journal of the Linguistic Society of America,* Vol. 30, No. 1 (Part 2), January–March 1954. Baltimore, Md.

POZAS, RICARDO

1962 *Juan, The Chamula, An Ethnological Re-Creation of the Life of a Mexican Indian.* University of California Press: Berkeley and Los Angeles.

REDFIELD, ROBERT

1930 *Tepoztlán, A Mexican Village.* University of Chicago Press: Chicago.

1941 *The Folk Culture of Yucatán.* University of Chicago Press: Chicago.

1950 *A Village That Chose Progress. Chan Kom Revisited.* University of Chicago Press: Chicago.

1962 *Chan Kom, A Maya Village.* Abridged edition, University of Chicago Press: Chicago, Ill.

RITZENTHALER, ROBERT E. AND F. A. PETERSON

1956 The Mexican Kickapoo Indians. *Milwaukee Public Museum Publications in Anthropology, No. 2.* Milwaukee, Wisconsin.

SAYLES, E. B.

1955 "Three Mexican Crafts." *American Anthropologist,* Vol. 57, No. 5, pp. 953-973.

SCOTT, ROBERT E.

1959 *Mexican Government in Transition.* University of Illinois Press: Urbana.

SIMPSON, LESLEY BYRD

1959 *Many Mexicos.* University of California Press: Berkeley and Los Angeles.

SPICER, EDWARD H. (editor)

1961 *Perspectives in American Indian Culture Change.* University of Chicago Press: Chicago.

SPICER, EDWARD H.

1962 *Cycles of Conquest. The Impact of Spain, Mexico, and the United States on the Indians of the Southwest 1533–1960.* University of Arizona Press: Tucson.

SUAREZ, VICTOR M.

1945 *El español que se habla en Yucatán Apuntamientos filológicos.* Mérida, Yucatán, México.

SWADESH, MAURICIO

1949 El idioma de los Zapotecos in *Los Zapotecos, Monografía histórica, Etnográfica y Económica.* Directed by Lucio Mendieta y Núñez. Instituto de Investigaciones Sociales, Universidad Nacional Autónoma de México. Mexico.

1959 *Indian Linguistic Groups of Mexico.* Escuela Nacional de Antropología e Historia, Instituto Nacional de Antropología e Historia, Mexico, D. F.

TAX, SOL (editor)

1952 *Heritage of Conquest, The Ethnology of Middle America.* The Free Press: Glencoe, Ill.

THOMPSON, J. ERIC

1954 *The Rise and Fall of Maya Civilization.* University of Oklahoma Press: Norman.

TOZZER, ALFRED M.

1921 A Maya Grammar with Bibliography and Appraisement of the Works Noted. *Papers of the Peabody Museum of American Archaeology and Ethnology, Harvard University,* Vol. IX, Cambridge, Mass.

VILLA ROJAS, ALFONSO

1945 The Maya of East Central Quintana Roo. *The Carnegie Institution of Washington Publication No. 559.* Washington, D. C.

WHETTEN, NATHAN L.

1948 *Rural Mexico.* University of Chicago Press: Chicago, Illinois.

WHORF, BENJAMIN L.

1946 The Milpa Alta Dialect of Aztec in Linguistic Structures of Native North America, edited by Harry Hoijer. *Viking Fund Publications in Anthropology,* Number Six. New York City.

We see there the physiognomy of the country, the aspect
of the sky, the form of the plants, the figures of the
animals, the manners of the inhabitants, and the kind of
cultivation followed by them, assume a different
appearance at every step of our progress . . .

— Alexander von Humboldt

Land, Man, and Time | DAVID A. HENDERSON

THE BOUNDARIES OF MEXICO are drawn around
strikingly different lands and ways of life. Features of
physical geography are extremely diverse. Within short
distances, the landscape may change from a low, hot
coastal plain to a high mountain basin, situated below
towering snowclad mountain peaks. In the great arid
basins of the north, intermittent streams flow through
arroyos, entrenched in mineral-rich alluvium, to pour
floodwaters into temporary saline lakes. These dry
lands are covered with desert and mesquite-grassland
vegetation, and are the homes of such wildlife as the
bighorn sheep, the antelope, lizards, and quails and
doves. By contrast, in the hot, moist lands of the south,
great sluggish rivers wind through broad floodplains
covered with tall savanna grass and verdant tropical
forest. Here is the domain of the tapir, the kinkajou,
the monkey, the tiny brocket deer, the iguana, and
tropical birds of many kinds. In the central high country, the basins and steep rocky slopes are in places
covered with oak and pine. In these highlands, deer,
rabbit, various upland game birds, and waterfowl on
the lakes, furnished food and skins and feathers for
the Indians, and today are still being hunted.

Culturally the geography of Mexico is as varied
as it is physically. The land offerings to man, and his
varied appraisals and appropriations of them, are diverse.
Thus the imprint of man on the land changes rapidly
from one part of Mexico to another. In the great open
country of the prosperous north, man is at home with
his herds of cattle and horses, and the *charro* cowboy
can today walk the streets of modern cities in the midst
of productive districts of irrigation agriculture. In contrast, in the densely populated rural areas of the south,
there are poverty-ridden little villages of farmers, many
of them Indian. These rural folk till tiny plots with
techniques employed centuries ago by their Indian and
Spanish forebears. Here the land is often tired and
unproductive from generations of misuse.

In the great city of Mexico, skyscrapers, traffic-
jammed boulevards, nightclubs, and the large Univer-

sity City represent the new, while Indian ruins, historic
buildings, and Spanish aqueducts turn thought to the
long past. An enormous polyglot population of *mestizos*
(persons of mixed Indian and European descent), Indians, Europeans, North Americans, and other residents
from all corners of the earth, lives and works in this
astonishing capital city — an immense urban agglomeration that now sprawls out across most of the Aztecs'
storied Valley of Anáhuac.

GEOGRAPHIC REGIONS

The Mexican landscape can be divided into regions
which have distinctive physical and cultural features
(Map 1, p. 104). The characteristics which man has
given to the land have evolved through a long history of
human occupancy. The regional names used here are
for descriptive convenience and not intended to establish a precise comparative system.

In the east-west oriented Central Volcanic Highlands, many of the high Indian cultures evolved. The
Spaniards first looked down from a high mountain pass
upon Tenochtitlan — the impressive capital of the
Aztecs. In the valleys of these favored volcanic highlands, the Spaniards settled to build cities, till the
land, and raise herds of livestock before moving outward to other parts of New Spain. It was here that
the Spanish left their greatest impression on Mexico
during three hundred years of colonial rule.

The three regions which follow the Central Highlands, or Volcanic Axis of central Mexico, are areas
into which the Spanish went — to settle in large numbers at certain places — soon after the initial colonization of the Central Volcanic Highlands. One of these
regions is the vast Meseta Central (Central Plateau)
which lies between the high Eastern and Western Sierra
Madres and slopes downward toward the Rio Grande
and the United States boundary from the Central Highlands (Map 1, p. 104). Precious metals first attracted
Spanish settlement into this frontier country of the

1. LANDFORMS AND REGIONS

MOUNTAINS AND LAKES

A MT. ORIZABA
B MT. COFRE DE PEROTE
C MT. IXTACCIHUATL
D MT. POPOCATEPETL
E NEVADO DE TOLUCA
F NEVADO DE COLIMA
G LAKE TEXCOCO
H LAKE PATZCUARO
K LAKE CHAPALA

BASINS AND VALLEYS

1 MEXICO
2 MORELOS
3 PUEBLA
4 TOLUCA
5 BAJIO
6 JALISCO
7 BARRANCA DE COBRE

⊚ DAMS AND RESERVOIRS
○ SINK HOLES
✳ HUASTECA AREA
❋ LAGUNA IRRIGATION DISTRICT

Pacific Ocean

Gulf of California

Gulf of Mexico

Bay of Campeche

YUCATAN PLATFORM

SOUTHEASTERN MEXICO

NORTHWEST MEXICO

MESETA CENTRAL

SIERRA MADRE OCCIDENTAL

S. MADRE ORIENTAL

GULF SLOPE

CENTRAL HIGHLANDS

SOUTHERN MEXICO

SIERRA MADRE DEL SUR

S. MADRE DE OAXACA

S. NORTE DE CHIAPAS

S. MADRE DE CHIAPAS

Soconusco Coast

Tehuantepec Isthmus

Bolson de Mayran

Bolson de Mapimi

Vizcaino Desert

Magdalena Plain

S. JUAREZ
S. PEDRO MARTIR
S.S. LAZARO

RIO GRANDE (BRAVO)
CONCHOS
NAZAS
AGUANAVAL
SALADO
JALAN
SAN J.
PANUCO R.
COATZACOALCOS R.
PAPALOAPAN R.
GRIJALVA R.
USUMACINTA R.
BALSAS R.
SANTIAGO-LERMA R.
ACAPONETA R.
BALUARTE R.
PRESIDIO R.
PIAXTLA R.
SAN LORENZO R.
CULIACAN R.
FUERTE R.
SINALOA R.
MAYO R.
YAQUI R.
SONORA R.
CONCEPCION R.

MEXICO

MILES
0   100   200   300

N

Compiled from existing maps and field studies by D. A. Henderson.
Drawn by Stephen Bahre.

fierce Chichimeca Indians. Mining has remained important here, as has ranching. However, irrigation agriculture and manufacturing now occupy much of the population — predominantly *mestizo* and much influenced by the culture of the United States.

In 1519, the ships of Cortés brought the conquering Spaniards to the tropical shores of Veracruz from which they invaded the highland realm of Moctezuma. However, it was not until the end of the sixteenth century that colonists began to settle widely and in appreciable numbers on the lower slopes of the mountains facing the Gulf of Mexico in the Gulf Slope Region. When the Spaniards entered the region, much of the land was densely settled. Today certain sections still contain many Indians. Although the mountain slopes are now occupied by a large population, much of the hot, wet coastal land has yielded to agricultural colonization only within the last few decades. Parts of the lowland are still very sparsely settled.

South of the Volcanic Axis lies a rough, broken, mountainous country leading from the higher Central Volcanic Highlands down to the Pacific Ocean and to the low Isthmus of Tehuantepec. Beyond the Isthmus, the highlands of Chiapas occupy the southernmost part of Mexico. Favorable valleys in this region of Southern Mexico were early occupied by the Spanish, as were certain port sites on the Southern Sea, or Pacific Ocean. However, much of the land was too isolated and rugged to attract Spanish colonists. The greatest concentrations of Indians in Mexico remain today in this most underdeveloped and poorest part of the nation where rural settlement is often dense.

The last two regions are those in which the Spanish early made contact with the Indian populations, but in which large areas remain unsettled and little utilized by man even today. Northwest Mexico faces the Pacific Ocean and Gulf of California (or Sea of Cortés), across the formidable barrier of the Western Sierra Madre from the Volcanic Axis of the Central Highlands and Meseta Central. Over much of this region, the Sierra Madre, aridity, and primitive and hostile Indians long retarded Spanish and Mexican colonization. However, over the last several decades, modern irrigation agriculture and American tourism — along with other newly developed sources of income — have made the Northwest Region a promised land. Thousands of Mexicans from the rest of the nation have migrated to this modern, booming region where few Indians remain today.

Southeastern Mexico is composed of the tropical forests and grasslands of the hot, low-lying Yucatán Peninsula and the coast of Tabasco. Although some of the more desirable areas became Spanish ranges and plantations during the colonial period, great numbers of Indians resisted Spanish encroachment. Moreover, the nature of the land did not invite extensive Mexican settlement at later dates. Large numbers of Mayan-speaking peoples remain in the region today. Since much of this region remains as one of the last frontiers for extensive agricultural settlement in Mexico, the federal government has instituted land development projects. The hope is that these may absorb some of the rapidly growing rural population from other parts of the nation.

THE CENTRAL HIGHLANDS

Mountain peaks towering above forest-clad slopes and shimmering blue lakes form a spectacularly beautiful natural landscape in central Mexico. Included within this region are the east-west Volcanic Highlands and such adjacent areas as the Bajío, the fertile, aggraded northern base of the mountains. The Central Highlands encompass all, or parts of, the states of Puebla, Tlaxcala, Hidalgo, Querétaro, Guanajuato, Morelos, Mexico, Michoacán, Jalisco, and the Federal District (*See* Political endpaper map and Map 1, p. 104). Within this mountainous region are large and small basins above which rise lofty peaks, many of which are volcanic cones.

Physical Geography: THE LAND

This highland country overlies the southern and more elevated end of the Meseta Central. Here, as along the Pacific shores of Mexico, there are zones of weakness in the crust of the earth. Where cracks, or faults, occur in the older rocks below, volcanic materials from the interior of the earth have been extruded to form the landscape of the Central Highlands. Volcanic peaks, cinder cones, crater lakes, mesas, and lava flows are visible evidences of the volcanic activity. Earthquakes are common in the Central Highlands and along the Pacific coast and are caused by slippage and earth movement along the faults.

The summits of the highest mountains extend above the tree line and are capped with perpetual snows. Near the eastern escarpment, where the mountainous region rises up sharply above the Gulf of Mexico coastal plain, stand the peaks of Citlaltépetl, or Orizaba, at 18,700 feet, the highest mountain in Mexico, and Nauhcampatépetl, or Cofre de Perote, at 14,048 feet (See Map 1, p. 104). Forming the eastern rim of the Valley of Mexico are the spectacular mountains of Ixtaccíhuatl, 17,342 feet, and Popocatépetl, 17,887 feet. At the western edge of the Volcanic Axis, the Nevado de Colima rises to 14,235 feet above the hot Pacific lowlands.

Erosional forces have cut deep gorges, descending toward lower country, into the edges of the highland, but the basins in the highlands are little dissected by stream action. The basins are separated by low ridges in some cases and high mountain masses in others. Around the Valley of Mexico the walls are high, except on the north. On the east, stand massive snowcapped Ixtaccíhuatl and Popocatépetl; on the south, a series of volcanic peaks, including Ajusco, form the divide between the Valleys of Mexico and Morelos. On the west, the valley is separated from lower country by high mountains crowned by the Nevado de Toluca (15,010 feet). Other major basins are those of Puebla, Morelos, the high Valley of Toluca, at 8,600 feet, and the huge basin of Jalisco (Map 1).

Volcanic mountains of the Central Highlands ring this large basin in northwestern Michoacán. Corn, the most important crop in Mexico, grows in a small field on the humid edge of this basin to supply the daily fare of local rural folk.

The floors of the basins are covered with materials derived from the beds of old lakes which have disappeared, deposits of volcanic ash, and weathered volcanic rocks. Such materials form rich, deep soils in many places. In the Valley of Mexico, the fill material is composed of beds of clay and jelly-like ash and water. This unstable floor accounts for the subsidence that has occurred in many sections of the capital city where water has been pumped out of the underlying strata, and the weight of the city has caused compression in the beds below. The lower places in many of the basins are filled with lakes which swell with the summer rains to create a most pleasing countryside during the season of greenness and billowing afternoon clouds. Some of the lakes — such as Chapala and Pátzcuaro — are large.

In the Valley of Mexico or Anáhuac, five interconnected lakes covered much of the valley floor in aboriginal times. It was on a mud flat in one of these lakes, Lake Texcoco, that the Aztecs built their city of Tenochtitlan (Map 1, p. 104). After long periods of draining by man, all that remains of these lakes today are marshes and a part of Lake Texcoco.

Many of Mexico's most important rivers have their headwaters in the lakes of the high basins or on mountain slopes of the Central Volcanic Highlands. The Lerma-Santiago, Balsas, and Pánuco Rivers all begin in these highlands and plunge toward the sea in deep *barrancas* filled with rapids and sometimes falls. Thus, in this part of Mexico, as in most other parts as well, no large rivers are navigable for any great distance.

CLIMATE AND VEGETATION ZONES

In ascending the escarpments into the highlands, or in climbing the mountain slopes within the high country, the traveler passes through lands of changing climate and vegetation. These changes are induced by profound differences in elevation. The names the Spaniards gave these vertical zones are in common use today. Along the eastern edge of the Central Highlands, the *tierra caliente* (hot country) ascends to an elevation of about 2,000 feet. Here, as in most of Mexico, except parts of the north, rainfall has tropical characteristics. It occurs during the summer when warm, moist air moves inland from the seas where atmospheric pressures are higher than over land. Rains generally fall in brief, intense showers. In the hot, low country at the eastern end of the Volcanic Highlands, annual rainfall is from 60 to 80 inches. Map 2, Table I, 20, pp. 108-09). Average monthly temperatures in summer are between 80 and 82 degrees Fahrenheit, while those of winter are between 70 and 75 degrees. The maximum temperatures are not as high as those in the northern deserts, but the humidity is much higher than in the deserts, and the nights do not cool off as much. Tropical evergreen forests and savanna grasslands cover much of the *tierra caliente* in Veracruz state, but where the land has been burnt over, scrub forests and savanna grasslands occur as second growth vegetation (Map 3, p. 110).

Above the *tierra caliente* the *tierra templada* (temperate country) extends up to 5,000 or 6,000 feet above sea level along the eastern edge of the Volcanic Axis. Annual rainfall in the eastern *tierra templada* is around 60 to 80 inches, but may rise to 200 inches in the cloud forests on some of the mountain slopes (Map 2, Table I, 22, 23, pp. 108-09). Average monthly temperatures are between 70 and 75 degrees in summer and between 60 and 65 degrees in winter. In the forests of the eastern *tierra templada,* oaks and other trees of temperate climates are mixed with the tropical evergreen forests which extend up the slopes from lower elevations (Map 3, p. 110).

Most of the Central Highland Region is high enough to be included in the *tierra fría* (cold country). However, the Basin of Morelos and parts of the Basin of Puebla are low enough to be parts of the *tierra templada.* The *tierra fría* on the east extends from some 5,000 to 6,000 feet above sea level to elevations of 12,500 to 13,000 feet, where the tree line is encountered and the zone of mountain meadows begins. Above 14,000 to 15,000 feet in eastern Mexico, snow fields occur on the mountain peaks. Annual precipitation varies much from place to place in the Volcanic Highlands of central Mexico because mountain barriers have such important effects in permitting or blocking the entry of moist air masses into the mountain basins. At Cuernavaca, in the low Basin of Morelos, and at Uruapan, in the western Volcanic Highlands of Michoacán, where in both cases the land is exposed to the entry of warm moist air masses from the Pacific Ocean to the southwest, average annual rainfall is about 41 and 56 inches, respectively (Map 2, Table I, pp. 108-09). In the high Basin of Toluca, uplift and cooling of air masses bring 31 inches of average annual precipitation. However, considerable variation in rainfall may occur within an individual basin, as in the case in the Valley of Mexico where rainfall is scant because the basin is walled off by high mountains on three sides. Air masses entering the valley from the open, north side pile up and cool and lose their moisture in precipitation as they travel southward in a *cul-de-sac.* Thus, north of the basin, at Pachuca, average annual rainfall is only about 17 inches, but rises to 23 inches in the capital city, and is 29 inches in Xochomilco at the base of the high mountains at the southern end of the basin (Map 2, Table I, pp. 108-09). On the rimming mountain slopes southeast of Mexico City, at San Rafael and southwest of the city at Huizquilucan, annual precipitation is about 45 inches. In most of the Central Highlands, average annual precipitation is between 20 and 40 inches, and thus that of Puebla, in the east, is 31 inches, and that of Guadalajara, in the west, is 40 inches (Map 2, Table I, pp. 108-09). However, even in areas where rainfall seems high, crops may fail in years of drought, for precipitation may vary greatly from one year to the next.

Moderate to cool temperatures are the rule in the *tierra fría* and upper *tierra templada* of the Central Highlands. Average monthly temperatures vary between winter and summer from the middle fifties to the middle sixties. However, as illustrated in Table I, at low places such as Cuernavaca the climate is warmer, and at high elevations, such as at Toluca, the climate is considerably cooler than at the other stations listed for the Central Highlands.

Most of the central volcanic country of Mexico was originally covered by forests in which oaks and pines were dominant (Map 3, page 110). In the higher country, pines and firs covered the slopes. Where forests remain, aztec pine — or *pino real,* various pines known as *ocotes* — including montezuma pine, Mexican white pine — known as *ayacahuite* or *pinabete;* and sacred fir, or *oyamel,* are the dominant conifers. Cypress trees also grow on the mountain slopes. A distinctive cypress which grows in the *tierra fría,* and in other parts of Mexico outside the true deserts and wet tropics, is a huge bald cypress, known as an *ahuehuete* or *sabino.* Notable examples are those in Chapúltepec Park in Mexico City, the largest example near the City of Oaxaca, and the *Noche Triste* tree, located in the Popotla section of modern Mexico City. At this last place Cortés is supposed to have wept on the night of June 30, 1520, when his army was expelled in defeat from the Aztec capital of Tenochtitlan. Today much of the forest has been cut off, except in the highest, least accessible, places. On many of the mountainsides left naked by timber cutting, farming and destructive erosion have left deep scars.

Along the western and southern descent down the slopes of the Central Highlands to the lower country of the *tierra templada* and *tierra caliente,* the land is dryer than in those climatic zones on the slope to the Gulf of Mexico. In the *tierra templada* and *tierra caliente* of much of the south and west, annual rainfall is only about 30 to 40 inches (Map 2, Table I, 11, 12, pp. 108-09). Summer temperatures are as high as on the east, but winters are a little warmer because there are fewer invasions of cold air, called *nortes,* from the northern parts of North America.

In the dryer *tierra templada* of the south and west, there are tropical, deciduous forests in which trees lose their leaves during the very dry winters (Map 3, p. 110). These forests are lower and more open than the tropical evergreen forests of the eastern low country. However, along the river courses these forests are dense and include many vines and epiphytes, such as orchids. In the *tierra caliente* of the west and southwest, because

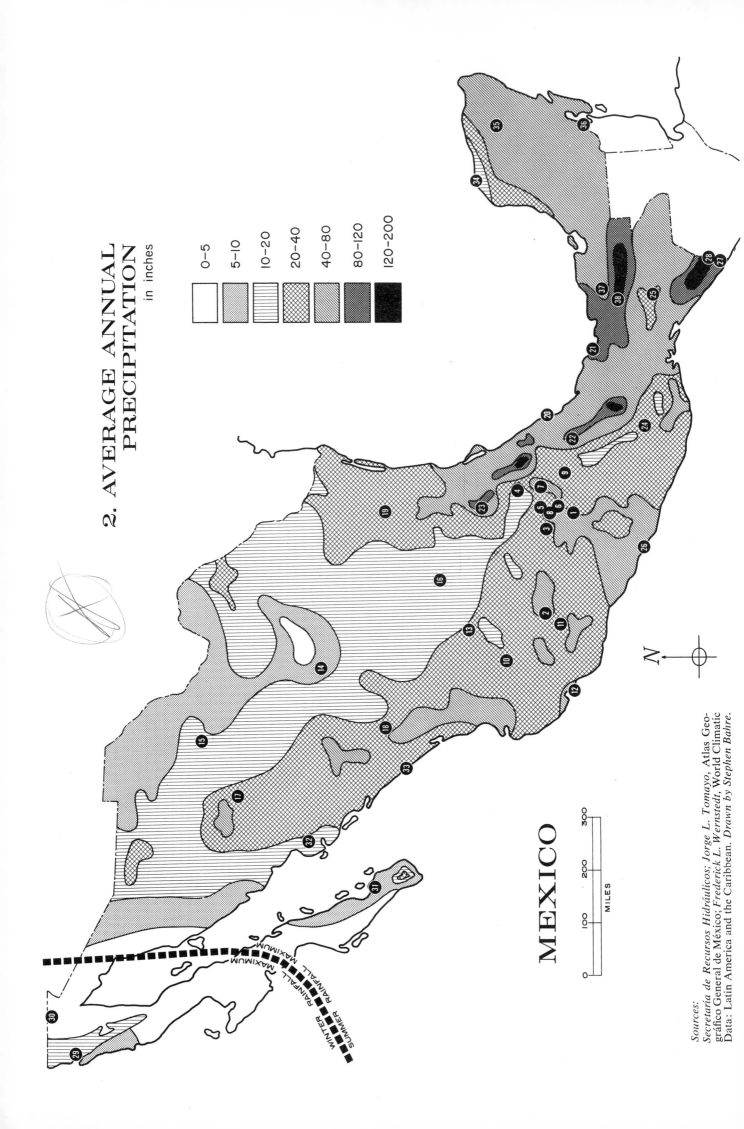

2. AVERAGE ANNUAL PRECIPITATION

in inches

0–5
5–10
10–20
20–40
40–80
80–120
120–200

MEXICO

N

WINTER RAINFALL MAXIMUM
SUMMER RAINFALL MAXIMUM

MILES

0   100   200   300

Sources:
Secretaría de Recursos Hidráulicos; Jorge L. Tomayo, Atlas Geo-
gráfico General de México; Frederick L. Wernstedt, World Climatic
Data: Latin America and the Caribbean. Drawn by Stephen Bahre.

TABLE I

CLIMATIC DATA FOR SELECTED MEXICAN STATIONS

Region and Station*	Elev.	N. Lat.	W. Long.		Jan.	Feb.	Mar.	Apr.	May	June	July	Aug.	Sept.	Oct.	Nov.	Dec.	Annual
CENTRAL HIGHLANDS AND ASSOCIATED STATIONS																	
1. Cuernavaca	5,059	18.55	99.14	T.	65.1	66.9	69.8	72.5	73.8	70.3	68.4	68.0	67.6	67.6	66.9	64.4	68.5
				Rf.	.12	.20	.28	.33	2.07	7.68	8.53	8.55	9.63	3.06	.32	.12	40.92
2. Uruapan	5,361	19.25	101.58	T.	60.8	62.6	67.3	70.7	72.3	71.2	70.0	69.6	68.5	67.5	63.5	61.9	67.1
				Rf.	.63	.83	.28	.16	1.26	10.75	13.65	12.97	15.99	7.04	1.47	1.24	66.27
3. Toluca	8,776	19.17	99.39	T.	49.8	52.0	55.4	57.7	58.8	57.9	56.1	56.3	56.1	55.0	52.3	50.5	54.8
				Rf.	.38	.34	.42	1.03	2.48	5.31	6.62	5.65	5.95	1.93	.77	.28	31.16
4. Pachuca	7,987	20.08	98.45	T.	53.2	55.0	58.1	60.6	62.1	60.4	59.4	59.2	58.8	56.3	54.0	54.3	57.6
				Rf.	.21	.50	.52	.71	1.31	2.28	2.31	2.10	3.05	1.93	.81	.24	16.51
5. Mexico City	7,349	19.26	99.08	T.	54.1	57.4	61.2	63.3	65.1	63.9	62.1	62.2	61.3	59.2	57.0	54.7	59.9
				Rf.	.02	.03	.05	.07	1.90	4.10	4.50	4.30	4.10	1.60	.05	.03	23.2
6. Xochimilco	7,382	19.16	99.06	T.	53.2	57.7	60.3	62.2	64.2	64.9	63.1	63.7	63.3	60.6	56.7	54.3	60.4
				Rf.	.50	.30	.30	1.30	2.30	4.30	6.00	5.80	5.70	2.00	.50	.40	29.4
7. San Rafael	8,298	19.13	98.49	T.	52.0	53.6	56.3	58.6	59.2	58.1	51.6	56.5	56.3	55.8	54.0	53.2	55.8
				Rf.	.43	.34	.50	1.63	3.38	7.06	10.64	8.85	8.72	2.82	1.24	.81	46.42
8. Huizquilucán	8,856	19.22	99.22	T.	52.2	54.7	58.8	60.3	61.0	59.4	57.6	57.7	55.6	55.2	53.4	53.2	56.7
				Rf.	.41	.41	.50	1.18	3.23	8.68	9.29	8.39	8.58	3.46	1.08	.41	45.62
9. Puebla	7,093	19.02	98.11	T.	55.0	58.1	62.2	64.9	66.0	64.2	63.0	63.3	62.2	60.8	58.5	56.5	61.2
				Rf.	.22	.24	.47	.51	2.85	6.10	5.40	4.78	7.35	2.24	.83	.34	31.33
10. Guadalajara	5,213	20.41	103.20	T.	59.9	62.4	66.0	70.5	73.9	72.1	69.4	69.3	68.4	67.1	63.9	59.9	66.9
				Rf.	.40	.20	.20	.20	1.10	8.80	9.40	8.50	7.20	2.20	.70	.70	39.6
11. Apatzingán	2,237	19.05	102.15	T.	77.5	79.9	83.5	86.4	88.9	87.6	83.5	82.4	82.8	83.1	81.0	77.7	82.8
				Rf.	.16	.28	.06	.04	.56	3.50	7.37	6.81	6.63	1.83	.32	.63	28.19
12. Manzanillo	1,010	19.04	104.20	T.	75.6	74.7	74.5	76.1	79.2	82.0	82.8	82.6	81.7	81.5	79.7	77.4	79.0
				Rf.	.92	.47	.00	.00	.18	4.03	5.39	7.24	15.19	5.01	.78	2.15	41.36
MESETA CENTRAL																	
13. Aguascalientes	6,259	21.53	102.18	T.	55.4	58.5	63.4	68.0	68.5	70.4	67.6	67.6	66.6	64.4	61.1	56.8	64.2
				Rf.	.45	.24	.14	.03	.70	4.36	5.34	4.19	3.52	1.32	.74	.69	21.72
14. Matamoros, Coah.	3,674	25.32	103.15	T.	54.3	60.4	64.6	73.9	80.6	83.3	80.4	81.7	80.2	74.3	64.4	56.1	71.0
				Rf.	.54	.16	.04	.19	.48	1.51	2.13	.95	1.46	.90	.54	.54	9.39
15. Chihuahua	4,669	28.38	106.04	T.	50.0	53.4	60.1	66.4	73.4	78.8	76.6	75.2	71.4	64.8	55.4	49.3	64.6
				Rf.	.20	.40	.30	.20	.20	1.70	3.60	3.70	3.30	.90	.50	.40	15.40
16. San Luis Potosí	6,157	22.09	100.58	T.	55.2	59.0	62.6	68.7	70.7	69.6	67.1	67.3	65.1	63.0	58.6	57.0	63.7
				Rf.	.45	.21	.40	.21	1.20	2.82	2.24	1.70	3.35	.69	.36	.57	14.20
17. Creel	7,724	27.46	107.39	T.	40.5	41.0	42.1	50.4	55.2	63.1	63.7	61.5	59.2	54.0	44.6	39.9	51.3
				Rf.	1.87	.31	.59	.55	1.11	5.37	5.31	5.47	1.14	2.66	1.34	1.86	27.56
18. El Salto	8,325	23.46	105.22	T.	43.3	43.7	46.4	51.1	55.2	61.9	59.7	59.9	59.4	55.0	48.7	45.0	52.5
				Rf.	1.45	1.35	.30	.09	1.43	6.03	7.60	7.43	5.08	2.40	.90	2.36	36.42
GULF SLOPE																	
19. Ciudad Victoria	1,053	23.44	99.08	T.	60.3	64.6	70.3	76.1	79.5	80.6	81.3	82.2	78.6	73.9	67.3	59.9	72.9
				Rf.	1.42	.94	.79	1.24	4.98	4.76	4.10	2.67	7.80	4.26	1.70	.61	35.55
20. Veracruz	52	19.12	96.08	T.	70.0	71.2	74.1	77.9	80.6	81.3	80.6	81.1	80.1	78.4	74.7	71.2	76.8
				Rf.	1.00	.60	.50	.60	1.70	11.40	13.00	10.70	12.00	5.70	3.10	1.00	61.30
21. Puerto México	46	18.09	94.24	T.	71.2	72.7	75.0	78.6	81.1	80.6	80.4	80.2	79.7	77.9	74.7	72.3	77.0
				Rf.	5.16	2.54	2.57	1.40	3.78	10.35	8.55	14.82	19.31	22.02	14.48	8.57	113.55
22. Córdoba	3,032	18.53	96.56	T.	61.9	63.7	67.3	71.6	73.6	71.8	70.1	70.1	70.1	68.2	64.6	62.7	68.1
				Rf.	1.83	1.50	1.51	2.17	4.33	13.64	15.58	15.53	18.18	8.95	3.72	2.38	89.32
23. Xilitla	3,396	21.24	99.00	T.	60.1	63.7	67.1	72.5	74.3	75.6	75.0	75.2	73.6	70.5	64.9	61.5	69.5
				Rf.	2.60	2.19	2.79	2.54	4.44	13.60	14.09	12.64	29.30	10.35	3.93	1.45	99.92
SOUTHERN MEXICO																	
24. Oaxaca	5,128	17.04	96.43	T.	62.8	65.8	69.4	72.5	72.9	70.7	69.4	69.8	67.1	65.3	68.8	63.0	68.1
				Rf.	.20	.20	.60	1.50	3.20	6.70	3.50	4.10	4.90	2.00	.40	.20	27.40
25. Tuxtla Gutierrez	1,759	16.45	93.07	T.	70.9	73.4	76.5	79.9	81.0	78.6	77.7	77.9	77.2	75.7	72.7	6.93	75.9
				Rf.	—	.02	.04	.22	2.97	9.27	6.89	6.11	7.91	3.20	.16	.25	37.04
26. Acapulco	10	16.50	99.56	T.	78.3	78.3	79.2	80.2	82.8	82.8	83.1	82.9	81.7	81.7	80.6	79.0	80.8
				Rf.	.36	.03	—	—	1.16	16.95	8.52	9.69	14.15	6.69	1.20	.45	59.20
27. Tapachula	551	14.54	92.16	T.	77.4	78.1	79.5	81.0	79.9	77.5	78.4	78.1	77.4	77.4	77.4	77.4	78.3
				Rf.	.28	.24	1.25	2.89	12.30	18.63	11.74	13.01	17.83	15.59	3.45	.45	98.02
28. Aurora	836	15.2	92.25	T.	75.0	80.6	82.8	82.6	82.9	80.8	80.1	81.0	80.4	80.6	80.4	79.0	80.4
				Rf.	1.33	.82	1.95	4.96	17.99	35.68	23.59	28.61	31.38	20.92	5.28	2.00	174.51
NORTHWEST MEXICO																	
29. Ensenada	46	31.51	116.38	T.	54.3	55.5	57.4	59.6	62.1	64.3	68.2	69.4	68.2	64.4	61.2	56.8	61.8
				Rf.	2.50	2.30	1.80	.90	.25	.10	.07	.09	.25	.60	.90	1.70	11.46
30. Mexicali	13	32.39	115.30	T.	53.9	58.5	63.8	70.9	77.5	85.3	91.8	91.1	86.4	74.9	62.4	55.5	72.7
				Rf.	.40	.30	.13	.12	.02	.01	.06	.33	.17	.30	.28	.40	2.52
31. La Paz	59	24.10	110.21	T.	64.2	67.5	70.5	73.9	78.7	81.1	87.8	87.6	84.7	80.4	72.0	60.4	72.2
				Rf.	.13	.45	.03	—	—	—	.25	1.64	2.05	.37	.54	1.35	6.81
32. Ciudad Obregón	131	27.29	109.55	T.	64.8	67.6	72.0	77.4	81.4	89.8	92.5	92.7	90.9	84.6	74.8	67.3	79.3
				Rf.	.27	.20	.06	.16	—	.07	.27	1.83	1.73	.57	.17	.51	8.31
33. Mazatlán	256	23.11	106.25	T.	66.7	66.9	67.5	70.3	74.8	79.5	81.5	81.7	81.5	80.1	74.3	69.1	74.5
				Rf.	.43	.38	.13	—	.07	1.16	6.56	9.53	10.58	2.42	.46	1.75	33.47
SOUTHEAST MEXICO																	
34. Progreso	46	21.17	89.40	T.	72.9	73.6	75.5	77.9	79.3	80.1	80.1	80.2	80.2	79.3	75.9	73.8	77.4
				Rf.	1.28	.67	.59	.70	2.17	2.86	1.78	1.81	2.18	2.72	.80	1.02	18.58
35. Valladolid	72	20.41	88.12	T.	70.0	73.4	76.5	79.9	81.0	79.7	80.1	79.7	79.3	77.4	73.6	72.9	77.0
				Rf.	2.15	1.09	1.06	2.92	4.74	5.81	5.53	6.31	7.03	5.72	1.91	2.22	46.49
36. Chetumal	13	18.30	88.20	T.	73.0	75.0	77.0	79.7	81.1	81.7	81.7	81.7	81.3	78.8	75.7	74.5	78.4
				Rf.	3.03	.86	1.14	1.18	5.45	6.93	5.16	4.23	5.57	8.41	3.41	3.76	49.13
37. Villahermosa	33	17.59	92.55	T.	72.0	74.8	76.8	80.2	82.8	82.8	82.4	83.1	81.7	80.1	76.5	73.2	78.8
				Rf.	5.53	3.92	1.82	1.81	3.22	8.05	7.64	7.67	10.69	11.51	5.61	7.12	74.89
38. Teapa	262	17.33	92.57	T.	71.2	73.0	75.4	79.3	81.7	80.8	80.2	80.4	79.3	74.4	73.8	72.5	77.0
				Rf.	14.40	9.82	8.15	4.47	7.79	14.86	13.53	14.76	22.51	20.00	12.15	13.60	156.04

Sources: Secc. de Climatología, Dir. Gral. de Hidrología, Sec. de Recursos Hidráulicos; Jorge A. Vivó and José C. Gómez, *Climatología de México*. Instituto Panamericano de Geografía e Historia, Pub. No. 19. México: 1946; Frederick L. Wernstedt, *World Climatic Data: Latin America and the Caribbean*. State College, Penn.: Dept. of Geography, Pennsylvania State University, 1961.

*The 38 stations, with records of at least 15 years each, can be located on Map 2.

3. VEGETATION ZONES

TEMPERATE

- DESERTS
- MESQUITE
- ACACIA
- CHAPARRAL
- PINE-OAK FOREST
- HIGH-CONIFEROUS FOREST

TROPICAL

- ARID TROPICAL SCRUB
- SAVANNA
- THORN FOREST
- TROPICAL DECIDUOUS FOREST
- TROPICAL EVERGREEN FOREST
- TROPICAL RAIN FOREST
- CLOUD FOREST

MEXICO

N

MILES
0   100   200   300

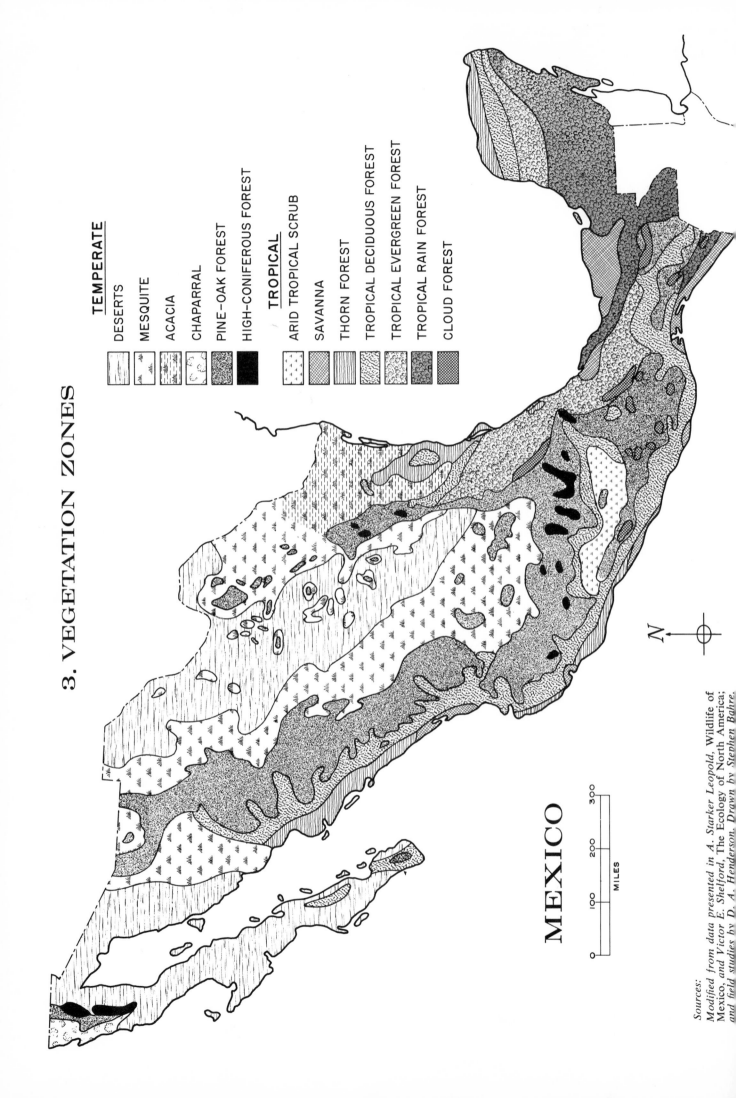

Sources:
Modified from data presented in A. Starker Leopold, Wildlife of
Mexico, and Victor E. Shelford, The Ecology of North America;
and field studies by D. A. Henderson. Drawn by Stephen Bahre.

vaporation of summer rainfall from the surface is apid, much of the lowland is covered with dense, crubby thorn forest and the cacti and shrubs of a opical arid scrub vegetation association. The trees of his vegetation association are only ten to thirty feet igh. Many cactus plants and leguminous acacia trees re found within the forest, an example of which may e seen inland from Acapulco. In both the forests of he *tierra templada* and *tierra caliente,* where clearing as taken place or where there is poor drainage, areas f tall savanna grasslands occur.

ultural Geography

The imprint made on the land by densely settled adian farmers was profound in central Mexico. With he arrival of the Spanish, the impact of western culture pon the lives and lands of the Indians set in motion rces which have continued to mold the amalgam of he Mexican landscape.

NDIAN CROPS AND FOODS

Agriculture has been the most basic occupation f Mexicans in the Central Highlands since the groups f Indians which settled in this high country first became armers. The earliest Indian invaders, who came down om the north, found the forests, grasslands, and lakes f the region full of plant and animal life which they athered or hunted to satisfy their needs. However, as me time went by, the Indians became sedentary farmers nd domesticated plants which grew in, or near, their ighlands. Some Indian crops which came from distant aces in the Americas were adopted by peoples of entral Mexico. Corn and *frijoles,* or kidney beans, were he most important crops cultivated by the Indians, and hese crops still occupy more farmland than any others n the Central Highlands (see Table II). Common idney beans and scarlet runner beans were grown by the adians and are still planted in the highlands. Other boriginal crops are also still important. Squashes, umpkins, and gourds are grown for food and for con- ainers. Pumpkin seeds, called *pepitas,* are still a com- on food. The *chiles, Capsicums,* have spread around he world as ingredients in the piquant dishes of many nds and are basic in the modern Mexican diet (Table). Red tomatoes, called *jitomates,* and green, or usk, tomatoes, called *tomates,* have also become im- ortant crops in many countries as they still are in Iexico (see Table II). The *chayote,* a vegetable hich grows on a vine often seen trailing over fences nd small homes in rural areas, and a large root with atery white flesh, called a *jícama,* are Indian crops hich are still seen in Mexican markets. Seeds of the uauhtli, or in Spanish, *bledo,* an amaranth; and seeds f the *chía,* or lime-leaved sage, were important in the ndian diet and are still crops in some areas. *Chía* seeds re used to make a refreshing soft drink. Indigo culti- ation, important to the Indians, has all but ceased in Iexico because synthetic blue dyes are superior and n be purchased cheaply.

TABLE II

PART A

PRINCIPAL MEXICAN CROPS*

Crop	Acres Under Cultivation in 1961 or 1960 in Nearest 100 Acres	Per Cent of Total Acreage
Corn	14,084,700 (1960)	50.06
Beans	3,212,300	11.42
Wheat	2,090,500	7.43
Cotton	2,026,200	7.20
Sugar Cane	790,700	2.82
Coffee	724,000	2.57
Sesame	622,700	2.21
Barley	607,900	2.16
Henequen	417,600	1.48
Garbanzos or Chickpeas	365,700	1.30
Rice	333,600	1.19
Sorghum	266,900	.95
Oats	244,600	.87
Alfalfa	237,200	.84
Melons and Market Vegetables (cantaloupes, watermelons, garlic, onions, peas, green beans, lentils, strawberries)	207,600	.74
Peanuts	187,800	.67
Coconuts	172,800 (1960)	.61
Tomates (red and green husk)	172,800	.61
Cacao	170,500	.60
Oranges	155,700 (1960)	.55
Safflower	138,400	.49
Chiles (dried and green)	138,400	.49
Tobacco	133,400	.47
Potatoes	123,600	.44
Bananas	116,100 (1960)	.41
Lima Beans	103,800	.37
Other Commercially Raised Fruits (avocados, mangoes, lemons, peaches, guavas)	42,000	.15
Sweet Potatoes	42,000	.15
Olives	39,500 (1960)	.14
Soybeans	29,700	.11
Castor Beans	29,700	.11
Grapes	27,200 (1960)	.10
Figs	27,200 (1960)	.10
Vanilla	22,200 (1960)	.08
Pineapples	22,200	.08
Jicama	7,400	.03
Total	28,134,600	100.00

Sources: 1960: "Progress in Mexican Agriculture," *Review of the Economic Situation of Mexico,* Vol. XXXVIII, No. 438 (May, 1962), pp. 6-7; 1961: Banco Nacional de Comercio Exterior, *Mexico 1963* (México: 1963), p. 108; Sesame: "Agriculture," *Review of the Economic Situation of Mexico,* Vol. XXXVIII, No. 433 (Dec., 1961), p. 8; Olives: "Olive Oil Industry," *Comercio Exterior,* English ed., Vol. VII, No. 3 (March, 1961), p. 5.

*Crops are listed in order of area under cultivation. Because some areas include commercial production only, and because some crops yield higher incomes than others per unit of area cultivated, the order of listing does not indicate the relative importance of some crops.

PART B

IMPORTANCE OF IRRIGATED FARM LAND IN MEXICO

Year	Harvested Area Irrigated by Federal Projects or Federally Controlled Waters	Percentage of Total Harvested Area in Mexico	Percentage of the Value of the Total Harvest in Mexico
1940	767,725 Acres	5.3	12.52
1950	2,122,935 Acres	10.0	22.50
1958	5,426,210 Acres	18.6	37.30

Source: Adolfo Orive Alba, *La Política de Irrigación en México* (Mexico: Fondo de Cultura Económica, 1960), p. 214.

Two large perennial plants, of much significance during the aboriginal period, are distributed widely over the landscape of the Central Highlands. The *nopal,* or prickly pear cactus, furnishes its fruits, called *tunas,* and its leaves when young and tender, as food. Moreover, the spines of the *nopal* have had a variety of uses, including those of needles and fishhooks. On the *nopal* lives a small scale insect called a cochineal, or *cochinilla,* from which red dye was extracted by the Indians. This dye became one of the important exports from New Spain during the Spanish colonial period. The *maguey, agave,* or century plant, is used for fences, as is the *nopal,* but also has other important uses. From the heart of this large plant is drawn a sweet juice which is rich in vitamins and minerals, and which was important to the Indians whose diet did not include many greens. The juice is called *agua miel* and when fermented, *pulque.* A concoction of pulque mixed with such things as brown sugar or pineapple is called *tepache.* When the heart of certain of the maguey plants is cooked and the extracted juice is distilled, intoxicating beverages which the Spaniards initiated in Mexico are produced. Among the regional designations of distilled maguey drinks, *tequila* and *mescal* are the best known. On some *maguey* plants live slugs or worms which were and still are eaten.

Some aboriginal tree crops which grow in the Central Highlands remain significant. Avocados are important as a source of vegetable fat in the Mexican diet (Table II, p. 111). This fruit is often made into *guacamole,* a food prepared by mixing smashed avocados with tomatoes, chiles, and the introduced European onions or garlic. The Indians sometimes included maguey slugs in this mixture. A small cherry, the *capulín,* is a native of the Central Highlands and was grown by the Indians. Other native tree fruits are guavas, *chirimoyas,* and *tejocotes,* the latter a small, yellow-orange fruit still found in highland markets.

Corn, or maize, the most important crop in Mexico, was prepared as food by the Indians in several ways that remain in use today. The preparation of corn foods ordinarily first involves heating and soaking the kernels in ashes, or lime, and water to soften them. In such a state the corn is called *nixtamal.* The white corn meal is then ground on a flat stone called a *metate.* To produce a dough called *masa,* women work the moistened meal between a cylinder-like rock held in their hands, called a *mano,* and the *metate. Tortillas* are made by roasting flattened cakes of masa on a thin, flat stone or earthenware griddle called a *comal.* As often as not, the modern *comal* is a thin sheet of metal. The *tamal* is made by cooking the masa dough without flattening it, often by steaming, and sometimes placing some other food inside the dough. *Pozole* is a gruel of *masa* and water, although in modern times it can be a soup of pork and hominy. *Atole* is made from masa mixed in water and cooked for a short while and sometimes flavored. *Pinole* is made from toasted corn kernels which are ground, and then sometimes mixed with water. Another, more modern, form of corn food is the *taco,* a tortilla with some other food wrapped inside before it is fried. The Tarahumara and Huichol Indians of the Sierra Madre Occidental in Northwestern Mexico used sprouted corn kernels or juicy stalks to make corn beer called *tesgüino.*

CHANGES IN AGRICULTURE

The Spaniards introduced many crops into the Central Highlands, and most of these crops are still being cultivated (Table II). Wheat and barley, better suited than corn to the coolness of very high altitudes, are of growing importance because they supply the flour for bread and malt for beer demanded by the growing middle class and urban workers of the cities. Barley and oats are produced to supply the growing animal feeding industry. Rye is grown but is of little significance. The Spaniards introduced alfalfa and other forage crops to feed the herds which grew from the animals imported from Spain, and these crops are extensively cultivated. Because swine fattening has increased much during the last several years, grain sorghum for swine feed is being planted in many areas, such as the Bajío of Guanajuato. (Map 1, Table II, pp. 104, 109). *Garbanzos* or chickpeas, garlic, and onions, have remained important since the times of their introduction by the Spaniards.

In the lower country of the highlands, for example, the Basin of Morelos, such crops as sugar cane, rice, and *ajonjolí,* or sesame, an Asian oil seed, have been planted since early colonial times. Potatoes, from South America, are an important crop in the higher parts of the Central Highlands, and in time of poor harvests are supplemented by less desirable native wild potatoes. The production of introduced fruits, like apples, peaches, and pears is of increasing significance as the demand for such fruits rises among the urban middle class. In a few areas of the Central Highlands farmers with large holdings now export off-season crops to the United States. Introduced melons of several kinds and strawberries are most important among these crops. The cultivation of market vegetables is expanding rapidly around cities. However, corn and beans remain most important in the daily fare of most Mexicans of the Central Highlands, and these two crops occupy more land in Mexico than all others combined (Table I, page 111).

One of the most dramatic changes wrought in Mexico by the Spanish was the turning of farm and untilled lands into ranges for livestock. Most of the species of livestock that are found in Mexico were brought by the Spaniards. The Indians had only the dog, which came with them from Asia, the turkey *(guajolote),* and a duck domesticated in the New World. The duck, known in English as a muscovy duck, was called a *pato casero* (house duck) by the Spaniard because in some parts of the New World they found it raised as a household fowl. Stingless bees provide honey for the Indians, but much of the honey produced in Mexico today comes from introduced European bees. Man was the Indian's beast of burden. Great herds of cattle, horses, burros, mules, sheep, and goats grew out of breeding stock imported by the Spanish, and these domestic grazing animals overran valleys, hillsides, and Indian farms to help cause famine among the population and erosion on the land. Swine and chickens were other important livestock imported by the Spanish. Oxen pulled the carts and plows on Spanish roads and farmlands.

Near the urban centers of the Central Highlands, and on some large ranches and farms, livestock production is now modern and intensive, but over much of the countryside, animal husbandry has changed little since colonial days. Around the cities there are new dairies and poultry and pig farms which supply their products to the urban middle classes. The livestock of the poor farmers and villagers are numerous relative to the amount of pasture available, but not relative to the needs of the dense rural population. Scrub cattle (*criollo* cattle) are the most numerous livestock in the Central Highlands as in much of Mexico (see Table III). They graze along with horses, burros, mules, sheep, and goats, on the hillsides and on the crop fields lying fallow. Beef is eaten irregularly by the poor farmers, and they may offer a few cattle for sale each year. The ox pulls the plow. The horse, once a prerogative of the Spaniard when the Indian remained afoot, is still common in the highlands, as is the burro. The mule driver, *arriero,* and his pack train, provided a basic means of transportation during the colonial period and nineteenth century. In the twentieth century, mules have declined in importance. Goats are especially common because they survive well on the tough, secondary vegetation of cutover areas and abandoned fields, and are easy to care for. Goat meat is a fare of the poorer people, and goat cheese is one of the few sources of animal protein consumed regularly by the poor rural folk. Sheep are numerous in parts of the highlands where wool replaced the cotton which the Indians had to import from lower, warmer regions.

Overgrazing to the point of causing pasture deterioration and erosion is more common in the agricultural areas of the highlands of central and southern Mexico, where man and beast alike press upon limited land resources, than it is in the range country of northern Mexico. In the villages and towns, along the roads, in the forests, indeed nearly everywhere that one may look, listen, or smell in central Mexico, scavenger pigs are evident. All too often, however, they must be sold for needed income rather than consumed by the farmers or villagers themselves.

When *aftosa,* or foot-and-mouth disease, was introduced into Mexico by way of Veracruz state, into which some diseased bulls were imported from Brazil after World War II, many Mexican cattle which had been exposed to the disease were slaughtered. Some of the oxen that were killed were replaced by mules, many of them imported into the central states from the northern states and from the United States. Mules, which are not subject to foot and mouth disease, became important again in some areas.

TABLE III
NUMBER AND PERCENTAGE OF VALUE OF PRODUCTION OF QUADRUPED LIVESTOCK IN MEXICO: 1960

Species Ranked According to Numbers	Number in 1,000's	Per Cent value of annual livestock offspring production
Cattle	24,675	70.30
Swine	11,824	2.69
Goats	7,042	1.98
Sheep	4,541	1.43
Horses	4,012	15.95
Asses or Burros	3,158	4.71
Mules	1,773	2.94
		100.00

Source: Banco Nacional de Comercio Exterior, Mexico 1960 (Mexico: 1960), pp. 119–120.

The Indians of the Central Highlands lived partially on wild game and used other game products for dress and ornament in their daily lives. They hunted small game like rabbits, squirrels, quail, dove, and *chacalacas,* the latter a chicken-like wild bird. On Texcoco and other lakes, fishing was important, wild ducks were killed with a spear thrown by a lever device known as an *atlatl,* and mosquito eggs were gathered for eating. The Indians hunted deer, wild pig-like animals known as peccaries or *javelinas,* coyotes, and cats, including the puma in the highlands and the jaguar, margay, and jaguarundi along the warmer edges of the highlands. They also hunted the *cacomixtle,* or ringtailed cat, a raccoon-like little animal. Animals which came northward from South America, after the Central American land bridge was established, and which were numerous in central and southern Mexico during aboriginal times, also were hunted by the Indians. These included opossums, porcupines, armadillos, and anteaters. On the southern and eastern edges of the Central Highlands, in the tropical forests, lived two large rodents from South America, the agouti and *tepescuintle.* All of these wild game animals are still present today, and in most places where they live, they are still hunted for food. Two other "game" foods in the highland Indian diet — very strange in our context — were ants covered with honey and grasshoppers.

The shooting of deer, ducks, and game birds still supplements the diet of many rural families. Fish from lakes and streams also provide a small amount of protein in the rural diet which is usually deficient in this respect. Since the days of the Spanish conquest, overhunting and fishing have gone on, and fish and game are badly depleted over most of the Central Highlands.

The Indian farmer worked small fields, fenced with maguey, nopal or stone walls, more as gardens than farms, with much attention given to individual plants. His basic tools were a *coa,* or digging stick, and his hands. The Spaniard introduced draft animals and simple iron-tipped wooden plows and these initiated erosion on hillsides formerly farmed as Indian gardens with erosion retarded by the planting of beans and squash among the corn plants. The wooden plow is still used in the Central Highlands. Large farms have, however, been mechanized.

Archaeological investigations begun in 1960 in the Tehuacán Valley of the southeastern borders of the Central Highlands indicate that irrigation agriculture, involving dams, ditches, aqueducts, and terraces, may have been much more important in Indian farming than was formerly supposed. During the colonial period, irrigation works were greatly expanded. Nevertheless, although irrigation has expanded much in this century, the great majority of all land is farmed under *temporal* conditions, or those of seasonal natural rainfall (Table II, B. p. 111). Since Indian times, crops have been planted in areas where the roots can reach a high water table, such as along lake shores, and this practice has become known as *jugo* farming. The Indians grew some crops in the lakes on rafts of woven branches, which were filled with earth and anchored, and known as *chinampas*. These raft gardens eventually became islands in shallow waters as is the case with the contemporary "floating gardens" of Xochimilco. Terracing of hillsides and mountain slopes was not characteristic among the Indians, and there is still very little of it on the slopes of the highlands. The use of fertilizer on farmlands is not common either, and many fields have become infertile through long years of misuse. However, some soils have remained fertile because they are derived from deep volcanic, alluvial or lake-bed materials.

Relative to the size of the population and the stage of agricultural technology, agricultural land is scarce in the Central Highlands as well as in the rest of the nation. Of all the land area in Mexico, only some seven per cent is cultivated, and another eight per cent is classified as cultivable. Areas classed as various kinds of pasture and range lands constitute about 44 per cent, and forest lands 17 per cent, of the national territory, while extremely arid and rocky areas, which are useless except for the most marginal kinds of grazing enterprises, make up about 24 per cent of the land area of Mexico. Although more land is classified as cultivable in the Central Highlands than in any other region of Mexico, the good farm land there was already being cultivated by 1950.

LAND TENURE

Ownership of land, the most basic natural resource of Mexico, has passed from one group of society to another, as power and ideology have shifted with history. Many of the Aztecs of the Central Highlands cultivated small plots *(tlalmilpas)* which they did not own, but which were owned by communities of *calpullis* or clans. In addition, the farmers of the clans sometimes worked public lands in common. When the Spaniards arrived there were, however, other lands owned by important warriors, and other landlords, which were farmed by serfs and sharecroppers and by Indian slaves taken in battles or raids.

The Spanish changed the land tenure system of Mexico greatly. Conquistadores and other Spaniards in favor with the crown were granted large tracts of land on which they were given rights to Indian labor and tribute from Indian communities. These Spanish holdings were called *encomiendas* and were granted only for the lifetime of the grantee or for that of the grantee and his son. However, by the early seventeenth century the powers associated with the outmoded *encomiendas* had been nearly abolished, and large properties had become concentrated in the hands of new owners represented chiefly by wealthy families and the church. The large estates, known as haciendas, were owned outright and were often legally indivisible and entailed. Their genesis was principally in the cattle country north of the Central Highlands where Indian lands protected by the Crown were few. As mining declined in the early seventeenth century, power in New Spain became concentrated on the great haciendas.

As the ability of the Crown and missionaries to protect the Indians waned, by the early seventeenth century, the aborigines became the major labor force on the haciendas. In the Central Highlands, even the Indians of poor villages which had retained their lands often became peons on nearby haciendas. Most of the Indian workers on the haciendas were not slaves but were held on the land through various means including a system of debt peonage. That is, Indian families became so indebted to the landlord that they could not repay their debts and were thus held on the hacienda. The haciendas became great, nearly self-sufficient, social and economic units which retarded the growth of commercial towns and an urban middle class. On the other hand, the hacienda was a place of refuge on which the poor country folk could find security in time of war or economic depression.

Freedom from Spain in the nineteenth century did not change the basic pattern of land tenure in Mexico. On the other hand, the Indians lost more and more of their traditional lands to the great estates, and as properties changed hands in repeated times of stress, land ownership became more concentrated than ever before. The church was the nation's most important landholder until just after 1850. The Juárez reforms then took church land, and other landlords incorporated it into haciendas. Toward the end of the nineteenth century, foreigners, mostly Americans, had acquired some of the large estates. By the end of the century, a great proportion of the natural and human resources of the nation was in the hands of a small part of the population.

It is little wonder that the battle cry of the Revolution of 1910 was *"tierra y libertad"* or "land and liberty." Mexico was essentially an agricultural nation; yet the most basic resource of such a country was not in the hands of those who worked it, nor were the farm laborers sharing in much of the yield from the land. Land reform became the heart of the revolutionary program. The great estates were, in most cases, broken up under new laws, into communal properties, and placed in the hands of those who tilled them. However, laws provided for the maintenance of various sizes of private rural properties according to conditions

TABLE IV
LAND TENURE
PART A
TENURE OF ALL LANDS
(Areas in Thousands of Acres)

Year	Mexican Total	Apparent Public Domain	Total Held Land	Percentage Mexico in Held Land	EJIDOS Acres	EJIDOS Per Cent	PRIVATE PROPERTIES 12.5 Acres and Under	PRIVATE PROPERTIES Per Cent	PRIVATE PROPERTIES Over 12.5 Acres	PRIVATE PROPERTIES Per Cent
1930	486,606	161,436	325,170	66.80	20,619	6.34	2,198	0.68	302,353	92.98
1940	486,606	168,467	318,139	65.40	71,468	22.46	2,860	0.90	243,811	76.64
1950	486,606	127,034	359,572	73.90	96,107	26.73	3,367	0.94	260,098	72.33

PART B
ARABLE LAND ON HELD PROPERTIES
(Areas in Millions of Acres)

Year	Total Held Land Classified as Arable	EJIDOS Acres	EJIDOS Percentage of Total Arable Land	PRIVATE LAND Acres	PRIVATE LAND Percentage of Total Arable Land
1930	36.1	4.7	13.3	31.4	86.7
1940	36.6	17.3	47.4	19.3	52.6
1950	49.1	21.7	44.1	27.4	55.9

PART C
HARVESTED LAND
(Areas in Millions of Acres)

Year	Total Harvested Land	EJIDOS Acres	EJIDOS Percentage of Harvested Land	PRIVATE PROPERTIES Acres	PRIVATE PROPERTIES Percentage of Harvested Land
1930	14.5	1.9	13.6	12.6	76.4
1940	16.6	8.2	49.0	8.4	51.0
1950	21.3	9.9	46.5	11.4	53.5

PART D
TENURE OF IRRIGATED LAND IN FEDERAL IRRIGATION DISTRICTS: 1958

Total Irrigated Land in Federal Irrigation Districts	Percentage of Irrigated Land on Ejidos	Percentage of Irrigated Land on Private Properties
4,896,000 Acres	41.9	58.1

PART E
VALUE OF CROP HARVESTS FROM EJIDO AND PRIVATE PROPERTIES

Year	Total Value of Harvest	Percentage of Total Value from Ejido Lands	Percentage of Total Value from Private Lands
1940	827,732,000 pesos	49	51
1950	5,902,204,000 pesos	32	68
	3,311,136,000 pesos*		

Sources: Adolfo Orive Alba, *La Política de Irrigación en México* (México: Fondo de Cultura Económica, 1960), pp. 203, 214; Banco Nacional de Comercio Exterior, *Mexico: 1960* (Mexico: 1960), pp. 109-110, Dir. Gral. de Estadística, *México en Cifras: 1959* (México: Talleres Gráficos de la Nación, 1959), Láminas 1, 23, 25; Ramón Fernández y Fernández, *Propiedad Privada versus Ejidos* (Ediciones conmemoratives del centenario de la Escuela Nacional de Agricultura, 1854–1954. México: 1953), p. 133.

*Value in 1940 pesos after devaluations in 1948 and 1949.

f moisture availability for crops, crop types, and ange-carrying capacities. Villages were given the right o apply for grants of land if their residents met certain qualifications, such as being essentially engaged in arming. As in the Indian days, the farmers were vested with only usufructuary rights in the land, in that they could not sell or mortgage their farms, and could rent he land only under special circumstances. These communal lands were called *ejidos,* and today there are in Mexico thousands of *ejidos* on which land has been distributed to nearly 2,200,000 *ejidatarios,* or heads of families. About 1,370,000 farmers have acquired private lands under Mexican agrarian reform. Of the some 100 million *hectares* (247 million acres) of public and private lands, both cultivable and non-cultivable, which have been distributed by the government since 1915, a little over one-half have been given to *ejidatarios.* About 44 per cent of all cultivable land in Mexico was within *ejidos* in 1950 (Table IV, B, above). Although the *ejido* lands are communal, that is, vested in the community, very few of the communal lands are worked as collective farms. Collective *ejidos* have not been particularly successful, and in some cases farmers participating in them have successfully petitioned the federal government to give them individual farms within communal structure. The collective *ejidos* that remain are located in areas of highly commercialized agriculture such as the cotton lands of the Laguna District in north central Mexico, the coffee region of Soconusco in the mountains near the southern coast, the sugar cane lands around El Mante, Tamaulipas, the citrus areas at Nuevo Lombardía and Nuevo Italia in southern Michoacán, and the cotton and wheat lands around the lower Río Yaqui (Front endpaper map and Map 1).

Most of the *ejidatarios* of Mexico farm their assigned plots of land or *parcelas*. The size of these is limited by federal law, as are the sizes of varying kinds of private farms. *Ejidatarios* are supposed to receive 10 *hectares* or about 25 acres of irrigated land, and 20 *hectares* or about 50 acres of non-irrigated land, called *temporal* land. Private farms of irrigated land, on which most crops are raised are limited in size to 100 *hectares* or about 250 acres. If irrigated cotton is grown, the maximum size increases to 150 *hectares* or about 370 acres. Non-irrigated private farms may contain up to 200 *hectares* or about 500 acres, while private farms on which perennial crops such as grapes, olives, sugar cane, coconuts, bananas, coffee, and cacao are grown, may include up to 300 *hectares* or about 750 acres of land. Private rangelands are limited to the area deemed necessary to maintain 500 head of cattle, horses, or other large livestock or their forage-consuming equivalent in smaller range animals. However, if there are no landless persons near a large ranch, nor any land on the ranch which could be effectively distributed to landless farmers, the private rancher may obtain a decree concession from the government which will permit him to hold more range than the specified legal limit for a period of twenty-five years. Thus, there are many ranches in Mexico which are within the law in size, but which contain much more land than is necessary to maintain 500 head of cattle. However, by the 1960's it began to appear that some of the large ranches would be made into collective ranching *ejidos* when their decree concessions expired. In 1962, there were several such ranching collectives as well as several forestry collectives in Mexico.

The *ejido* land system was slow in being implemented after the Revolution. In 1910, before the Revolution, some 97 per cent of all land was held on haciendas, two per cent in small private holdings, and one per cent in village and Indian pueblo lands. A small amount of land distribution occurred early in the revolutionary period, but the process of creating communal *ejidos* was resisted by many of the politicians from the north who commanded the Revolution between 1915 and 1934, and who favored small private properties over *ejidos*. At one time *ejidos* could be even limited to designated *Ejido* Districts so that the better lands of haciendas would not be affected by land reforms. By 1930 only 13 per cent of the cultivable land and six per cent of the held land of Mexico was on *ejidos* (Table IV, A, B, p. 115). However, after President

Lázaro Cárdenas came to power in 1934, he institute a rapid and far-reaching distribution of estate land. B 1940, 22 per cent of all held land, 47 per cent of a cultivable land, and 49 per cent of all harvested lan in the nation was on *ejidos* (Table IV, A, B, C, 115). As the extension of small and medium-sized pr vate farms took place in many colonies after 1940, b 1950, *ejidos* contained only 44 per cent of all cultivab land (Table IV, B, p. 115). In 1950, of all Mexica land not in the public domain, 72 per cent was private held and 27 per cent was on *ejidos*. This situation illus trates the fact that most range land not in the publi domain is still private. However, much public land also utilized as range by *ejidatarios*.

Unfortunately, in the Central Highlands there we so many families which were given *ejido parcelas*, farms, that the farm size could not be maintained the designated amount of land. Many such farms in th Central Highlands are tiny in size and cannot produc enough to provide either full employment or fu stomachs for their tillers. The *ejido* is more prevale in the Central Volcanic Highlands than in any of th other regions of Mexico. Nevertheless, there are s many persons within the rural population that th region contains more day laborers on farms than a found in any of the other regions.

The *ejido* land tenure system has been very im portant in accomplishing some of the goals of tl Revolution and in bringing major changes in the who of the Mexican economy. It has been the basic mear by which the old hacienda system has been broken up and through which, landless farmers have been give land and thereby a stake in, and identification with, tl operation of their nation. By destroying the mear through which economic and political power were co centrated in the hands of the few, the *ejido* system wa able not only to release land for redistribution, but al to set free the other factors of production from the restricted utilization in the old order. New outlets f investment began to be sought by capital, even in tl hands of small businessmen, who became the prototyp of the new growing middle class in Mexico. Labor w. set free and became more mobile. Young men ar women now could often seek the kinds of jobs th attracted them most, anywhere in the nation. Since tl control of the economy was wrested from the o regime, a new class of managers and technicians aro to make Mexico one of the few Latin American natio with a sizable corps of such individuals. Moreover, primary schools were built on many of the *ejidos*, the communal organizations offered the first means of brin ing a rudimentary education to a large proportion the rural population.

In spite of the favorable accomplishments of tl *ejido* system, great problems remain in making tl form of agricultural production efficient. In this sens land reform has not, in most cases, been accompani with the increases in productivity needed to keep pa with a growing population such as that of Mexico. 1958, the average corn yield in Mexico was only

Clinging to the hillsides in both the Central Highlands and Southern Mexico are many tiny subsistence farms whose owners have neither technical training nor access to agricultural credit. Subsistence crops, oxen, and wooden plows leave the sloping fields wide open to the damages of erosion.

bushels per acre, or about one-fourth that in the United States. However, the average wheat yield, which comes in large measure from private and irrigated land, was 23 bushels per acre, or 85 per cent of the United States yield. Had the population of Mexico been static, the *ejido* farms might have served the nation better.

Problems on the *ejidos* have been many, but the most basic is probably the small size of the farms which obviates the economies of larger scale operation. In many cases the inefficiencies of *latifundia,* a system of large estates, have been exchanged for the inefficiencies of *minifundia,* a system of tiny farms. On many *ejidos* the farmers have not been secure in their tenure and local bosses have run the operation for their own ends. In such cases there has not been incentive to husband the resources of the land, and crop fields have been allowed to deteriorate and common ranges to become overgrazed. *Ejido* farmers have lacked adequate training, capital, equipment, and farm credit. In fact, the problem of adequate investment has plagued all farmers in Mexico because, since the Revolution, insecure tenure in agriculture and the attractiveness of investment in other sectors of the economy have diverted funds away from farming. Another problem within the *ejido* system has been the graft connected with political operation of some farms and the credit system designed to serve them.

An important impediment to production on *ejidos* has been the absence in the farmers of the kind of acquisitive spirit which seems necessary for increased production in either a capitalistic or socialistic society. Until recently, most of the farmers had to be satisfied with the meager rewards of the peon laborer on an estate. Thus, the concept of saving for reinvestment in order to increase production for a market economy is foreign to many of the *ejido* farmers. In many parts of Mexico, *ejidatarios* have sold or rented their land to other persons who hire them back as laborers. Thus, in contravention of Mexican agrarian law, the ancient relationship between landlord and peon has been surreptitiously re-established. Finally, the *ejido* program has committed the government to a policy of free land for all those legally qualified persons who apply for it. The problem of *minifundia* which accompanies this policy has already been mentioned. Another aspect of the free-land policy has been the placement of *ejidos* in areas of marginal, and sometimes completely unsuitable, farm land. Such places serve essentially only as home sites, and in order to gain a living the farmers must find other employment, such as seasonal labor in the United States. The free-land policy has also created a problem of squatters, landless persons who settle on lands owned by others in the hope that the government will confirm their right to remain.

The low productivity of *ejidos* in 1950 is demonstrated by the fact that, although 47 per cent of all harvested land was on *ejidos* and 53 per cent on private lands, 68 per cent of the value of farm production came from the private farms (Table IV, C, E, p. 115). Time and money are expended by the government and the farmers in trying to settle unproductive lands where such expenditures would undoubtedly increase total agricultural productivity more if made on already existing farms.

Hence, although the *ejido* land tenure system has contributed to the attainment of revolutionary goals, it has been attended with very grave problems. In the battle cry of *"tierra y libertad"* the two goals were really inseparable. Without the elimination of the hacienda system, which has been accomplished mostly through the *ejido* system, there could have been little liberty of either human beings or the factors of production in Mexico. Such liberties have been essential to the progress made in Mexico since the Revolution. However, the land on *ejido* farms has not been made as productive as it someday must be made, in order to feed the rapidly growing population of the nation.

The moderate-sized farms in the private sector of Mexican agriculture have contributed most to farm productivity since the elimination of the haciendas, especially since 1950 (Table IV, C, E, p. 115). The farmers with moderate-sized holdings enjoy the advantages of large scale operations, considerable capital investment in land, good technical training, and access to agricultural credit. There are, however, many tiny private farms in Mexico, especially in the Central Highlands and in Southern Mexico. On these farms the owners may till the fields with an ox and a wooden plow, and may be even less efficient than the *ejido* farmer who enjoys a certain amount of government patronage. Problems of insecurity of land tenure and insufficient agricultural credit have plagued some of the private farmers as they have *ejido* farmers.

In spite of attempts since the Revolution to raise farm yields and free men from the soil, most Mexicans are still employed as farmers, and agricultural productivity is below that of other sectors of the economy. In 1930, 70 per cent of all Mexican laborers were farmers, and by 1960, the percentage of the Mexican labor force in agriculture was, at about 52 per cent, still high. Although official estimates of the agricultural portion of the gross national product are probably much too low, about 12 to 13 per cent; nevertheless, the proportion of the population engaged in farming is much greater than the percentage of the gross national product contributed by agriculture. However, rural conditions are improving nearly everywhere, and in some areas of the nation they are improving rapidly. Between 1950 and 1960, cultivated land increased by some 38 per cent, and the value of agricultural production by about 45 per cent, while the population grew by 35 per cent. Ever since the 1930's, increases in Mexican agricultural productivity have outstripped those in most Latin American nations. Between 1953 and 1963, percentage increases in total and *per capita* agricultural production, and in total and *per capita* food production in Mexico, exceeded those in all other major Latin American nations. Total agricultural and total food production nearly doubled in Mexico between 1953 and 1963. In contrast to former years, when most of Mexico's exports were minerals, about one-half of all exports are now agricultural products. In spite of large agricultural exports, *per capita* daily consumption of calories in Mexico rose from 2,050 in the early 1950's to a respectable 2,680 in 1963, and the increase in the caloric value of the diet in Mexico between 1955 and 1963 was greater than in any other major Latin American nation.

CENTRAL HIGHLAND MINING

New Spain and Mexico are both names calling to mind visions of fabulous wealth pouring forth from silver and gold mines; however, precious mineral production has not been present over much of the Central Highlands, and the nation's most important mining districts lie outside the volcanic country. The mountain slopes of the Central Highlands are largely covered with young basaltic volcanic rocks and residues of cinders and ashes which are not mineralized. Thus the volcanic highlands have given up precious minerals to the Indians and later miners only where veins have been discovered along faults in underlying older andesite or rhyolite volcanics or other buried rocks, such as at Pachuca and El Oro-Tlalpujahua (Mexico-Michoacán border). Some mines have been located in canyons cut by streams below the sterile surface of basalt or along the edges of the Central Highland where the basaltic cover is incomplete or absent. Sites of the latter kind are found at Guanajuato, Taxco, and the old placer works on the Pacific slope in Colima where Indian and early colonial miners obtained gold weathered out of quartz veins in rocks without a basalt cover. The Indians of the highlands mined and worked gold, copper, tin, and a little silver. The Spaniard appropriated Indian mining areas and discovered new deposits. Silver became the most important mineral product of New Spain. In the first few years of the Conquest, Spanish mines were opened at Taxco, Zumpango (Guerrero), Sultepec (Mexico state), and Tlalpujahua. Shortly thereafter (1552) Pachuca became a mining center. Prior to the ascendancy of silver at Taxco, tin and copper from that place were used to produce bronze for Cortés's cannon at Tenochtitlan. Because of the richness of some of the veins, the ease of accessibility in shallow veins, and the cheapness of labor, some of the mines in the Central Highland proved to be real bonanzas from which certain families attained great wealth.

Many mines in the areas of Spanish discoveries have continued to be worked. However, many are now so marginal that only intervention by the federal government, or circumvention of tax and labor laws by companies, have kept the mines open. Minerals are no longer the major exports of Mexico as once they were.

TABLE V

MINERAL PRODUCTION

PART A

VOLUME AND VALUE OF MINERAL PRODUCTION IN MEXICO: 1960

Mineral	Volume of Production in Metric Tons	Value of Production in 1,000 Dollars	Per Cent of Total Value
Petroleum	108,772,000 Bbls.	128,278	29.60
Zinc	262,425	77,810	17.95
Lead	190,670	50,665	11.69
Silver	1,385	40,764	9.40
Copper	60,330	40,195	9.28
Sulphur	1,242,794*	28,836	6.66
Iron	521,356	11,678	2.69
Gold	9	10,429	2.42
Coal	1,776,693	9,613	2.16
Manganese	71,856	9,542	2.21
Fluorite	398,514*	6,693	1.55
Mercury	693	4,271	.99
Cadmium	1,181	3,690	.86
Barite	248,709*	2,786	.64
Antimony	4,231	2,378	.55
Graphite	34,316	2,086	.48
Bismuth	272	1,348	.31
Arsenic	12,131	1,203	.28
Tin	371	826	.19
Tungsten	105*	188	.04
Molybdenum	100	166	.04
Selenium	3	48	.01
		433,493	100.00

Sources: Banco Nacional de Comercio Exterior, *Mexico: 1963* (Mexico: 1963) p. 148; Dirección General de Estadística, *Compendio Estadístico: 1960* (México: Talleres Graficos de la Nación, 1962), 82–83.

1961

PART B

PETROLEUM PRODUCTION FOR SELECTED SIGNIFICANT YEARS

Year	Production in 1,000 Barrels
1901	10
1907	1,005
1911	12,533
1916	40,546
1920	157,069
1921	193,380
1925	115,515
1927	64,121
1932	32,805
1938	38,500
1948	58,500
1954	85,000
1960	108,772
1962	112,000

Sources: Dir. Gral. de Estadística, *Compendio Estadístico: 1960* (México: Talleres Gráficos de la Nación, 1962), p. 83; Banco Nacional de Comercio Exterior, *México: 1962* (México: 1963), p. 126; Ricardo Torres Gaitán ed., *La Industria Petrolera Mexicana* (México: Escuela Nacional de Economía, Universidad Nacional Autónomo de México, 1958), pp. 19, 54; U. S. Dept. of Interior, *Minerals Yearbook: 1962* (Washington: Government Printing Office, 1963), Vol. II, p. 511.

INDUSTRIAL DEVELOPMENT

The rapid growth of large scale manufactural industries in the Central Highlands has come about in only the last three of four decades. The Indians had many handicraft industries which were located where the natural resources — certain kinds of stone, minerals, wood, crops, or animals — were propitious for the making of trade articles. Early Spanish accounts of the great Indian market places, like that of Tenochtitlan, the capital of the Aztecs, describe the great variety of textiles, metal objects, skin and feather articles, and other goods which were displayed in the markets. Some of the Indian handicraft products are still for sale in the highlands, but most of these articles have been modified over the centuries as to materials used and techniques involved in manufacture.

The Spaniards introduced new industries to Mexico, most of which involved the processing of agricultural products or the smelting of ores. Sugar and flour mills were erected over the countryside. Spinning mills processed cotton and wool, and dye factories extracted blue coloring from indigo and red dye from the cochineal or *cochinilla* insect. The process of distillation brought by the Spaniard fostered the establishment of *maguey* distilleries from which came such products as *tequila.* Sugar was distilled into a clear drink, known in Spanish America as *aguardiente.* During the late nineteenth and early twentieth centuries, manufactural industries of some significance were established in the Central Highlands. Foreign investment in these industries was important. Included within the new industries were small steel and other metal foundries, cement plants, cigarette, match, and shoe factories, and breweries.

Manufacturing industries are of increasing importance in the Central Highlands as they are in all of Mexico. Although great new modern factories are rising at certain places throughout the region, age-old craft industries remain important. A resurgence in the handicrafts was initiated in about 1920, when tourists began to come to Mexico in large numbers. There are reportedly some two million persons in all Mexico involved as full-time or part-time laborers in the craft industries. Many of these artisans earn only a precarious living because they are at the mercy of middlemen who market their products. Some sixty-two kinds of *sarapes* (blankets, often worn as clothing) are produced in Mexico, and there are ninety-six kinds of *sombreros* (hats) made by craftsmen in Mexico. Some seven hundred towns and villages are involved in pottery making. The most famous of these places are in the Valley of Atemajac, in which Guadalajara is located. In this valley there are five pottery towns, the most famous of which are Tonalá and Tlaquepaque. In the valley there are reportedly 20,000 workers involved in some way in the pottery industry. At and near La Piedad de Cavadas, located in northwestern Michoacán, there are 7,000 persons engaged in making *rebozos* (women's shawls). At Uruapan and Quiroga, in Michoacán, the townsfolk are famous for their lacquer work, and at Paracho, also in Michoacán, guitars and mandolins are made by craftsmen. At Toluca, wool sweaters, baskets, and cotton clothing are made in handicraft industries. Saltillo, capital of Coahuila, is famous for its *sarapes*. At Puebla pottery, tiles, and objects of onyx are products of craft industries. Glass works, leather works, metal-working shops, and small furniture factories are found at certain places throughout the nation, especially in the central and southern areas. Taxco, in Guerrero, has long been the home of silversmiths. In 1960, it was estimated that 18 per cent of all tourist expenditures in Mexico went to buy goods made by the folk art industries. In that same year, exports of these products were valued at two and one-half million dollars. The United States, Japan, Canada, and even African countries were importers of Mexican craft products. The most important exports have been sombreros, brooms, baskets, and clay articles. As the years go by, craft industries are less orientated toward the making of a great variety of objects for local town and regional use, and more directed toward making fewer products, in special centers of production, for widespread distribution.

Some of the large, important industries in the Central Volcanic Axis are old, but the greater proportion of them have been established since the Mexican Revolution. The textile and paper mills in the Valley of Mexico are old industries, as are the leather works, including shoe factories, at León in Guanajuato State. The *ate* (fruit paste) factories in Morelia and Zamora in Michoacán are other examples of older industries. *Pulque*-making is no longer important except in the states surrounding the Valley of Mexico where there are poor folk who cling to this traditional beverage, and where there are eroded lands on which the government has promoted *maguey*-growing because the crop need not be cultivated as are annual crops. In Jalisco around the town of Tequila, however, the making of *tequila* has continued to flourish, and many fields are planted with the *tequila maguey* plants.

Although the new industries are scattered at places throughout the Central Highlands, their greatest concentration is in, and adjacent to, the Valley of Mexico where 55 per cent of the value of all Mexican industrial production originates. At the northwestern edge of Mexico City there is a large industrial area centered around the town of Tlalnepantla. The new factories of central Mexico produce both new kinds of products and those that have been made in the country for some time. Some of the major consumer goods industries include cigarettes, matches, soap and detergents, clothing, processed foods, soft drinks, and beer. With rising incomes, the latter two industries have grown tremendously to replace traditional drinks concocted in the marketplace. Between 1943 and 1956, beer consumption in Mexico increased by 102 per cent. Light industries which produce for industrial consumers include plate glass, paper, drugs and chemicals, textiles, and cement. New heavy industries in the Central Highlands, most of them located in the Valley of Mexico, include steel production, automobile assembly and production,

all kinds of metal working, rubber tire and other industrial rubber production, and even the manufacture of railroad cars. The rapid growth in the demand for power sources has caused petroleum refineries and electric power plants to rise across the Central Highlands. All cities, and most towns of any size, are now served with electricity.

The concentration of industry in the Valley of Mexico and in nearby areas is likely to continue for many reasons. Power and water are cheaper, and transportation facilities are better, in and around the capital city. More skilled labor and better credit facilities are available in the nation's metropolitan area. A system of centralized administration for government regulation of business also is a strong influence in encouraging industry at the political heart of the nation. If Mexico is to reverse the centralization of industry, the advantages available to industry in the Valley of Mexico must be made accessible in other areas of the nation. This may be accomplished by improving the transportation, credit, and public service facilities of the country, by the training of skilled labor in the hinterlands, and through the decentralization of federal administration to areas outside of the capital city.

CENTRAL HIGHLANDS FORESTRY

Despite the denudation of hillsides for agriculture and firewood that has been going on for centuries, there are still considerable stands of pine in the more inaccessible mountain areas. Mexico now has laws to protect her timber resources, but destructive, illegal cutting is flagrant. To meet the needs of the new industrial Mexico, many of the pine forests are now being commercially exploited. In the Central Highlands commercial cutting is important in Jalisco, Michoacán, and the state of México. In many deforested areas of the Central Highlands grows a plant called zacatón, the roots of which are widely used for brooms and brushes both in Mexico and in the export market.

TOURISM AND COMMUNICATIONS

The impressive scenic beauty and fascinating differences in ways of life in Mexico have attracted droves of tourists southward from the United States. Tourism is now a major source of income. Foreign exchange earned from border transactions with the United States and tourist expenditures in the interior is now equal in value to about two-thirds of the foreign exchange earned from Mexican exports of goods. Border and interior tourist expenditures in Mexico in 196 amounted to some 819 million dollars. In 1962 some 918,000 tourist cards for entry into the interior of the nation were issued to foreigners; and in 1960 there were 61 million border crossings, most of them by Americans. Tourism along the frontier with the United States is much more important than tourism in the interior. Border-transaction earnings are about double tourist expenditures in the interior. Net income to Mexico from tourism and border transactions is, however, only about one-half of total earnings because

Mexican tourists and border residents spend the other half of total earnings abroad, chiefly in the United States. Nevertheless, many tourists, almost all of them Americans, do come to the Central Highlands, mostly by automobile or air. Motels, hotels, restaurants, shops, and many other businesses all profit from the tourist business in the highlands of central Mexico.

The transportation network of the Central Highlands, and other regions of Mexico as well, is much better than that of most of Latin America. There are more paved, and all-weather unpaved, roads in Mexico than in any other Latin American nation. The total length of such roads is three times that in Brazil, a much larger country.

In the past, Indian trade and military operations entailed a widespread network of footpaths over which human porters traveled great distances with heavy loads. There are still villages in Mexico which are connected to the outside world only by the traditional footpath. The mule train became the basic means of transporting goods and persons over the rugged central Mexican countryside during the colonial period. Cart roads were few. Royal roads (*caminos reales*) — usually only trails — crossed the Central Highlands and led out of this region northward to the mining country of the Meseta Central, up the west coast to the Northwest, eastward to the Port of Veracruz, and southward to Guatemala. The China Road connected Mexico City with Acapulco, the port at which exotic goods from the Far East were landed off the famous Manila Galleons. During the latter nineteenth and early twentieth century, railroads were built throughout the Central Highlands and across the mountains from the Gulf to the Pacific sides of the nation. The first railroad in

Mexico connected Mexico City with Veracruz in 1873.

Since the beginning of the Revolution, transportation facilities in, and to and from, the Central Volcanic Axis have improved tremendously. Although little new rail mileage has been constructed, the railroads which serve the Central Highlands still carry much of the freight cargo which moves into and out of the region. The railroads are now owned and operated by the federal government. Since 1910, the trunk rail lines in the Central Highlands have been supplemented by branch lines which connect places of economic importance with the main routes.

The automobile, bus, and truck have transformed the way of life in the Central Highlands by making it possible for farmers and villagers, as well as city folk, to ride to market, to work, or to seek new employment over distances undreamed of only twenty years ago. Moreover, commercial goods now move by truck in and out of what were once remote and isolated places. Automobile roads reach almost all places of any importance in the Central Highlands today. Although some of the roads may be no more than truck and jeep tracks, nevertheless, they serve the countryside and villages far better than did the horse and mule trails.

Four major highways lead northward out of the highlands to the United States boundary, one along the west coast, two up the Meseta Central, and one east of the Eastern Sierra Madre. Paved roads lead southward all the way to Guatemala. The highway to the southwest coast leads to Acapulco, and the highway to the Gulf of Mexico leads to Veracruz. From Veracruz a paved road has just been completed all the way through the tropical forests and swamp lands to Yucatán. By 1960, in all of Mexico there were 25,000 miles of

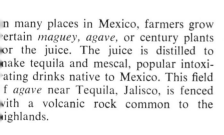

n many places in Mexico, farmers grow ertain *maguey, agave,* or century plants or the juice. The juice is distilled to nake tequila and mescal, popular intoxiating drinks native to Mexico. This field f *agave* near Tequila, Jalisco, is fenced vith a volcanic rock common to the ighlands.

paved and all-weather unpaved roads, and about 80,000 miles of *brechas* or dry-weather roads. One of the outstanding achievements of the governments since the Revolution has been the construction of a modern highway system linking all corners of the nation. As paved roads and city streets have become numerous, a minor revolution in the poor man's means of transportation has been accomplished by the spread of bicycles over the countryside and in the cities. Most of these bicycles are now made in Mexico.

Major Mexican and foreign airlines fly into Mexico City and to some other large cities, and many of the smaller cities and towns are served by local airlines.

CENTRAL HIGHLANDS POPULATION

The Central Highlands constitute, on the whole, the most densely populated part of the nation. Moreover, about one-half of all the Mexican population lives in these highlands (Table VI, below). Among the seven most populous states in Mexico, only Oaxaca does not have all or a large portion of its territory in the Central Volcanic Highlands (Table VI, below). As the more primitive Indians came southward into the highlands and settled there to evolve a sedentary agricultural population, population became much more dense in many of the basins and valleys. At the time of the Spanish conquest, the population of the Central Highlands and adjacent parts of the Meseta Central and Southern Mexico may well have been approximately twenty-five million. However, by 1605, so many Indians had died from introduced European diseases and the disruption of their way of life that perhaps less than ten per cent of the aboriginal population remained. By 1960, the areas which once had contained twenty-five million Indians had a population of about twenty-one million. It may well be that since aboriginal times, these areas have never again been so densely populated.

TABLE VI
MEXICAN POPULATION: 1960

Entity	Population of Entity	Percentage of Mexican Population	Percentage Rural*	Population of Capital and cities over 100,000
MEXICO	34,923,129	100.00	49.30	
Central Highlands	16,845,797	48.26	41.65	
Federal District	4,870,876	13.95	4.39	
Mexico City				2,832,133
Jalisco	2,433,261	6.97	41.48	
Guadalajara				736,800
Puebla	1,973,837	5.66	60.84	
Puebla				289,049
Mexico	1,897,851	5.44	61.39	
Toluca				77,124
Michoacán	1,851,876	5.30	59.40	
Morelia				100,828
Guanajuato	1,735,490	4.97	53.58	
Guanajuato**				28,212
León				209,469
Hidalgo	994,598	2.85	77.59	
Pachuca				64,571
Morelos	386,624	1.11	46.78	
Cuernavaca				37,144
Querétaro	355,045	1.02	71.86	
Querétaro				67,674
Tlaxcala	346,699	.99	56.11	
Txlaxcala				7,545
Meseta Central	6,083,702	17.42	49.75	
Chihuahua	1,226,793	3.51	42.84	
Chihuahua				150,430
Ciudad Juarez				261,683
Nuevo León	1,078,848	3.09	29.64	
Monterrey				596,939
San Luis Potosí	1,048,297	3.00	66.36	
San Luis Potosí				159,980
Coahuila	907,734	2.60	33.25	
Saltillo				98,839
Torreón				179,955
Zacatecas	817,831	2.34	72.82	
Zacatecas				31,701
Durango	760,836	2.18	64.48	
Durango				97,305
Aguascalientes	243,363	.70	40.10	
Aguascalientes				126,617
Gulf Slope	3,752,081	10.75	54.90	
Veracruz	2,727,899	7.81	60.43	
Veracruz				66,296
Tamaulipas	1,024,182	2.94	40.17	
Ciudad Victoria				50,797
Tampico				122,197

Entity	Population of Entity	Percentage of Mexican Population	Percentage Rural*	Population of Capital and cities over 100,000
Southern Mexico	4,289,302	12.29	73.80	
Oaxaca	1,727,266	4.95	75.63	
Oaxaca				72,370
Chiapas	1,210,870	3.47	75.56	
Tuxtla Gutíerrez				41,244
Guerrero	1,186,716	3.40	74.25	
Chilpancingo				18,022
Colima	164,450	.47	38.19	
Colima				43,518
Northwest Mexico	2,613,470	7.48	47.54	
Sinaloa	838,470	2.40	61.80	
Culiacán				85,024
Sonora	783,378	2.24	42.42	
Hermosillo				95,978
Baja California	520,165	1.49	22.32	
Mexicali				174,540
Tijuana				151,939
Nayarit	389,929	1.12	57.36	
Tepic				54,069
Baja California	81,594	.23	63.70	
Territorio Sur				24,253
La Paz				
Southeast Mexico	1,328,777	3.80	53.23	
Yucatán	614,049	1.76	40.20	
Mérida				170,834
Tabasco	496,340	1.42	73.35	
Villahermosa				52,264
Campeche	168,219	.48	36.81	
Campeche				43,874
Quintana Roo	50,169	.14	68.56	
Chetumal				12,852

Sources: Banco Nacional de Comercio Exterior, *México 196.* (Mexico: 1963), p. 90; Dirección General de Esta dística, *Octavo censo general de Población, 1960, resu men general* (México: Talleres Gráficos de la Nación 1962). pp. XLV, 68–69.

*Rural dwellers live in settlements of fewer than 2,501 inhab tants.

**Where two cities are listed in one entity, the capital is give first.

By the nineteenth century, the Mexican population began to grow rapidly, and during that century the number of Mexicans doubled to become about fifteen million by 1910. An even more rapid increase in the Mexican population has taken place in the twentieth century. Between 1910 and 1950, the population of the country grew from fifteen million to twenty-five million, and in the ten years between 1950 and 1960, the population increased to nearly thirty-five million (Table VI, p. 122). All during this evolution of the Mexican population, the Central Highlands have remained the most populated part of the nation.

During the colonial period the Mexican population was changed in composition as Spaniards settled in New Spain, as Negro slaves were introduced into some areas, and as Spanish and Indian blood was mixed to produce a new race, called in Mexico, the *mestizo*. Although *mestizos* outnumber persons of other racial groups in most of Mexico today, the real surge to numerical dominance by the *mestizo* did not occur until after independence came to the nation in the nineteenth century.

The Indian population of Mexico has remained large, especially in the Central Highlands, where about one-fourth of the Indian population of the country lives. In 1960, eight per cent of the Mexican population still could speak Indian tongues, and about 1,100,000 persons were monolingual. Most of the surviving Indian language speakers have changed their way of life in important ways from that of their ancestors, and many of them are not racially Indians anymore. However, their presence is a strong and fascinating reminder of the heritage of the Indian in the Central Highlands.

The *per capita* production in the states within the Central Volcanic Highlands is, in most cases, lower than elsewhere in Mexico, except in some parts of southern Mexico. In spite of much progress, many rural families are still outside the effective national economy. Many persons have little or no formal education. And still confined within the so-called "traditional sector" of the Mexican economy are many rural and village folk who live with their families in one-room homes, do not wear shoes, sleep on mats rather than on beds, and never consume wheat bread.

Many of the important, large urban centers are found in the Central Highlands, although, excluding the Federal District, there are other parts of the nation where a greater proportion of the population lives in cities (Table VI, p. 122). However, only in the last three decades have these highland cities become really large. Although there were some large Indian cities like Teotihuacán and Tenochtitlan, most of the Indians lived in villages. Indian cities were, however, impressive, and the Spaniards have described Tenochtitlan for us as a city of imposing pyramids, plazas, great marketplaces, granaries, and landscaped gardens. Many towns and some cities, often located at centers of Indian population, came into existence during the colonial period and later during the nineteenth century. However, most of these urban centers remained small, so that Mexico until

rather recently could well have been called "a nation of villages." During part of the colonial period, and again for a time in the nineteenth century, towns in Mexico were precisely planned by officials in Spain or Mexico City. Where there was planning, towns were laid out in a grid pattern with a central plaza around which were grouped important buildings, such as the church, the *palacio de gobierno* (government palace), and the better residences and stores of the place. Such remains the pattern of many urban Mexican places today.

About one-third of the Mexican population has made the transition into the so-called "modern sector" of the national economy, and this represents a great stride forward from pre-Revolution days. In the cities a much greater part of the population is so designated; and it is in the urban centers that the growing middle class is concentrated. However, the cities have been faced with the most difficult problem of absorbing great numbers of poor rural folk who have migrated to the urban places when the countryside could not support them. With the huge influx of persons into the cities, the growth of urbanization has been striking. For the first time in the history of census-taking in Mexico, in 1960, it was reported that just over one-half of the population had become urban (Table VI, p. 122).

Most important by far of all the urban centers in the nation is the capital city of Mexico. This great city is the heart of every phase of the Mexican economy. Population growth in Mexico City since the Revolution has made it one of the major cities of the world. In 1887, there were only 230,000 inhabitants in the capital city, and eleven Mexican states had larger populations than the city. By 1910, the population had approximately doubled to 471,000. Between 1950 and 1960, the population increased by some 21 per cent to 2,832,000 in the latter year (Table VI, p. 122). However, the population of the Federal District, over which the city and its suburbs spread, increased by 58 per cent between 1950 and 1960, and the total number of inhabitants by 1960 was 4,870,000. In 1960, the Federal District was twice as populous as any Mexican state, and one-seventh of the total Mexican population lived in the great urban agglomeration in the Valley of Mexico.

Summary

Standing above the rest of Mexico, the cool seasonally moist Central Volcanic Highlands have provided man with the resources of forests, grasslands, lakes, varied wildlife, mineral deposits, and the good earth of basin floors and mountainsides. Through long occupance of these favored highlands, man has left the imprint of his culture nearly everywhere. Impressive Indian ruins, small villages settled into hillsides of which they seem a part, and everpresent fields of corn represent the old. Skyscrapers, long, paved highways, and tractors in the fields represent the new. The vista, whatever it may be, in these ancient lands, represents that which is most Mexican in a given age.

THE MESETA CENTRAL

A vast expanse of dry, interior country slopes downward from the northern edges of the moist volcanic highlands of central Mexico toward the Río Grande and the international boundary between Mexico and the United States. This interior plateau, or *Meseta Central,* is enclosed by the high Eastern and Western Sierra Madres, and is divided by lower mountains into a series of basins. Here the Spanish initiated mining on the mountainsides and livestock grazing on the basin slopes to give character to the land as the richest mining and cattle country of Mexico. The southern reaches of the region lie north of the rich agricultural lands of the Bajío, at the northern edge of the central volcanic mountains, but include the transitional lands of Aguascalientes where history and physical geography seemed weighed in favor of the northern region. Included with the Meseta Central are all, or parts of, the states of Guanajuato, Jalisco, Aguascalientes, Zacatecas, San Luis Potosí, Durango, Chihuahua, Coahuila, Nuevo León, and Tamaulipas (endpaper maps and Map 1).

Physical Geography: MOUNTAINS AND BASINS

One of the outstanding landform features of Mexico is the formidable barrier of the Sierra Madre Occidental, or Western Sierra Madre, which forms the western rim of the Meseta Central. The Sierra Madre rises westward rather like the upturned edge of the Meseta Central but descends precipitously as a great escarpment along much of its Pacific slope. Much of the summit area in these mountains is rolling to nearly level plateau country comprised of volcanic strata. Above the tablelands stand peaks of between 7,000 and 10,000 feet in elevation. The barrier nature of the range results from the high, steep slopes of its edges, especially on the west, and from the highlands having been cut up by streams which flow through deep canyons. Steep, narrow, and long north-south valleys have been eroded downward into strata of rocks weaker than those which cap the summit tablelands. Many of these valleys are along fault traces. To reach the outer edges of the mountains, the streams have had to cut transverse valleys eastward and westward. The most spectacular canyons, or *barrancas,* in the range are those leading westward as part of the Pacific drainage system. Some of these steep-walled chasms are thousands of feet deep, and the country through which they pass is known as the *barranca* country. Most renowned of these canyons is the Barranca de Cobre in southern Chihuahua along the upper edges of which grow needle-leaf evergreens and in the depths of which are tropical flora and fauna (Map 1, page 104).

Throughout most of the history of New Spain and Mexico, the barrier of the Sierra Madre Occidental was pierced only by foot and pack-animal trails leading down to the Pacific coast. Plans for a railroad through the Sierra Madre were made in the 1880's because such

a route would have reduced the distance from Kansas City to the Pacific by 400 to 600 miles. Several attempts to finish this route, known at one time as the Texas, Topolobampo, and Pacific Railroad, were made. However, the line did not actually go into operation until 1962. Several years before this, a paved highway was completed through the Sierra Madre from Durango to Mazatlán on the Pacific.

The Sierra Madre Occidental is of great significance to the lowland irrigation districts both west and east of the range because in the moist highlands rise the rivers which supply irrigation water to the desert and semiarid country below. On the west, the rivers include the Yaqui, Mayo, and Fuerte, and on the east are the Conchos, Nazas, and Aguanaval.

The barrier nature of the Sierra Madre has made it important as a refuge for some of the few surviving Indians in the *mestizo* north country. Among the Indian groups in the mountains, from north to south, are the Tarahumara, Tepehuán, Huichol, and Cora.

East of the Meseta Central the Sierra Madre Oriental, or Eastern Sierra Madre, extends as a continuous range from the Central Volcanic Highlands northward to the city of Monterrey. That city is located on the route which leads around the northern end of the sierra to the Gulf of Mexico coast. Beyond Monterrey the mountains extend as a discontinuous belt of desert ranges northwestward into the United States. The Sierra Madre Oriental consists of folded sedimentary rocks, largely limestone, with deep north-south valleys between the ridges. These are high mountains; the summit of Cerro Peña Nevada, west of Ciudad Victoria, is 13,300 feet in elevation. In the southern part of the range, deep gorges, which are part of the Pánuco River drainage system, run eastward to the sea. However, this range has not been as great a natural barrier as has the Sierra Madre Occidental.

There is a railroad through the mountains which leads from San Luis Potosí to Tampico on the Gulf of Mexico. A highway also follows this route. Farther south a highway leads from Pachuca, on the northwestern edge of the Central Highlands, through the Sierra Madre Oriental to Tuxpán on the Gulf coast. Many Indians survive in the southern part of the range, although their lands are no longer so isolated as they were twenty-five years ago.

On the Meseta Central, individual basins are separated from one another by mountains which, in general, extend in a northwest-southeast direction (Map 1, page 104). The basins are higher in the south than in the north. Zacatecas is located at an elevation of 8,500 feet above sea level; Durango at 6,000 feet in elevation; Saltillo, in eastern Coahuila, at 5,200 feet above the sea; Chihuahua City at 4,668 feet in elevation and Juárez, on the south bank of the Río Grande, is only 3,700 feet above sea level. On most of the Meseta Central there are isolated fault block mountain ranges, the bases of which are buried in deep mineral-rich alluvium. The large basins filled with the alluvium are called *bolsones*. Most famous of these basins are the Bolsón de Mayrán, east of Torreón, and the Bolsón de Mapimí, northwest of that city (Map 1, p. 104).

Some streams which flow through the basins of the Meseta Central reach the sea as tributaries of larger rivers. However, many of the streams flow into basins of interior drainage where their waters, if not utilized for irrigation, run into the sands or into saline lakes. In the north, three important rivers descend from the Western Sierra Madre into the Meseta Central. The waters of the Río Conchos, in Chihuahua, reach the sea by way of the Río Grande, or Río Bravo as the Mexicans call it (Map 1, p. 104). The Río Nazas and the Río Aguanaval, however, flow down into the low area at the juncture of the Bolsón de Mapimí and the Bolsón de Mayrán where their waters are used to irrigate crops in the Laguna District. In the northeast, a few rivers, such as the Salado, flow out of the desert ranges into the Río Bravo. In the southern part of the Meseta Central, some rivers flow southward to join the Lerma-Santiago system which leads to the Pacific Ocean around the southern end of the Western Sierra Madre.

DRY COUNTRY AND ITS EDGES

Except in areas along the fringes of the mountains at the southern end of the Meseta Central, the climate is either semiarid or arid. In Mexico only about 10 per cent of the total area has sufficient rainfall to grow crops throughout most of the year. Most of the Meseta Central lies within the 50 per cent of all Mexico where rainfall is deficient throughout the year.

The Central Plateau is cut off on both the east and the west from moist air masses coming from the Gulf of Mexico or the Pacific Ocean. However, during the summer, some moist air from the seas is pushed inland over the hot country from areas of higher pressure over the water. As in all of the nation, except the far northwest, summer is the season of maximum precipitation (see Table I, p. 109). During the winter, polar fronts occasionally cross the region and bring some rainfall or, in the higher mountains, snowfall. Rainfall decreases from the higher southern part of the region toward the north, and inward toward the central part of the plateau from the bordering Eastern and Western Sierra Madres. At Aguascalientes, in the south, average annual precipitation is 22 inches, while in the Bolsón de Mapimí in the Laguna irrigation district, at Matamoros, Coahuila, near Torreón, the average annual rainfall is only nine inches (Map 2, Table I, pp. 108-09). On the higher, outer edges of the Meseta Central, as at Chihuahua City on the west, and San Luis Potosí, on the east, average annual rainfall is about 15 inches. The rainfall barriers presented by the mountains which border the Meseta Central are well demonstrated by the contrast in annual precipitation at San Luis Potosí, on the inland side of the Eastern Sierra Madre, and at Xilitla, just north of Tamazunchale along the Pan-American highway on the windward side of the Sierra Madre, in southeastern San Luis Potosí state. At the latter place, annual rainfall is nearly 100 inches (Map 2, Table I, pp. 108-09). In the Sierra Madres, summer rains and

winter snows may equal up to 30 to 60 inches of annual precipitation. At Creel, on the Chihuahua-Pacífico Railroad in the Sierra Madre Occidental, yearly precipitation is about 28 inches. Along the Durango-Mazatlán highway at El Salto, annual precipitation is 36 inches.

Average monthly summer temperatures in the basins of the north are high (in the low 80's), and during the day the temperatures may rise to over 100 degrees. In the higher country on the edges of the central basins, or south of them, summer temperatures are about 10 degrees cooler than in the hot, lower areas (see Table I, p. 109). Winters are moderate except when the cold air of the *nortes* sweeps down from the higher latitudes of North America. In the surrounding mountains, winter months are cold.

The vegetation of the dryer, lower parts of the Meseta Central is desert scrub (Map 3, p. 110). Creosote bush, yucca, mesquite, and prickly pear cactus are common plants in the desert scrub plant association. A plant called *candelilla* is collected in the deserts of the Meseta Central for the wax it secretes. *Candelilla* wax exports form a marginal supplement to the incomes of poor rural folk. Vegetation on the moister edges of the Meseta Central is mesquite-grassland in which gramma grasses are common. On the lower, dryer slopes of the mountains, oaks, junipers, and piñon pines may be found growing alongside *agaves* (century plants). In the higher mountains there are large pine and oak forests surrounding mountain meadows, while in the highest places, fir trees and aspens grow. In the Western Sierra Madre, Chihuahua pine, Arizona pine, limber pine, and Lumholtz pine, or *pino triste,* are the common conifers in the north, and montezuma pine is common in the south. White pine, known as *ayacahuite* or *pinabete,* extends from Chihuahua southward through the Mexican highlands to Guatemala. Cypress trees also grow on the mountain slopes ringing the Meseta Central.

Wildlife survives in abundance in parts of the Meseta Central because there have not been great numbers of hunters in such areas as the great tracts of uninhabited desert, the desert mountain ranges, and the higher areas of the Eastern and Western Sierra Madres. In the desert and semiarid country, lizards, snakes and rodents are common. In these lands dwell also quail, doves, rabbits, foxes, ringtail cats, raccoons, badgers, and skunks. Predators found here are the coyote, puma or mountain lion, and bobcat. Large game animals are the collared peccary and white-tailed deer. The Mexican black mallard lives in Chihuahua and Durango, and migratory ducks and geese fly southward to and across this land in winter.

In the higher country of the two bordering sierras and of some of the desert ranges, in addition to some of the species found on the desert, such as the puma, bobcat and coyote, there are also wild turkeys, squirrels, and coatimundis. In the Eastern Sierra Madre the armadillo extends its range northward. Wolves inhabit the Western Sierra Madre and the desert ranges of Coahuila. The black bear lives in the Sierra Madres and in some of the desert ranges. In the most northern desert ranges and in the Sierra Madre Occidental, there are mule deer. The last strongholds of the grizzly bear in Mexico are in the mountain ranges, some fifty miles north of the city of Chihuahua. The bighorn sheep lives in the mountains of the northernmost part of the desert. On the plains of northwestern Chihuahua and out on the desert of the Bolsón of Mapimí, there are still herds of antelope. The wildlife of Meseta Central supplies a certain amount of the food of the local rural folk. Goat herders often carry an ancient shotgun in the hope of shooting a quail, dove, or squirrel for the evening meal. The game also attracts Mexican and American sportsmen to the less well-hunted areas.

Cultural Geography

It was mining that first attracted the Spaniards northward from the Central Highlands onto the Meseta Central where there lived wild and hostile Indians who were mostly hunters and gatherers known collectively as the Chichimecas. The Spaniards did not break through into the Chichimeca country until 1541 when several groups of Chichimeca Indians were defeated in the Mixtón War north of Guadalajara. Throughout most of the history of New Spain and Mexico, much of the Meseta Central has been a frontier land. On this frontier, unions between Spanish miners, ranchers, farmers, and soldiers and the local Indians, and gangs of highland Indians and Negro slaves brought northward to work the mines, created a population which today is almost entirely *mestizo*. Much of the semiarid and desert country in the far north of the Meseta Central was so scantily populated by Mexicans that it was lost to the United States when American frontiersmen moved westward into the ill-defined border zone.

HISTORY OF MINING

After the Mixtón War, the Spanish miners moved quickly northward along the eastern edges of the Sierra Madre Occidental and the western edges of the Sierra Madre Oriental to establish flourishing mining towns. Mining camps sprang up in the high country of the Sierra Madre Occidental. Zacatecas, Guanajuato, Sombrerete, Aguascalientes, Durango, Santa Bárbara, Parral, Chihuahua, and San Luis Potosí all began as important Spanish towns at or near mines. North of the Central Highlands ore veins are, in most cases, not covered with the basaltic volcanics. The fabulous veins which are exposed in shaley sediments at Guanajuato made that city the richest mining community in the colonial New World. Moreover, mineralization of other kinds is common on the Meseta Central. Vast low-grade deposits of ore-bearing rocks were created, as replacement mineralization took place where beds of limestone were followed by mineral solutions which replaced the limestone. In other places, deposits occur as contact metamorphic mineralization where molten rocks welled up from great depth and made contact with overlying rocks to create great irregular mineralized areas along the zones of contact.

In the Sierra Madre Occidental, veins at great depth were discovered in such abysmal canyons as that of the Urique River (Barranca de Cobre) where silver, lead, zinc, and iron are all exposed in slates. Spanish miners preceded our modern "explorers" into this great *barranca* by centuries. The famous silver mines at Batopilas, Chihuahua, were discovered in a nearby deep canyon. Other veins in volcanic rhyolites are at less depth in the Sierra Madre.

The value of silver was much greater than that of other minerals exploited, but gold mining was also important in the Sierra Madre Occidental. By the eighteenth century, many of the high-grade ores had been worked out. However, in the latter decades of the nineteenth century, industrial minerals increased in value relative to precious metals. During the reign of the dictator-president Porfirio Díaz, foreign mining companies, chiefly American and British, brought new equipment and techniques to mining in Mexico. Mining of industrial, as well as precious minerals, was given new impetus and the mines of the Meseta Central and Sierra Madre Occidental again boomed.

As in the past, the Meseta Central is still the most important mining region in Mexico. Although silver mining remains important and Mexico remains the most important producer of silver in the world, silver is often extracted from the same ores as lead and zinc, both of which are produced in far greater quantity than silver (Table V, A, p. 119). Much of the mineral production is exported. Near Durango, silver, lead, gold, and iron are all mined. At San Luis Potosí, lead, zinc, and silver are mined. The United States obtains considerable amounts of its antimony imports from mines near San Luis Potosí. Near Fresnillo, in Zacatecas state, silver and lead are mined. At Guanajuato, the federal government has assumed control of the old, nearly exhausted mines in order to maintain employment in a marginal business. In Coahuila, at Sabinas and Lampazos, the coal for the steel industry at Monterrey is mined. Formerly these coal fields were more important suppliers of fuel for Mexican railroads than they are in this age of diesel locomotives. The state which leads all others in Mexico in the production of metallic minerals is Chihuahua where lead, zinc, silver, and gold are mined. All of the large ore smelters, *fundiciones,* of Mexico are located on the Meseta Central except two copper smelters in the Northwest. Large smelters are located at Chihuahua City; Monterrey; Piedras Negras, Monclova, and Las Rosita in Coahuila; Torreón; and San Luis Potosí. Ores or concentrates from mines in other regions of the nation are often transported over long, circuitous routes to the large smelters of the Meseta Central. With the exception of the steel smelters, most of these *fundiciones* represent large foreign investments in Mexico.

The mines that once produced a large share of the wealth of New Spain and Mexico, and most of the value of exports, now employ only a small portion of the labor force and contribute only about two per cent of the gross national product. Agricultural products

Guanajuato on the Meseta Central was the richest mining community in the colonial New World. Located in the high country of the Sierra Madre Occidental, today Guanajuato is a picturesque town often visited by tourists. The federal government has taken over the old and nearly exhausted mines to help maintain employment in a marginal business.

have overtaken minerals as the most important exports of Mexico. In order of percentage of the total value of production, the most important minerals in Mexico are petroleum, zinc, lead, silver, copper, sulphur, iron, gold, coal and manganese (Table V, A, page 119). With the exception of iron, gold, and coal, all of these minerals are exports, as are also antimony and tungsten. Mineral trade is chiefly with the United States. The future of petroleum and sulphur mining in Mexico is promising because of the large internal demand for oil and the good export market for sulphur. However, the future of mining of some metallic minerals is not bright unless larger internal demand can be stimulated, and mining methods, as well as mining laws, modernized.

LEADING LIVESTOCK REGION

As the Spanish mines were opened on and along the edges of the Meseta Central, ranches and livestock haciendas, some of which were huge, became established on the vast tracts of dry countryside. It was, in fact, in this north country that the great Mexican hacienda had its genesis. The haciendas supplied meat, wool, horses and mules, hides, and tallow to the mining centers and the markets in the Central Highlands. In the nineteenth century some of the ranches became as large as European kingdoms, and many were owned by foreigners.

Within the states on the Meseta Central, the value of livestock is greater than in any other region. Cattle are most important. Since the days when the Spanish introduced cattle onto the vast ranges, the numbers and quality of the animals have increased greatly. Many of the cattle in the northern tier of Mexican states are high-grade beef breeds, among which the Hereford is most important. Much of the cattle production is exported to the United States. With the exception of Sonora, across the Sierra Madre Occidental on the Pacific slope, the northern states of the Meseta Central contribute almost all of the export cattle to the nation's foreign trade. In fact, by federal law, the 350,000 to

500,000 live cattle that are included within the annual export quotas may legally come only from the Mexican states along the international border with the United States, or from Durango or Baja California Sur. Other Mexican cattle are reserved for home consumption. The export quota law respects the long established trade in cattle along the international frontier.

When foot-and-mouth disease struck Mexico in 1946, the export trade was shut off by the United States government, although the disease never reached the northern exporting states. To remedy this great loss in income, meat-canning plants were established in some of the northern cities; for the cooked, canned meat could not spread the disease. Much of the canned meat was exported to Western Europe as part of the Marshall Plan aid. Today some of these canning plants are closed, and the flow of live cattle across the boundary into the United States has been resumed since 1954.

Not only on the Meseta Central, but in the nation, cattle are the most valuable livestock. The value of annual production from nearly 25 million cattle in Mexico constitutes 70 per cent of the value of production from all Mexican livestock (Table III, p. 113). According to value of production, horses, burros, and mules follow cattle. These riding, draft, and pack animals are still important in a nation in which mechanization in many rural areas is only beginning. Swine are rapidly increasing in number and value as the feeding of these animals on scientific diets increases. Pork products from the large-scale, modern pig farms provide the best meat consistently available in Mexican cities. Goats, many of which are milked, are more numerous in Mexico than any other livestock except cattle and swine. Found everywhere in the country, goats are easy to keep, can browse on inferior range land, and thus are useful to the poor folk. Sheep and their wool are important in parts of the Central Highlands and in the mountains and basins of the Meseta Central. However, as the northern lands of Mexico are no longer the great sheep country of the New World — as they were during the colonial period — much wool must be imported. Poultry farms have increased greatly in importance in the last several years, and imports of chickens and eggs have been reduced as part of a government program to promote domestic production. However, the indigenous turkey has to be imported in significant quantities from the United States during holiday seasons. As during and since aboriginal times, beekeeping, especially in the Central Highlands and in the tropics of Veracruz and Yucatán, is important on farms and in towns, and honey is a major Mexican export.

The future of the livestock industry in Mexico portends shifts away from the raising of riding, pack, and draft animals, and the increased production of high-grade livestock for domestic food consumption and export. Already there are many large chicken and pig farms near cities and in some of the rich farming districts. Cattle feeding is largely unknown, but is beginning around some of the northern cities. Although the great tracts of uncultivable land, which exist on the Meseta Central and in other parts of the nation, will remain as important ranges, the greatest promise for the expansion of the livestock industry seems to lie in the intensive production of meat, milk, and eggs on animal farms.

FARMING AND FORESTRY

Farmers followed the miners northward onto the Meseta Central. In the moister southern part of the plateau, dry-farming was initiated, and small areas of irrigation farming were established in the deserts. Late in the nineteenth century some large irrigation projects were undertaken, and much farmland was acquired by foreigners.

Agriculture on the Meseta Central experienced a great increase in crop area and a great change in land ownership after the Mexican Revolution began in 1910. Irrigation districts were established or increased in size. The most important irrigated areas have become those of the Laguna District around Torreón, those along the Río Conchos of Chihuahua, those along the Río San Juan in Nuevo León and Tamaulipas, and those on the south bank of the lower Río Bravo (Map 1). Corn and beans remain important crops in the southern part of the Meseta Central, but in the north, especially in the cities, the people have become essentially wheat eaters. The two great commercial crops are among the four most important crops in Mexico — not the corn and beans of the Central Highlands — but wheat and cotton (Table II, page 111), the latter raised almost entirely for export to Europe or Japan. Market vegetables have increased greatly in area of production and are sold in Mexican cities, or in the United States. Potatoes are a crop of increasing importance. Alfalfa and other animal feeds are important because of the large livestock industry of the north. Thus, throughout much of the Meseta Central, the traditional Mexican crop patterns have been greatly altered. Around Mon-

terrey, the old orange groves are still in production, and in the south, in Aguascalientes and Zacatecas, the commercial production of chiles is more important than anywhere else in Mexico.

Land reform on the Meseta Central has not been as far-reaching as in the more southern parts of Mexico. As the region was one of important commercial agricultural and livestock production, in most cases, there was no effective way in which the large farms and ranches could be redistributed without greatly disrupting production, some of which was badly needed to earn foreign exchange through export. Moreover, there were fewer landless farmers in the north country, and in some cases there were no villages on or near the great ranches among which the land could have been divided. In many cases the nature of the crop or livestock production required a large-scale operation. Finally, a great many of the northerners were opposed to communal land tenure. Although there are ejidos on the Meseta Central, most of the agricultural and ranch land is held under private ownership. Some of the ranches are very large, and many of the farms are of the maximum, or larger than maximum, size permitted under ordinary circumstances. Some of these properties are held legally under the protection of special laws, but others are held extra-legally.

In the Laguna District of irrigated agriculture one of the experiments in collective farming on ejidos has been carried out. Since the expropriation of the private lands in 1936 the collective ejidos around Torreón have suffered many organizational and production problems. One of the problems has been the reassignment of ejido lands, by their holders, to private operators in contravention of the law. However, in the last several years there seem to have been adjustments made in the organization of the Laguna ejidos, and production is apparently on the upswing.

Since the Second World War, several of the large cattle ranches in the northern part of Mexico have been expropriated and divided among landless families. Some of these ranches were owned by Americans. In at least one case the foreign-owned ranch was within sixty-two miles (100 kilometers) of the international boundary, a location prohibited, along with the foreign ownership of real estate within thirty-one miles (50 km.) of the sea, by Article 17 of the Mexican Constitution of 1917.

From the forests of the Sierra Madre Occidental comes the greater part of the nation's timber production. Chihuahua and Durango alone account for one-half of all timber production in Mexico.

TRANSPORTATION AND TRADE

The great distances up and down and across the Meseta Central over which goods and people moved during the colonial period, and until toward the end of the nineteenth century, were covered by mule trains and wagons. These slow and often punishing means of transport were augmented in the late nineteenth century by the construction of some of the first railroad

In the frontier-like north of the Meseta Central, vast stretches of countryside gave rise in colonial times to the Mexican hacienda, which supplied meat, wool, horses, mules, hides, and tallow to mining centers and urban markets. The kingdom-size ranches of the nineteenth century are now rare, but much land is still privately owned, although holdings may be modest and equipment primitive.

lines in Mexico. These tracks ran between the United States and Mexico City along the eastern and western sides of the Meseta Central. As mining recovered, much of the rail freight became ores, mineral concentrates and metals, especially on the feeder lines built into the mountains.

The modern transportation network of the Meseta Central includes the long rail lines established prior to the Revolution, and several shorter new lines. Most important in railroad development has been the completion in 1962 of the Chihuahua-Pacific Railroad by which the Meseta Central is linked to the markets and supplies across the Western Sierra Madre on the Pacific slope. This railroad passes through some of the breathtaking *barranca* and high pine country of the Sierra Madre, and an American tourist trade of considerable size has developed between Ojinaga, on the Texas boundary, and Los Mochis, near the Pacific shore.

Paved highways and lesser roads are extensive on the Meseta Central. Agricultural areas are served by secondary paved roads, and three of the four paved highways between the United States and Mexico City enter Mexico by crossing the Río Grande. The oldest is the Pan American Highway which connects Laredo with Monterrey before heading east of the Sierra Madre Oriental. Another paved highway enters Mexico at Juárez and runs along the foothills of the Sierra Madre Occidental to reach the Central Highlands. The third, the newest and fastest north-south trunk highway, enters Mexico at Piedras Negras and passes through Saltillo, San Luis Potosí, and Querétaro, along the eastern side of the Meseta Central, on the way to Mexico City.

East-west paved highways connect the north-south highways between Saltillo, Torreón, and towns to the west, and at several places south of San Luis Potosí. Surfaced dirt roads and automobile tracks lead to almost all communities of significance. Thus, on the Meseta Central, trucks have all but replaced mule trains, even in out of the way areas.

The port at Brownsville, Texas, serves the northern Meseta Central as a two-way window for international trade. Cotton and some of the mineral products of the region are exported from that American port through which they move, under bond, duty-free. However, the Mexican government now has plans underway to develop a port across the Río Bravo from Brownsville at the Mexican town of Matamoros. Out of Matamoros would move not only cotton and mineral products from the Meseta Central, but also oil from fields near the Gulf Coast. Moreover, by linking the new port with Monterrey by a new highway, it is hoped that some of the manufactured products of that industrial city could be shipped to world markets, especially those in the Latin American Free Trade Association (ALALC) of which Mexico is a member. When completed, the port may become the second most important in Mexico, exceeded in significance only by the port of Veracruz.

INDUSTRY IMPORTANT

Industry has long been important at places on the Meseta Central. Early in the colonial period, smelting, metal working, and craft industries grew up around the mines. In the late nineteenth century, iron from

Durango and coal from around Sabinas and Lampazos in Coahuila were combined at Monterrey in a steel industry, and the processing of wheat and cotton began on a large scale in agricultural areas.

A good transportation system and increasing consumer demands have contributed to the growth of industry in the region of the Meseta Central. Monterrey is second only to Mexico City in concentration of industry in the nation. The steel mills of Mexico are still mostly at Monterrey and north of there. At Monclova and Piedras Negras, both in Coahuila, there are steel mills. In the last two decades, the Mexican steel industry has grown rapidly. Since 1945, in none of the significant steel producing nations of the world has the rate of increase in steel production equaled Mexico's. Between 1958 and 1963, Mexican steel production doubled. By 1963, the nation had a production of a little over two million metric tons, and was second only to Brazil in steel production in Latin America. However, *per capita* production in Mexico exceeds that of Brazil. In 1963, for the first time there were no net imports of steel into Mexico — that is to say — steel exports equaled imports. Breweries and cigarette factories are important in Monterrey. New metal-working industries in Monterrey provide durable consumer goods for Mexico's growing middle class. At Saltillo and near Monterrey, there are branch factories of American agricultural machinery companies. In many other towns and cities of the Meseta Central, there are manufacturing industries which have been established since the beginning of the Mexican Revolution.

A PROSPEROUS REGION

On the Meseta Central, where the *mestizo* population was Spanish-speaking and had already taken considerable part in the modernization of Mexico, the Revolution changed the way of life more than it did in parts of backward Indian Mexico of the south. The gap between the urban industrial worker of Monterrey and the backward farmer of the central and southern mountains was widened by the effects of the Revolution. As the factors of production were set free to seek new and increased employment in the north country, industrial and rural production rose rapidly. All of the northernmost Mexican states were members of this prosperous part of the nation. The rapid growth of cities has accompanied industrialization on the Meseta Central. Monterrey, Ciudad Juárez, Torreón, and San Luis Potosí are among the larger cities of Mexico (Table VI, page 122).

The people of the Meseta Central have lived in a frontier society, and they have had the industriousness, energies, and adaptability often found in such a group. Moreover, the northerners have lived in close contact with the culture of North Americans from which they have borrowed, and to which they have given, ideas. Little of the conservatism of the Indian has remained in the Spanish-speaking *mestizo* of the north country.

Differences in the culture of the northern Meseta Central from that of central and southern Mexico are

many. The standard of living is considerably higher than to the south and is the highest in all Mexico, with the exception of the northwestern areas on the Baja California Peninsula and in Sonora. The population is more urban than in other parts of the nation where so many families depend on the low productivity of traditional agriculture. Agriculture is mechanized on the large *ejidos* and private farms. Manufacturing industries are common. The man of the central north eats wheat bread and considerable quantities of beef. He wears factory-made shoes, blue denims and often a *tajano*, or felt cowboy hat. He sleeps in a bed, and unless he is out on the more rugged parts of the range, he rides about in an automobile, truck, jeep, or bus. Although his way of life is becoming more common in other parts of the nation, his own land remains one of the two most prosperous modern regions in Mexico.

THE GULF SLOPE

The Gulf Slope Region is a land of steep mountain slopes and humid, tropical mountain valleys facing eastward toward a coastal plain which is crossed at places by broad river valleys. The region is not more than one hundred miles in breadth at the widest place. Almost all of the large state of Veracruz and some of the eastern part of another large state, Tamaulipas, are included in this region which extends for some six hundred miles in a north-south direction (endpaper map and Map 1, page 104).

Physical Geography

The east-facing Gulf Coastal Plain extends through the region from the Río Bravo on the north to the Isthmus of Tehuantepec on the south. Mountain promontories extend eastward from the main range across the narrow coastal plain in many places. In the north the plain is wider than in the middle section of the region, and along the seacoast there are lagoons protected from the sea by offshore sandbars extending for many miles. In the southern part of the region, the plain widens again, but there the volcanic mountain mass of Los Tuxtlas rises up off the hot plain along the seashore (Map 1, page 104). This cluster of volcanic cones extends upwards into the *tierra templada* to elevations of just over 6,000 feet. Broad rivers which rise in the moist highlands to the west, wind across the coastal plain through floodplains covered with swamps or tropical grasslands and forests. In the north, the Río Pánuco reaches the sea at Tampico while in the south the courses of the Papaloapan-San Juan and Coatzacoalcos river systems meander across the low plain.

Except in the most northern part of the region in Tamaulipas, the coastal plain is faced on the west by mountains which rise abruptly from the lowlands. The northern highlands are the eastern slopes of the Sierra Madre Oriental. Deep gorges cut by the rivers of the Pánuco system are incised into these mountains.

The highlands which face the coastal plain in the middle part of Veracruz state are the eastern edges of the Central Highlands. Rising upward above fertile mountain valleys along the eastern slopes of these highlands are volcanic cones such as Orizaba, or Citlaltépetl, and Nauhcampatépetl or Cofre de Perote. A continuation of the Sierra Madre Oriental, south of the area where the volcanic materials of the Central Highlands have been extruded over the surface, is the Sierra Madre de Oaxaca. In these moist uplands, composed chiefly of limestones and other folded and faulted rocks, the deep valleys of the Papaloapan-San Juan river systems have been cut headward back into the rough mountain country of Oaxaca. Except where petroleum and sulphur deposits are located on the coastal plain, or where important ports have developed, most of the population is concentrated in the *tierra templada* on the slopes and in the valleys of the east-facing mountains, or in the Los Tuxtlas mountains.

Rainfall, which comes mostly in the summer, is lowest along the northern coastal plain where average annual precipitation is between 20 and 30 inches (Map 2, page 108). Inland at Ciudad Victoria, on the Pan-American Highway in Tamaulipas, where the elevation is about 1,000 feet, annual rainfall is 36 inches (Table I, page 109). Throughout the lowlands of the region, average monthly summer temperatures are in the low 80's, but average monthly winter temperatures vary from the low 60's in the north to the low 70's in the rest of the region (Table I, p. 109). The high evaporation rates present during the period of summer rainfall are reflected in the acacia-grassland vegetation which covers the semiarid country of the northern coastal plain (Map 3, p. 110). In the coastal and lower mountain areas north and south of Tampico, average annual rainfall increases to between 30 and 50 inches. Although evaporation is still intense, the increased rainfall brings a vegetation response of tropical thorn forest. Thorny leguminous trees, such as acacia and mesquite, are dominant in this forest in which most of the trees lose their leaves in the dry winter. On the mountain slopes above the thorn forest, where temperatures are lower and rainfall greater, there are tropical deciduous forests of low, stocky, broadleaf trees in rather open stands.

South of the dryer northern country, throughout most of the lowlands of Veracruz state, average annual rainfall is between 50 and 70 inches (Table I, 20). In the lowlands, where moist air decreases the effectiveness of the sun's rays, summer temperatures are several degrees lower than in the dryer lands to the north, but winters are warmer. Relative humidity is high during the summer, and thus summer days may be uncomfortable. In this lowland *tierra caliente* country, the vegetation is tropical broadleaf evergreen forest.

In the lowlands of the most southern part of Veracruz state, average annual rainfall rises to between 80 and 120 inches (Table I, 21). This is one of the few parts of Mexico where rainfall is dependable from year to year. Thus, the region has a good potential as a place for hydroelectric power development and irrigation during the rather dry winter season. Great tropical rain forests extend into this southern part of the region from the southeast. On the coastal plain of the south there are also vast areas of tall, tropical savanna grasslands (Map 3, page 110). These grasslands probably do not reflect climatic conditions, but poor soil drainage, or hundreds of years of burning by hunting Indians or Spanish and Mexican ranchers.

The mountain backdrop to the coastal plain is struck by the trade winds which bring heavy rainfall to the highland slopes (Map 2, p. 108). At Córdoba average annual rainfall is about 90 inches and at Xilitla, in eastern San Luis Potosí state, nearly 100 inches (Table I, p. 109). In this *tierra templada* country, summer and winter temperatures are about ten degrees lower than in the lowlands near Veracruz City, and the climate is comfortable the year around. The tropical evergreen forest here is mingled, at its upper levels, with the species of the oak-pine forests of the Central Highlands.

On the wettest, high mountain slopes above the tropical evergreen forest, annual rainfall rises as high as 150 to 200 inches. The runoff created by such copious rainfall forms the great rivers which cross the lowlands to the east of the mountains. In this high, wet country, grow luxuriant cloud forests which are above 5,000 feet in elevation on the east-facing slopes where the mountain lands are constantly blanketed by moist air masses from the Gulf of Mexico (Map 3, p. 110). The dominant tree species in this wet, cool country are those of temperate regions, such as the pine, oak, gum, beech, tupelo, basswood and dogwood of Appalachian flora. Mingled with the temperate species are giant ferns, begonias, bromeliads, orchids, and lianas of the tropical flora.

In the tropical parts of the region, heavy rainfall percolates downward through the soil. Aided by high temperatures and the presence of acids, the water carries away soluble matter, calcium, other base minerals, and nitrates, in a process called leaching. Thus, the tropical soils are deficient in the assimilable plant nutrients necessary to the growth of many crops. These soils of the hot, wet country are acidic in chemical reaction and contain much iron and aluminum. It is from their high iron content that the tropical soils acquire their red or yellow cast.

Organic matter that falls to the ground from the forests becomes humus when acted upon by bacteria in the soil. The humus adds nitrogen to the soil, and also makes the soil friable so that the ground may be tilled easily. However, tropical soils are usually low in humus because soil bacteria are so active in the warm, moist ground that decomposition of organic matter is very rapid.

Under ordinary circumstances, when tropical forests are cleared for cultivation, the soils deteriorate rapidly. The leaching process is accentuated when the forest cover has been removed, and thus the loss of plant nutrients is accelerated. Exposure of the ground to the heavy rains and intense heat from sunshine also causes accelerated decomposition of humus in the soil and the removal of organic matter from the surface through runoff. With the removal of humus, the ground becomes compact and difficult to till, and the soils are deprived of nitrogen. Thus, unless special farming techniques are employed, soon after the tropical forests have been cleared away, soil fertility for ordinary shallow-rooted crops begins to decrease rapidly.

Not all soils in the region are as infertile as those which have developed in place under the rainy, hot conditions in most of the forest lands. Where rich alluvium has been transported downstream year after year to be spread out over flood plains, the soils may be very rich. Also, in some of the highlands, where soils are derived from volcanic materials, the land may be much more fertile than it is throughout much of the region.

Wildlife in the Gulf Slope region is abundant. Many species that are found elsewhere in Mexico are numerous in the region, and the tropical forests and grasslands are the habitats of many animals found only in the tropical, southern parts of the nation.

Among the birds that are found elsewhere in the country are migratory ducks and geese, tree ducks, the muscovy duck, and pigeons and doves. Mammals which also have habitats in other parts of Mexico include opossums, the armadillo, squirrels, the coyote, the gray fox, a ringtailed cat, the raccoon, the coatimundi, the collared peccary, the white-tailed deer, and three cats — the puma, the jaguar, and the ocelot.

The tropical forests and savannas are the homes of many species which are either not found or not numerous in cooler or dryer parts of Mexico. Tropical birds include the tinamous, which scurry about on the forest floor and fly only when flushed; macaws, parrots, the fowl-like curassow, the crested guan, and the *chacalaca*. In the coastal area of Tamaulipas live wild turkeys. Included within the abundant mammalian life of the tropical lands, especially in the southernmost part of the region, are howler and spider monkeys, and the white-lipped peccary, Other tropical mammals are the anteater, tropical forest rabbit, and porcupine. Especially important as game animals are the forest rodents from South America, the *tepescuintle*, or paca or cavie, and the agouti. Two small cats inhabit the tropical forest lands, the margay cat and the jaguarundi. In the trees dwells the kinkajou, or *martucha*, a wide-eyed, long-tailed small nocturnal animal which is much valued as a pet by the people of the forest lands. The smallest North American deer, the brocket deer, or *temazate*, inhabits the wet forest lands. Together the head and body of this reddish-brown deer are only some three to four feet long. Although the brocket deer is hunted intensively, it continues to survive because the forest floor provides such a good cover for this furtive creature.

Reptiles are numerous in the region. Alligators, snakes, iguanas, and turtles all inhabit the rivers and forests. Along the shores of the Gulf of Mexico are a variety of warm water game fish including red snapper, or *huachinango*, (jewfish) or *mero*, and pampano.

Cultural Geography

The east-facing mountain slopes and plains below which border the Gulf of Mexico, constitute an important part of the Mexican nation today, but these land went largely undeveloped by Spaniard or Mexican until the latter nineteenth century. Although Cortés landed at Veracruz, the Spaniards moved up into the Central Highlands and north and south of those mountain where they were able to find Indian labor, minerals and climates more suitable for their crops and livestock. Many Indians in the tropical forests had little contact with the Spaniards, and the Indian population of the region is still large today.

CULTIVATION OF THE LAND

Since man learned the art of cultivation, agriculture has always been the dominant basis of livelihood in the region. The economy of many of the Indians was based upon shifting cultivation in the forests. A clearing was made in the forest by burning, and the ashes left by the fires were worked into the soil. When the crop yields declined because of encroachment of weeds and brush from the forests, and because the scarce mineral nutrients and humus in the soils had become depleted another plot was cleared. The old clearings were abandoned and left to nature, to recuperate for possible use at some time in the future. The crops typical of Mexican Indian agriculture in the Central Highlands were also grown by the Indians of Veracruz. Corn was the basic staple, and must have given high yields, for the hot, humid country of the lower elevations has the best climate in Mexico for corn. Beans, squash, chiles, tomatoes, and *magueys* were also important crops. Other crops were those of the lower country. Sweet potatoes, or *camotes*, pineapples, sweet manioc, and tobacco were Indian crops. Cotton, which grew as woody shrub, was planted by the Indians, and this perennial is the ancestor of the majority of the herbaceous annual cottons grown throughout the world today. Tropical tree fruits, significant in the diet, included *zapotes* (also called *mameys* in central Mexico), *chico zapotes*, avocados, cherimoyas, and guava. The cacao tree, source of the chocolate bean, was valuable Indian crop. The Indians around Misantla and Papantla, in the country north of Veracruz City cultivated a climbing orchid in the wet, shady forest and from this plant they harvested vanilla beans. Rubber tapped from trees of the forests was also utilized by the Indians of Veracruz. Tropical products were carried inland to the peoples of the Central Highland.

There were fewer Spanish *encomiendas* in the Gulf of Mexico tropics than in the interior highlands, and Spanish settlement was concentrated at the port of Veracruz and at way stations along the trails into the highlands at such places at Jalapa, Orizaba, and Córdoba. The Indians cultivated cotton, cacao, and vanilla and sold these crops to the Spaniards for consumption and export. Indigo and tobacco became important crops on Spanish farmlands. Although it is probable that some kinds of sugar cane and bananas grew in the Americas (including tropical, eastern Mexico) before the arrival of Europeans, these two crops were carried by the Spaniards from the Old World to the hot country bordering the Gulf of Mexico. The cooking plantain was introduced into the Caribbean region and Mexico very early in the Spanish period. Bananas eventually became a significant food crop in the wet Mexican tropics, but the most important period of commercial banana growing and diffusion seems to have been delayed until the introduction of the Roatán or Gros Michel banana into Tabasco from the island of Roatán, off Honduras, in the late nineteenth century. During the colonial period, the Asian mango was first introduced into Mexico by way of the West Indies to Veracruz, rather than from across the Pacific to the Mexican west coast. Yams probably were first brought to the New World by the Portuguese from Africa, where, like sugar cane and bananas, this root crop had been taken from tropical Asia. The yams grown in tropical and subtropical Mexico are sold throughout the country under the same name as the native sweet potato, the Nahua *"camote."*

In the latter nineteenth century, increased local and export demand for tropical products and the stable government of Porfirio Díaz greatly stimulated agriculture and settlement in the tropical lands east of the Central Highlands. By 1910, Veracruz had become the second most populous state in Mexico, exceeded in population only by Jalisco. Indian production of cacao and vanilla was intensified and commercialized. Mexican plantations of cacao and sugar were expanded. Introduced rice, restricted by the Spanish in favor of wheat in the highlands, was widely planted. Tobacco cultivation increased, especially around the cigar manufacturing center of San Andrés Tuxtla. However, the most important agricultural development was the great expansion in plantings of coffee, a crop that had been introduced in a few places at the end of the colonial period. Coffee plantations were established in much of the area of intermediate elevation in the east-facing highlands. The crop also became important in the *tierra templada* of the mountains of Southern Mexico.

Since the Mexican Revolution, increased demand for market crops, sold both in Mexico and overseas, has brought about expansion of commercial agriculture. By 1950, over four times as much sugar was produced in Veracruz state as in any other Mexican state. The El Mante Region of southern Tamaulipas has become one of the nation's leading sugar sources. Coffee production in the intermediate altitudes of the highlands has become more important than in any other state in the nation. By 1960, sugar cane and coffee were respectively fifth and sixth in acreage among all Mexican crops (Table II, p. 111). Commercial banana growing became intensified when railroads, trucks, and port developments made it possible to get this perishable fruit to market. By the late 1930's, banana exports from the area along the shores of the Bay of Campeche had become so large that Mexico was the leading

banana exporting nation of the world. However, banana diseases and insect pests reduced production for export, and consumption in Mexican markets rose rapidly to the point where Mexican banana exports are now small. Veracruz has remained the leading Mexican state in banana production. Tobacco growing has remained important, although in 1950, more tobacco was produced in Nayarit, where cigarette making and tobacco exports are of more substance than in Veracruz. The vanilla industry has remained significant to some 10,000 Totonac Indians who produce the bean on family plots at Misantla and Papantla. However, most of the world's commercial vanilla production is today carried on in the tropical areas of former European colonies, especially Madagascar, to which the plant was taken from Mexico. In the hot, moist lowlands small amounts of cacao, coconuts, and rubber are grown. Rice is a major crop, and twice as much of this grain is grown in Veracruz as in any other Mexican state. Many kinds of tropical fruits are grown commercially for local and other Mexican markets. Such fruits include mangos, *zapotes,* papayas, *mameys,* guavas, cherimoyas, avocados, and oranges and limes. Although the commercial production of certain export and specialty crops has increased greatly, the traditional Mexican crops — corn, beans, tomatoes, and chiles — remain most important. For instance, in 1950 about twelve times as much land was used for corn production as was planted to sugar in Veracruz.

Slash-and-burn agriculture, in which the only tools employed may be the *machete* (large, heavy knife) and the hoe, is still carried on in the forests. Where enough unoccupied land remains so that farmers may move about from one plot to another every few years, the productivity of this primitive agriculture is often greater than that of the permanently occupied farmlands on the Central Highlands. However, as the population increases, this shifting kind of agriculture becomes less practicable. On many properties farming is carried on with the ox and wooden plow. Mechanized agriculture employing modern farming techniques is usually confined to the larger farms where plantation agriculture is practiced.

LIVESTOCK RAISING

The various kinds of livestock brought by the Spanish were introduced into the lowlands and mountain slopes of the region and became numerous in Veracruz. Much of the low, tropical grassland and forest area, which was frequently inundated, was suitable only for range, and here cattle and horses became especially numerous in the latter nineteenth century.

Although the livestock of Veracruz are not of as high a grade as some in the northern states, Veracruz does have more cattle, horses, pigs, and chickens than any other state in Mexico. The cattle business is the largest livestock enterprise, and much of its importance is attributable to the fact that in the rainy, tropical low country, there is still so much land which cannot be effectively utilized for farming. The poor tropical range of the Huasteca area, north of Veracruz City, is one of Mexico's most important cattle regions, and from there large amounts of beef from low-grade *criollo* cattle enter the markets of the Central Highlands (Map 1, p. 104). In the last twenty years, ranchers and the government have imported many cattle of breeds which are resistant to the heat, insects, and diseases of the tropical ranges. Most important are the Brahmas or Zebus originally from India, but Charolais and Santa Gertrudis cattle also have been introduced. It was, in fact, the introduction of Brahma cattle from Brazil in 1946 which brought *aftosa,* or foot-and-mouth disease, to Mexico by way of Veracruz. The epidemic of this highly contagious disease spread rapidly to all but the northern and southern states of Mexico. At first all infected and exposed cattle were slaughtered, but such a control program proved disastrous in a nation so dependent on beef cattle and oxen. Later, the largest animal vaccination program ever undertaken anywhere was carried out in Mexico. By 1952, sixty million cattle vaccinations had been given because each animal had to be vaccinated several times a year. With the help of United States funds and technicians, the disease was finally eradicated, and the international boundary with the United States, which had been closed to Mexican cattle, was finally permanently opened to Mexican cattle exports again in 1954.

LAND DEVELOPMENT

Since the beginning of the Mexican Revolution, land reform and land development have been extensive in Veracruz. By 1950, more *ejidos* had been formed in Veracruz than in any other state; however, the area within *ejidos* was not as great as in some of the northern states where *ejidos* and individual farm plots on *ejidos* are large. The southern part of Tamaulipas also contains many *ejidos*.

In the south of Veracruz state, the federal government has undertaken a large land development project in some ways similar to the Tennessee Valley Authority project in the United States. In the drainage basin of the Papaolapan River where farmers on *ejidos* and private farms (in the upper basin, Indian communal lands) lived and worked in isolated and backward conditions, a broad program of improvement was undertaken. A large dam has been constructed on a tributary of the Papaloapan, the Río Tonto, and electric power from the dam has become available in the river basin as well as in Puebla in the Central Highlands. Flood control and road building have been major aspects of the project, while improvements in health, education, and urban conditions have been lesser components of the undertaking. The establishment of two agricultural colonies failed, and the resettlement of 22,000 Mazatec Indians from the reservoir basin has certainly not been wholly successful. Nevertheless, a backward area is now on the way to incorporation within the modern sector of the Mexican nation. The Papaloapan Project represented one of the first measures taken by the federal government to direct the nation's eyes toward the hot, moist lowlands of southeastern Mexico as places worthy of economic development and, in some cases, of agricultural colonization.

FISHING AND FORESTRY

Commercial fishing is not as important along the coasts of Veracruz and Tamaulipas as it is in several other Mexican coastal states, especially those of the Northwest. Shrimp are caught for export, and snook *(robalo),* grunts *(mojarrones* or *roncadores),* bass *(cabrilla),* croakers *(corbina),* mackerel, pompano, and red snapper *(huachinango)* are caught for local consumption and by sportsmen. Along the shore, oysters, crabs, and clams provide food for the coastal population. Much of the fishing is carried on by cooperatives organized under Revolutionary laws which have attempted to create *"ejidos* of the sea." However, in many cases, the cooperatives have lacked equipment and marketing channels and have become dependent upon fish canning and processing companies for their boats, equipment, and sales outlets.

Timber cutting is extensive. However, most of the wood is utilized locally for construction and firewood or *leña*.

PETROLEUM AND SULPHUR DEPOSITS

In the northeastern portion of Mexico, including the Meseta Central and the Sierra Madre Oriental, sedimentary rocks are predominant, and the chief oil resources of the nation are stored in some of these rock beds. In Mexico's most important oil district, near the Gulf coast between Tampico and Tuxpán, limestones are the reservoir rocks. Some of the limestones are so compact that oil exists only in fractures and fissures. At places, along the contact zone with volcanic rocks which have intruded the compact limestones from below, the oil has flowed to the surface to form the seeps which have been known since Indian times. South of the Tampico field, brought into production in 1904, porous and even cavernous limestones contain oil underlain by salt water under high pressure. Here in the Golden Lane field, gusher wells were drilled around 1910, one of which yielded 100,000 barrel a day! The Poza Rica field, just southwest of Tuxpán, is now the most important field in the nation.

Another Mexican oil district, dating from just after the turn of the twentieth century, is located near the north shore of the Isthmus of Tehuantepec around Minatitlán. Here the oil is located in sandstones arched upward into oil traps by salt core domes which penetrated the sandstones from below. Petroleum and sulphur, which rest on the salt domes, were discovered here in a search for cheap fuel oil for the Tehuantepec Railroad in the first decade of this century.

By 1921, the peak year of Mexican output (Table V, B, p. 119), the nation produced 21 per cent of the world's oil and was second only to the United States in production. However, since that date, Mexico has dropped to a position of minor importance in world oil trade because old wells have played out, explora tion has not uncovered any bonanza fields, and, most importantly, production in the Middle East and Venezuela has far outstripped Mexico's output. Until 1938, when the Mexican government expropriated foreign oil holdings, most of the fields were controlled by United States and British companies. Under Mexican law, as derived from Roman and Spanish law, subsurface minerals were considered to be the property of the state, and so considerable litigation developed after expropriation because the companies claimed that they should have been compensated for unutilized oil reserves beneath the surface.

Oil production and marketing are now in the hands of the national petroleum monopoly called *Petroleos Mexicanos (Pemex)*. Mexico is still an exporter of petroleum products, although net exports are small, partially because of the rapid growth of the domestic market. Oil production has increased greatly since the low level of output in the early 1930's (Table V, B). However, production is still considerably below the year of peak output in 1921.

Several new fields have been brought into production in the last two decades. Just west of the Golden Lane is the Moralillo field, and in the Tehuantepec district there are new fields in northern Tabasco. At Reynosa, just south of the Río Grande, oil and gas were discovered in sandstones in the 1940's. The gas is of particular importance because it supplies power to the industrial city of Monterrey.

Petroleum is the most important mineral product of Mexico. The value of production represents about 80 per cent of the value of all mineral output in the nation (Table V, A, page 119).

The most important development of several decades in Mexican mineral production began in 1944 on the northern side of the Isthmus of Tehuantepec. Exploration for sulphur began in the Jáltipan area, in which old, capped oil drillings into salt core domes had turned up brimstone corings. A number of domes with sulphur were found. Using the Frasch process of pumping very hot water into the brimstone rock and bringing the molten material to the surface to solidify, Mexican sulphur production has so increased that since 1954, sulphur has become one of the major minerals produced in the country (Table V, A). Most of the sulphur has been exported, and Mexico is now second only to the United States in sulphur exports. However, because of concern over the rapid depletion of reserves and the growing needs of the domestic economy, the government has instituted controls over exports and encouraged exploration for new deposits.

INDUSTRY AND TRANSPORTATION

Industry, although important at certain places in the region, has always been concerned with the processing of certain crops, minerals, or fish. The Indian had, and still has, his craft industries. The Spaniard established sugar mills, indigo, and tobacco factories, and distilleries where *aguardiente,* or sugar brandy, was made from cane. In the nineteenth century, coffee *beneficios,* or hulling and drying plants, were constructed on the major coffee plantations, and in the twentieth century, the first oil refineries were established. Large oil refineries, petrochemical industries, and sulphur-extracting plants are now located in the region. In 1963, the first aluminum smelter in Mexico began production at the city of Veracruz. This plant will soon use electric power generated at installations to the south in the Papaloapan and Grijalva river basins. Most of the rest of the industry consists of agricultural processing of sugar, coffee, tobacco, rice, and other crops for market. Only a small percentage of the total population is, as yet, employed in industry.

Although most of the lowland and mountain country of this region was situated off the major travel arteries of the Spanish and later Mexican economies, the region was crossed by some of the most important roads and railroads in the nation. The royal mule train and cart roads, leading down from Mexico City to the port of Veracruz — the colonial window to the European world — passed through the region. In the latter nineteenth century, railroads followed these same routes and were also built southward to the Isthmus of Tehuantepec, and inland from Tampico oil fields.

The railroads are still important in the transportation of bulky petroleum, sulphur, and agricultural products, but highways have become very important in the movement of goods and persons alike. Paved roads now link the region with all parts of the nation, including the long isolated Yucatán peninsula. The city of Veracruz remains the most important seaport in Mexico.

STILL A RURAL REGION

By 1960, the growth of the economy and population, which had begun to accelerate in the mid-nineteenth century, made Veracruz, with 2,727,900 inhabitants, the most populous state in Mexico (Table VI, p. 122). The southeastern part of Tamaulipas also had become rather densely populated. Most of the population, however, has remained rural. There are few large cities in the region (Table VI). Off the beaten tracks, in the forests of the hills and mountains and in the low, hot coastal areas there are still Indians and other rural folk in great numbers who have not yet moved out of the traditional sector of the Mexican economy. The earth, corn and beans, the ox, and the footpath are still important in the lives of these people.

SOUTHERN MEXICO

In Southern Mexico, the Spaniard early settled in some of the interior valleys, and blazed trails down to Pacific port sites and into Guatemala; however, the region has remained less affected by Spanish and modern Mexican culture than all other parts of the nation, with the possible exception of Yucatán. Southern Mexico contains the states of Colima, Guerrero, Oaxaca, Chiapas, as well as the southwestern part of Michoacán (Endpaper Maps and Map 1, p. 104). All of these states reach the Pacific shore, but only in Colima does a large proportion of the population live along the coast. The interior highlands north and east of the bold coast contain most of the villages, towns, and farms where the preponderantly rural population lives. Much of the region is still Indian country. Transportation is less well developed than in other parts of the nation. The poorest people of Mexico live in the backlands of the region, and there has been little participation in the industry and urbanization which have characterized the more prosperous parts of the country. This is a picturesque region, but one which presents most challenging problems to the national government.

Physical Geography

South of central Mexico, the land slopes off toward the Pacific Ocean through the dissected borderlands of the more elevated Central Volcanic Highlands. The surface, which is mostly devoid of volcanic areas, has been extensively cut by stream erosion. Much of the country is what the Mexican calls *pura sierra,* where little level land remains. The deep river valleys which drain the mountainous country enter the tropical world as they approach the warm land of the Pacific coast. The most important of these valleys is that of the Mexcala or Balsas River (Endpaper Maps and Map 1, page 104).

On the northeast, the southern extension of the Sierra Madre Oriental, called the Sierra Madre de Oaxaca, divides Southern Mexico from the Gulf Slope. Southwest of the Sierra Madre de Oaxaca lies the large fertile Central Valley of Oaxaca where the Spaniards, in the person of Cortés himself, very early appropriated some of the best land in Southern Mexico. Near the Pacific coast of Guerrero, Oaxaca, and Michoacán, known as la Costa Grande, a mountain range called the Sierra Madre del Sur stands higher than the rough country of the interior and reaches the sea in headlands and cliffs (Map 1, page 104). In southwestern Oaxaca, the southern end of the Isthmus of Tehuantepec contains low mountains in back of the broad low coastal area, which is fringed by lagoons.

The highlands of Chiapas, which are part of the mountain system of Central America, begin southeast of the Isthmus of Tehuantepec. These mountains trend more west-east than north-south. The southern range, the Sierra Madre de Chiapas, like parts of the Sierra Madre del Sur (of which it is a continuation beyond the Isthmus of Tehuantepec), is composed largely of a crystalline mass, rare elsewhere in Mexico outside northern Baja California. This range rises to elevations of 9,000 and 10,000 feet immediately behind the moist, narrow, Soconusco coastal lowland. In the mountains of Chiapas, volcanic country reappears and continues southeastward into Central America. On the border with Guatemala, the volcanic cone, Tacaná, rises to an elevation of 13,300 feet. In northern Chiapas, a continuation of the folded and faulted sedi-

ments of the Sierra Madre Oriental appears again as the Sierra Madre del Norte de Chiapas. In this range of rather level summits with elevations of close to 10,000 feet, limestones are the predominant rocks. Between the two highlands of Chiapas, there is a broad rift valley where earth movement along fractures left the valley floor at an elevation of only some 3,000 feet. The valley of Chiapas is drained off to the Gulf of Mexico by the Río Grande de Chiapas or Río Grijalva, which flows through the narrow, deep Canyon of Sumidero on the way to the *tierra caliente* country of Tabasco.

Except at the higher elevations, the climate of Southern Mexico is subtropical or tropical. However, there is great variation in the amounts of rainfall received annually at different places. As in almost all of the rest of the nation, the season of maximum rainfall is summer. Downslope from the Central Highlands, the rough mountain country to the south is mostly in the *tierra templada.* At Oaxaca City, the average temperature of the warmest month, June, is 73°F. while that of the coldest month of the year January, is 63°F. Average annual rainfall at Oaxaca is 27 inches (Table I, p. 109). In the hot coastal lands and in the Valley of Chiapas, the warmest months of summer have average temperatures in the low 80's while the coldest months of winter have average temperatures in the 70's. The lowest areas are *tierra caliente* country. Rainfall in the Valley of Chiapas is more abundant than in the lower areas in central Oaxaca. At Tuxtla Gutiérrez, average annual precipitation is 37 inches. Much of the coastal area has about 40 inches of rain a year. However, at Acapulco, annual average rainfall is nearly 60 inches, while on parts of the coast of Oaxaca yearly rainfall is only about 23 inches (Map 2, p. 108). Along the Pacific, or Soconusco, coast of Chiapas, annual rainfall in front of the high Sierra Madre de Chiapas is very heavy. Tapachula has 98 inches and Aurora 175 inches of annual precipitation (Map 2, Table I, pages 108-09).

Much of the interior mountain country of Oaxaca and Guerrero is covered with the rather dry, open, low broadleaf tropical deciduous forest. This forest becomes denser along the river courses. However, north of the Sierra Madre del Sur, in the rain shadow of those mountains, lower precipitation and high evaporation rates reduce much of the vegetation to the cacti and shrubs of the arid tropical scrub association. On the highest slopes of the Sierra Madre del Sur, and in the highland country of Oaxaca, pine-oak forests extend southward from the Central Highlands (Map 3, p. 110). The coastal areas north of the Isthmus of Tehuantepec are also covered in the wetter places with tropical deciduous forest and in the dryer places with thorn forest. In both the tropical deciduous forest and the thorn forest leguminous trees are abundant. Mimosa-like acacia and mesquite, are common, as are trees of the Senna subfamily. Along the Pacific, there are long stretches of tropical savanna grassland on the coast of Guerrero and Soconusco. In the mountains behind

A New World portal for trade with Asia in colonial times, Acapulco in the state of Guerrero, Southern Mexico, was reawakened in the 1930's from sleepy fishing-port existence to become the most important resort in Mexico. Its tourist attractions include water sports, game fishing, and a concentration of hotels, motels, vacation residences, and entertainment centers.

he Soconusco coast, in the area of extremely heavy rainfall, the slopes are covered with tropical rain forest (Map 3, page 110). The Valley of Chiapas contains a tropical deciduous forest, but the slopes of the surrounding mountains have, at higher elevations, the continuation of the oak-pine forest which carries on southward all the way into Nicaragua. The conifers of these highlands include the various species called ocotes; the white pine, or *ayacahuite;* the aztec pine, or *pino-real;* and cypress. The tropical evergreen and rain forests of Southeast Mexico extend into the areas of lower elevation in northern and eastern Chiapas.

The shallow, loose, porous soils on so many of the mountain sides of Oaxaca and Guerrero provide a poor agricultural base for the dense rural population. In many areas erosion is severe. The leached soils of the moist tropical areas are also poor soils for the kind of farming carried on in the densely populated areas. However, in the valley bottoms and along the river courses there are good alluvial soils which support the most productive agriculture in the region of Southern Mexico.

Wildlife in Southern Mexico is characterized by those species which are found throughout much or all of the nation and other species which are peculiar to the hot, wet, forested lands found in parts of the region. Quail, doves, and pigeons occur throughout the region. Migratory ducks are found on the south coast along the Pacific flyway, while tree ducks and the muscovy duck occur in the lowlands of Southern Mexico. Among the mammals, opossums, armadillos, rabbits, squirrels, porcupines, raccoons, skunks, and the coyote, coatimundi, collared peccary, white-tailed deer, gray fox, ring-tailed cat, and puma are found over most of the region. In the forests of the wet, tropical lowlands live the paca, or *tepescuintle,* agouti, kinkajou, and five cats — the jaguar, ocelot, margay, jaguarundi, and puma. Along the Soconusco coast there are tapir, brocket deer, spider monkeys, and anteaters. Reptiles in the wet country include lizards, snakes, turtles, and alligators.

Cultural Geography

In turn, the Spaniards and Mexicans in their development and settlement of Mexico have been attracted chiefly to the Central Highlands, the mining country of the north, the plantation lands of the tropics, and the irrigable lands of the northern deserts. Thus, the mountains and valleys of Southern Mexico have become, in a sense, a storehouse of culture traits which have disappeared, or are rapidly disappearing, in other parts of Mexico. Indians are numerous, and something of the way of life of the Indian at the time of the Conquest still remains, as do many customs which date back to the colonial period. Nevertheless, superimposed upon the old are modern cities, highways, and methods of doing things that portend widespread change toward the newer Mexican way of life.

SMALL FARMS AND PLANTATIONS

Cultivation of the land has been by far the most important tradition of life in almost all of Southern Mexico. Throughout much of the highland area of the region, the Indians practiced sedentary agriculture in which they farmed small plots with a digging stick, and raised corn, beans, squash, chiles, tomatoes, *nopales, maguey,* and other crops familiar to the Indians of the Central Highlands. In the tropical forests, shifting agriculture was common, and, in addition to staples of the higher country, lima beans, cotton, pineapples, tropical fruits, and cacao were raised by the Indians of the warmer country. Lesser crops of Indian Southern Mexico were the grain *quinoa,* more commonly associated with Andean Indians of South America, and the peanut or *cacahuate.*

Some of the important early Spanish *encomiendas* and later haciendas were located in the fertile valleys of Southern Mexico. However, in the isolated, high, rough mountain lands, the Indians were able to escape life as a peón on the hacienda. Indian crops, such as tobacco, pineapples, indigo, and cotton, became important on Spanish haciendas, while sugar cane was a Spanish crop on the estates. The coconut was introduced into southwestern coastal Mexico from the south in the early 1500's. This palm is probably native in Southeast Asia, but had somehow reached the west coast of Central America and Colombia before the arrival of the Spaniards in the New World. However, important utilization of the coconut did not occur until Asian techniques of tapping the inflorescences for their sap arrived by way of the galleon trade between Acapulco and Manila. The sap was used in making *tuba —* a coconut wine. This wine industry was especially important in Colima in the seventeenth century. The *tuba* industry is essentially forgotten today, and, as elsewhere in Mexico, coconuts are raised commercially for the oil from the meat of the nut. With the nineteenth century came the establishment of coffee as a major crop, especially in Chiapas where production greatly increased in the early twentieth century.

Since the Mexican Revolution began in 1910, most of the large haciendas in Southern Mexico have been broken up into smaller properties. However, because in the Indian and other rural areas away from the mainstreams of Mexican life there were already many small private properties, the formation of *ejidos* has not been as important as in the Central Highlands. Within Southern Mexico there were in 1950 more small private properties of five *hectares* and under (about 12.5 acres and under) than in any other region in the

nation. On the other hand, because many of the crops of the region are plantation crops for which the maximum legal size of private holdings is larger than for ordinary fields crops, there are many large farms in Southern Mexico. Farms on which such crops as coconuts, cacao, coffee, bananas, and fruit crops are raised may contain legally, under Mexican law, up to 300 *hectares* (about 750 acres) of land.

Although the *ejidos* of Mexico are, in general, less efficient than the larger private properties, they are probably more efficient than the tiny private farms where government aid is less likely to be applied than on *ejidos.* With a land tenure system characterized by so many small private farms, the region of Southern Mexico contains the poorest agricultural economy in Mexico.

In 1950, the value of machinery, vehicles, and implements on farms was far below that value in any other region in the nation. The value of irrigation works was below that of any other census region, and the number of farms without tractors and with draft animals was higher than in any other census region in the country. And even with the large number of small farms, the region still contained, in 1950, a great number of rural day laborers. Thus Southern Mexico, which is essentially a farming region, is the poorest part of Mexico.

The traditional crops, corn and beans, remain the most important in terms of harvested land. Avocado plantings are many in the warm parts of the region. In the highlands of Oaxaca, wheat, important here since colonial days, is still a principal crop. Bananas, an important Mexican crop, are a staple food crop in the lowlands (Table II, page 111). There are large commercial plantings of bananas in Chiapas and on the coast of Guerrero. Other commercial plantation crops are important. Sugar cane is grown in the Balsas River Valley.

Tobacco farms occupy some of the warmer parts of the region. Tomatoes are grown in large quantity on the coast of Guerrero for shipment to urban markets, and there are large amounts of oranges produced in central Oaxaca and in the Central Valley of Chiapas. The old Indian and colonial cacao region on the Soconusco coast is still important, but more cacao is now grown in Tabasco than in Chiapas. As an area in which coconuts are grown, the coast of Guerrero is second only to the coasts of Tabasco and Campeche on the Gulf of Mexico. Only in Veracruz are more pineapples grown than in the lower, warmer valleys of Oaxaca. Southern Mexico leads all other regions in the production of two crops, coffee and sesame. Among Mexican coffee-growing states in 1962, production in Chiapas was second, in Oaxaca third, and in Guerrero fifth.

The oil seed sesame is one of the most important crops in Mexico because in many places where animal products are scarce, it provides a source of fat in the diet (Table II, p. 111). All sorts of tropical fruits are grown in the warmer areas, both for family consumption and commercially. Such fruits include mangos, *mameys,* guavas, *zapotes,* and *granadillas. Agave* or century plants, grown to produce *mescal,* are now more numerous in Guerrero, and in the Central Highlands, than in Oaxaca where distilling was more important in earlier days.

ANIMAL AND LIVESTOCK PRODUCTS

Because the more level lands, and even many of the mountainsides, are covered with farms, and because the climate and range conditions of the tropics are not propitious for livestock raising, Southern Mexico is not one of the important livestock regions of Mexico. The Indians had their dogs, turkeys, and *patos caseros* (house ducks). They collected cochineal insects from the *nopal* to make red dye, and gathered honey made by stingless bees in the forest. In Indian Mexico, a hairless dog, called in Nahua *xoloiscuintli,* somewhat larger than the modern Chihuahua, was bred for fattening and eating. These dogs had religious significance, and ceramic figures of fat, hairless dogs have been found in considerable quantity at archeological sites in Colima. All of the various species of domesticated livestock brought by the Spaniards were introduced into Southern Mexico. As elsewhere, except in the north, oxen pulled plows and carts. Thomas Gage, an English Dominican who was one of the few foreigners to report from the carefully guarded New Spain of the Spanish, reported that sheep were numerous in the highlands of Oaxaca in 1625. Indigenous stingless bees were common in Gage's time, and honey production and collection have remained important. During the colonial period, the cochineal dye business became very important in the export trade. Although all kinds of livestock are found in the region now, there are few areas where animal production is a major business.

From the forests of the tropics come rubber, fruits, fibers, and some tropical hardwood. In the highlands there are softwood pines. In the mountains of Guerrero, pine is cut in areas where concessions on timber land have been issued by the federal government. In Oaxaca and Chiapas, there is also commercial pine cutting.

MINES AND MINING POTENTIAL

Southern Mexico has never been a major mining region of Mexico. The Indians worked small deposits of the soft metals, gold and copper. The first Spanish mining activities in New Spain included the mining of copper, tin, gold, and silver at Taxco and the washing of placer gold in Colima. There were Spanish iron mines in the *Mixteca Alta* of Oaxaca (highlands of the Mixtec Indians). However, the mines of Southern Mexico have never matched the fame of those of the Meseta Central, Northwest Mexico, or certain bonanza works in the Central Highlands. For instance, German mining activity proved unprofitable in the Sierra Madre de Oaxaca near Ixtlán, in the first half of the nineteenth century. As a reminder of that enterprise, incidentally, the region still has some steep-roofed, shingled wooden dwellings.

Taxco, however, has been an exception. The rich silver mines there were located largely outside the cover of volcanic rocks so common to the north. The mines penetrated veins in sedimentary and metamorphic rocks, and areas in limestone, where rich replacement mineralization astonished the German geographer, Alexander von Humboldt, in 1803. Most mines in Southern Mexico are now marginal, and mineral production is small.

The future of mining in the region could be bright along the southern coast from Jalisco into Guerrero. This area is an outlier of the zone of mineralization caused by contact metamorphism, most pronounced in Northwest Mexico, but running also down the west coast. Here, as in the Northwest, where molten rocks welled up from depth and contacted overlying rocks, large irregular mineralized areas occur along the zones of contact. Moreover, along this coast the young volcanic basaltic rocks do not obscure the underlying rocks. Most prominent among the minerals along the Pacific coast are iron and other ferrous minerals located beneath limestones. As new hydroelectric and other economic developments continue to progress in this coastal region, it seems probable that important mining will follow.

FISHING

Commercial fishing is not as important along the south Pacific coast as in the northern Pacific area of Mexico. *Huachinango* (red snapper), *robalo* (snook), *mojarra* (grunt), and *pargo* (porgy) are caught along the seacoast. Game fish caught by tourists at places like Acapulco include *sabalo* (tarpon), *aguja* (marlin), *pez espada* (swordfish), and *pez vela* (sailfish). Salina Cruz, on the southern shore of the Isthmus of Tehuantepec, is an important Mexican fishing port where the shrimp catch is especially important.

RETARDED INDUSTRIALIZATION

Southern Mexico is today a region with little industry. During aboriginal and colonial times, the country included within modern Oaxaca was the center of blue dye-making from indigo, and red dye production from the cochineal insect. Certain very old Indian craft industries still exist. The Spanish established sugar-milling and chocolate-processing which are still important. With the nineteenth century came the coffee *beneficios.* In addition to these older food-processing industries, copra and sesame oil mills are now located in the region.

There are also sawmills, fish canneries and processing plants, textile mills, and handicraft shops where products like straw hats are made on a rather large scale. Probably the most significant new development for industry in Southern Mexico is the large hydroelectric project now under construction about thirty-five miles from the mouth of the Balsas River at a narrows called Boquilla de Infernillo (Map 1, p. 104). This is said by the Mexican government to be the largest such project in Latin America, and a lake thirty-nine miles long will be created behind the dam. Power will be used locally and in the Federal District. Based upon this new source of power, an industrial complex is contemplated in the southwestern lowlands of Michoacán as well as in that part of the state located in the Central Highlands. Most important in this future industrialization may be a steel industry based upon plentiful ferrous mineral deposits found along and near the Pacific coasts of Jalisco, Colima, and Michoacán, among which are those of manganese at Autlán, Jalisco, and of iron at Las Truchas in southwestern Michoacán. Until the project began, this area was in isolated country in the *tierra caliente*. The degree of success of the project will demonstrate the possibilities of economic development in one of the poorest parts of the nation.

ISOLATION AND CONTACT

Some of the most important travel routes in Mexico have crossed Southern Mexico; but, on the other hand, much of the region has suffered from isolation. Spanish mule trails to Guatemala and the Southern Sea, as the Spanish called the Pacific Ocean, followed Indian footpaths along tortuous routes through the highlands and valleys. Along the Pacific coast the Spanish early established a series of ports from which ships set out for exploration in northwest New Spain or across the Pacific to the Far East. When the famous Manila Galleon (or China Ship) trade with the Far East got underway, Acapulco became the eastern terminous of the route. Exotic goods from the Orient bought with Mexican silver were carried from Acapulco to Mexico City over the China Road which followed essentially the route traversed by the modern highway. Asiatic influences which entered Mexico through Acapulco, although not numerous, are rather intriguing. They include motifs on the *cerámica poblana* (ceramics of Puebla) and on the *lacas* (lacquer work) of Michoacán and Guerrero, the techniques of palm wine making once widely used in Colima, and a form of Mongolian still used by the Huichol and Cora Indians. Less certain in their Asiatic origins are the palm-leaf rain capes (*chinos*) of southwestern Mexico and the wooden plank and shingled cabins (*trojes*) of the Tarascan Sierra. It is possible that both of these items may owe their Mexican beginnings to the first visits of Japanese to Acapulco in 1610 and 1614.

In the late nineteenth and early twentieth centuries, railroads were built down the east side of the mountains in Veracruz, across the Isthmus of Tehuantepec, and down Soconusco coast to Chiapas to reach Guatemala. However, although rail lines were built southward into northern Guerrero and Oaxaca, no railroad has ever been built through the southern highlands in either Oaxaca or Chiapas. For a few years, before the opening of the Panama Canal in 1914, the Tehuantepec line carried a great amount of interoceanic freight. At the height of the traffic many trains a day were reported to have crossed the Isthmus carrying such goods as Hawaiian sugar.

Railroad building has not been important in Southern Mexico since the Revolution, but automobile roads have now been blazed through the forests and rough mountain country to villages that were linked with the outside world only by mule trails twenty, even ten, years ago. Many of the roads are most rudimentary, but jeeps and trucks pass over them daily to transport people and goods back and forth across distances formerly undreamed of. Paved highways now also join Southern Mexico to the commerce and culture of the outside world. A four-lane super-highway has been completed over much of the distance between Mexico City and Acapulco. A paved road crosses the Isthmus of Tehuantepec, and the Pan-American highway extends to the Guatemalan boundary through the Central Valley of Chiapas. Airplanes fly to landing fields at almost all towns of any size. Thus, isolation, one of the gravest obstacles to economic development, but a condition which kept much of Southern Mexico picturesque, is being eliminated.

At Acapulco, tourism, one of the several largest industries in Mexico, supports a good-sized city and brings much dollar exchange to the nation. About two-thirds of Mexico's tourist dollars are earned along the international boundary with the United States. However, important amounts of the approximate six to eight hundred million dollars earned each year from tourism and border transactions are spent by Americans at such places in the Mexican interior as Acapulco. It is the most important resort center in the nation, and many Mexican tourists annually visit the seaside city, along with Americans and other foreigners. The small fishing and port town, which had badly declined in importance since colonial days, was revived by the tourist business during the 1930's. Acapulco is now the largest urban place in Guerrero and contains many hotels, motels, vacation homes, and entertainment centers. Sporting opportunities include swimming, water skiing, fishing, hunting, and golf. The thousands of visitors who come to Acapulco each year have created a real estate boom which surely would have surprised the rich merchants of the galleon days.

REGION REMAINS RURAL

The population of Southern Mexico remains the most rural among the regions of the nation (Table VI, page 122). None of the larger cities of the nation is located in the region (Table VI, p. 122). The village and farmstead are still the most important forms of settlement. Indians are still more important, as a percentage of the total population, than in any other part of Mexico. The rate of population growth was below the national average from 1950 to 1960, and Oaxaca was next to last among the Mexican states in rate of growth. Young people tend to leave the region and fewer babies survive to increase the population than elsewhere in modern Mexico. In spite of changes since the Mexican Revolution, which have greatly altered the old order of things, Southern Mexico has come into the modern world less rapidly than other parts of the nation, in part because much of the region was so near to colonial culture when the Revolution began.

NORTHWEST MEXICO

The gap between the way of life in the Northwest and in some parts of Southern Mexico is as wide as the difference between the twentieth and the eighteenth centuries. This difference has developed, however, only within the last century, and much of it within the last two or three decades.

The Northwest was long an isolated frontier in a far corner of Mexico. Some of the very early Spanish *entradas* (explorations) and sea voyages were made in, and along the coasts of, the primarily arid lands of Northwest Mexico. However, because both the land and peoples of the Northwest proved hostile to settlement, effective occupation of much of this region by the Spanish, and later by Mexicans and foreigners, was long delayed. In fact, on the Baja California Peninsula, the population remained small until some thirty years ago. The region includes the states of Sinaloa and Sonora, which became states shortly after Mexican independence; the state of Nayarit, one which did not become important enough for statehood until 1917; the state of Baja California, which had attained a large enough population for statehood by 1952; and the Southern Territory of Baja California, which is still very sparsely populated and remains a federal territory (endpaper map and Map 1, page 104).

Physical Geography: THE LAND

Northwest Mexico is separated from the rest of the nation by high and spectacular mountain barriers. In the south, the northern edge of the volcanic country of the Central Highlands reaches the Pacific Ocean to rise above the lower country that extends into the Northwest. On the east, the formidable barrier of the Western Sierra Madre stands between the Northwest and the Meseta Central. Because the coast of the Gulf of California, called as well the Sea of Cortés, bends southeastward, and the barrier wall of the Sierra Madre Occidental extends more directly southward, the area between the high sierra and the sea becomes pinched off in the south into a narrower and narrower belt of westward sloping country.

West of the Sierra Madre Occidental in Sonora and Sinaloa there are lower, parallel fault block mountain ranges which trend in a north-south direction (Map 1, p. 104). Rivers flow between the ranges and turn westward to the sea, where they have been able to break through the mountains, often in gorges, in zones of weaker rocks. In the east, the basins between the ranges have rolling surfaces which have been dissected by the eroding streams. However, in the west, the basins nearer the coast are depositional lands where the streams have spewed forth the alluvial materials which they have carried out onto the great desert plains. North of southern Sonora, during most of the year, the streams disappeared into the sands of the dry basins of the west before reaching the sea even prior to the appropriation of water for irrigation. However,

In the volcanic lands of Mexico's peninsular northwestern extremity of Baja California, the landscape sometimes approaches fantasy. Characteristic of the plant association in the central part of the peninsula are tall, slender *cirios* or "boojum trees" and squat elephant trees.

where water is available for irrigation, and where natural rainfall is sufficient for crops farther south in Sinaloa and Nayarit, the alluvial lands along the river courses make excellent agricultural soils which are high in water-soluble mineral nutrients. Along the coasts of southern Sonora and northern Sinaloa the alluvial soils along the rivers have been deposited on elevated marine terraces, but in southern Sinaloa and in Nayarit, the coastline is subsiding and there are large drowned areas covered with lagoons, marshes, and swamps.

The lifeblood of the agricultural Northwest is supplied by the waters of a series of major rivers which rise in the wetter country in the mountains to the east. In the deserts of the north these rivers are, from north to south, the Colorado, Concepción, Sonora, Yaqui, Mayo, Fuerte, and Sinaloa (Endpaper Maps and Map 1, p. 104). South of these rivers, where winters are dry and even some summers are dry enough to make irrigation desirable, there are other great rivers which rise in flood stage after the summer rains, but may be nearly dry in winter. Some of these rivers are also sources of irrigation water, and others may someday supply needed water for winter and more secure summer crops. The rivers south of the Sinaloa are, from north to south, the San Lorenzo, Piaxtla, Presidio, Baluarte, Acaponeta, San Pedro, and Río Grande de Santiago, the latter of which rises, as the Lerma, near Toluca, five hundred miles upstream in the Central Highlands.

The Baja California peninsula is a huge fault block tilted upward on the eastern side and sloping rather gradually downward to the sea on the Pacific side. On the eastern side of the peninsula a high escarpment drops off precipitously to the desert on the Gulf of California coast. Vertical displacement from the crest of the escarpment to the down-faulted floor of the Gulf is of great magnitude. Spectacular views of the lands and sea to the east may be had from vantage points in the northern granitic Sierras Juárez and San Pedro Mártir which form the crest of the fault block at the summit of the escarpment. The highest point on the peninsula is in the San Pedro Mártir range where the peak, Picacho del Diablo, rises up to about 10,100 feet in elevation. Along a considerable part of the Pacific coast, elevated terraces and seacliffs present a most scenic coastline.

In much of the central part of Baja California, the granitic core of the peninsula is not exposed, as in the north, but is covered with volcanic rocks. There, many of the mountains are tablelands, and unlike the landscape of western Sonora, there are few large plains covered with alluvial materials. Two worthy of mention, however, are the Vizcaíno Plain, on the western side of the peninsula between about 27 and 28° N. latitude, and the Magdalena Plain, on the Pacific coast behind Magdalena Bay (Map 1, p. 104). Irrigated agricultural land has already been opened to production by deep wells in the Santo Domingo area of the Magdalena Plain, and there may be enough water beneath the Vizcaíno Plain to support some farming.

At the southern end of the peninsula, the granitic core is again exposed in the Sierra de San Lázaro. This sierra rises up to about 7,000 feet in the cape district south of La Paz.

There are few streams which flow for any considerable length of time during the year, except in the northwest of the peninsula where there are rainy winters. In the northwest, enough runoff pours from the northern highlands to keep many small streams flowing over much of their courses to the sea during a large part of the year. Small irrigated valleys and coastal plains benefit from the runoff in the northwest. Small streams flow down the escarpment on the east through narrow palm canyons, to be lost in the desert sands beyond the canyon mouths. The only river of large size in Baja California is the Colorado which rises in the Rocky Mountains to flow to the sea over a delta at the head of the Gulf of California in Mexico.

All but the southern part of the Mexican Northwest is dry country. The dryness of far northwestern Mexico is related to its location between the rain-forming mechanisms of the low latitudes of tropical Mexico and those of the higher latitudes of the west coast of North America. High and complex terrain cuts off the Northwest from most summer moisture originating in the Gulf of Mexico. However, summer rainstorms also form in the tropical Pacific, but most of these either intersect land only in humid Nayarit and southern Sinaloa or move out to sea without affecting the Northwest. In the autumn, occasional inflows of tropical air arrive from the southwest in the form of tropical hurricanes called *chubascos* or *cordonazos de San Francisco*. These hurricanes are more common along the Mexican Pacific Coast south of the Northwest, but rarely their effects are felt as far north as central California. Nevertheless, it is the air of southwesterly origin in the warmer months that brings most of the scanty rainfall to southern Baja California, Sonora, and northern Sinaloa.

Northern Baja California is the only part of Mexico with a winter rainfall maximum. The northern part of the peninsula, which has little summer precipitation, shares in the easterly-moving frontal storms of winter which account for so much of the rainfall of the Pacific Coast of the United States. Although these winter storms also bring some cool season precipitation to other parts of the Northwest, their frequency and/or effectiveness decreases southward and eastward into the deserts.

In the absence of the rain-bearing winter storms, northern Baja California is usually dry. For the most part, the air flowing along the coast of the peninsula comes from the northwest off the cool sea. The air arrives in a cool, humid, and even foggy condition. However, most of the time the lower air is overlaid by a thick stratum so warm and dry that even the heat of summer cannot induce the processes of rising and cooling necessary for precipitation.

In northwestern Baja California, where there is a climate nearly moist enough in the winter to be called

Mediterranean, average annual rainfall is about eight to twelve inches. In the highlands it may be as much as twenty-five inches (Map 2, p. 108). As illustrated by the climatic data for Ensenada in Table I, summers and winters have mild temperatures. The warmest months of summer have average temperatures of only 65 to 70° F., and the coolest months of winter have average temperatures of only 55 to 60°. East of the escarpment and in the south of Baja California, annual rainfall is very scanty, only about two and one-half to five inches, except in the Cape District of the extreme south where annual precipitation is about six to ten inches (Table I, 30, 31). In the mountains of the extreme south there may be as many as twenty inches of annual rainfall. The deserts of the peninsula have mild winters, in which the coldest months have average temperatures of about 55 to 65° F. However, the summers are intensely hot. The hottest months of summer have average temperatures of between 85 and 92° F., and maximum temperatures may reach 120°. Summers near the Pacific coast are cooler than elsewhere in the deserts of Baja California.

The deserts of western Sonora have mild winters and extremely hot summers like most of the desert areas of Baja California. Rainfall is under five inches a year in northwestern Sonora, but rises to eight to twelve inches in the Hermosillo-Guaymas area. In the irrigated agricultural district at Ciudad Obregón, annual rainfall is eight inches (Map 2, Table I, pp. 108-09). Annual rainfall increases in eastern Sonora because of rises in elevation up into the Sierra Madre Occidental. On the western slopes of the high mountains, annual precipitation may be as high as 30 inches. Rainfall increases south of Sonora where invading summer air masses pass over warm, stagnant offshore waters which extend far out into the Pacific. At Mazatlán, annual precipitation is 33 inches (Table I, p. 109), while in southern Nayarit it is 40 to 50 inches (Map 2, p. 108). In the humid tropical country from Mazatlán southward, winters are dry and mild, with the average temperature in the coldest month being in the high 60's, or low 70's. These summer-moist tropical lands do not get as hot as the deserts during the hot season because the humid air retards insolation or the receipt of the sun's energy. The hottest months of summer have average temperatures in the low 80's. In the fall both Baja California and the coasts of Sonora, Sinaloa, and Nayarit may be visited by the hurricanes known as *chubascos* or *cordonazos de San Francisco*.

VEGETATION IS DIVERSE

In the winter-moist region of northwestern Baja California the natural vegetation is characterized by small trees and brush known, as in Southern California, as chaparral (Map 3). In the canyons and on the moister hillsides there are live oak trees. The high sierras of northern Baja California have forests of pine and other coniferous trees, and, indeed, there are aspen in the highest parts of the Sierra San Pedro Mártir. In the Sierra Juárez, Jeffrey pine is dominant, while in the

Sierra San Pedro Mártir, there are also stands of lodgepole pine, sugar pine, incense cedar, white fir, and cypress. Across the mountains eastward into the extremely dry desert of northeastern Baja California and northwestern Sonora, vegetation is sparse and consists mostly of two species, creosote bush and burro weed. In central Baja California the deserts are replete with unusual forms of vegetation which make the region a land of fantasy. There are squat, fat, contorted elephant trees; tall *cirios*, or boojum trees, which look like huge inverted carrots; giant cactus, or *cardón*, the largest of all cactus plants; tree yucca plants called *datillos*; large branched ocotillos, and many other species. Near the foggy Pacific coast these plant forms have moss draped over their shapes. In southern Baja California there are many species of plants, such as flowering thorn trees, which are characteristic of mainland Mexico across the Gulf of California.

In western Sonora as far south as Guaymas, the desert contains organ pipe cactus and the famous sahuaro which grows only in southern Arizona, far southeastern California, and Sonora. North of Hermosillo there is a large area of desert trees, chiefly mesquite,, growing over grasses (Map 3, p. 110). In the foothills of eastern Sonora, oak trees appear and in the high mountains there are junipers and pines. In the highest parts of the Sierra Madre, even spruce and fir trees appear. Extending southward along the lower foothills of the Sierra Madre in Sonora and out onto the lowlands farther south, where it is rainier, there is a large thorn forest. The dry thorn forest is a dense growth of trees from ten to thirty feet high, within which there are many thorny, leguminous trees mixed with cactus. In the winter, most of the trees are bare, but in the spring and summer the green forest is decorated with an array of white, yellow, red, and purple flowers. Some of the trees in the forest have been reduced in number because, like the Brazilwood, they are dyewoods which were cut off during years when natural dyestuffs could still compete with the newer synthetic dyes.

Along the rivers of northern Sinaloa, the vegetation of the wet tropical areas to the south invades the semi-arid country. Huge tropical trees like the *guanacastle* and *higuerra*, the latter of which is a banyan-like tree with hanging aerial roots, are found along the river banks. The trees are covered with vines and orchid-like flowers. In much of southern Sinaloa and in Nayarit there are savanna grasslands dotted with palm trees. Around San Blas, on the coast of southern Nayarit, there is a tropical evergreen forest in which the dominant tree among the forest giants is the *corozo* palm. This palm is called locally *coquito de aceite,* and bears a small oil nut which is both eaten and used for making soap. At many places, the coasts of Nayarit, Sinaloa, and Sonora, as far north as Tiburón Island, are covered with mangrove swamps. Some introduced trees, such as the *tamarindo* from southeast Asia and the *tabachín* or flame tree, of Madagascar, grow so abundantly that they appear to be native in parts of the region. The coconut palm, from farther south along the Mexican west coast, has been planted in many of the warmer parts of the Northwest. On the other hand, the leguminous *guamúchil* tree of the Mexican thorn forests was carried to the Philippines and mainland Far East by the Spaniard, and in some Asian places the tree retains names similar to the Mexican name of Nahua origin. The *guamúchil* illustrates the importance of native plants to the Indian, Spaniard and Mexican, and the transplantation of valuable plants from one part of the world to another. This tree is valuable because it is good for construction, it yields a yellow dye, it contains tannin, medicine, and mucilage, and the pods are esteemed as a sweet food and in the preparation of a soft drink.

WILDLIFE STILL PLENTIFUL

Some kinds of wildlife are still abundant in Northwest Mexico, especially where isolated mountain areas or the protective vegetative cover of the thorn forest exist; but some species have been badly decimated by hunting. In the arid lands of Sonora and Baja California, desert birds, rodents, and reptiles are the most numerous animals. Among the interesting reptiles are the desert tortoise, the gila monster of Sonora, and the Mexican beaded lizard whose northern range is southern Sonora. Of the same genus these are the only two lizards in the world known to be poisonous to man.

Game birds in the Northwest include quail, bob-whites, pigeons, and doves. The Sierra Madre Occidental is inhabited by wild turkey, and the chicken-like *chacalaca* is found from southern Sonora southward. Migratory ducks and geese fly south in winter along the Pacific flyway, and alight on the rivers and in the lagoons and bays along the Pacific coast. A few migratory waterfowl may be found along the Pacific coast of Baja California, and on the lower Colorado River Delta there are waterfowl in winter. Mexican tree ducks inhabit the coastal regions, especially the large river valleys, from southern Sonora southward.

Among the small mammals of the Northwest, foxes, raccoons, rabbits, and hares dwell throughout the region, the opossum is found on the mainland south of middle Sonora, and squirrels inhabit the high mountains of the mainland and northern Baja California. The coatimundi has migrated up from the moister tropical lands, following the wetter areas in the mountains and foothills of Sonora. The ring-tailed cat or *cacomixtle* is found throughout most of the region, and the badger lives along the rivers in the arid north.

Larger mammals of importance include the coyote, found throughout the region, and the wolf and black bear of the Sierra Madre Occidental. The puma lives throughout the region as does the bobcat. The jaguar and ocelot are found in the humid tropical parts of northwest Mexico and in the foothills of southern Sonora. Jaguar are hunted in the Sierra de Bacatete, a former Yaqui Indian redoubt near the coast north of the Yaqui River. The collared peccary inhabits all of the northwest except the Baja California peninsula. Mule deer are found in northern and western Sonora,

and as three separate races in Baja California. White-tailed deer live in all of the region, except Baja California. Bighorn sheep survive in some abundance on the more desolate, rocky slopes of the deserts of Baja California and northwestern Sonora. Antelope have been severely decimated, but survive in northwestern Sonora and at a few places in the central and northeastern deserts of Baja California. There were once many antelope as far north as San Felipe on the Gulf coast of Baja California. Escaped domesticated livestock, called feral animals, may be hunted in some areas. Feral burros are common in Baja California and in the Sonoran desert areas, and feral goats survive on the islands off the Gulf coast of southern Baja California and on Guadalupe Island in the Pacific.

In the humid tropical parts of the region, live animals not found in the deserts. Tropical birds, including the crested guan, parrot, parakeet, and the muscovy duck, live mostly south of Sonora. The armadillo's range extends only into southern Sonora. River otters inhabit the streams and their banks in Sinaloa and Nayarit. The margay cat and jaguarundi are found only in the humid tropical parts of the Northwest.

The rivers of Northwest Mexico do not, in general, contain good game fish. However, along the lower Colorado River, where the fish fauna of the river has been nearly completely altered through changed river conditions and fish planting, there is a good sportsman's fishery. Native rainbow trout are found in a few small streams in the Sierra San Pedro Mártir in northern Baja California. From Sinaloa southward, where some river systems have cut headward to capture streams of the Gulf of Mexico drainage system, there are good game fish of the Mississippian fauna in the west coast rivers.

In contrast to the river fauna of the Northwest, the sea fauna is abundant and of great commercial value. The most valuable fish catch of the nation comes from the shrimp in the warm waters off the coasts of Sonora and Sinaloa. Along the cold-water coasts of western Baja California, sardines, clams, abalone, and spiny lobsters are taken commercially. Oysters are found in the warm waters near La Paz in southern Baja California, where there was once an important pearl fishery, and along the mainland coast. Some game fish, such as the *corbina* and *totoaba* of the Gulf and the tuna of the Pacific, are taken in commercial quantities. Green turtles are fished commercially by harpooning, and they are taken out of isolated desert ports alive by trucks to the cities of the Northwest.

Game fish in the northwestern waters include barracuda, *cabrilla* (bass); *roncadores* (croakers) like the *corbina, totuava,* and white seabass; *dorados* (dolphin fish); flatfish, like the halibut, flounders, soles, and sanddabs; jacks, including the yellowtail and pampano; mullet; *sierra* (mackerel); snappers; and *majorrone* (grunts). There are also marlin, sailfish, and swordfish. Tuna are for the most part in the Pacific.

Sea mammals have been important in the Mexican Northwest and were especially so during the nineteenth century when some species were hunted to near extinction by New Englanders and other foreign seafarers. Most important has been the California gray whale which winters and calves in Mexican bays in Baja California, southern Sonora, and northern Sinaloa. The winter grounds of the California gray whale have included Black Warrior Lagoon, Scammon's Lagoon, Ballenas Bay, San Ignacio Lagoon, and various lagoons or *esteros* in, and near, Magdalena Bay, all on the west coast of Baja California. Several years ago, wintering grounds were discovered at Yavaros Bay, in southern Sonora, and in Reforma Bay in northern Sinaloa. When the gray whale was finally protected by international treaty, in 1938, there were only several hundred of the species left. In the last century, at the same time when whale oil was so important for lighting, the sea elephant and the sea lion and harbor seal were hunted for oil in the Pacific Ocean off Baja California. The huge sea elephants, some of which weigh around 5,000 pounds, are found along the southwest coast of Baja California and on Guadalupe Island in the Pacific Ocean. Sea otters were pursued down the west coast of America by Russians because the pelts of this little sea mammal were much valued in the Far East. Later, British and Americans hunted the sea otter nearly to extinction. The Guadalupe fur seal was thought to be extinct from overhunting until it was rediscovered in the mid-nineteen-fifties. All of the sea mammals that were commercially important still exist, and their numbers are increasing from the days when some of them were thought to have become extinct.

Cultural Geography

The cultural geography of the Mexican Northwest is fascinating because so many different groups of adventurers and settlers have lived in, or exploited the resources of, the region. In one way or another, all of these groups have left their mark.

Northwest Mexico today is one of the most important agricultural regions of Mexico. The great increase in the productivity of agriculture has come only in this century. Some of the Indian tribes of the northern part of the region and in most of Baja California did not practice agriculture but were hunters, fishermen, and gatherers of wild plants. However, agriculture was basic to the way of life of most of the Indians of Northwest Mexico; and some groups, such as the Cócopa Yumans on the lower Colorado River, carried on agriculture in overflow basins adjacent to river channels. Important Indian crops in the Northwest were corn, beans, pumpkins, the amaranth, *huauhtli*; and cotton. Particular kinds of beans and pumpkins associated with Indian farming, in Sonora and northward, are the tepary or Papago bean, and a pumpkin with a stalk which forms a turban over the top of the fruit. In addition to those already mentioned, many other crops of the Indian agriculture of the Central Highlands extended up the coast of Northwest Mexico.

The Spaniards entered the Northwest very early in the colonial period, but chiefly as explorers on land and sea. Nuño de Guzmán, Cabeza de Vaca, Fray Marcos de Niza, and Coronado had all traversed parts of the Northwest by 1540. Explorations by sea were carried out by Cortés, Ulloa, Alarcón, Cabrillo, and Vizcaíno. However, because of the isolation of the region from the Central Highlands, the aridity of the climate, and the many hostile Indians, Spanish agricultural settlement was limited and many colonies failed. In Sinaloa, south of the Fuerte River, there were Spanish haciendas on which cattle-raising was important, but on which crops were also raised. North of the Fuerte and in Baja California, Spanish irrigation agriculture was introduced by the mission system of settlement. Farming did not maintain many of the missions, especially in Baja California, and food and other goods had to be shipped northward to the missions with deficit economies. Almost all of the crops which are now important in the far Northwest were introduced by the Spanish farmers and missionaries. The arid climate and desertic soils of the northern part of the region were not unlike dryer parts of the Iberian Peninsula, and thus crops typical of the lands around the Mediterranean Sea — wheat, barley, grapes, olives, figs, dates, citrus fruits, garbanzos, peaches, and apricots — as well as less typical crops — rice, sugar cane, and apples — were all introduced with varying degrees of success by the Spanish. The Spaniards also brought Mexican crops, such as corn, beans, squash, *nopal,* and *maguey* to parts of the Northwest where they had not been previously cultivated.

AGRICULTURE GREATLY EXPANDED

In the late nineteenth century, the real "opening" of agricultural settlement occurred in the Northwest. Small irrigation projects were built along the major rivers. Foreigners, especially Americans, came to the Northwest as farming colonists, but also as filibusters (soldiers of fortune) who invaded this distant corner of a Mexico greatly weakened by war with the United States. The foreigners left their imprint in farming techniques, buildings, race, and in many other aspects of the culture of the Northwest of Mexico.

Northwest Mexico was isolated from the main currents of the Mexican Revolution and hence little affected by the ravaging battles and disturbed economic conditions which plagued much of Mexico after 1910. The social and economic conditions which gave impetus to the Revolution in many other parts of the nation were largely absent, for, in the northwest, debt peonage and land hunger were not acute problems. While so much of Mexico was plunged into experimentation with socialistic policy and enterprise by the Revolutionaries, the people of the Northwest were largely carrying on development by free enterprise. Although many of the leaders of the Northwest supported the Revolution, these northerners opposed the land reform policies which produced communal *ejidos,* and favored the creation of small private farms. When, after 1920, men from Sonora took command of the Revolution for some fifteen years, the extension of the *ejido,* and of other more sweeping reforms of the Revolution, was fore-stalled in much of the Northwest. Thus, although many reforms came to the Northwest after President Cár-denas took charge of the Revolution in 1935, the region has continued in a general course of development which was already set by the end of the nineteenth century.

The expansion of irrigated land has been the most significant agricultural development. In Mexico, irrigated farms are held predominantly as private lands (Table IV, D, p. 115), and the dominance of private farms in the irrigated areas of the Northwest is especially important. The organized colony method of establishing private farms on the public domain or an expropriated estate lands has been more significant in the Northwest than in other parts of the nation. In 1952, out of 379 colonies in Mexico, 105 were in Baja California Norte, 64 were in Sonora, and 10 were in Baja California Sur. The colonies were less important in Sinaloa and Nayarit where land tenure conditions and problems were more akin to those of central Mexico. For seventeen years, much land was distributed at low cost to colonists through the implementation of the Federal Law of Colonization of 1946. However, in 1963, a revision in the Mexican Agrarian Code closed the public domain to agricultural colonies and left such public land open for distribution to only the communal *ejidos*. Many private farms and ranches were small enough so that revolutionary land tenure laws did not affect them. Moreover, some of the large ranches still exist because there has been no way to divide them up effectively, and some of the owners of the large ranches have decree concessions which exempt their properties from expropriation for periods of twenty-five years.

In the major irrigated areas of the Northwest, the *ejidos* are more like private properties than in most of Mexico. The large collective *ejidos* have either been divided up into individual *ejido* farms, or modified so that their operation is almost like that of a large co-operative of private farms. The individual *ejido* farms are large, relative to those in most of the nation. Fifty-acre farms are the rule in Baja California. The *ejido* farms are mechanized in Sonora and Baja California, the *ejido* farmers receive agricultural credit from private and government banks, and their farming practices are essentially like those on small private farms. There is little difference in the efficiency of operation of *ejido* farms and small private farms, although the large private farms are operated much more efficiently than either of the other two. Some private farms are larger than the area permitted one farmer by law because, legally or otherwise, land registered in the names of several persons is cultivated by one family. Although primitive methods of agriculture are still employed away from the main currents of economic life, the farming of the major agricultural districts in the Northwest is modern.

OUTSTANDING IRRIGATION DISTRICTS

The major irrigation districts of Northwest Mexico include, from north to south, the lower Colorado Delta;

the Caborca District, on the Magdalena (Concepción) River; the Costa de Hermosillo, located on the alluvial lands where the Sonora River disappears underground near the Gulf coast; the Sonora River Valley at Hermosillo; the Guaymas Valley; the deltas of the Yaqui, Mayo, and Fuerte rivers; and the region around Culiacán (Endpaper maps and Map 1, p. 104). The greater part of the irrigation water comes from the rivers, but in some areas, such as the Costa de Hermosillo, the Caborca district, and the Guaymas Valley, deep wells are the major source. The irrigation districts of the Northwest, and of other regions in Mexico, have come to encompass much of the farmland and agricultural productivity in a country with so many regions of aridity. The development of irrigation has been especially rapid since 1940. By 1958 about 19 per cent of the harvested land in Mexico was within areas served by government irrigation works, and 37 per cent of the value of the crop harvest came from such irrigated areas (Table II, B, page 111).

CROP PRODUCTION

Statistics from the 1960's point up the role of the Northwest as one of the nation's most important agricultural regions. In 1963, one-half of all cotton grown in Mexico came from there, and in that same year, 6 per cent of all the wheat produced in Mexico was raised in the Northwest — 51 per cent of the total in Sonora. Influenced by increased Mexican wheat consumption and a program of government stimulus to growers, Mexico's international trade position in wheat has changed spectacularly from that of an importer, between 1940 and 1958, to that of a significant exporter (1963). However, cotton has still provided the most dramatic among Mexican increases in crop production since 1939 (Table II, page 111). Between 1939 and 1956, Mexican cotton production increased tenfold, and since 1956, production has remained at about ten times that of 1939. In 1963, Mexico was in sixth place among cotton-producing nations, and cotton exports from Mexico were second only to those from the United States. About 75 per cent of all Mexican cotton production is exported.

Besides cotton and wheat there are other crops which are particularly important in the Northwest. Barley, like wheat, is a crop which grows better in the dry air of the Northwest than elsewhere in the nation. Demand from breweries and livestock feeders has made barley a major crop of Mexico and the Northwest (Table II). Since animal feeding is an important enterprise in this prosperous region, alfalfa is a major crop and grain sorghums are becoming increasingly important. In northwestern Baja California, Mediterranean crops grow well and that area produces more olives than any other part of the nation. Although more grapes are grown in Coahuila and Aguascalientes than in Baja California, wine production in Baja California is larger than elsewhere in the nation. As there is a large market in the United States for off-season winter vegetables from the warmer parts of Northwest Mexico,

Near San Blas on the coast of southern Nayarit, a village nestles at the very edge of a tropical evergreen forest, its vegetation in sharp contrast to that of the other more arid regions of the Northwest. The forest is dominated by the *coquito de aceite* or *corozo* palm, which bears a small oil nut useful for food and for making soap.

vegetable-growing is important in the major agricultural districts from Hermosillo to Culiacán. Tomatoes are the most important vegetable, and nearly one-half of all that acreage in Mexico is in the Northwest. Other important vegetable and melon crops include watermelons, cantaloupes, cucumbers, bell peppers, squashes, and peas. By June of 1960, 11,339 railroad carloads of Northwest Mexican vegetables, valued at about forty million dollars, had passed through Nogales, Arizona, on the way to American and Canadian markets. On the west coast of Baja California near Ensenada, chili peppers and market vegetables are raised for Mexican and American markets. In the Yaqui-Mayo districts, rice, garbanzos, and flax are raised, and soybeans are becoming a significant crop. In the warmer lands of Sinaloa and Nayarit, other crops are important commercially. In 1950, Sinaloa was second only to Veracruz in the production of sugar, and was a leading Mexican state in the production of sesame. By 1950, cigarette tobacco production had become so important in Nayarit that the state led all others in tobacco production and contained nearly one-half of all the tobacco acreage in the nation. The traditional Mexican crops, corn and beans, are hardly grown at all in Baja California, are minor crops in Sonora, but more important in Sinaloa and Nayarit.

Although corn and beans are not major crops in most of the Northwest, many of Mexico's outstanding crops are chief crops of the Northwest (Table II, page 111).

In addition to cotton, wheat, and sugar cane, animal feeds as well as soybeans are particularly well developed crops in Northwest Mexico. As the consumption of animal products has risen with increases in Mexican incomes, animal feeds have become a much more vital element in Mexican agriculture.

LIVESTOCK RAISING

Once the Spaniards reached the Northwest, livestock production became established over the vast dry areas of desert and dry thorn forest range where crop farming could not be carried on successfully. The production of cattle, horses, and mules was most important. In the latter nineteenth century, cattle raising prospered in the far Northwest as the Indian menace disappeared and as the market for cattle in the adjacent southwest of the United States increased. Americans held some of the large ranches at that time.

Livestock production has remained important in Northwest, especially in Sonora which is one of the nation's leading areas of cattle production. Many cattle from Sonora, as well as from other Mexican states along the international boundary, are exported to the United States. The cattle of northern Sonora and northern Baja California are "improved Mexican" cattle in which strains of Hereford, Angus, and Holstein are dominant. In Sinaloa and Nayarit, Mexican *criollo* (lower grade, scrub) cattle are most numerous.

In response to the high incomes of the Northwest, especially in Sonora and Baja California, there are many dairy cattle. As in much of northern and central Mexico, new chicken farms and pig farms are also becoming numerous (Table III, p. 113). Nevertheless, many animal products are imported from the United States, especially into Baja California. Commercial live-stock production flourishes in Northwest Mexico because there are export markets for cattle and high incomes within the region so that much of the populace can afford to eat meat, eggs, and dairy products.

MINING FORMERLY MORE IMPORTANT

Before the burgeoning of farming and industry in the Northwest at the turn of the twentieth century, mining was the most significant sector of the frontier economy. Areas prospered and declined, and the population shifted with the fortunes of the mines. Sonora and Sinaloa, in particular, were thought of as treasure houses of precious minerals. Spanish adventurers opened silver and gold mines in veins exposed below the volcanics, in the canyons of the Sierra Madre Occidental and in the desert block ranges west of the main mountain barrier. Mining began at Alamos, Sonora, by the late seventeenth century. The silver mines at San Antonio in southern Baja California were opened in the middle of the eighteenth century. By the latter nineteenth century, gold rushes brought miners from California and elsewhere to the mountains of northern Baja California where both veins and placers were worked. Gold rushes to placer works in the deserts of northwestern Sonora and parts of Baja California occurred into the twentieth century. In the desert of northwestern Sonora great lumps of silver continued to be found from colonial times into the nineteenth century. As elsewhere in Mexico, towards the end of the nineteenth century, foreigners gained control of many important mines.

The major kind of mining in the Northwest today began in the latter nineteenth century when deposits of copper and other minerals created by contact metamorphism began to be exploited. All down the west coast of Mexico there is a zone of mineralization created by contact metamorphism; in fact most of the metamorphic rocks of Mexico are located along the Pacific coast. At Cananea the copper deposits are in a zone between layers of sedimentary and volcanic rocks and the granite rocks which were intruded below these. In central Baja California there are large low-grade deposits of contact metamorphic copper, as well as iron, deposits created in the same way. The tungsten deposits of northern Baja California are found along the zone of contact between the granite mountain mass and blocks of limestone resting on the granite.

Except for Cananea, Sonora, however, mining is no longer as important as it was before 1910 in North west Mexico. In Baja California, the mining of precious metals has effectively ceased. The copper mines are still open at Santa Rosalía; but the French company which opened the mines in the latter nineteenth century sold the property to a Mexican quasi-governmental concern which maintains marginal production in order to keep the town from deteriorating. However, just southeast of Santa Rosalía on San Marcos Island in the Gulf of California, the mining of gypsum, for export to cement factories in California, has become a large enterprise. Salt is mined from deposits along the shores of Black Warrior Lagoon in the middle of the peninsula on the Pacific coast. The salt is exported for paper pulp processing in the Pacific Northwest of the United States and for this and other purposes, at other places on the shores of the Pacific Ocean. Tungsten mining flourished during, and for a while after, World War II in northern Baja California, but when the United States stopped stockpiling this metal, production ceased with the disappearance of the only market. The search for oil in southern Baja California by the national petroleum monopoly has proved futile thus far.

Cananea, Sonora, is one of the most important mining centers in Mexico. About one-half of all the copper produced in Mexico comes from Cananea (Table V, A, p. 119). With the exception of the isolated operation at Santa Rosalía, the only large smelter west of the Western Sierra Madre is located in that Sonora city. In the deserts of Sonora and in the foothills and highlands of the Sierra Madre Occidental, in Sonora, Sinoloa, Nayarit, and bordering Durango, there are mining operations which still garner precious, and other metals from the earth. The important minerals of the foothills and highlands of the Sierra Madre Occidental are silver, gold, and lead. More gold is mined in this area than in any other in Mexico. Tayoltita, Durango is today the leading gold mining center of the nation. Mines of various ores are located at San Ignacio, Ixpa lino, Cosalá, La Rastra, and La Joya in Sinoloa and Tamazula in northwestern Durango. In some of these mountain communities gold dust and little gold balls still serve as money. Gold is still mined in the Sierra Madre foothills of Sonora at El Tigre, Bavispe, Mula tos, and Sahuaripa. Tungsten is mined in middle Sonora and fluor spar in northeastern Sonora. There are lead mines near Santa Ana and manganese mines near Magdalena in northwestern Sonora. At Alamos the old silver mines have been closed since the days during the Revolution when the mines were abandoned and allowed to flood, and then invaded by *gambucinos* (prospectors who stripped out supporting pillars of high-grade ore). However, studies of mine conditions at Alamos are being made in the hope of reopening the silver mines. Although copper is smelted in Sonora, the other ores and concentrates of the Northwest must be transported the long distances to the smelters, *fundiciones*, of the Meseta Central or to El Paso, Texas.

There is some mining potential in the Northwest

but new ventures will have to await other developments, such as the growth of markets. In the desert of northern Baja California, around San Fernando, there are iron ore deposits of considerable size, and in the Yaqui River Valley, around Tónichi, there are coal deposits. Thus, if reserves, grades of ores, and accessibility should prove adequate, there exist the resources for a steel industry in the Northwest. In northern Baja California limestone of high quality is abundant, and at Punta China, on the coast south of Ensenada, limestone is mined for cement manufacture in Ensenada.

MARINE RESOURCES VALUABLE

The exploitation of marine resources in the ocean waters off Northwest Mexico has been substantial during some periods in the history of the region. Many of the Indians of the Northwest camped along the seashores to collect shellfish from tidal waters. Among the first attractions of the Northwest for the Spaniards were the pearl beds along the eastern shore of the southern part of the Baja California Peninsula. Long before mission settlement began on the peninsula in 1697, pearling expeditions from the mainland to the Baja California beds were common. In the nineteenth century, whalers and hunters of the other sea mammals were active in Northwest Mexico, especially along the west coast of Baja California.

Northwest Mexico is now the most significant fishing region in the nation. In order, Baja California, Sonora, and Sinaloa are the states where the fish catch is most valuable in Mexico. Largely because of the high value of shrimp for export, 62 per cent of the value of the fish catch comes from the waters off Northwest Mexico. Coastal places of standing as fish camps or ports with canneries or icing plants are, on the Pacific coast of Baja California, Ensenada, San Quintín, Cedros Island, Bahía de Tortugas, Bahía Asunción, San Juanico, Isla Margarita, Puerto Ulloa, and Cabo San Lucas. La Paz and San Felipe are fish ports on the Gulf shore of Baja California. In Sonora and Sinaloa, Puerto Peñasco, Guaymas, Yavaros, Topolobampo, Altata, Mazatlán, and San Blas are fishing ports. The Mexican government has initiated a program to promote fishing and fish-eating among Mexicans because fish offer an excellent source of the animal protein which are deficient in the diets of most Mexicans. However, fish-eating is not now a culture trait in very many parts of the nation. Only 25 per cent of the Mexican commercial catch is destined for domestic consumption, and in the state of Campeche, where a large portion of the Mexican fish catch is taken, some 62 per cent of the population never eats fish. The percentage is even higher in most parts of the country.

LUMBERING IN THE SIERRAS

Commercial logging in the pine forests of the Northwest is not very important. In Baja California there is a forest *ejido* in the Sierra Juárez with a sawmill, but production of lumber is small. No commercial logging exists in the more heavily timbered Sierra San Pedro Mártir, but it has an excellent potential. Some commercial timber cutting is located on the Pacific slope of the Sierra Madre Occidental.

INDUSTRIES, TOURISM, AND TRANSPORTATION

Many of the industries which have come to characterize Northwest Mexico were begun in the late nineteenth and early twentieth centuries when agricultural settlement and foreign colonization became substantial. These were agricultural processing industries such as sugar mills, cotton gins, flour mills, leather working factories, and wineries, the latter located in northwestern Baja California where grapes had been grown since the mission period. Cotton ginning and flour milling are now the most important industries in the Northwest. Breweries, malt factories, and feed-grain mixing plants have become large industries, and olive packing as well as wine making are significant in northwestern Baja California. Sugar mills are common in Sinaloa and cigarette manufacture and packing leaf tobacco for export have become large industries in Nayarit. Fish canneries and icing plants are found along the coasts. There are several cotton spinning mills, and a cotton textile mill is located in Hermosillo. Many small industries supply local manufactured goods for the prosperous local inhabitants.

Tourism is one of the most vital industries in Northwest Mexico, and income from tourism is probably larger than in any other region in the nation. Because two-thirds of all tourist dollar earnings are derived from the zone along the boundary with the United States, and because Baja California is so close to the great population concentration in Southern California, Tijuana has become the most important tourist city along the international frontier. In 1960, there were 21 million human and 5,600,000 automobile border-crossings from the United States into Tijuana. Total dollar earnings in Tijuana in 1960 were 115 million dollars, and net dollar earnings, after the respending of dollars in the United States by Baja Californians, were 51,120,000 dollars. Other places where tourists from the United States contribute much to the local economies are Ensenada, San Felipe, Guaymas, Alamos, Mazatlán, La Paz, and the nearby region, and San Blas.

Rapid transportation of freight and large numbers of persons were slow in coming to the Northwest where the barrier nature of the Sierra Madre Occidental isolated the region from the heartland of the nation and where, within the region, there were such vast stretches of unsettled arid land. Mule trains moving over tortuous mountain trails and across desert wastelands were the leading means of transportation over much of the region right up into the twentieth century. Sea travel was also widely used. Launches plied the mainland coast and crossed the Gulf of California with goods and frontiersmen during the colonial period and the nineteenth century. The railroad age directed the course of trade and travel northward toward the Southwest of the United States because the railroads were built into Northwest Mexico from that region rather than from interior Mexico. The railroads were one more manifestation of American influence in the Northwest. Although the first railroads were built southward from the United States boundary in the 1880's, the railroad to Guadalajara and Mexico City was not completed up the escarpment into the Central Highlands in Nayarit until 1927, and Baja California was not connected with Sonora and interior Mexico by rail until 1947. Although a rail route across the Sierra Madre Occidental from Chihuahua to northern Sinaloa was surveyed in the 1880's, as part of the shortest route from Kansas City to the Pacific Ocean, the line was not inaugurated until 1962.

Transportation facilities in Northwest Mexico are now as well developed as anywhere in the nation. During the years between 1956 and 1962, as much as one-half of the navy and maritime budget of Mexico was expended in improving the ports of Ensenada and Guaymas, out of which cotton is the most important export.

Automobile roads, of one kind or another, exist almost everywhere in the Northwest. Even remote and isolated ranches and farms have unimproved *brechas,* or automobile tracks, running to them. Important paved highways include the west coast highway between Nogales and Guadalajara; the Mexicali-Santa Ana, Sonoran highway, which links Baja California with the west coast highway; the Tijuana-Arroyo Seco highway down the west coast of Baja California; and the Mexicali-San Felipe highway. In the major agricultural areas, there are grids of paved roads throughout the farmlands. Trucks now carry most of the winter vegetables and melons to markets in the United States. Airlines serve all the major cities of the Northwest. Tijuana has the second busiest airport in Mexico, and the route between Tijuana and Mexico City is the most traveled air course in the nation. As early as 1958, there were some twenty-three flights a week between Mexicali and the nation's capital.

FREE-TRADE AREAS IMPORTANT

A highly significant feature of the cultural geography in Northwest Mexico is the existence of areas of free trade with the United States. All along the international boundary between Mexico and the United States, there is a free-trade perimeter some twenty kilometers wide, but the whole Baja California Peninsula and northwestern part of Sonora, south to Puerto Peñasco, are in a free-trade zone. These free-trade areas have been established and augmented at various times in the past because the northern border zone, especially in the far Northwest, has been so isolated from the rest of the nation that it has been most difficult to supply the region with goods made in Mexico. Thus, most American goods enter these areas duty-free. Such an economic situation has meant that the factors of production in the free-trade areas have been channeled into the most efficient kinds of production and that supplies of many items, expensive in the rest of Mexico, have

been imported cheaply from the United States. However, at the present time, manufacturers in places such as Monterrey and Mexico City are putting pressure on the federal government to reduce the effect of the free-trade areas. Some goods are no longer duty-free, especially if they can be produced by local industry near the international boundary, and reductions in rail rates are given to manufacturers of goods being shipped from the interior to the boundary area. The Mexican government would like to save many of the dollars earned by tourism near the international boundary by having Mexican merchants and manufacturers supply goods to the border population which now buys so many ordinary household items in the United States.

Dollar foreign exchange earned along the international frontier with the United States is extremely important to Mexico because the United States is the chief supplier of imported goods; and there have been only four years since 1940 in which Mexican exports of goods to the United States have exceeded imports from that nation. Much of the excess of import over export goods is paid for in dollars earned by tourism, and as it has been pointed out earlier, some 65 per cent of all American tourist expenditures in Mexico are made in border transactions along the international frontier. Total gross earnings from American tourism increased from 234 million dollars in 1950 to 819 million dollars in 1962. Many of the dollars earned in border transactions are quickly spent back in the United States by Mexicans who live along the international frontier; however, the net balance of border dollar transactions is weighted heavily in favor of Mexico. As stated earlier in the chapter, net earnings from tourism along the border and in the interior of Mexico amount to about one-half of gross earnings. By 1962, some nine hundred thousand Americans had traveled beyond the immediate international boundary as tourists, and 61 million border crossings were made into Mexican border cities, most of them by Americans.

POPULATION INCREASE

As a percentage of the total Mexican population the population of Northwest Mexico has increased since 1910. Since the region has been so prosperous, thousands of immigrants from other parts of the country have come to the Northwest. Between 1950 and 1960 the population of Northwest Mexico increased by about 49 per cent, a greater percentage increase than was recorded in any other Mexican region. In the state of Baja California, the increase in population between 1950 and 1960, of about 130 per cent, was the highest in the nation. With immigration at a peak, the birth rate high in a young population, and the death rate low in a relatively healthy population, it is understandable that the state would have a great proportional increase. Nevertheless, this frontier still contains a smaller percentage of the Mexican people than any other region except the Southeast (Table VI, p. 122). As the economy of the Northwest is characterized essentially by mechanized agriculture, industry, and the services of a modern society, the population of the region is more urban than that of most of the rest of the nation. Moreover, the two border cities of Baja California — Mexicali and Tijuana — are among the larger cities of Mexico (Table VI). After the Revolution, many foreigners left the Northwest or became Mexican citizens. Because so many Indians died at and near the missions, and because in many settlements Spanish women were few or absent, the population of the Northwest is almost entirely *mestizo*.

LEADS IN PROSPERITY

The people of Northwest Mexico have continued to be prosperous. *Per capita* income in Baja California and Sonora is higher than in any other states. In 1960, the gross product *per capita* in Baja California, 952 dollars, was higher than that in any other Mexican state, and was ten and one-half times as much as in Oaxaca, the state with lowest gross produce. In order, Tijuana, Nogales, and Mexicali are the three border cities of Mexico with the highest *per capita* incomes, and incomes in these three cities range between two and one-half and three and one-half times the national average. Income is better distributed among the population in the Northwest than in other regions of Mexico. Minimum wages and taxes are higher in Baja California and Sonora than in other states. In 1955, while the average *per capita* bank deposit in Mexico was 62 pesos, in Baja California it was 1,046 pesos!

Prosperity in Northwest Mexico is reflected in the material well-being and culture traits of the population. In Baja California and Sonora there are more motor vehicles, both *per capita* and absolutely, than in any other Mexican states. The use of electricity is common, even in many villages, in the Northwest. Educational facilities are better than in most parts of the nation. The population, especially in Baja California, is healthier than in other parts of the country. Most of the inhabitants of the Northwest wear manufactured shoes, rather than *huaraches* (sandals) made at home or by craftsmen. Housing is better in most of the Northwest than in other regions, and most of the population sleeps in beds rather than on mats *(petates)* on the floor. The consumption of meat and wheat is more common than the consumption of corn and beans in most of the Northwest. Most of the population of Northwest Mexico lives in a manner which would indicate that the region is thoroughly involved in the modern world.

SOUTHEAST MEXICO

In the southeastern part of Mexico, tropical lands and their hostile Indian inhabitants long conspired toward isolation from the mainstreams of Mexican life. Although Yucatán was the first part of what is now Mexico to become known to the Spaniards, most of the Southeastern Region remained for centuries without effective occupation by either Spaniard or Mexican. Moreover, in the nineteenth century and after the Mexican Revolution, attempts were made by governments on the Yucatán peninsula to secede from Mexico.

In several ways, the Mexican Southeast remained isolated from the rest of the nation until the last twenty or thirty years. Transportation connections between the region and the rest of the nation have been carried on mostly by sea and by air. A railroad into the region was not completed until 1948, while an all-weather paved highway between southern Veracruz and Yucatán was not finished until 1961. Since World War II, with available capital and techniques necessary for the effective development of tropical lands, this region, so early the site of high Indian civilization and contact with the Spaniard, has become a frontier of economic development. Within the tropics of Southeastern Mexico are three states, Tabasco, Campeche, and Yucatán, and the federal territory of Quintana Roo (Endpaper map and Map 1, page 104).

Physical Geography: TROPICAL LOWLANDS

The eastern part of Southeastern Mexico has been called a country without land or water. In Yucatán, Quintana Roo, and eastern Campeche, the surface is that of a limestone platform which was uplifted late in geologic history and extends out across the Caribbean to rise from the sea in Cuba, Florida, and the Bahamas. The surface of this limestone plain is covered with thin and extremely porous soil through which rainwater and runoff sink to pass through fissures in the limestone to the groundwater table. This downward movement of water is so rapid that there are very few surface streams in the limestone area. Thus, good soil and surface water are scarce. However, the groundwater table is rather close to the surface, and in many places the cap rock of limestone has been dissolved by the groundwater to form sink holes, or *cenotes,* in which groundwater is exposed at the bottom of the steep-walled hollows. In other places, windmills are necessary to obtain enough water for cattle in a region of moderate-to-heavy rainfall.

In western Campeche and in Tabasco, vast areas are covered with alluvial materials carried downstream and deposited by great rivers which rise in some of the rainiest lands of Mexico. The seaward portion of Tabasco is made of a series of river deltas, of which two belong to the largest rivers in Mexico. In volume, the Usumacinta River is the largest, and the Chiapas-Grijalva River system is the second largest, in the nation (Map 1, page 104). In fact, about 50 per cent of the stream flow in Mexico is contained in the great rivers which enter the sea along the southern shore of the Bay of Campeche. Lagoons and swamps are common on the low lying delta lands of Tabasco where annual floods inundate enormous areas. While there is a deficiency of surface water in Yucatán, a basic problem in much of Tabasco is flood control.

The north coastal region of Yucatán lies along a line of diverging surface tradewind air traveling northwestward across the Caribbean from Trinidad to the mouth of the Río Grande. Such air does not release moisture except where it flows against mountains as in Veracruz, or piles up because of drag over level surfaces, as in interior Yucatán. Thus rainfall increases along the east coast and in the interior part of the Yucatán peninsula, and is heavy there and in Tabasco. Maximum rainfall in Southeastern Mexico is in the summer, when the moist, warm air masses from the warm seas drift inland over Tabasco and the southern part of the Yucatán peninsula where heavy thundershowers occur. Destructive hurricanes may pass over the region in autumn. In northern Yucatán, average annual precipitation is from about 20 to 40 inches (Map 2, p. 108). On the dry north coast at Progreso, annual rainfall is only 18 inches, but increases rapidly inland so that at Valladolid, only sixty miles from the north coast, annual rainfall is 46 inches (Table I). At Mérida average annual precipitation is 35 inches. Farther south, and along the east coast of the Yucatán peninsula, in coastal Campeche, and in eastern Tabasco, annual rainfall is from about 40 to 80 inches (Map 2, Table I, 36, pp. 108-09). The rainiest parts of Mexico, with the exception of some east-facing mountain slopes in Veracruz, are in a belt extending from western coastal Tabasco inland and eastward into northern Guatemala and the southern part of the Yucatán peninsula. Annual rainfall in this belt is from about 70 to 170 inches. At Villahermosa, capital of Tabasco, annual rainfall is 75 inches, while at Teapa, thirty miles to the south in front of the northern Chiapas Mountains, yearly rainfall is 156 inches (Table I).

The region has very mild winters and hot, humid summers. Average monthly temperatures are in the middle and low 70's in winter, and in the low 80's in the summer.

FROM THORN FOREST TO RAIN FOREST

Following the increase in annual rainfall, eastward and southward in Yucatán and westward in Tabasco, the vegetation of Southeastern Mexico changes from the dry thorn forest of northern Yucatán to more luxuriant plant associations in the wetter areas (Map 3, p. 110). The thorn forest is in appearance like those of other parts of Mexico and, along with the tropical deciduous forest which begins south of Mérida, contains leguminous tropical trees. In the wetter interior of the Yucatán peninsula and on the coast of northern Campeche, there is a belt of tropical evergreen forest like that of so much of the state of Veracruz. However, much of the original evergreen forest has been destroyed by cutting and burning, and where this has occurred the forest has been replaced by scrub growth. In the evergreen forest there are large *ceiba* trees; *zapote* trees which bear edible fruits, sometimes called *mameys;* the *chico zapotes* from which comes the latex *(chicle)* of which chewing gum is made, and palms. Along the east coast, and in the southern and interior parts of the Yucatán peninsula, as well as in coastal Campeche and in parts of Tabasco, is found the only true tropical rain forest of Mexico. The rain forests of the tropics are the most luxuriant and profuse of the vegetation associations of the world, and they contain literally hundreds of species of plants. The top of the forest is a sea of green, intertwined crowns of gigantic trees which shade sunlight from the forest floor. Smaller trees grow below the forest giants, and vines and orchids are attached to the trunks and limbs of the trees. The floor of the forest is usually free of tangled underbrush, but in many places may be covered with standing water. Plant species in the rain forest of Southeastern Mexico include mahogany, *zapote,* and breadnut trees; bamboo and palms; and parasitic and epiphytic plants. In the poorly drained lands of coastal Tabasco, there are vast areas of swamp and savanna grassland where scattered trees grow among the tall, coarse grasses.

Soil conditions throughout much of Southeastern Mexico are inferior, and where productive soils exist there are other problems which make farming difficult. Over much of the Yucatán peninsula the soils derived from the underlying limestone are thin, dry, and stony. In the moister areas, beneath the more luxuriant forests, soils are deeper, but are lateritic and therefore deficient in water-soluble plant nutrients. When such land is cleared for farming, the humus in the topsoil is destroyed by intense heat, leaving the soils poor in structure and deficient in nitrogen. In many areas where alluvial soils would be good for farming, the land is inundated much of the year. However, with flood control many of the floodplain areas can (and in fact have), become lands with productive soils.

FORESTS AND WILDLIFE

Wildlife is abundant in much of the Southeast because there are many areas where human habitation is sparse and many places where the forests give good protective cover to wildlife. All along the coasts there are migratory ducks and geese in winter. Tree ducks also inhabit the coasts, and the muscovy duck lives in the Southeast. Quail, doves, pigeons, bobwhite, and a wild Yucatán turkey are found in the region. Tropical forest birds include curassow, guan, and *chacalaca.*

In the forests live many animals which have come northward from tropical lands to the south. The agouti and paca *(tepescuintle),* small forest rodents, spider and howler monkeys, the kinkajou, and the tapir are all found in this region. Primitive animals from the south include the opossum, porcupine, armadillo, and collared anteater. Other animals include a ringtailed cat, the raccoon, coatimundi, squirrels, tropical forest rabbit, and the gray fox. Both the collared peccary, common in much of the rest of Mexico, and the white-lipped peccary dwell in the Southeast. The white-tailed deer and the small brocket deer are wildlife inhabitants of the region. All of the Mexican cats, except the bobcat — that is — the jaguar, puma, ocelot, margay, and jaguarundi are found in Southeast Mexico. The wildlife of the region provides important items in the diets of some of the local inhabitants and is also sought after by sportsmen.

In northern Yucatán as well as in the foothills of the Sierra Madre in Sonora and the lowlands of northern Sinaloa, there are large thorn forests, characterized by a mixture of thorny leguminous trees and cactus. Bare and bleak in winter, the green thorn forest in spring and summer is brightened by an abundance of colorful flowers.

ABUNDANT SEA LIFE

The coastal waters of Southeastern Mexico team with many kinds of game and commercial fish. Important species on the north-facing coast are those already mentioned as being found along the Veracruz coast: shrimp, snook *(robalo),* grunts *(mojarra),* jewfish *(mero),* croakers *(roneadores),* mackerel, pampano, and snappers. Of increasing importance for sport fishing are the coastal lagoons and offshore waters of the east coast of Yucatán and of Quintano Roo. Off the eastern shore are barracuda, groupers, tarpon, snook, snappers, mullet, king mackerel, amberjack, and the larger pelagic fish: sailfish, marlin, dolphin, and tuna. Along the east coast the fish are often concentrated above upwellings of fresh water which comes from the groundwater beneath the limestone surface of the Yucatán peninsula. These upwellings of fresh water within the sea are called *ojos de agua,* and were a curiosity commented upon by the Spaniards who found Indians from the streamless land obtaining fresh water at sea.

Cultural Geography

Man has been a farmer or has lived from products of the forests in most of the areas in which he has settled in the hot, low tropical lands of the Mexican Southeast. However, particular kinds of agricultural practices and crops have evolved in this region where, in many places, climate and land have not been propitious for farming. Today, problems resulting from the difficult natural environment and from isolation are rapidly being overcome, and southeastern Mexico has become a new frontier of the modern nation.

MAYA AND SPANISH ECONOMIES

The Maya Indians built an astonishing civilization, first in damp rain forests where many plant nutrients are leached out of the soils, in northern Guatemala and in the southern part of the Yucatán peninsula; and later in the thorn forests of the region of dry, porous limestone-derived soils in northern Yucatán. Yet, Maya culture was based on an agriculture which supported a rather dense population. Indian farms were kept productive in a system of shifting agriculture in which the ashes from the cleared and burned forest added fertility to the soil, and land was abandoned after some years of cultivation. One of the worst hazards of modern farming in Yucatán, keeping noxious plants of the surrounding forest from encroaching on fields, was apparently avoided for long periods of time by hand-weeding in the garden farming of the Maya. The agricultural society of the Mayas, in which metallurgy was unknown and the dog was the only domesticated animal, was closely knit together and sustained by religion and a priestly class. Revolt against control by the priests in the great cities is probably a better explanation for the decline of the Maya civilization by the time the Spaniards arrived, than are natural catastrophe or the exhaustion of soils from too many years of farming in a tropical environment.

Many of the crops grown in central Mexico were important in Indian agriculture and are still the chief crops today. Corn, kidney beans, squash, *chayotes,* tomatoes, *jícamas,* and chiles are among the traditional crops of the region. The small black beans of southern Mexico are more important than the reddish bean of central Mexico. Tropical crops grown since Indian times are *camotes,* or sweet potatoes, cotton, and cacao (Table II). The forests of the Southeast have supplied Indian, Spaniard, and Mexican alike with many products. Tropical fruits include papaya, avocado, *anonas,* one of which is the *chirimoya,* vanilla, *granadillas,* guavas, *zapotes* and *chico zapotes,* and breadnut fruits, the seeds of which are boiled and eaten. The papaya and *chico zapote* are fruits which probably originated as domesticates within the Maya culture area. The leaves of the *chaya* plant, boiled and eaten, are a source of vitamins and minerals. The orange-red juice and outer covering of seeds from the *achiote* tree are used as coloring and flavoring. Tobacco, rubber, and *copal,* the latter used for incense, can be gathered in the forests. Honey, gathered in the woods, in Indian times from the stingless bee and now from the introduced European bee as well, can be mixed with water and the bark of the *balche* tree and fermented into an alcoholic drink.

In addition to the gathering of plant products of the forests, hunting has been an important source of food and other products. Deer, tropical fowl-like birds, the forest rodents, and jaguars are all game animals. The *quetzal* bird of the highlands to the west and south of the lowland Maya area has been highly prized for its colorful plumage, and thus has been hunted nearly to extinction in some areas.

Even after the Spanish had finally secured southeastern Mexico by conquest, between 1541 and 1546, Indian revolts continued to occur during the colonial period. Nevertheless, the Spaniards established many indigo plantations and processing factories in the region. Indian production of cacao in rainy parts of the Southeast was supplemented by crops from Spanish plantations. The cultivation of native tobacco and introduced sugar also became important in the wet areas of the region.

HENEQUEN IMPORTANT CROP

Since the middle of the nineteenth century, the most significant development in agriculture has been the large-scale, commercial production of fibers from henequen. This species of *agave* or *maguey* grows well in the dry area of porous soils in the northern part of the Yucatán peninsula. The Indians had used the *maguey* fibers for making such articles as shoes, rope, and bags, and the Spanish added saddle gear to the uses of the fibers. However, it was not until the 1870's that large-scale production and exports stimulated the spread of henequen over much of northern Yucatán and Campeche. By that date, hand-decorticating had been supplanted by mechanical decorticators powered by steam engines, and a great demand for strong binder twine made from henequen had been created by the invention of the self-binding harvester in the United States. The rise of the henequen industry brought great prosperity to traditionally poor Yucatán. Mérida grew to be an important city.

Until World War I, henequen growers on the northern part of the Yucatán peninsula were able to maintain a virtual monopoly on world production, thus assuring themselves high prices most of the time. However, during World War I the Germans managed to get the production of sisal, a Mexican *agave* similar to henequen, started in their East Africa colonies which later became British. Since the end of the First World War, planters in other areas in the semiarid tropics have instituted the cultivation of this fiber, and Mexican henequen production has been plagued by low prices and problems attendant to land reforms of the Revolution. However, henequen remains one of the most important crops in Mexico (Table II, page 111).

In 1937, President Cárdenas expropriated most of the henequen plantations, and established collective *ejidos* on land that had been privately owned. These unschooled collective farmers proved unable to manage commercial farming, and production suffered. Now, much of the production on the *ejidos* is actually managed by former landowners and other capitalists who also run processing plants for the *ejidatarios* and share in the profits of production. Because the henequen *ejidos* are large, and because so much of the agriculture of Southeastern Mexico follows traditional patterns of land tenure in the shifting cultivation of the forests, *ejidos* are less numerous in the Southeast than anywhere else in Mexico except in the Northwest.

THE RURAL ECONOMY

The staple crops of the Southeast remain those of the Indians. One third of all sweet-potato production in Mexico originates in Yucatán and Tabasco. Henequen is by far the most important commercial crop, and 95 per cent of all Mexican production comes from Yucatán and most of the rest from Campeche (Table II, p. 111). Sixty per cent of all cacao grown in Mexico comes from

Tabasco, and the coastal lands of the Southeast contain about one-half of all the cocoanut plantation land in the nation. In Tabasco, there is considerable commercial production of bananas, rice, and sugar in the northern lowlands, while in the interior highlands, coffee is grown on lands contiguous with the coffee highlands of Chiapas.

Commercial collection of certain plant products of the forests of the Southeast has been important since the colonial period, but especially since the middle of the nineteenth century. Dyewoods, gums, and tropical log woods are taken from the forests for local use and for export. One of the important forest products is chicle which is used in making chewing gum. Chicle is gathered by tapping the *chico zapote* tree for its latex, much the way a rubber tree is tapped. Chicle gatherers, who live short, unhealthful lives in the tropical forests, bring large balls of chicle out of the forests for processing in world chewing-gum industries, especially in Mexico and the United States where the chewing-gum habit is widespread. Most of Mexico's chicle comes from Quintana Roo and Campeche.

Unlike most of Mexico, coastal, lowland Tabasco and Campeche suffer excessive rainfall and floods as major agricultural problems. Nevertheless, some of the best farming soils in the nation lie in the flood basins of the great rivers of the Southeast. With river control, agriculture on these floodplains can absorb large numbers of Mexican farmers from parts of the nation where the rural populations are now excessive. With proper though expensive control of rivers, soils, insect pests, tropical plant and human diseases, and weed growth, these alluvial plains promise to be a new frontier for Mexico. On the Mal Paso stretch of the Grijalva River in northwestern Chiapas state, the Raudales de Mal Paso Dam is now under construction (Map 1, p. 104). This huge dam, and downstream hydraulic projects, will provide flood control and irrigation works for some 850,000 acres of land which will be divided about equally between crop fields and pastures, and thousands of new families will be settled on newly created agricultural lands.

Moreover, the dam will bring about the creation of a lake twice the size of Lake Chapala. Not only will this provide electric power for industry, but it will maintain water levels permitting navigation of the lower Grijalva River all year. Such development projects as are forecast by the Raudales Dam will be prerequisites to the "opening" of the hot, moist, lowlands of Southeastern Mexico.

When the Spaniards placed European livestock, especially cattle, on the tropical savanna grasslands and forest lands of the Southeast, animal husbandry was first established in the region. Because so much of the land could not be farmed successfully, large cattle haciendas came to cover much of the rather poor range country in Southeastern Mexico. During the nineteenth century, except in the Indian forest country of Quintana Roo, land became increasingly concentrated on the great haciendas. Nevertheless, because of the low carrying-capacity of the ranges and because of the absence of a tradition of animal husbandry among the many Indians, the Southeast is not one of the major livestock regions of Mexico. Beekeeping, more in harmony with tradition, is still important.

FISHING, MINING, AND INDUSTRY

Commercial and sport fishing, for the species listed in the section on the physical geography of Southeastern Mexico, is significant along the long shoreline of the Southeast. Commercial fishing has the most standing in Campeche, especially at Ciudad Carmen, on Isla Carmen, which forms the seaward limit of the Laguna de Términos. Among all Mexican states, Campeche stands only behind Baja California, Sonora, and Veracruz in the tonnage of fish taken annually. Off the east coast of Yucatán, Isla Mujeres and Isla Cozumel are the chief sport fishing centers.

Mining does not exist over most of the Southeast where so much of the surface is underlain by limestone or covered deeply with the alluvium of the great rivers. However, in northern Tabasco, there are small oil fields, and oil exploration has been active along the Gulf coast in the last decade.

Manufacturing is not strong yet in Southeastern Mexico. Some Indian villages still maintain craft industries, and the agricultural processing industries begun in colonial times still provide such products as sugar and cacao for Mexican and world markets. The preparation of henequen fiber for market is still a major industry in Yucatán. With the penetration of the Southeast by railroad and paved highway, and with the promised introduction of cheap hydroelectric power, there is developing an important impetus to the future of manufacturing.

TOURISM AND TRANSPORTATION

Over the last twenty-five years, tourism has been a growing industry in Yucatán. Tourists have come to view the Maya ruins at places such as Chichén Itzá and Uxmal, and to fish in waters along the coasts, especially off Isla Mujeres and Isla Cozumel. Now that there is at last a railroad and a paved highway between central Mexico and Yucatán, tourism is increasing. Such formerly out-of-the-way places as the Maya ruins at Palenque in northeastern Chiapas are convenient to modern transportation routes. Airways have, of course, placed many small fishing ports and isolated Indian ruins within tourist reach.

Thus the isolation of southeastern Mexico from the rest of the nation has now been partially overcome. The Maya Indians maintained a system of stone roads between some of their cities; but it was a long and difficult trail that led westward toward the other high Indian cultures. Although during the henequen boom of the late nineteenth and early twentieth centuries, a system of rail lines was built throughout the northern part of the Yucatán Peninsula, during the colonial period and the nineteenth century, only mule trails and sea routes connected the Southeast with the rest of the nation. Airplane flights first made rapid transportation links in the nineteen-thirties. The railroad of the Southeast finally linked Yucatán with the other railroads of Mexico in 1948. Now a paved highway leads eastward from Coatzacoalcos in southern Veracruz across the swampy lowlands of Tabasco and Campeche to Yucatán, and before many years have passed, there should be good roads leading into the interior of the Yucatán Peninsula all the way to southern Quintana Roo, which, incidentally, is a free-trade zone with cheap British goods, along the boundary with Belize or British Honduras.

Thus geographic isolation, which for so long maintained strong regionalism, fostered separatist movements, and retarded economic development, has finally become a thing of the past. Effective transportation to southeastern Mexico portends cultural changes that have probably not been equaled since the arrival of the Spanish in the region.

POPULATION GROWTH LAG

The "opening" of this region with projects for economic development and new transportation routes has only just begun to bring about major changes in the population and settlement patterns. Yucatán, Quintana Roo, and even Campeche have remained strongly Indian. On the Yucatán Peninsula, the Mayas remained an important force until after their unsuccessful uprising in the War of the Castes in the mid-nineteenth century. In 1895, seventy per cent of the population of Yucatán was still classified as speaking Indian languages. Many of the rural Indian and *mestizo* folk remain effectively outside the urban market economy. Population growth in the Southeast has not kept pace with the national rate. However, in Quintana Roo a small population nearly doubled between 1950 and 1960. The total population of the region was only about 1,300,000 in 1960, and was smaller than that of any of the other regions in the nation (Table VI, p. 122).

Much of the countryside remains nearly or completely unsettled, and thus both Yucatán and Campeche are two of the most urban states in Mexico (Table VI). However, it would appear that, like the Northwest three decades ago, the Southeast stands on the verge of important increases in population and significant changes in the structure and cultural characteristics of population which accompany economic change.

THE MEXICAN PEOPLE: THEIR LAND AND THE FUTURE

Great changes have taken place in both the land and people of Mexico over the long history of man's settlement. Natural resources have been sometimes developed and sometimes abused, and some of the more favorable parts of the country have become densely populated. The physical geography of parts of Mexico which remain sparsely settled has greatly limited the ease with which these lands can be developed economically. Cultural geography also reveals problems limiting the facility and speed with which change can occur in a nation where many people cling to traditions of Indian and colonial forebears. Moreover, the rapidity of population growth makes the increase of prosperity difficult even though economic productivity is increased. Contrary to much popular opinion, the natural resources of Mexico are not abundant, in relation to the size of the growing population and the manner in which the resources are being exploited in much of the country.

The problems of physical geography faced by Mexicans relate to the particular kinds of natural resources available to man in Mexico. In the expansion of agricultural area, farmlands will have to be extended into the arid lands of the north and the tropics of the south. In both of these parts of the nation, cultivation is difficult or impossible without great expenditures for irrigation works and/or improved systems of tropical agriculture. The rehabilitation of farms in the older agricultural areas and the conservation of soil throughout the nation must be undertaken on a massive scale if the Mexican land is to continue to feed its people and industries and provide exports to pay for important agricultural and industrial imports. Other natural resources, such as those of the seas, forests, and mines, must be exploited more efficiently, while being husbanded carefully, in order to support properly more people in a better way of life. Terrain, climate, and dense forests, in many parts of Mexico make road and railroad building most difficult. Nevertheless, the expansion of the modern transportation network must be pushed back farther from the trunk routes into the countryside in order to bring all Mexicans within the national commercial economy. The features of physical geography present both opportunities for, and impediments to, economic development.

With respect to cultural geography, important factors in change will be man's ability and desire to utilize more effectively the natural and human resources of the country. Such desire must come to exist within the two-thirds of the population still remaining in the "traditional sector" of society. They must, somehow, be brought into the "modern sector" if Mexico is to continue modernization. Change is naturally slow in a nation where regional cultural and economic differences are pronounced, where millions of citizens still do not speak the national language in their daily lives, and where the knowledge of the possibility of a better way of life remains unawakened in much of the population. Moreover, substitutes for an older order of life may be fraught with unforeseen and unpleasant conditions, such as industrial slums, quite as undesirable as a more primitive state of affairs.

Since one of the basic needs of Mexico is a better-educated population, it is encouraging and commendable that the largest single item in the federal budget over the last several years has been education. The literate proportion of the population is increasing steadily. In 1960, some 62 per cent of Mexicans over five years of age knew at least the rudiments of reading nd writing. However, in the poorer states of central nd southern Mexico only about 40 per cent of the opulation was literate, while in the rich northern states, 5 to 80 per cent of the population was literate. The aste of human resources from poor health conditions as also been greatly remedied, but much remains to e done. The disease rate in the years, 1955–59, was ut half that in the years 1929–31, although certain iseases indicative of an inadequate standard of living, uch as gastrointestinal ailments and influenza and pneu- nonia, are still most prevalent. Nevertheless, the disease ate continues to drop, and the incidence of some dis- ases, such as malaria, has been reduced drastically by overnment health programs. These problems of poor ducation and health, and general inefficiency within he "traditional sector" of society are of course most ronounced on the farmlands in central and southern Mexico. When living standards are raised for the people here and for the majority of the farmers of Mexico hrough better farming methods, and, perhaps, changes n land-tenure organization, there will be a greater mass narket for the products, services, and continued growth f other sectors of the Mexican economy.

The improvement of the Mexican standard of liv- ng, difficult enough if the population were static, is nore complex a problem because, with an increase of bout 3.1 per cent a year, Mexico has one of the most apidly increasing populations in the world. After cen- uries of slow growth and periods of severe decline, occasioned by disease and civil war and strife, the Mex- can population nearly doubled between 1940 and 1963. n 1960 the census placed the Mexican population at ust under 35 millions, and the population was estimated o be about 38½ millions in 1963. While the deathrate as been drastically reduced over the last thirty years, he birthrate remains among the highest on earth. Thus, ttempts to increase the standard of living in Mexico nust keep pace with the rapidly increasing population vhich includes an extremely high percentage of depen- lent young persons. Nevertheless, because the gross ational product trebled between 1939 and 1959, *per apita* income nearly doubled between those years, and n 1961, was approximately 3,500 pesos or 280 dollars.

Population increase has been greatest in the cities vhere it creates all kinds of real and potential prob- ems. As late as 1930, only one-third of the Mexican opulation was urban, but by 1960, fifty-one per cent f the population lived in settlements of over 2,500 opulation. In just ten years, between 1950 and 1960, he population of the Federal District increased by 58 er cent while that of Monterrey grew by 80 per cent, hat of Guadalajara by 100 per cent, that of Juárez by 40 per cent, that of Tijuana by 150 per cent, and that f Mexicali by 165 per cent! The creation of decent iving conditions of these vast new urban populations s a monumental task.

Considering the nature of all of these problems, he Mexican nation has made great progress over the ast several decades. The economy is now well diversi- ied compared to most Latin American economies.

Mexico is one of the few of the so-called emerging nations in which population growth has not offset gains in the gross national product. In Mexico, as we have seen, there have been significant gains in real *per capita* income.

The efficiency which comes with mechanization will enable increasing numbers of Mexicans to raise their standard of living. This must take place not only in the industrial centers but mechanization must also raise crop yields and free fields from producing feed for unneeded draft animals. Trucks, buses, and auto- mobiles must be able to travel roads where now only paths or jeep trails lead. Fishing and forestry also need the efficiency of the machine. In fact, if properly employed, the machine in Mexico, as everywhere in the world, can help to bring about a better life, wherein the resources of the land and sea are not abused nor the vital ways of life and values destroyed; and the natural and human resources are conserved for the benefit of millions yet unborn.

As mechanization progresses in Mexico, the hope will be also for a more equitable distribution of income, a measure that will promote the mass market and increase the number of enterprisers necessary for grow- ing productivity.

In addition, the road to a better life in Mexico must be paved with imports of items necessary for economic development, including some foodstuffs. In- come derived from remittances of *braceros* (migrant laborers employed in the United States) and from heavy capital investment by Americans in Mexico has been declining; yet the need for foreign exchange to pay for the excess of imports of goods over exports of goods remains. So that needed imports may be maintained, it appears that the tourist industry must be increased as much as possible. Although Mexican trade with Japan, Western Europe, and South America has in- creased over the last decade, there appears to be little chance that a major shift in the direction of Mexican foreign trade away from the United States will occur. In 1963 some 68 per cent of all Mexican imports came from the United States. These imports could be paid for readily, because in 1963, about 61 per cent of all Mexican exports went to the United States and addi- tional dollar income was derived from tourism, *bracero* remittances and capital investment from the United States. Continued dollar, and other foreign exchange, income is of utmost importance in Mexico, and the imports should continue to be those which will aid in economic development.

Regional differences in Mexicans and their land will not be erased easily by economic progress. In fact, only by taking account of these regional variations in physical and cultural geography, will the people of Mexico be able to make a rational approach to im- proving their lives. The varied appeal of the Mexican countryside, from the great desert basins of the north to the rugged mountains and verdant tropical plains of the south, will remain, as will the charm of the Mexi- cans who live in those lands.

BIBLIOGRAPHICAL NOTES

The reader has been spared the frequent interruptions which would have been injected into the preceding chapter through the use of footnotes. However, as the author has drawn extensively upon certain source materials, these sources are presented here. This selected list of literature includes many publications which are not geographies; but which, nevertheless, deal with the relationships between man and land in Mexico. Thus, in addition to providing a list of sources, the bibliography is designed to serve the reader as a guide to further reading in Mexican geography and allied subjects. Sources of statistical information provide references to data which may not have been presented completely in the chapter text. As an aid to those unfamiliar with the authors of the publications listed, the bibliography is arranged according to subject groupings. Publications in Spanish, and a few of those in English, are annotated. Works which constitute, in the author's view, a basic reading list of geographical material for the English speaking student, traveler, businessman, or sportsman are preceded by an asterisk.

General Geography

JAMES, PRESTON E. *Latin America*. 3rd ed. New York: Odyssey Press, 1959. Chapter XX, pp. 584-655.

TAMAYO, JORGE L. Geografía General de México. 2nd ed. México: Instituto Mexicano de Investigaciones Económicas, 1962. 5 vols. Vol. I: *Geografía Física*, 562 pp. Vol. II: *Geografía Física*, 648 pp. Vol. III: *Geografía Biológica y Humana*, 633 pp. Vol. IV: *Geografía Económica*, 777 pp. *Atlas Geográfico General de México*, 22 plates and text. (The most detailed modern geography of Mexico. Includes a large atlas. Best used as a reference. Contains errors in details.)

VIVO, JORGE A. *Geografía de México*. 4th ed. México: Fondo de Cultura Económica, 1958. 349 pp. (A text designed for use in secondary schools. Contains much statistical data.)

Physical Geography

GENTRY, HOWARD S. *Rio Mayo Plants*. Carnegie Institution, Pub. No. 527. Washington: 1942. 328 pp.

PUBLICATIONS OF THE INSTITUTO MEXICANO DE RECURSOS NATURALES RENOVABLES, A.C. (Publications concerned with such subjects as arid lands, forests, and water resources by the Mexican Institute of Renewable Natural Resources.)

*JAEGER, EDMUND C. *The North American Deserts*. Stanford, California: Stanford University Press, 1957. 308 pp.

*LEOPOLD, A. STARKER. *Wildlife of Mexico. The Game Birds and Mammals*. Berkeley: University of California Press, 1959. 568 pp.

MARTINEZ, MAXIMINO. *Plantas útiles de la flora méxicana*. México: Ediciones Botas, 1959. 621 pp. (A manual of the useful plants of Mexico.)

NELSON, EDWARD W. *Lower California and its Natural Resources*. Memoirs of the National Academy of Science, Vol. XVI, No. 1, Washington: Government Printing Office, 1921. 194 pp. (A basic book on Baja California. Good source for physical geography and cultural geography in the early twentieth century.)

*PESMAN, M. WALTER. *Meet Flora Mexicana*. Globe, Arizona: Dale S. King, 1962. 280 pp. (A plant manual designed for use by the layman. Plants are grouped according to geographical plant associations.)

RAISZ, ERWIN. *Landforms of Mexico*. Physiographic diagram with text. Cambridge, Massachusetts.

SHREVE, FORREST, AND IRA L. WIGGINS. *Vegetation of the Sonoran Desert*. Stanford, California: Stanford University Press, 1964. Vol. I, pp. 1-840; II, pp. 841-1740.

STANDLEY, PAUL C. *Trees and Shrubs of Mexico*. Contributions from the United States National Herbarium Vol. 23, Parts 1-5. Washington: Smithsonian Institution, Part 4, 1924, Parts 1-3, 5, reissued in 1961. 1721 pp.

SYKES, GODFREY. *The Colorado Delta*. Joint publication of the American Geographical Society, Special Pub. No 19, and the Carnegie Institution of Washington, Pub No. 460. New York: 1937. 193 pp. (The classic work on the physical geography of the Colorado Delta. Includes much historical cultural geography.)

VIVO, JORGE A., AND JOSE C. GOMEZ. *Climatología de México*. Instituto Panamericano de Geografía e Historia Pub. No. 19, Mexico: 1946. 80 pp. (A climatology of Mexico containing climatic data and many climatological maps.)

WERNSTEDT, FREDERICK L. *World Climatic Data. Latin America and the Caribbean*. State College, Penn: Geography Department, 1961. Mexico, pp. 53-65.

Cultural Geography

HISTORICAL GEOGRAPHY

BARGALLO, MODESTO. *La minería y la metalurgia en la América española durante la época colonial*. México: Fondo de Cultura Económica, 1955. 433 pp. (The story of mining and metallurgy in the Spanish colonial New World. Includes major sections on Mexico.)

*CHEVALIER, FRANCOIS. *Land and Society in Colonial Mexico. The Great Hacienda*. Trans. by Alvin Eustis. Edited by Lesley Byrd Simpson. Berkeley and Los Angeles: University of California Press, 1963. 334 pp. (The evolution of land tenure and land use, and their effects upon society during the colonial period in Mexico.)

CORTES, FERNANDO. *Fernando Cortés: His Five Letters of Relation to the Emperor Charles V*. Trans. and ed. by Francis A. MacNutt. Cleveland: The Arthur H. Clark Company, 1908. Vol. I, 354 pp.; Vol. II, 374 pp.

DUSENBERRY, WILLIAM. The Mexican Mesta. *The Administration of Ranching in Colonial Mexico*. Urbana: University of Illinois Press, 1963. 253 pp.

GAGE, THOMAS. *Thomas Gage's Travels in the New World*. Edited by J. Eric Thompson from *The English-American his Travail by Sea and Land: or, A New Survey of the West-Indies*. Norman: University of Oklahoma Press, 1958. 379 pp.

GUZMAN-RIVAS, PABLO. "Geographic Influences of the Galleon Trade on New Spain," *Revista Geográfica* of the Instituto Pan-Americano de Geografía e Historia Vol. XXVII, No. 53, (Julho-Dezembro, 1960), pp 1-81.

McNEELEY, JOHN H. *The Railroads of Mexico.* Southwestern Studies, Vol. II, No. 1. El Paso: Texas Western College Press, 1964. 56 pp.

MORLEY, SYLVANUS G., AND GEORGE W. BRAINERD. *The Ancient Maya.* 3rd ed. Stanford, California: Stanford University Press, 1959. 494 pp.

PETERSON, FREDERICK A. *Ancient Mexico. An Introduction to the Pre-Hispanic Cultures.* New York: G. P. Putnam's Sons, 1959. 313 pp.

ROBERTSON, THOMAS A. *A Southwestern Utopia.* Los Angeles: The Ward Ritchie Press, 1947. 261 pp. A second edition published in 1964. (The story of American colonization in the Fuerte River Valley of Northern Sinaloa in the latter nineteenth century.)

SAHAGUN, FRAY BERNARDINO DE. *A History of Ancient Mexico.* Trans. from the Spanish edition of Carlos María de Bustamante by Fanny R. Bandelier. Nashville, Tennessee: Fisk University Press, 1932. 315 pp.

SCHURZ, WILLIAM L. *The Manila Galleon.* New York: E. P. Dutton and Co., 1959. 453 pp.

*SIMPSON, LESLIE BYRD. *Many Mexicos.* Berkeley: University of California Press, 1952. 349 pp. (An history of Mexico which includes a great deal of cultural geography.)

_____. *The Encomienda in New Spain. The Beginning of Spanish Mexico.* Berkeley: University of California Press, 1950. 257 pp.

VAILLANT, GEORGE C. *Aztecs of Mexico.* Garden City, New York: Doubleday, Doran and Co., 1941. 340 pp.

WOLF, ERIC R. *Sons of the Shaking Earth. The People of Mexico and Guatemala, Their Land, History and Cultures.* Chicago: University of Chicago Press, 1959. 303 pp.

NATIVE AND INTRODUCED CROPS AND LIVESTOCK

SAUER, CARL O. *Agricultural Origins and Dispersals.* Bowman Memorial Lectures, Series Two. New York: The American Geographical Society, 1952. 110 pp.

_____. "Cultivated Plants of South and Central America," *Handbook of South American Indians,* Julian H. Steward, editor. Smithsonian Institution, Bureau of American Ethnology. Bulletin 143. Washington: Government Printing Office, 1950. Vol. VI, 487-543.

_____. *Plant and Animal Exchanges Between the Old and New Worlds. Notes from a Seminar Presented by Carl O. Sauer.* Ed. and comp. by Robert M. Newcomb. Los Angeles: 1963. 87 pp.

MODERN MEXICAN ECONOMY AND SOCIETY

BANCO NACIONAL DE COMERCIO EXTERIOR. *México 1960* and *México 1963.* Mexico: 1960 and 1963. 1960, 366 pp. 1963, 354 pp. (Concise references for historical, political, economic, and social information about Mexico.)

PUBLICATIONS OF THE DEPARTAMENTO DE INVESTIGACIONES INDUSTRIALES OF THE BANCO DE MEXICO.

MOSK, SANFORD A. *Industrial Revolution in Mexico.* Berkeley: University of California Press, 1954. 331 pp.

ORIVE ALBA, ADOLFO. *La política de irrigación en México.* Mexico: Fondo de Cultura Económica, 1960. 292 pp. (Chiefly concerned with the history of the development of irrigation in Mexico during different political periods.)

PUBLICATIONS OF THE SECRETARIA DE RECURSOS HIDRAULICOS. Generally in Spanish.

*WHETTEN, NATHAN L. *Rural Mexico.* 3rd ed. Chicago: University of Chicago Press, 1958. 671 pp. (The outstanding book on rural sociology in modern Mexico.)

YATES, PAUL L. *El desarrollo regional de México.* 2nd ed. México: Departamento de Investigaciones Industriales, Banco de México, 1962. 271 pp. (Regional patterns of economic development in Mexico.)

AGRARIAN REFORM AND LAND TENURE

CODIGO AGRARIO DE LOS ESTADOS UNIDOS MEXICANOS. 3rd ed. Mexico: Editorial Porrúa, S.A., 1957. 318 pp. (This publication contains the Mexican Agrarian Code as well as the text of other Mexican laws concerned with rural properties.)

FERNANDEZ Y FERNANDEZ, RAMON. *Propiedad privada versus ejidos.* Ediciones comemorativas del centenario de la Escuela Nacional de Agricultura 1854-1954. México: 1953. 135 pp. (A critical analysis of land reform in Mexico by a university professor and former government official.)

MENDIETA Y NUÑEZ, LUCIO. *El problema agrario de México.* 6th ed. México: Editorial Porrúa, S.A., 1954. 564 pp. (Historical, political and legal treatment of land tenure and agrarian reform in Mexico.)

SENIOR, CLARENCE. *Land Reform and Democracy.* Gainesville: University of Florida Press, 1958. 269 pp. (A case study of agrarian reform in the Laguna District of Coahuila and Durango.)

SIMPSON, EYLER N. *The Ejido, Mexico's Way Out.* Chapel Hill: University of North Carolina Press, 1937. 849 pp. (Contains much information concerning rural economic and social conditions during the early years of land reform. The optimistic views of land reform prevalent among American writers at the time of the initiation of that reform are evident in this book.)

TANNENBAUM, FRANK. *Mexico, the Struggle for Peace and Bread.* New York: Alfred A. Knopf, 1950. 293 pp. (A basic book on land reform in Mexico.)

Statistical Materials

DIRECCION GENERAL DE ESTADISTICA. *Anuarios estadísticos de los Estados Unidos Mexicanos.* Mexico: Talleres Gráficos de la Nación. (Statistical annuals published yearly by the Mexican federal government.)

DIRECCION GENERAL DE ESTADISTICA. *Censo Industrial, 1956. Resumen General.* Mexico: Talleres Gráficos de la Nación, 1959. Vol. I, 212 pp.; Vol. II, 202 pp.; Vol. III, 222 pp. (Summary volumes of the 1956 industrial census.)

*DIRECCION GENERAL DE ESTADISTICA. *Compendio Estadístico, 1960.* Mexico: Talleres Gráficos de la Nación, 1962. 165 pp. (Mexican statistics of all kinds condensed into a single volume.)

DIRECCION GENERAL DE ESTADISTICA. *Cuarto censo de transportes, 1955. Resumen General.* Mexico: Talleres Gráficos de la Nación, 1959. 73 pp. (Summary volume of the 1955 census of transportation.)

DIRECCION GENERAL DE ESTADISTICA. *Estadísticas Sociales del Porfiriato, 1877-1910.* Mexico: Talleres Gráficos de la Nación, 1956, 249 pp. (Demographic and cultural statistics for the period of the Porfirio Díaz dictatorship, 1877-1910.)

DIRECCION GENERAL DE ESTADISTICA. *Octavo censo general de población, 1960. Resumen General.* Mexico: Talleres Gráficos de la Nación, 1962. 652 pp. (Summary volume of the 1960 population census.)

DIRECCION GENERAL DE ESTADISTICA. *Tercer censo agrícola ganadero y ejidal, 1950. Resumen General.* Mexico: Talleres Gráficos de la Nación, 1956. 256 pp. (Summary volume of the 1950 agricultural and livestock census.)

Periodicals and Serials which contain materials on physical and cultural geography

AMERICAS. Washington: Pan American Union. Published monthly in English, Spanish and Portuguese. The section "Facts and Figures of the Americas" was especially important as a source for this chapter.

ANNALS OF THE ASSOCIATION OF AMERICAN GEOGRAPHIES. Washington: Association of American Geographers. Quarterly.

UNIVERSITY OF CALIFORNIA PUBLICATIONS IN GEOGRAPHY. Berkeley and Los Angeles: University of California. (Published in series.)

COMERCIO EXTERIOR. Banco Nacional de Comerco Exterio. Published monthly in English and Spanish. (In additio to information concerning Mexican foreign trade, th publication includes a wealth of economic, politica and social data about Mexico.)

ECONOMIC GEOGRAPHY. Worcester, Massachusetts: Clar University. Quarterly.

THE GEOGRAPHICAL REVIEW. New York: American Geographical Society. Quarterly.

IBERO-AMERICANA. Berkeley and Los Angeles: Universit of California. Published in series.

MEXICO AGRICOLA. México. Agricultural journal publishe monthly in Spanish.

*REVIEW OF THE ECONOMIC SITUATION OF MEXICO. Banc Nacional de México. Published monthly in Englis and Spanish.

Bibliographic Material

BASSOLS BATALLA, ANGEL. *Bibliografía geográfica de Mé. ico.* Mexico: Dirección General de Geografía y Meteo rología, 1955. 4,600 entries, 652 pp. (Bibliography o geographical materials concerned with Mexico. Organ ized topically and regionally.)

To create in Mexico a democracy with some aspects
of authenticity is of course a task that would discourage
any sensitive man. It is so complex, so arduous, and
so slow that it should be conceived as the consequence
or end of many other changes and not as a task in
itself, to be met head on, let us say.

— Daniel Cosío Villegas

A Developing Democracy | PAUL KELSO

CITIZENS OF THE UNITED STATES who measure governmental virtue on a democratic scale may be gratified to
learn that the Republic of Mexico has democratic objectives. But the initial gratification of some may be modified
when they discover that democracy is broadly interpreted
to include economic and social as well as political objectives, and that in seeking these ends, the government
participates in the national economy and in many respects
is building a welfare state.

It is essential that we recognize, however, that
democracies — or emerging democracies — while resting upon similar basic assumptions, may legitimately
differ in institutions, processes, and policies. Since the
Republic of Mexico does accept the values and processes of democracy, and for fifty years has worked to
make them reality, its system of government and politics may properly be measured by democratic standards.

Mexico is a "federal, democratic, representative Republic," according to the Constitution of 1917, and "all
public power originates in the people and is instituted
for their behalf." The Constitution states that democracy shall be considered "not only as a legal structure
and a political regimen, but as a system of life founded
on a constant economic, social, and cultural betterment of the people." Thus the Constitution reflects
two lines of thought: traditional political democracy,
as we know it in the United States, and a better material
and cultural life, with government playing a positive
role in the economy and in other areas of Mexican
society. Democracy in the second sense is also present
in the United States, although not given explicit constitutional expression.

Since the Revolution, Mexico has been moving
toward its democratic objectives but still cannot qualify
as a full-fledged member of the democratic family. For
all practical purposes it is a one-party state, and the
official party, the Institutional Revolutionary Party, with
no effective opposition from its rivals, dominates both
elections and legislative bodies. The level of popular
participation in government and politics, while rising,

is still low. Presidential power and influence are the
controlling elements in a government whose three
branches are equal only in theory. The judiciary dis-
penses substantial justice in most cases, but is less
than independent of the executive. Administration,
while improving, has much to learn about efficiency
and expertise, and the *mordida* remains an essential
part of doing business with the bureaucracy at all levels.
Standards of living are low, and there is an appalling
gap between the income of the few and the many.

But social and political change is taking place,
with the national government stimulating, directing, and
controlling, and the movement is toward the democratic
goals set by the Constitution. The Mexican government,
albeit at times hesitantly and uncertainly, is trying to
create conditions basic to democracy. Its interrelated
programs of industrialization, public works, agricultural
improvement, better transportation and communication, education, health and sanitation, and national integration, are not only raising living standards, slowly,
it must be recognized, but are building the economic
stability and sense of national community prerequisite
to a working democracy.

Professor Russell H. Fitzgibbon of the University
of California at Santa Barbara on four occasions has
attempted to measure trends in democratic or undemocratic change in Latin American states. He was joined
in his last study by Kenneth F. Johnson. In each study
Mexico was assigned a relatively high position when
rated on the basis of democratic criteria. It was ranked
seventh in 1945 and 1950, fourth in 1955, and fifth
in 1960. While Mexico occupied a lower relative position in 1960 than in 1955, yet its overall democratic
rating was higher than ten years earlier.

ROADBLOCKS TO DEMOCRACY

Those seeking democracy have learned that the
search demands intelligence, flexibility, perseverance,
and unflagging optimism and patience, for the obstacles

[161]

are numerous and stubborn, and often monumental. Political democracy has surely been a familiar enough expression in Mexican constitutions since 1824 but relatively absent from the process of government until recently. Social and economic democracy, if anything, has been even more foreign to Mexican experience. In the Mexican culture were numerous elements alien and sometimes hostile to the democratic ideal, and hence cultural change, seldom easy, has been a *sine qua non* for democratic development. Economic and social change, and with it, changes in the individual Mexican, are being effected as conditions essential to democracy.

The Topographic Barrier

Topography has divided the Mexicans into separate communities isolated from one another and from the national capital by mountain and desert barriers

Opened in November, 1961, and tagged by President López Mateos as a "means of national integration," the 938-kilometer Chihuahua-Pacific railroad crosses the Sierra Madre Occidental, a rugged range of mountains which defied crossing by any wheeled vehicles until the completion of the Durango-Mazatlán highway several years ago.

and has thus contributed to the spirit of "localism," or identification with the local community rather than the larger national entity. This spirit has kept many from participating in the national political life and supporting national democratic objectives. Because of localism many Mexicans have been unable to comprehend the idea of the nation; this has been particularly true of the Indians who are members of an Indian tribe or community and speak only an Indian language. Localism is less a barrier to national integration today than fifty years ago, but it has not disappeared. Physical isolation has been compounded by an inadequate system of transportation and communication.

Democracy—an Alien Practice

For many and probably a majority of the Mexicans at the outbreak of the Revolution in 1911 democracy was an alien practice. Mexico had been denied the opportunity to evolve the skills and understandings of political democracy by three centuries of Spanish viceregal rule and, after independence, almost fifty years of *caudillismo,* broken only by the Reform and the presidency of Juárez, and thirty-four years of *porfirismo.* Although there may have been some belief in individual dignity, this was not generally construed

— Courtesy Mexican Government Department of Tourism

is it is today, as the right of the individual to a voice in the formation of major governmental policies and to share equitably in the values — economic and social — produced by his society.

The Revolution meant not only the rejection of old ruling classes and values but also many of the symbols connected with them; and consequently the new regime was faced with the necessity of adapting familiar symbols which still retained some vitality and developing newer ones in support of democratic goals. Hidalgo, Morelos, Juárez, and other traditional heroes have been installed in the Revolutionary pantheon, and properly so, and they have been joined by newer heroes, Cuauhtémoc, Serdán, Madero, Obregón, and others, created since 1911.

The Economic Barrier

Other conditions for the development of democratic institutions and processes — industrialization, urbanization, literacy, and greater national wealth — were absent or else present only in attenuated form when the Querétaro convention spelled out the goals of the new Mexico. National wealth was comparatively low and per capita income both relatively and absolutely low. The preoccupation of a majority with the business of staying alive precluded any deep involvement, and in many instances any at all, in the national political process.

Industrialization had begun under Díaz, but Mexico was still predominately an agricultural country, without the economic means to achieve its economic and social ends. Economic development, with emphasis upon industrialization since about 1940, has been one of the major objectives of government since 1917. A scarcity of technical, scientific, and managerial skills, less acute today than formerly, has hindered the growth of science and industry.

As part of its economic program, the Mexican government has attempted to create a system of agriculture capable of producing the surpluses essential to an urban, industrial society, but has been handicapped by the primitive methods of subsistence farming and a paucity of land and water resources. A recent study estimated that only approximately 14 per cent of the national territory has enough rainfall for farming.

At the time of the Revolution, approximately 80 per cent of the population was illiterate and consequently poorly equipped to acquire the information and understanding basic to effective, democratic political action or the skills needed for the creation of a modern economy. Despite the persistent efforts of national and state governments, approximately 29 per cent of the Mexicans are still classified as illiterate.

For many Mexicans, illiteracy supplemented physical isolation as a barrier to their grasping the idea of nationhood, and contributed to the spirit of "wantlessness" which tended to make economic and social goals relatively meaningless. Until fairly recently, a majority of the population lived in rural areas, a condition which probably did not advance the cause of democracy. As rural dwellers they were isolated from the educational and democratizing influences produced in urban areas by the interaction of groups and ideas, and the exposure of individuals to the diverse media of communication.

Like other underdeveloped states which have attempted to build a modern, industrial society, with government taking a leading role as promoter and participant, Mexico discovered that its bureaucracy, which like bureaucracies everywhere, must translate policy into reality, was ill-prepared for its heavier responsibilities. In 1917, when the Constitution become effective, the bureaucracy largely lacked the necessary skills and attitudes, and, moreover, was demoralized by the disruptive forces of revolution. Appointments were determined more by the traditional influence of family and by partisan ties than by competency, and as a consequence the managerial and technical skills needed for the new Mexico were in short supply.

As a relatively poor state, Mexico was unable to pay salaries which would attract in sufficient numbers able administrators, technicians, professional people, and scientists. Low salaries, as well as cultural traits, were responsible for the *mordida* being part of the bureaucratic way of life, as the income obtained from the "little bite" often was a necessary supplement to official pay. The expression "little bite" can be misleading, for it can amount to millions of pesos when higher governmental officials are involved. But small or large, by adding to the cost of government and contributing to a cynical attitude toward officialdom, it has interfered with the attainment of democratic goals. The Mexican bureaucracy has been improved, and its greater effectiveness is seen in its ability to operate an increasingly complex modern state. But it still is handicapped by nepotism, partisan influence, and corruption, and further changes are in order, a need which official sources recognize from time to time.

The Population Barrier

One of the most formidable barriers to economic and social development is the rapidly expanding population of Mexico, which has one of the highest rates of growth in the world today. Between 1910 and 1960 the population increased 130.4 per cent, and the rate of growth has been climbing in recent years. The population grew 18.7 per cent between 1930–1940, 31.2 per cent between 1940–1950, and 34.6 per cent between 1950–1960. The 1960 census revealed that the total population had grown, at an annual rate of almost 3.5 per cent, from 25,791,017 to 34,923,129 during the decade. At the end of 1964 the population was estimated at approximately 40,000,000.

While relatively high, and reflecting various social factors, including religion, the birthrate has remained fairly constant in recent years. Public sanitation and health programs, while lagging behind need, have reduced infant mortality rates and expanded longevity to trigger the population explosion. The live births per 1,000 population were 43.5 between 1935–1939 and 46 between 1955–1959. In 1960 they were 45.5 per 1,000 population. Infant deaths under one year per 1,000 population declined from 127.6 for 1935–1939 to 83.2 for 1955–1959. In 1964, according to President López Mateos, there were 64.6 infant deaths per 1,000 population. The general death rate per 1,000 population dropped from 23.3 for 1935–1939 to 12.6 for 1955–1959. For 1964, as given by López Mateos, it was 9.6.

If there is to be no retreat from present standards of living, a substantial portion of each year's economic gain must be invested in the needs of the growing population and hence is not available for capital investment. The Red Queen's remarks to Alice seem to fit Mexico as well: "It takes all the running *you* can do, to keep in the same place. If you want to get somewhere else, you must run at least twice as fast as that." Fortunately, the Mexican economy usually has run almost "twice as fast as that," producing a surplus for capital investment. In 1961, however, when the gross national product grew only 3.5 per cent, and population by the same percentage, government and business officials were seriously worried. Despite this concern, national planning for economic and social development continues to emphasize industrial and agricultural growth to the exclusion of other approaches, probably because some aspects of religious dogma are still a potent force in Mexican life.

Urbanization, industrialization, higher standards of living, and the continued expansion of the middle class in the long run will lower the birthrate. A study in 1956 by Robert G. Burnight, Nathan Whetten, and Bruce Waxman of differential urban-rural fertility rates reported 505 children per 1,000 women of child-bearing ages in urban places of 50,000 or more, in contrast to 698 per 1,000 in rural places. Despite the long-run impact of these factors, however, the population currently is growing rapidly and from the standpoint of national goals, alarmingly. A United Nations population study states that a decrease in birth rates "can hardly be expected to occur before 1980." Population projections for 1980 made by the same source range from a low of 48,239,000, through 55,469,000, to a high of 64,425,000. It is now estimated by some authorities that actual population in 1980 will be remarkably close to the high figure, and that the population in the year 2000 will be well above 100 million.*

Mexico's multiplying population has become more urban in character, and this change, though in part a corollary of the industrial approach to improved living standards, has further augmented the problems of the Republic. Industrialization is only one cause of the urbanization trend; others include natural increase, the inability of the land to support all of the growing rural population, in part because of the small area of *ejido* plots, the color and drama of urban centers, and the greater educational and cultural advantages of urban living.

The urban population — all persons living in communities of more than 2,500 — constituted 51 per cent of the total population in 1960, in contrast to only 3? per cent in 1930. Between 1930 and 1960, the urban population more than tripled, expanding from approximately 5.5 to 17.7 million. The rural population was only one and one-half times larger in 1960 than thirty years earlier.

In 1960, slightly more than 30 per cent of the population was concentrated in cities of above 50,000 in contrast to 18 per cent in 1930. Mexico in 1960 had five cities of more than a quarter million — Mexico City, 2,932,133; Guadalajara, 736,800; Monterrey 596,939; Puebla, 389,049; and Ciudad Juárez, 261,68?. The growth rate of the Federal District, 96 per cent urban, where Mexico City is situated, is higher than for the country in general. District population was nine times greater in 1960 than it was in 1900. expanded from 1,758,000 in 1940 to 4,871,000 1960.

Cities of Mexico are not only growing, but they are growing at a rapid tempo, and these two factors combination have seriously strained the facilities of urban government. They have led to the expansion and further overcrowding of city slums, already appalling, to overloaded transportation facilities, to new demands for electric power and water, and to increases crime and disease. Some of the proletarian settlements and squatter villages are without electricity, sewerage and running water. The number of persons crowding into urban areas has exceeded the needs of industry commerce, and the service trades, and living for those without steady employment is precarious indeed. As result, government — national, state, and municipal — faced with unprecedented demands, far from being met, for more services of all types and for enlarged regulatory and control programs.

Urbanization and National Unity

In the long run, urbanization, with its various political and cultural cross-currents, will assist the one-time *campesino* to become part of the nation political and social community; in the short haul, however, the former peasant now living on the politic and cultural fringe of the city is a potential recruit for extremist groups because of his lack of cultural moorings and his extremely unsettled economic status doubly onerous because of the visible abundance of the city. The national government has devised a number of programs to help the urban proletariat. The city as well as the industrial and commercial expansion,

---

* The Mexican press is showing some interest in the problems related to population growth and the subject of birth control. See, for example, the supplement, "Demografía y Desarrollo," to *Comercio Exterior,* June, 1965; "Opiniones Femeninas: El Control de la Natalidad," *Impacto,* No. 811 (Sept. 15, 1965), p. 45; "Población: Control o Catástrofe," *Hispano Americano,* vol. XLVIII (Nov. 8, 1965), pp. 30-36; and Jacobo Zabludovsky, "Se Cree Usted Muy Macho Pues Tenga Menos Hijos!" *Siempre,* No. 647 (Nov. 17, 1965), pp. 12-13.

Residents of the Federal District point with pride to Unidad Independencia, Social Security's low-rent housing project with modern architecture and educational and recreational facilities. Growing population and the continued existence of slums emphasize the need for many more such urban projects.

stimulating the growth of an urban middle class. This class, together with its rural counterpart, with moderate values and concern with stable government and economic conditions, tends to further the cause of democracy.

MEXICO'S EVOLVING REVOLUTION

The Revolution which erupted in 1910 against the dictatorship of Porfirio Díaz and the small ruling group he headed was an unavoidable prelude to the development of a political and economic system committed to the goals of economic growth, social justice, and the establishment of democratic institutions and practices. The Revolution was a bloody, violent, bitter, and protracted struggle against the traditional order. Tens of thousands lost their lives, much property was destroyed, and the existing patterns of trade and industry were disrupted. While the Revolution apparently was the only road to change, the destruction which it brought complicated enormously the labor of reconstruction and evolutionary growth.

It would be idle to pretend, however, that all the revolutionary generals and other leaders had a clear picture of what they were fighting for. For some, the objective was the overthrow of Porfirio Díaz and later Victoriano Huerta; for others, it was the defeat of rival generals with whom they were competing for power. In the instance of minor leaders, the end may have been the toppling of the local *jefe político* or the *hacendado*. For many peons the Revolution was an opportunity to vent their frustrations against the ruling oligarchy. The goals later given constitutional expression emerged slowly and even at the time of the Querétaro convention of 1916–1917 were in dispute.

Wellsprings of the Struggle

As logically might be expected, one must look to the long years of *porfirismo* for the wellsprings of the Revolution. The dictatorship had created enemies by its disregard of personal rights, its alienation of much of the national domain to a small handful of landowners, its generosity to foreigners, its maltreatment of the peon, its rejection in fact of the Constitution of 1857, and its failure to enforce the Laws of the Reform and their restraints upon the power of the clergy. Moreover, the Díaz government and the *científicos* associated with it, in their emphasis upon economic development, had fostered the growth of new groups and interests who were denied admission to the small ruling class. A new group of intellectuals appeared who furnished much of the post-Revolutionary economic, social, and political leadership.

Another major cause of the Revolution was the hacienda system, which had concentrated much of the cultivable area in relatively few hands. The system denied the peon the small farm for which he longed, condemned him to work for the *hacendado* through debt peonage which was enforced when necessary by the *rurales,* and rewarded his labors with a subsistence standard of living. With this background in mind, one is better able to understand the violent outburst of the peon against constituted authority which is portrayed so vividly by Mariano Azuela in *The Underdogs,* one of the great novels of the Revolution. The hacienda system also contributed to the Revolution by standing in the way of economic development. With the peon working for subsistence wages and perpetually in debt, Díaz' Mexico had an extremely limited market for manufactured products. The hacienda was devoted to an agricultural pattern which was basically uneconomic in character. Traditional crops were cultivated by traditional methods, and a goodly part of the land lay idle much of the time. As the *hacendado* tended to channel whatever profits he made to the acquisition of more land or to consumer's goods, the system was incapable of contributing to the capital formation needed for the industrial development of the Republic.

Madero as an Instrument

Francisco I. Madero was the immediate instrument through which the ruin of Díaz was accomplished. That many dissident elements accepted his leadership is a measure of the widespread discontent, for Madero stressed political objectives to the neglect of the economic and social problems of the country. He first won public acclaim in 1909 following the appearance of his book, *The Presidential Succession in 1910,* in which he proposed a return to the Constitution of 1857 and the free choice of a vice president. In 1910 he ran for the presidency as the candidate of the Anti-Reelection Party, and the Díaz election officials awarded him 196 votes. Madero sounded a call for revolt against the dictator in his Plan of San Luis Potosí. The uprising was to occur on November 20, which is now the official date of the beginning of the Revolution.

Numerous armed uprisings at various places in the Republic, some breaking out on November 20 in accord with Madero's plan, marked the start of the military phase of the Revolution. Public sentiment mounted for the resignation of Díaz and the election of Madero as president. Madero and representatives of the Díaz government, early in May, 1911, signed the Treaty of the City of Juárez which provided for the resignation of Díaz and his vice president and, pending the election of Madero in the fall, a provisional government headed by Francisco León de la Barra, Díaz' secretary of foreign affairs. Díaz resigned on May 25.

Unfortunately for Mexico and for himself, Madero was woefully unable either to understand or to control the revolutionary forces which he headed. He failed to grasp the underlying sentiment for social and economic change and the need for a strong president, supported by loyal cabinet officers and generals, who would initiate vigorous reform measures. Madero was deposed on February 19, 1913, by General Victoriano Huerta and, along with his vice president, Pino Suárez, assassinated several days later. General Huerta assumed the presidency and in effect launched a counterrevolution to restore the "good old days" of the *porfiriato.* The movement to unseat him went far beyond the revolt which toppled the Díaz regime, to become a genuine social revolution. Huerta finally was forced to flee Mexico in August, 1914, by a combination of forces which included Venustiano Carranza, Alvaro Obregón, Francisco Villa, and Emiliano Zapata. The victors quarreled among themselves, but Carranza managed to establish himself as the head of a provisional government which commanded considerable but not unanimous support among the revolutionary groups. The Querétaro convention of 1916–1917 was called to draft a constitution incorporating the gains of the Revolution which would provide the legal basis for a more enduring government.

An Ongoing Process

Whether or not the Revolution has ended is a question which is often debated. Some contend that the Revolution ended at a given time; for example, at the close of the presidency of Lázaro Cárdenas, who during his six years in office instituted a program — more extreme than that of his predecessors — which included agricultural reform, nationalization of the railroads, and expropriation of the petroleum industry. Those who insist that the Revolution was terminated as of 1940 or some other date obviously interpret it in limited and selective fashion. As a social myth, standing for social justice for all Mexicans, to be attained by democratic processes, the Revolution remains a potent force and commands the allegiance of most citizens. Few can remain in Mexico for long without becoming aware of the constant references to the Revolution and its goals by the president and other officials, the newspapers, and the leaders of labor, agricultural, and other functional groups.

The Revolution has a broader significance, which must be mentioned, for it is uniquely a native Mexican revolution, not an importation from abroad, even though some of its participants were well-read in the European political, sociological, and economic thought of the day. The techniques and programs painfully developed during the past fifty years, the admixture of state capitalism and private enterprise, and the inevitable mistakes, may be studied with profit by the underdeveloped states of Latin America and the new nation-states of Africa and Asia.

The Foundations — Constitution of 1917

Political, economic, and social aspirations of the Revolution are expressed in the Constitution of 1917, which formally is the law of the land today. The Constitution reflects the divergent doctrines and goals of the troubled period between 1910 and 1917, and is a marriage of nineteenth-century liberalism and twentieth-century economic and social democracy. In its provisions for the institutions and processes of political democracy and guarantees for the protection of traditional civil rights, the Constitution bears witness to the influence of the Constitution of 1857. But it also includes guarantees for the protection of new economic and social rights and charges the state with a positive role in furthering national and individual welfare. The Constitution, moreover, was the first in Latin America to acknowledge the relationship between economic and social problems and stable, popular government, and the importance of striving for both as two sides of the same problem.

The Constitution was drafted by a convention which met at Querétaro in December, 1916, and completed its task by early February the next year. General Venustiano Carranza, first chief of the Constitutional Army, issued the convention call; he was recognized as provisional president by most of Mexico, with notable exceptions such as Villa and Zapata. His immediate objective was a lawful basis for his position, but beyond that was the desire of numerous groups, after six years of turmoil, to get along with the business of building law and order within a definite constitutional framework. There was the feeling, too, that the economic, social, and cultural aspirations which had emerged from the revolutionary struggle ought to be given constitutional expression. These aspirations were to be voiced, not in a new constitution, but in a revised and up-to-date version of the Constitution of 1857.

Carranza on several occasions had spoken fulsomely of various social reforms, but apparently with him the word was equivalent to the deed, for the constitution he proposed was essentially a refurbished version, with only minor changes, of the 1857 document. His draft recommendations offered a stronger chief executive, which (aside from the general's personal ambitions) events proved desirable, but slighted the issue of social change. Though *zapatistas, villistas,* and other opponents of Carranza were absent, the First Chief did not have everything his own way.

MAJOR RADICAL INFLUENCES

The main protagonists were the so-called radical and moderate factions, which clashed over the questions of education, property rights and mineral re-

sources, the rights of labor, and other issues. The radicals, led by General Francisco J. Múgica, had considerable influence, not only because they spoke for the social objectives of the Revolution but also for the more practical reason that they were backed by General Obregón, without whose armies the Carranza government would have collapsed. The radicals persuaded the convention to adopt Articles 27 and 123, the most significant parts of the Constitution, because they laid the foundation for radical modifications in the political, social, and economic structure of the country. Other notable articles were 3 and 130, which restated and extended the anticlerical restraints of the Laws of the Reform, and Article 3, which directed establishment of a public education system, free, secular, democratic, and, through the sixth-grade level, compulsory.

Article 27 was radical because it struck at certain existing property and contractual relationships and defined a theory of land and subsoil mineral ownership as a basis for government regulation in this area. The article in effect empowered the government to correct some of the worst abuses of the Díaz regime — the transfer of Indian *ejidos* or communal land to private ownership, the granting of generous mining and oil concessions to foreigners, and the distribution of much of the public domain to a few favorites. The article was clearly intended, moreover, to prevent the recurrence of these abuses, which had concentrated much of the ownership of land and minerals resources — and with them political power — in relatively few hands.

BROADENING THE BASE

To provide a legal basis for public control, Article 27, borrowing from the theory of the Spanish period, declares that the nation originally owned all lands and waters and that, though it had transferred title to private persons, thereby creating private property, it retained the right to protect the public interest by imposing limitations upon private property and regulating the use of other natural resources. In line with this theory, Article 27 directs that steps be taken to break up the large landed estates and thus bring about a more equitable distribution of the public wealth. In acting upon this injunction — some national administrations more enthusiastically than others — the national government undoubtedly has broadened the basis of its support and thus contributed to political stability. Article 27 also declares null and void certain transfers, concessions, and sales of communal land.

The article vests in the nation ownership of all subsoil minerals. A private person or company wishing to exploit or use these resources, first must get a concession from the federal executive and then abide by express legal rules and conditions. The right to own lands and waters or obtain concessions for the exploitation of mineral resources is limited to Mexicans or to foreigners who agree to accept Mexican law and to renounce appeal to their own governments.

Article 123 is the Bill of Rights of Mexican Labor. Indicative of its high importance was the action of the

Mexican government in naming a section of one of the principal downtown streets in Mexico City "Articulo 123." "Articulo 123" is linked to another section of the same street named "Venustiano Carranza," and it is interesting to speculate whether the tie disturbs the ghost of the former *primer jefe,* who as president failed to implement this and other radical sections of the Constitution. In providing guarantees for workers in all branches of the economy, the article deviates radically from tradition and practice, not only in Mexico but in many other states as well. The protections were indeed advanced for a country still largely agricultural, and their full realization, if it ever comes, must await the development of an industrial and agricultural economy which can pay for the long-promised benefits. Though it has been said, with some justice, that the industrialization of Mexico is being achieved at the expense of the worker, the government is sensitive to his needs and has given him various protections in accord with Article 123.

The article fixes maximum hours for workers and directs the enactment of minimum wage legislation. It recognizes the right of workers to organize and to strike. Employers too may organize, but the constitutional right of lockouts is stringently limited. Employers are liable for injuries or diseases suffered in course of employment. The principle of equal pay for equal work, regardless of sex, finds a place in the article, which also singles out pregnant women employees and new mothers for special protection. The *tienda de raya,* the Mexican equivalent of the company store, is banned. The article directs the enactment of a social security law.

RESTRAINING THE CLERGY

Anticlerical provisions of the Constitution clearly demonstrate the determination of the men who met at Querétaro to prevent the clergy from standing in the way of change. In wording, these provisions are of general application, but they obviously were intended to restrain the dominant and almost the only clerical group, that of the Roman Catholic Church. With a deep sense of history, the *constituyentes* recognized the clergy as a conservative force which, throughout the colonial period and afterwards, almost invariably opposed liberal or progressive measures, and they decided to place drastic limitations upon its power.

In an effort to destroy the political power of the clergy, the Constitution in Article 130 — which invoked the wrath of many of the faithful — forbids members of the clergy to criticize the fundamental laws or governmental authorities in any assembly, acts of worship, or religious propaganda. Clergymen are denied the right to vote. Periodicals of a religious nature are forbidden to "comment on national political matters or publish information on acts of the authorities of the country or of private persons directly related to the functioning of public institutions." No political group may in its name include any word or other indication that it is related to any religious denomination. A member of

Congress may not be a minister of any religious group, and the President may have neither ecclesiastic status nor be a minister.

The Constitution designates clergymen as professional people, subject to governmental regulation, including licensing. It gives state legislatures the power to fix the maximum number of ministers who may function within their boundaries. Monastic orders are forbidden. Freedom of religion is guaranteed.

Recent activities by some members of the Catholic hierarchy may fairly be questioned as possible violations of the constitutional ban upon clerical interference in political matters. These activities concern the right of Mexican Catholics to join designated left-wing organizations and through them attempt to influence official policy. In July, 1962, a "Declaration of Catholic Principles" was issued over the signatures of forty-eight members of the Catholic hierarchy, including the primate of Mexico and the archbishop of Guadalajara. The document warned communicants against Communist Party membership, possession of Communist literature, and the danger of possible excommunication for Communist activities. The main burden of the declaration, however, was that Catholics should campaign against Communism through religious instruction and advocacy of the principles of social justice.

In February, 1963, a tract distributed by the diocesan conference of Mexican Catholic Action warned that Catholics who "freely and with knowledge beforehand" join groups considered Communist by the church would be automatically excommunicated. Groups listed included the Independent Campesina Central, organized in 1963, the Popular Socialist Party, and the General Union of Peasant Laborers. The Bishop of Zamora in January, 1963, forbade Catholics in his diocese to join either the Independent Campesina Central or the National Liberation Movement, which had been organized in 1961, with the blessing of ex-President Lázaro Cárdenas. The national government has taken no action against the clergymen, possibly because their campaign against Communism serves official ends, but clerical criticism of the free textbook program, which involves major national policy, may meet with vigorous national resistance.

Foreseeing that efforts might be made to indoctrinate youth contrary to the objectives of the Constitution, Article 3 requires all public education to be secular, "maintained entirely apart from any religious doctrine" and "based on the results of scientific progress . . ." Churches, ministers, and groups devoted to the propagation of any religious creed are specifically forbidden to participate in any way" in institutions giving elementary, secondary, and normal education, and education for laborers or field workers." With the passage of time and more tolerant attitudes, the church has quietly reentered the field of education. Private persons and institutions may conduct schools of all kinds and grades, but they must first receive express authorization from the government and comply with constitutional provisions applicable to the public schools.

ATTENUATED FEDERALISM

Formally Mexico is a federal republic. Article 40 of the Constitution declares that "it is the will of the Mexican people to organize themselves into a federal, democratic, representative Republic . . . " The official name of the republic, confined largely to coins and public documents, is *Estados Unidos Mexicanos*. Mexicans customarily refer to their country as the "Republic" and reserve the term "Mexico" for the national capital, Mexico City.

Twenty-nine states, the Federal District, and two territories comprise the Republic. The states are Aguascalientes, Baja California, Campeche, Coahuila, Colima, Chiapas, Chihuahua, Durango, Guanajuato, Guerrero, Hidalgo, Jalisco, México, Michoacán, Morelos, Nayarit, Nuevo León, Oaxaca, Puebla, Querétaro, San Luis Potosí, Sinaloa, Sonora, Tabasco, Tamaulipas, Tlaxcala, Veracruz, Yucatán, and Zacatecas. The Federal District, where Mexico City is situated, is the political, economic, and social center of the Republic. Similar to the District of Columbia, the Federal District is under national jurisdiction. The two territories are Baja California Sur and Quintana Roo. President López Mateos, in the course of a visit to Quintana Roo late in 1961, announced that he would propose to Congress that the Territory be admitted to statehood but apparently did nothing about the question on his return to the capital.

Whether or not Mexico is in fact a federal republic is a moot question. Certainly, when compared to the United States, it seems less than one. Mexican constitutional authorities question whether federalism exists in other than a formal sense; Felipe Tena Ramírez, for example, refers to federalism as "precarious and fictitious." Professor J. Lloyd Mecham of the University of Texas, who has written extensively on Mexican federalism, denies that the states exist "in other than a purely formal sense," but Professor August O. Spain feels that "federalism, however, different or . . . weaker than in comparable systems elsewhere, remains an important factor." The weight of opinion, however, seems to support the thesis that Mexico in fact is a unitary state, governed from Mexico City. This thesis may require modification in view of the emergence of a new crop of more effective governors in recent years, such as former governors Juan Gil Preciado of Jalisco, Carlos A. Madrazo of Tabasco, and others, who have tended to inject new life into state government. Industrial decentralization, currently stressed by national planners, calls for a more active role by state government.

Goal of Centralization

If one reads the Constitution of 1917 carefully, he cannot escape the conclusion that the men of Querétaro wanted to set up a system of government in which national authority predominated. The logic of the situation as well as the facts of history pointed in this direction. National action — although this did not debar state cooperation — would be indispensable in working for the goals delineated in the constitutional articles dealing with education, religion, land and mineral resources, and labor, as well as with the later goal of industrialization. Historically, after independence, the development of rival centers of power on the state level had been a serious obstacle to national political stability. State authority, moreover, ever since independence, generally had failed to develop a reputation for a keen sense of the public interest and a capacity for separating private from public welfare. In 1917, in the light of the hatreds and rivalries created by the Revolution and the fact that the goals of the Querétaro convention were not accepted by many leaders and groups, there were strong reasons for believing that these diverse forces could be successfully countered only by central power and a large measure of central control over the states.

When the delegates to the Querétaro convention designated Mexico as "a federal, democratic, representative Republic composed of free and sovereign States in all that concerns their internal government," they were not cynically engaged in an exercise in constitutional hyperbole. Obviously, the states were neither free nor sovereign, and the delegates did not intend that they become so. But federalism had value as a symbol because of its historical association with liberalism and democracy, and by paying deference to it, the delegates could broaden popular support for the new constitution. Furthermore, numerous delegates probably accepted the validity of the federal principle. Since Mexico is sometimes downgraded as an emerging democratic country because of the hollow nature of its federalism, it is legitimate to ask whether the democratic ends of the Constitution would have been better served by federalism or the present system. A persuasive case can be made for centralism.

Similar to the Constitution of the United States, the Mexican Constitution delegates specific powers to the national government and reserves the remainder to the states. "The powers not expressly granted by this Constitution to federal officials are understood to be reserved to the states." But the range of powers granted to the national government is broader than those granted to ours, including a number which in this country belong to the states. The restrictions upon the Mexican states, however, are more extensive.

In Mexico, the national government has, in addition to powers similar to those possessed by Washington, jurisdiction over hydrocarbons, mining, the motion picture industry, games of chance and lotteries, credit institutions, and electric power. It is directed to enact laws to implement the labor provisions of the Constitution and to protect the general health of the country. Central authority enforces constitutional restraints upon religion, although the states are empowered to fix the number of clergy within their borders. The guarantees of the Mexican Constitution for the protection of individual liberties apply not only to the central government but, unlike the bill of rights of the United States Constitution, to the states as well.

DIRECTIVES FOR STATE GOVERNMENT

The Mexican Constitution goes far beyond that of the United States in its provisions concerning state and local government. Our Constitution, aside from guaranteeing to the states a republican form of government, is silent on structure, organization, and qualifications for office and makes no mention at all of local government.

The Mexican Constitution directs the states to adopt "the popular, representative, republican form of government." It limits state governors to one elected term, which in no instance can be more than six years, and it establishes several qualifications for the office. The Constitution forbids legislators to serve for two consecutive terms, and, classifying states on the basis of population, fixes the minimum number of legislators for each class.

With respect to local government, the Constitution gives the states no choice but to establish "the Free Municipality as the basis of their territorial division and political and administrative organization." The structure of municipal government and the election of officials are subject to constitutional provision.

The national government has broad constitutional powers to intervene in state government and has employed them on numerous occasions, but less today than formerly. For every Pullman strike, Little Rock, and Oxford, there have been numerous instances of national interference in Mexico, because of domestic violence, widespread and flagrant corruption, political disloyalty, violations of state or national constitution, illegal administration, illegal elections, and conflicts between state authorities. Our professional states' righters might indeed find life intolerable in the Republic, or perhaps they would enjoy the greater latitude given by the Mexican scene for inveighing, admonishing, and viewing with alarum.

The Mexican national government is charged with protecting the states against domestic violence when asked to do so by the legislature or, if that body is not meeting, by the governor. The President has the general obligation of enforcing the Constitution and national statutes, which in the past sometimes served as a basis for intervention. The Supreme Court of Justice has exclusive jurisdiction in all controversies "between the powers of one State concerning the constitutionality of their acts, and in disputes between the Federation and one or more States . . . " It is also directed to investigate, on its own volition or at the request of the President, Congress, or state governor, "any act or acts which may constitute a violation of any individual guarantee, or the violation of the public election, or some other crime punishable by Federal law." The Court has made investigations when prompted by national authority — usually the President — and on several occasions when petitioned by political parties, but has consistently turned down requests from state officials, despite constitutional directives to act. The Supreme Court is apt to avoid controversies of a political nature.

Unquestionably the most important basis for direct national intervention is Article 76, which indicates beyond peradventure the fear of the constitution-makers that the ambitions, allegiances, and practices of state authority might not always contribute to national political unity. The article authorizes the Senate, or during adjournment the Permanent Committee of Congress, to take the drastic step of declaring that "the constitutional powers of a State have disappeared," an action which has often meant the removal of the elected governor. The Senate appoints a provisional governor from a list of three submitted by the President, and the provisional governor must call an election for the replacement of officials who are out of jobs because of Senate action. The Senate seldom exercises initiative in this matter; instead, it customarily acts after the President, through his Ministry of Government, has already looked into the situation. Most problems are settled at this level. But if differences persist, the President may refer them to the Senate, with the findings and recommendations of the Ministry of Government.

Record of Intervention

Between 1918 and 1957, the national government intervened in state affairs on approximately fifty occasions by the findings of the Senate or the Permanent Committee of Congress that "the constitutional powers of a State have disappeared." This may be illustrated by the action of President Ruiz Cortines in 1954, in using Article 76 as a lever to remove all three branches of the government of the state of Guerrero because of notorious and wholesale corruption.

Another governor of Guerrero lost his job in January, 1961, because his misconduct had provoked serious local disturbances and embarrassed national authority. The governor's misdeeds included the appointment of approximately sixty relatives to state jobs, and the acquisition, along with other members of his family, of substantial property holdings in Chilpancingo, the state capital, and in Acapulco and Mexico City. For a time it seemed nothing would be done, and the mayor of Acapulco, who had clashed with the governor, was forced to resign, but as local unrest mounted, and the situation was widely reported by the press, the Senate on December 30, 1960, appointed a special commission of investigation. This body went immediately to Guerrero to make on-the-spot inquiries, and on its return, reported widespread misgovernment and violation of individual rights. The Senate on January 3 found that the powers of the state had disappeared and petitioned the President to name a *terna,* or slate of three, from which it would designate a provisional governor.

Article 76, however, has been used infrequently in recent years because national authority has other and better ways of keeping state governments in line. The acceptance of the Constitution — and of the oligarchy which rules Mexico — by more and more groups has meant that Article 76 no longer need be used against rebellious state governors, as in the early 1920's, or against governors who gravely offend public opinion by their avariciousness or arbitrary behavior.

Today, when a state governor offends or embarrasses the national government and the problem cannot be resolved short of his removal, the governor customarily is persuaded to ask the state legislature for an indefinite leave of absence. The legislature always grants the request and then appoints a successor more palatable to central authority. This is the pattern that presidential intervention took during the administration of Ruiz Cortines, with the exception noted above, when five governors were induced to ask for leave, and again in 1956, during the term of President López Mateos, when a governor of San Luis Potosí requested leave. More recently, in October, 1964, the governor of Puebla was granted indefinite leave after he had aroused public opinion and caused public demonstrations by a series of unpopular measures.

THE ONE-PARTY SYSTEM*

Mexico for all practical purposes is a one-party state, which some observers consider a demerit from the standpoint of democratic values. The Institutional Revolutionary Party (PRI) dominates national, state, and local elections and the corresponding levels of government. Minor parties exist, participate in politics, occasionally elect a few representatives to legislative office, but nonetheless fail to offer the voter a genuine alternative to the candidates and program of the PRI. Because of the preeminent position of the PRI in government and elections, the voter lacks an effective choice. Voters and interest groups in reality have no place to go if dissatisfied.

Pragmatic Growth of Party

Although the leaders of the PRI often talk about the Revolution and insist that the government and its programs are revolutionary, the growth of the single-party system has been essentially pragmatic and experimental, in response to concrete problems and situations. It has not proceeded from any theory concerning the desirability of an elite group's leading Mexico into the promised land of the Constitution, or from any other theory. Because it is pragmatic, the PRI has been able to keep up with social change by reinterpreting and broadening its goals and by assimilating many but not all the new groups which social change has produced.

The official party today is an important force in politics and government because of its traditional monopoly of political power, because a broad range of interests is represented in its membership, because it is headed by the President, and because its policies in the main are accepted as promoting the goals of the Revolution as currently interpreted.

Development of the official party began in March, 1929, with General Plutarco Calles as its organizer and patron. Before this date there were numerous parties. They went under a variety of labels which generally included a word such as socialist, labor, worker, revolutionary, or liberal. They were headed by *caudillos* and civilian *políticos* whose ambitions were a standing threat to political and economic stability. To restrain and channel these divisive forces, General Calles united many of them into an easy confederation, the Partido Nacional Revolucionario (PNR). For the first several years the component state and local groups kept their organizational integrity but under the direction of a national executive committee.

Housed in a towering structure in downtown Mexico City, the National Lottery adds to national revenues for health and welfare, and offers a chance for rapid economic improvement to the thousands of Mexicans who daily buy tickets. Ticket sellers are more numerous than newsboys and bootblacks in Mexico City.

* Sources of particular value to the writer in the preparation of this section were Frank R. Brandenburg, *The Making of Modern Mexico* (Englewood Cliffs, N. J.: Prentice-Hall, Inc., 1964), chaps. 1, 5, 6; "Mexico: An Experiment in One-Party Democracy," (Unpublished Ph.D. dissertation, University of Pennsylvania, 1956), and "Organized Business in Mexico," *Inter-American Economic Affairs,* XII (Winter, 1958), 26-52; L. Vincent Padgett, "Mexico's One-Party System: A Re-Evaluation," *American Political Science Review,* LI (Dec., 1957), 995-1008; Karl M. Schmitt, "Communism in Mexico Today," *Western Political Quarterly,* XV (March, 1962), 111-124; and Robert E. Scott, *Mexican Government in Transition* (Urbana: University of Illinois Press, 1959), chaps. 5-7.

In his last presidential message to Congress, in September, 1928, shortly after the assassination of President-elect Álvaro Obregón, Calles declared that Obregón was the last *caudillo,* as the time had come for Mexico to move from its historic position as a government of one man to a government of institutions and laws. Thus, in organizing the PNR, Calles was moved by a desire for a more permanent and stable basis for Mexican government. This was essential in a country where consensus on political ends and means was notoriously lacking. Calles also was impelled by the less laudable aim of maintaining his grip upon the political power which he could no longer control directly as president. Events proved this the stronger of his two motives. Instead of writing an end to dictatorship, the PNR, in the short run, served Calles admirably as an instrument for furthering his ambitions.

In the long term, however, the party contributed to responsible presidential power, rather than to the power of a behind-the-scenes dictator. It also served the purpose of neutralizing and then undermining the power of state and local political groups. All public employees found themselves members of the PNR, whether they liked it or not, and were required, without prior consultation, to hand over one day's pay in months of thirty-one days to the party treasury. By contributing to the financial independence of the party, these exactions weakened the influence of the component political groups and were an important factor in their replacement in 1932 by a party structure consisting of national, state, and local conventions.

General Lázaro Cárdenas became president in 1934 and set about wresting control of the party, and of the government, from Calles. To counter the influence of party groups loyal to Calles, he encouraged the formation of new organizations of workers and farmers, and their inclusion, under faithful leaders, in the official party. When one of the organizations, the Mexican Federation of Laborers (CTM), made up of both industrial and farm workers, threatened to become too strong, he offset its power by throwing his weight behind the formation of state Peasant Leagues and their consolidation into a National Farmers Federation (CNC). By early 1936, President Cárdenas had captured control of the PNR. Calles, shorn of much of his influence but still dangerous, was exiled. Cárdenas made skillful use of the machinery of party and government to establish himself as master of both party and state.

Reorganization Into Sectors

In 1938, the official party was reorganized under the name of the Partido Revolucionario Mexicano (PRM). The various organizations supporting Cárdenas were grouped formally into four sectors — agriculture, labor, popular, and military — which had been developing during the closing years of the PRN. Party affiliation for most members was acquired, not directly, but through membership in a local labor union, agricultural association, or professional group. These, through their respective state federations, were united into national sectors. The party in the main was an organization of economic and social interest groups, not of individuals. Individuals, however, might affiliate directly by joining the Popular Sector.

The extensive control of the political process by the PRM, and the president's leadership of the official party, created a political environment which favored further action by the national government to carry out its program of reform. Not all was well with the PRM, however, for it became the target of a swelling volume of criticism, especially from the newer economic and social groups not included in the sector organizations and hence denied a direct voice in the political process. Dissatisfaction was aggravated by high-handed party tactics in some of the municipal elections of 1945. The party leadership responded in January, 1946, by changing the name of the official party to Partido Revolucionario Institucional (PRI) and by attempting to reduce the political power of the sectors. The sectors were to be stripped of their function of making nominations for public office; the voters, including members of the newer interest groups, were to choose candidates in direct primary elections. The new system proved unsatisfactory, partly because Mexico was not yet ready for the open display of interfactional rivalry in primary elections and partly because of the opposition of sector leaders, who resented their loss of authority. As a consequence, sector nominations were restored in 1950. The party's new name reflected broader membership, increasingly middle-of-the-road programs, and the institutionalization of party and governmental procedures.

Three of the four sectors formed in 1937 — the military sector was dissolved in 1940 — continue as the basic components of the PRI, but with more numerous and representative membership than formerly. The Agrarian Sector, largest of the three, consists mainly of the National Farmers Confederation (CNC), which represents the *ejido* farmer and farm laborers, and the Mexican Agronomy Society (SAM), a group of professional agronomists.

Of more diverse character is the Labor Sector, made up of the Confederation of Mexican Workers (CTM), the largest labor combination, the Revolutionary Confederation of Workers and Farmers (CROC), the second largest group, other federations, and a number of unaffiliated, individual unions. Sector diversity is reflected in serious differences over ends and methods. The moderate federations and groups, under the leadership of the CTM, have coalesced into a Labor Unity Bloc (BUO). The more radical but less numerous associations and unions, including the CROC, form the opposition to the BUO.

The Popular Sector is the most disparate of the three, its membership representing a wide variety of labor, agricultural, professional, and nonvocational groups. To coordinate sector activity more effectively, the National Confederation of Popular Organizations (CNOP) was organized in 1943. The largest units of the CNOP are the Federation of Government Employees' Unions (FSTSE), which are forbidden to affiliate with unions outside government, the Federation of Cooperatives, and the National Confederation of Small Farm Proprietors. Other groups include small merchants, small industrialists, professionals and intellectuals, artisans, women's organizations, and diversified or unaffiliated persons.

Today many of the major economic and social groups in Mexico are represented in the PRI and share in the decision-making process through their sector organizations. President Adolfo López Mateos, like his predecessor Adolfo Ruiz Cortines, has encouraged broader participation in the PRI. Economic interests not represented in the party are consulted by the government through their functional groups. The three sectors first organized in 1938 — agrarian, labor, and popular — remain the principal components of the party, but, as indicated above, with broader membership and hence greater representativeness than before. The Popular Sector not only is the most heterogeneous of the three but is also the most powerful, having elected a majority of the members of the Chamber of Deputies since 1943 and maintained an important role in the nomination and election of recent presidents.

Contribution to Stability

The official party has contributed significantly to the representative quality of Mexican government and to political stability. It has been a steadying influence because it has permitted, even encouraged, an ever-widening range of interests to participate in the political process through its sector organizations. It has served as a training school for party and government leaders and has given groups and individuals invaluable experience, in the light of the democratic objectives of Mexico, in the give-and-take of party politics.

Domination of the political process by party and President has facilitated the peaceful transfer of power from one chief executive to another. Probably the only alternative would have been a dreary succession of *caudillos* and periodic disturbances as rival strong men battled for the presidency, as in various other Latin American states. The party to some extent has functioned as an agency through which the government and ruling oligarchy could curb the dissatisfaction of the *campesinos* with the slow pace of agrarian reform and the unrest of industrial workers whose purchasing power has been curtailed to permit greater capital formation for industrial development. The party program, however, has led to various benefits for workers and farmers, and the several sectors have received symbolic rewards in the election of leaders to public office.

Recent efforts to inject democratic elements into the selection of PRI officials and nominees for local office, to rid the party of spoilsmen and time-servers, and in general to raise the moral level of the organization, may have ended, at least for the time being, with the resignation of Carlos A. Madrazo, the president of the national executive committee, on November 17, 1965. President Díaz Ordaz, who had appointed Madrazo in December, 1964, apparently decided that the party president had become a liability and asked for his resignation.

The Work of Madrazo

Madrazo has a reputation as a liberal in politics and economics. As governor of the state of Tabasco, from 1958 to 1964, he built a substantial reputation for the economic and social programs of his administration. His failure as PRI president has both substantive and procedural causes. The reforms he championed posed a threat to powerful interests within the party, and his uncompromising and shrill attacks — seemingly upon every possible occasion — on the shortcomings of the PRI and its members, alienated not only the proper targets of his strictures but also many persons who normally would have sided with him. Madrazo's public and impolitic censures of the party may have been a matter of temperament. On the other hand, there is the possibility he despaired of reform through established party channels and deliberately chose to take his case to the people, in the hope of enlisting the support of the public and that of the rank and file PRI members.

The PRI, as Madrazo defined its role, should function as the guardian of the Revolution, elucidating its ideals and disseminating them among the people, especially the newer generation. The party has the obligation to work out programs for the attainment of revolutionary objectives, including long-range plans for the social and economic development of the Republic. In line with the last objective, the PRI, in 1965, appointed a national commission for economic and social planning, and charged it with the preparation of a general plan of national development, divided into six-year periods, for the remainder of the century.

Taking a first step toward internal democratization, the PRI in March, 1965, used new and experimental procedures to nominate its candidates for municipal office in the states of Baja California and Durango. Madrazo explained that the new processes were designed to purify the municipal electoral process and to end the monopoly of a few persons over nominations.

Each PRI sector nominated its precandidates for municipal office. Later the party members as a whole, meeting in local assemblies and voting by secret ballot, chose the candidates to represent the PRI in the municipal elections in August. Madrazo favored the entry of more women into politics and government, and as a consequence the new nominating procedures required the inclusion of women among the precandidates for nomination.

Madrazo met serious resistance when he attempted to apply the new methods of selection to the state of Sinaloa. Governor Leopoldo Sánchez Celis apparently was determined to maintain his hold over nominations, even though to do so was to injure the spirit and practice of democratic elections. Because of irregularities in the selection of PRI nominees for the office of municipal president in the cities of Culiacán and Rosario in September, PRI national headquarters annulled the nominations, thus provoking a clash with the governor. The governor closed the PRI offices in the two cities, and the official party decided not to run candidates for the municipal presidencies. The governor's choice for the presidency of Culiacán, whose nomination had been revoked by national authority, ran as an independent in the November general election and won the office.

Members and chairmen of the PRI municipal committees, in harmony with the democratic theme, were chosen in party elections held in July in 1,608 communities of twenty-six states. Local party officials formerly were appointed by the national executive committee in Mexico City on the recommendation of state or territorial committees. In July rank and file *priistas* of the sections into which municipalities are divided elected delegates who, meeting in municipal assemblies, nominated and elected by secret ballot the municipal committeemen and chairmen.

Not long after Madrazo became president of the PRI executive committee, he stated that the party would create a commission of honor and justice with the broad function of rewarding and encouraging the faithful and punishing the transgressors. The commission is charged with granting honors or recommending promotions for meritorious members and meting out sanctions to those who have failed to demonstrate sufficient probity in the discharge of the public functions entrusted to them — that is, those who dispose illegally of the goods or funds of the PRI, who engage in divisive activities, who propagate principles antithetical to those of the party, and who betray party interests through deals with other parties. In view of the tolerance of the Mexican political system for deviant political behavior, it is anticipated that the commission, if it outlives Madrazo, will busy itself in the main with honors and rewards.

Madrazo stirred up a political tempest. He made numerous enemies, some of whom accused him of "creating problems," the worst charge that can be leveled at a Mexican politician, since unwonted problems menace political stability. Some critics said his vision of a more active role for the PRI in policy leadership was unrealistic, since the ruling oligarchy wants a subordinate, not a relatively independent, party. Specific programs based upon economic and social planning, it was feared, might cause irreparable division among the broad range of interests represented in the PRI.

The insistence of Madrazo upon the democratic selection of PRI officers and nominees was regarded as a threat to the traditional structure of power. Governor Sánchez Celis was only one of a large number of state governors unwilling to see control of party organization and local government slip through their fingers. Madrazo's repeated references to party undesirables and archaic procedures are said to have offended General Alfonso Corona del Rosal, his immediate predecessor, who reportedly, with substantial support from several other cabinet members, worked for the removal of the PRI president.

Madrazo unquestionably provoked dissension within the party and, worse still, from the party's viewpoint, the conflict was conducted openly and publicly. Just as earlier, Madrazo had recommended dropping the constitutional amendment to permit two consecutive terms for deputies because it was disrupting party and national unity, so the ruling oligarchy decided to abandon Madrazo for similar reasons.*

The PRI represents the large majority of Mexicans but by no means all of them: important groups and individuals are found outside of the sector organizations. Gustavo Díaz Ordaz, whom the official party selected as its presidential candidate for the 1964 elections, acknowledged in his acceptance speech that party membership is somewhat less than all inclusive, although he indicated his aspiration to be president of all Mexicans. Numerous groups operate politically outside the PRI, sometimes from choice, for they have developed their own approaches to policy and administration, and sometimes because of hostile elements in the official party. These groups include the larger commercial, industrial, and agricultural interests, whose economic significance has mounted with the growth of industry and with the stress by the central government since 1940 upon industrialization and foreign trade and investment. Given the economic and social significance of these groups, their absence from the PRI seriously lowers its representative quality.

Commercial, industrial, and banking interests have a voice in government through semi-official functional groups and through a number of less formal but nonetheless influential associations consisting of the principal financial and industrial enterprises of the Republic. Industrial enterprises are represented through the Confederation of Industrial Chambers of Mexico (CONCAMIN), in which membership is compulsory if an enterprise is capitalized at $40 or more. Merchants with like capitalization must join the Confederation of National Chambers of Commerce (CONCANACO), which serves as their official channel of communication. Bankers are grouped into the Mexican Bankers Association, which is represented on various public financial agencies. The Employers' Confederation has official status. Other functional groups also work closely with politicians and bureaucracy. By one means or another, the government seeks the views of these confederations and their member organizations on proposed legislation and administrative changes and on state-operated industry.

Of at least equal importance as channels of communication with government are the less formal associations of banking and industrial interests, which have learned that joint endeavor best promotes their search

---

* See p. 185.

Busy centers of finance such as Guadalajara's modern Banco Industrial de Jalisco find a voice in government through the Mexican Bankers' Association or other semi-official functional groupings from the world of finance.

for protection, credits, contracts, and other concessions from government. These associations are exemplified by the National Bank of Mexico group, the Monterrey group and its financial ally, the Bank of London and Mexico, and groups headed by Carlos Trouyet, Antonio Sacristan, and other individuals.*

Professor Frank R. Brandenburg, an acute and knowledgeable student of the interrelations of government and business in Mexico, has stated that practically every important business group has close working relations with an appropriate agency of government, and that probably there are similar interrelations involving religious groups, large agricultural interests, and the military. Through these relationships and through the official party, the Mexican government today is largely representative of the nation.

MINOR PARTIES

Minor parties are a familiar part of the Mexican political scene. In general they have been short-lived, appearing briefly to compete for political power and then vanishing with the defeat of the leader around whom they were built. Between 1940 and 1952, several efforts were made to assemble a broadly based party comprised of functional groups splintered away from the official party, but they were relatively ineffective. With the development of formal and mutually advantageous relations between functional groups and the PRI, it is extremely difficult today to persuade any of the former to risk certain benefits for the dubious profits of political adventure.

If minor party leaders are realistic, they entertain even less hope than their counterparts in the United States of ousting the PRI from its control of public office or even attaining any position of influence as a minority voice in politics and government. President López Mateos in July, 1962, in responding to a question on the Mexican party system — one of a series of questions from the *United States News and World Report* — stated that "in reality we have five parties that offer to the voters a broad range of platforms for approaching the problems of Mexico, and the

people enjoy the most complete liberty to select candidates of their choice in secret elections." The President's reply was correct as far as it went, but it omitted the obvious fact that the PRI's almost complete monopoly of power, plus the related fact that support of the official party pays off in economic and social dividends, leave the voter with little freedom of choice in reality.

Evidence of Weakness

Election results offer tangible evidence of the weakness of the minor parties, and the strength of the PRI. The minor parties won approximately 7 per cent of the popular vote in the 1940 presidential election, 21 per cent in 1946, and 26 per cent in 1952. The Partido de Acción Nacional (PAN) was the only minor party to oppose the PRI presidential candidate in 1958 and 1964; in the former year its nominee received about 10 per cent of the total presidential vote and in the latter approximately 11 per cent. After report of the victory of Gustavo Díaz Ordaz in the presidential election of July 5, 1964, the president of PAN, Adolfo Christlieb Ibarrola, and PAN's defeated presidential candidate, José González Torres, in an unprecedented action recognized that Díaz Ordaz had won in a free election. The Mexico City daily, *Novedades*, stated that this represented "an extraordinary case in the history of the Mexican people" . . . and "a progressive advance in our democratic discipline."

In the congressional elections of July, 1961, the minor parties polled 34 per cent of the popular vote

* Vernon, Raymond. *The Dilemma of Mexico's Development. The Roles of the Private and Public Sectors* (Cambridge, Mass.: Harvard University Press, 1963), pp. 20-21. For a description and analysis of the powerful economic groups which cluster around the large banks of deposit, see the series of articles by José Luis Ceceña in *Siempre,* No. 644 (October 27, 1965), pp. 20-21; 645 (Nov. 3, 1965), pp. 18-19; 646 (Nov. 10, 1965), pp. 20-21; 647 (Nov. 17, 1965), pp. 20-21; 648 (Nov. 24, 1965), pp. 20-21. Ceceña characterizes the leaders of these groups as an oligarchy which exercises a pervasive decision-making power not only in the business sector but also in government. In his opinion this oligarchy "constitutes a type of cabinet without portfolio."

in the Federal District, a little more than 5 per cent in the remainder of the Republic, and 14 per cent for the entire country including the Federal District. The PRI at first was reported to have filled all 178 seats in the Chamber of Deputies, but when the defeated parties cried foul, PAN was granted five deputies and the Partido Popular Socialista (PPS) one. In the 1964 Chamber elections, PAN was victorious in only two electoral districts and PPS in only one.

Despite the poor showing of the minor parties in the 1964 congressional election, all have more representation than formerly in the Chamber of Deputies, as a consequence of recent changes in the election laws based upon constitutional amendments initiated by President López Mateos in December, 1962. The gains, however, were basically in the nature of a gift from the President and the PRI, rather than a prize which the minor parties were able to seize because of their political power.

A party, according to the electoral reform, is entitled to five deputies if its candidates receive at least 2.5 per cent of the total vote for Chamber candidates throughout the Republic, even though the party fails to elect a single candidate by majority or plurality vote. It moreover qualifies for one additional deputy for each 0.5 per cent of the total vote it receives over the 2.5 per cent level, up to a total of twenty deputies. If a minor party does not succeed in electing as many as twenty deputies by majority or plurality vote, it may still fill twenty seats if its total popular vote in the Republic is sufficiently large.

The reform classifies deputies under two headings — *diputados de mayoría,* elected by majority vote, and *diputados de partido,* designated by virtue of a minor party's having attracted 2.5 per cent or more of the total vote. In harmony, perhaps, with the spirit of the reform, but not with the letter of the law, the Chamber of Deputies, sitting as an Electoral College in August, awarded eighteen deputies of party to PAN, nine to PPS, and five to the Partido Auténtico de la Revolución Mexicana (PARM). Only PAN was eligible for deputies of party. Neither PPS nor PARM polled sufficient votes but nonetheless they obtained their *diputados de partido* because of the sentiment of the Electoral College that "without interference by a purely arithmetic question . . . all currents of opinion ought to be represented in the Chamber of Deputies" and that "the electoral reform should not operate to the benefit of a single party in detriment to the other established parties." The PPS and PARM may have earned the deputies for which they did not qualify on the basis of their voting strength by their support of the candidacy of Díaz Ordaz.

According to some sections of the capital press, the electoral reform was designed to inject more life and controversy into the usually torpid proceedings of the subservient Chamber of Deputies, without at the same time seriously impairing the power of the majority to govern. López Mateos, in commending the reform to Congress, declared that it would further the growing democratic maturity of the Republic by permitting th representation of a broader range of opinion in th Chamber. The reform may mirror presidential an party sensitivity to the criticism that the lopside majority of the official party in the Chamber is essen tially undemocratic and that the Chamber is little mor than a sounding board for the President.

Standards for Registration

Whether a political party may compete in nationa and state elections is determined by a national agenc of cabinet rank, the *Secretaría de Gobernación.* If, i the judgment of Gobernación, the party meets certai legal standards, including a membership of not fewe than 75,000 distributed among at least two-thirds c the states, it will be registered as a legal party. Gobe nación also may cancel a party's registration for viola tions of the election laws or other reasons; for example it ended the legal existence of the Popular Force Party the political arm of the reactionary Sinarquista move ment, after a group of Sinarquistas in December, 1948 had reviled the memory of Benito Juárez during demonstration at the Juárez hemicycle in Alamed Park in Mexico City.

Four parties — PRI, PAN, PPS, and PARM - participated in the national election of July, 1964. Th registration of the Partido Nacionalista de Méxic (PNM), active since 1927, was cancelled before th election because the party had split into three cor tending factions which were unable to reunite, an none was able to demonstrate its ability to meet th standards for party registration. One of PNM's prir cipal objectives was "to unite the Mexican Revolutio with Christianity."

Characteristics of the Parties

Two new political groups, the Frente Elector del Pueblo and the Partido Demócrata Cristian wanted to take part in the 1964 election but wer refused registration by Gobernación. Some Mexica political writers speculated on what would happen t the registered parties, with the exception of PRI, Gobernación applied the same tests to them as to th 1963 candidates for registration. The Frente Elector del Pueblo is a left-wing group organized under th sponsorship of the Communist Party of Mexico. Th Partido Demócrata Cristiano is a part of the Christia Democratic movement in the Republic. Althoug denied a place on the ballot, the Frente nominated presidential candidate, Ramón Palomino Danzos, who campaigning, it was hoped, would help the party mai tain its identity and disseminate its propaganda.

PAN is the strongest and most influential of th minor parties. Its membership consists in the main representatives of middle and upper-class econom and social interests — business, industry, and the pr fessions, and its programs generally are conservativ Since its organization in 1939 by Manuel Gómez Mori

PAN has been regarded as a special pleader for the Catholic Church, though not officially identified with it. It has sought, for example, revisions of Article 3 of the Constitution to permit teaching of religion in elementary and secondary schools. PAN has been afflicted by a certain amount of political schizophrenia, the result of internal dissension over the question of whether it should become a broad-based party similar to PRI or a small, militant party of opposition.

PARM is closely associated with PRI, from which it splintered after the election of President Alemán because of the objections of a group of older revolutionists to what they regarded as the subversion of revolutionary goals to personal and frequently dishonest gain. The party is unimportant from the standpoint of membership and influence, and may ultimately commit suicide because of its reluctance to admit younger members to positions of leadership. It has taken part in presidential and congressional elections since 1958.

The only recognized party to the left of the PRI is the PPS, which was formed in 1947 by Vicente Lombardo Toledano and others formerly active in the PRI. They charged that the official party was corrupt and had betrayed the Revolution. Lombardo Toledano was the most influential labor leader during the presidency of Cárdenas and was still powerful when he broke with the PRI, unhappy about various changes which he feared would undermine the influence of labor in party councils.

Lombardo Toledano denies personal membership in the Communist Party, but the PPS has rather consistently walked the official Communist line, giving credence to its frequent identification as a Communist-front organization. Lombardo Toledano recently defined the membership of the political and economic left, with which he identifies himself, as consisting only of those who publicly declare themselves Marxists-Leninists.

In general the party endorses the domestic programs of the Mexican government but goes somewhat further than the government when it proposes the nationalization of private credit and other key sectors of the economy. The party is not too happy about friendly relationships between Mexico and the United States, and the investment of United States capital in the Republic. It supports without reservation the Castro regime in Cuba "since he is constructing the first socialist rule of America." The party regards the Catholic hierarchy as a threat to the values of the Revolution, and Lombardo Toledano on at least one occasion protested because some public officials attend mass.

Mexico, until 1963, had two other Communist parties, the Communist Party of Mexico and the Mexican Farmers and Workers Party (POCM), but the latter affiliated with the PPS in April of that year. The Communist Party, organized in 1919, has been relatively unimportant from the standpoint of influence and size of membership. Its recent petitions for registra-

tion as a legal party have been rejected by Gobernación. Its sponsorship of the Frente Electoral del Pueblo was an obvious attempt to bolster the influence of left-wing political groups.

POCM was formed in 1950 as a product of the chronic internal dissension within the Communist Party. Its influence was negligible because of limited membership, estimated at not more than 1,500, inept leadership, and the narrow range of interests represented in its ranks. On the occasion of the consolidation of the PPS and POCM, Lombardo Toledano grandiloquently referred to the union as the first step in the formation of a great Marxist-Leninist party.

The rise of the Castro dictatorship and the domestic agrarian discontent have created situations which the Communists currently are attempting to exploit. It is a safe guess, however, that most Mexicans who oppose intervention in Cuba, and perhaps are sympathetic to the Cuban revolution, are neither Communists nor fellow travelers. Their attitudes are more the outgrowth of the revolutionary and anti-intervention traditions — still strong in Mexico — than of any ideological attraction to Communism. Attitudes also may be colored by latent anti-gringoism.

Members of the Catholic hierarchy evidently suspect Communist influence in the Independent Campesina Central, the General Union of Peasant Laborers, and the National Liberation Movement. Communists undoubtedly have been active in the left- and right-wing clashes at the University of Puebla and the University of Michoacán.

The Revolution, and the persistent efforts of the government to realize its economic and social goals, have served to immunize the country against Communism. The government and party officials have monopolized the terms "revolution" and "revolutionary," which tends to negate the "revolutionary" propaganda of the Communist parties and other Communist groups. The strong nationalism of Mexico's continuing revolution, too, is antithetical to international Communism. The immunization, however, will last only so long as most groups are convinced that the government is trying to meet their most urgent needs and to build a society which will progressively better their lot.

Outlook for the Two-Party System

What are the chances for a two-party or multi-party system in Mexico in the near future? Conditions for a viable two-party system are slowly appearing — broader consensus on ends and means, more political maturity, more cross memberships in interest groups, more individual memberships in the Popular Sector of the official party, and rising national wealth — but have not yet reached the point where they would support genuine interparty rivalry for position and power. Given this situation, a two-party system as present is neither desirable nor workable. Unless the tempo of political evolution quickens, there seems little likelihood of a two-party system in the foreseeable future.

In his penetrating group analysis of Mexican politics, *Mexican Government in Transition,* Professor Robert E. Scott of the University of Illinois writes that, given proper conditions, a two-party system might result from the inability of the PRI to work out programs satisfactory or acceptable to all the powerful interest groups within its ranks. As the party grows more diverse with industrial and social change, the balancing and adjusting of conflicting interests becomes more difficult. Dissatisfied groups might abandon the PRI and be absorbed by another party; the resultant new combination might be sufficiently powerful to compete on relatively even terms with the formerly dominant PRI. This situation might well mark the end of one-party rule.

THE PRESIDENT AND THE PRESIDENCY

In the Mexican system of government, the President is a central and commanding figure who towers far above the legislature and the courts. There was a period from 1928 to 1935 when the incumbent president — Emilio Portes Gil, Pascual Ortiz Rubio, or Abelardo Rodríguez — was the puppet of ex-President Calles, but today the President is not only the titular but also the functioning head of the oligarchy which rules the country and makes the basic decisions concerning government and the economy. It has been said that the President is the government, a statement which one can accept as true if it refers to the key role of the chief executive in policy formation and major administrative decisions and as head of state.

The President exercises a decisive influence upon policy making as chief executive and as head of the official party. In the former role he also directs the activities of the expanding national bureaucracy. Though the presidents of the United States and of Mexico are by all odds the outstanding public figures in their respective countries, the Mexican President, in much greater degree than his counterpart north of the border, represents for the average citizen the government and the state.

By design, the *constituyentes* at the Querétaro convention of 1916–1917 created a strong executive; they attributed the Díaz dictatorship in part to the failure of the Constitution of 1857 to endow the President with sufficient authority. The powers of the President since 1917, however, have grown far beyond those granted in the basic law. The Constitution to be sure confers substantial powers upon the chief executive, but in addition he has those powers which inhere in his leadership of the official party.

Presidential authority, furthermore, is enhanced by cultural traits which cause many Mexicans to equate the President, a single, definite figure, with the national government and to look to him for personal leadership — similar to that of the father in the family or the patron on the hacienda or in business. Many Mexicans find it difficult to grasp the concept of national government or to understand its several branches, but on the other hand they can identify with relative ease with the President of the Republic. A persuasive case, too, can be made for the thesis that presidential powers have expanded in response to Mexico's need for a leadership strong enough to compensate for internal disagreement on the bases and objectives of government and for the dearth of experience in the rivalry and compromise of democratic law-making.

Constitutional Powers

The Constitution has equipped the President with generous powers of appointment and removal. These powers, which he may use to control administration, as well as to influence the political process, with respect to certain offices, exceed those of the President of the United States. For example, the Mexican President appoints the secretaries of the major departments of government as well as certain other high officials, without going to the Senate or other agency for approval. He also has a free hand in removing diplomatic agents and high treasury officials. The Constitution directs the President "to promulgate and execute the laws enacted by the Congress . . . providing for their exact enforcement in the administrative sphere"; and the President, in discharging this duty, has made extensive use of the rule-making authority through the issuance of *reglamentos.* The President has broad powers over the conduct of foreign affairs and the armed forces, the latter of which is used on occasion to back presidential decision and in general to contribute to political stability.

Under the Constitution, the President exercises a privilege which may seem unusual to observers of United States government, that of introducing laws or decrees directly into Congress; and in practice he or the departments under him originate most important bills coming before the lawmaking body. As a matter of academic interest, it might be mentioned that the President also has a veto but, since he is the fount of major legislation, almost no occasion for using it. Two bills, for minor, technical reasons, have been vetoed since the Revolution.

Congress also accepts without change or criticism the President's budget, through which the executive exercises a pervasive control not only of government spending but also of the substantive programs underlying the spending proposals. Lest it be thought that this acceptance is somehow unique, at least as compared to practice in this country, it should be pointed out that our Congress, despite the very vocal criticisms by individual congressmen of specific items, usually accepts the President's budget without comprehensive examination of the whole and without major change. But there *are* criticisms and minor changes, both absent in Mexican legislative practice.

Until recent years, the President frequently ruled by decree; and, as a matter of record, executive decrees were the source of a major share of the more signifiant legislation between 1920 and 1938. President Lázaro Cárdenas, for example, proved himself to be a master of government by decree, utilizing this convenient device to set up new departments, establish new laws and codes and amend existing codes, and to regulate industry and agriculture. Congress and the courts have always accepted these decrees.

Article 29 of the Constitution indicates that the power may properly be conferred upon a President only when the country is faced by grave emergency. In this event, the President, with the consent of his cabinet and of Congress, or the Permanent Committee of Congress if Congress is not in session, may suspend throughout the Republic or in a specific region "the guarantees which present an obstacle to a rapid and ready combatting of the situation." Congress then grants in specific manner and for specific periods the powers needed by the President to cope with the emergency. Despite the explicit wording of the Constitution, Congress between 1920 and 1938 often granted decree powers in the absence of real emergency and without prior suspension of individual guarantees.

President Cárdenas in 1938, possibly because of an uneasy conscience or criticisms leveled at his extensive use of decrees, had the Constitution amended to prevent the granting of extraordinary powers to the executive except "in accordance with provisions of Article 29." Though extraordinary grants have not been made in peacetime since 1938 — they were made to President Avila Camacho during World War II — one wonders whether the amendment, if a President wanted to disregard it, would be a serious obstacle to the bypassing of Article 29.

Though the President has imposing powers, today he cannot rule by personal whim, in disregard of established rights and ways of doing things. Mexico's increasingly complex economic and social system requires an environment of determinative rights, privileges, and procedures for its continued development, and this need is exerting a subtle pressure upon the President for orderly, constitutional government.

Need of Broader Support

The desire of recent Presidents for support from a broad range of interests, and their practice when faced with a difficult problem of consulting all sectors of the party as well as outside economic and social interests, have tended to limit executive power by narrowing the range of choice. As the government becomes more representative, the capacity of the President to inaugurate bold, new programs seemingly becomes more limited, at least in the short run. In the long run, however, a broadly representative government may contribute to a more general consensus on goals and means and to a greater willingness to accept innovative decisions, even on the part of interests which would prefer different policies.

The President is finding that he has neither the time nor the expertise for dealing personally with many of the issues confronting government. The functions of the national government have grown as it has assumed an ever-widening range of responsibilities for the economic development of the country and the social welfare of its people. The perennial demand for the better coordination of the policies and activities of the more than two hundred decentralized agencies — Pemex, Nacional Financiera, and others — with those of the regular administrative establishment is indicative of the growing difficulty of personal presidential control of many aspects of administration. As a consequence, the chief executive is turning more and more to the bureaucracy for help. Individuals and business organizations might prefer to see the President in person about their problems, and often do, when they have unusual influence or their problems are of major proportions; but to an increasing extent, in compliance with established procedure or informal practice, they are taking their problems to the bureaucracy. As a result, the presidency is becoming institutionalized. Today Mexico is governed not by the President alone or by the President and official party; it is governed by the President with growing assistance from the bureaucracy and relatively less from the party.

One notable result of the bureaucracy's success in handling substantive administrative problems which formerly were reserved for presidential decision is the growing volume of respect from affected citizens. Such respect undoubtedly will contribute to a further expansion of this function of the bureaucracy. The practical knowledge gained by the bureaucracy of economic and social problems, reinforced by its mounting technical and professional expertness, has enhanced its capacity to advise the President on policy questions. It is not unreasonable to expect the bureaucracy to assume a progressively important role in administrative and legislative policy making, all of which will contribute to the further institutionalization of the presidency.

Survival of Personalismo

Such institutionalization and the growth of esteem for the institution itself, as well as the traditional respect for the man, have added to the stability of Mexican government. *Caudillismo* seems to be dead, at least on the national level, although *personalismo* is still very much alive, albeit less vigorous. The decline of *caudillismo* has been paralleled by a rise in the influence of civilian politicians; the last four presidents, including Díaz Ordaz, have been civilians. Given political stability and a continued minor role for the military, as denoted in part by its share of the national budget, there is no good reason for anticipating a revival of *caudillismo* on the national level. There are recurrent charges in the Mexican press, however, of *caudillismo* on the state and local levels.

Personalismo is relatively less important than formerly because the President, as pointed out above, finds it impossible to hear all individuals who would like to lay their causes before him in person, because of the greater need for the application of expert knowledge to problems, and because political and economic stability require the handling of many problems on the basis of established rules and procedures. However, the crowded anterooms of executive offices on all levels of government testify to the continued strength of *personalismo* in Mexican government.

When Mexicans have problems which may call for public solution, they seemingly have a compulsion, which some writers refer to as "señorpresidentismo," to lay them before the President and to bypass the administrator within whose purview they fall. Thus, when the interns and resident physicians of fifty-nine hospitals in the Federal District and forty-eight in the states went on strike in January, 1965, they appointed a commission to present their requests directly to President Díaz Ordaz. The President received the delegation, explaining, however, that "he was doing it as an exception, since his obligation to deal with the more serious national problems prevented his handling each and every one of the concerns of the different sectors of the people" and that the strikers should have addressed themselves to their immediate superiors.

The ordinary Mexican has a lively interest in the President as a person, an interest which is indicated by the large amount of space which newspapers and periodicals allot to presidential activity. On the occasion, for example, of President López Mateos' last state-of-the-union address in 1964, *Tiempo,* a weekly news magazine, described in no little detail the activities of the President during the morning hours preceding the address, including his breakfast with Señora López Mateos and their daughter.

> With Doña Eva and Avecita, President López Mateos passed to the dining room . . . A bouquet of roses decorated the center of the table. The dishes were porcelain; the glasses and pitchers of cut crystal; and the place settings of silver. The rector of the national life drank slowly a glass of grape juice which his wife served. Following, he ate slices of watermelon, cantaloupe, mango, and grapefruit, and drank a half cup of coffee. Then he was served fried eggs with tomato sauce, and he finished the cup of coffee and took a few sips of another. He finished breakfast with three slices of cheese, *chilaquiles,* and *frijoles refritos.* He smoked a dark cigarette at the same time that he enjoyed a little more coffee. He had time during the breakfast conversation to smoke another cigarette. Finally, on leaving the table, he drank some more grape juice. Outside, he kissed Doña Eva and Avecita on the cheek and took leave of them.

Immunity to Restraints

A feature of Mexican government which may seem unique and even dangerous to observers farther north in the hemisphere is the lack of effective formal restraints upon presidential power. Congress is obedient and critical, and the federal courts either accep national policy which, after all, is representative c presidential policy, or else maintain a hands-off atti tude, holding that certain disputes are political in natur and hence outside their realm.

In the main, however, recent presidents hav wielded power in responsible manner, with a high degree of sensitivity to the national interest, as define by party, outside interest groups, and the presidency and to established political and constitutional proce dures. Through a period of apprenticeship in officia party and in government, presidents today have ac quired an understanding and appreciation of th evolving Mexican constitutional system which ten both to guide and restrain their official acts.

The attitudes and expectations of interest group with recognized, established roles in the political pro cess also set limits to authority. No doubt the capacit of the bureaucracy to check the President, in the sens of a tempering influence upon administrative and legis lative decisions, will grow with the institutionalizatio of the office. As a result of these forces, the Presiden usually does what is expected of him, though his tangi ble awards may exceed official salary. Public opinio seems willing to accept, as part of the customary orde of things, that most presidents will finish their term better off financially than when they started. Never theless, Alemán and his principal associates wer widely criticized after they left office for unjustifie enrichment.

Mexico in general has a free press, but pres criticism stops short of the President. His appointee and programs which have his blessings may draw th fire of the press, but the President, never. Subsidie possible reprisals, genuine respect for the office, an the fear of impairing governmental stability are factor which stay criticism.

Leaders of opposition parties and other publi figures, similar to the press, treat the President wit deference. The leadership of the leftist peasant organ ization formed in 1963, the Independent Campesin Central, although critical of official agrarian policie promised to respect the office of the President. Th belief that reprisals may follow criticism is illustrate by the rumor, true or not, that the famous artis David Alfaro Siqueiros, who was sentenced to eigh years in prison in March, 1962, for violation of th ambiguous Law of Social Dissolution, had arouse official ire by his strictures on President López Mate in speeches in Cuba and Venezuela. Possibly in respons to numerous petitions, López Mateos pardone Siqueiros in July, 1964, for the ostensible purpose c allowing him to carry on his painting for the benef of the national culture.

Ex-presidents too are generally treated gently b the press, but their immunity is less than that of th incumbent. The President and others who have a han in running the country also strive to present to th public a picture of harmony, or at least not of discor among the family of ex-presidents. In the light c

Special new schools in the Federal District and elsewhere are part of a long-range plan for vocational training of young Mexican men and women to meet the Republic's needs for a much larger skilled work force. President López Mateos was honored guest at the dedication of one of the government centers near Mexico City.

public dissension between Cárdenas and Alemán, this has not always been an easy task. Cárdenas, for example, lent the weight of his considerable prestige to the *Movemiento de Liberación Nacional,* organized in 1961, which is sympathetic to the Castro government and in general has a leftist orientation. To counter MLN influence, Alemán and a number of associates organized the *Frente Revolucionario de Afirmación,* anything but a revolutionary group, which enjoys the backing of more conservative interests. Fearful that dissension would harm both government and official party, President López Mateos assigned public responsibilities to all seven ex-presidents (Pascual Ortiz Rubio has since died), and designated them collectively as a National Consultative Committee. He appointed Cárdenas executive director of the Balsas River Development Commission and Alemán chairman of the Tourism Advisory Board.

The Process of Election

Candidates for the presidency are formally nominated by convention seven or eight months in advance of the sexennial election held on the first Sunday in July. In the PRI, spokesmen of one of the party's component groups customarily identify the candidate shortly before the convention. On November 3, 1963, for example, the directors of the Mexican Labor Confederation (CTM), the railroad workers' union, the electricians' union, the miners' union, and other labor organizations pronounced for Díaz Ordaz, secretary of Gobernación, as the party's candidate. The railroad workers' union earlier had asked Díaz Ordaz if he would accept the nomination. Díaz Ordaz was for-

mally nominated on November 16 at the party convention in Mexico City. "For his definite qualifications of a civic nature, for his proved revolutionary conviction, and his brilliant political career, the candidate for the Institutional Revolutionary Party for the next six years, 1964–1970, is Gustavo Díaz Ordaz."

The nomination of Díaz Ordaz was the culmination of a process of *auscultación.* Similar to a physician who seeks to learn the state of his patient's health by listening to sounds in his chest and abdomen, the higher echelons of the ruling oligarchy, working in part through the PRI sector organizations, sound out party and public attitudes toward various precandidates. The opinions of workers, farmers, bureaucrats, merchants, industrialists, ex-presidents, and other political figures are solicited. The rules of the game forbid party and public officials publicly to discuss possible candidates during the period of *auscultación.*

The President is able to speak with a decisive voice in the choice of his successor. Since he is in a position to veto the chances of any man who displeases him, the candidates at the very least must be acceptable to the chief executive. But the President cannot impose his personal choice upon the ruling oligarchy over the determined opposition of its other leaders. For the sake of internal unity and harmony, he must be ready to accept another candidate if other members of the oligarchy strongly favor him.

Ex-presidents are consulted, and their disapproval may be sufficient to kill the opportunities of a presidential hopeful, as happened in 1952 when Cárdenas objected to two right-wing candidates. The Mexican press reported that Cárdenas opposed the candidacy of Díaz Ordaz, but, if he did, his objections did not carry enough weight to block nomination. Cárdenas, however, did not publicly oppose Díaz Ordaz either before or after the nomination, but, on the contrary, after months of silence, endorsed him for the presidency not long before the election.

As in past years, the leadership of the PRI early in 1963 warned its members against *futurismo,* or premature maneuvering for nomination for the presidency, or for lesser offices. Although the public and the press were fully aware that the official party was occupied with the consultations and trades incident to nomination, they received no enlightenment from the party itself. A writer in the Mexico City daily, *El Universal,* of October 24, 1963, stated that the official party "considers that preelectoral activity is treason to the government; that the legitimate aspiration of a minister or official is a crime of *lesa patria;* that propaganda concerning one's own work must be interpreted as an act of open rebellion; that the expression of one's ideas in a discourse is equivalent to dangerous self-promotion; and that the only politics permitted to cabinet members is to devote themselves completely to their work." The party and the ruling oligarchy believe that open competition for the nomination would be a disruptive force dangerous to keeping party harmony and government stability. Within the party there are some who contend that a few leaders are best qualified to select the presidential candidate and that the injection of more democracy in the nominating process would threaten national stability.

In contrast to the silence of the PRI is the large volume of speculation in newspapers, periodicals, and politically-aware groups concerning the official party's choice for the nomination. Mexicans refer to the unidentified candidate of the PRI as *el tapado,* the hidden one, and newspapers and magazines use him as a subject for cartoons and cover pages. For months in 1963, the identity of *el tapado* was a favorite topic of conversation, and even bootblacks were able to rattle off the list of eligibles and name the favorites. Leading candidates, in addition to Díaz Ordaz, who was a front runner from the start and whose nomination was generally regarded as a certainty as early as September, were Antonio Ortiz Mena, secretary of the treasury and public credit, who has been reappointed to the position by the new President; Donato Miranda Fonseca, secretary of the presidency; Benito Coquet, director of the Mexican Institute of Social Security; and Alfredo del Mazo, secretary of hydraulic resources. Ernesto Uruchurtu, whom Díaz Ordaz has appointed for another six years as regent of the Department of the Federal District, was also considered a candidate.

President Díaz Ordaz

When it became apparent in September that Díaz Ordaz would be the PRI nominee and next President, numerous leftists desperately tried to head off the nomination by condemning him as an ultra-conservative and a friend of reactionary clerical interests who would do irreparable harm to the forward march of the Revolution. *La Política,* a Communist semi-monthly magazine of news and opinion, pointed out that he was a practicing Catholic and a member of the Knights of Columbus. Conservatives, on the other hand, were inclined to support Díaz Ordaz as a friend of private business, of the clergy, or of the United States, and as an enemy of Communism. In the United States *Time, U. S. News and World Report,* the *Wall Street Journal,* and the *First National City Bank of New York,* described Díaz Ordaz as anti-Communist and "slightly right of center" and reported that private business generally was happy with the prospects.

From his many speeches after his nomination in November, one is able to put together a picture of the new President which differs markedly from that painted by the leftists and to a lesser degree from that sketched by American news magazines. Díaz Ordaz emerges as a strong nationalist dedicated to the revolutionary objective of a better life for all Mexicans and especially for the majority who still lack adequate income, housing, clothing, and other values. In working for this goal, he accepts the programs supported by López Mateos — continued agricultural reform and industrial development, expansion of educational opportunities, and broader social security, health, and other benefits. Government will continue to have a guiding but not exclusive role in economic development.

Díaz Ordaz is a practicing Catholic in a country where more than 90 per cent of the people are at least nominally of the same persuasion. His devotion provokes suspicion in some circles, however, because of the hostility of the church hierarchy for more than four centuries to practically every forward-looking proposal for change. Although some Mexican clerics still reject the Revolution, the church today tends to accept the political and social programs of the government, and the government in turn consults church leaders on matters of mutual concern. It is of course impossible to delineate with any certainty the course that Díaz Ordaz will take with respect to church-state relations. But it is relevant to point out that he not only is a son of the church, but that he also is the product of a powerful political and bureaucratic organization, which has had its profound influence upon his beliefs and attitudes. It is conceivable, although it certainly is not inevitable, that the presidency of Díaz Ordaz may further improve church-state relations and contribute to greater political stability through more comprehensive clerical acceptance of the Revolution.

The new President has pledged that he will "increase the harmony of our foreign relations," especially with the United States because of geographic, economic and social reasons. His meeting with President Johnson in November, 1964, was a partial fulfillment of this promise. But since his primary concern is Mexico, Díaz Ordaz also can be expected to continue López Mateos' policy of closer ties with other Latin American and with European states as a means of expanding sources of foreign credit and trade opportunities as well

Early in 1962 the Mexican government launched a National Border Program designed to promote the economy by improving tourist facilities, establishing new commercial centers, and in general creating closer ties between the national economy and that of the frontier cities. Through the arch, which is one of two spanning the highway into Nogales, Sonora, the tourist can see a part of the new border commercial center. The Mexican national insigne of eagle and serpent is shown to the right of the archway.

is increasing Mexico's economic independence of the United States.

During his campaign for the presidency, Díaz Ordaz won the endorsement of a number of prominent Mexican leftists, which further weakened the conservative character given him by the extreme left and by various conservative interests. Lombardo Toledano early in the campaign declared for Díaz Ordaz, but there was nothing startling in this, as he had supported all PRI candidates since Avila Camacho. But it was significant when General Heriberto Jara of Veracruz, a highly respected leftist and member of the constitutional convention of 1916–1917, Jacinto López, leader of peasant invasions of large estates in Sonora, and Lázaro Cárdenas aligned with the PRI candidate.

If Díaz Ordaz is indeed more conservative than his predecessor, his speeches and the appraisal of left-wing leaders belie the fact. But if the event should fulfill early prognoses, it does not follow that the new President will be a counter-revolutionist. To the average observer north of the border, the programs of a "rightist" president could appear strikingly liberal and to the remnants of the ultra-conservative wing of the Republican Party nothing short of Communism. Díaz Ordaz' particular task could be the consolidation of the gains of the López Mateos government, but such a role is not necessarily conservative. Mexico, however, has numerous unresolved problems. Its industry is producing at about 50 per cent of capacity. Its average per capita income is approximately $300 per year, and that of the peasant considerably lower. A broad gap

remains between agrarian problems and the programs designed to cope with them. Pressures arising from this milieu alone are likely to give Mexico a president at least slightly left of center.

Díaz Ordaz has the personal and political traits which in aggregate gave him a high degree of availability, or appeal to the ruling oligarchy and to the public, in the Mexican political scene. He was born in 1911 in San Andres Chalchicomula, Puebla, shortly after the outbreak of the Revolution, and thus belongs to a new generation of public servants who by now have largely replaced the old revolutionaries. His background is middle-class and he is trained in the law. While still a university student, he began his career as administrator and politician as an intern in the department of government in the state of Puebla. Later he filled several judgeships in Puebla, and between 1941 and 1945 was secretary general of the government of the state. As a reward for public service and party loyalty, he was elected first to the national Chamber of Deputies and then to the Senate. President Ruiz Cortines brought him to Mexico City for an important position in the Secretaría de Gobernación, and López Mateos appointed him to head this agency.

Díaz Ordaz married in 1937 and has three children. The weekly *Reporter* of November 30, 1963, described him as of medium stature, thin, of clear color, and possessing the physical traits which provide unmistakable evidence of his crossbreeding (*mestizaje*). He was pictured as a model husband, a very affectionate head of family, and a man fond of sports and of the simple life in the warmth of his home. He also was characterized as the prototype of a middle-class Mexican.

For a time in November, 1963, it looked as if Díaz Ordaz might run for the presidency without opposition, and PRI leaders feared that the absence of a challenger might lend support to the accusation that Mexico does not have free, democratic elections. PAN, the only possible opponent, was racked by internal dissension over the question of taking part in the presidential race. One group contended that PAN should limit its efforts to congressional and local elections and that its participation in the presidential contest would lend the appearance of genuineness to what was essentially a farce. The other faction, whose views prevailed, maintained that a presidential candidate would improve the chances of PAN candidates for election to the Chamber of Deputies and would contribute to party unity. PAN nominated José González Torres, a forty-four-year-old lawyer and native of Michoacán, who had been secretary-general and national head of PAN and on several occasions had represented Mexican Catholic intellectuals abroad. A charge was made that the PRI was subsidizing the campaign of González Torres. Both parties issued a vehement denial.

Value of the Campaign

Nomination by the PRI of a candidate for the presidency is tantamount to election, but nonetheless the candidate will conduct a vigorous campaign throughout the Republic. Far from being a cynical gesture toward democratic practice, the campaign has several positive values: it gives the next president an opportunity to broaden popular support for his coming administration, to work for greater party unity, and to learn first-hand more about the problems of the Republic.

Qualifications for Office

Almost any Mexican citizen, if he lives long enough, can meet the constitutional qualifications for the presidency, but, as in this country, only a few have the traits which in varying combination give their possessors a high degree of "availability" for the office. Formal qualifications are more limiting than those of the United States. Reflecting the strong spirit of nationalism of the Querétaro assembly, the Constitution requires a president not only to be a native-born Mexican citizen but also the son of native-born Mexican parents. He must be at least thirty-five years of age, as in the United States, and have lived in the Republic for a full year prior to election day. The anti-clerical bias of the Constitution again is noted in the clause which disqualifies a man for the presidency if he has ecclesiastical status or is a minister of any cult. Army personnel, heads of national administrative departments, the attorney general of the Republic, and state and territorial governors cannot be president if they fail to resign at least six months before the day of the election.

No Mexican president can serve for more than one elected term of six years. "No-reelection" was one of the watchwords of Madero in his struggle against Díaz, and the Querétaro convention, moved by its fear of a recurrence of a Díaz-type dictatorship, gave "no reelection" constitutional statement. The ambitions of General Alvaro Obregón, who had been president from 1920 to 1924, led him to seek a second term in the 1928 election, and President Calles furthered these ambitions by having the Constitution amended to remove the ban against reelection. Obregón won a second term but was assassinated by a religious fanatic before he could serve again. Today the Constitution not only denies a second term to an elected president but states that any person who has held the office by appointment cannot again fill it. The presidential term was four years until 1928, when it was extended to the present six.

Mexico does not have a vice president. If the elected president suffers "absolute disability" during the first two years of his term, Congress appoints an interim president and issues a call for the election of a president to fill the remainder of the term. If the disability occurs during the last four years, Congress designates a substitute president to finish the term.

CONGRESS — THE THIRD BRANCH

In the Mexican national government the legislative branch is at the bottom of the political peck order and is likely to remain so for some time. If the three branches of government, presumably co-ordinate if one interprets the Mexican Constitution correctly, were arranged on a power-prestige scale, the presidency would be at the top, Congress at or near the bottom, and the judiciary somewhere between. Recent presidents have treated Congress with respect, somewhat similar to that which a family of fifty years ago accorded to a noncontributory maiden aunt, but have granted it little authority. But unlike the maiden aunt who scolded, admonished, and helped raise the children, Congress is docile and shows a due regard for its proper station in the political order of things.

The official party and the President designate all but a few of the deputies and senators, and the designees, men who know their duties, seldom shatter the faith reposed in them. When six PRI candidates who thought they had won seats in the Chamber of Deputies in the 1961 election later were notified by the Electoral Commission (which conducted an investigation after protests by the PAN and PPS) that they had not been elected, they accepted their fate without too much audible grumbling. Such behavior would be incomprehensible in a state where the legislative branch is a vital force. Congressmen representing other parties are hesitant to oppose presidential legislative initiatives for fear that their parties will lose official recognition and with it the right to compete in elections.

President López Mateos encouraged Congress to show more initiative in considering bills, but this action, while it may have long-term benefits, was in itself a measure of the low estate of the legislative branch. In sponsoring the constitutional amendments to allot more deputies to minor parties, President López Mateos looked to a Congress which mirrored more faithfully the principal political currents of the Republic and in which the expression of various shades of opinion would add more life and content to debate.

The Chamber of Deputies elected in July, 1964, is showing some signs of life independent of the President, perhaps because of the larger number of minor party deputies and possibly too because President Díaz Ordaz, like his predecessor, is supporting greater legislative enterprise. Several significant policy proposals have been introduced without presidential imprimatur. PRI deputies affiliated with the Mexican Confederation of Labor (CTM), for example, during the second session of Congress which opened in September, 1965, introduced several controversial measures, reportedly without prior clearance with the President. The CTM deputies proposed the amendment of Article 123 of the Constitution to establish a forty-hour week; to recognize as a proper cause for striking, the failure of an employer to comply with the profit-sharing law; to prevent discrimination in employment against workers over forty years of age; and to improve worker housing by requiring employers to supply housing at reasonable rents.

Vicente Lombardo Toledano and other PPS deputies made the Chamber of Deputies the target for a large volume of vociferous criticism from press and politicians because of their successful advocacy, within the lower house, of a proposed constitutional amendment to make deputies eligible for immediate reelection. As introduced by the PPS deputies, the proposal recommended election for an indefinite number of consecutive terms, the arrangement of the original constitutional text until it was changed in 1933, but the Chamber limited eligibility to two consecutive terms. Not only PPS but also PRI and PARM deputies voted for the amendment. PAN deputies cast negative votes because they preferred unlimited reelection.

Opponents stated that the amendment violated a basic tenet of the Revolution, that of no-reelection, that it would open the door to presidential reelection, and that the deputies were more concerned with keeping their jobs than promoting national interest. The weight of public opinion seemed to be against the amendment. Carlos Madrazo told the delegates attending the Fourth Ordinary National Assembly of PRI in April, 1965, that the amendment, although not without merit, was disrupting national and revolutionary unity and suggested abandonment. The Senate killed the amendment in September, 1965, by unanimous vote.

PPS deputies also commended to the Chamber, in October, 1965, a new article to the Constitution to be entitled, "De la economía nacional." Of far-reaching significance, the article would expand the role of the national government in economic development, require a general plan of development, applicable both to the public and private sectors of the economy, provide for the expropriation of the property of monopolies, levy a single tax, limit business profits, and establish a flexible wage scale based upon the cost of living.

Both Chamber and Senate assumed the role of spokesman in the field of foreign affairs, a prerogative of the President, when they rejected the resolution of the United States House of Representatives of September 20, 1965, affirming the right of signatories of the Treaty of Rio de Janeiro to unilateral intervention in Latin American republics to keep communism outside the hemisphere. In the Chamber, deputies representing all parties inveighed against the resolution. The Senate, in somewhat more sedate fashion, reaffirmed its support for non-intervention.

Subordination of the Legislature

Despite these stirrings of parliamentary life, the Mexican system, if the forces behind presidential ascendancy have been correctly identified and assessed, has no choice but to relegate the legislative branch to a subordinate position. The organization of the official party in 1929 and its control of the electoral and legislative processes contributed to the subordination of Congress. Another contributory factor is the needless "no-reelection" provision of the Constitution — Díaz, not Congress, was the dictator — which, by denying two consecutive terms to a legislator, means a complete turnover in the membership of the Chamber every three years and in the Senate every six. In any given Congress, however, there will be numerous members who served in the past. Each chamber, moreover, appoints a new presiding officer each month, a practice which further discourages the growth of strong legislative leadership. The PRI leader in each chamber, however, has considerable authority.

If Mexico is to continue to move toward its democratic goals, Congress apparently must become a more influential body, representative, along with the President, of the sovereign people and their various constituent interests. Presidential support for legislative initiative may help raise Congress from its lowly status. But its acquiring any significant amount of power will have to await the more general acceptance of the underlying assumptions of Mexican government and greater maturity in democratic processes. With consensus and maturity may come the mutual respect and the greater willingness to compromise and adjust differences which are indispensable to the legislative process. This situation doubtless will facilitate some redistribution of political power, with Congress the chief beneficiary. The appearance of a two-party system, by encouraging interest groups to place more reliance upon the legislative approach to policy formation, will enhance legislative power and prestige.

However, in the light of the numerous contingencies involved, the emergence of Congress as a powerful lawmaking body is still far distant. When it occurs, it probably will not be marked by the legislative-executive relations delineated by formal constitutional provision; rather, it seems more likely to resemble parliamentary democracy in some respects, with a popularly elected President functioning in effect as a first minister but without the power of dissolution. The President's role today in the legislative process, including his direct introduction of bills, and support of administrative measures by cabinet officers on the floor of Congress, suggest this line of development.

The inability of Mexican interests to find effective representation in Congress is offset to some extent by the system of functional representation which has developed as a significant part of the policy-making process. Through the three sectors of the official party, through legally-established functional groups, and through informal clusters consisting of industrial corporations and financial institutions, as well as through other means, practically every substantial interest has access to decision-making centers. Possibly in this area lies the hope of representative government, rather than in the Congress of the Republic.

Structure of the Legislature

The structure of Congress is similar to that of its counterpart in the United States, with the states and the Federal District each having two senators in the upper chamber, and the states, Federal District, and territories being represented in the Chamber of Deputies on the basis of population. In one limited area the Mexican Constitution is more democratic than ours, for it allots representation in both chambers to the Federal District, while under the United States Constitution the District of Columbia is without representation in Congress and only recently, through the Twenty-third amendment, won the right to vote for presidential electors. Congress presently consists of two hundred and ten deputies and sixty senators.

Though lacking in power, the Mexican Congress is not without distinctive characteristics. For each proprietary or regular legislator, the voters elect an alternate or substitute, who, under specific circumstances, serves during the absence of his principal. Not only may members introduce bills, the sole method in the United States Congress, but also the President and the state legislatures. The impact of Mexican nationalism upon the Constitution is seen again in the stipulation that only Mexican citizens by birth are eligible for membership.

When Congress is not in session, the Permanent Committee mentioned above is on hand to perform designated functions. As a legislative device, such committees are thought to have originated in Spain; they also are found in several other Latin American republics. The Mexican committee consists of fifteen deputies and fourteen senators. Various constitutional authorities are of the opinion that it could be eliminated without any great harm except to itself.

FEDERAL COURTS AND LAW

In Mexico the federal courts have substantial powers, exercised with the tacit understanding that they cannot be used against major policies or other political matters of concern to the ruling elite. Though a major branch of the federal government by provision of the written constitution, the courts customarily play the role assigned to them by constitutional convention, a role which is subordinate to that of the President. The Mexican political system apparently does not yet have sufficient stability or sophistication to tolerate a court system with the power to impose substantial restraints upon presidential authority.

Relations between judiciary and President might seem strange indeed to an uninformed observer accustomed to the relative independence of the two branches in the United States. During the 1964 presidential campaign, for instance, the chief justice of the Supreme Court accompanied Díaz Ordaz, at the latter's invitation, on a swing through the northern part of the state of Veracruz. Shortly before López Mateos left the presidency, the justices of the Supreme Court held a banquet in his honor at which Justice Felipe Tena Ramírez thanked the President for having respected the independence of the judiciary. He asserted that the President had not made even the slightest hint concerning court decisions but on the contrary has respected both the dignity of the court and that of its members.

Influence of the Judiciary

Operating within the bounds delineated by the Mexican political system, the federal judiciary has attained a position of influence markedly above that of Congress but below that of the President. In deciding controversies between private individuals, the courts dispense substantial justice on the basis of established law and procedures, a development which has come in response to the needs of a complex society for order, fairness, and certainty in the adjudication of rights.

The courts furthermore, and for similar reasons, show a due regard for individual rights in the large majority of criminal cases. Through the writ of *amparo*, which will be discussed later in more detail, the courts offer the citizen an opportunity to protect himself against the arbitrary acts of public officials or the wrongful application of the law, though some observers charge that the courts are more inclined to check state than national authority.

Unlike the federal judiciary of the United States, the courts do not invalidate national laws by finding them in effect unconstitutional. This restraint is a product of the traditions of the civil law, Mexico's system which frown upon judge-made law and demand compliance with the precept that a law can be invalidated or repealed only by another law enacted by the legislature. In numerous cases the Supreme Court of Justice has upheld the competency of Congress to make laws without restriction by the judiciary.

In adjudicating civil cases, Mexican courts may constitutionally fill gaps in the law by interpretation. This power does not extend to criminal matters. The courts, however, do not follow the common law rule of *stare decisis.* They regard past decisions as persuasive and on occasion may follow them; on the other hand, they are free to ignore either individual decisions or an entire line of decisions bearing upon the case at hand, except in the instance of a *jurisprudencia,* discussed below. When faced with a gap in the civil law, the judges are more apt to be influenced by *doctrina,* or the learned opinion of legal authorities, than by past decisions.

In structure and subject-matter jurisdiction, the Mexican federal courts resemble our own, reflecting influence from north of the border, but the law applied, as suggested above, is alien in some respects to the Anglo-American system of common law. The courts have jurisdiction over controversies involving the Constitution, national statutes and treaties, admiralty law, and two or more states. Unlike our courts, they may decide controversies between a state and residents of another state and between the different branches of state government when the constitutionality of their acts is questioned. Jurisdiction arising from national statutes is extensive because of the broad range of legislative powers delegated to Congress. The courts have exclusive jurisdiction over civil rights controversies.

The Writ of Amparo

For the protection of the individual guarantees of the first twenty-nine articles of the Constitution, the Constitution has armed the federal courts with the highly significant writ of *amparo* for bringing cases involving personal and property rights before them for decision or review. The Mexican writ of *amparo* — the word means protection or shelter — is unique to the Republic and has been in process of development for more than a century. It is similar but not quite the same as our writs of *habeas corpus,* injunction, *mandamus,* error, and *certiorari.* Only federal courts may issue the writ and try or review *amparo* cases; state courts are specifically barred from this legal area.

Federal courts have *amparo* jurisdiction over three classes of cases: those arising from statutes or official acts which violate personal or property rights, federal law or action which restricts or invades the rights and privileges of state government, and state statutes and actions which trench upon the federal domain. The law of *amparo* as well as court practice, with a wholesome respect for the actual structure of power, exclude political matters from *amparo* jurisdiction. By far the largest number of cases come before the courts because a law or official act has injured an individual by purportedly invading his constitutional rights. Numerous cases arise out of court action in civil, criminal, and labor cases because of alleged errors in procedure or violation of the laws in the final judgment or award, to the injury of individual rights. *Amparo* also is a remedy for administrative acts causing individual injury which cannot be corrected by other legal means.

In all instances the principal parties to *amparo* cases are state or national officials on the one hand and individual persons on the other. The law offers other correctives for the invasion of individual rights by private action. In all three categories of *amparo,* even controversies between national and state authority, the courts are concerned only with the injury or damage to the individual.

The judgment of the court in *amparo* is confined to private individuals, "being limited to affording them redress and protection in the specific cases to which the complaint refers." The courts, moreover, are forbidden by the Constitution to make "any general declaration as to the law or act on which the complaint is based." Since decisions are limited to the immediate case and the parties involved, they ordinarily cannot serve as precedents for the same court or other courts in later cases of a similar nature. Whenever a court finds that a law has damaged an individual by violating one of the individual guarantees of the Constitution, it obviously is of the opinion that the application of the law is unconstitutional. But the court, unlike those of the United States, does not nullify the law; its decision on the contrary goes no farther than suspending the operation of the law with respect to the party immediately concerned.

Fortunately, the law of *amparo* does permit the Supreme Court of Justice to set up a sort of precedent, in the form of *jurisprudencias,* for the direction of the courts of the Republic in cases involving interpretations of the Constitution, national statutes, and treaties. A *jurisprudencia* is established when the full Supreme Court or one of its four divisions, by stipulated majorities, makes the same interpretation of the same point of law in five consecutive decisions without an interrupting contrary decision. A *jurisprudencia* of the full court binds future action of the Court and its divisions; *jurisprudencias* of the divisions control their future action. The *jurisprudencias* of the full Court and its division are binding not only upon other federal courts but also upon the courts of the states, territories, Federal District and upon boards of conciliation and arbitration. The Supreme Court, of course, may set aside or modify a *jurisprudencia.* Though the Supreme Court refrains from making a general statement concerning the constitutionality of the law involved, the effect of a *jurisprudencia* is to negate the law. The Congress often recognizes this fact by repealing or amending the statute.

The large volume of requests for *amparo* is a partial index to the high regard in which it is held by litigants and their attorneys. As a matter of record, many cases in the district courts and a majority of those crowding the dockets of the Supreme Court are *amparo* cases. To lighten the load of the Supreme Court, the Mexican government in 1951 established five collegial courts of appeals for the sole purpose of reviewing *amparo* petitions from the decision of federal trial courts and the awards of boards of conciliation and arbitration. In 1954, the number of collegial circuit courts was raised to six with the organization of a second in Mexico City and more recently to seven with the creation of one in Guadalajara.

Relief provided by the 1951 changes was only temporary because of the long-term pressures stemming from population and economic growth. At the end of 1964, the Supreme Court's backlog consisted of about 15,000 unresolved pieces of business. As a result, the President in November, 1965, after a study by a Supreme Court committee of the problem, recommended to Congress a number of amendments to the law of *amparo* and to the Constitution for the purpose of limiting the *amparo* jurisdiction of the highest court to cases of major importance. The jurisdiction of the collegial courts of appeal would be broadened and their number increased.

Through *amparo*, the Mexican federal courts have served democratic ends well by protecting individual rights guaranteed by the Constitution against unjust or arbitrary infringement by state or national authority. This conclusion is not invalidated by the fact that numerous *amparo* proceedings represent more an abuse of the right of *amparo* than of individual guarantees. By protecting rights against unjust laws and the arbitrary acts of officialdom, the national courts have created greater confidence in the administration of justice.

The use of *amparo* protection for individual guarantees and its denial by law and practice to violations of political rights constitute another of the contradictions of Mexico's emerging democracy. It is held that political rights do not fall within *amparo* because they are not part and parcel of the individual guarantees of the Constitution; however, if the PRI or the chief executive were not involved, the Court conceivably might extend *amparo* protection to political rights through interpretation of the "due process" clause of Article 14, as it has done in numerous cases involving taxation and individual rights.

The Federal District Courts

Most cases originate in the federal district courts, the general trial courts of the system. There are from one to three in each state or territory and seven in the Federal District. Before collegial circuit courts appeared in 1951, the intermediate appellate level was occupied solely by six, single-member circuit courts of appeals (*tribunales unitarios de circuito*). These latter courts remain, but with jurisdiction confined to non-*amparo* appeals. Judges of the intermediate appellate level are called *magistrados*.

At the apex of the judicial hierarchy, the Supreme Court of Justice is comprised of twenty-one *ministros*. The court functions either *en tribunal pleno* (as a full court) or in four *salas* or divisions — criminal, administrative, civil, and labor — which were created to speed up the operation of the judicial process and to bring the weight of special knowledge to bear in the adjudication of cases. A fifth auxiliary division operated from 1951 to 1955, applying a judicial hand to the reduction of the *amparo* backlog. The Supreme Court as a whole, and each of its divisions, annually elect one of their number to serve as president during the year; and he, unlike the President of the Republic, is eligible for reelection.

The President of the Republic appoints the ministers of the Supreme Court, subject to the approval of the Senate, which is always given. The Supreme Court in turn not only makes appointments to district and circuit courts but may transfer judges from one area to another and promote them from district to circuit court. District and circuit court judges do not enjoy tenure during their first four years on the bench, but if afterwards they are reappointed or promoted to a higher position, they can be removed only for misconduct by a vote of the majority of the members of each house of congress. Several years ago the president of the Supreme Court explained to the author that Supreme Court designation of inferior court judges minimized the influence of partisan politics in the appointive process. At the very least it eliminates the diversity of influence which characterizes appointments in the United States, where members of the Senate, in the main, control district and circuit court judgeships. Because of the method of appointment, Mexican jurists probably represent the national viewpoint even more strongly than those of this country.

District and circuit court judges need not be residents of the state or area in which they function. An acquaintance of the author, for example, began his judicial career in the state of Chiapas, from there went to a northern border state, was later transferred to the Federal District, and a little later was elevated to a circuit court. No assignment was in his home state.

In appointments to the federal judiciary, the President and the Supreme Court in one sense have less discretion than the President of the United States, for the Constitution and statutes prescribe minimum standards of choice. Mexican nationalism again crops out in the requirement that judges must be citizens by birth. To insure minimum standards of professional competency, the law requires judges to be attorneys with degrees from accredited institutions and to have practiced for a given number of years. Minimum ages for the several courts are established. Whether because of the theory that judicial arteries begin to harden with the onset of age or for other reasons, the Constitution fixes an upper age limit of sixty-five for ministers of the Supreme Court. This is unique in that there is no corresponding disability for other officers of the government, and no doubt on occasion it has deprived the Republic of the services of able men.

The president of the Supreme Court in 1959, in his report at the end of the year, complained that the items in the federal budget for the courts did not permit decent salaries for judges and court employees or proper housing for the courts. "From the budget of expenditures of the Federation we received only approximately 0.43 per cent for the discharge of our duty. A federal judiciary on which is spent less than one-half *centavo* of each peso of the budget is not able to satisfy the Mexican people's hunger and thirst for justice." The president also indicated that the poverty of the moral climate and the lack of voluntary attachment to moral and legal standards are recognized as circumstantial causes interfering with the administration of justice.

Improvement of Justice

The Supreme Court is showing a serious concern with improving the administration of justice by trying to recruit young men of demonstrated professional ability and promise for careers as federal judges. When vacancies occur today in the lower courts, the Supreme Court frequently fills them with men who have acquired some experience as judges in courts of the Federal District, as clerks of the Supreme Court and lower federal courts, and as attorneys in the Public Ministry (somewhat similar to our Department of Justice). Ministers of the Supreme Court are putting more stress upon their constitutional duty of making periodic visits to circuit and district courts as another means of insuring compliance with Supreme Court rules and in general improving the administration of justice.

To the person suspected or accused of crime, the Constitution extends various protections against arbitrary police action and various guarantees for a fair trial. In the case of the poor, and Mexico has many, others without influence, and persons arrested on criminal charges in the big cities, constitutional rights not infrequently are trampled upon by untrained police officers whose ignorance of modern police methods is matched only by their hazy notion of the rights of the accused.

The writ of *amparo* frequently serves to shield the individual against disregard of legal rights and procedures, but too often it is beyond the resources of the Indian, *campesino,* or urban poor. Official efforts, it should be noted, are being made to upgrade the quality of police officers; the Federal District, for example, has organized a police academy with a formal program of training for recruits. The smart, young police officers now appearing in greater numbers on the streets of Mexico City are graduates of this school.

The Constitution forbids officialdom to molest a person or his family, home, papers, or other possessions, unless it has a written order from competent authority stating the legal grounds for the action. Only competent judicial authority can issue orders of arrest, after a formal accusation has been filed indicating the probable guilt of the accused. As in Anglo-American law, a man's home is his castle, free from unreasonable searches and seizures, at least so far as the Constitution is concerned. Police officers may obtain search warrants, but only from competent judicial authority, and the warrants must indicate the place to be searched,

the person or persons to be arrested, and the objects sought. After taking a person into custody, police officers are not supposed to detain him for more than three days without a formal order for commitment. The Constitution bans the ill-treatment of prisoners during arrest or confinement, any molesting without legal authority, and any exaction or contribution levied in prison.

In criminal trials the accused has procedural rights similar to those in the United States. He is entitled to bail, if the offense is not punishable by more than five years' imprisonment, to know the identity of his accuser and the nature of the charge, to confront witnesses against him and subject them to cross-examination. His trial must be public. The judge decides the question of innocence or guilt. Jury trials are mandatory, however, for persons tried for press offenses against the public peace or the domestic or foreign safety of the nation or for public officials or employees whose official acts or omissions have injured the public interest or the proper conduct of administration. Juries consist of seven persons and decide by a simple majority vote.

GOVERNMENT AND THE ECONOMY

Though Mexican presidents since 1917 have differed in their zeal for reform (but not substantially in their protestations), and several, including Carranza and Calles, have become downright conservative, the government and the people in general have been faithful to the economic and social aspirations of the Constitution. To pursue these ends, even though program content may vary, is to be "revolutionary" in today's Mexico. In their annual reports to Congress and in other public statements the Presidents pay tribute to these aspirations and more important still lend the weight of their enormous power and prestige to mediating programs. The Immediate Action Program, for example, worked out by the Mexican government for 1962–1964 in accord with the Punta del Este charter, stressed objectives long basic to national policy — low-cost housing, sanitation, extension of the social security system, expansion and improvement of public education, construction of rural and urban welfare centers, and continued agricultural reform.

Successive national governments have underlined economic development as indispensable to a better life, and their efforts, in conjunction with those of private business, have stimulated substantial growth in the economy. Figures presented by different sources may not jibe on the exact increase for a given period, but they all agree on the fact of growth. The Banco Nacional de Comercio Exterior reports that between 1939 and 1959 the gross national product practically tripled in size, that in 1961 it was 167 per cent higher than in 1950, and that the average annual increment between 1950–1955 was 5.4 per cent and between 1955–1961, 5.7 per cent. The annual increase in the GNP slumped to 3.5 per cent in 1961, to the consternation of public and business officials alike, but subsequently improved to show a gain of 4.8 per cent for 1962, 6.3 per cent for 1963, and, according to the Bank of Mexico, approximately 10 per cent for 1964. In terms of 1950 prices, the GNP grew from more than 20 billion pesos in 1939 to almost 85 billion in 1963.

Practically all sectors of the economy have shared in this growth, though some are relatively less important than they were. Manufacturing, emphasized in recent years as part of the industrialization program, in 1960 accounted for 25.6 per cent of the gross national product, as compared to 16.4 per cent in 1940. Agriculture's share for the same period remained relatively constant at about 20.5 per cent. The petroleum industry produced 1.7 per cent in 1940 and 4.5 per cent in 1960. The relative contribution of mining declined during the twenty year period, from 4.4 to 2.2 per cent. The contribution of other economic activities to the GNP for the two years, 1940 and 1960, was as follows: electric power, 0.6 and 1.3 per cent; construction, 1.8 and 3.5 per cent; transportation and communications, 5.8 and 5.3 per cent; commerce, 25.1 and 20.9 per cent; and other activities including government, 22.4 and 16.3 per cent.

The Federal Role

Anyone who reads the Mexican Constitution cannot escape the conclusion that its framers decided upon an active role for the national government in the country's economic development. The framers were impelled more by a realistic assessment of the shortage of capital resources and other obstacles to higher standards of living than by doctrinaire economic theory. In response both to constitutional directive and to economic need, the national government has indeed played an important part in the economic growth, planning, stimulating, directing, restricting, and in some areas owning and running a number of business enterprises.

The government draws its authority from sections of the Constitution dealing with land, mineral, and water resources, the powers of Congress, and labor and social security. Amendments to the Constitution in 1960 enlarged national economic powers by giving the government the exclusive right to exploit petroleum and solid, liquid, or gaseous hydrocarbons and "to conduct, transform, distribute, and supply electric power which is to be used for public service."

In its participation in the economic development of the Republic, the central government has followed closely a policy of economic nationalism, the major components of which are Mexicanization of industry and agriculture, and in given areas, when deemed necessary, government ownership or controlling interest in private corporations. As part of its program, the government has adopted a policy of import substitution, partly to conserve foreign exchange and partly to encourage the development and expansion of the skills and processes essential to an expanding industrial system.

The Meaning of Mexicanization

Mexicanization has several meanings. According to a law of 1931, it means that 90 per cent of the skilled and unskilled workers of any enterprise must be Mexican. The government normally will not grant immigration permits to foreigners when Mexicans are available for managerial, technical, and specialist positions. Public policy also favors foreign concerns which are willing to teach their technical processes to Mexican personnel.

Mexicanization also means, according to the Constitution, that Mexicans "shall have priority over foreigners under equality of circumstances for all classes of concessions and for all employment, positions, or commissions of the Government in which the status of citizenship is not indispensable." Since 1944, the President has possessed the discretionary power, which has not been applied to all classes of corporations, to stipulate that 51 per cent of the ownership of Mexican companies be in Mexican hands. The 1960 mining law reserves new mining concessions to government enterprises, mixed corporations, or Mexican corporations 51 per cent of which is owned by Mexicans, offers a reduction in production and export taxes to existing corporations with at least 51 per cent Mexican ownership, and provides for the termination without compensation at the end of twenty-five years of the concessions of existing corporations in which Mexicans do not have a controlling interest. Economic necessity, however, has compelled national authorities to accept foreign corporations, foreign skills, and foreign capital. The government generally prefers foreign credits to foreign corporations, since it has greater freedom in channeling the former to areas where they will do the most good, and since they are more in harmony with the Mexicanization program.

Program of Industrialization

Both public and private capital are sensitive to the fact that the per capita income of underdeveloped or semi-developed states, in which agriculture is the principal economic interest, is generally low; and that income levels tend to rise as industry becomes a significant factor. Hence, the central government during the past twenty years has stressed the development of industry, a term which includes manufacturing, construction, and the production and distribution of electricity, water, and gas, but has not neglected agriculture.

The volume of industrial production between 1939 and 1957 expanded by 130 per cent. Industry accounted for 20 per cent of the GNP in 1940 and 30.5 per cent in 1961. A major share of recent advances is owed to the petroleum industry, though gains in manufacturing and electric power also are noteworthy. Growth may be measured, too, by the increase in the percentage of industrial workers in the total working force, from an estimated 12 per cent in 1940 to about 16.7 per cent in 1960. The major emphasis has been on capital investment for producer goods, but industries serving the consumer also have grown in number and output.

Public spending constitutes a crucial part of the total new investment each year and compensates in part for the shortage of private investment capital, which is aggravated by the reluctance of many Mexicans with savings to invest in the national economy. Private capital's share of the total annual new investment, however, exceeds that of government; but even here at least part of the private spending must be credited to public incentives. The policy of President Díaz Ordaz with respect to the relative roles of public and private investment is essentially a continuation of that of López Mateos. In a press conference in January, 1964, during his presidential campaign, Díaz Ordaz explained his proposed policy.

> With respect to economic activities, I repeat that Mexico needs more and better private enterprise and more and better state initiative, that the two are able and ought to join their forces harmoniously for attaining a more rapid economic development.

> I think that the State ought to limit itself in this area, to act in the area that the Constitution reserves in a formal manner: hydrocarbons, coal, electricity, or in general terms, energy; general means of communication, etc., as a general rule. But this is not to mean that the State abstains from intervening in other branches when there are unsatisfied collective needs and private enterprise omits or neglects them.

Public investment between 1939 and 1950 came to 40 per cent of the total invested and to 39 per cent between 1950 and 1959. Federal budgets since 1961

have allocated approximately 39 per cent of total budgeted expenditures for economic development. In the main, federal investments have gone to stimulate further economic growth through the expansion of transportation and communication facilities and the supply of petroleum products, including industrial chemicals, and electric power and water.

Budget expenditures are supplemented by the investments of decentralized agencies and state-run concerns, such as Petroleos Mexicanos, Federal Electricity Commission, National Railways, Federal Toll Roads and Bridges, and the Mexican Social Security Institute, which for 1961 supplied more than half of the total public investment. The Immediate Action Plan of economic development for 1962–1964 recommended a total public and private investment of approximately 80 billion pesos, of which slightly more than half was to come from the national government, decentralized agencies, and partly government-owned enterprises.

Nationalized Industries

The central government has nationalized the electric power industry, a process completed in 1962 with the purchase of the stock of Compañía de Tranvías, Luz y Fuerza Motriz of Monterrey. It had acquired in 1960 the two largest private power companies, American and Foreign Power and Mexican Light and Power. Mexico maintains a government monopoly in petroleum through Pemex, which, in addition to gasoline, lubricants, and other traditional products, is turning out a mounting list of petrochemicals for Mexican industry. In 1959, Pemex began the construction of eighteen plants for the production of basic petrochemicals, and it is participating with private enterprise in other industrial enterprises. Pemex also has constructed pipelines which are transporting gas from various oil fields to Mexico City, Monterrey, and a growing number of other urban places.

Service stations bearing the legend Pemex sell the products of the government-owned petroleum industry. The stations, however, are a small segment of the industry permitted by government to remain in private hands. This typically busy station in the northwestern agricultural region displays a Mexican highway map over the doorway.

— Ray Manley Photo

HIGHWAY NETWORK OF MEXICO

Source: MEXICO 1963: Facts, Figures, Trends, *courtes* *Banco Nacional de Comercio Exterior, S. A.*

In 1962, national authority acquired control of its second major airline by buying 80 per cent of the stock of Guest Aerovías México. The first nationally owned and operated airline was Aeronaves de México. With certain minor exceptions, the railroads have been nationalized, and the government administers the larger part of the total through National Railways of Mexico. The national government owns and operates the telegraph system and the larger portion of the facilities for the distribution and exhibition of motion pictures.

The central government owns or has a controlling interest in the largest steel corporation, Altos Hornos de México; in Constructora Nacional de Carros de Ferrocarril, which manufactures boxcars, cabooses, and gondolas; and in numerous other industries. It is significant to note that the central government and private capital, both Mexican and foreign, are the joint owners of many enterprises. Through the direct investment of public funds and through loans, the Mexican government has promoted the establishment of essential industries, motivated not by a master plan of socialization but a desire to industrialize the Republic as rapidly as possible.

Approximately twenty national development banks supply credit for general and specific types of economic growth. This number includes the Bank of Mexico, Nacional Financiera, National Bank of Foreign Commerce, National Farm Credit Bank, and National Ejidal Credit Bank. Nacional Financiera, the principal development agency, lends money both to public and private

enterprise, guarantees security and bond issues, own: a majority interest in various companies, and on occasion will manage business concerns. The Small Merchants' Bank, possibly the smallest of the credit institutions, lends at relatively low interest rates to smal retailers of Mexico City. The federal government also offers incentives in the form of tax exemptions or reductions, tariff protection, and import controls to stimulate private investment in new industries, particularl those whose products will permit import substitution and augment the exportation of manufactured goods

Under the Treaty of Montevideo, effective Jan uary 1, 1962, Mexico, along with eight other states became a member of the Latin America Free Trade Association, which it is hoped will broaden the market for exports and eventually lead to a Latin Americar common market.

An important current import substitution program has as its objective the domestic manufacture of autos The auto program was started in 1960 with the levying of heavy taxes upon imported vehicles in order to encourage auto assembly in Mexico, and with the prohibition of certain luxury models. National law required that by the end of 1964, not only must auto be manufactured in Mexico but not less than 60 per cent of their parts, by cost, must be produced within the country. The program is designed to create new employment opportunities, stimulate the developmen of industries which produce parts, provide autos a lower prices — although it now appears that auto price will be higher than before — and conserve foreign exchange.

The Department of Industry and Commerce has approved plans submitted by eight companies for the manufacture of autos, including one all-Mexican company which bought outright the patents and machinery for the manufacture of the Borgward and removed the machinery from Germany to Mexico. There has been some speculation as to the capacity of the Mexican market, and of the export trade, to absorb the output of the new auto industry. Fábricas Automex, a Chrysler-Fiat affiliate, on June 18, 1964, completed the first auto built under the new plan, and President López Mateos drove it from the assembly line of the Automex plant at Toluca.

TRANSPORTATION AND COMMUNICATION

The national government has spent heavily for the improvement and expansion of communication and transportation facilities, which in 1961, 1962, and 1963 absorbed about 6.5 per cent of budgeted expenditures. This spending has been prompted by recognition of the key position of these facilities in economic growth and in the social and political integration of the country.

The Mexican highway system between 1929–1964 expanded from 9,900 to 56,399 kilometers of "all-weather" roads — paved, surfaced, and unsurfaced. Experience indicates that some unsurfaced "all-weather" roads in Mexico be avoided during the rainy season.

Highway transport has reacted to this growth to the point where public service vehicles chartered by the national government in 1959 carried 165 million passengers, as compared to about 31 million reported by the railroads, and more than 3 million metric tons of freight, compared to about 13 million transported by rail. Highway transport reported 182 million passengers in 1960. In 1961 the railroads carried 32.6 million persons and more than 34 million metric tons of freight.

The total length of Mexican railroads has varied little in recent years; however, one impressive addition came in November, 1961, with the opening of the 938-kilometer Chihuahua-Pacific Railroad, from Ojinaga, Chihuahua, over the rugged Sierra Madre Occidental mountains, until recently not crossed by any road for wheeled vehicles, to Topolobampo, Sinaloa, on the Pacific. Significantly, President López Mateos, who rode the first passenger train which officially crossed from Chihuahua to the Pacific, described the

Source: MEXICO 1963: Facts, Figures, Trends, *courtesy Banco Nacional de Comercio Exterior, S. A.*

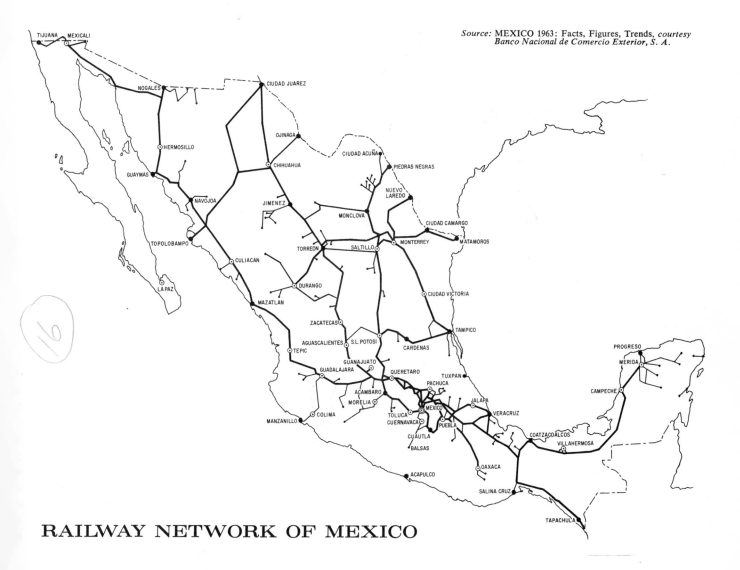

RAILWAY NETWORK OF MEXICO

The populous Valley of Mexico and other industrial centers consume a large part of the electricity generated by hydroelectric and other power plants. The Mexican government is attempting to further increase the nation's total output of electricity (which more than doubled in the decade from 1950 to 1960) and extend lines to rural as well as urban areas.

Dams such as this have helped to new lands, increase agriculture's p tive power, and somewhat to relieve co's population pressure. The feder ernment has supported many irr and hydroelectric projects as p regional development, under the a of river valley commissions similar TVA in the United States.

basic purpose of the new line as "one of national integration." The rail system of Mexico in general has been upgraded by the acquisition of modern rolling stock and the installation of more durable roadbeds and heavier rails.

The aviation industry, with government help, has expanded rapidly and now ranks, on the basis of invested capital, third in the transportation world. In 1960, the airlines flew 1,780,000 passengers and 72,707 metric tons of freight. Mexico in 1960 listed 880 airports and landing fields, including twenty-three federal airports. President López Mateos in September, 1964, reported twenty-nine federal airports. The airport at Mexico City is considered one of the world's best, but already, as a result of heavier traffic and city growth, there is discussion of a new facility.

MULTIPURPOSE DAMS AND OTHER HYDRAULIC PROJECTS

Since 1928, the federal government has been building a series of hydraulic works consisting of dams, irrigation canals, tunnels, and hydroelectric plants to supply the additional water and power basic to economic development. The economic meaning of these projects, in a country where only about 15 per cent of the total area receives sufficient rainfall, is denoted in part by the increase in hectares irrigated by federal-controlled water from 20,000 in 1930 to 2,610,000 in 1958.

The Raudales dam on the Grijalva River in Tabasco, which is considered one of the major public works of the López Mateos administration, will open new lands to cultivation and settlement and possibly

offer some relief to the population pressure of other parts of Mexico. The President, in November, 1964, as part of the grueling program of dedicating public works started by his administration which kept him occupied for the last several months of his term, officiated at the formal opening of the Presidente Adolfo López Mateos dam on the Humaya River in Sinaloa, described by one journal as the most "audacious" hydraulic work in his administration, which will supply water for the cultivation of 120 thousand hectares of new land and complete the irrigation of an additional thirty thousand hectares.

The production of electric power in the Republic has been boosted by the generating facilities of multipurpose dams, the erection of other dams whose main purpose is electric power, and the construction of new thermoelectric plants. The national government, through the Federal Electricity Commission, Empresas Eléctricas Nacional Financiera, Industrial Eléctrica Mexicana, and other agencies, has taken a leading part in expanding the nation's power generating facilities. Installed capacity was increased from 1,400,000 kilowatts in 1951 to 5,290,000 by December, 1964, thus slightly surpassing López Mateos' target of 5 million kilowatts by the end of his administration. Per capita consumption grew from 171 kilowatt hours in 1951 to 315 in 1961.

Two major hydroelectric projects of the López Mateos government were inaugurated by the President in November, 1964. The Infiernillo project on the Balsas River, on the border between Michoacán and Guerrero, will be the largest hydroelectric installation of Latin America when all its generating equipment i in place. It will have an installed capacity of 672

housand kilowatts when fully completed. The project s a part of the President Adolfo López Mateos Hydrolectric System, which will include other installations. At the site of the project, a heroic bust of López Mateos protrudes from the solid rock of the mountainide, and under it is the legend, "Al Presidente Adolfo López Mateos, Electrificador de México. Los Trabaadores."

The second project, President Plutarco Elías Calles n the Yaqui River in Sonora, will have an installed apacity of 100,000 kilowatts. Like the Infiernillo 'roject, it was a work of the Federal Electricity Comnission. The dam, El Nivillo, also dedicated by López Mateos in November, 1964, is 443 feet high, only lightly under the 490-foot height of Infiernillo.

Numerous irrigation and hydroelectric projects ave been part of more comprehensive programs of egional development by river valley commissions, imilar to the T.V.A. in the United States. The Papabapan Commission, the first of these, was organized n February, 1947, to administer the government's rst comprehensive program of agricultural developnent in tropical Mexico. The commission is charged vith the agricultural development, and related industrial nd colonization projects, of the valley of the Papabapan River and its tributaries in Oaxaca, Puebla, and

Veracruz. Other commissions are the Tepalcatepec Commission in Michoacán, created later in 1947 (consolidated with the Balsas Commission in 1960); the Fuerte Commission in Sinaloa, 1951; the Grijalva and Usumancinta Commission in Tabasco and Chiapas, 1951; and the Balsas Commission, 1960, whose writ runs through the entire state of Morelos and areas in the states of Puebla, Tlaxcala, Mexico, Michoacán, Jalisco, Guerrero, and Oaxaca.

AGRICULTURE

Despite the weight given to industrialization and the relative scarcity of land for cultivation, Mexico has enlarged its agricultural output to the point where it is able to feed itself in normal years and to produce a growing volume of products for Mexican industry and for export. Between 1945 and 1957, agricultural output doubled and consistently accounted for approximately 20 per cent of the gross national product each year. The most pronounced increases have been in export crops, which today comprise approximately 60 per cent of all exports and produce earnings essential for further economic development.

While the total number of persons working in agriculture has grown, from 3.6 million in 1930 to approximately 6.3 million in 1960, the percentage of the economically active population in this sector of the economy has declined, from 70.5 to 52.8 per cent for the same years. Agriculture remains, nevertheless, the major source of employment.

In agriculture as in most other branches of the economy, government and private enterprise have joined hands to raise and diversify the yield, but gains would have been considerably less impressive without extensive public participation. In the Immediate Action Plan for 1962–1964, the central government assigned a larger percentage of the total amount for public investment to agriculture, with emphasis upon irrigation works and agricultural rehabilitation. Public hydraulic projects, as indicated above, have opened new lands to cultivation and in some sections have brought an adequate and more certain supply of water to established farmlands.

The National Bank of Mexico states that "agricultural progress is measured mostly in increases in areas under cultivation, and seldom is due to greater efficiency; yields per hectare, or per worker, are still low; mechanization is still meager, in most places." Still a part of the gain must be credited to the national programs of education and research designed to boost agricultural production and improve its quality.

Two Types of Landholding

The Constitution recognizes only two types of landholdings — the small private farm and the *ejido*. Since the hunger of the Mexican peasant for land was a major cause of the Revolution, it was to be expected that the various "revolutionary" governments would be forced to change the system of land tenure. The *ejido* program, attended by the division of large estates and public lands among landless peasants, was started in 1915 and given constitutional status in Article 27 of the fundamental law. The title to *ejido* farms belongs to the community, not to the individual members. *Ejido* plots, however, are farmed in the main by individual families, but woodlands and pastures are held communally. The typical *ejidatario* is a cultivator of the soil, but a growing number are found on cattle and forest *ejidos*. President López Mateos in September, 1964, in his annual report to Congress, announced that eighty-six cattle *ejidos* had been organized in the six years of his administration.

The upper limits of the size of small private farms, the second type of landholding, are fixed by the Constitution. The small agricultural property consists of 247 acres of first-class moist or irrigated land under cultivation, 494 acres of seasonal land, 988 acres of good quality pasture land, or 1976 acres of arid pasture. Irrigated cotton farms in private hands may be as large as 370.5 acres. Holdings up to 741 acres are allowed for the growing of bananas, sugar cane, coffee, henequen, rubber, coconuts, grapes, olives, vanilla, quinine, cacao, or fruit trees. Small holdings for stock raising cannot be larger than the area needed to main-

tain as many as 500 cattle or their equivalent in small animals.

Between 1915 and November, 1958, the central government distributed 107,445,000 acres among the *ejidos*. President López Mateos reported in September, 1964, that his administration had distributed a total of 39,629,100, or more than one-third of the land distributed since the initiation of the program in 1915. Frank Brandenburg, in *The Making of Modern Mexico*, states that lands redistributed by the national government, beginning with Alemán's administration, "have been predominantly grazing, forest, and 'mixed' lands," and that López Mateos between 1958 and 1961 left arable areas "virtually untouched." If correct this may explain rising agricultural output.

Effects of Redistribution

The political effects of land redistribution match and possibly exceed those of an economic character. The destruction of the hacienda system shattered the basis of the economic and political power of one of the most important components of the pre-Revolutionary power structure. While the program is not without its shortcomings, it has contributed to political stability by removing inequities in the distribution of land, by broadening the popular basis of government, by giving many peasants a sense of hope which was denied them by the hacienda system, and by better integrating the rural dweller with the national economic and political system.

There are numerous landless peasants, however, who have been bitterly critical of the government's reform program, charging that it is not moving fast enough and that there are still many large estates in the Republic, thanks to official protection and concessions. In recent years, landless peasants on a number of occasions have invaded private lands, especially in Chihuahua, Sinaloa, and Sonora. One of their leaders, Jacinto López, supported Díaz Ordaz for the presidency. He now represents the Popular Social Party in the Chamber of Deputies.

In January, 1963, the Independent Campesino Central, an organization of landless peasants, was formed to bring concerted pressure upon the government for an accelerated program of agrarian reform. About a week later, President López Mateos announced that his administration intended to partition all the remaining large estates by the time he left office.

A nine-point program of agrarian reform had been announced in December, 1962 by the secretary of agriculture, who later reported that his department was taking various steps to speed up the land distribution program and had demanded that "the generals and colonels" voluntarily hand over the land they possessed. He pointed out that the certificates of exemption from partition granted by former governments had meaning when they were "only 15 million Mexicans and much land to divide but at the present moment . . . constitute an obstacle to basic agrarian reform."

In a lecture in October, 1965, before the PRI's Institute of Economic, Political, and Social Studies, Edmundo Flores, agricultural economist, stated that there still are approximately 500 large estates in Mexico ranging from 50,000 to 150,000 hectares in size. These are found in the main in remote, semi-desert, or tropical areas, or else belong to influential politicians.

Production tends to be low on many agricultural plots not only because of antiquated methods which numerous farmers still employ, through ignorance, lack of capital, or the two factors in combination, but also because many farms are so small that they can scarcely return a subsistence livelihood to the families which cultivate them. Too small for economical cultivation, largely unaffected because of their size by the reforms aimed at higher productivity, these farms have created the problem of *"minifundia."* Minifundia farming involves slightly more than one million *ejidatario* families existing on plots which on the average are about fifteen acres in size, not all of which are cultivable, and a similar number of private farms. The *ejido* phase of the problem has been caused by the failure of past governments to distribute sufficient land of good quality to the *ejidos*. It should be stressed, however, that the growth in the Republic's agricultural production indicates that many *ejido* and private farms are economically viable.

Both opinion and statistics, when the latter are available, differ on the relative productivity of privately owned farms and *ejidos,* although the weight of opinion supports the belief that much of the credit for higher output must go to the private sector. However, Professor Robert Barrios, former head of the Department of Agricultural Affairs, stated in February, 1963, that the *ejidos* grow 58 per cent of the cotton and 60 per cent of the sugar cane harvested in the Republic. The attention directed to agricultural rehabilitation in the Immediate Action Program for 1962–1964 indicates that production on numerous *ejidos* is sufficiently low to warrant a fuller measure of public help.

Education and Research

Land redistribution is but one phase of agrarian reform in Mexico. The rise in production cited above is attributable not only to an increase in the total area under cultivation but also to the various national programs of education and research, some conducted by the Mexican government alone, others conducted in cooperation with agencies of the United States government, with other Latin American states, and with the Rockefeller Foundation, which have encouraged the use of improved seeds, livestock, and land management, the application of fertilizer to the soil, and more effective measures against plant and animal diseases. The new national agricultural center at Chapingo, near Mexico City, is indicative of the government's concern with agricultural problems. In the course of his campaign for the presidency, Díaz Ordaz recognized agriculture as the nation's foremost problem.

Division of the remaining large holdings into *ejidos* is but the final act in the first stage of a two-stage program of agrarian reform. The government, moreover, will continue organizing *ejidos* in new centers of population — particularly in the southeastern part of the Republic — for landless peasants from overcrowded, older sections where all available land has been partitioned. López Mateos in September, 1964, announced the establishment of twenty-eight new population centers in the area of Panuco, seven in Alto Candelaria in Campeche, twelve in Quintana Roo, forty-five in Veracruz, and sixty in Oaxaca.

The second stage calls for the treatment of the problems of the *ejidatario* and the small proprietor, not in isolation, but as an integral part of the national economy and society. During the 1964 presidential campaign, the National Farmers Confederation (CNC) used the slogan, "If it is not integral, it is not agrarian reform." To raise output per hectare, greater stress will be given to improved, technical methods of cultivation and to production for the market rather than for subsistence. The central government promises that more credit will be available.

To the greatest possible extent, the *ejidos* will be industrialized in the sense that they will conduct at least the primary manufacturing processes in preparing their products for the market. One important objective is higher living standards in the *ejido* village through basic urban services, such as potable water, electricity, and health and social programs. The government will persist in its efforts to remove the *caciques* or bosses who have held sway in some *ejidos,* subverting democratic political processes and arrogating to themselves a disproportionate share of the values produced. By creating new jobs and making rural life more attractive, the new program may help in the solution of problems stemming from the high rate of urban growth.

López Mateos stated in his 1964 report to Congress that sugar mills had been installed on *ejidos* in San Luis Potosí, Jalisco, Michoacán, Oaxaca, and Quintana Roo. The state of Michoacán, according to an announcement in 1963, was to be divided into eight resin-producing zones which would include one hundred fifty-four *ejidos* and fifty-two Indian communities. A resin-producing plant was to be constructed in each zone for direct exploitation of this product. No new contracts were to be signed with private companies, and existing contracts on termination were not to be renewed. *Ejidos* were to organize credit associations, and these were to be grouped into a Union of Regional Associations to handle the processed resin in domestic and foreign markets. The precedent for the new industry is the reportedly successful operation of a pitch and turpentine factory in El Chaparro *ejido* in Ciudad Hidalgo.

The state of Oaxaca has formed a decentralized organization, the Forest Improvement Association of Oaxaca, which will plan and direct the development and use of the forest resources of the *ejidos* and Indian communities of the state. Guanajuato, in 1963, became the first state to adopt a comprehensive approach to its agricultural problems, including those of the *ejido*. Under the initial part of the plan, which calls for national participation, the state will be divided into seven zones, each with a brigade of technicians headed by an engineering section and including topographers, economists, draftsmen, and other specialists. The national government is encouraging other states to adopt similar plans.

Another objective of the second-stage program is a more attractive way of life for the *ejidatario* and his family through the organization of urban zones, improved housing, and elementary community services. President López Mateos shortly before he left office stated that his administration had organized 2,858 urban zones since 1958. At Ejido Higuerón in Morelos, for example, the President in March, 1963, dedicated a new kindergarten, primary school, library, market, and facilities for electricity and potable water. The *ejido* also obtained better breeding stock for its cattle and pork industry. At *Ejido* Forestal, also in Morelos, the new regime includes a health center, school, improved housing, a mill for *nixtamal* or corn *masa* (from which tortillas are slapped together), a store, electricity, and shops for the production of *huaraches,* textiles, and articles of wood. The López Mateos administration also sought to supply an example for *ejido* self-improvement through the organization of seventy model communities.

Price Support Program

Through the National Company of Popular Subsistence (CONASUPO), the federal government administers a price-support program as one of its measures to improve rural income. When the prices of specific farm items are threatened by surpluses or other dangers, CONASUPO may attempt to maintain prices at a stable level by buying large quantities of the products from the *ejidatarios* and small proprietors. A portion of the more durable products are stockpiled as reserves in case of scarcity. The remainder, along with the eggs, are sold at lower-than-market prices through the retail outlets which CONASUPO maintains in urban areas as part of the national program to improve diet and raise the standard of living.

PRESENT LEVELS OF LIVING

Mexico is moving toward its economic and social goals, but progress is painfully slow. The Republic has a growing middle class which is winning more of the material values generally associated with a higher standard of living and a small upper class whose general affluence and conspicuous expenditures are in striking contrast to the general poverty. All too many Mexicans, while they have managed to improve their lot, are still too close to the subsistence level for comfort, and numerous others have yet to attain this condition. Ana María Flores in her study, *La Magnitud del Hambre en*

Mexico, reports that in 1958, the average daily diet consisted of 1,985 calories, 21 per cent fewer than the 2,500 calories recommended by nutritionists, and that 15 per cent of the people went hungry. The Banco Nacional de Comercio Exterior commented in one of its publications in 1962 that "the rural population has a very low standard of living," and noted the disparity between the cost of manufactured goods and agricultural prices.

Given its present production capacity, Mexico at best could not raise living standards appreciably even though it were able to effect a more equitable distribution of national wealth. Moreover, there has been a chronic need for capital formation — most of the money for new investment is domestic — and as a consequence this need has tended to depress wages. Daniel Seligman in an article in *Fortune* in January, 1956, referred to the Mexican worker as "the true hero of the . . . investment boom, whose acceptance of a declining real income has in effect 'subsidized' much of the nation's new building."

Per capita income, however, has been rising; during the twenty-year period from 1939 to 1959 it climbed, in terms of constant prices, from 304 to 544 pesos, but is still very low in relation to need and to the per capita income of industrial nations. On the other hand, prices have risen more rapidly, at least until quite recently, as illustrated by the increase in the worker cost of living for Mexico City from 100 in 1939, the base year, to almost 700 in 1959 and 755.1 in 1963. López Mateos claimed, however, in his last annual message to Congress in 1964, that rises in wages and salaries during his six years left price increases far behind. He said that prices increased an average of 14.3 per cent, while wages and salaries climbed 96.7 per cent. The percentage increase for wages and salaries seems incredibly high.

Housing facilities are grossly inadequate, especially in urban areas, and the problem, like all Mexican problems, is compounded by the rapidly growing population. It has been estimated that only about 25 per cent of the population is properly housed, and that the other 75 per cent "lives in highly precarious conditions." For the entire Republic, the accumulated housing deficit was placed in 1962 at 2 million dwellings, a figure steadily growing because of an annual deficit of between 35,000 and 45,000 dwellings. Mexico needs at least 200,000 new units each year, according to expert calculations, but during the past several years, public efforts have added only 20,000 units annually and those of private enterprise about 10,000 houses and 2,000 apartments.

A number of knowledgeable observers of the Mexican scene believe that national economic and social programs have raised living standards. Professor Howard F. Cline states that "a vast and growing body of Mexicans" are considerably better off today than they were as recently as 1940, in terms of nutrition, rising standards of living, job opportunities, and other values. Oscar Lewis, while fully cognizant of the grinding poverty afflicting many families in Mexico City noted the presence of a growing number of gas stoves, washing machines, televisions, autos, and other symbols of rising material standards. He might also have pointed to the large number of small, transistor radios of whose presence in busses and other public places one is painfully aware, and to the apparent affluence of the crowds in Chapultepec Park on Sundays and fiesta days. In all fairness, the economic programs of the central government should be assessed not only on the basis of their short-run impact upon living standards, but also in terms of long-run promise. But if mounting expectations are too long delayed and income disparities become too pronounced, the political stability of the country will be seriously endangered.

PUBLIC FRINGE BENEFITS

Low living standards are offset to a limited extent by social security benefits for workers in private industry and the public service, various public health programs, free breakfasts for primary and pre-school children, free textbooks and notebooks for school children, public housing projects, price ceilings on basic articles of diet, and the sale of foodstuffs and clothing at below-retail prices to low-income groups.

Although Article 123 of the Constitution directs the national government to enact a social security law, the system was not set up until 1943. The Mexican Social Security Institute (IMSS) administers the program, which at the end of 1964 covered a total of 6,565,551 persons, as compared to 2,500,000 in 1958. Approximately 1,000,000 persons were added to the system in 1964, including for the first time more than one-half million farm workers, employed in the cultivation and processing of sugar cane. President López Mateos, like most of his predecessors, declared that the government plans "to extend social security services and general welfare to all Mexicans." During his administration, the IMSS established 135 new medical units, eighty-four of them in rural areas, and constructed seventy-four social security centers and fifty-four clubs for juveniles with 270 classrooms and 366 workshops.

Under the programs administered by the IMSS, the worker has some protection against the risks of occupational accidents and disease, general sickness, and old age. The system also pays maternity and death benefits. A *"dote matrimonial,"* or dowry, is available to insured women and the widows or concubines of deceased workers. IMSS constructs and operates low-cost housing projects for its members. Through Social Security Centers for Family Welfare, IMSS seeks to raise the cultural level of the Mexican woman and to improve the home by educational programs in hygiene and sanitation, improved dietary methods, arts and crafts, civic education, recreation, physical education, and sports.

Insured workers and their families are entitled to a broad range of medical services and hospitalization through a growing system of Social Security hospitals and clinics. As might be expected, facilities and services vary in quality and number from place to place, but in general are being improved and expanded. At the apex of the system is the impressive National Medical Center in Mexico City, whose numerous specialized units not only offer medical care and treatment to thousands of outpatients and inpatients every year, but also are engaged in extensive research programs and in education in medicine, nursing, and hospital administration. The medical services of the Social Security Institute go far beyond the limited "Medicare" program for the aged in the United States.

The national government is alert to the significance of the social security program, not only as a means of providing the worker with at least minimum guarantees in designated areas but also as an instrument for bringing about a more equitable distribution of national wealth. The program also is justified in terms of its contributions to greater worker productivity. The Banco Nacional de Comercio Exterior in its January, 1963, number (in English) of *Comercio Exterior de Mexico* stated that the social security program "can efficiently divert to the great masses of workers a portion of the national income." But the same number on another page quoted "expert" opinion to the effect that the extension of social services in underdeveloped countries, by failing to increase economic resources and productivity, in the long run weakens their economic position.

Employees of the national government, the Federal District, and territorial governments are protected by a social security system administered by the Social Security and Services Institute for Government Workers (ISSSTE), which had its origins in a Civil Pensions Bureau created in 1925. Under the ISSSTE program, the state assumes the responsibility for on-the-job accidents and occupational illnesses and insures the worker against non-occupational diseases. Public employees may rent, when available, low-cost housing owned by the ISSSTE, or procure mortgage loans up to $8,000 at not more than 8 per cent interest. Pensions are reviewed every six years to adjust them to the cost of living. Since September, 1964, the ISSSTE has offered up to $3,200 in life insurance, without examination, to all federal employees, with the government paying half the cost.

Protection of Public Health

Low-income groups are singled out as special beneficiaries of some of the programs falling within the jurisdiction of the Department of Health and Social Work, although a major share of that department's energies are directed to the protection and improvement of the health of the general population. Free medical services are available to low-income groups in many areas. The department wages unremitting war against epidemics and endemic diseases, constructs and maintains hospitals and maternity and child welfare centers, and is bringing potable water and sewerage systems to more and more communities each year.

Malaria, not so many years ago one of the leading killers in the Republic, has been eradicated from all but a small portion of the areas in which it formerly was endemic. Between September, 1963, and September, 1964, no Mexican died of the disease, according to López Mateos. The Department of Health and Social Work for the same period administered 23,000,000 immunizations, including 7,500,000 smallpox vaccinations.

Oral vaccinations against polio for "recently born children" have been obligatory since November, 1963; and 75 per cent of the six-year-olds have been immunized. As part of its attack against goiter, the government decreed in 1963 that salt for human use must be iodized. In his annual reports to Congress, López Mateos remarked on the steady expansion in the number of urban, rural, and regional hospitals, health centers, day nurseries, and hospitals for mental illness. Among diseases the principal causes of death are still diarrhea-enteritis, respiratory ailments, and diseases of early infancy.

A major share of the responsibility for the welfare of infants and pre-school children belongs to the National Institute for the Protection of Infancy. In its more than a hundred centers of nutritional training, it teaches sewing, sanitation, first aid, cooking, and principles of dietetics. It offers various services to expectant mothers, infants, and pre-school children. Its most publicized activity consists of the distribution of approximately three million free breakfasts daily, to children in the primary grades in 24,468 localities of the Republic. A complementary program is administered by the Department of Health and Social Work which, in addition to its free breakfasts for children, supplies milk to nursing and pregnant women. In the Federal District, the National Institute operates a rehabilitation center for handicapped children, and it is planning also an institute for problem children.

Doña Eva Sámino de López Mateos, wife of the President, assumed the role of patroness of the Institute after its organization in 1961, and her sponsorship persuaded the wives of numerous governors, as well as other notables, of the great merit of the Institute and its programs. Señora Guadalupe Borja de Díaz Ordaz, the wife of the new President, is now the patroness.

Unidad Independencia, a low-rent housing project constructed in Mexico City by the Mexican Social Security Institute, with its ultramodern architecture, kindergartens, primary schools, and sport center, is an internationally known "showpiece" which is usually included on the tours officially arranged for distinguished foreign visitors. It offers some relief to the Republic's critical housing shortage and increases the purchasing power of the incomes of its tenants, who must be IMSS members. Nevertheless, the slum areas, in the immediate neighborhood and in other parts of the Federal District, indicate that this and other projects, while commendable, fall far short of need. In explanation of plans for a large public housing project southeast of Mexico City, it was stated that "since private enterprise is interested in profits and the government . . . is not, only the government is able to solve the problem . . .'

During the six years of López Mateos' presidency the various public housing agencies constructed 48,121 dwellings — houses and apartments. The largest of these is the Unidad Nonoalco-Tlaltelolco, which replaces the large part of a former slum area not far north of Avenida Juárez in downtown Mexico City. The project consists of 102 high rise, multiple family units with a total of 11,916 apartments which will house an estimated 69,000 persons. In addition the project includes nine primary, two secondary, and one technical preparatory school, thirteen nurseries, three clinics, three clubs, a cultural center, and a museum.

Another major housing project is the Unidad San Juan de Aragón, opened late in 1964 in the Federal District. Of its 10,000 houses, 3,000 are reserved for indigent paper and garbage collectors, other non-salaried workers, and low-paid government employees. The project, like Unidad Nonoalco-Tlaltelolco a complete urban community, includes six kindergartens, ten primary schools, four markets, a children's hospital, three sport centers, and a wooded area with fountains and a zoological park.

Government Merchandising

Low-income groups can make their money go further by buying basic items of food, clothing, and footwear at under-the-market prices from stores operated by a public corporation organized by the national government. In addition to items of food, these stores sell complete outfits of clothing for school children and for workers and, in an attempt to battle the problem of nutrition, packets of fourteen basic foods designed to last a family of five for one week. The price of the latter was thirty-five pesos or $2.80. During the 1964 Christmas season, as in past years, it offered a special food packet at a cost of thirty-five pesos containing items for a Christmas or New Year's dinner for seven persons.

The program is administered by the National Company of Popular Subsistence (CONASUPO), which appeared in March, 1961, as successor to the more familiar Mexican Import Company, whose trade mark CEIMSA, still identifies articles sold. The new title is more descriptive of function and, because of its social and economic connotations, is apt to have more political merit than the old one. The new corporation, moreover, has been endowed with fuller administrative and financial means to accomplish its three objectives: (1) raising farm income; (2) stockpiling reserves of specific foodstuffs for use in event of scarcity; and (3) helping raise living standards and indirectly regulate prices by its sale of items of basic necessity at discount prices to low income groups.

A subsidiary corporation, the Distributive Company of Popular Subsistence (CDSP), is in charge of sales. The CDSP inherited a chain of CEIMSA stores and outlets for CEIMSA milk, *la leche rehidratada*

Since the early 1960's, discount-priced merchandise has been offered to the working man and his family in Mexico City by government-sponsored stores such as the one on the right which offers not only food items but clothing for every member of the family. Many low-income neighborhoods are also served by a fleet of 52 supermarkets on wheels which bring staple items to working families.

which is concocted from powdered milk bought in the United States. On the assumption that these outlets did not adequately serve the consumer, the CDSP in July, 1961, began bringing its discount food and clothing to proletarian neighborhoods of Mexico City in a fleet of fifty-two supermarkets on wheels, which officials believe are unique to the Republic. These mobile stores, equipped with shelves, refrigerator, electrical generator, and checking stand, are installed in huge tractor-drawn trailers and driven from station to station in lower-income neighborhoods. Customers who can read are handed leaflets instructing them how to prepare more nutritious and appetizing meals.

The CDSP also operates a growing chain of mills in the Federal District for grinding corn into masa for tortillas, a basic food for many Mexicans, and sells it to tortilla stores and directly to the public. The CDSP assists the small farmer by buying his corn, beans, rice, wheat, eggs, and other products at prices higher than those offered by regular wholesalers or middlemen.

A profit-sharing plan which became effective in April, 1964, is expected to boost the income of four million or more workers. The Constitution had long authorized profit-sharing, but the national government did nothing about it until 1962, when it initiated a series of amendments to Article 123 directed toward this objective, and in 1963, organized a national commission for the participation of labor in business profits on which business, labor, and government were represented. Mounting pressure from left-wing groups for more labor reform, and the approach of the 1964 presidential election may have spurred the government into action. On the other hand, the government may have adopted the plan because it judged it to be in harmony with "revolutionary" objectives and considered that the economy had sufficient maturity to support it.

The plan, published in the *Diario Oficial* of November 13, 1963, asks business to distribute 20 per cent of its profits to workers, after a deduction of 30 per cent for reinvestment and return to capital, and another deduction of varying size as a corrective factor for the relation in different businesses between the elements of labor and capital. Smaller enterprises are exempt. The right of the workers to dip into profits does not include participation in management.

Wage and Rate Controls

For some years now the government has offered the worker some protection against exploitation in the form of minimum wages. Although the rates often are criticized as too low in relation to profits and to worker needs, it is generally recognized that without these safeguards wages would be lower. New rates for the biennium 1966–1967 went into effect January 1, 1966. According to the president of the National Commission on Minimum Salaries, these rates are designed to raise worker purchasing power and to broaden the market for products of Mexican manufacture. It has been estimated that a majority of the manufacturing enterprises of the Republic operate at only 50 per cent of capacity.

The National Commission divided the country into one hundred and eleven economic zones and, in cooperation with Regional Commissions on Minimum Salaries, fixed urban and rural rates for each zone. Rates vary considerably among zones because of differences in the economic factors on which they are based.

In the latter part of 1962, the national government — as part of a general overhaul of the rate structure of the nationalized electric power industry — lowered charges for the benefit of the poorer consumer groups. It is estimated that 52 per cent of the consumers of electricity benefited. On the other hand, the cost of electricity was increased for "the sectors having greater economic potential," a classification which included not only many industrial and commercial enterprises but also many individual consumers of moderate incomes. The government plans to apply the anticipated higher profits to the expansion of the system in order better to meet the growing demands of industry and agriculture to bring electricity to more communities.

PUBLIC EDUCATION

Both the Constitution and successive national governments have recognized a better educated populace as central to political and social democracy and economic development. In the Constitution, the primacy of this goal is underlined by its inclusion among the individual guarantees and by its treatment in Article 3 at the very beginning of the document. The Constitution directs the organization of a system of secular education in which elementary education is compulsory and all public education is free. Education must be democratic, "considering democracy not only as a legal structure and a political regimen, but as a system of life founded on a constant economic, social, and cultural betterment of the people"; it must be national, in the sense of contributing to the Republic's economic, political, and social development; and it must be directed to better human relationships and to the development of the individual.

The national government, unlike that of the United States of America, has been the prime mover in the development of the educational system. It has the constitutional power to establish, organize and maintain schools on all educational levels and to fix standards for the administration of public schools. Its grants-in-aid to state and local governments give it additional powers.

The Eleven-Year-Plan

Mexico is currently carrying out an "Eleven-Year-Plan" in an effort to narrow the gap between educational resources and need. Instituted in 1959, the plan has two principal objectives: (1) to expand opportunities for primary education until by 1970 not a single child of school age will be deprived of an elementary school education; and (2) to provide higher grades as needed. During the eleven-year period, Mexico hopes to construct 36,265 new classrooms, including 11,825 in urban and 27,440 in rural areas, and to create 51,900 new teaching positions, a slight majority of which will be in rural schools. The plan also calls for an expansion of opportunities on the intermediate and advanced levels. Shortly before he left office in 1964 President López Mateos stated that the Republic would attain and go beyond many of the goals before the end of the eleven-year period.

Since the launching of the "Eleven-Year-Plan," the central government has allocated a larger share of the national budget to education. In 1950, the budget figure for education amounted to 11.5 per cent of the whole and was only slightly larger in 1955. But in 1960, under the stimulus of the "Eleven-Year-Plan," 18 per cent of the national budget was earmarked for education. The percentage has slowly risen, and in the budget for 1965, it came to 23.42 per cent. President López Mateos, in his last state-of-the-union message, reported that "today, including the amount for construction, the budget for education is . . . more than three and a quarter times greater than in 1958; almost ten times more than in 1952, and twenty-two times more than in 1946."

As further evidence of the Republic's progress in education, the President cited the 30,200 classrooms, or more than one each two hours, constructed during the six years of his administration. Despite this achievement, to which the President pointed with justifiable pride, the Republic's school building program probably is still lagging behind need, in view of the population increase of more than one hundred persons per hour. Mexico's performance in school building was a major factor in the establishment in Mexico of the Regional Center of School Construction for Latin America under the sponsorship of UNESCO and the OAS.

The national government prides itself on the fact that it is spending a great deal more for education than for national defense, and that the nation's teachers outnumber members of the armed forces.* These spending patterns reflect not only the stress upon education but the growth of political stability and the decline of *caudillismo*. The size of the armed forces of Mexico's neighbor to the north also is a factor.

In an effort to provide more equitable educational opportunities, the national government in 1960 began supplying free textbooks and notebooks to elementary school children. President López Mateos pointed out that the Republic, with its numerous low-income families, cannot have primary education which is really free, as commanded by the Constitution, without free textbooks.

In his state of the union message of September, 1964, he announced that the central government had distributed 114,000,000 copies of free textbooks and notebooks since 1960. The program has run up against stubborn opposition, much of it centered in Monterrey, where the Grupo Industrial Cuauhtémoc-Vidriera and the Union of Heads of Families of Nuevo León have charged that the textbooks contain Marxist-oriented, totalitarian, anti-religious, and anticlerical materials and, moreover, that they fail to stress fundamentals.

The National Action Party in conferences and in its official organ, *La Nación,* has attacked the program, and some members of the clergy, according to items in the press, have spoken against it. The government has refused to budge and has attacked critics as enemies of public education and the poor. It has promised, however, to work constantly for the improvement of the textbooks and to correct any mistakes they may contain, all of which offers little comfort to those hostile to the program. Meanwhile, elementary pupils read *Mi libro de cuarto año. Historia y Civismo.* and textbooks prepared for other elementary grades and subjects.

Diminishing Illiteracy

Analfabetismo or illiteracy continues a major problem, although under the impact of national and state programs it becomes less so each year. Progress has not been faster because of the scope of illiteracy, estimated at about 80 per cent of the entire population in 1910; the limited resources of the Republic and the competition of other urgent programs for funds; indifference or hostility in some areas, which will remain until the Indians and peasants have been more fully integrated into the national culture and rising living standards lower the importance of school-age children as breadwinners; lingual and cultural diversity; and the rapidly growing population, 44 per cent of which was under 15 years of age in 1960.

In 1944, a year in which 53.26 per cent of the population six years of age or older was classified as illiterate, the central government started a national campaign against illiteracy. By 1960, at the time of the decennial census, the percentage had declined to 36.39. On the occasion of the observance in 1964 of the twentieth anniversary of the anti-illiteracy campaign, the number of illiterates was placed at 28.91 per cent of the total population. President López Mateos stated in September, 1964, that since 1961 there had been an absolute decline in the number of illiterates each year.

Because of the shortage of classrooms, many children cannot attend school, and thus, in terms of their own and the national interest, constitute a lost generation. In the rural areas there are fewer schools than in the cities and towns, and it is the unusual rural school which offers work beyond the fourth grade. Professor Jaime Torres Bodet, López Mateos' minister of education, reported early in 1963 that approximately 983 of each 1,000 children who enter primary school withdraw before reaching the sixth grade.

More children, however, are going to school. UNESCO estimates that 50 per cent of them between the ages of five and fourteen were in elementary school between 1956–1959, as compared to 47 per cent between 1950–1954 and 43 per cent between 1930–1934. A Mexican source calculates that in 1958, 52 per cent of the children between five and fourteen were enrolled in primary schools. The "Eleven-Year-Plan" aims at an elementary education for all children of school age by 1970. The primary grade enrollment of 6,600,000 in September, 1964, was ahead of the interim goal set by the plan.

The secondary level is beyond the reach of most, and as recently as 1958 only 9 per cent of the population between 15 and 19 were in secondary or technological schools. By September, 1964, however, the enrollment in these schools was more than 140 per cent higher, or a total of 261,000 students.

Mexico in 1964 had thirty-nine universities and other institutions of higher learning, with a combined enrollment of 232,000. The student body of the National Autonomous University of Mexico, one of the oldest of the New World, grew from 44,794 in 1958

---

* Mexican youth are required to undergo military training for one year. This consists largely of drill once a week, usually on Sunday in the local community. The Minister of Defense, in November, 1965, proposed that conscripts be placed in military installations beginning January 1, 1967, for one year of intensive training. Critics pointed out Mexico needs more schools, not barracks.

to approximately 71,000 in 1962. The latter figure included 24,483 students in the seven preparatory schools affiliated with the university. In September, 1964, a total of 145,327 students were enrolled in technical programs of various levels of difficulty, as compared to 46,000 in 1958. The National Polytechnic Institute in 1964 had 47,700 students.

Schools vary widely in quality, even more so than in this country, from the ultra modern National University, with its thousands of square meters of murals and mosaics, to the poorly equipped and staffed state university; and, below this level, from schools such as the magnificent Centro Escolar Niños Héroes de Chapultepec in Puebla to the poverty-stricken rural school found throughout the Republic. Crude statistics on illiteracy fail to show fully the dimensions of the educational problem. Many classified officially as literate on the basis of one or two years of schooling have little more than the illiterates to offer their country in the way of special training or the ability to learn.

Need of Special Training

The Republic has an urgent need not only for a population better equipped for the duties of citizenship but also one containing an ever-expanding percentage of persons with the technical, scientific, and professional skills needed by agriculture, industry, commerce, and the public bureaucracy. The sale of more manufactured goods in international markets, as currently planned, requires improvements in product design, greater and more economical production, better methods of distribution and financing, and higher levels of managerial competency. Mexico, however, is not fully meeting these conditions. One source reports that today 85 per cent of the factories do not employ technical personnel. In the remaining 15 per cent, which would include the largest industrial enterprises, only 39 per cent of the technical personnel are professional; 7 per cent are semi-professional, and the others have acquired their training through job experience.

The increase in the number of persons receiving technical education from 46,000 in 1958 to more than 145,000 in 1964 is one manifestation of the recognition by both government and the private sector of the mounting needs of industry for more and better trained personnel. The government responded to the need, too, by organizing in 1962, with a grant from the United Nations, the National Preparatory Center for Technological Teaching (CNCET) for the purpose of preparing instructors to teach in technical schools and to train industrial workers. In recent years there has been an increase in the number of degrees and titles awarded by the educational system in agronomy, veterinary medicine, architecture, engineering, nursing, pharmacy, dentistry, science, economics, and the social sciences.

The needs of the economy promise to be a major factor in the extension of educational opportunities to more Mexicans. Minister of Education Torres Bodet announced in May, 1963, the initiation of a far-reaching program of vocational training aimed in part at the numerous children who drop out of elementary school before the sixth grade. By the end of 1963, the government planned to have in operation ten industrial training schools in six states and the Federal District, and twenty agricultural training schools in rural areas in eighteen states. Youth will be trained for jobs on modern farms and in industry.

A POINT OF PERSPECTIVE

In sizing up Mexico as a developing democracy, we must view not only the distance traveled since the Revolution but also the distance yet to be covered before democracy is attained. Progress to date has been remarkable, but much remains to be done before the Republic can enter the democratic family of states. If present trends last, the day will come, though probably not in the near future, when knowledgeable observers recognize the essentially democratic quality of the Republic.

Meeting Complex Needs

The institutionalized presidency, with mounting bureaucratic influence, is meeting in reasonably acceptable fashion the needs of a complex society for continuity, predictability, and equity in policy formation and execution. *Personalismo* is still a force, but a more responsible force than formerly. The institution of the presidency, however, may prove a more formidable obstacle to the evolution of legislative power than a more personal presidency. Congress formally is more representative than before, but its role in the policy-making process continues minuscule. Most important interests, however, have access to decision-making centers through the system of functional representation which has grown up outside the tripartite structure of government.

A large measure of freedom of expression exists in Mexico. Along with the adulation of the President, there is genuine criticism of government by some sections of the press which on occasion do not hesitate to assail cabinet secretaries and Supreme Court justices. The Law of Social Dissolution is represented as a threat to civil liberties by both leftist and rightist groups, which claim that its ambiguous provisions make it possible for the government, in the absence of substantive evidence of misdeeds as defined by other laws, to arrest and imprison persons for words or activities offensive to the ruling current elite. The relative freedom from official and unofficial harassment enjoyed by the PAN presidential candidate during the 1964 campaign may be indicative of a growth in freedom of assembly in the Republic. As compared to past years, the 1964 campaign was peaceful, aside from a few arrests of PAN partisans, the occasional turning off of the lights in halls where PAN rallies were in progress, and the burning of a PRI rostrum in Ciudad Chihuahua, perhaps justifying the claim of PRI and government offi-

The National Medical Center in Mexico City is an outstanding example in the nation-wide system of social security hospitals and clinics for insured workers and their families, under the program of the IMSS. Specialized units of the Center not only treat outpatients and inpatients by the thousands annually, but participate in extensive research and education in medicine, nursing, and hospital administration. Social security benefits recently were extended to about 6 million *ejidatarios* and small private farmers.

cials that the Republic was maturing democratically.

Caudillismo seems a thing of the past on the national level but has not yet disappeared from state and local government. Editorial acclaim of the governors inaugurated early in 1963 as competent executives may possibly denote that the PRI and President have recognized the need for change in this area. The national government has promised to continue its efforts to eradicate *caciquismo* from the *ejidos*. National encouragement of industrial decentralization is premised upon the desirability of extensive cooperation by state government, and this of necessity may stimulate the upgrading of state executives and the development of more vigorous state government in general.

The *mordida* is deeply imbedded in Mexican culture, and the ordinary Mexican seems to believe that both elective and administrative officials regard it as a proper reward for public service, in addition to the prestige, power, and official income normally due those in politics and administration. If so, it adds a new dimension to the concept of economic gain as one of the rewards of public service. Seemingly the theory is that the Republic benefits from the service of able men whose talents would be denied *la patria* but for the opportunities for pecuniary gain outside the legal emoluments of office. It should be obvious that the incompetent and the time-servers, too, expect this extra

incentive. The contrary theory is that the *mordida* is essentially undemocratic, as it subverts the idea of public service and the democratic ideal of equality of treatment and furthermore retards progress through additional costs and pervasive public cynicism. Many public servants, and possibly a majority, it should be noted, do their work without expectation of any gain outside official pay.

Mexico is now sufficiently industrialized to be ranked as a semi-developed country. Mexico City, with its industrial suburbs and pervasive smog, Monterrey and its factories, and other industrial centers are taking on some of the characteristics of the industrial cities of more economically advanced nations, though they still retain a uniquely Mexican flavor, a compound of pre-Spanish, Spanish, and contemporary cultures.

Dilemma of the Present

But the Republic is faced by a dilemma consisting on the one hand of the pressing need for investment capital and, on the other, the imperative of higher wages and purchasing power stemming from the revolutionary goal of social justice and the need of a developing industry and commerce for broader markets. Because the government has accepted the theory that industrialization is Mexico's chief hope for a higher standard of living, official policy during the past twenty-five years has been more sensitive to the need for investment capital, but has granted some wage increases, a profit-sharing scheme, and various public fringe benefits to the workers. If industry is to continue to expand, purchasing power must be raised to create the consumers for a growing range and volume of industrial products.

The conspicuous expenditures of the higher income groups might indicate that they are receiving disproportionate rewards in the name of capital formation. It should be noted that as industry and foreign trade grow, the Mexican economy becomes more susceptible to world economic conditions, and that a major depression would seriously threaten the economic and possibly the political stability of the Republic.

A standing threat to this stability is the poverty of the majority. Despite Mexico's status as a semi-developed nation, and some improvements in living standards, millions of Mexicans are still underfed, poorly clothed, and inadequately housed. Rural poverty is endemic, as frequently acknowledged by the government, and the various public agricultural programs have not yet alleviated it. Cline and others believe that the lot of the urban worker may have been improved, but the gap between his level of living and that of the growing middle class and the wealthy is broad. But is it not fair to ask how long the *campesino* will continue to support a system, or at least accept it, which has yet to make any substantial change in his income, his diet, his housing, his general mode of life? The urban worker's impatience with the status quo may be aggravated by the relatively few improvements which have come his way and by his constant proximity to the higher material standards and conspicuous expenditures of the middle and wealthy classes. Unless the system brings more material benefits to farmer and worker, the growing expectations of both groups, aroused by the repeated statements concerning social justice for the masses and by the visible signs of a better life enjoyed by the few, could undermine the present political stability of the country.

Solutions in View

Industrialization also is serving the ends of democracy as an instrument of national integration. The network of roads, railroads, and airlines developed in part in response to economic needs is helping to erode the isolation of many communities by bringing them in touch with national economic and political currents. Cities and towns not only are assisting in the integration of the former *campesino* into the national society — though there is usually a period in which the newcomer is in limbo between two worlds — but as centers of trade and commerce they disseminate economic goods and with them more intangible values to the rural communities. Industrial and urban growth is stimulating the rise of a middle class, whose values tend to be moderate and democratic and whose interest in getting ahead constitutes a politically stabilizing factor and a spur to further change.

Despite the distribution over the years of millions of hectares of land to landless peasants and programs for upgrading the quality and output of Mexican agriculture, the problems of agriculture and the rural population are far from solved. During his campaign for the presidency, Díaz Ordaz gave a position of prime importance to the problems of agriculture. Rural unemployment has been aggravated by the action of the United States Congress which ended the *bracero* program. The second phase of the *ejido* program pledges a better rural life. By stressing production for the market, the growth of *ejido* industries, and urban amenities, it may raise levels of living, create more jobs, and inject more color and vitality in rural life. These developments may help check the population flow from farm to city and alleviate rural discontent.

Other obstacles to democracy linger on but generally are less serious than formerly, with the one notable exception of population growth. Eventually, urbanization, the growth of the middle class with its itch for self-improvement, and more education and sophistication will exert a braking force.

The Catholic hierarchy seemingly has accepted the Revolution and most of its goals, a position which is reinforced by the influence of the social doctrines of the great papal encyclical, *Mater et Magistra*. Cardinal Garibi y Rivera, for example, speaking in February, 1964, to a group of businessmen in Guadalajara, praised the breakfasts-for-scholars program of the national government and activities designed to raise the standard of living of the needy classes, including the official minimum wages. The central government apparently is ambivalent in its attitude toward church political activities. It usually holds the line with respect to those directly banned by Constitution or statute. On the other hand, church spokesmen before the 1964 presidential election urged Mexicans to fulfill their duty as citizens by voting on election day, and the government quite correctly raised no objection. Cardinal Garibi y Rivera advised the citizens of Guadalajara not to welcome Tito when he visited the city as the official guest of the national government; there were no political repercussions. Political activities of the clergy aimed at Communism are potentially dangerous, especially if the definition of Communism becomes too inclusive. The church hierarchy favors amendment of the Constitution to permit the open establishment of parochial schools, which in light of the educational needs of the country does not seem unreasonable. The commitment of successive administrations to Article III of the Constitution, however, probably will mean that the government will not go beyond its unofficial policy of accepting the establishment and operation of church schools under the names of revolutionary heroes and in other guises.

Individualism Reinterpreted

The traditional Latin-American belief in the dignity of the individual is being reinterpreted to include economic and social amelioration. This new meaning, as indicated above, is explicit in the Constitution and numerous public programs; it also is being accepted by more and more Mexicans as a goal which is both valid and desirable. It was present in the statement of the Sonora businessmen, representative, it is hoped, of a growing number of middle-class Mexicans, who supported a wage increase not only because of its impact upon rate of sales but also because of its influence upon the material welfare of the worker.

Discrimination based upon color or ethnic background is largely absent, and thus the Republic in this area comes closer to the democratic concept of individual dignity than many parts of the United States, south and north. Mexico has a *mestizo* population made up largely of persons of mixed Indian and white ancestry in varying proportions, and the absence of color bias reflects this fact. There are a few who place a premium upon a light skin, and the author remembers the restaurant in Mazatlán with the sign, "we reserve the right to refuse service," which probably reflected *norteamericano* biases, but these are exceptions to the general air of tolerance.

SUGGESTED READING

BRANDENBURG, FRANK R. *The Making of Modern Mexico.* Englewood Cliffs, N. J.: Prentice-Hall, 1964.

_____. "Organized Business in Mexico," *Inter-American Economic Affairs,* XII (Winter, 1958), 26-52.

CLAGETT, HELEN. *The Administration of Justice in Latin America.* New York: Oceana Publications, 1952.

CLINE, HOWARD F. *Mexico. Revolution to Evolution: 1940–1960.* New York: Oxford University Press, 1963.

Comercio Exterior de Mexico. Published monthly in English and French by the Banco Nacional de Comercio Exterior. Essentially a condensed version of the more comprehensive *Comercio Exterior,* published in Spanish.

DULLES, JOHN W. F. *Yesterday in Mexico: A Chronicle of the Revolution, 1919–36.* Austin: University of Texas Press, 1961.

GLADE, WILLIAM P. and CHARLES W. ANDERSON. *The Political Economy of Mexico.* Madison, Wis.: University of Wisconsin Press, 1963. The volume includes two studies: Glade, "Revolution and Economic Development: A Mexican Reprise," and Anderson, "Bankers as Revolutionaries: Politics and Development Banking in Mexico."

GOODSPEED, STEPHEN S. "Mexico: President and Constitution," *Mid-America,* 36 (April, 1954), 96-115.

LEWIS, OSCAR. *The Children of Sanchez.* New York: 1961.

_____. *Five Families. Mexican Case Studies in the Culture of Poverty.* New York: Science Editions, Inc., 1962.

_____. "Mexico Since Cárdenas," *Social Change in Latin America Today: Its Implications for United States Policy.* New York: Vintage Books, 1961, 285-345.

Mexico, 1963. Facts, Figures, Trends. English translation by Mildred Russell. Mexico City: Banco Nacional de Comercio Exterior, 1963.

PADGETT, L. VINCENT. "Mexico's One-Party System; a Re-evaluation," *American Political Science Review,* LI (December, 1957), 995-1008.

POLEMAN, THOMAS T. *The Papaloapan Project.* Stanford, Calif.: Stanford University Press, 1964.

Review of the Economic Situation of Mexico. A monthly publication of the Banco Nacional de México, S. A.

SCHMITT, KARL M. "Communism in Mexico Today," *Western Political Quarterly,* XV (March, 1962), 111-124.

SCOTT, ROBERT E. *Mexican Government in Transition.* Urbana: University of Illinois Press, 1959.

TAYLOR, PHILIP B., JR. "The Mexican Elections of 1958: Affirmation of Authoritarianism?" *Western Political Quarterly,* XIII (September, 1960), 722-744.

TUCKER, WILLIAM P. *The Mexican Government Today.* Minneapolis: University of Minnesota Press, 1957.

VERNON, RAYMOND. *The Dilemma of Mexico's Development. The Role of the Private and Public Sectors.* Cambridge, Mass.: Harvard University Press, 1963.

_____. ed., *Public Policy and Private Enterprise in Mexico.* Contains studies by Miguel S. Wionczek, "Electric Power: The Uneasy Partnership"; David H. Shelton, "The Banking System: Money and the Goal of Growth"; Calvin P. Blair, "Nacional Financiera: Entrepreneurship in a Mixed Economy"; and Rafael Izquierdo, "Protectionism in Mexico." Cambridge, Mass.: Harvard University Press, 1964.

Seafoods, especially shrimp and sardines, are regionally important in Baja California, Sinaloa, and Sonora, on the west coast, and in Campeche on the east. Guaymas, Sonora, is a well-known port for shrimp boats that unload their cargoes at processing plants within view of the resort center.

— *Ray Manley Photo*

Where steel mills roar and wooden plows
till a land beset by thirst;
Where new dams rise and a new wave vows,
We will be first.

—*G. E. Beinhorn*

An Economy of Contrasts | GEORGE F. LEAMING & WALTER H. DELAPLANE

THE BROAD OBJECTIVE of Mexican economic policy, since 1940 and even earlier, has been industrialization. In this way the nation has hoped to increase employment, production, and income, not only to support projected population increases, but also to improve the material standards of large masses of the Mexican people. Mexico has made notable progress in all phases of its economy since the outbreak of World War II. Both the productivity of its workers and real income per capita have substantially increased.

In 1961, however, a slowing down of this rate of production increase led one writer to call it a "year of stagnation." Despite subsequent growth, such occasional stagnation serves to highlight the need of the Mexican nation to emphasize the activities and investments that will foster continued growth of real income per capita — investments in the means of production — in factories, highways, transportation, power, irrigation, and health and education.

The problems in achieving the aims of national economic policy have been manifold. Supporting policies have included:

1) nationalization of a few basic industries and the requirement of a majority ownership of corporations by Mexican citizens;

2) strict use of foreign loans to open new sources of production;

3) the maintenance of reasonable stability in both the internal and external value of the peso, keeping the budgetary deficits within fairly close limits to avoid inflationary consequences of such financing;

4) encouragement of greater economic independence from the United States through regulations of investment holdings, efforts to expand trade with other areas of the world, and arrangements for technical and financial assistance from sources other than the United States;

5) negotiation of agreements with the United States Treasury and the International Monetary Fund to buttress its monetary reserves and assure stability of the peso abroad, thus protecting itself against flights of capital;

6) continuation of redistribution of land and the use of improved techniques and machinery in its cultivation;

7) amendment of the tax system so that it is less regressive in its effects, bearing more lightly on low-income earners and more heavily upon those with higher incomes in accordance with the principle of ability to pay;

8) allocation of increasing amounts for housing, health, and education to improve the situation of the population and of the nation.

Intensified efforts to increase production and spread its benefits through all sectors of the economy are required by the continuing great numbers of the poor, especially in Mexico's rural areas, and by the rapid growth of population and reduction of the death rate among Mexicans of all ages, as medical care has become more generally available.

Basic to the task are human resources — in short, a greater spread and depth of education, and improvement of health. Mexico's physical resources are limited, but much has been and can be accomplished by raising the level of individual skills and knowledge. These processes are at work in Mexico now, through more extensive training in agricultural, vocational, and health programs, and also through general and professional education.

Before 1940, the Mexican economy ran much of the time in low gear, when it was not completely stalled by internal political problems, international economic difficulties, or war. Mexico was then almost entirely a producer of agricultural exports and mineral products, which were the source of the foreign exchange needed to finance the importation of most of the manufactured consumer goods available in its markets. Significant and rapid development of power, roads, railroads, industry, and even agriculture, has come only since the end of World War II.

Up until that time, Mexico was preponderantly a country of small villages upon which modern ideas had made little impression. Both agriculture and industry were small-scale, and commerce was mainly in the hands of small shopkeepers, peddlers, and sellers in the marketplace. Primitive tools were employed on the farms, and virtually all of the requirements of a modern economy were lacking.

A measure of Mexico's strides forward was recorded early in 1965, however, when the International Monetary Fund elevated the Mexican peso to the status of one of the world's "hard" currencies, permitting its use by other nations in multilateral transactions with the Fund. The peso thus became the first Latin-American monetary unit to be so designated. It is reasonable to expect that, granted political stability and freedom from international economic depression, Mexican economic improvement will continue.

AGRICULTURE

Agriculture today, as it has been for hundreds of years, is the foundation of the Mexican economy. Despite eras of rapid expansion in other industries — mining in the nineteenth century, manufacturing in the twentieth — the economy of Mexico is principally one of farms and ranches. Even considered as two economies — that of the Federal District and its immediate environs and that of the rest of the country — Mexico is predominantly agricultural. In the area around the capital, this situation has been changing rapidly since World War II, and in the not too distant future, the region dominated by the Federal District may no longer be characterized by farming. In the rest of the Republic, however, agriculture is still paramount, as it was in the nineteenth century. Indeed, in some areas — particularly those where a once prosperous mining industry has declined — agriculture has assumed even greater importance.

In 1960, agriculture, forestry, and fishing provided the principal means of livelihood for about 55 per cent of the economically active population (a term roughly equivalent to our "labor force"). In the United States the same year, the proportion of the labor force employed in similar pursuits was less than 10 per cent. The United States has not had half of its labor force employed on farms since the 1870's.

The agricultural sector is also of considerable importance in the Mexican economy as an earner of foreign exchange. In 1963, crude and processed products of agriculture, fishing, and forestry accounted for almost 54 per cent of the total value of export goods, and more than 31 per cent of total exports of goods and services. Slightly more than 25 per cent of all United States exports were in that category in 1963.

In terms of contribution to national income and product, Mexican farms are not nearly as important as they are in providing employment and goods for export; still they overshadow other parts of the economy. In 1958, about one-fourth of national income was attributed to farms, forests, and fisheries, but in more recent years, agricultural products have comprised less than one-fifth of the country's net domestic product. A comparable figure for the contribution of the agricultural sector to net domestic product in the United States is about one twenty-fifth.

GROSS NATIONAL PRODUCT 1960
by sector of origin

Source: MEXICO 1963: Facts, Figures, Trends, Banco Nacional de Comerc Exterior, S.A.

Agriculture becomes even more important if th income earned by Mexican farm workers — braceros - in the United States, is included. Total remittances b Mexican workers abroad in 1963 exceeded 30 millio dollars and accounted for almost two per cent of th country's foreign-exchange earnings. In the peak yea of 1956, such remittances reached almost 38 millio dollars, and accounted for almost three per cent c Mexico's total foreign exchange.

Five Commodities Important

The agriculture of Mexico is based largely on fiv commodities — corn, cotton, cattle, coffee, and can (sugar). Corn is the basic element of the averag Mexican diet and the principal product of Mexica agriculture. Somewhat more than half of all land unde cultivation is devoted to its raising, and most of th small farms take part in its growing. Even in value c total production, corn has consistently exceeded it nearest competitor — cotton — in recent years, by a much as 25 per cent. The largest amount of this grair however, comes from the small plots of the commun; farms and the private landowners, and is intended fc domestic consumption. Practically no corn is exportec

Cotton, Mexico's second most important far product in terms of value of total production, is th principal "cash crop." It is also Mexico's most impor tant export commodity. Productivity in value per acr is also far greater for cotton than for many other crop since — although in recent years the value of cotto produced has exceeded 20 per cent of the value of a agricultural production — it has taken only about six per cent of the land to raise it. Nearly all of the cotton is raised on irrigated land, and this cotton land constitutes about 40 per cent of all irrigated farmland in Mexico.

The third most important segment of Mexican agriculture is the raising of livestock, primarily beef cattle. Judging by the value of the product, the raising of cattle has accounted for almost one-fourth of total agricultural production in recent years. Beef, usually on the hoof, has also been a substantial item in the country's exports, in most recent years taking third place behind cotton and coffee.

Very little local fattening of beef is done in Mexico. Most of the animals which are raised on the large ranches in the semiarid northern states are exported as feeder cattle to the United States. In the southern and central parts of the country, the livestock segment of the agricultural industry has been concerned mostly with beasts of burden, dairy cows, and meat animals other than beef.

Like most of Mexican agriculture, cattle raising has had persistent if not perennial low productivity, and has been hampered to a considerable extent by periodic drought and foot-and-mouth disease.

An exception to the chain of "C" commodities that tends to dominate Mexican agriculture is wheat, the country's second most important grain and an item that is becoming increasingly prominent in domestic food consumption. For many years it was necessary for Mexico to import wheat, but lately it has achieved self-sufficiency in this grain. Wheat has become Mexico's third most important crop in terms of total value. In 1962, wheat accounted for 7 per cent of the total value of farm production. Growing wheat took up 6 per cent of the total area under cultivation, much of it in the irrigated regions of the northwestern states. Today 80 per cent of all wheat grown in Mexico is grown on irrigated land.

The nation's fifth most valuable farm product and its second most important export commodity is coffee. Coffee accounts for about 7 per cent of the value of all agricultural production in Mexico, but a much larger portion of the farm labor force. Because of depressed prices in recent years in world and United States markets, the Mexican government has arranged for the granting of a flexible subsidy on exports of raw coffee (actually a flexible reduction in export tariffs), a reduction in the support price from seven pesos per kilo to six pesos per kilo (25c U.S. per pound to 22c U.S. per pound), standardization of state tax systems to allow free interstate transit of coffee exports, and other measures designed to increase productivity. The intention, in the translated words of the Ministry of Finance and Public Credit, is that, "the cultivation of this crop will be profitable even when prices are relatively low on the international market, and growers will be encouraged to improve their crops and increase their productivity as has occurred in the case of cotton in response to a policy of variable subsidies."

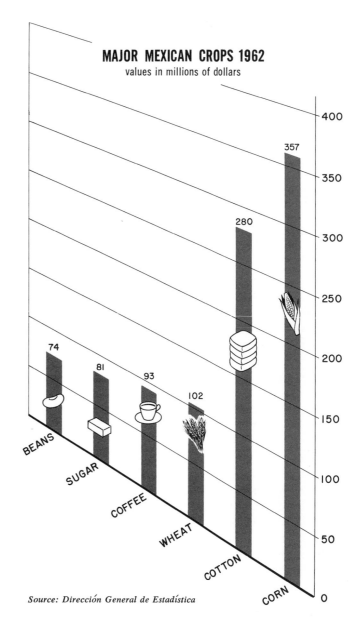

MAJOR MEXICAN CROPS 1962
values in millions of dollars

Source: Dirección General de Estadística

Sugar is another of Mexico's more important crops, both domestically and in her export trade. The growing and processing of sugar cane supports more than seventy refineries scattered throughout the producing regions of the country, and provides employment for about 2 per cent of the economically active population. It ranks fourth in production and in foreign exchange.

Also important in the average Mexican diet, and likewise in agriculture, are beans, which rank sixth (representing about 5 per cent of total value), and occupy 14 per cent of all land devoted to farming.

Still relatively minor but increasingly influential commodities in Mexican agriculture are fresh fruits and vegetables, largely for export to the United States during the winter season. To date, tomatoes have dominated this sector of agriculture, but other vegetables are becoming increasingly important. The principal fruits grown and exported are citrus and bananas.

Other products of significance, both for domestic consumption and export, include copra, alfalfa, henequen fiber, and rice. It is rather ironic that although cacao is native to southeastern Mexico, and the early Aztec emperors were drinking *chocolatl* before the coming of the Spaniards, this particular commodity has long been relatively insignificant in Mexican agriculture. Moreover, chiefly as a result of cheap competition from Africa on world markets, Mexico has not been a factor in the world production of cacao. Only within the past few years has any concerted effort been made, either by government or private interests, to increase productivity and exports to make cacao a more prominent item in the Mexican economy.

Land Ownership Changing

For hundreds of years after the coming of the Spaniards, Mexican agriculture operated under a feudal system of large haciendas, owned by the wealthy, and worked by resident laborers and sharecroppers who lived in virtual serfdom. In 1910, one per cent of the population owned 97 per cent of the land. Small independent farmers owned only 2 per cent of the land, and villages and cities comprised the remaining one per cent. Ninety-six per cent of those engaged in agriculture were either small farmers or residents of small villages, and 55,000 of the nation's 70,000 villages were situated on large haciendas. Although the commonly held view is of the resident laborer as the chief component of the work force on the haciendas, estate owners actually made much more extensive use of the equal share, sharecropping arrangement, thereby avoiding the necessity for investing the capital required had they managed the farms themselves and employed day labor. The Revolution of 1910 was aimed primarily at destroying this traditional system of land ownership. Today the hacienda is no longer a major force in the agriculture of Mexico.

The absence of the hacienda in the current agricultural scene, however, should not give rise to the picture of a country dotted with numerous small, medium, and large commercial family farms — the traditional structure in the United States. Rather the picture is one of many very small, privately owned, subsistence-level farms and many large cooperatives of commonly owned or worked land — the outgrowth of the redistribution of the land taken from the haciendas. With these are found a very few large ventures of a commercial nature, particularly in the livestock segment of the industry.

Since the beginning of the breakup of the large estates in 1915, a distinct form of farm ownership not found to any extent in the United States has assumed (or re-assumed) considerable importance in the agriculture of Mexico. This is the *ejido* or communal farm. According to most recently available figures, *ejidos* comprise almost half of all land under cultivation in Mexico.

Some writers have attributed the *ejido* system and its growth since the Revolution to the ideas of agrarian reformers and advocates of cooperative movements in Europe and the United States. It is generally conceded, however, that the *ejido* is in fact a revival of a system of land tenure used by the Aztecs and continued into the colonial period. In attributing the *ejido* to the ancient Aztec system of communal farm land, on should also note that another Aztec system of land tenure, applied by the Indians to conquered lands and peoples, was sharecropping, the system adapted by the Spanish conquerors of the Aztecs to the pre-revolutionary haciendas.

In Mexico today, an *ejido* is comprised of communal land assigned to a village and set aside essentially for farming. Although most of the land involved is assigned for crop raising, many *ejidos* also contain pastures and woodland, and most of them have certain areas set aside for light commercial structures and schools. The cropland of each *ejido* is actually divided in most instances into land grants to individual farmers with ownership retained by the community, but with the legal tenancy of the farmer permitted to continue (and even to pass on to his heirs) as long as he or his family works the land. The maximum size of each individual grant is now slightly less than twenty-five acres for naturally watered or irrigated land and slightly less than fifty acres for other land. However, because of the large number of former farm workers considered to have rights to *ejido* land, and the limited amount available for distribution to them, the average size of *ejido* holdings is much less than the legal maximum. Several years ago it was estimated that the average *ejido* grant was only about fifteen acres, for the country as a whole, and only about eight acres in the more heavily populated sections. In recent years the government has taken steps to make the tenancy of the *ejido* grants more permanent, and deeds and certificates of farming rights, which make the tenure conditional only upon its being worked by the grantee himself, have been awarded.

Although nearly all *ejidos* are based on the system of individual grants, some are farmed collectively either because it has been found to be extremely uneconomical to work them on an individual basis, or because the law requires that certain *ejidos* in specified areas and commodities be operated as collective farms. These collectives are found chiefly in the Laguna cotton-producing region and in the henequen and rice growing sections of Yucatán and Michoacán, but the collective farm has become an important element throughout all of Mexican agriculture. Even though some *ejido* land is operated on a collective basis, a sizeable portion of it is also farmed by the individual grant holder much as though he were a small farm owner, regardless of the fact that, strictly speaking, ownership is retained by the community.

The majority of *ejido* lands, then, are farmed either collectively or as individual grants by the *ejidatarios* themselves, but some *ejido* lands are also worked by hired labor or leased out, generally on a sharecrop basis. Although the law under which the communal lands are administered stipulates that the *ejidatario* must work the land himself, exceptions are made for holdings pertaining to women and children, children who have inherited the right to *ejido* land, and disabled persons unable to perform farm labor. Nevertheless

Man and animal together in the field, without machinery or modern tools, still account for much of Mexico's farm production, especially in the central and southern areas. To the northwest, however, are several major areas of irrigation agriculture, where farming has become highly mechanized. The fiber in these cotton bales being loaded for transport from a modern gin was grown in the state of Sinaloa.

there are indications in some parts of the country, particularly where water is in short supply and the land is poor, that other *ejido* holdings also are often worked with hired labor or leased out under a sharecrop arrangement.

The other half of Mexico's farm lands, that is the half not included in the *ejidos,* consists of privately held small and medium-sized farms and a number of farm cooperatives which might be regarded as collectives operated by groups of private individuals. Many of these farms are found in new lands only recently cleared and cultivated. Not all of such farms, which by law are limited to a maximum of 370 acres, are worked by the landowners themselves. In fact, in some areas where arable land is scarce and/or farm labor is cheap, some of the lesser landowners of only a few acres are able to rent their land or lease it to sharecroppers and live on the proceeds. Moreover, many holders of *ejido* grants additionally cultivate sizeable portions of privately owned land.

Thus the two main sources of Mexican agricultural production are very small, privately owned farms and large collectives and cooperatives. The hacienda has virtually disappeared, the family farm as we know it has never existed, and the Aztec tradition of sharecropping has proved to be quite persistent.

The Role of Government

As in the United States, government in the twentieth century has played an important part in Mexican agriculture, although along somewhat different lines. Probably the greatest area of government participation in agriculture in Mexico has been in the realm of agrarian reform, i.e., land redistribution after the Revolution of 1910. The land of the large haciendas was redistributed among the rural laboring class, beginning slowly in the 1920's, gaining momentum and reaching a high point in the administration of President Cárdenas in the 1930's, when over seven million acres were distributed to former peons and sharecroppers. Such reform activity has decreased noticeably in recent years, in large part because of the relative scarcity of large landholdings remaining.

In addition to redistributing land, the government has continued unabated a number of programs for resettlement of the rural population — the landless farm laboring class — on newly developed lands.

On the other hand, there has been little federal participation in the direct production of agricultural products, although of course the government does give strong support to the collective *ejidos*. An autonomous government corporation, however, does participate directly in the purchasing and marketing of agricultural products. This corporation, the *Compañia Nacional de Subsistencia Popular, S.A.* (CONASUPO), operates several hundred of its own stores throughout Mexico, besides serving as wholesaler for several hundred privately owned retail stores selling farm products at prices determined by CONASUPO. Within recent years, the agency has been expanding its operations as well in the retailing of agricultural products.

CONASUPO has also served as the government's agency in providing price supports to various agricultural commodities, primarily those for domestic consumption, e.g., corn, wheat, beans, and eggs. Although some export commodities, such as coffee, are involved in the price support program, government actions are aimed primarily at holding up the prices paid to growers, but keeping down prices paid by Mexican consumers at the retail level. Through CONASUPO, the government operates to some extent as a middleman in direct competition with commercial distributors of farm products.

In addition to price supports for commodities consumed at home, the government also maintains a subsidy program designed to promote the export of certain goods. Many of the subsidies take the form of reduced export taxes, rather than payments to producers; in other words, the subsidy is effected by decreasing the restrictions on exportation rather than by providing a positive incentive. Furthermore the Mexican program varies subsidies from one producing area to another. Higher subsidies go to regions that have shown higher productivity; and decreases in productivity are accompanied by decreased subsidies, i.e., higher export taxes. In contrast with the United States, Mexico's problem is one of underproduction of agricultural products, and the government programs are designed to correct such deficiency. As in other countries, the agriculture policies of the Mexican government do contain some contradictions. Likewise, as in many other countries, the government levies import duties on numerous farm products, in the stated hope of promoting domestic production.

Government investment in, and financing of, agriculture has been greatest in irrigation where extensive programs accounted for approximately 15 per cent of total expenditures during the 1950's and over 90 per cent of expenditures on agriculture during that decade. Many of these projects were not designed solely for irrigation − the production of electric power was often a prime consideration.

The Mexican government has also been active in extending credit to farmers, principally through two agencies. The *Banco Nacional de Crédito Agrícola y Ganadero* grants crop or equipment loans to small and medium-size private farms which have been organized into local agricultural credit organizations; and the *Banco Nacional de Crédito Ejidal* grants credit to the *ejidos*. Another federal bank, the *Banco Nacional de Comercio Exterior,* has served as a means of providing government aid to agriculture, chiefly where export commodities are involved, although it has also served as the source of financing for CONASUPO. The bulk of farm credit in Mexico, however, is provided by private firms and individuals, with usurious rates of interest not uncommon.

As an additional service to farmers, the federal government, in 1955, began a system of crop insurance. Destruction due to insects and drought has long been a problem in Mexican agriculture. Since institution of the crop insurance program these hazards have not materially diminished, and payments to farmers have been substantial in some years.

Since the early 1950's, the government has also provided aid to agriculture through an extension service and a research program which conducts investigations at a number of experiment stations in the more important farming areas. The Rockefeller Foundation, in conjunction with the Ministry of Agriculture, has provided considerable assistance in this activity. The Bank of Mexico has also supported agricultural research chiefly by financing special projects and by technical assistance.

The Remaining Challenge

Although the problem of land tenure has received far more attention and publicity than any other area of Mexican agriculture, a number of other problem areas still exist and are of greater importance to the country's economic well being. The most persistent of these problems is the existence of antiquated methods and extremely low productivity in agriculture. On the whole, the redistribution of land after the Revolution of 1910 has not improved the primitive techniques used on Mexican farms with their attendant low productivities. Farm implements generally are of the most primitive type, and oxen, horses, and mules still provide the greater part of farm power. The use of fertilizers and improved grades of seed is still severely limited, and in many places crop rotation is virtually unpracticed. These are generalities, however, and like most generalities, they do not provide a complete and accurate picture. In the north, for example, much has been done to increase productivity. Today more than three-fourths of the farming in that part of Mexico is done by up-to-date methods. In the southern coffee growing regions, fertilizer is being used advantageously. In addition, the manufacture and use of insecticides are increasing as are the domestic manufacture and use of tractors and other mechanical farm equipment. Hence improvement has begun in recent years and may be expected to continue. Modernization has been primarily in the areas devoted to the commercial growing of export crops. In the central valley and elsewhere where production is for limited domestic consumption methods are still primitive and are likely to remain so as long as labor is cheap, capital expensive, and land holdings small.

Rainfall has been another problem − both the lack of it and the destructive results of it. The former as resulted in the extensive promotion of numerous irrigation projects, both public and private, in recent decades. By far the major proportion of government assistance to agriculture has been in the form of irrigation facilities, and since the need still exists, this emphasis is expected to continue for some time. Erosion, the destructive result of rain, has not received much emphasis, and the waste resulting from denuding previously forested land without practicing effective conservation practices is a formidable problem, reducing still further the amount of already scarce land suitable for cultivation.

The lack of an effective distribution system for its products is another major problem of Mexican agriculture. This has been remedied to a certain extent in some areas where the construction of farm access roads and railroads has helped to increase availability of markets. Lack of adequate rolling stock and storage facilities, particularly those providing refrigeration, and an antiquated system of marketing, still hamper the distribution of the products of Mexican farms and ranches.

Forestry

Forested area, exclusive of brushland, covers 17 per cent of Mexico, mostly in tropical lowlands, where there has been little development of commercial forestry. The industry, as it exists, should probably be considered a minor facet of agriculture, the value of its output being equal to less than 2 per cent of the total value of farm and ranch production.

In the absence of any other readily available source of energy, Mexican forests have been of greatest use in providing firewood and charcoal. About 10 per cent of the total production from the nation's woodlands is in the form of firewood or charcoal, mostly for use by the rural population. About one quarter of the forest products are non-wood items, principally naval stores, *chicle, candelilla* wax, and a few others. The remaining 65 per cent of the value of forestry production is comprised of numerous and varied types of wood for construction and manufacturing. Despite the fact that Mexico's forests are largely tropical, most of the wood and lumber produced are softwoods from the relatively sparse conifer forests found at higher elevations, and the output of tropical hardwoods is very small.

Actually, Mexican forestry's most pressing problem is not insufficient or inefficient production; it is reforestation and conservation. The once extensive forests of temperate-zone hardwoods have all but disappeared, destructively exploited as the handiest source of supply for early producers of firewood and charcoal. There is evidence that the remaining forests of conifers are being exploited in the same manner.

Villagers on the shores of Lake Pátzcuaro still use simple boats and the ever-present burro for transporting wood and other needed materials.

Mexican forest products are relatively insignificant in the country's export trade. The exploitation of timberland by foreigners is severely restricted, as is the exportation of unfinished lumber. The leading forest product that is exported is *chicle,* almost all of which is shipped to the United States.

Fishing

In terms of monetary value, fishing is of even less importance to the Mexican economy than forestry, the extensive coastline notwithstanding. In 1962, the value of the total output of the fishing industry was only about one per cent of the value of total agricultural production. In terms of employment, the industry is of even less significance, since in 1960 it employed only two-tenths of one per cent of the economically active population.

Despite this insignificant relationship to the national economy, the production of seafoods is of great importance regionally, particularly in Baja California, Sinaloa, and Sonora, on the Pacific, and in Campeche on the Gulf of Mexico. The industry is also important in Mexican export trade, since approximately three-fourths of the total production is shipped to other countries, principally the United States. In 1963, products of the sea, mostly shrimp, accounted for over 5 per cent of the total value of export goods.

Cooperation is particularly strong in this industry, with most of the production controlled by fishery cooperative societies. This affords some combining of resources, although more than three-fourths of the boats in the industry are smaller than ten tons.

In addition to the fleet itself, there are about fifty freezing plants in the more important producing areas, supported by the harvesting of seafoods, and concerned primarily with the freezing of shrimp for export. The same regions also have some canneries to process the sardine catch, primarily for domestic consumption.

Shrimp and sardines account for over half of the value of Mexican fishery production. The remainder includes other food fish and some oysters and lobsters. Although tuna are fairly abundant off the west coast of Mexico, most of them have been caught in the past by United States boats and landed at United States ports. In recent years, the operations of United States firms in these waters have declined, but they have not yet been replaced by Mexican equivalents.

Mexican fishing industry problems are similar to the problems of the other extractive industries. Fishing is heavily dependent upon exports and therefore upon external market conditions. To serve a domestic market, there is a dearth of distribution facilities from the coast to inland population centers; and both inland and on the coast there are not enough satisfactory cold-storage facilities. There has also been a deficiency of modern equipment, although expansion of the fishing fleet since World War II, in terms of tonnage, has been more than tenfold. In some contrast to the other extractive industries, however, fishing has been and is being hampered by severely limited resources. Mexico's tropical waters are not as abundant in commercial seafoods as the colder seas, and even the principal warm-water products — shrimp and sardines — are limited in supply.

MANUFACTURING

Despite the continuing absolute dominance of the extractive industries in Mexico, manufacturing has grown considerably in relative importance since World War II and has today become a significant factor in the economy. In 1960, manufacturing enterprises employed about 13 per cent of the economically active population and provided 26 per cent of national income. In the United States that year, 27 per cent of the labor force was engaged in manufacturing, more than double the proportion in Mexico.

Manufacturing also has increased its contribution to the value of Mexico's export trade. While still accounting for much less than crude commodities, in 1960, manufactured products comprised 5 per cent of the total value of exports. It is notable, however, that most of this amount was composed of items that would still be considered as industrial raw materials rather than as finished articles, even though considerable value had been added by manufacturing. The more important exports of such items included binding twine, henequen fiber, molasses, textiles, and basic metal manufactures such as copper wire and lead pipe. The amount of consumer goods manufactured and exported was negligible.

Characteristic of Mexican manufacturing is an intense geographic concentration, considerably greater than one finds in the United States, in the New York and Chicago areas, for example. In Mexico, the capital is the center of population, but even more the center of manufacturing. According to a recent study made for the Bank of Mexico by the U. N. economist, Paul Yates, the area around the capital in the Valley of Mexico (primarily the Federal District and the state of Mexico), has a population of five million persons or roughly one-seventh of the nation's people, but it also has over half of the manufacturing capacity. Other studies show that the same area, in 1960, included over 60 per cent of the manufacturing workers, paid over 60 per cent of all manufacturing payrolls, and produced almost 60 per cent of the total value of manufactured goods. The number of separate manufacturing establishments in the area, however, was only 33 per cent of the nation's total, indicating that the size of industrial enterprises in the region around the capital tends to be larger than in the rest of the country.

In the United States and other highly industrialized nations, industrial firms in recent years have shown a tendency to locate new factories away from the original centers of concentration. In Mexico, however since World War II, there has been a trend toward even greater concentration of manufacturing facilities in the Valley of Mexico. Since 1940, the proportion of the country's manufacturing employment and payrolls accounted for by the Valley of Mexico has more than doubled, and the percentage of the total value of the nation's manufacturing output in that area has almost doubled. The size of establishments is also undoubtedly on the increase, since, during the same period of time, the number of factories in the district rose by only a half.

Mexico City and its environs are not the only part of Mexico in which industry is concentrated to any degree; the country has a number of other urban industrial centers. Most prominent of these is Monterrey, the "Mexican Pittsburgh," in the northern border state of Nuevo León. Yates estimated at the time of his study that Nuevo León and the other relatively industrialized northern border states contained 16 per cent of the country's population, but 23 per cent of the manufacturing capacity. Other manufacturing centers include Veracruz, Puebla, and Guadalajara, none of them as important in this respect, however, as Mexico City or Monterrey.

Dominating, both in numbers employed and in the value of product, are two basic industries and two consumer-goods industries. Textiles is Mexico's leading manufacturing industry in number of employees. In 1960, cotton, wool, and synthetic textile manufacturers provided jobs for about 3 per cent of all workers engaged in manufacturing. The basic iron and steel industry is the second largest employer in manufacturing. Firms producing iron and steel and those producing basic steel products — sheet, tubing, and structural shapes — in 1960 employed a little more than one and a half per cent of the manufacturing work force. The motor vehicle assembly industry, third in rank of employees, accounts for little more than 1 per cent of the total manufacturing work force, as does the food processing industry. Other principal industries from the standpoint of numbers employed are beer, tobacco products, glass, cement and other building materials, paper and pulp, and rubber goods — principally tires and tubes for Mexico's growing motor vehicle registration.

In terms of value of product, the first- and second-ranking employing industries reverse their positions. Basic iron and steel is the leading industry here, closely followed by textiles. Motor vehicle assembly remains in third place, and food-processing fourth, the value of its product being about one-half the value of the iron and steel output. Other manufacturing industries of significance for the economy of the nation as a whole are beer, rubber goods, cement, tobacco products, soaps and detergents, and paper.

Cotton Dominates Textiles

Cotton dominates the Mexican textile industry, just as it does the agricultural scene, with 85 per cent of textile employees engaged in making cotton thread and cloth. A similar percentage of the total value of textile output is attributable to cotton goods. In contrast to its role in agriculture, however, cotton in the textile industry is of considerable importance to the

Age-old methods and equipment are used in such places as this Oaxacan village to produce beautiful woven cloth that is used by local inhabitants, and greatly prized by discriminating tourists.

internal economy but of little export consequence. Only one per cent of total output is exported. The cotton cloth industry is of considerable significance, however, as a provider of raw material for other Mexican manufacturing.

The making of cotton cloth is, in fact, one of Mexico's oldest manufacturing industries, dating back to the 1830's. Of all Mexican industries, it has come the closest to providing the country with substantial self-sufficiency in its product. Today the cotton textile industry is not dominated by any one firm but is composed of many large and medium-size plants, i.e. about five hundred separate factories averaging two hundred workers each, according to latest available figures. Comparable figures for the United States show the existence in this country of about 1500 similar plants averaging a little less than three hundred workers each.

Unlike the cotton-based segment of the textile industry, the wool sector is made up of a large number of very small firms with much of the output of woolen goods being produced in small handicraft shops for local consumption. Latest records show that about eight hundred separate plants, averaging only thirty employees each, are responsible for Mexico's woolen cloth production. Also unlike cotton, nearly all of the raw material for woolen textiles must be imported, since Mexico's domestic production of wool is inadequate both in quantity and quality.

The fastest growing segment of the textile industry is the manufacture of synthetic fabrics. Synthetics assumed second place in importance from woolens about 1950, and are already approaching cotton in terms of value of total product. The industry manufactures mostly rayon and acetate fabrics. Nylon production was started in 1957 and has expanded rapidly, although production is still far short of domestic demand. Except for nylon, most synthetic fibers are produced locally, and imports are negligible. As in the case of cotton and wool, most production is for the satisfaction of a growing domestic demand, and exports are of little consequence. So far the synthetic textile industry has only a few medium-size plants of about 150 workers each. Among the leading producers are Mexican subsidiaries of a number of prominent United States firms. Foreign investment in this area of the Mexican textile industry has been relatively heavy.

Steel Industry Long-established

Mexico's basic iron and steel industry is one of the oldest in Latin America, having been established in 1903 with the formation of *Cia. Fundidora de Hierro y Acero de Monterrey* (Iron and Steel Smelting Company of Monterrey), today Mexico's second largest steel producer. Despite the later construction of steel plants in the central Valley of Mexico and on the Gulf Coast, the center of the industry has remained at Monterrey, in relative proximity to the country's iron and coal deposits. During World War II, Mexican steel production was increased substantially with the founding of *Altos Hornos de Mexico* (Blast Furnaces of Mexico) by the government investment agency, *Nacional Financiera,* which still owns more than 50 per cent of the company and effectively controls it.

Altos Hornos, as the largest producer of iron and steel, and the pioneer *Cia. Fundidora,* have dominated the iron and steel industry in Mexico. The government blast-furnace operation, in 1959, bought out and has continued to operate *La Consolidada* — the third largest Mexican steel producer. The latter company has been a fully integrated steel manufacturer, producing an extensive line from raw iron ore through structural steel and industrial hardware. Thus the government enterprise has acquired full integration and a substantially greater market. Outside of these major enterprises, most industrial areas of the nation — the mining centers in particular — have small independent foundries and fabricators of steel products.

In 1954 a private firm, *Tubos de Acero de Mexico* (Steel Tubing of Mexico), began production in a plant near Veracruz to supply seamless steel tubing to Pemex, the government oil monopoly. Today, the company also supplies pipe and tubing to the chemical, sugar, and mining industries and is responsible for about 10 per cent of the country's total production of steel billets. A significant feature of *Tubos de Acero* is that one of its leading stockholders is *Fondo de Inversiones Rentables Mexicanas,* (FIRME), one of Mexico's leading investment trusts, which are roughly the equivalent of mutual funds in the United States.

Mexican steel production has grown rapidly in recent years, with a high percentage of the output used by the steel companies themselves in expanding their facilities. Since 1950, steel production has quadrupled in volume, with the highest increase, from 1960 to 1961, being about 7 per cent. Although they have grown considerably in the past two decades, the Mexican companies, like steel firms in other parts of the world, have their problems. With present capacity in excess of domestic needs, the industry has experienced difficulties in obtaining short-term domestic credit, and has faced strong foreign competition in marketing its product. Trouble from foreign competitors has not been limited to the industry's export trade, however, for, according to the president of the National Chamber of the Iron and Steel Industry, in 1961 domestic sales suffered because many Mexican government agencies had been able to purchase iron and steel products abroad with long-term credit at low rates of interest. The domestic steel industry had been relegated to the position of a secondary supplier because it was not, said the Chamber president, "in a position to compete with credits dispensed from abroad with the customary largess."

Automotive Assembly Industry

Although a government-owned firm was established in 1954 to make complete motor vehicles, Mexico's present automobile and truck industry consists almost entirely of plants for the local assembly of components imported from the United States and Europe. Even the plant of *Diesel Nacional,* the government enterprise, has been used primarily to assemble automobile parts imported from France. At recent count, local assembly plants controlled by foreign companies numbered about fifteen and were responsible for producing about thirty different makes for the Mexican market. Some such plants have been forced to close down in the past several years, however, as the result of a government program started in 1961 to reduce the number of foreign makes assembled in Mexico and to reduce the importation of vehicle components. Some parts and accessories have been made in Mexico, but the new government program is designed to require that an even greater proportion of auto and truck components be domestically manufactured. For the most part, only the smaller United States and European companies have ceased Mexican operations as a result of the program while such firmly entrenched giants as General Motors and Ford remain and are expanding their local fabrication of parts.

The assembly of automobiles in Mexico grew slowly following its beginning in 1926, not receiving any great impetus until after the end of World War II. Since 1950, the number of plants and firms has not expanded appreciably, but the number of units assembled has more than doubled. The annual output is about equally divided between private passenger cars and commercial vehicles, i.e., trucks and buses, although in recent years there has been a trend toward greater relative production of trucks and buses. In

1961, the number of these vehicles assembled was slightly in excess of the number of private automobiles.

Virtually all motor vehicles assembled in Mexico are used in Mexico. While the industry has no export significance, it has been of considerable significance to the import trade. Despite high tariffs and other restrictions, in 1962, the importation of finished vehicles accounted for almost 10 per cent of the total value of the nation's imports. The importation of motor vehicle components and spare parts for the same year, however, was only a third of the value of finished vehicle imports, accounting for a little less than 3 per cent of the total value of goods imported. The government's program of greater local production of auto components, then, may curtail the smaller import category but increase the need for expanding the larger import class of finished vehicles.

Production of Pulp and Paper

Also becoming significant in Mexico's rapidly industrializing economy is the production of pulp and paper. Domestic output has expanded rapidly since 1940, with most increase in the production of kraft and semi-kraft papers. In 1960, the industry was composed of twenty-two different firms operating forty-two sep-

arate plants producing pulp, paper, and paper products. Thirteen of these twenty-two firms operated exclusively in the Federal District and the state of Mexico.

Although nearing self-sufficiency in the kraft and heavier papers, Mexico still imports most of its special papers and newsprint, as well as a large amount of its pulp requirements. In 1960, over 90 per cent of the newsprint consumed in the country was imported, and the imports of pulp and paper formed almost 2 per cent of the total value of goods imported. Sugar cane bagasse is being promoted — although not yet extensively used — as a source of pulp to limit the need for wood pulp, which has to be brought in for the most part from Canada, northern Europe, and Chile.

Other Manufacturing

Along with steel, paper, and automobiles, indoor plumbing is an accepted symbol of both higher living standards and an industrial economy. The plumbing fixtures industry often reliably reflects the status of the construction industry; and while not significant in the numbers employed or value of product, it is typical of the many lesser manufacturing industries that in recent decades have been forming the base for a Mexican industrial economy.

Mexico's automotive manufacturing largely involved the assembly of components imported from the United States and Europe until the early 1960's, when a government program directed at increasing the proportion of Mexican-made auto and truck parts was begun. General Motors and Ford have fabrication and assembly plants in the Valley of Mexico.

The plumbing fixtures industry includes three firms, two in the Valley of Mexico, and one in Monterrey. The first of these was opened in 1932 in Mexico City, the second just outside the capital in 1948, and the third in Monterrey in 1951. One other firm failed in 1949. Financing of the three existing companies has been domestic, although the government industrial investment agency, *Nacional Financiera,* has actively supported one of them. Since establishment of the newest of the three firms, (1951), investment in the industry has increased by 25 per cent, and production by about 50 per cent.

The production of the plumbing fixtures industry is able to meet the domestic demand and provide for some exports as well. Exports have diminished in recent years, however, because of heavy competition from the United States and Japan, and at present the industry is operating at about 75 per cent of capacity. Although its products are relatively insignificant in Mexican export trade, the industry is heavily dependent upon imports. Over half of the industry's raw materials consists of clay and enamel, and more than 80 per cent of these items must be imported because of the poor quality of domestic resources.

The plumbing fixtures industry could in many ways be considered typical of small and medium manufacturing industries in Mexico today. Many of its traits are typical of the larger industries as well, for it is composed of a small number of small or medium-sized firms, most of which came into existence after World War II; financial aid has been given to at least part of the industry by the government; productive capacity is currently in excess of domestic requirements; and it is dependent upon the country's foreign commerce either for essential raw materials or for the marketing of excess output.

The rate of growth in Mexican industry since the early forties has been one of the highest in Latin America. The greatest increase in physical production has been in the building materials industry, which produced in 1960 almost ten times what it produced in 1939. Substantial gains have been pointed out also in food-processing and the production of rubber goods, paper and chemicals. In the manufacture of textiles and shoes — Mexico's only major commodities with manufacturing histories reaching back to the early nineteenth century — the nation has come close to self-sufficiency.

Since the 1930's, the federal government has actively encouraged manufacturing in Mexico with long-term financing, protection from foreign competition with tariffs and other import restrictions, and the granting of tax concessions. *Nacional Financiera* has been an extremely active element in Mexican industrialization, owning and controlling a noticeable portion of industry, although most manufacturing enterprises are still in private hands.

Foreign investment in Mexican manufacturing has been substantial, despite the fact that domestic investment and ownership have been encouraged and the production of certain goods, e.g., motion pictures, beverages, and rubber goods, has been restricted by law to "Mexicanized" (at least 51 per cent Mexican-owned) firms. Actually, more investment capital from the United States and Western Europe has gone into manufacturing in Mexico in recent years than into the areas traditionally dominated by foreign spending before World War II — mining, power, and transportation.

MINERAL INDUSTRIES

Despite Mexico's reputation as a producer of nonferrous metals, petroleum and natural gas and their products now constitute the country's most important mineral industry and a rapidly growing factor in the economy. In 1960, the petroleum industry accounted for almost 5 per cent of national income — two-thirds of the amount accounted for by all mineral industries — and provided slightly more than 1 per cent of all non-agricultural employment. Far greater than the exact number of people the industry employs, however is its influence in the employment world in general *Petróleos Mexicanos* (Pemex), the huge governmen

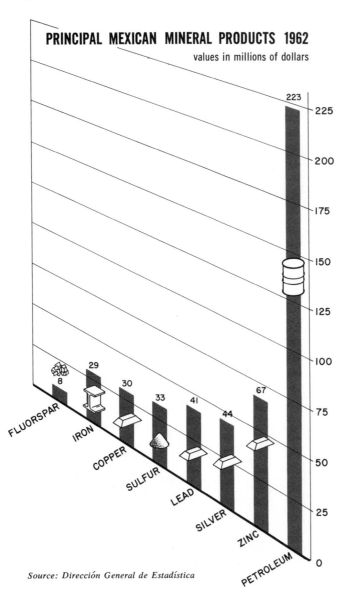

PRINCIPAL MEXICAN MINERAL PRODUCTS 1962

values in millions of dollars

FLUORSPAR 8
IRON 29
COPPER 30
SULFUR 33
LEAD 41
SILVER 44
ZINC 67
PETROLEUM 223

Source: Dirección General de Estadística

monopoly controlling the industry, has long had a reputation for liberal treatment of its workers and has been upheld by the government as a standard for other Mexican companies. The Pemex reputation was indicated by the results of a survey conducted for Sears Roebuck de Mexico among the upper economic half of the population in Mexico City in the early 1950's. Almost half of those surveyed stated that they would rather work for Pemex than for any other major employer in Mexico.

As an earner of foreign exchange, Mexican oil is also significant, but its importance is declining. In 1963, nevertheless, petroleum products — mostly fuel oils — were still among the ten most valuable of the country's export commodities, accounting for about 4 per cent of the total value of export goods. Although Mexico was the first nation in Latin America to become an important oil producer, it is now in second place — far behind the leader, Venezuela. Even second place is sufficient, however, to make Mexico one of the world's major oil producers.

Despite the fact that petroleum comprises only about 4 per cent of goods exported and provides only a small percentage of income and employment, the industry is critical to the Mexican economy. With coal reserves distant from the major population centers and hydroelectric resources not yet fully developed, oil provides the country's major source of energy.

Virtually all production and distribution of oil and natural gas in Mexico have been controlled by the government owned corporation, *Petróleos Mexicanos* (Pemex), since nationalization of the private oil companies by President Cárdenas in 1938. In 1961, this huge autonomous agency had a budget almost two-thirds as large as all the rest of the federal government. Private enterprise has not been completely excluded from Mexico's oil industry, however. Private firms under contract to Pemex have played a substantial role in exploratory drilling and in the erection and installation of plant and equipment for the government monopoly. In addition, a few private firms have engaged in the production and marketing of lubricating oils with the crude petroleum purchased from Pemex.

At present Mexico's oil comes chiefly from the producing areas along the Gulf Coast from Tamaulipas to Tabasco. Pemex operates eight refineries scattered throughout this area and in the Central Valley. From its refineries, Pemex also handles all distribution throughout the country, except in the extreme northwest where oil is imported from the United States. Since 1938, Mexican production of crude oil and refinery products has increased almost three times, just enough to keep up with the country's demands, except in the far northwest.

Pemex also produces some natural gas, mainly in the Isthmus of Tehuantepec, where output has increased about five times since production began in 1950. A recently completed pipeline brings the fuel from the producing area to Mexico City, but lack of an urban distribution system prevents its utilization by household consumers and limits its use to industrial firms. In the far northwest, demands for natural gas are met by imports from the United States.

The government monopoly also operates a number of plants for the production of basic petroleum derivatives for the petrochemical industry, and more such plants are planned. Providing a base for a growing chemical industry operated primarily by private enterprise appears to be the present aim of the federal petroleum authorities. Another avowed aim of Pemex for the near future is to make the nation, including the northern border areas, completely self-sufficient in oil and gas products.

The Non-ferrous Metals

Second in importance to the production of petroleum and natural gas as a mineral industry is the mining and smelting of nonferrous metals. This is also the oldest non-agricultural industry in Mexico, silver and gold having been mined by the Indians long before the coming of the Spaniards. Metal mining in recent years has provided jobs for about 1 per cent of the economically active population and accounted for approximately 2 per cent of the national income, although the latter proportion has been decreasing steadily. In 1837, nonferrous metals, mostly silver and gold, comprised 90 per cent of Mexican exports. In 1963, nonferrous metals comprised only about 8 per cent of the nation's exports of goods and 5 per cent of total exports. Despite the fact that it is no longer of principal importance to the country as a whole, the mining and smelting of nonferrous metals has been, and still is, of major significance in certain areas. Indeed, in some states, namely Chihuahua, Durango, Guanajuato, Guerrero, San Luis Potosí, and Zacatecas, mining was responsible for initial economic development and still is a prime factor in their economies.

Historically, the nonferrous metal mining industry in Mexico has been controlled by private capital, largely from Great Britain and the United States. In the mid-1950's it was estimated that 85 per cent of the investment in Mexican mining was controlled by United States and British interests, including some of mining's largest and best known companies (Anaconda, American Smelting and Refining, American Metals Climax, and others). Although the proportion of foreign investment in Mexican mining has declined of late, its historical prominence is exemplified by the story, which is probably apocryphal but often told. The notorious revolutionary, Pancho Villa, when asked if he spoke any English, replied that he did, and promptly recited two phrases, one a profanity, the other the name of a large United States mining and smelting firm with widespread operations in Mexico.

Undoubtedly, however, the day of the foreign capitalist in Mexican metal mining has passed, for, in 1961, the government adopted the principle of "Mexicanization" of mining. This consisted in granting extremely favorable tax concessions to enterprises owned at least 51 per cent by Mexican citizens, and in prohibiting the granting of new mining concessions to any company not owned by a majority of Mexican individuals or firms.

As in other aspects of the Mexican economy, the cooperative has also had a place in mining. Many of the older mines, no longer able to make a profit for their private owners, have been acquired (in many cases by outright gift) by worker cooperatives in order to save jobs and prevent the industrial base of a particular locale from disappearing. Operated in most cases with substantial government subsidies, many of these cooperatives have fulfilled their purpose for many years, but even some of them have been forced to cease operations for one reason or another. Only a few years ago, the El Oro and Tlalpujuhua district, one of the oldest mining districts in Mexico, was dealt a severe economic blow by the closing of *La Cooperativa Minera Dos Estrellas* (The Dos Estrellas Mining Cooperative). The Dos Estrellas Mine, along with others in the district, reached its peak production in the 1920's but had remained a leading gold producer up to 1938 when the private firm that owned it turned it over to the workers because of its inability to show a profit. Other mining cooperatives throughout the country, although not a dominant factor in the industry, continue to operate to preserve jobs and towns.

The federal government has also become an element in the metal mining industry's operations. Just as some unprofitable mines have been operated by worker cooperatives, others have been taken over and operated by the government in an attempt to save jobs and protect particular localities. Federal subsidies to mining companies, particularly silver producers, are likewise a prominent feature of the industry's operations. In addition, the government provides technical assistance and physical and monetary aid to small mining enterprises through its Commission for Mining Development and the Office of Non-Renewable Natural Resources, both under the *Departamento de Patrimonio Nacional* (Department of the National Endowment).

Despite decreasing emphasis on mining, Mexico is still the world's leading producer of silver, supplying about one-fifth of total free-world output. Nearly all of the country's silver is exported; only about 5 per cent of total production is used internally. Its consumption of the metal for coinage purposes is one of the lowest in the world, although a significant amount of Mexican silver is made into coins for other countries, particularly certain Arab nations. The value of silver produced in 1961 was about 13 per cent of total mineral production (exclusive of petroleum) and two-thirds of this was produced as a by-product in the mining of lead and zinc. Many of the country's silver mines, once fantastically rich, now operate at a loss and are subsidized heavily by the government.

Mexico is also one of the world's important sources of gold. Today this metal, like silver, is produced largely as a by-product in the mining of lead and zinc.

Aside from being sources of the precious metals, lead and zinc are themselves important mining commodities. The nation is one of the world's leading producers of these two base metals, exporting about 70 per cent of its output each year. In combination, they account for over 5 per cent of the value of export goods. Although lead and zinc are usually produced jointly from the same mines, lead is also mined for itself along with its silver content. Lead production has declined since its 1938 high and is presently only about two-thirds of the 1938 figure. Zinc production, on the other hand, has been on the increase in both absolute and relative terms. Efforts are being made to increase the value added by fabrication in Mexico and to promote domestic consumption of zinc. In 1960, a concern was formed jointly by the Mexican government and private Belgian interests to refine high-grade zinc domestically.

Copper, another important metal in Mexican mining, is one of the country's ten most valuable export commodities. Over half of the present output comes from one property — the Cananea operation of the Anaconda Company's Mexican subsidiary. Elsewhere in the country, copper is mined frequently as another joint product with lead, zinc, gold, and silver. Half of the red metal mined in Mexico is exported. Of the half which is fabricated domestically, one-third is exported, so that actually two-thirds of all of the copper produced in Mexico is shipped to world markets. Copper production in Mexico reached a peak in 1929, and has fallen ever since, although not steadily. Production in 1959 was only three-fourths of the 1929 maximum.

Mercury and antimony are also mined in Mexico and recently a joint United States-Mexican firm was organized to build and operate an aluminum smelter at Veracruz on the Gulf Coast. To date, however, the country has not been an important source of bauxite, the aluminum ore so abundant in the Caribbean area.

Iron Reserves Substantial

Unlike the nonferrous metals, iron is of great internal importance to Mexico and has been of practically no export significance. The country has substantial reserves of adequate-grade iron ore which are considered sufficient for its domestic steel industry. Most of the deposits are found in the northern states and along the Pacific Coast. However, as elsewhere in Latin America, Japanese steel firms have recently expressed interest in Mexico's Pacific Coast ore deposits, which are presently unexploited. As a result, iron may soon rank with the nonferrous metals as an important export commodity. While no Mexican iron ore is currently shipped to other countries, some basic steel products are, as are concentrates of other metals such as manganese, used in steel production. Today all of Mexico's iron mining is controlled by the country's major steel companies, and all ore produced goes to their blast furnaces.

Copper is one of Mexico's ten most valuable export commodities. More than half of the nation's output comes from the modern operations of the Anaconda Company's Mexican subsidiary in northern Sonora. The 16,000 tons per day concentrating plant at Cananea is shown above.

Mexico's coal mining industry is similar to its iron mining in that the principal operations are captive mines owned by the steel companies, and the product again goes almost exclusively to the blast furnaces. Coal resources, found chiefly in the north, near the center of the steel industry at Monterrey, are considered sufficient in tonnage and coking quality to meet the needs of domestic industry. Mexican coals are not used to any extent for electric power production or for transportation, however, both because of their quality and the distance from population centers.

Sulfur Important to World

Second to petroleum, Mexico's most important mineral in terms of tonnage produced, is its principal nonmetallic mineral, sulfur. Mexican sulfur is of consequence, not only to Mexico, but to the world. The country is the second-ranking producer of elemental sulfur among the non-Communist countries, and accounts for almost 9 per cent of total free-world sulfur production. The yellow mineral, an important raw material for the chemical industry, is also one of the country's ten most valuable export commodities,

comprising almost 4 per cent of the total value of goods exported in 1963. (That year zinc accounted for slightly more than 2 per cent, lead almost 3 per cent, copper 2 per cent, and oil 4 per cent.) In recent years, more than three-fourths of Mexican sulfur production has been exported, one-third of it to the United States. Domestic consumption is increasing, however, and more and more of Mexico's sulfur output is being used at home.

Sulfur mining, most of it by the Frasch process, is a relatively new process in Mexico, pioneered in the early 1950's by United States capital and personnel. Today, the means of production of elemental sulfur in Mexico are privately owned, the most important companies being subsidiaries of United States firms. Some by-product sulfur is also produced by Pemex and certain integrated metal-mining companies which handle sulfide ores.

Other nonmetallic minerals of importance in the Mexican economy are graphite, fluorspar, and barite, which are produced almost exclusively for export.

Because the bulk of mineral production is exported, Mexico's mining industry — except for coal, oil, and iron — is largely at the mercy of price fluctuations in the world markets, which have been downward in recent years and considerably so. This is particularly true for the nonferrous base metals, lead, zinc, and copper. Despite the fact that government subsidies have taken up some of the brunt of world price variations for Mexican producers, the effect on the economy as a whole has been noticeable and has tended to perpetuate instability.

Despite statements of contrary intent and certain area subsidies, official government policy toward mining has resulted in discouraging new investment, by both foreign and Mexican capital, in the more established branches of mining, (e.g. base metals). The tax system as applied to mining is generally burdensome, transportation has long been inadequate, and sufficient power facilities for successful mineral exploitation are lacking in many areas. In addition, certain metals have been subjected to progressive rates of taxation which have made increased production even less attractive.

The most recent and most significant development in Mexican mining has been the previously mentioned "Mexicanization" law which, together with regulations of the government's fiscal authorities, was designed to give majority ownership and control of industrial enterprises to Mexican citizens. Under the law, new mining concessions are to be granted only to firms with at least 51 per cent Mexican ownership. The law and the regulations also grant a 50 per cent reduction in both production and export taxes to "Mexicanized" firms, in effect doubling the tax rate for non-Mexican companies. A number of firms in the industry have already complied with the new legislation while others are negotiating with Mexican financial interests for the transfer of at least part of their ownership.

Since 1938 and the expropriation of the petroleum properties, the mineral industries of Mexico have lost a good deal of their traditional position of prominence in the nation's economy, and they have also lost a great deal of their traditional character — control by British and United States capital. These industries have also become less a source of supply for more industrialized nations, turning instead to the provision of basic raw materials for Mexico's own industrialization.

CONSTRUCTION

Since World War II, Mexico has had one of the highest rates of industrial growth in the Western Hemisphere, as well as one of the world's highest rates of population increase. Accompanying these has been a traditional deficiency in adequate housing. Recent estimates are that fully 75 per cent of the country's rapidly growing population is without sufficient housing, and that an additional 200,000 dwellings per year will be needed merely to hold the currently estimated deficit of two million dwelling units.

Despite this state of affairs — and yet causally related to it — Mexico's contract construction industry has been and is of relatively minor importance in the national economy. In recent years, less than 3 per cent

of the economically active population has been employed in contract construction, and only about [...] per cent of national income and 3 per cent of gross domestic product came from this activity in 1960. In the same year, contract construction in the United States provided about 8 per cent of the gross domestic product and employed more than 6 per cent of the labor force. In 1961, the value of total building construction in Mexico City and the Federal District (with a population of about three million) was approximately the same as the value of total building construction in Salt Lake City, Utah, which has a population less than one-fifteenth that of the Mexican capital.

Mexico's contract construction industry is composed primarily of a great many small firms, privately owned and operated, but heavily dependent upon government contracts. It has been estimated that about 65 per cent of total construction expenditures in Mexico are made by the government, either directly or through its numerous autonomous agencies. Government control of building expenditures is probably even greater than this estimate suggests, as exemplified by a housing project recently undertaken near Mexico City. Of the one billion peso total cost of the project, 300 million pesos were provided by private sources, mainly insurance companies, and 700 million by government sources. Although private sources provide 30 per cent of the financing, the project is administered completely by the government, a kind of joint arrangement which has become increasingly popular in recent years.

The government's principal participation in construction, aside from the industrial and public works projects of its autonomous entities (such as Pemex, the Federal Electricity Commission, and the National Railways, to name only a few) is through the National Housing Institute. The Institute was formed in 1954 and operates chiefly as a coordinating agency, working through and with other government bodies, labor unions, housing cooperatives, and private construction companies. The federal agencies involved in housing construction include the Social Security and Service Institute for Government Workers, which administer some 60 per cent of all public housing expenditures. Other important federal activity in construction is exercised by the Mexican Social Security Institute and the *Banco Nacional Hipotecario Urbano de Obras Públicas*.

Government influence is not limited solely to its own activities, however. By law, Mexican employers are required to provide housing for their workers at nominal monthly rentals. It is doubtful, however, that this requirement is very strictly enforced.

A heavy dependence on government contract awards is not the only problem facing the many small firms and the few larger ones that make up the building industry. Most of their problems, however, are financial. Private bank financing of construction, particularly housing, is almost non-existent, and other sources of credit are difficult to obtain. In addition, rents are kept artificially low in many areas, thus discouraging private investment in housing except under special circumstances. Despite its problems, the industry's output has grown at an average rate of 6 per cent per year since 1950, and, at present, according to a former president of the National Chamber of the Construction Industry, the combined productive capacity of the industry is greater than the demand for its services, a condition also claimed for other Mexican industries.

ELECTRIC POWER

The production of electric power is a vital but relatively small industry in Mexico. The entire industry employs less than one-third of 1 per cent of the economically active population, and its direct contribution to national income is little more than 1 per cent. Electricity itself, however, as the prime mover for the nation's growing industrial enterprises, contributes far more to the country's total output than these percentages indicate. By far the greatest portion of electrical output is sold to industrial users, most of these concentrated in the Valley of Mexico and the other centers of manufacturing. At present there is little in the way of rural electrification.

In 1959, installed generating capacity in Mexico was less than 2 per cent of total United States capacity, and the country's per capita consumption of electricity was less than 7 per cent of the per capita consumption in the United States. About half of the country's electrical generating capacity is provided by hydroelectric plants. Among the Latin American republics, Mexico ranks eighth in per capita consumption of electric power, despite its relatively advanced state of industrialization.

Early in 1962, the federal government acquired the *Compañía de Tranvías, Luz, y Fuerza Motriz de Monterrey* (Electric Railway, Light, and Power Company of Monterrey) to complete the nationalization of the country's electric power industry. Before beginning to acquire private power companies in 1960, the government had been responsible for producing about one-third of the nation's electrical energy through the facilities of an autonomous agency, the *Comisión Federal de Electricidad*. While a number of smaller companies were also acquired in the nationalization program, of primary importance were the purchases of the two foreign-owned corporations which had been responsible for about half of the nation's total electrical output. The first of these to become government-owned was *Compañía Impulsora de Empresas Eléctricas*, a subsidiary of American and Foreign Power Company. The purchase of this firm (then controlled by United States capital) was greatly facilitated by a loan of $100 million to the Mexican government by another United States company, Prudential Insurance. This became, then, an act of government acquisition significantly different from the expropriations of foreign holdings in oil and railroads which took place in Mexico in the late 1930's. The second major firm to be nationalized — one that had been the country's largest producer of electric power with facilities concentrated in the Valley of Mexico — was the Belgian- and British-owned Mexican Light and Power Company. Since completion of the nationalization program, the government has established a special super-agency to administer the entire power industry, including its own producing agency, the *Comisión Federal de Electricidad*.

Because the provision of adequate power is essential for industrial expansion, the Mexican government, since World War II, has strongly emphasized the expansion of electrical generating facilities. Up to the end of 1961, over half of all money loaned to Mexico by the World Bank and the Inter-American Development Bank went for construction of electric power facilities, including the huge Miguel Alemán hydroelectric system, which provides power to the Valley of Mexico. Although most of this money was loaned to the government's *Comisión Federal de Electricidad* for projects throughout the country, more than one-third went to the Mexican Light and Power Company for expansion of its facilities in the Mexico City area. Partly as a result of the stress by both public and private interests on the development of generating capacity, the total output of electricity in Mexico has more than doubled since 1953.

TRANSPORTATION AND COMMUNICATIONS

Transportation and communications are of much less direct importance in the economy of Mexico than the equivalent sectors are considered to be in the economy of the United States. In 1960, transportation and communications enterprises in Mexico provided employment to less than 3 per cent of the economically active population, while in the United States these activities occupied more than 7 per cent of the labor force. The sector's contribution to national product, however, is more comparable to that of this country. In Mexico in 1960, transportation and communications contributed more than 5 per cent of the value of net domestic product. In the United States that year they accounted for about 6 per cent of net domestic product.

Like other parts of the Mexican economy, the transportation and communications industries are a mixture of both public and private ownership, as they are also in many other countries. Also like other sectors of the Mexican economy, certain segments of the transportation and communications sector have grown rapidly in recent years while others have been relatively stagnant or even deteriorated. It should be noted, however, that Mexico is not the only nation in which this is true.

Highway Transportation

Long dependent on railroads for its land transportation, Mexico's modern highway system has been developed for the most part only since the early 1940's.

Even today a large part of the nation's network of state and federal highways is unpaved, although Mexico has more miles of surfaced roads than any other country in Latin America. For the most part, the federal highways are adequate and well kept, but there is a serious lack of feeder roads and even many of those that exist are not properly maintained. The lack of farm-market roads and roads linking various parts of the country outside the Valley of Mexico has been a serious handicap to the economic development of many areas.

Truck transport is one of Mexico's fastest growing industries. The trucking firms, ownership of which is limited by law to native-born Mexican citizens, are already numerous and still multiplying rapidly. All truck transportation operates under federal franchise and under both federal and state regulations.

Bus transportation is also one of the country's rapidly growing industries and has assumed a significant role in domestic passenger travel. Approximately 80 per cent of all interstate travel in Mexico is by bus and a very large percentage of urban traffic is by the same means. In recent years, the bus lines have substantially increased their share of total passenger traffic, largely at the expense of the railroads, despite the fact that bus fares are slightly higher than rail fares.

Almost three-fourths of all buses in Mexico are engaged in local transit. The remaining 6,000 are owned by the 750 private firms which provide all interstate bus service. Small companies dominate the interstate travel field. Over 80 per cent of the companies have fewer than ten buses while only three firms have more than 150 and none has more than 200 vehicles. Most Mexican bus lines provide both first and second class service on the same bus, although a few operate only single-class accommodations. The principal interstate bus routes, of course, radiate from Mexico City. The most important is the Mexico City–Nogales route and the second is the Mexico City–Veracruz route. Also of importance are the routes from the capital northward to Ciudad Juárez and Laredo on the Texas border. There is little bus transportation in the southeastern part of the country, not for lack of passengers, but rather for lack of roads.

Railroads

An extensive system of rail transportation was developed in Mexico in the latter part of the nineteenth century and the early years of the twentieth, by British and United States interests, including the mining companies. Within the last thirty years there has been little increase in the country's total miles of track but there has been extensive reconstruction of existing lines. An exception to the lack of new track was the completion in 1961 of the 580-mile Chihuahua–Pacific Railroad extending from the Texas border at Presidio to the Pacific Coast port of Los Mochis, providing a new rail connection between the agricultural region of Sonora and Sinaloa and the central part of Mexico, as

well as better access to rail connections with the mid western United States. In 1960, Mexican railroad carried the second largest freight ton mileage in Lati America, more than 25 per cent of the total for th area. All this was done, however, with only 10 per cer of Latin America's railway rolling stock.

Rail transportation in Mexico today is provide by fourteen different railroads, all of which are owne and operated by government or autonomous govern ment agencies. The largest of these separate railroac is the *Ferrocarriles Nacionales de Mexico,* which wa expropriated from its foreign owners in 1937 and currently operated as an autonomous agency of th Federal Government. *Ferrocarriles Nacionales* carri 70 per cent of the country's rail freight and 80 per cer of its rail passenger traffic, on lines that extend in a directions from Mexico City and reach as far as Ciuda Juárez and Laredo on the north to Guatemala on th south.

Autonomous federal agencies also operate th nation's two other principal railway systems, the *Ferro carril del Pacífico* and the *Ferrocarriles Mexicano* The *Pacífico* is probably the nation's most modern rai road in terms of roadbed, track, and equipment, havin been almost completely rehabilitated since 1954. Th system, which until its nationalization in 1951 was th Southern Pacific of Mexico, extends southward alon the Pacific Coast from Nogales on the Arizona borde The other of Mexico's three major railroads, *Ferro carriles Mexicanos,* was nationalized in 1946. Th country's minor railroads are operated directly by th federal *Ministerio de Communicaciones,* except for th *Ferrocarriles Unidas de Yucatán,* which is owned an operated by the state of Yucatán. The nation's onl privately owned rail facilities are a few short lin owned by some of the mining companies and operate for their own use.

Until the mid-1950's Mexico's railroads wer sadly inadequate to meet the needs of the nation growing economy. In 1955, a loan of $61 million fro the World Bank was used to completely revamp th *Ferrocarril del Pacífico,* including relaying about thre fourths of the system's track, installing better commu ications facilities, repairing rolling stock, and replacin its older locomotives with diesel equipment. The cou try's only other relatively modern railroad is the pr viously mentioned *Ferrocarril Chihuahua al Pacífic* completed in late 1961. Elsewhere, roadbed, track an equipment are in generally poor condition. In son areas traffic handling is unable to prevent serious co gestion during peak operating time. Most of the line however, have been or are rapidly being converted diesel, and railroad cars are now being manufactured Mexico, some even being exported.

Despite their problems, Mexican railroads hav been able, since the middle 1950's, to steadily increa the tonnage of freight they carry. In 1960, total freig tonnage hauled on the nation's railroads was almo 50 percent more than that carried in 1953. They hav been faced with a continuing erosion of their passeng raffic, however, as a result of competition by the numerous bus lines, which generally provide faster, though higher priced service, and the importance of the railroads in Mexican passenger travel has declined steadily.

Water Transportation

Despite its long coastline with many ports, Mexico has few naturally good harbors and water-borne transportation has not become of major importance in the nation's economy. With its long, common land border with the United States of greater significance in the country's foreign trade, less than 50 per cent of Mexico's exports and imports are shipped by sea. Of its overseas trade, fully three-fourths is shipped through ports on the Gulf of Mexico and a sizable portion of this is shipped in coastwise trade with ports along the United States' Gulf coast.

By far the great bulk of Mexico's overseas trade is carried in foreign flagships. The country's merchant fleet is small, having only about fifty seagoing vessels of any consequence at all for cargo purposes. Most of these are tankers owned by Pemex, and bulk cargo vessels owned by CONASUPO, the government's agricultural marketing corporation, *Guanos y Fertilizantes de México,* a firm harvesting and shipping guano on the Pacific Coast and offshore islands, and a few smaller concerns engaged in coastwise traffic. Several years ago the government placed in service two passenger liners for international traffic, apparently more as a prestige measure than as an economically sound venture.

Air Transportation

With the rough terrain and long distances characteristic of Mexico, air transportation has historically been of considerable significance in the nation's economic life. While air transportation is of greatest importance in passenger travel, the use of air transport for the movement of freight has been noticeably greater in Mexico than in the United States. Air freight, however, is still not a serious competitor with rail, truck, and water transportation within the country. In 1960, Mexico ranked second among the Latin American countries in passenger miles flown and third in cargo ton miles flown.

The Mexican air transport industry is dominated by *Compañía Mexicana de Aviación,* a private firm in which Pan American World Airways holds a minority interest. *Mexicana* is the country's most important domestic as well as international air carrier. Second in importance in both domestic and international air service is *Aeronaves de México,* a government-controlled concern. Also of importance in international traffic is *Guest Aerovías México,* a private company until mid-1962, when 80 per cent of its stock was acquired by *Nacional Financiera.* Foreign flag airlines are of considerable importance in the country's international air traffic, which accounts for almost one-fifth of all air-line flights in Mexico. Domestic traffic is handled not only by *Mexicana, Aeronaves,* and *Guest,* but also by more than twenty secondary airlines carrying passengers and cargo only on domestic routes.

Mexico City is the center of Mexican airline transportation, as it is the center of the country's railway and highway systems. From the capital, routes extend to more than fifty major cities throughout Mexico and to major cities in the United States, Canada, and the rest of the Americas.

Government is involved in Mexico's airline industry much less than in the railroad or maritime industries but to a greater extent than in truck or bus transportation. In addition to its outright control of two of the country's major airlines, *Aeronaves* and *Guest,* the federal government has also provided financing to *Aerolíneas Mexicanas,* a short-haul domestic carrier. Unlike many other countries, Mexico does not subsidize its privately owned airlines, and they are required to carry mail at about regular cargo rates. All Mexican airlines operate under franchises and regulations of the federal government, and the government does operate some facilities for airline use in that it owns and administers airports at most of the principal cities. Such facilities, however, comprise only about 10 per cent of all airport installations in the nation. The remainder are for the most part owned and operated by the airlines themselves.

Unlike the railroads, and more like the truck and bus lines, Mexico's airlines have relatively few problems, and face good prospects for continued growth and development. Some air routes, however, have suffered competition from automobile travel where newly constructed highways have proved popular. The advent of large capacity and expensive jet planes has created problems for one of the international airlines but such problems apparently have been solved by the other two.

Telephone and Telegraph

One company, *Teléfonos de México,* dominates this Mexican industry. Now owned by private domestic interests, prior to 1958, the firm was owned partly by the Swedish Ericsson Group and partly by the International Telephone and Telegraph Corporation which had created it in an earlier merger of their separate Mexican affiliates. In addition to *Teléfonos de México,* there are five other private telephone companies in various parts of the country, but they operate strictly on a local basis. The federal government maintains telephone service in some of the more isolated areas of the nation, and also operates some public telephone facilities in connection with its other communications activities.

Teléfonos currently serves all of Mexico's major population centers, although almost 60 per cent of its telephones are located in the federal district. Recently, the company began another expansion program to provide service to new areas and to increase and improve service in those areas in which it already operates. A substantial part of this program involves the installation of microwave relay equipment for long distance service, and the replacement of manual switchboards with automatic exchanges. Although the company has undertaken a number of expansion and improvement programs in past years, telephone facilities for the country as a whole are still far from adequate. With an average of fifteen telephones per thousand persons, Mexico ranks eighth among the Latin American countries in per capita telephones. Argentina ranks first with an average of sixty phones per thousand inhabitants. (The United States has about 400 telephones per thousand persons.)

Telegraph service in Mexico is provided by a government monopoly, *Telégrafos Nacionales de México.* International radio-telephone service is also provided by federally owned and operated facilities. In addition to this direct participation in the communications industry, the federal government, through the *Ministerio de Comunicaciones,* regulates both the private and public concerns engaged in telephone and telegraph communications.

MAJOR CATEGORIES OF IMPORTS AND EXPORTS 1962

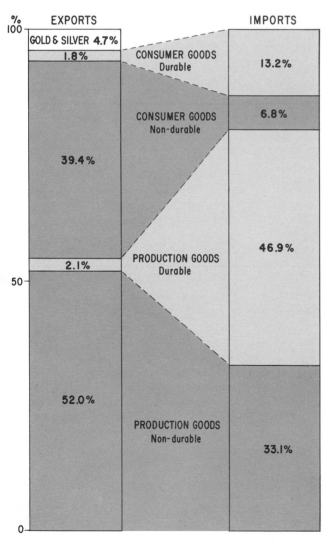

Source: Banco Nacional de Comercio Exterior, S.A.

Radio and Television

Although television has made rapid gains in popularity in Mexico and has already become what could properly be called a mass medium, radio remains the more important means of mass communication. Compared to other Latin American nations, however, Mexico, with an average of about ninety radio sets per thousand persons, makes by no means as extensive use of this medium as the United States, with almost 950 radios per thousand persons, or even Uruguay and Argentina, which have about 200 radios per thousand persons. At present, the Mexican radio broadcasting industry is composed of two major chains of about ninety stations each, a minor chain of about thirty stations, and a multitude of independent stations scattered throughout the country.

Mexico was one of the first of the Latin American nations to adopt commercial television. The first station was established in Mexico City in 1950. By 1960, the country had ten commercial television stations variously distributed throughout most of the large centers of population. Mexico uses television more than most Latin American countries, but with only eighteen sets per thousand persons in 1960, the nation still lagged far behind the leading television country of Latin America, Cuba, which had an average of fifty-five sets per thousand persons in 1960. Both television and radio enterprises in Mexico are privately owned and operated, with government regulation.

Other Communications Media

Despite the rapidly growing acceptance of television in Mexico, the motion picture is still an extremely popular form of entertainment and mass communication. The nation has more motion picture theatres than any other country in Latin America and is a leading cinema producer for the Spanish-speaking world.

Newspapers are also of importance in Mexico, although their influence is concentrated in the metropolitan areas because of the relatively high rate of illiteracy among the rural population. Today, Mexico is second only to Argentina, among the Latin American republics, in the number of newspapers published.

COMMERCE

Foreign Trade

Mexico is dependent mainly on the United States for its imports, and as a market for its exports, condition natural between neighboring countries with production in one country so vast, and income so high. The same observation could be made with respect to Canada and the United States and, in fact, to most contiguous countries, where one is much larger in population, income, and wealth than the other. Argentina, for example, has a similar relationship to Paraguay, and other comparable situations could be cited

FOREIGN TRADE BY CONTINENTS 1964
in millions of pesos

1,142 10.1%
446 2.4%

EXP. 291 2.6%
IMP. 895 4.8%

EXP. 1,410 12.5%
IMP. 3,983 21.3%

EXP. 7,610 67.4%
IMP. 12,779 68.5%

EXP. 151 1.3%
IMP. 6 .05%

EXP. 46 0.4%
IMP. 8 .05%

EXP. 29 0.2%
IMP. 268 1.4%

EXP. 625 5.5%
IMP. 276 1.5%

Source: Banco Nacional de Comercio Exterior, S.A.

In recent years, approximately four-fifths of Mexican imports have come from the United States, compared with three-fifths before World War II. About 90 per cent of Mexico's tourist earnings, almost all the remittances from Mexican workers abroad (mostly *braceros,* employed on United States farms), and most of the capital coming into Mexico — whether as private investment or as official grants or loans — originate in the United States.

By attempting to increase trade with other nations, the Mexican government has sought to minimize any resentment that some Mexican leaders might have toward the United States as a result of the financial relationship described above. Recently, for example, an agreement was negotiated with Italy for financial assistance and technical aid. In December, 1950, the Mexican government abrogated the reciprocal trade agreement with the United States to give Mexico more freedom in setting tariff rates on imports of American goods. Likewise, the government of Mexico has avoided involvement in such organizations as GATT (General Agreement on Tariffs and Trade) in order to remain free to pursue those policies it regards as necessary to protect its own industry. Mexico has entered into trade agreements with a number of western and eastern Euro-

pean nations, as well as with Canada and various Latin American countries.

During World War II, the shortages of many goods in world trade permitted Mexican exports to Latin America to increase (mostly to neighboring countries in Central America) and to reach $36 million, or 12 per cent of the total. By 1950, however, following restored production of consumer goods, in the United States and restoration of the European economies, Mexican exports to this area fell to $25 million, 6 per cent of the total. In the same interval, imports into Mexico from Latin American countries fell from $42 million to $5 million, or from 8 per cent to 1 per cent of total imports. In 1962, Mexican exports to Latin America were slightly more than 3 per cent of the total, while imports from that region were only 1 per cent.

The Latin American free-trade area, established under the Montevideo Treaty of February, 1961, has had little time to show results. Electrical equipment plants of United States corporate affiliates in Mexico and Brazil are prepared to make much of the electrical equipment needs of Latin America, but are handicapped by the liberal credit terms available from United States and European manufacturers. It is still too early to say what the accomplishments will be of the Free Trade Association in competition with the burgeoning production of the European common market countries, but the probability is that the increase in inter-American trade will not be appreciable. Just as significant toward such growth of trade as the reduction in tariff barriers among the participating countries will be the accumulation of capital and technical accomplishments of management and labor. Nevertheless, from 1962 to 1964, Mexican trade with other LAFTA nations more than doubled.

Historically, Mexico has been quite different from most Latin American nations in its freedom from dependence upon two or three commodities as sources of foreign exchange. By a certain amount of diversification it has been able to avoid such serious effects from price fluctuations upon its exports as have been felt by some nations that are dependent on one or two products, for example, coffee or sugar. Yet, Mexico has been basically an exporter of unfinished products and minerals and an importer of manufactured goods.

In 1964, mineral exports amounted to less than 20 per cent of the total value, but agricultural commodity exports had increased more than sevenfold over the 1939 level and were equivalent to almost 52 per cent of total exports. By 1959, the volume of cotton production in Mexico was 275 per cent above 1939 and 110 per cent above 1948, and Mexico had become fourth among cotton exporting countries of the world. Between 1950 and 1959, the value of cotton exports rose 50 per cent and the volume by 150 per cent. Coffee comprised 8 per cent of exports by 1950 and 14 per cent by 1959, but by 1964 had dropped again to 8 per cent. In 1964, cotton and coffee together provided 25 per cent of Mexican exports.

In recent years, with the continuing expansion of irrigation to new and productive areas in the north, and increased investment in fisheries, tomatoes and shrimp have each assumed a more important place among Mexican exports. Sugar exports have likewise become more significant.

Contributing to the rise of Mexican exports of agricultural products have been the high prices for such export crops as cotton, coffee, and oil seeds, in contrast to the prices for crops produced for home consumption. Other factors have been the increase of irrigation and the general improvement of farming methods on newer lands.

Although zinc, lead, copper, sulphur, and oil are still among the ten leading export commodities of Mexico, as the export trade of the nation has grown, these products have comprised a steadily declining percentage of total exports. In the last decade, lead shipments declined by 50 per cent in value. Copper exports doubled in the middle of the decade, but again declined by 1959 to the level of 1950. Sales of zinc abroad have remained fairly stable, but there has been a substantial development in production and exports of sulphur in the last five years. As Mexican internal demand for oil products has grown, its shipments abroad have declined to a rather low level. Shipments of all these minerals aggregated less than 20 per cent of total exports in 1964.

Exports of manufactures, which increased fifteenfold between 1939 and 1946 and comprised 35 per cent of total exports, fell by 1950 to less than half the 1946 dollar value and to an even smaller proportion of total export trade. By 1959, manufactures represented almost 10 per cent of the total of commodity exports.

In the late 1940's and early 1950's, the salient feature of Mexico's import trade was the inflow of capital goods and the decline in imports of consumer goods and of raw and semi-processed materials. By 1950, the volume of capital goods imports had risen over 3.6 times, and the value by more than 6.5 times to more than 38 per cent of the value of imports, compared with 1943. In 1959, capital goods, consisting of unprocessed and processed raw materials and investment goods, comprised 80 per cent of Mexican imports — investment goods alone being 44 per cent of the total. Nearly 13 per cent of total imports consisted of durable consumer goods.

In general, this trend in imports is the consequence of the emphasis, in Mexican economic policy, on industrialization, on government and private investment – domestic and foreign — in power, transportation, manufacturing, and on other kinds of development requiring the importation of machinery.

Domestic Commerce

Marketing in Mexico operates simultaneously under two different systems, one close to the modern procedures of more industrialized nations, the other relatively unchanged since pre-Columbian times. Although no specific figures are available, the greater volume of goods sold in Mexico is probably handled through the older, indigenous system.

The more modern marketing structure includes chain stores, some of them affiliated with United States companies, which have developed rapidly and now account for a significant portion of the country's total sales of both durable and non-durable goods. Many large department stores exist in Mexico City and other major metropolitan areas. In recent years, these have changed swiftly from nineteenth-century facilities and practices to an approximation of present-day retailing in the United States. Self-service food markets have become accepted in the more important cities, although a far greater portion of food sold in Mexico is sold in the general markets, many of which are still operated in the open air. The small, family grocery store that was common in the United States prior to World War II is today a standard feature of Mexican retail trade.

As in other areas of the Mexican economy, cooperation is important in marketing, although not of major importance. Consumer cooperatives are widespread throughout the country and are a noticeable factor in retail trade. Even more numerous and of greater

Although canvas roofing, basket containers, and tropical fruits are still characteristic of many open-air markets operating in the interior of Mexico, the modern supermarket has come into being as well. Its varieties of canned goods and display of fresh meats in refrigerated cases reflect both the increasing demands and purchasing power of the Mexican today, and the correspondingly rapid development of retail merchandising.

significance are the many producer marketing cooperatives found in a wide variety of industries.

The government plays a substantial role in retail and wholesale trade just as it does in nearly all other areas of the Mexican economy. The government's agricultural marketing corporation, *Compañía Nacional de Subsistencia Popular* (CONASUPO), is an active retailer among the nation's working classes, not only of agricultural commodities but also of other household necessities. CONASUPO operates a chain of several hundred retail stores throughout Mexico supplying certain food items and household goods (matches, soap, etc.) to the lower income groups, primarily in the larger cities. Within the past few years, the corporation has begun the use of large vans, which serve as traveling retail stores and make regular rounds through the working-class sections of Mexico City. CONASUPO also operates in the domestic wholesale phase of Mexican marketing, serving as a bulk distributor of agricultural commodities to several hundred privately owned retail establishments throughout the country.

Government's part in Mexican marketing, however, is not limited to providing competition to privately owned retail stores or to serving as a low-cost wholesaler of farm products. The federal government imposes direct price controls on certain necessities — many foods, medicines, and worker housing. In many instances, however, particularly in the case of foods, the government-imposed price ceilings are widely violated.

Mexican trade today is adopting certain practices long customary in retail and wholesale trade in the United States. Consumer credit, formerly available only to high income persons with excellent credit rating, is becoming much more widespread, particularly in connection with the purchase of higher priced consumer durables. Interest rates, however, are very high. Trade credit is commonly used, frequently with much longer terms than are usual in the United States. Discounts for prompt payment, though occasionally offered, are generally ineffective, and the slowness with which trade accounts are settled, tying up considerable amounts of working capital, is often a serious problem for wholesalers and producers alike. Advertising is (as it is in the United States), a thoroughly accepted and widely used business practice. Generally, the advertising media used are the same, although the billboard and the poster are probably used to a greater extent and, of course, television and newspapers to a somewhat lesser extent, in Mexico than in the United States.

THE RECORD OF GROWTH

Frank Tannenbaum has remarked that Mexico was a poor country comparable to the Balkans or to India. In 1929, he states, the average annual income per inhabitant was 123 pesos, or 34 centavos per day — the equivalent of approximately 17 cents in American money. Most of the things used in the rural household were produced locally.

Following the revolution against Díaz in 1910, leaders in Mexico strove to bring the nation into the twentieth-century economy. Throughout the 1920's, multiple projects were begun, including the agrarian reform movement for redistribution of land and the framework of a nationwide transportation system. Colonization and irrigation projects were initiated, a new policy for construction of highways and feeder roads was adopted, the financial system was reorganized into a modern banking system, and improvements were made in public administration and finance.

Progress was retarded by the world economic crisis in 1929 and the subsequent economic depression. The contraction in demand for raw materials during the depression and the severe decline in their prices caused exports and general economic activity to fall. In 1931, Mexico dropped the gold standard and in the next two years undertook again the revision of its credit system with the aim of avoiding the effects of the world depression. Agrarian reform continued in the 1930's, and new labor legislation was enacted. In addition, educational reforms were carried out, particularly for the rural areas. In 1935, President Cárdenas developed a six-year plan, which aroused controversy both at home and abroad. He redistributed more than twice the land parcelled out by all previous administrators and expropriated foreign oil holdings, the latter action under the article of the Constitution declaring the government's right to mineral and other deposits below the surface of the land. Mexican government action with respect to oil contributed to a sharp reduction in foreign investment.

Prior to that time, American investment in Mexico had increased steadily, as it had elsewhere in the hemisphere. J. Fred Rippy estimated that of a total of $320 million of investment in Latin America in 1897, two-thirds was in Mexico and more than half of that was in railroads. From then until 1914, the flow of capital from the United States increased rapidly and on the eve of World War I, total United States investment in Latin America exceeded $1.6 billion, slightly more than half of which was in Mexico. Roughly one-fifth of United States Mexican investment consisted of portfolio holdings, mostly government and government-guaranteed bonds. The balance was in direct investment. Approximately $85 million were in oil wells and refineries, $202 million in mines, $110 million in railroads, and $266 million in portfolio bonds.

During World War I and the 1920's, foreign investments of the United States rose at an unprecedented rate, and by 1930 the United States had $695 million

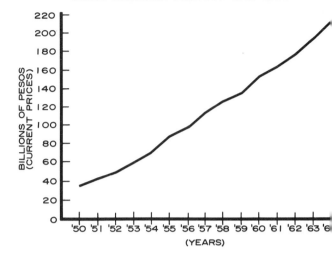

GROSS NATIONAL PRODUCT 1950-1964

of direct investment in Mexico alone. By 1943, however, this had fallen to $422 million. This decline apparently can be attributed to the depression, to growing nationalism in Mexican policy with respect to industrialization, and to increasing uncertainties in Mexican finance.

For several years before 1936, Mexican governmental finances had been fairly well balanced, and money for public works had been provided from tax revenues. The launching, in 1937, of a large-scale program of public works with central bank financing led to a sharp monetary expansion. Subsequently the federal government borrowed increasing amounts from the Bank of Mexico. Moreover, the government undertook support for a broad program of agricultural credit through new banking institutions, inducing further expansion of credit. Under pressure from the inflationary forces operating in 1938, the government devalued the peso from 3.6 to 4.85 to the dollar. In the judgment of T. C. Call, (*The Mexican Venture*, 22), Cárdenas' social and economic experiments did little actually to raise Mexican living standards. Nevertheless, his enforcement of land redistribution and reassertion of Mexican sovereignty were basic to future national development. His example of sincerity, integrity, and morality in high office and his ability to rule through a troubled period without resort to open force served to raise, it is hoped permanently, the low standards of Mexican politics.

Post-War Development

The outbreak of World War II brought to Mexico as well as to most of the countries of this hemisphere a quickening of economic development that has continued to the present day. Inability to obtain any longer the manufactures of Europe and the United States provided an unparalleled degree of protection for Mexican industry. Even under the protective Mexican tariff policy, limitations upon ability to obtain capital goods prevented growth that would otherwise have been possible; it was largely by utilizing more fully the producive facilities already existing that Mexico was able to increase its production rapidly.

Between 1940 and 1945, for example, while electric power capacity increased by 20 per cent, power generated rose by one-third. Exports doubled and imports nearly tripled in terms of dollars, the greatest growth in imports occurring in 1944 and 1945. The wholesale price index in Mexico City nearly doubled while the index of consumer prices rose by about 125 per cent. National income rose from 6.4 billion pesos to 18.6 billion, and per capita income from 325 to 338 pesos. Notwithstanding the inflation that was taking place universally, per capita income in real terms gained by nearly 33 per cent. Federal government receipts went from 500 million to 1.23 billion pesos, and the employment index rose by 40 per cent. The wartime situation enabled Mexico, like other Latin American nations (although at a slower pace) to increase its monetary reserves. While reserves of gold and foreign exchange of several South American countries multiplied several times between 1939 and 1945, those of Mexico expanded by only 16 per cent. This moderate increase of reserves reflects somewhat the fact that Mexico's terms of trade with the United States remained quite stable throughout the war years, and exports did not increase faster than imports by any significant margin. Capital movements in the form of grants did not grow appreciably during the period, and, although there was some increase of net receipts from tourist travel, the major part of such growth came after the war ended.

Although Mexico has maintained a much higher degree of stability in the value of its currency than a number of countries in South America, the purchasing power of the peso since 1940 has declined more rapidly than that of the dollar and of currencies of several neighbors to the south. The inflationary spiral, begun in 1936–1937 with deficits of the Cárdenas administration for financing public works and agricultural development, continued with increased intensity during World War II, when the wholesale price index in Mexico City doubled. Pressures, which earlier were mainly of internal origin, became external after 1940 with the influence of war demands added to those of the industrialization program.

During the war a flood of money poured into Mexico far in excess of goods and services available. Like other Latin American nations, as Mexico's exports grew, especially until 1944, exporters had more dollars to sell than importers needed for payments. Purchases of foreign exchange by the central bank increased, its reserves accumulated, and the pesos it paid for dollars flowed into the monetary stream. According to one source, the monetary reserves increased by 1.6 billion pesos, or 16 per cent, between 1939 and 1945, providing the base for a much larger expansion of bank credit. Bottlenecks extended the lag of production behind investment. Other forces causing the monetary expansion to run ahead of increase in output were transportation difficulties, labor troubles, fuel shortages,

and difficulties in importation of machinery. Between 1939 and 1945, deficit financing by the government brought cumulative debts of more than 800 million pesos, covered by the issuance of internal bonds and treasury certificates. While the Bank of Mexico began using reserve requirements in 1940 as a means of checking undue expansion of credit, these actions were rather ineffective as a curb, and monetary expansion exceeded one-half billion pesos annually through the war years. Metallic money gradually disappeared, with paper currency coming to substitute; by 1945 more than half of the total money supply was in the form of bank deposits.

After the conclusion of hostilities in 1945, with price controls removed on many commodities, with tremendous pent-up demand for consumer goods of all kinds from the United States and Europe, and with inadequate facilities to supply goods in the quantities demanded, inflation took hold more firmly in Mexico. With the exception of 1953, some slowing down in 1959 and 1961, and an actual decrease in 1963, rising prices persisted through 1965. As happened so commonly in Latin America after 1945, the Mexican inflation during the first few years of peace was accompanied by a new surge of imports and the loss of reserves behind the currency. Also, the cessation of demand by the United States for the products of Latin America for prosecuting the war, and the ability of those nations to pay for consumer goods from abroad out of accumulated foreign exchange reserves led to increasing imbalance in the foreign trade of Mexico, as well as in all Latin America. The Mexican trade deficit rose from $92 million in 1945 to $255 million in 1946. As a result of the increase of exports exceeding considerably that of imports in 1947 and a substantial decrease of imports in 1948 as well as improvements in prices of Mexican exports, the deficits diminished to $246 million in 1947 and to $133 million in 1948. The increase in tourist travel that occurred during these years failed to offset the trade deficit. The high level of the deficit on current account from 1935 through 1948 occurred, notwithstanding improvement in Mexico's

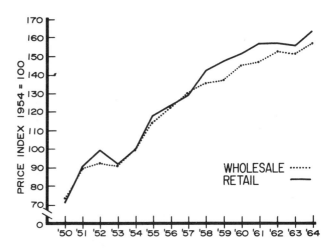

RETAIL-WHOLESALE PRICE INDEX 1950-1964

DISTRIBUTION OF MEXICAN FEDERAL REVENUES AND EXPENDITURES 1962

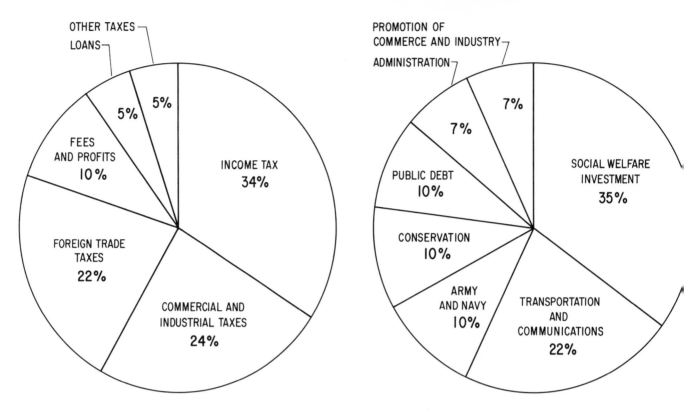

Source: MEXICO 1963: Facts, Figures, Trends, *Banco Nacional de Comercio Exterior, S.A.*

terms of trade, as the ratio of export prices to import prices rose from 100 in 1946 to 113 in 1947 and 120 in 1948.

An important factor explaining the growth of imports in 1946 and 1947 was the increase that took place in national income and in the proportion of it spent on imports. In a study made for the International Bank for Reconstruction and Development, the observation was made that a small proportion of the population of Mexico generated most of the increased demand for consumer goods. The high rate of investment and the insufficient level of voluntary savings produced a price inflation which altered the distribution of incomes in favor of the upper income class, the group having the greatest tendency to import. Moreover, as inflation developed at a faster pace in Mexico than in the industrial nations, it made imports relatively cheaper and stimulated purchases from abroad.

The rise of imports was, of course, not the consequence simply of consumer goods being purchased in larger quantities, but was also the result of the government's determination to foment industrialization in Mexico. Public works took 36 per cent of the federal budget in 1946 and 38 per cent in 1949. Investment in machinery, virtually all imported, rose rapidly after 1945, with large sums being directed to the textile industry in 1947 and 1948, and with investment in electric power nearly quadrupling between 1945 and 1947, and again doubling in 1948.

Some of the demand for foreign exchange to pay for imports of industrial equipment was met by foreign loans. To advance its industrialization program, the government tapped the United States Export-Import Bank for $54 million in 1947 and 1948. Nevertheless, the changes in foreign trade after the war brought about a significant reduction in the reserves behind the currency. The adverse balance of payments during 1946 and 1947 had totaled roughly a quarter of a billion dollars, the excess of imports over exports being nearly equal to the reserves accumulated from 1939 to 1945. From a peak of $390 million in early 1946, the Bank of Mexico's reserves fell to $42 million in the next twenty months. Despite loans of over $40 million in 1947 and $17 million in 1948 from the International Monetary Fund and the United States Stabilization Fund, reserves reached such a point that the government found it expedient in July, 1948, to set the peso free to find its own level on the foreign exchanges. From 4.85 to the dollar it fell to more than six to the dollar and in June, 1949, was given a new parity of 8.65 to the dollar.

In its effort to establish a new equilibrium and stabilize the currency, the government, in addition to the devaluation, imposed new restrictions on imports to limit the outflow of dollar exchange and to guide purchases into productive enterprise by manipulation of tariffs. It sought additional credits from international finance agencies and to provide encouragement to long-term private foreign investment. It endeavored to shift credits away from imports of consumables toward productive investment in domestic industrial enterprise and agriculture. Concurrently, the government made new efforts to stimulate the tourist business, with considerable success.

Following the devaluation and these supplementary measures, there was improvement in the balance of payments, especially after the outbreak of the fighting in Korea and the renewal of characteristic wartime demand by the United States for Mexican exports.

The resumption of the favorable balance of payments increased the nation's monetary reserves by $60 million in the second half of 1949, by $11 million in the first half of 1950, and by $100 million in the last half of 1950. Monetary expansion took place and the wholesale price index in Mexico City rose by 11 per cent between July and December of 1950. Renewed inflation brought on another building boom comparable to that of 1944–1946.

To combat the resumption of inflation, the government and the central bank again imposed some economic curbs, but without marked results. Emergency legislation in December, 1950, gave the executive direct power to control prices and the distribution of goods — an authority difficult to enforce, however, without strict rationing in the relatively unorganized markets of Mexico. He was also empowered to raise or lower tariff rates as an economic control measure. Except for loans required for industrial and agricultural operations of high priority, bank credit expansion was virtually frozen by June, 1951. The government urged greater savings upon the public, and in 1950–1951 floated an issue of savings bonds to the amount of 100 million pesos. Trust and participation certificates of *Nacional Financiera* more than doubled to 934 million pesos, and money in circulation dropped some 300 million pesos between March and July, 1951. Through 1951, the government continued a fiscal policy of budgetary surplus and reduction of the public debt.

Tariff Flexibility Gained

In its foreign trade policy, Mexico relaxed its direct restrictions on imports early in 1951, but by terminating the reciprocal trade treaty with the United States on January 1 of that year it gained flexibility enabling it to impose high tariffs, both to protect new industry and to limit non-essential imports. During the eight months ending in May, 1951, agricultural and industrial machinery and other capital goods accounted for 76 per cent of imports, as the government tried to protect itself against a shortage of such goods from the United States. It also tried to regulate exports to conserve the domestic supply and hold down prices at home. With the strengthening of its monetary reserves, the government even restored, in July, 1952, a small part of the previous devaluation of the peso by revaluing it upward from 8.65 to 8.50 to the dollar. Concurrently, it renewed the stabilization agreement with the United States Treasury, committing the latter to support the peso to the extent of $50 million if necessary. Inflation resumed in 1954 with a 10 per cent increase in price levels and a still greater increase in national

Table I

TOURIST RECEIPTS

Year	No. of Tourists	Gross Tourist Receipts (million dollars)	No. of Mexicans Abroad	Mexican Tourist Expenditures Abroad (million dollars)	Net Tourist Receipts (million dollars)
1939	139,010	30.7	N.A.	9.0	21.7
1945	164,782	60.9	N.A.	10.0	50.9
1950	390,097	162.4	N.A.	6.3	156.1
1957	711,809	591.5	N.A.	242.2	349.3
1958	735,357	541.6	46,381	237.6	304.0
1959	749,390	636.7	54,432	295.7	341.0
1960	782,028	670.4	63,610	296.8	373.6
1961	813,370	708.2	69,387	322.8	385.4
1962	917,637	788.2	N.A.	340.6	477.6

Sources: (1) International Bank for Reconstruction and Development, *The Economic Development of Mexico* (Baltimore: Johns Hopkins University Press, 1953, p. 377), cites data provided by the Department of Economic Studies of the Bank of Mexico.

(2) For 1957–1961, data from Annual Reports of the Bank of Mexico, in *Mexico, 1963*, Banco Nacional de Comercio Exterior, p. 238.

(3) For 1962, Banco Nacional de Comercio Exterior, *Comercio Exterior de Mexico*, Apr. 1963, pp. 5, 28.

income. By April, 1954, the government felt obliged to devalue the peso further and established a new exchange value at 12.5 pesos to the dollar. Since that time it has maintained a stable value at that level. Early in 1965, the International Monetary Fund elevated the Mexican peso to status as one of the world's "hard" currencies in permitting its use by other nations in multilateral transactions with the Fund. The Mexican peso thus became the first Latin American monetary unit to be so designated.

While the peso had been constant on the foreign exchanges since 1954, prices have continued to go up within the country. Between 1950 and the end of the decade, the wholesale price index in the capital rose by 80 per cent and the cost of living index by 110 per cent. In the United States, on the other hand, wholesale prices rose by only 16 per cent during the decade, and consumer prices rose in the same limited range. The Mexican inflation, however, has been rather modest in comparison with those of Argentina, Chile, Brazil, Bolivia, and Paraguay. National income and value of product kept rising at an even faster rate, moreover, with the result that per capita income at the end of the decade was more than double that of 1950 and per capita real income was approximately 12 per cent higher. The annual rate of growth in real terms was substantially above that of most other nations in the hemisphere.

Following the devaluation in 1954, monetary reserves again increased for two years and have held quite steady since 1956, rising by 862 million pesos in 1959, falling by 820 million in 1960, and increasing again in 1961. An important factor in explaining the favorable position with respect to reserves and the recent stability of the peso has been the substantial growth of tourist receipts. Between 1950 and 1959, the number of visitors to Mexico rose by 92 per cent, the increase being steady except for a slight reversal in 1953-54. Tourist expenditures increased from $162 million to $637 million, interrupted only slightly in 1958. Net revenues from tourist and border transactions in 1959, amounting to $341 million, exceeded by $57 million the entire trade deficit. The vast majority of these tourists were from the United States — the principal source of Mexico's imports — and their numbers reflect the rapid growth of personal incomes and prolonged high level of employment in the United States, as well as the increased opportunity for comfortable traveling over new roads in Mexico, the construction of new hotels and motels, and the greater efforts of the Mexican Tourist Bureau to attract more travelers.

Since 1955 and particularly since 1958, the inflationary trend has been very moderate. The increase that has occurred in the monetary circulation appears to have approximated the needs of a growing nation, and the economy, while expanding, has been free of economic pressures on the exchange value of the peso that were so prevalent in preceding decades. New investment and rising employment have brought forth a continuing expansion of goods and services and improvement of per capita income and individual well-being. Even though this improvement may not be affecting all areas and individuals equally, as population and national income have grown, the domestic market for increased industrial products has broadened, permitting more efficient levels of operation and promising continuing economic improvement.

The emphasis on industrialization, which became particularly pronounced in the administration of Ávila Camacho and which was continued by Miguel Alemán and his successors, Ruiz Cortines, López Mateos, and Díaz Ordaz, appears to be bringing favorable results. In the view of these men and many other Mexican leaders, Mexico faces a constantly increasing need for industrial job opportunities to support a growing population and to permit higher income levels than usually prevail in an agricultural economy. Mexico has considered itself to be at a disadvantage in relying so heavily upon agricultural and mineral production for exports, because these products are subject to the mercy of economic fluctuations abroad, especially in the United States, and feel the impact much more heavily of varying world prices. By achieving better balance between manufacturing on the one hand and agriculture on the other, Mexico could be expected to withstand better the dislocations in world trade that have accompanied war, depression, and inflation. Only through industrialization have many Mexican leaders considered it possible to raise national income to the point necessary to supply the nation's capital requirements for public works, health, and education, since the possibility of expanding mineral and agricultural production is limited. As in most of the developing countries, controversy in Mexico is not centered upon industrialization *per se,* but on its speed and direction.

Progress Better Balanced

While the problem of increasing production and consumption at a faster rate than the increase in population is a real one that will continue to require attention in the years ahead, and, although per capita income is still low (4,530 pesos in 1963 or $362 at the rate of 12.5 pesos per dollar), the government, through its fiscal and other policies aimed at industrial development, has contributed to the improvement recorded to date and to the basis for future economic growth. While its policies have added directly at various times to the difficulties of the peso in the foreign exchange markets, it would appear to have attained somewhat better balance in its progress in recent years. Furthermore, while Tannenbaum in his *Mexico, The Struggle for Bread and Peace,* presents a gloomy outlook based on the ratio of a growing population to limited physical resources, development since 1954 in Mexico gives reason to believe that future progress can and will occur. One can be like Malthus and have forebodings of the future, but account should be taken of the ingenuity of man in overcoming the obstacles of his environment.

FINANCE

Monetary and Banking System

Mexican coinage and currency are issued under law by the Bank of Mexico, the nation's central bank. Reserves behind the currency are required to equal 25 per cent of the bank notes and other demand liabilities of the central bank, with at least 80 per cent of it in the form of gold and foreign exchange and the remaining 20 per cent in coined or barred silver. For many years the peso has been freely convertible on the foreign exchanges, with the current par value of 12.50 pesos per dollar established in 1954. The Bank of Mexico has the exclusive right of note issue, as well as of ordering new coinage and of regulating the circulation of the currency. It also regulates the circulation of foreign exchange and operates as a central bank and clearing house for associated institutions, establishes and manages the reserves of member banks, and acts as fiscal agent for the federal government in dealing with international agencies.

The Bank of Mexico and the Ministry of Finance and Public Credit are the monetary authorities. They direct monetary policy, handle the public debt commitments of the federal and district governments, and exercise jurisdiction over operations involving the use of public credit.

Bank credit is handled by two types of institutions, the private banking system and government credit institutions. Privately owned banks include commercial, savings, trust, mortgage, capitalization and investment banks, all operating in accordance with carefully defined legislation and under the supervision and control of the Bank of Mexico and the National Banking Commission. The latter, created in December, 1924, by federal executive decree, acts as an agency of the Ministry of Finance and Public Credit and has the function of inspecting and exercising vigilance over all operations of national or private credit institutions to insure compliance with existing legal requirements. In 1961, there were approximately 2,954 banks and branches operating in Mexico.

Of fourteen national credit institutions, the most important are the Bank of Mexico, *Nacional Financiera, Banco Nacional de Comercio Exterior, Banco Nacional de Crédito Agrícola y Ganadero, Banco Nacional de Crédito Ejidal,* and the *Banco Nacional Hipotecario Urbano y de Obras Públicas. Nacional Financiera,* created in 1933, regulates the national securities and longterm credit market, acts as the federal government's agent and advisor for public debt issues and transactions, negotiates and manages loans from foreign institutions, whether governmental or private, and provides institutional support for investment firms. In practice its resources have been directed toward creating and strengthening basic enterprise in the national economy and toward promoting industrialization.

The principal purpose of the *Banco Nacional de Comercio Exterior* is to finance Mexican foreign trade and promote exports. It supports government programs aimed at increasing production of agricultural goods and livestock for export and for replacement of imports, and supports financially official agencies charged with maintaining minimum prices on certain agricultural products or price ceilings on consumption goods. The bank promotes diversification of foreign trade with respect to products, markets, and sources of supply, and prepares compensation or barter agreements with other nations. It also assists in controlling imports.

The *Banco Nacional de Crédito Agrícola y Ganadero* was established in 1926, with the primary function of granting commercial crop-secured or equipment loans to small and medium farmers organized in local agricultural credit associations. The *Banco Nacional de Crédito Ejidal* was founded in 1936 as part of the agricultural credit system to promote communal farm production by granting credit to local communal farm associations. The *Banco Nacional Hipotecario Urbano y de Obras Públicas* was created in 1933, to promote public housing, works, and services.

Combined assets of all types of banking institutions increased between 1955 and 1959 from approximately 26 billion pesos to 42 billion pesos, but the assets of the private banks remained approximately constant at about 50 per cent of the total, the rest being divided between the Bank of Mexico and the national credit institutions.

Bank credit in Mexico is still expensive as compared with the United States. Not long ago average rates on loans registered with the National Banking Commission ranged from 8 to 12 per cent, with farm crop loans at the lower part of the range and mortgage loans at the higher figure. These rates may be moderate in relation to many other Latin American countries, but remain characteristic of a nation that is short on credit and capital accumulation with respect to the demands of all kinds of businesses and consumers.

Public Finance

Since the end of World War II the Mexican government has operated most of the time at a deficit, although in many years the difference between receipts and expenditures was small. Overall expenditures rose nearly eight-fold between 1939 and 1951, and in the last ten years again more than doubled. Receipts increased nearly seven times in the earlier period and nearly tripled in the last decade. After 1939, in which a small surplus was reported, outlays increased faster than revenues and, in terms of fixed prices at the 1939 level, doubled, whereas receipts grew by only 80 per cent up to 1951. The growth of the nation, with increased efforts by the government to foster economic development and to provide for the greater need for social services, explains in large part the rise of the budgetary level.

From 1940 to 1945, the entire deficit was financed by domestic credit, mainly from the Bank of Mexico. During 1945–1948, on the other hand, new external loans, principally from the Export-Import Bank of the United States, equalled indemnities and amortization of the foreign debt, and, in addition, financed nearly 20 per cent of the public deficit. In 1949–1951, grants from the United States Government for the eradication of foot-and-mouth disease in cattle, together with loans from the Export-Import Bank and the International Bank for Reconstruction and Development, raised the share of foreign financing of the deficit to over 50 per cent.

In some years the budgetary deficit undoubtedly exercised an inflationary influence, but to a considerable extent the growth of national production required expansion in the monetary system. It may be said, therefore, that the frequent existence of deficits contributed to the maintenance of growth, and that the rising national product would have constituted a deflationary force but for the existence of deficit financing. Substantial deficits in 1947 and 1948 — 204 million and 305 million pesos respectively — undoubtedly contributed to inflation in those years and to the need for devaluation of the peso in June, 1949.

The distribution of federal disbursements offers an interesting contrast with that of the United States and of other Latin American nations. A surprisingly moderate amount of federal government expenditures in 1960, approximately 11 per cent, was allocated to the army and navy. Thirty per cent, on the other hand, went for social welfare and 25 per cent for investment in communications and transportation. Agricultural and livestock development absorbed 11 per cent, industrial and commercial promotion 7 per cent, and only 8 per cent applied against the public debt. Administrative costs took the remaining 8 per cent.

The Mexican public debt is relatively a moderate one. At the end of 1959 it totaled $650 million, of which $93 million was funded and $555 million represented non-funded obligations. Most of the funded debt arose from commitments contracted between 1886 and 1913, and were the subject of the 1942 and 1946 agreements between the Mexican Government and the International Committee of Bankers. In May, 1960, notwithstanding much later maturities, the government decided to redeem the major portion of these debts.

Like other nations in the hemisphere, Mexico's history has been marked by defaults on its obligations, with the entire debt defaulted in 1914 and remaining so until 1942, in the case of the government debt and until 1946, in the case of the railroad debt. Between 1946 and 1950, loans of the United States Export-Import Bank to Mexico totaled 115 million pesos and from 1947 to 1952 external financing from all sources increased considerably.

Since 1949, foreign loans have been negotiated with the United States Export-Import Bank and with various international lending agencies. Beginning in 1949, the International Bank for Reconstruction and Development made a series of eight loans to Mexico, totaling $245 million, primarily for the development of power ($125 million), for railroads ($61 million), and for roads and irrigation. In October, 1960, the Bank lent $25 million through *Nacional Financiera* to enable the government to construct or reconstruct two thousand miles of the most important roads in Mexico. In its program for 1960–1964, the government aimed to construct or reconstruct about 8,700 miles of highways with needs for foreign exchange costs provided by the International Bank for Reconstruction and Development loan.

In January, 1961, a loan of $15 million was made to *Nacional Financiera* to allow the government to carry out the completion and rehabilitation of four irrigation districts suffering from faulty drainage, involving 1,438,000 acres near the Gulf of California. In these ways international lending is contributing significantly to the development of the nation. Products from irrigated land now represent more than one-third of the total value of agricultural products and nearly one-third of total commodity exports. The loan for highways, railroads, and power all make possible the continued increase of national production.

Although federal revenues climbed from approximately 2.3 billion pesos in 1950 to 8.7 billion in 1959, and total fiscal revenues of government in Mexico from five billion to twelve billion pesos, the burden of taxes as represented by the relationship between them and gross national product has remained fairly steady at around 10–12 per cent. This is a relatively low tax level by today's standards in industrial countries.

During the past two decades there have been improvements made in the tax structure, which provide more equitable treatment among the people of the nation. While only 30 per cent of revenues came from direct taxes in 1939, nearly 50 per cent came from such tax sources in 1951 and about the same percentage in 1959. The income tax has assumed increasing importance, providing 30 per cent of total revenues in 1951 and fluctuating slightly above and below that percentage ever since. Indirect taxes, in contrast, decreased correspondingly in their relative importance to the fiscal system, from 67 per cent in 1939–1941 to slightly less than 50 per cent by 1951. Import duties, which approximated 20 per cent of total governmental revenues in 1939–1941, furnished only 13 per cent of the total ten years later. Although sales and consumption taxes rose from 9.5 per cent to about 13.5 per cent, industrial excise taxes fell from 17 per cent to 5 per cent of total receipts in this period. As a consequence, Mexico appears to have taken the lead in Latin America in introducing greater reliance in its tax system upon the principle of ability to pay and to have anticipated reform principles of the Alliance for Progress.

LABOR

The Labor Force

In 1960, Mexico's economically active population (labor force) numbered slightly under twelve million, almost 34 per cent of the country's total population of 35 million. In the United States that year, the labor force comprised more than 40 per cent of the total population. Although the percentage of Mexico's total population included in the labor force is low compared with the United States and the countries of Western Europe, it is comparable with that of other Latin American nations, and it has shown some increase over the previous ten years. In 1950, the economically active population represented only 32 per cent of the total Mexican populace. The relatively low Mexican percentage is generally attributed to the high proportion of children in the population and to the traditional resistance of women working outside the home, which keeps the number of women in the work force much lower than in the United States.

Another significant difference between the labor force of Mexico and that of the United States is that the proportion of wage and salary workers is only about half in Mexico what it is in the United States. In 1960, only 46 per cent of the economically active population in Mexico were employed on a wage or salary basis, while about 80 per cent of the labor force in the United States were so employed. In Mexico, a little over 40 per cent of the economically active population were considered to be self-employed, a classification that apparently disguises much unemployment and underemployment. Employers comprised about one per cent of the economically active population, and about 12 per cent were unpaid family workers. In the United States in 1960 less than one per cent of the labor force were classed as unpaid family workers, the much higher Mexican percentage being chiefly a reflection of the greater importance of agriculture and small handicraft shops in the Mexican economy.

Mexico's total population is concentrated regionally and so, of course, is the economically active population. Approximately half of the nation's entire labor force is found in the central valley with another fifth living in the northern border states. About half of all of the nation's people are found in rural areas, and, as mentioned previously, about 55 per cent of the economically active population are engaged in agriculture, forestry, or fishing. Only about 17 per cent, however, are engaged in what could be called industrial enterprises, i.e., manufacturing, mining, construction, and electric power production. In the United States more than 27 per cent of the labor force is so engaged.

Despite the view often held of Mexico as a land where personal servants are numerous and government employees are legion, the part of the labor force employed in service occupations, including government, in Mexico is only 13 per cent, while in the United States it is over 20 per cent. The percentages of the economically active population of Mexico devoted to transportation and communications and to commerce are also somewhat different than in the United States. In Mexico, transportation and communications account for about 3 per cent of the labor force; in the United States they account for about 5 per cent. In Mexico, finance and trade occupy only 9 per cent of the economically active population; in the United States the percentage is over 19.

A difference in the composition of the United States and Mexican labor forces that is often noted, but which is actually more apparent than real, is the percentage unemployed. Latest available figures for the economically active population of Mexico show an unemployment rate of only 1 per cent, while figures for the same period show the United States with an unemployment rate of almost 5 per cent. However, the same figures for Mexico list fully 4 per cent of the labor force as being in "unspecified" occupations, and there are other reasons, which will be discussed later, to question the 1 per cent unemployment figure.

The Mexican labor force has a number of characteristics typical of emergent and rapidly developing nations. There are shortages of skilled workers and technical personnel, although both public and private facilities exist for vocational and technical training. For skilled laborers there are no general and well-organized apprentice training programs. A large number of firms, particularly the industrial companies, however, do have on-the-job training programs. Although schooling is compulsory in Mexico up to the age of fourteen, the

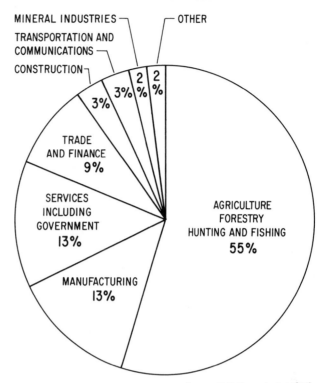

EMPLOYMENT OF THE ECONOMICALLY ACTIVE POPULATION 1960

Source: 1960 Censo de Población

requirement is only nominal in many areas. Approximately 43 per cent of the population over fourteen years of age are illiterate, and this lack of educational background makes difficult, if not impossible, the absorption of advanced vocational training.

There are few reliable statistics available on the productivity of Mexican labor. It is generally thought to be considerably lower than that of comparable labor in the United States, but it should be remembered that this is a generality and exceptions are numerous. The reasons for the lower productivity of Mexican labor, where it is lower, are usually inadequate training and antiquated methods of production. Ill health, excessive absenteeism, and over-staffing are also common causes of the comparatively low productivity of a large portion of the country's workers. As has been noted elsewhere, productivity in agriculture is extremely low, even when compared to other Latin American countries with similar labor force characteristics. Of course, this is not all due to the nature of the labor force but also to soil and climatic conditions. The productivity of Mexican labor is also very low in clothing manufacture, food processing, and construction. In the more highly mechanized industries, however, where equipment and methods are similar to those used in the more industrialized nations, productivity is similar or higher.

Employment and Income

Unemployment in Mexico in 1960 was only one per cent of the economically active population. It should be noted, however, that the Mexican statistical definition of unemployed differs markedly from the United States definition. While in the United States, those who have been without work for at least one week and are actively seeking employment are counted as unemployed, the Mexican statistics consider only those who have been without work for at least thirteen weeks, and no figures are available for those jobless for less than three months.

Although long-term, complete unemployment only affects one per cent of the Mexican labor force and is not considered a pressing problem, disguised unemployment and underemployment are greater and are believed to be a serious problem by responsible Mexican authorities. Undoubtedly many of the 41 per cent of the economically active population that were classified as self-employed in 1960 were in reality underemployed or temporarily unemployed. Disguised unemployment through overstaffing and underemployment are also prevalent in a great many industries, and notably in agriculture.

With employee turnover relatively low and most of the labor force relatively immobile, Mexican labor markets have developed on a very informal basis, with the possible exception of the Monterrey area. Most workers gain employment by personal initiative through friends and relatives, or through their union. There are no effective government employment services, and private agencies are not widely used. The federal government does operate an employment service of sorts, but it is mainly concerned with agricultural labor, including *braceros* hired for work in the United States, and the resettlement of rural workers.

Promotions in Mexican business enterprises are based largely on seniority or family. The latter is particularly true for managerial personnel, since most Mexican business firms are still family owned and managed. If promotion is difficult in a Mexican firm, dismissal is even more difficult. Legal requirements for justifying discharges are strictly defined and the burden of proof of sufficient cause for dismissal is often quite heavy. Dismissal benefits to discharged workers are extremely high, so high, in fact, that they have for the most part eliminated any pressing need for unemployment insurance. Labor turnover is generally low and the government at present has no formal program of unemployment insurance, although one is being considered.

Wages and salaries in Mexico vary considerably between industries, between areas, and between companies. Even within a given firm there may be considerable variation in compensation to persons doing more or less equivalent jobs. On the average, however, the wages for skilled crafts, technical work, and the more responsible clerical jobs are about double the wages paid for unskilled labor. In 1960, average monthly earnings in manufacturing were 849 pesos (US$68), and by the first quarter of the following year this had risen to 880 pesos (US$70). These are overall averages, however. Differences between different manufacturing industries are often quite marked. In 1960, average earnings in manufacturing industries varied from about 390 pesos per month (US$31) in the food processing industry to 1,300 pesos (US$104) per month in the rubber goods industry. Even higher average wages were paid in petroleum, mining, and by the railroads.

Mexico has a system of legal minimum wages which are established every two years in each state by the state's Central Board of Arbitration and Conciliation. Early in 1962, the Board of the Federal District set the minimum wages in that area at 17.50 pesos (US$1.40) per day for urban workers and 17.00 pesos ($1.36) per day for rural workers. In practice, actual wages paid by employers are well above the legal minimum, although in many outlying areas, skilled craftsmen may work for the equivalent of two dollars a day and common laborers for as little as a dollar and a quarter a day.

Fringe benefits have become extremely important in the compensation of Mexican workers as they have in most of the countries of Latin America. The benefits often represent a considerable labor cost to the employer over and above direct wage payments. Such benefits obtained as the result of collective bargaining vary widely, and most often result in a highly paternalistic relationship between employer and workers. Some of the more commonly obtained benefits include low-cost food, low-cost housing, free medical care, subsidized transportation, free recreational and educational facilities, retirement benefits, and bonuses for various reasons, ranging from increased efficiency to getting married.

In addition to an extensive system of fringe benefits obtained by collective bargaining, Mexico has an elaborate social insurance program providing benefits to both workers and their dependents. Administered by the *Instituto Mexicano de Seguro Social,* the program is supported by contributions from employers (5 per cent of payroll), workers, and the federal government. Provisions are made for compensation to workers and their dependents for industrial accidents and disease, old age, sickness, disability, maternity, forced retirement, and death. Coverage is far from complete, however, for in 1960 only about 7 per cent of the population were eligible for benefits and most of these were in urban areas. There is a special social security program for government workers, administered by a separate agency. This provides principally the same benefits as the general program, plus making low-cost housing and credit available at relatively low interest rates.

Working conditions for Mexican labor, besides being the subject of collective bargaining agreements, are minutely prescribed by law for both organized and unorganized workers. Standards which have been set up in detail under federal law involve age of employment (no one under twelve years old), hours (the eight-hour day and the 48-hour week are the legal standards), holidays (one day off with pay for every six days worked, plus a number of legal national holidays), vacations, the employment of women, safety and hygiene, and provision of primary educational facilities.

With inflation in Mexico relatively mild compared to the rest of Latin America, real incomes as well as money incomes have risen over the past decade. For the year 1960, per capita national income in Mexico was 3,474 pesos (US$278), which in real terms was about 12 per cent higher than the 1950 figure. Furthermore, rents, interests, and profits are a far greater factor in Mexican national income than in the national income of more industrialized nations. In 1960, the proportion of national income in Mexico attributable to wages and salaries was only about 30 per cent, while in the United States that year more than twice that percentage of national income was composed of wages and salaries.

Although the term "real income" has been used above, actual determinations of changes in real income for Mexico are difficult, because of a serious lack of reliable data on changes in the cost of living. The only currently available measure of the cost of living in Mexico is an index of the cost of a limited number of items of worker consumption in Mexico City. This so-called general index covers food, household goods, and clothing, weighted on the basis of 1939 consumption patterns. Many of the items included in the index are subject to officially controlled prices, but presumably a large volume of these goods is sold at prices above the ceiling. In addition, the index omits many manufactured items that have become common consumer expenditures since 1939. This general index has risen by about 50 per cent since 1954. The special index of food items alone has also risen by about half since 1954.

Industrial Relations

Since its beginnings in the nineteenth century, the Mexican labor movement has had a strong political orientation, a tendency which still exists. The nation's first real labor union was formed by railroad workers in Laredo in 1887, but organized labor in Mexico has achieved its greatest growth since the Revolution of 1910, with strong participation in and assistance from the government.

The country's first national labor federation of any consequence was the *Casa del Obrero Mundial* (House of the Workers of the World), an anarcho-syndicalist group formed in 1912. This organization, similar in many ways to the I.W.W., existing in the United States at that time, was displaced from prominence in Mexican labor in 1918 by the formation of the *Confederación Regional Obrera Mexicana* (Mexican Regional Labor Federation, CROM). In the early 1920's a faction of the CROM disassociated itself from the parent body and formed the *Confederación General de Trabajadores* (General Federation of Workers, CGT), but the older organization continued to dominate the labor movement until the 1930's.

In 1936 the *Confederación de Trabajadores de México* (Federation of Workers of Mexico, CTM), was formed in competition with the already existing federations, CROM and CGT, and soon became the leading national labor organization. Originally under communist influence, control of CTM was seized by non-communists in 1941, and the federation has remained non-communist although leftward-leaning ever since. Today, CTM is Mexico's largest labor federation with member unions representing workers in a variety of manufacturing industries and construction, transportation, and service enterprises. Total membership in CTM's unions is estimated at about one and a half million, or 35 per cent of the non-agricultural work force.

The two older labor federations, CROM and CGT, have retained only a portion of their former prominence. Today, the unions that form the *Confederación Regional Obrera Mexicana* are estimated to represent only about 5 per cent of the non-agricultural labor force, and the *Confederación General de Trabajadores* represents even less. The membership of both federations is concentrated in only a few regions and industries, and the influence of the CGT is confined almost entirely to Mexico City.

Mexico's second most important labor federation at present is the *Federación de Sindicatos de Trabajadores al Servicio del Estado* (literally, Federation of Unions of Workers in the Service of the State, FSTSE), an independent federation of twenty-five national unions representing employees in various departments of the government. Total membership in FSTSE unions is estimated at about 6 per cent of the non-agricultural labor force.

In 1949, these four federations – CTM, CROM, CGT, and FSTSE – formed the *Bloque de Unidad Obrera* (Labor Unity Block, BUO) in an attempt to unite non-communist segments of the labor movement. Most of Mexico's major independent unions are also participants in this extremely loose confederation.

In addition to the federations mentioned, three other small federations exist in the Mexican labor movement. All three either are avowedly communist or considered as communist dominated. Their membership comes mostly from agriculture and the basic manufacturing industries processing agricultural products. As in the United States, there are also a number of large independent unions in Mexico. The more important of these are found among the railroad workers and in the mining and metal working industries. There are also a few smaller communist-affiliated independent unions, chiefly among the country's electrical workers.

A high percentage of Mexico's industrial labor force and most government employees are organized. Those unorganized are chiefly, as in most other countries, among the retail trade, service, and farm workers. Most Mexican unions are *sindicatos* or industrial unions organized on a plant-wide basis. Craft unions or *gremiales*, although permitted by law, are few. With the exception of those independents noted above, most of the *sindicatos* are organized into national unions, as well as state or district federations, which in turn are organized into one of the national federations mentioned, four of which are now loosely associated in the Labor Unity Block. A notable exception to this hierarchy is the labor movement in the traditionally conservative Monterrey area. Many unions in "Mexico's Pittsburgh" have remained independent of national affiliation but have federated on a local basis in close association with the Monterrey Chamber of Commerce and the local association of employers.

Collective bargaining has long been recognized in Mexico, and the government's part in it is also of long standing. In bargaining for determination of contract terms, the government can, if two-thirds of the employers in an industry arrive at common terms with their employees' representatives, declare those same terms to be valid and binding on the rest of the employers in that industry. In the administration of collective bargaining agreements, the government maintains a system of boards of conciliation and arbitration, which function simultaneously as labor courts. For employers, submission of grievances to these tripartite government boards is mandatory if the workers involved so request. For workers, submission of disputes to the boards is voluntary. The detailed and expressly required procedures involved in using the labor courts, however, have led both labor and management in recent years to turn to the use of the separate mediation service established by the Federal Ministry of Labor.

The closed shop is legal in Mexico and is the prevalent contract arrangement. Lockouts are prohibited and certain types of strikes are illegal. The major difference between a legal and an illegal strike apparently lies in the procedure followed by the union before calling the strike, and depends primarily on the opinion of the Board of Conciliation and Arbitration, which rules on the legality of walkouts. The difference for the workers and employers involved is not merely procedural, however. By law strikers receive pay for the time they are out in a legal strike but need not be paid for the time they lose in an illegal shutdown. An exception to this practice is the sympathy strike, which, though legal, does not entitle the striker to receive pay for time off the job.

LOOKING FORWARD

Switzerland, Denmark, and other European countries have demonstrated the possibility of attaining a rather comfortable living standard with little poverty, even without rich natural resources. Closer to home, Puerto Rico made great economic progress since World War II.

Fundamental economic factors needed for expanded production are transportation, electric and other forms of power, and communications. In Mexico, the development of these resources presents financial hazards for the peso and the entire economy if imbalance in planned progress occurs as a result of excessive concentration on industrialization at the expense of the other economic sectors. In 1950, S. A. Mosk *(Industrial Revolution in Mexico, 310)* stated:

In some degree the industrialization process i bound to be painful. Economic and social dislocations cannot be prevented. But a modest amoun of planning by the government, to give direction to the process and to keep the rate of industrial development in line with other branches of the economy, and especially with the capacity of the market to absorb manufactured goods, will keep the pains of readjustment at a minimum. Such planning, of course, cannot be infallible. Errors of judgment will be made. But the greater error would be for the government to refrain from mapping out a broad program of economic development leaving the industrial fate of the country entirely to the decisions of private firms.

In essence, Mosk's statement remains true today There must be balance in the growth of the Mexican economy if severe dislocations are to be avoided. The government will have to channel public investmen funds into developments which would ordinarily have little appeal to private enterprise or for which private funds would not be adequate. In its fiscal policy, however, the government needs to avoid discouragement of private investment. What constitutes suitable areas of investment for private and public funds will differ in Mexico and other nations from those in the United States, but investment funds from both sources are needed if the desired rate of development is to be realized. If Mexico can maintain political stability judiciously combine state and private investment, and promote understanding of technology and business, one can reasonably expect continuing economic development of the nation, increased benefits for its people and growing importance in the world economy.

BIBLIOGRAPHY

Banco Nacional de Comercio Exterior. *Comercio Exterior de México,* monthly. Mexico, D.F.:
_____. *Mexico, 1963.* Mexico, D.F.: 1963.

Banco Nacional de Mexico, S.A., *Review of the Economic Situation in Mexico,* monthly. Mexico, D.F

Bank of Mexico, *Annual Report.* Mexico, D.F.:

Blanco, Gonzalo. *Agriculture in Mexico.* Washington D.C.: Pan American Union, 1950.

Call, Tomme Clark. *The Mexican Venture; from Political to Industrial Revolution in Mexico.* N. Y. Oxford University Press, 1953.

Cavers, David F., and James R. Neelson. *Electric Power Regulation in Latin America.* Baltimore: Johns Hopkins Press, 1959.

Center of Latin America Studies. *Statistical Abstract of Latin America.* Los Angeles, California: UCLA 1961.

CLARK, MARJORIE R. *Organized Labor in Mexico.* Chapel Hill: University of North Carolina Press, 1934.

COMBINED MEXICAN WORKING PARTY. *The Economic Development of Mexico.* Baltimore: published for the International Bank for Reconstruction and Development by the Johns Hopkins Press, 1953.

DIRRECCION GENERAL DE ESTADISTICA SECRETARIA DE INDUSTRIA Y COMERCIO. *Revista de Estadística.* Mexico, D.F.:

DUNBAUGH, FRANK N. *Marketing in Latin America.* New York: Printer's Ink Book Co., 1960.

INTERNATIONAL BANK FOR RECONSTRUCTION AND DEVELOPMENT. *Annual Report,* 1946 to date. Washington, D.C.

INTERNATIONAL BANK FOR RECONSTRUCTION AND DEVELOPMENT AND THE INTERNATIONAL DEVELOPMENT ASSOCIATION. *The World Bank and the IDA in the Americas.* Washington, D. C.: 1962.

INTERNATIONAL LABOR OFFICE. *The Landless Farmer in Latin America.* Geneva: 1954.

_____. *Minimum Wages in Latin America.* Geneva: 1934.

_____. *Yearbook of Labour Statistics.* Geneva: 1964.

INTERNATIONAL MONETARY FUND. *Annual Report.* Washington, D. C.:

_____. *International Financial Statistics,* monthly. Washington, D. C.:

JAFFE, ABRAHAM J. *People, Jobs and Economic Development; a case history of Puerto Rico, supplemented by recent Mexican experiences.* Glencoe, Illinois: Free Press, 1959.

MOSK, SANFORD. *Industrial Revolution in Mexico.* Berkeley: University of California Press, 1950.

PAN AMERICAN UNION. *Mexico.* Washington, D. C.: 1957.

POBLETE TRONCOSO, MOISES AND BEN G. BURNETT. *The Rise of the Latin American Labor Movement.* New York: Bookman Associates, 1969.

RIPPY, JAMES FRED. *Globe and Hemisphere.* Latin America's Place in the Post War Foreign Relations of the United States. Chicago: H. Regnery Co., 1958.

RYAN, JOHN MORRIS. *Handbook for the Foreign Investor in Mexico.* Mexico, D.F.: 1961.

SILVA HERZOG, JESUS. *El agrarismo mexicano y la reforma agraria. Fondo de Cultura Económica.* Mexico, D.F.: 1959.

TANNENBAUM, FRANK. *Mexico, The Struggle for Peace and Bread.* New York: Knopf, 1956.

UNITED NATIONS. *Monthly Bulletin of Statistics.* New York:

_____. *Statistical Yearbook.* New York: 1948-1964.

UNITED STATES DEPARTMENT OF COMMERCE, BUREAU OF INTERNATIONAL COMMERCE. *Basic Data on the Economy of Mexico.* Washington, D. C.: 1964.

UNITED STATES DEPARTMENT OF COMMERCE, WORLD TRADE INFORMATION SERVICE. *Civil Aviation in Mexico.* Washington, D. C.: 1957.

_____. *Market Indicators for Latin American Republics.* Washington, D. C.: 1962.

UNITED STATES DEPARTMENT OF LABOR. *Labor in Mexico.* Washington, D. C., 1963.

_____. *Labor Developments Abroad,* monthly. Washington, D.C.:

Choreographers of the dance for the Ballet Folklórico have returned to the wellsprings of Mexico's Indian past for many of the ballet sequences performed by the company. The versatile troupe is in great demand at the Palacio de Bellas Artes in Mexico City, and on international tours.

— *Courtesy S. Hurok*

Mexico is in my songs.
Most cruel sweet is she,
All hearts she does transform
To rounded drops of honey.

And one day you will know her,
Friends of another land:
Her colors are of gladness,
Her taste is bitter-sweet.

— *Jaime Torres Bodet*

The Legacy of Literature and Art | RENATO ROSALDO

MEXICO IS AT ONCE blessed with a wealth of literature and beset with a continuing critical dispute as to when that literature actually began. There are critics who insist that it started with the arrival of the Conquistadores in 1519; others who would postpone the beginning of literature until the renaissance of Modernism toward the end of the nineteenth century. In the view of a third group, literature in Mexico can scarcely be judged apart from the abundance of pre-Conquest material. This seems a telling point, considering the depth and breadth of Indian cultures before the coming of the Spaniards.

PRE-COLUMBIAN LITERATURE

There were three major groups that could have participated in Mexican literary development: the Toltecs, the Mayas, and the Aztecs. The Toltecs who left such magnificent representations of art in many sections of Mexico, were studied by Fernando de Alva Ixtlilxóchitl. Descendant of the kings of Texcoco, Ixtlilxóchitl was a *mestizo* who finished his Chichimec history about 1648. One feels that a group as civilized as the Toltecs would have left literature for posterity; and in these terms one hopes that more information may some day come to light about Toltec literature as such.

Most civilized of Indian groups in the Americas — the Mayas — have left a written legacy of which the paramount work is the *Popol Vuh*, or the *Book of the Counsel*. This book by an unknown Quiché Indian was written in the Quiché language with Latin characters, about 1554. Father Francisco Ximénez discovered the manuscripts and translated it into Spanish in 1701. The padre was acquainted with the language, having lived among that tribe for many years. Often miscalled the "Maya Bible," the *Popol-Vuh* includes history, mythology, tradition, fable, and the story of migrations, and has been translated into French, German, and English. The first part deals principally with the origin of the world and the creation of man, and depicts also the constant struggle between good and evil as expressed by the many different gods of the Mayas. Symbolism and religiousness are the two main characteristics. In lofty language, its depth and wisdom make it comparable to the great books of other civilizations, such as the Scandinavian sagas, and the Hindu primitive epics. Parallelism, repetition, and eloquence are frequently used, as they are in our Bible. The noble tone of the work may be judged from its very beginning:

This is a tale of how everything was in suspense, everything calm, and silent, everything motionless, quiet and empty the extension of the sky. This is the first narrative, the first speech, there was not a man yet, not an animal, birds, fish, crabs, trees, stones, caves, ravines, weeds nor forests: only the sky existed. The face of the earth was not manifest. Only the quiet sea and sky in all its extension existed. There was nothing together, that might make noise, nor anything that moved, nor anything that agitated, nor anything that made noise in the sky. There was nothing standing; only the water in repose, the peaceful sea, alone and tranquil, there was nothing endowed with existence.

The *Popol-Vuh* is, thus, a veritable encyclopedia of Maya religion and thought. Its complete and full significance is yet to be deciphered.

The Mayas also left us the *Books of Chilam Balam* which are among the most important parts of American indigenous literature. Composed after the Conquest, these sacred books deal with religious, historical, medical, chronological, and astrological material and are often attributed to a Maya priest, Chilam Balam, who prophesied the coming of a new religion. The books are frequently known by the name of the place from which they originated. The best known are the *Books of Chiam Balam of Chumayel* translated into Spanish in 1930 and into English in 1933. Their compilation is attributed to Juan José Hoil, a native of Chumayel, in 1782.

A characterizing feature of these books is the section on prophecies having to do with the dispersion and the overthrowing of the people through what the authors call "the empire of greed." Mysticism and esoterism are outstanding qualities.

The *Annals of the Xahil,* written in the Cakchiquel dialect, constitute an interesting document. Although they are first and foremost legal records to prove the right of property in a lawsuit, these annals contain historical data, genealogical information, and tradition. They deal with the struggles and vicissitudes of the first inhabitants of the Mayan peninsula, their pilgrimages, their search for an adequate place for their civilization, their constant struggle against disease, nature, and adverse gods.

It is among the Maya that we first find traces of a dramatic literature. The *Rabinal-Achí* is their only dramatic work now extant; however, there does seem to have existed among them a taste for theatrical performances. Historians and chroniclers tell us that the Indians took great pleasure in these representations and in the mimic ability displayed in their spectacles, especially those of comic nature, and often accompanied by music. Surviving through oral tradition for many centuries, the text was eventually written in 1850. Essentially, the function of the dance and the song are explained in a symbolic manner as are the instruments they used in their ceremonies. The play has two principal characters: the Varón de los Quiché and the Varón de Rabinal. The Varón de los Quiché has been captured and eventually is killed. The traditional ceremonial ritual used in the sacrifices of important prisoners, and the steps leading up to the death of the victim are portrayed by means of dialogues between the two main characters.

The literature of the Nahuatl or the Aztecs has been studied thoroughly by the humanist, Angel María Garibay, whose work is fundamental to the knowledge of this type of literature.

Nahuatl civilization, flourishing in the central part of Mexico, had as important cultural centers Texcoco, Tenochtitlan, and Tlaxcala. Father Garibay insists that there are Texcocan, Tenochcan, and Tlaxcalan cycles of epic poetry; and from a careful study of historians and chroniclers of the times, he has pointed out the main themes of these epics.

Since the life of the Aztecs centered around religion, it is to be expected that religious poetry would have had a great importance for them. Huitzilopochtli and Coatlicue were the two main gods to whom these poems were dedicated. More than two thousand poems have been found to date, the majority of which are hymns of praise characterized by religious feeling. Although the greater part of Aztec poetry is of a collective nature, lyric poetry written on the themes of lyric poets of all times is also found among them, expressing their feeling towards the ephemeral nature of life, the enigma of death, the joy of living, the beauty of spring, the mission of man on earth, and fear before

supernatural powers. They employed parallelism, repetition, and refrains as stylistic devices. Their poetic symbols were not numerous: flowers, birds of rich plumage, precious stones and mythical allusions. Their poems are full of symbolic references difficult to interpret even for the modern Mexican since his state of mind is remote even from that of the present-day Indian. Existentialist anguish is expressed at times, as in the following poem:

> In vain was I born, in vain did I come to
>   sprout on this earth:
> I am unfortunate, although I was born
>   and sprang up on this earth:
> I say: what will the children do who are to survive

The ephemeralness of life is noted:
> We only come to sleep, we only come to dream:
> it is not true, it is not true that we come to
>   live on earth.
> We come to be converted into the grass of spring
> our hearts come to turn green, they come to
>   open their crowns, our body is a flower:
> giving off many flowers and withering.

Sometimes a poet expresses a desire for immortality
> I am like a drunkard, I cry, I suffer,
> I do know, I say and I have in mind:
> Would that I would never die,
>   would that I would never perish!
> There where there is no death, there where
>   one triumphs, there I shall go:
> Would that I would never die,
>   would that I would never perish!

THE SIXTEENTH CENTURY

The contribution to Mexican literature of the Indian peoples seems unquestionable, but it lies in a shadowy past from which the known highlights gleam with surprising brilliance. As Mexico passed from the Conquest and domination into the colonial period, and through the stresses of revolution and independence, the elements become more clearly traceable which were to combine and produce a tremendously varied literature.

Generalizations regarding these elements are bound to be hypothetical, but of interest. For example, the role of the clergy in Mexican literature, by simple enumeration appears enormous. From the Conquest on, here was a unifying factor in Mexican culture. Yet paradoxical effects arose from the differing stamps placed upon the face of clerical writing by the uniqueness of circumstance, the variation in holy orders, and the individual personalities of the writing clergy. Their vast range of types is exemplified by Las Casas, "Apostle of the Indians," who accompanied Cortés as a kind of social conscience; Sor Juana Inés de la Cruz, the gifted nun of the seventeenth century who wrote intense and polished love poetry from the convent; historian Father Clavijero of the 1700's who was a forerunner of the modern social scientist; Father Mier whose fighting career in the cause of independence at the turn of the century reads like an historic novel.

Gradually, with the secularizing of modern life, the quantitatively great role of the church in letters was modified, and Mexican literary figures began to emerge from the fields of medicine and law, from government posts, from journalistic offices, and often from the diplomatic service.

The number of Mexican literary men who were diplomats leads to speculation as to what other cultures were influencing Mexican literature. Considerable influence seems to have come from southern Europe. Through foreign service, travel, or European education, many cultivated Mexicans knew Europe — not just ancestral Spain but France and Italy as well. But there seems at no time to have been much impress on letters exerted by Mexico's sprawling, youthful neighbor on the north.

Any historical journey through Mexican letters seems likely to be biographical in tone. In a nation of many regions, many dialects, and many heritages, one of the powerful unifying factors must have been the dynamic, effective, and vividly human lives that were lived by Mexico's writers. In general these men were neither sedentary, aloof, nor in any sense passive commentators on the development of their nation. They were part of it, and their histories give the literary story that kaleidoscopic quality of diversity within unity that has characterized Mexico through the centuries and continues to do so in modern times.

Shortly after the conquest and occupation of the old Tenochtitlan on August 13, 1521, the Conquistadores began the reconstruction of the city that was to become the capital of the viceroyalty of New Spain. They set up a political organization and established a foundation for immigration to Mexico.

Now came a task much more difficult as well as complex: incorporation of the Indian groups into Spanish civilization. In fact, the task was the creation of a civilization. There was an implication here of primary purpose: conversion of the Indians to Catholicism and to Christian morality. Naturally, spiritual conquest meant essentially religious conquest. Conversion to Catholicism translated itself primarily into knowledge and teaching. The missionaries had to become familiar with the language of the Indians, their customs and their character, and to establish an intimate bond with them. They had to seek out Indian sentiments and ideas, feelings, way of life, and spirit; thus it was above all the missionaries who undertook the tremendous work of civilizing, incorporating the Indians into the non-Indian world. This overwhelming and Herculean work, which had to be undertaken through research, conversion, and teaching, was carried out by the missionaries under extremely difficult circumstances. The Indians, with their many dialects, had to be led to accept the missionaries after having just undergone the trauma of the Conquest. Violence, roughness, abuse could not be easily forgotten. Another obstacle was the fact that there were only a few missionaries compared to the millions of Indians scattered all over Mexico.

This was an exceptional challenge, but the missionaries were exceptional men. They were compelled to be researchers, teachers, and social workers, as well as apostles. They had to be endowed with physical as well as spiritual vigor and thoroughly instilled with the spirit of heroism.

The socio-religious work of the missionaries took them all over Mexico. Their "field" was not only cities, churches, and monasteries, but the totality of the vast expanse that was Mexico at that time. As part of their approach to this problem, the missionaries began the founding of schools. It was Father Pedro de Gante who established, in 1523, the first school in the Americas, La Escuela de San Francisco in Mexico City. With as many as a thousand students at one time, it also housed many of the members of the Indian nobility. Later on, Father de Gante added a trade school where he trained sculptors, painters, embroiderers, stone-cutters, tailors, carpenters, shoemakers, and other similar tradesmen. The first Bishop of Mexico, Father Juan de Zumárraga, wanted to do something more for the Indians, so founded a school of higher studies, catering to the formation of select groups. Hence, the School of Santa Cruz de Tlaltelolco was founded in January 6, 1536, with a group of sixty Indian students, and an excellent Franciscan faculty. This institution graduated the Indian teachers who were to teach Nahuatl to the Spaniards and who provided information about ancient customs, rites and histories, scribes, collaborators, and typographers who made possible the books of philology and history of the sixteenth century. The first viceroy of Mexico, Antonio de Mendoza, founded the school of San Juan de Letrán, which was to serve both as an orphanage for *mestizo* children and as a school for teachers who were to continue the work of founding schools of the same type all over New Spain. The *criollos,* or white men born in Mexico, also had their own private schools.

In 1583 the Jesuits combined their schools of St. Michael and St. Bernard into one to which they gave the name of St. Ildefonso. In later centuries this was to be the site of the university high school of the University of Mexico. The Colegio Máximo of St. Peter and St. Paul, founded by the Jesuits in 1573, was destined exclusively for the *Criollos* and later competed advantageously with the University.

Higher education was not imparted at any of the Jesuit school systems. Indians, *mestizos,* and *criollos* were segregated from each other. At the same time, young men who wanted to complete their education had to travel to Spain. This fact made education unnecessarily expensive and forced the city of Mexico to request the foundation of the University. Antonio de Mendoza was the first public official to make an attempt at creating a university by endowing it with some cattle ranches of his own. He requested from the King of Spain the official creation of a university, but it was not until the administration of his successor, Luis de Velasco, that in 1551, Charles V ordered the founding of the Royal and Pontifical University of Mexico. This institution was inaugurated the twenty-fifth of January, 1553, but courses of study were not officially open until the third of June of that year.

To the cultural forces of school and university, a third force had been added, the printing press. Mexico City has the distinction of having been the place where the first printing press operated in the Americas. Juan Cromberger, a famous printer from Seville, sent a press to Mexico City at the request of Viceroy Antonio de Mendoza and Bishop Zumárraga. It arrived in 1536, and early in 1537, the first book printed in the Americas was off the press: the *Escala espiritual para llegar al cielo* of San Juan Climaco, translated from the Latin by Father Juan Madalena. Other printing presses were to follow.

Linguistic Literature

Of necessity, the majority of the books that came from the printing presses of the sixteenth century were religious in nature. They included primers, books of doctrine, vocabularies and grammars of the Indian dialects, prayer books and missals. Since the main impediment to achievement of the goals that the missionaries had set up for themselves was lack of knowledge of the Indian dialects and languages, it was understandable that the learning of these languages was among the first things that they set out to do. The task was enormous. Indian languages and dialects were different from those spoken by the Europeans and offered many differences among themselves as well. Learning the basic languages was indispensable; later on the subtleties and nuances could be mastered. After such knowledge had been gained, books had to be written to facilitate the learning of these languages for the missionaries who were to follow. Publication of these linguistic works was, then, an aspect of literature that cannot be neglected. It is true that it is a literature of necessity, but it became extremely useful, almost indispensable, to future missionaries.

Father Andrés de Olmos was probably the first of these philologists. He learned several dialects of the Chichimec, as well as Nahuatl, Huastec, and Totonac. His *Gramática Mexicana* was finished in 1547 although not published until the latter quarter of the nineteenth century.

Father Alonso de Molina printed in 1555 his *Vocabulario Castellano-Mexicano* with a second edition in 1571 to which was added the Mexican-Castilian vocabulary. His *Nahuatl Grammar* was published in 1571.

Numerous other individuals of the clergy studied Tarascan, Zapotec, Mixtec, the languages of Chiapas, and many others. The translations of religious books were destined to indoctrinate the Indians into the Catholic religion. Some included prayers, some liturgy, some lives of the saints, catechisms and others; some

appeared in Spanish, some appeared in the Indian languages. The extraordinary wealth of publication available in the Indian dialects and languages, and compiled essentially by the sixteenth and seventeenth century clergymen was to be extremely valuable to missionaries who arrived in subsequent centuries.

Scientific Books

The presses of Mexico also published works of philosophy, theology, and science, or, rather, books of a scientific nature. The outstanding philosopher of the sixteenth century was Father Alonso de la Veracruz. His works *Recognitio Summularum*, 1554, *Dialectica Resolutio*, 1554, and *Physica Speculatio*, 1557, are essentially examples of the dialectics of scholasticism of the time. Much more interesting is the *Speculum Conjugiorum*, 1556, which discussed marriage among the Indians and attempted to find a solution for some of the more difficult cases of those marriages.

Books of a scientific nature included a *Cedulario*, 1563, by Dr. Vasco Puga, the first legal compilation in the Americas and highly important for the early history of Spanish domination in Mexico.

Among the books published in the sixteenth century, we might select *Primera parte de los problemas y secretos maravillosos de las Indias*, 1591, by Doctor Juan de Cárdenas, pointing out the state of the natural sciences in that century.

Chronicles and Histories

The sixteenth century in Mexican literature was an epoch of exploration, discovery and conquest: a time of action. The Renaissance had come to Spain shortly before the Conquistadores to Mexico in 1519 contributing to Spain a spirit of restlessness which was imbued in Cortés's men. The deeds of the ancient world, both Greek and Roman, were uppermost in the minds of the Conquistadores when they arrived on Mexican shores. The exotic nature of the geography of Mexico with tropical lands, immense rivers, majestic mountains, snow-clad volcanoes, immediate contrast between lowlands and highlands, deserts next to fertile valleys, all these factors inflamed the imagination of the Conquistadores. The new empires discovered and conquered in Mexico were reminiscent of the empires the Greeks and Romans had overpowered. The heroic deeds of the Conquistadores were conceived as similar to the deeds of the ancient heroes of Greece and Rome. It is easily understandable, then, that a main type of literature in the sixteenth century would occupy itself with these conquests and these heroes. The writing of chronicles and histories became very popular.

The chroniclers of Mexico in the sixteenth century and part of the seventeenth century may be divided into four main groups: peninsular, Conquistador, missionary, and Indian.

The peninsular chroniclers or historians were essentially men of humanistic background drinking from

The Pyramid of Quetzalcoátl is one of the major structures in the great pre-conquest city of Teotihuacán, where extensive archaeological excavation and research have taken place under Mexican government auspices in the 1960's.

he fountain of Greek and Roman inspiration. They were men familiar with the histories of Tacitus and Herodotus; among the many we can point out two: Francisco López de Gómara (1511–1566), the chaplain of Cortés, and Antonio de Solís, (1610–1686). Primarily official chroniclers, they wrote chiefly from documents from the Mother Country and from information supplied by men who had been in the New World; and, although they had not visited the new lands, they e-created their history and conquest from hearsay, document, and testimony.

Among the Conquistadores who wrote about the history of Mexico were Hernán Cortés himself and Bernal Díaz del Castillo. The works of Cortés are comprised in the five *Cartas de Relación*, now in Vienna. Written between 1519 and 1526, the dispatches of Cortés to the young Charles V, Emperor of the Holy Roman Empire and King of Spain, show the historical, political, and human aspects of the Conquistador of Mexico. The most famous of the missives was the second one. We must remember that Cortés

had attended the University of Salamanca and had been exposed to the study of good classical models. His letters have often been compared to the *Commentaries* of Caesar, and there is, in truth, a great deal of parallelism between these works. Both captains were writing while the campaigns were going on, both took part in the conquest of these territories, and both were not aware of the outcome of their campaigns at the time of their writings. Spurred on by fame, Cortés plunged into adventure and described in detail the feelings and events that would lead to the conquest of Mexico. There is no question that Cortés was trying to influence favorably the young King of Spain, and also no question that the greatness of Cortés as a leader of men shows frankly and clearly in these dispatches. Customs of inhabitants, violence of battles, disappointment at defeats, concessions to the enemy, all appear in the dispatches of Cortés.

Another eyewitness of the conquest of Mexico, Bernal Díaz del Castillo, (1492–1580?), had taken part in the 1517 and 1518 expeditions to Mexico before he joined up with Cortés. He accompanied the latter in triumph and defeat and eventually was rewarded as a city councilman in Guatemala; but, incensed at the glorification that López de Gómara made of Cortés in his history, Bernal Díaz decided to write his *True History of the Conquest of New Spain,* edited in 1632. His aim was to give the foot soldier of the Conquest his due. At seventy years of age, veteran of more than one hundred ten battles, without the aid of documents and trusting only his marvelous memory, Bernal Díaz began to compose his history of the Conquest. He then read, among others, the history of López de Gómara, and decided to point out the merits of the companions of Cortés. This outstanding work, the only one of its kind in all literature, was roughly written, for Bernal Díaz was not a man of letters. However, a naturalness, a warmth, a joy of living, a feeling of truth make the book easy reading to the very end. It might be called a history book *par excellence,* a testimony of fact, for without taking away from the glory of Cortés, Bernal claims for himself and for his companions the glory that is due them. Both conquerors and vanquished are portrayed with sympathy; he paints battles, praises the conquered and glorifies the conquerors. Devoid of rhetoric and lacking in literary vanity, the book has the spontaneity associated with the restlessness of Renaissance man. This is the true history; this is, in truth, the authentic epic of the Conquest of Mexico: the struggle of two cultures, two wills, two destinies confronting one another in a world that up to this time had been unsuspected.

The missionary or religious historians may be divided into two types: active and passive.

Most of the missionary chroniclers are of the passive type, the great exception having been Father Bartolomé de las Casas (1474–1566). Great defender of the Indians, Las Casas devoted himself to protecting Indians throughout his life, thus earning the title, Apostle of the Indies. After becoming acquainted with the *encomienda* system in the Caribbean Islands, he dedicated his life to its elimination. He wrote, he preached, he argued for the Indians; and eventually, he persuaded the King of Spain to permit a debate on the *encomiendas.* His opponent was Father Juan Ginés de Sepúlveda. The debate took place in Spain, with Sepúlveda bringing forth all the arguments in favor of imperialism and Las Casas denouncing them; for Las Casas wanted to establish colonies that, by example, would induce the Indians to civilization and to conversion to Catholicism. Not believing in the right of conquest, Las Casas attacked imperialism and was thus, in a way, the founder of liberalism in Mexico and the Americas. Although Las Casas was the official victor in the Valladolid debate, the *encomienda* system, unfortunately, persisted. His writings were a constant argument in favor of the human rights of the Indians and were used by other European nations in the establishment of the Black Legend of the conquest of the Latin-American colonies. As late as the Spanish-American War, the writings of Las Casas were still being used as propaganda denouncing the cruelty of the Spaniards in the treatment of the Indians.

Among the passive missionaries was Father Toribio de Benavente, better known as Motolinía, also a defender of the Indians, a founder of cities and monasteries, and an authority on Indian languages. His main work is the *Historia de los Indios de Nueva España,* considered the oldest of such histories, since he began writing it in 1536. The passive missionary historians are not interested in portraying the violence in the conquest of Mexico; they rarely depict the deeds of arms of the Conquistadores but rather concentrate on recreating the life, custom, tradition and ritual of the ancient Indian civilizations.

Probably more outstanding than Motolinía in this respect is Father Bernardino de Sahagún who wrote *Historia General de las Cosas de Nueva España.* Father Sahagún had in mind a careful study of the customs and religion of the Indians, with the aim of abolishing pagan customs in order to convert the Indian to Catholicism. He set about learning the Nahuatl language and spent most of his life in a monastery devoted to the study of history, tradition, and custom of the Aztecs. He gathered together a whole corps of Indian informers on all aspects of Indian civilization to compile an encyclopedia of Nahuatl culture. His book deals with religion, superstition, intellectual life, social life, economics, vices and virtues of the Indians, plants, animals, and minerals of the country. His is the first attempt at a systematic gathering of an encyclopedia of historical and anthropological interests.

The last group of historians included the Indian chroniclers, writing about their own people. Among them, one of the most important is Fernando de Alvarado Tezozómoc. A nephew of Moctezuma, he wrote *Crónica Mexicana* in Spanish in 1598 and *Crónica Mexicáyotl* in 1609, in Nahuatl. The first work deals with the conception of life of the ancient Mexican, and the second contains sections of tradition and epic poems that now are lost in their first composition.

Fernando de Alva Ixtlilxóchitl was a descendant of Netzahualcóyotl, one of the kings of Texcoco and the only Nahuatl poet that we know by name. His Chichimec history is based on documents, paintings, songs, etc., and deals primarily with the Toltecs and pre-Hispanic times. Although the work was considered unreliable and exaggerated, the newest findings are giving it more and more credence.

At this point, the *Historia de los Indios de Nueva España y Islas de Tierra Firme* by Father Diego Durán (1538?–1588), was left unfinished. Father Durán was a *mestizo,* and his chronicle is a good example of the fusion of cultures as well as of a first attempt to interpret Indian texts while seeking to transmit purely Indian emotion expressed through the Spanish language.

The Novel

During this time, the novel, so popular in Spain in the form of romances of chivalry, was unknown in Mexico. By decree of the fourth of April, 1531, it was forbidden to have "books of romances, of fictional stores, or profane, as are those of *Amadís* and others of that type, because it is a bad exercise for the Indians, and a thing that is not right that they occupy themselves in nor read." This decree, of course, included not only the Indians but also the peninsular Spaniards and the *criollos* in the Colony; and soon the novels that came into Mexico were smuggled.

Poetry

Poetic manifestations in the sixteenth century were expressed mainly through epic poetry and lyric poetry. Epic poetry had become popular in Spain as a result of the Renaissance. The new learned epic, with a known author, had its influence in Spain principally through Ariosto and Tasso. The outstanding epic poem written in Spanish in the sixteenth century was *La Araucana* by Alonso de Ercilla, depicting chiefly a rather unimportant event in the conquest of the Americas, the conquest of Chile. Regrettably, Cortés did not inspire a great poet to sing his praises and heroic deeds in the conquest of Mexico, thereby omitting one of the most significant phases in the conquest of Latin-American colonies.

Francisco de Terrazas, probably the foremost Mexican lyric poet of the sixteenth century, is supposed to have written a long epic poem "New World and Conquest," which was left unfinished because of the death of the poet. Fragments of it have been found and identified by various critics, although apparently it circulated in manuscript form among his contemporaries and found great favor with them.

Antonio de Saavedra Guzmán was born in Mexico. He took some seven years to gather the materials for his epic poem *El Peregrino Indiano,* 1599, and the seventy-day trip from Mexico to Spain was used by Guzmán to compose this poem, according to his own confession. Some critics argue that this epic poem belongs under history, rather than under poetry, since it only has meter to recommend it.

Captain Gaspar Villagrá wrote his *Historia de Nueva Mexico,* printed in Madrid in 1610. Also considered more of a chronicle than a poem, it is interesting because the captain was one of the discoverers of the Rio Grande.

Antagonism between the *peninsulares* and the *criollos* is notable from the beginning of the Colony in Mexico. The *criollos* felt themselves relegated to a secondary position when they saw that the *peninsulares* were appointed to the highest posts in government, church, and army. As sons of Conquistadores, they firmly believed that they had a greater right to this land and its government and its wealth than the often bureaucratic peninsular Spaniard, a Johnny-come-lately

who was taking back with him the richest plums available. The sixteenth century was the beginning of this rivalry and it was to continue until the time of Independence. The *criollos* aspired, as was the custom, to public offices which more often than not were taken away from them by the peninsular Spaniards who quickly became examples of "nouveau riche."

And here we have another type of literary product. The *criollos* wrote anonymous poetry, usually in the form of a sonnet, criticizing the peninsular Spaniard; we find bitter criticism indeed in most of this poetry. They buffoon and satirize the lack of education of the peninsular Spaniard, his rapid rise to power, his newly found wealth, and as one of the sonnets says

> And the other one who shoelaces and pins
> sold on the street, now is a Count
> in quality and in quantity a banker.

It is also pointed out that the peninsular Spaniard then abominates Mexico:

> And he abominates afterwards the place where
> he acquired esteem, taste, and fortune.

No doubt lyric poetry in New Spain was affected by the arrival of three Spanish poets in Mexico City: Gutierre de Cetina, Juan de la Cueva, and Eugenio de Salazar. Gutierre de Cetina came to Mexico City in 1546. A well-known sixteenth-century Spanish poet, no one knew why he left Spain for Mexico. His literary formation had already taken place before this. One of the best-known representatives of the Italian-Spanish school which had been introduced in Spain by Garcilaso and Boscán, and although only twenty-six when he arrived in Mexico, Cetina's definitive poetry had already been written. He lived in Mexico for eight years, and it is to be presumed that during that time he composed some literary work which has not yet been discovered. There is no doubt that his stay in Mexico also must have had some influence on the Mexican poets of his time.

Flores de Baria Poesía, an anthology of poetry compiled in Mexico in 1577 in manuscript form, is now at the National Library in Madrid. The manuscript is not complete, but in its present form contains over three hundred and fifty poems, almost one-fourth of which belongs to Gutierre de Cetina. It is almost certain that there were others written by Cetina during his stay in Mexico which were lost. Cetina's life was very romantic. He had been at the court in Spain, Italy and Germany. The friend of noblemen and literary men, he fell in love with a Countess Laura de Gonzaga whom he glorified in his verses.

On the night of the first of April, 1554, at the city of Puebla, he was stabbed by a jealous husband as he passed under the windows of a lady. Mortally wounded, he was chivalrous to the end and refused to reveal who his assailant was. Critics who have studied the life of Cetina believe that he was killed by mistake.

Unlike Cetina, Juan de la Cueva left a literary legacy of his stay in Mexico. He was born in Seville, probably around 1550, and came to Mexico accompanying his brother, who was later to become inquisitor. He stayed in the capital of New Spain from October, 1574, to the early part of 1577. Again unlike Cetina, he did not enjoy a literary reputation when he came to New Spain. His poetic production was to come later. Better known as a playwright, Cueva probably did not write any plays before his arrival in the New World since his first play was presented in Seville in 1579 and the others in the same city in 1581. His other works date from the time of his return to Spain to 1609 at which time all traces of him seem to be lost.

Part of the poetic production that appears in his *Obras,* (works) published in 1582, had already been included in the *Flores de Baria Poesía.* Therefore, they must be attributed to his youth.

During his short stay in Mexico, Juan de la Cueva cultivated two types of poetry: poetry describing everything that seems different and exotic to him in New Spain to make it known to his friends in Spain or to comment on it with his new friends in Mexico; and poetry based on memories, nostalgia, and tenderness. He wrote a long *epístola* to the first corregidor of Mexico, in which he described fruits and flowers he was encountering for the first time such as bananas, mamey, guavas, anonas, etc. He was also interested in the character and picturesque customs of the Indians, but nostalgia overcame him and he returned to Spain. Although I have not been able to make a complete study of the handwriting of the poems of Juan de la Cueva and the handwriting of the 1577 manuscript of *Flores de Baria Poesía,* from a preliminary study I have published, I am very inclined to regard Juan de la Cueva as the compiler. In a study printed in Mexico, I have suggested that the manuscript may have been left unfinished because of the magnitude of the work. Then too, for lack of time or some other reason, it is probable that Juan de la Cueva could not have finished the manuscript before leaving Mexico. Very likely his return to Spain prevented him from finishing the manuscript as he had first intended; and once in Spain he may have been overwhelmed by the lengthy original plan.

Of the three hundred and fifty-nine poetic compositions included in the extant anthology, one hundred and seventeen are anonymous. The most popular form of poetry used in the manuscript is the sonnet. There are some thirty-two compositions by Juan de la Cueva in the compilation, of which twenty-five are sonnets.

The manuscript was originally divided into five books, the first containing religious poems; the second, love poems; the third, epistles; the fourth, satirical poems; and the fifth, "indifferent things that could not be applied to any one of the other books." Unfortunately, the manuscript as it stands contains only the religious and the love poems; the others are missing, probably they were never compiled. Among the better known Spanish poets appearing in the anthology are Fernando de Acuña, Baltasar del Alcázar, Cetina, Juan de la Cueva, Francisco de Figueroa, Fernando de Herrera, Juan de Malara, Diego de Mendoza, among others.

Among the possible Mexican poets, we have Martín Cortés, the son of Hernán Cortés, Hernán González, who could well be Fernán González de Eslava, Carlos de Sámano, and Francisco de Terrazas. Many of the unidentified poets in the collection could well be *criollos* from New Spain. Martín Cortés, son of the conqueror, appeared in Mexico in 1563 and remained until 1568. It is very likely that the octaves in this manuscript were written in Mexico during that time. The poem deals with the love of a poor shepherd for a shepherdess and his subsequent death, a theme common to Spanish poetry of the sixteenth century written in the Italian fashion.

Although a minor poet by comparison to Cetina and Cueva, Eugenio de Salazar lived in New Spain longer than they, occupied a higher position in government and university, and very possibly had a greater influence on the poets of Mexico. He was born in Madrid in 1530 and attended the universities of Alcalá, Salamanca, and Sigüenza. He was appointed to government posts in Spain and the Canary Islands, and served as a judge to Santo Domingo and later prosecutor to the court of Guatemala. He came to Mexico as a prosecutor in 1581 and was later a judge. In 1591 he obtained a doctor's degree from the University of Mexico. Later Philip III made him a member of the Council of the Indies where he served in 1601. The date of his death is not known.

His "Epístola," written in tercets, refers essentially to the state of culture in the capital of the viceroyalty of New Spain, describing the Lake of Texcoco, Tenochtitlan and frequently using Indian names.

Although born in Plasencia, Spain in 1534, in 1561, Pedro de Trejo was already in Morelia and later in Zacatecas and Lagos. In 1575, he fell into the clutches of the Inquisition, condemned to four years in the galleys and ordered forever to abstain from writing poetry. His manuscript "Cancionero," 1570, and other poems that were found during his trial, recommended him as a religious, love, elegiac, and satirical poet. He was as well versed in the fashion of Jorge Manrique as he was in the new Italian style. In 1559, to mark the death of Emperor Charles V, great celebrations were held at the Church of San Francisco. The big catafalque built for the occasion was thoroughly described by Francisco Cervantes de Salazar in his work *Túmulo Imperial de la gran ciudad de México a las obsequias del invictísimo César Carlos V,* 1560. The tomb contained a wealth of the customary inscriptions in Latin and Spanish prose and verse. Many critics believe it all to be the work of Cervantes de Salazar, but others think that he wrote only the Latin. Sonnets and royal octaves in the Italian manner are in this collection. This litterateur was inextricably tied to the cultural life of the Colony. He was born in Spain, probably in 1515, and came to Mexico to become the first professor of rhetoric of the Royal and Pontifical University, twice its president, and received a doctorate in arts and theology there. His *Mexico en 1554* is a collection of dialogues of inestimable historical value.

Composed as an exercise for his Latin students to learn the language through verbalization of familiar situations, the dialogues antedate a technique used in modern language teaching. The first exercise describes the University of Mexico, the functioning of the institution, its professors, and the life of the students. In the second dialogue, the participants walk through the city and describe it. The third dialogue portrays the area surrounding the capital. On these "walks" with his interlocutors, we see the streets of Mexico at the time, the homes built like fortresses, the former royal palace, the main square or tianguis with the bustle of the market days, the myriad types of merchandise, the boat-studded canals that crossed the city, the monasteries and the churches.

Bernardo de Balbuena has been called by a Spanish critic "one of the greatest Spanish poets" and "the true patriarch of American poetry." He was born in Spain probably in 1561 and came to Mexico as a child, but because of his education, Balbuena belongs to Mexico. He occupied different posts in the church and in 1604 published his *La Grandeza Mexicana*. He left for Spain in 1607 and received a doctor's degree from the University of Sigüenza. Returning to the New World, he devoted himself to his religious tasks as abbot of Jamaica, 1610, and bishop of Puerto Rico from 1622 until his death in 1627. His three works include the already mentioned *La Grandeza Mexicana, El Siglo de Oro en las Selvas de Erifile,* a collection of eclogues published in 1608, and *El Bernardo* or *La Victoria de Roncesvalles,* 1624. *Grandeza Mexicana* is a descriptive poem, depicting the capital of New Spain towards the end of the sixteenth century. As he himself expresses it in one of the octaves of the work, he will deal with the origin and greatness of the buildings, horses, streets, treatment, compliments, letters, virtues, variety of trades, gifts, occasions for rejoicing, immortal spring, illustrious government, religion, and state. In short, Balbuena attempts to depict Mexico in all its aspects: external, spiritual, political, and social. His poem probably contains the greatest praise of Mexico up to his time. Menéndez Pelayo, the great Spanish critic, called it a kind of poetic topography. Father Rafael Landívar was to sing of the glories of Mexico again in the eighteenth century.

Francisco de Terrazas (1525?–1600?) is the oldest known Mexican poet. The first son of a Spanish Conquistador by the same name, he was a "man of quality, lord of pueblos and great poet," praised by Cervantes as a new Apollo among the "sovereign geniuses of the Americas." He wrote in Latin, Italian, and Spanish. His sonnet "Dejad las hebras de oro ensortijado" has become a classic and is considered by many to be the most exquisite jewel of Petrarchism in Mexico. Although his epic poem "Nuevo Mundo y Conquista" was lost, enough fragments were published to show that Terrazas was a poet of a good school and that his work would not detract from the epic poems of the sixteenth century about the Conquest of the New World. Five of his sonnets are included in the *Flores de Baria Poesía,* a collection published in 1577.

Fernando de Córdoba y Bocanegra was born in Mexico in 1565 of a family akin to poets, warriors, explorers, and even to Ferdinand the Catholic. At fourteen he was already a musician and an excellent poet in Spanish and Latin, as well as a painter and a singer. At twenty-one he gave his worldly goods to the poor, and in Texcoco devoted himself to a life of poverty and charity toward the sick Indians. He died in 1589 and was considered a saint. His two surviving poems — to divine love and to the name of Jesus — are perhaps the best of the sixteenth century because of their classical form, the depth of thought, the emotion and sincerity expressed in them.

The very interesting man who was Mateo Rosas Oquendo, was born in Seville about 1559. Sometimes soldier, sometimes rogue, he travelled through Italy and France, took part in the Conquest of Argentine territories, was later an *encomendero* and studied arts and necromancy. He became an attendant to the viceroy in Lima and from 1598 to 1612 lived in Mexico. Essentially a satirical poet, he has described the life in the Americas, criticizing the peninsular Spaniard because

> All are fine noblemen
> from well-known families . . . ;
> as if it were not known
> that over there they were dying of hunger! . . .

Other times he criticizes the *criollo* ladies in Mexico. He portrays a caricature of the *mestizo* who is already speaking with scorn of the peninsular Spaniard. His language often is a parody of the Spanish spoken by the Indians of the Americas. Nature as he found it in Mexico, however, has an undeniable influence on Oquendo, and from satirist in Peru, he turned to a contemplator in Mexico.

Drama

Very soon after the conquest, the missionaries discovered the Indians' great inclination towards performances and dances, celebrated during festivities of their religious rituals. The missionaries were inspired to convert this pageantry and spectacle into an appropriate channel for educating the Indians along the paths of the Catholic faith. Their objective presentation of religious topics stimulated the public to attend these performances; and, soon, these ceremonials constituted the most efficacious means of propagating Christian doctrine.

Teotihuacán, Cholula, and Tlaxcala were most commonly used by the Indians for conducting their performances before the Conquest; the missionaries took advantage of the same locations. They performed these plays inside the temples, in the atrium of churches and monasteries, on outdoor platforms built especially for this purpose, in open chapels or schools. Frequently, the actors were people from the town and clergymen. As in many of the European theatres, the roles of the girls or women were played by young boys. These performances sought to substitute plays based on Christian dogma and morals for the frequent and numerous festivals of their bloodthirsty religion of the past. In a way, these plays were derived from the *auto sacramental* of Spain. The friars themselves either wrote the plays or adapted them. If not originally written in an Indian dialect, they translated them, often with the help of the Indians, into the Indian dialect of their anticipated audience.

These plays were not necessarily the main part of a religious festival. In such festivals the ceremonies usually started with a procession. The priests carried the Holy Sacrament and the faithful carried images of saints of their devotion. The public carried crosses and flags and thousands of candles. There were flowers in the path of the procession, as well as a shower of flowers for the paraders. There were also triumphant arches made of flowers, similar to the ones that are used nowadays in the processions of the Virgin of Zapopan in Guadalajara. From time to time, they had chapels with altars that were well decorated where the Holy Sacrament rested while dancers and singers honored Him with dances and songs. If there was enough time, they would put on pantomimes on outdoor platforms; these pantomimes usually reproduced some episode from the Scriptures. When these tableaux were not shown, usually plays in Nahuatl were performed. Apparently these processions and festivals led to abuses of several kinds and forced Bishop Zumárraga, the first Bishop of Mexico, to suppress them during his term of office. Although they were continued later on, they finally were regulated by the Third Mexican Council of 1585. The performances usually took place during the celebration of Corpus Christi, and Zumárraga himself, on speaking about how these processions must be carried out with reverence and devotion, said "It seems a thing of great shame and disrespect to have before the Holy Sacrament men with masks and dressed as women, dancing and jumping with dishonorable and lascivious walk, making noise, hampering the church songs, representing profane triumphs, such as that of the God of Love, so dishonorable and so shameful to look at even to persons who are not honorable."

The first play of this type was performed in Santiago Tlaltelolco in 1533, and was entitled "Auto del Juicio Final." This play was nothing more than the play of the Final Judgment, by Father Andrés de Olmos. This type of play, usually anonymous, often written in the dialect of the Indians where the play was performed, was close to medieval theatre because of its religious subject matter and its purpose. It became very popular throughout Mexico during the century and was found from the northwest in Sinaloa to the southeast in Oaxaca. In spite of the fact that it was so popular, and that these performances extended through a large part of New Spain, very few examples have come down to our day; in fact no more than three or four. The primary purpose of these plays was to preach the Gospel to the Indians, to convert them, to catechize. They were not written for artistic purposes and therefore were probably not fine examples of play writing.

The first and one of the most brilliant fetes in New Spain was celebrated by the people of Tlaxcala on the Day of Corpus of 1538. Motolinía describes it thoroughly. Four plays were presented with such titles as: *La Anunciación de la Navidad de San Juan Bautista, La Anunciación de Nuestra Señora, La Visitación de la Santísima Virgen a Santa Isabel,* and *La Navidad de San Juan Bautista.*

Along with this current of plays written in Indian dialects, there were usually other plays written in Spanish or in Latin and normally performed at the schools of the Jesuits during great celebrations.

Two famous events gave rise to plays of this type. On the eighth of December of 1574, Pedro Moya de Contreras was made archbishop with all the usual ceremonies in the Cathedral of Mexico City. As part of the festivities, a play was presented called "Spiritual Wedding between the Pastor Peter and the Mexican Church," composed by Juan Pérez Ramírez. Born around 1554 or 1555, he was a native of Mexico and a son of a Conquistador. He was proficient in Latin and Nahuatl, and was considered to be a good poet. We might classify Pérez Ramírez as the first dramatist born in Mexico. His play had a simple plot: it is the mystic wedding of Contreras to the church, told in pastoral fashion. Among the characters appearing are the church, Pedro, the virtues, and divine love. Here for the first time the *bobo* or the simpleton is introduced, giving thus a comic element to the play.

Much more solemn and of greater splendor was the ceremony that took place in 1578. The occasion was a reception given to the holy relics sent by Pope Gregory XIII to Mexico. There was a parade of students of the Jesuit colleges or schools; many were on horseback dressed as Spaniards, Englishmen, and Turks; some pretended to be princes, others kings. The parade ended on the main square where there were the usual arches with flowers and inscriptions in different languages, dances, angels, Indians or symbolic figures reciting poetry. During the first six days of the celebration, plays were presented, among which the outstanding one was "Triunfo of the Santos," played by students. As usual, we have no idea of who the author of the play is, although we suspect that many authors collaborated in it. The plot is essentially the persecution of the church by Diocletian and the splendor that the church achieved under Constantine. In the cast among other personages appeared Pope Silvester, St. Peter, St. John, St. Gorgonius, the Church, Faith, Hope, Charity, Idolatry, and Cruelty, among others. The very subject matter as well as the mixture of characters gives us an idea of the relative literary merits of the play.

There was also *criollo* theatre, following the patterns of the Spanish theatre of the time, and written by Mexican authors, with a *casa de comedias* in which these plays were presented. This type of theatre, however, never achieved the popularity of the early religious theatre.

By the middle of the sixteenth century, we already find Spanish plays of Lope de Rueda being performed.

Festivities of any type are used as excuses to present plays: the arrival of a new viceroy, the arrival of a new archbishop, the birth of a new heir to the Queen, the Feast of Corpus, etc.

Fernán González de Eslava, although born in Spain, and most likely in Seville, is considered a Mexican dramatist. He was born probably around 1535, and by 1567 he was in Mexico. While in the capital of New Spain, he wrote his *Coloquios espirituales y sacramentales*. It was not until 1610, after the death of the author, that his plays were published. That 1610 edition also announced sacred poems in the title. They were in the tradition of the usual sacred anthologies of the times. The editor of the 1610 work promised to publish soon his "human works" which were never published or the edition of which has been lost.

The plays are sixteen in number, probably written between 1567 and 1600. Although similar to the *autos sacramentales,* they differ from them in the structure and subject matter. The dialogue that Eslava uses is of a familiar type; the plot is not particularly complicated. Humor is used throughout even to the point of grotesqueness. His characters often take on a popular air, and he argues theological points with plainness. His sixteen plays are religious, moral, historical, and those commemorating a special event. They are all written in verse and are one act long, with the exception of two. His *Coloquios* are all of a religious nature, which makes it difficult at times for the author to introduce religion when dealing with a special event. In his speech, he has been influenced by the *criollos* and by the Indians. He often describes customs, ways of thinking and the feelings of the inhabitants of New Spain; and he frequently alludes to contemporary events.

SEVENTEENTH CENTURY

Seventeenth-century literature in Mexico can be characterized as essentially the epoch of *gongorismo* or *culteranismo*. Luis de Góngora, 1561–1627, a Spanish poet, founded the cultivated style of the school which he was to develop. He was the poet who gave the most extreme expression to the formal and the artificial in Baroque literature. Although he wrote in a popular vein, Góngora is mostly known for his poetry in somber tones, somewhat haunted, and full of anxieties. Death, pain, fickleness of fortune and human attachment are some of his themes. Dámaso Alonso said of his work "here we find a most extreme form of authentic convention concerning a language of metaphorical allusions which put an unreal wall between the meaning and the object it refers to." Góngora revitalized poetry and gave new orientation to it as Mallarmé, Stefan George, and T. S. Eliot were to do later. Góngora tried to mold Spanish to Latin, introducing many Latin terms, and altering Spanish syntax to emulate Latin syntax. He sought also to paraphrase the direct meaning of words. He abounded in artificial metaphors which had subtle relationships among themselves almost impossible to perceive, except by the author himself. He reveled in obscure allusions and references to classical mythology. Thus poetry was hermetic, for the initiated few, a banquet for the erudite, forbidden to the comprehension of the general populace. It would be, perhaps, an oversimplification to say that *gongorismo* was obscurity of style, that the gongorists preferred form to contents.

Later on another literary manner appeared: conceptism. Conceptism was more concerned with the concept, the idea itself, contents rather than form; to oversimplify once more, obscurity of contents. In Mexico the two schools assimilated each other and became fused so that in the years to come it was difficult to distinguish gongorists from conceptists. All were obscure, extravagant, and for the most part, empty.

Culteranismo found great opposition in Spain, but soon it spread like an epidemic and affected other countries. It was the manifestation of the Baroque literature, and it was Góngora who stood out as the originator of this literary fashion. The gongoristic disease spread to the Americas and affected seventeenth-century literature in Mexico, surviving longer in Mexico and in the Latin-American colonies than in Spain. There it was still prevalent through part of the eighteenth century, long after it had died as a literary vogue in Spain and elsewhere.

There are two factors, nevertheless, that might explain the persistence of *culteranismo* in Mexico. The Spanish government, through its administrative machine established in Mexico, kept a very rigorous censorship in the country, carefully examining the books that were to be shipped into Mexico, as well as the books that were to be published in that colony. This censorship by political administrators also prevented the development of thought along liberal lines.

We must not forget also the censorship imposed upon Mexico by the church. The ever-present threat of the Inquisition prevented intellectuals from engaging in philosophical discussions that might eventually conflict with the theological beliefs of scholasticism. Fear of this dichotomy hindered a man of intellect from exploring political thought or engaging in philosophical discussion. It was natural, then, that the intellectual would turn to ineffectual poetry in which the emphasis, whether on style or on concept, did not lead him to controversies with church or state. There was little incentive for *criollos* to enter the field of literature, for the most part difficult and far from lucrative. Very often the would-be-writer would rather join the church to be assured of its protection and its benefits in a clerical post that would allow him to write. Thus, we find that the majority of the writers of the seventeenth and eighteenth centuries were priests or clergymen, and the literature of these times took on a religious aspect. Unlike the sixteenth-century clergymen who often were vigorous historians, capable of knowledge, dedicated anthropologists, and careful linguists, the religious writers of the seventeenth and the first half of the eighteenth centuries tended toward a false and artificial rhetoric expressed in theological books or books of devotion, books which were far from expressing the

The Cathedral of Mexico City, begun in the period and style of the Renaissance, acquired a baroque character during the one hundred and fifty years of its building. Today it is a landmark for tourists on the busy square of Zócalo and a center of religious life in Mexico City.

mystic enthusiasm of some of the sixteenth-century Spanish writers.

This was a century of monotony; a century in which the great deeds of the Conquistadores were only a repercussion. Empires had already been conquered, discoveries had been made, except for the areas in the northern deserts away from the capital of New Spain. These were no longer heroic times, but times in which colonizer, settler, and bureaucrat prevailed. It was natural that such a silent and monotonous society should not offer much incentive to literary activity. It was also natural that literature hindered by censorship, both political and religious, should take on a rather artificial and tedious aspect. Theology prevailed over philosophy, history, science, and literature. The uni-

versity, which from its beginnings remained aloof from intellectual Renaissance currents, was and continued being a verbalizing school for dialectics. It was only natural that the literary man of the seventeenth century would gravitate towards *culteranismo*. Cleverness was to be applauded over true genius; stylistic exercises were placed above inspiration.

Poetry

In poetry it was the gongoristic fashion that predominated. Arias de Villalobos was born in Spain in 1568 but came to Mexico at a very early age. He received a degree in Arts in 1585 at the age of seventeen and later studied theology from 1592 to 1594

From 1589 on, the City of Mexico drew up a contract for his plays of Corpus and his Octave, and in 1594 we find him receiving an annual pension as a paid author for the festivals of San Hipólito. The Audiencia of Mexico placed him in charge of *La obediencia que México dió a Felipe IV* in 1623. By this time he was known as "the most celebrated poet of New Spain." He wrote numerous plays, songs to the trip of the Count of Monterrey, epitaphs to the Marchioness of Guadalcázar, the praise of the Marquis de Gelves, the treaty of the House of Austria, and the prologue to the *Antigüedad de la lengua Vasca* of Baltasar de Echave. All of these works, with the exception of the latter, have been lost. In his book to Phillip IV, he mentioned Mexico City in a sonnet as the "Rome of the New World." He also penned a *Canto intitulado Mercurio histórico y descriptivo de esta gran ciudad de México — Tenoxtitlán* dedicated to the viceroy Marquis of Montes Claros, in two hundred and thirty-three octaves where he described the ancient history of Mexico, in the pomp of the court of his times. This is similar to the *Grandeza Mexicana* of Balbuena, but does not compare in greatness although it seems to be more enthusiastic than the works of Salazar and Cueva. Villalobos' portrayal of the Conquest has powerful realism: he describes the festivals of Moctezuma, the Sad Night, the joy of the Indians, the glorification of San Hipólito and Cortés. The whole work is a mixture of Baroque elements and Aztec words. He seems to have been a famous lyric poet, the initiator of gongorism in New Spain and one of the best epic singers of Cortés.

Juan de Palafox y Mendoza, 1600–1659, was not only an ascetic, apostolic, exemplary, wise, and dynamic governor but also a genuine poet. He was born in Navarre of a noble family, became a priest in 1629, and travelled through Germany, Italy, France, Bohemia, Flanders, and Sweden. He became a member of the Council of the Indies and in 1639 was made a bishop of Puebla. He was a protector of the Indians, the judge of three viceroys, viceroy himself, and chosen as Archbishop of Mexico, a position which he declined. He returned to Spain in 1649 and died there in 1659. He was the instigator of the building of the Cathedral of Puebla, built other temples there, founded seminaries with courses in Nahuatl, and donated his library of some six thousand volumes to the Seminary of Sts. Peter and Paul. He was viceroy of Mexico in 1642 without pay, and outstanding in his sense of justice, prudence, initiative, and integrity. Palafox performed the miracle of leaving over seven hundred thousand pesos in the royal treasury which had previously been exhausted. In 1691 his investigation for beatification was begun in Rome; in 1767 they approved his "famous sanctity, heroic virtues and miracles in general," proclaiming him Venerable. In poetry he left his religious work *Poesías Espirituales,* his "Cánticos," and two other books of verse. His complete works number fourteen volumes. His poetry shows traditional conceptism, the style of the Salamanca school, and reminiscences of St. John of the Cross. Unlike most of the poets of his time, he makes meaning crystal clear in many of his poems.

Miguel de Guevara was probably born in 1585 and died about 1646. He was an Augustinian monk in the province of Michoacán and served as a missionary among the Aztecs, the Tarascans and the Matlalzingos. In the manuscript of 1638 for his *Arte doctrinal y modo para aprender la lengua Matlalzinga para administración de los Santos Sacramentos,* among other poems is included the famous sonnet "I am not moved to love Thee, my Lord God," which has been attributed to many other authors.

Father Matías de Bocanegra was born in 1612 and died in 1668. A native of Puebla, the famous Jesuit was highly regarded by viceroys and bishops. He became a clergyman in 1628 and published sermons and poetical works such as "El viaje del Marqués de Villena," 1640, and the "Teatro jerárquico de la Luz," 1642, as well as an unpublished play, now lost, called "Sufrir para merecer." He has been saved from oblivion by his "Canción de un desengaño," which was imitated again and again both in Mexico and in Spain. Except for Sor Juana, he is perhaps the only one deserving to be remembered for this particular poem. His version, which stands out among all those of his time, first develops a theme of freedom and later resolves it, along the theological lines which were characteristic of the period.

Captain Agustín de Salazar y Torres was born in 1642 in Spain and came to Mexico in 1645 with his uncle, the Bishop of Yucatán who was later to be viceroy. He died in 1675. He studied theology and law at the University of Mexico. In the poetic contest of 1654 he won first place. In 1660 he returned to Spain with the Duke of Alburquerque, married well, became a friend of Calderón, the Spanish playwright, and travelled through Germany to the viceroyalty of Sicily. He died in Madrid and his work was published in two volumes in 1681 and 1694. He left several plays which have been highly acclaimed, fables on Venus and Adonis, humorous sonnets and a "Soledad," an imitation of Góngora. In 1653 he published in Mexico his "Descripción en verso de la entrada del Duque de Alburquerque," and left among his manuscripts a "Drama Virginal para la Universidad de México," and "Metamorfosis mexicana," an imitation of Ovid.

Luis de Sandoval Zapata published from 1645 to 1665. He was born in Mexico of a noble family, descended from the Conquistadores, and considered an excellent philosopher, theologian, historian, politician and poet. His philosophical prose includes "Panegírico a la Paciencia," 1645. If scholars could find a manuscript of his with the title translated as "Castilian Miscellanea, many human and divine verses, the political Tiberian Caesar, the apology for novelty, the panegyrical information for origins, the Christian Epictetus, and some Latin works, etc." a comparison could very well be drawn with his great contemporary Quevedo. He left a ballad on the "Degollación de los Avilas" and several sonnets. One of these brought him renown, his original Guadalupian sonnet on the Phoenix, published in 1725. In 1937, twenty-nine of his sonnets were found. Spiritually, he is closer to Quevedo than to Góngora. His verbal energy, his love for the subtle, even to the metaphysical depths of scholasticism, his predilection for effective figures and his repetition of such favorite themes as death, are among his main characteristics. Called the prince of Mexican baroque, he was qualified by one critic as the "immortal phoenix of the Americas."

Mathematician, historian, astronomer and cosmographer was Carlos de Sigüenza y Góngora who was born in 1645 in Mexico City and died in 1700. He studied at the University of Mexico and in 1672 became professor of astrology and mathematics. In 1680 he edited the *Glorias de Querétaro,* a contest called to celebrate the construction of a new temple to Our Lady of Guadalupe. That same year he also published his *Teatro de virtudes políticas,* which was the triumphant arch to the Counts of Paredes. Likewise he published his *Manifesto filosófico contra los cometas* in which he carries on a campaign against superstition which was to be continued in his *Belerofonte matemático contra la Quimera Astrológica* and his *Libra Astronómica* in which he refuted Father Kino, explorer and missionary of the Southwest. He exchanged letters with many of the learned scientists of Europe of his time. In 1683 he edited the famous *Triunfo Parténico* and the next year published the *Paraíso Occidental,* a chronicle of the convent of Jesús María. By 1690 he had written *Los infortunios de Alonso Ramírez,* a sketchy picaresque novel based on historical facts. His *Trofeo de la justicia española* was published in 1691 to celebrate the victory of New Spain against the French in Santo Domingo. During the riot of 1692, which came about as a result of rivalries between the viceroy and the archbishop, he entered the burning buildings of the City Hall to save books and manuscripts. He occupied positions as expert in fortifications and drainage, general examiner of artillery men, cosmographer for His Majesty, historian of the ancient civilizations of Mexico, and devoted singer of Our Lady of Guadalupe. Sigüenza y Góngora died shortly before the publication of his poem to St. Francis Xavier, the *El oriental planeta evangélico.* He has been condemned both as a gongorist and as an opponent of gongorism. There is no question that he was enthusiastic about the poetry of his relative Luis de Góngora about whom he reminisced many times in his verses. He did not possess the originality or the exquisiteness, the impetus or the balance that his Spanish relative had. Well acquainted with the innovations of gongorism, Sigüenza used them frequently in his poems, to bring about exquisite synesthesia of melody and color at times or in the tonic changes of vowels. *Triunfo Parténico* is the story and compilation of two contests in honor of the Virgin Mary, held by the University of Mexico in 1682 and 1863. To the first contest alone, over five hundred poems were submitted, but seventy-nine poems by forty-seven authors received an award in both contests. As a Jesuit, Sigüenza studied in the College of Tepotzotlán and, although he had differences with the Company of Jesus, and abandoned it for seven years,

he nevertheless glorified St. Frances Xavier, the Jesuit's saint, in his writings. He considered the Jesuits his teachers and donated to them his excellent library, his collection of manuscripts, and his scientific instruments.

Towards the end of the seventeenth century, there was an awakening of interest in the history of pre-Cortesian Mexico, and Sigüenza y Góngora played a very prominent part in this development. He studied the laws of the languages of the Indians as well as their archaeological objects of art. He intended to write a complete history of the former kingdom of the Chichimecs, utilizing the manuscripts he had inherited from Fernando de Alva Ixtlilxóchitl. In this work he made use of astronomical knowledge to interpret the historical dates of events, correlating the Indian dates with the Christian calendar. Unfortunately, most of his works of this type have been lost. His longest work was the *Paraíso Occidental,* while the rarest is probably the *Piedad heroica de Fernando Cortés.* The latter work has been kept only in fragmentary form but must have had great historical interest and information, not only about the Christian gospel but also events and people of the times. In his "Fénix del Occidente," which was never published, he attempted to identify the legendary figure of Quetzalcóatl, a Toltec and Aztec personage, with the Apostle St. Thomas. Sigüenza y Góngora was typical of the savant of the seventeenth century; rather, indeed he was a forerunner of the eighteenth-century intellectual. Sigüenza's love for the arts and history of ancient Mexico and his interest in science testify to his wide range of knowledge as well as to his stature as a modern man; although in his poetry he was often plagued by the rhetorical devices of the gongoristic era.

Juan de Guevara, born in Mexico, was a chaplain of St. Ines, was a collaborator of Sor Juana Inés de la Cruz and possibly a cousin. He was secretary of the University poetry contest of 1654, was awarded a prize in the 1665 contest, and received three awards for his 1682–83 poems (for the poems that he submitted to the *Triunfo Parténico* of 1862–83). His ballad to the Marquis of Laguna is reminiscent of Sor Juana. He collaborated with Sor Juana in *Amor es más laberinto,* and probably contributed the second act to her play.

Captain Alonso Ramírez de Vargas, whose works were published between 1662 and 1696, was born in Mexico of noble parents. He compiled the *Descripción poética de las fiestas . . . por el nacimiento del Príncipe D. Carlos,* 1662, as well as the *Zodíaco Ilustre* referring to the arch of the cathedral to the viceroy, the Count of Moctezuma. He was also the compiler of two other arches: "Eneas" to the Marquis of Mancera, 1664, and "Cadmus" to the Count of Galve, 1688. He is famous likewise for his song to the funerals of the Bishop of Yucatán, 1695, his poem to the Immaculate, 1665, a sonnet to St. Francis of Borja, 1672, and many others. As a dramatist he took part in the University of Mexico festival of 1683 with an *auto* entitled "El mejor triunfo de Diana" which was played for three successive days during the celebrations. He also wrote humorous poetry with lyric grace, rich description of customs, and a wealth of Aztec words. His best gongoristic manner shows in an elegy to the "Fama póstuma y gloriosa del Capitán Retes Largache," with its lofty thoughts, daring imagery, forceful language, and deep sincerity.

The greatest poet of colonial Mexico and Latin America was Sister Juana Inés de la Cruz. She was born Juana Inés de Asbaje in the hacienda of San Miguel Nepantla, a ranch some miles from Mexico City, on the twelfth of November, 1651. She was a precocious child who learned to read at three and wrote her first poetry when she was eight. She heard about the University and insisted on being sent there, even suggesting that she wear men's clothing in order to attend. Her mother opposed this, and the future nun had to be content with reading the books in the family library and taking Latin lessons. In twenty lessons she completely mastered Latin. At the age of eight, she went to the capital of New Spain with her parents. It was her custom to set herself a time limit for learning something, and failing, cut off her hair; for she said it was not just "that a head should be dressed with hair when it was so devoid of knowledge, which was a more desirable ornament." That she was beautiful, we can judge by the painting left to us by Miguel Cabrera. By 1665, her reputation for beauty and talent had grown, and we find her as the lady-in-waiting of the Vicereine. The Viceroy, Marquis of Mancera, was astonished at the knowledge that Juana Inés had accumulated. To test her, he gathered in his palace all the professors of the university and as many experts in arts and sciences as there were in Mexico. Some forty theologians, philosophers, mathematicians, historians, humanists, and poets were brought together. She was examined by the savants and defended herself as "a royal galley would defend itself against the few canoes that might charge against it." For two years, she remained at the court where she must have tasted love and disillusionment. Her sudden decision to enter a convent has never been fully explained. Some critics believe that it was an unrequited love affair, although she claimed "total negation for matrimony." Other critics have sought an explanation in the fact that she was an illegitimate daughter. As she herself stated, because of the conventions of the time, she could not prefer to live alone and devote her life to studies. In August of 1667, she entered the Convent of Santa Teresa la Antigua, but after being there for a few months, she could not stand the rigid rules, and, her health being affected, she left. On February 24, 1669, however, she entered the Convent of San Jerónimo, to remain there for the rest of her life. She was an accountant and an archivist for the convent, but she twice declined the post of Mother Superior. In the convent, at any rate, she found the necessary peace to quench her thirst for knowledge and to carry on the experiments, reading and writing which were to bring her an even greater reputation. In spite of objections from some of the other nuns, she lived in the cloister among her books, maps and musical and scientific instruments.

She gathered a library of some four thousand volumes since she was interested in all fields of knowledge, especially philosophy, theology, astronomy, painting, humanities, and music.

She was placed in charge of the triumphal arch to the entrance of the Count of Paredes described in 1680 in the *Neptuno Alegórico*. She won two prizes in the contest of *Triunfo Parténico,* and she often wrote poetry for civil and religious festivals. Her poems circulated in manuscript until Juan de Camacho Gayna began to collect them and published the first volume in Madrid in 1689, with the baroque title of *Castalid Flood of the Only Poetess, Tenth Muse, Sor Juana Inés de la Cruz, Nun in the Monastery of San Jerónimo of the Imperial City of Mexico; where in various meters, idioms and styles, she fertilizes several matters with elegant, subtle, clear, ingenious, useful verses for teaching, recreation and admiration.* In 1692 the second volume appeared in Seville, and the third and last in Madrid in 1700 posthumously.

Towards the end of her life an incident took her away from her studies. She decided to question the theological thesis of the celebrated Portuguese Jesuit, Antonio Vieyra. The Bishop of Puebla, Manuel Fernández de Santa Cruz, wrote a letter to her praising her rebuttal but at the same time he exhorted her to withdraw from studies to devote herself completely to religion. The Bishop ended up by saying, "You have spent much time in the study of philosophers and poets." In her reply, Sor Juana gave us the best information about her character, literary inclinations, and life in general. She defended educated women and sustained her right to discuss the sermon she had rebuffed. She created both a biography and a psychological portrait of herself. However, the letter of the Bishop had a profound effect on her, and she sold library, musical and scientific instruments, and maps for the benefit of the poor. Perhaps the disastrous events of New Spain between 1690–91 — storms, floods, hunger, epidemics, and riots — set her to thinking about the imminence of death and the ephemeral quality of terrestrial glory. She led an ascetic life from then on until an epidemic of fever invaded the convent. Full of charity, she devoted herself to care of the sick sisters and, falling ill herself, she died at forty-four on the seventeenth of April, 1695.

Her restlessness of spirit, always avid for knowledge and research, the universality of her culture, the temper of her intelligence, the overflowing fantasy, and the sincere sentiment that appear in her poetry, all isolate Sister Juana and place her above the literature of her times, saving her from dying in that environment. Being influenced by gongoristic and conceptistic currents, she also succumbed to the taste of her times. She followed Góngora, whom she admired, in her *Primero Sueño* where she describes knowledge on a limitless trip, an exercise in pure and free intellectual enjoyment. Philosophy, mythology, erudition, history, science, and artistic description are all intermingled in this work.

She was not absolutely gongoristic although we can say that she gongorized. Her gongorism had something of literary virtuosity, but it was not a sincere and genuine expression of her spirit, usually clear and diaphanous.

The poems of worldly love of Sister Juana, according to a Spanish critic, "are the softest and most delicate that have come from the pen of a woman." It is this poetry that has made some critics suspect that she suffered from a passion as ardent as it was mysterious, that filled her life. The request for love, the painful complaints, the jealous fits, the sorrow expressed almost in sobs which appear in such poems cannot be artificial, but sincere. They have the mark of truth in them. Using the translation of Samuel Beckett, we can become aware of her love poetry when she describes rationally the irrational effects of love and says,

> This torment of love
> that is in my heart,
> I know I feel it
> and know not why.

Her love sonnets can be included among the best of such poetry written. Examples of these sonnets are "Tarry, Shadow of my Scornful Treasure," "Diuturnal Infirmity of Hope," "This Colored Counterfeit that Thou Beholdest," "Divine Rose, Led in a Pleasant Garden," "Crimson Lute that Comest in the Dawn," "Green Enravishment of Human Life," etc. Her depth of feeling, and her jealousy can be seen in the sonnet, "This Evening when I Spake with Thee, Beloved," when she says,

> Enough of cruelty, beloved enough:
> let my heart's jealousy torment thee not
> nor vile suspicion violate thy virtue.
> With foolish shadows, vain appearances,
> since now in aqueous humor thou hast seen
> and held between thy hands my broken heart.

The roundels, "Foolish Men Who Accuse Women" and her "Reply to Sister Filotea" exemplify her beliefs in the rights of women.

She also wrote three *autos sacramentales,* "El Cetro de José," "El Mártir del Sacramento," and "El Divino Narciso," following in the footsteps of Calderón, whom she admired greatly. Also influenced by Calderón were her two plays in the contemporary fashion. *Los empeños de una casa* is in the manner of the sword and cloak play, so popular in the Spanish theatre of the seventeenth century. Somewhat more affected by gongorism is another of her plays, *Amor es más laberinto,* written with the collaboration of Juan de Guevara.

Drama

The theatre had continued to develop, and undoubtedly performances were better and more numerous, emphasizing the works of Spanish and a few Mexican authors. We know that a theatre with a regular company existed before 1673. It was located inside the Royal Hospital and burned down in 1722, and the Old Coliseo followed. Hence, although there is no doubt that theatre as well as theatrical companies existed, information on the plays and playwrights is scanty.

One of the most outstanding playwrights of Mexico, Juan Ruiz de Alarcón y Mendoza, spans the sixteenth and seventeenth centuries. The exact place of his birth is unknown, although he himself asserted that it was the city of Mexico. Others insisted that it was Taxco, the silver-mining town where his parents lived before and after their marriage. His grandparents came to Taxco in 1535 and were well-known members of that community. At least two of his brothers were born there. Some critics place the date of Juan's birth as 1581; others insist that it might be as early as 1575. Paternally he descended from a noble family of Cuenca with titles going back to the twelfth century. On his mother's side were even more illustrious ancestors, the House of Mendoza, with such forebears as Antonio de Mendoza, Chancellor López de Ayala, the Marquis of Santillana, Jorge and Gómez Manrique, Garcilaso de la Vega and Hurtado de Mendoza.

The father of Alarcón was a miner. Although perhaps not too prosperous, the family enjoyed an excellent social position. Juan entered the Royal and Pontifical University of Mexico in 1592 to study arts. His brothers Pedro and Gaspar also enrolled there, the first, to study geology and the second, jurisprudence. After finishing the four-year course in arts, Juan began a course in law and almost finished the requirements for a degree. Then, despite the fact that the University of Mexico enjoyed an excellent reputation, young Alarcón decided to go to the University of Salamanca to obtain a Bachelor of Laws degree which he had by 1602. At this time, a relative gave him an annual pension of 1,650 *reales,* and it may be conjectured therefore that the Alarcón family had become impoverished. Since it was expensive to obtain a degree at the University of Salamanca, Alarcón decided to return to Mexico City. En route he stopped in Seville and took the examinations required to practice law before the *Audiencia.* For the first time he participated in a poetic event in Seville, his literary debut consisting of *décimas* written under a pseudonym "to console the lady who was sad because her hands perspired a great deal."

In 1607 he decided to join Father Pedro Godínez Maldonado, being sent as a bishop to the Philippines through New Spain. Unfortunately, the fleet that was to be used to transport the Bishop was destined instead to fight Dutch pirates. So Alarcón embarked instead with the new Bishop of Mexico, Father García Guerra, accompanied by the Spanish picaresque novelist Mateo Alemán, on May 13, 1608. The destination of the fleet was New Spain.

Alarcón finally obtained his law degree from the University of Mexico in 1609, attempting unsuccessully to be excused from all the pomp accompanying he doctoral rites. Between 1609 and 1613 he applied n vain for three different professorships. He was unlucky in his university career, as in his applications or government employment.

Alarcón's father died between 1607 and 1608; his mother probably by 1612.

Who can say what might have become of the literary career of Alarcón had he remained in New Spain?

Not having succeeded in his applications, and being forced to accept the position of lawyer for the Royal Audiencia of Mexico, he finally decided to return to Europe. He left Mexico in 1613 and arrived probably at the end of that year in Madrid. For a while he became a friend of Lope de Vega; they later clashed and made violent allusions to each other in their work.

Alarcón's literary life was active, contentious, and frequently bitter. It is a measure of his greatness that although he was a foreigner, and wrote very little by comparison to the dramatists of the Golden Age of Spain, he nevertheless stands out as an original personality among them. Few literary figures have been attacked as bitterly as Alarcón; few have been so mocked and maligned. The majority of the writers of the Golden Age of Spain took up arms against him. His physical deformity, a hump on his chest and on his back, lent itself to ridicule and criticism. Góngora, Quevedo, Lope, Tirso de Molina, among many others, were his attackers. *Criollos* were often ridiculed for pretending to be of noble birth as Alarcón actually was, and proudly so, but his adversaries could not forgive him his pride in the family name. They harassed him constantly and made fun of him for using the "don" before his name.

Alarcón's theatrical works were published in two parts; the first in 1628, with eight plays, and the second in 1634 with twelve. Others were published individually.

Counting those of doubtful paternity and those he wrote in collaboration, there may be as many as thirty-six plays. For the purposes of comparison we can recall that Lope de Vega claimed to have written over fifteen hundred plays, Tirso de Molina four hundred, and Calderón close to five hundred.

In 1626, through the president of the council of the Indies, Alarcón was able to obtain the post of temporary relator of the Council and in 1633 he was given the position permanently. Perhaps somewhat disillusioned with literary failures, he devoted himself to bureaucracy and abandoned letters. Finally he reached a certain stage of comfort, with a carriage, servants, and some money. He died in Madrid on August 4, 1639. Even in death he was mocked. The only epitaph to Juan Ruiz Alarcón was written by the gazetteer Pellicer de Tovar, who said that he died, "as famous for his plays as for his humps."

Whereas in Calderón or in Tirso, moral sentiment is a consequence of religious dogma or scholastic philosophy, in Alarcón it stems from man. In his plays, and possibly for the first time in the Spanish theatre, morality appears in a secular sense. Alarcón is concerned with friendship, generosity, forgiveness, the keeping of promises, the avoidance of gossip and of lying. These virtues are not heroic but they are attainable and more useful for man in general. A reflective man, his heroes and heroines, maids and servants, have an inner life that is difficult to find in the theatre of the times. Outwardly, his heroes appear typical heroes of the Spanish theatre of the Golden Age: adventuresome, quarrelsome, discreet, enamored, brave, handsome; inside they are endowed with a more noble fibre and with feelings of generosity. Heroines are frequently treated more rigorously than heroes by Alarcón. Most of them have nasty dispositions and are rather commonplace. As some critic has said: ". . . they act in an evil fashion in cold blood." Often these ladies prefer money to love, titles of nobility to talent. Unfortunately, very little is known of the intimate details of the playwright's life that might explain these attitudes. We do know that he had a love affair with Angela Cervantes by whom he had a daughter Lorenza.

Servants are everpresent in the theatre of Alarcón, and in some cases become main characters in the play. They are not licentious, impertinent, nor shameless, but often become valuable counselors to the hero.

In speaking of Alarcón, Pedro Henríquez Ureña has said that over and above ". . . the impetus, the prodigality of the European Spaniard who created and divulged the mechanism of the Comedia, there has been imposed, as a moderating force, the prudent sobriety, the discretion of the Mexican."

Alarcón is, as a Mexican, believed by critical admirers to have had the malicious and sharp powers of observation that his countrymen keep to themselves, and release at the unexpected moment. The courtesy of Alarcón was also proverbial. His plays abound with expressions of courtesy and amenability by contrast with the sparsity of those characteristics in the dramas of his contemporaries. The critic Usigli feels that Alarcón's sensibility corresponds directly to the pessimism of a subjugated Mexico combined with the effervescence of a conquering Spain. Other critics have commented that Alarcón, the moralist, was created by the study of law in his youth and the professional activity to which he devoted a good part of his life. Whereas in Calderón and in Tirso, the moralist is derived from the theologian, in Juan Ruiz de Alarcón, the moralist is derived from the jurist, a jurist of ugly appearance who is also ambitious, who has failed in part but is generous and good. The critic Jiménez Rueda lists certain elements that he believes affect Alarcón's literary work: In the first place, his origin and his upbringing are different from that of the Spaniard. *Criollos, mestizos,* and Indians indubitably influenced the young playwright. In the second place, his classical and legal studies made him acquainted with antiquity and disciplined his spirit. His studies in law put him in contact with the casuistry of Roman or church law, thus preparing him for the casuistic morality found in some of his protagonists. In the third place, his physical deformity isolated him from others. An inferiority complex, along with Mexican upbringing, fostered the habits of reserve and courtesy and adaptation to hostile environment. At times, however, Alarcón's pride burst forth in violent form, as with reference to Lope de Vega. In the fourth place, the literary battles of the time in Madrid made him a target for insulting attacks and permitted him no illusions as to some of the harsher realities of human nature. The name of Juan Ruiz de Alarcón was not to lose in the long run. Many of the authors celebrated during his lifetime have been forgotten, probably forever.

The plays of Alarcón, however, still register intensity and actuality of feeling, and his influence on the French theatre of the seventeenth century is undeniable.

The relatively small number of plays he wrote can be explained in part by two factors: the precarious life that he led while writing, and the hostility of the public.

Alarcón often spoke of the public as "fierce beasts." He instructed, ". . . treat them as you usually do; not as it is just, but as it is your pleasure, for they look upon you with scorn and without fear, as those who have already gone through the danger of your whistlings, and those which can now only go through the danger of your rancour."

With Alarcón, improvisation, so common to dramatists of his time, stepped aside for reflection, serenity, and polish. He took the ambivalence of literature seriously: to entertain and to teach. He denounced such vices as ingratitude, gossip, lying, and lack of constancy in love. He exalted the virtues of piety, sincerity, gratitude, and loyalty. Yet he did not preach. Moral purpose was implicit in his development of plot. He had no peer in the creation of characters, in the logic of development, and in the penetration and minuteness of psychological analysis of his characters.

Simplicity and economy characterized Alarcón's plays. His plots were often not as complicated as those of his fellow dramatists. He used few superfluous characters, his monologues were concise, and his dialogues brief. Having started as an imitator of Lope de Vega, he eventually developed his own comedy which dealt with morals as well as with customs. Influenced by Terence, he was to leave his own imprint on Corneille and Molière in France, and Moratín in Spain.

Although the Spanish theatre of the Golden Age claims Juan Ruiz de Alarcón as its own — one of the Big Four — we must remember that Alarcón was born, educated, and spent his early youth in Mexico. His literary talent first revealed itself there. And since this talent differed from that which was dominant in Spain at the same time, showing sensibility and expression akin to that of the Mexicans, we must therefore consider Juan Ruiz de Alarcón as the greatest literary figure of the Mexican theatre.

Among those who composed religious *autos* were Juan Ortiz de Torres, Jerónimo Becerra and Alfonso Ramírez Vargas. We also know that Agustín Salazar y Torres as well as Eusebio Vela composed plays during the seventeenth century. Salazar y Torres was born in Spain and came to Mexico as a child. No doubt he composed some of his theatrical plays in New Spain and returned to Spain later on to become known as a dramatic author. Beristáin, a bibliographer of the early part of the nineteenth century, said Vela was a dramatic poet, "if not equal to Lope and Calderón, he was superior to Montalván and to Moreto in the decency of his humor." Vela was born in New Spain and is supposed to have composed up to 14 plays, some of which were printed but have probably been lost. The Spanish Golden Age playwrights had a great deal of influence on Vela.

Historical Writing

The interest in historical writings continued in the seventeenth century with a new orientation. Most of the histories at that time concerned the religious provinces of New Spain. Philology was still studied in the seventeenth century, but not to the extent it had been during the 1600's when first contact was made between the Indians and the preaching missionaries. Some of the lesser-known Indian dialects were studied, however, among others those of the Tepehuanes and the Tarahumaras.

An outstanding historian, Father Agustín Vetancurt, was born in Mexico in 1620. He spent his life in the service of the church, became chronicler of his province and served as Commissary General of the Indies until his death in 1700. He published a work on the Aztec language in 1663 and religious books in both Spanish and Aztec. His best-known work is *Teatro Mexicano: Descripción breve de las sucesos ejemplares, históricos, políticos, militares y religiosos del Nuevo Mundo,* published in Mexico in 1698. The first part deals with natural history of Mexico; the second, with political events from ancient times until the arrival of the Spaniards; the third, with military events from the discovery of the New World until the capture of Mexico City; the fourth part is a chronicle of the Province of the Holy Gospel, complemented by the *Franciscan Menologio.*

Among the historians, we come again to the versatile Carlos de Sigüenza y Góngora, expert on Indian language, history, and antiquities. Unfortunately, we know his historical works only by reference, as they were unpublished. He wrote an "Historia del imperio de los Chichimecas," "Genealogía de los reyes mexicanos," "Calendario de los meses y fiestas de los mexicanos," and "Teatro de la grandeza de Mexico." He lent even greater service to history by collecting Mexican documents which, in twenty-eight volumes, he donated to the Colegio Máximo de San Pedro y San Pablo. When Gemelli Carreri, the Italian traveler, was composing *Giro del Mondo,* printed in 1700,

Sigüenza y Góngora very generously gave him all the information he had available about Mexico. Later on, Father Clavijero, the foremost eighteenth-century historian of Mexico, also made use of the documents of Sigüenza y Góngora to write his masterpiece, *Historia antigua de México.*

Gil González Dávila wrote *Teatro eclesiástico de las iglesias de Indias,* which is not very accurate. In 1688, in Madrid, Father Diego López de Cogolludo wrote *Historia de Yucatán.* Matías de la Mota Padilla (1688–1776) wrote the *Historia de la Nueva Galicia* (Jalisco), not printed until 1871.

Among the valuable histories are the chronicles of religious provinces. They narrate the activities of the various orders and the biographies of the members, whether famous or not. These are worthwhile for a picture of colonial customs and beliefs. For certain regions of Mexico they are the only existing historical accounts of culture. An Augustinian, Father Juan González de la Puente wrote a chronicle of Michoacán, printed in 1624. Father Francisco Burgoa, Oaxaca-born (1605–1681), wrote several religious works and left unpublished an "Itinerario de Oaxaca a Roma y de Roma a Oaxaca," but his most famous works are his *Palestra Historial* or the *Historia de la Provincia de San Hipólito de Oaxaca* in 1670, and the *Geográfica Descripción de la America Septentrional y de la Nueva Iglesia de Occidente,* 1674. Another Augustinian, Father Diego de Basalenque, born in 1577 in Salamanca, Spain, authored a chronicle of Michoacán in 1673.

Born in Colima, in 1559, Dominican Father Juan Grijalva wrote *Crónica de la Provincia de México* in 1624. Also a Dominican, Father Antonio Remesal of Galicia went to Guatemala in 1613 and wrote the *Historia de la Provincia de San Vicente de Chiapa y Guatemala,* printed in 1619.

Franciscan Father Alonso de la Rea, born in 1624 in Querétaro, was the author of the *Crónica de la Provincia de San Pedro y San Pablo de Michoacán,* published in 1643. In 1891 was published the seventeenth-century chronicle of Father Antonio Tello, *Crónica Miscelánea en que se trata de la conquista espiritual y temporal de la Santa Provincia de Xalisco.*

In 1694, the first part of the *Historia de la Provincia de la Compañía de Jesús de Nueva España* appeared. It was written by Father Francisco de Florencia, a native of Spanish Florida, and president of the Colegio Máximo of Saint Peter and Saint Paul, the foremost Jesuit institution for higher studies in New Spain. This history was to be rewritten in the eighteenth century by another famous Jesuit, Father Francisco Javier Alegre.

The Novel

The real Mexican novel awaited the beginning of the nineteenth century and the movement for Independence, although in the 1700's, there were recognizable forerunners. In the sixteenth century, one recalls, was issued the royal decree of April, 1531, prohibiting novels being shipped "to the Indies." Admittedly this helped to account for the paucity of novels a century later.

Although the same regulation persisted in Spain, control was easier in the overseas dominions. With the exception of clergymen and scholars, the settlers who came to New Spain were not distinguished for their love of books and reading, and the Indians, of course, were not familiar with the novel, perhaps because the conditions of their lives curtailed to a certain extent their initiative and their imagination. At any rate they were imaginatively stimulated by illegal remembrance of their ancient rites and some of the dramatic performances put on for their conversion.

Nonetheless, in spite of the prohibition, novels *were* introduced and probably even written in New Spain. Inventories of certain convents and monasteries reveal these forbidden books as early as the beginning of the seventeenth century. Novels that were written surreptitiously and on a secular theme have remained in manuscript — an indication of the effectiveness of censorship during colonial times.

What many critics have called the first example of the novel in New Spain is *Los sirgueros de la Virgen sin original pecado* (1620), by Francisco Bramón, a councillor of the Royal and Pontifical University of Mexico. Little is known about his life except that he had a bachelor's degree and wrote poetry and as a participant in a literary contest concerning the Immaculate Conception, won fourth prize. Bramón's novel has a rather weak and conventional plot often overshadowed by a sermon. In keeping with the spirit of these times, the doctrinaire element almost floods the narrative thread. The clergyman who approved the publication of the book referred to the honest and holy entertainment found in it. The plot of the *Gold Finches of the Virgin without Original Sin* tries to follow the lines of the pastoral novel, praising the Virgin Mary, not only through lyric poems, which would account for the title, Gold Finches or singers, but also through apologetic dialogues, explanation of symbols, construction of triumphal arches, dramatic representations and other means. The book ends with festivals in honor of the Immaculate Conception.

The next ancestor of the novel appeared in 1662 by Antonio de Ochoa, *Sucesos de Fernando o La caída de Fernando.* In 1690, Carlos Sigüenza y Góngora wrote the *Infortunios de Alonso Ramírez,* an historical narrative which could have been a picaresque novel. Alonso, the hero, is a naïve narrator in the typical autobiographical style of the picaresque. He speaks of his birth in San Juan de Puerto Rico, of his good and Christian mother and his Andalusian carpenter father. He leaves home to seek his fortune and goes from one master to another. Captured by pirates in the Philippines, he finally makes his way to the coast of Yucatán, having navigated almost around the world. This may come closer to being a first Mexican novel than the work of Bramón.

EIGHTEENTH CENTURY

Gongorism or *culteranismo* began its decadence during the first half of the century. Although already vanished in the Peninsula, it persisted in Mexico until the middle of the eighteenth century when neoclassicism drove it out. The eighteenth century was characterized by its scientific inclination and its critical spirit, although some earlier writers such as Sigüenza y Góngora and Sister Juana already showed the intellectual thirst of the savant that was to typify the 1700's. By 1700, the Jesuits had acquired great cultural, political, and economic prestige. In their schools developed the humanistic movement of the eighteenth century. In the main seminary at Tepozotlán were students from all the Americas, attracted by important innovations from the thought of Descartes and Leibnitz, among others in scholastic philosophy. Letters, history, sciences, the study of Greek and Latin for direct knowledge of the classics, were among the higher studies of the Jesuits. They looked upon the classics as an inexhaustible source of inspiration and teaching, and possessing the values which compose the humanistic ideal. The theory was that harmony, proportion, and clarity were the ideal of good taste, best to be acquired by translating and imitating the great Greek and Latin authors. The efforts of the Jesuits, together with the influence of Spanish neoclassical writers who had introduced French taste into Spain, brought about the reaction against the gongorism which had plagued Mexico during almost all the seventeenth century and part of the eighteenth. As so often happens, the pendulum swing had been too great, and writers reacting against gongorism, with few exceptions, fell into the vicious exaggerations of neoclassicism: prosaism. With the advent of the Bourbon kings to Spain in the 1700's, there developed a conflict between the highly centralized government of the enlightened eighteenth-century kings and the power that the Jesuits had accumulated. In 1767, Charles III ordered the expulsion of the Jesuits from New Spain and the Latin-American dominions by a decree posted in several places in the capital of New Spain, on the twenty-sixth of June, 1767. The Viceroy, the Marquis of Croix, informed his subjects of the royal decree and threatened to execute those who did not obey and who did not respect the "always just resolutions of their sovereign." The Mexicans were reminded that as subjects of His Majesty, they were born "to be quiet and obey and not to dispute and opine in the high matters of government." From their missions, their churches, and their schools, the Jesuits were sent to Italy, leaving Latin America without its prime spiritual tutors. Reaction against this type of censorship expressed itself through pamphlets, ballads, and *corridos* (popular ballads). This was to be one of the major grievances of the *criollos* which culminated in the movement for Independence at the beginning of the nineteenth century. The arbitrary, violent, and authoritarian measures taken by the Spanish government against the Jesuits served to make salient the privileges that the Peninsular Spaniards enjoyed.

Although the work of the Jesuits indicated essentially the synthesis of a new humanism, another factor contributed signally to the creation of a national spirit. The Jesuits were the first to notice that the people of Mexico were neither Indians nor Spaniards, but simply Mexicans. They devoted themselves zealously to the study of the Indian past, and tried to explain the customs of the Indians from the religious point of view. Since missionaries and Conquistadores were both responsible for the destruction of several valuable manifestations of pre-cortesian cultures, the Jesuits complained against their excessive fervor. They also condemned slavery as much for the Indian as for the Negro because it is contrary to divine and human right. They considered the philosopher a "citizen of the world." In accepting the theories of Bacon, Leibniz, Galileo and Descartes, they discarded the old scholastic philosophy. The origin of authority they attributed to the people, using as their premise the social nature of man.

Because of their exile, they portrayed the faraway land of home with nostalgic memories, describing it and exalting it. Such manifestations seem to have been directly related to the search for a national spirit.

Poetry

Among the gongoristic poets of the eighteenth century, we can point out Francisco Ruiz de León, born in Tehuacán. He left several volumes of poetry in manuscript. In 1755 he published a heroic poem, *Hernandía Triumphos de la Fe y Gloria de las armas españolas* dealing with Cortés. In Bogotá, Columbia, in 1791 (probably after his death), was published a religious poem entitled *Mirra dulce para aliento de pecadores*. Probably the best epic poem praising Cortés, *The Hernandía,* written in octaves, relates the history of the Conquest from the expedition of Juan de Grijalva to the imprisonment of the last Aztec emperor, Cuauhtémoc. His religious poem, narrating the sorrows of the Virgin Mary at the foot of the cross, is superior to heroic verse.

A native of Jiquilpan, Michoacán, Diego José Abad (1727–1779), taught philosophy, law, and theology in Mexico and was a student of medicine and mathematics. He also wrote a Latin poem in hexameters, *De Deo Deoque Homine.* Agustín Castro (1728–1790) described the Oaxacan ruins of Mitla in Latin, and wrote a fragment of an epic, *La Cortesíada.*

The foremost Latinist in Mexico was Father Francisco Javier Alegre who was born in Veracruz in 1729 and at 17 joined the Jesuit order and devoted his life to the study of theology, history, and classical literature. He was exiled to Italy and died in 1788, leaving many printed works and manuscripts. His poetical work includes a small epic on the conquest of Tyre by Alexander the Great, Latin translations of the Iliad which were printed in 1776, and the *Batracomiomaquia.* He translated into Spanish several satires and epistles of Horace and the three first cantos of the *Poetic Art* by Boileau as well as several original Latin poems. His prose work includes *Theological Institutions* where he speaks of slavery as an unjust and iniquitous exploitation, and *Historia de la Compañía de Jesús* en la Nueva España (Mexico, 1841). This Jesuit history is endowed with ample documentation, excellent methodology and good style. The first volumes were published in 1841 in Mexico, leaving the fourth one unpublished.

Although born in Guatemala, which then (1731) belonged to the Viceroyalty of New Spain, Father Rafael Landívar belongs to Mexico where he received his intellectual education. He taught philosophy, rhetoric, and poetics, and died in Italy in 1793. His *Rusticatio Mexicana* was written in Latin hexameters in fifteen cantos with an appendix. It is an agricultural poem discussing nature and life in the country of Mexico. He portrays the Mexican lakes, the eruptions of a volcano and the cataracts in Guatemala. He describes the countryside in Oaxaca, the production of cochineal, the planting, cultivation, harvesting, and manufacturing of anil, the customs of the beavers and different

ways of hunting them. He also talks about the mines, pictures the cultivation of sugar cane, and depicts cattle, springs, birds, beasts, the popular games, such as cockfights, bullfights and pelota, etc. The wealth of local color places the book next to the *Grandeza Mexicana* of Balbuena. It was published first in Italy in 1781 and in a definitive edition in 1782. A prose translation into Spanish in 1942 comes closest to reflecting the spirit of the work.

José Manuel Sartorio (1746–1829) was born in Mexico, studied Latin and other languages, and became a priest distinguished for his preaching. When Independence came, he was suspect because he did not denounce from the pulpit the insurgents who disobeyed the commands of the viceroy. Sartorio signed Mexico's Declaration of Independence. He left some twenty volumes of sermons. His sacred and secular poems were published posthumously in Puebla in 1832. Sartorio is a typical example of prosaism. He wrote poems on familiar themes, congratulatory poems, epigrams, roundels to collect alms, extravagant epitaphs, fables, songs, poems to persons and animals, to noble ladies, to Mother Superiors, to the Archbishop, to the viceroy,

— Courtesy Mexican Government Tourism Department

Transplanted to Mexico from Spain, the highly sculpturesque and dynamic baroque architectural style of the eighteenth century produced some of the New World's most fascinating architectural treasures. This is the church of San Francisco Atapec, in the state of Puebla, east of Mexico, D.F.

to landladies, etc. His best effort deals with his poems praising the Virgin Mary.

The most important of the Mexican neo-classical poets was Father José Manuel Martínez de Navarrete, born in 1768 in Zamora, Michoacán. He became a Franciscan at nineteen, was a professor of Latin in Querétaro, and died in 1809. In 1823 his *Entretenimientos Poéticos* were published. Between 1806 and 1810 he published his poems in *El Diario de México*. Actually, he represents the transition between neo-classicism and romanticism. As a poet he imitated Meléndez Valdés, the most popular of the neo-classical Spanish poets of his time. His love poetry, rather than showing real and sensual passion, seems a candorous rhetorical exercise. In his nature poems, however, he let his contemplative tenderness loose. He was endowed with spontaneity, freshness, sensitive delicacy, and "a certain melancholy fervor that is like a lukewarm dawn of romantic sentiment." His poetry represented the neo-classical taste reaching its maturity.

History

Father Francisco Javier Clavijero stands out as the first historian of Mexico who used rigorous methods, a critical spirit, and solid erudition in portraying ancient history of the Aztecs and the history of the Conquest. He was born in Veracruz in 1731 and spent part of his life in the country. He studied Latin, philosophy, and theology in Puebla, and in 1748, he joined the Jesuit order. He possessed the solid and ample culture typical of the Jesuits of his times. He studied exact physical and natural sciences, music, and literature of the Latin as well as the Spanish classics; he was also well versed in Greek, Latin, and Hebrew, in the principal European languages, in Náhuatl, Otomí, and Mixtec, and besides this knew the grammar of some twenty dialects of Mexico. He withdrew from peripatetic philosophy, orienting his students toward a more rational scholasticism because of his thorough acquaintance with the philosophies of Descartes and Leibniz (as shown by the *Diálogos entre Filateles y Paliófilo*). When he was expelled from Mexico in 1767, he undertook the study of navigation, physics, and astronomy on the very ship that took him to Europe. He died in 1787. His *Historia Antigua de México* was made up of ten books dealing with the physical geography, the people that inhabited the valley of Mexico before the Aztecs, the departure of the Aztecs from Aztlán and their pilgrimage to Mexico City. He also pictured the political and military life of the Aztecs and the other principal peoples of Mexico. Discussing their religion, customs, culture, social organization, occupations, and wealth, he established, for the first time, the chronology of Indian peoples. His account ends with the history of the Conquest from the arrival of the Spaniards to the imprisonment of Cuauhtémoc. In the *Dissertations,* a corollary to the *History,* he considers such matters as the origin of the population of the Americas, the geographical peculiarities of Mexico, the physical and moral constitution, the culture and religion of the Aztecs, and the limits and population of the Aztec empire. He wrote the original text in Spanish but put it into Italian with the title, *Storia Antica del Messico,* publishing it in 1780–81. He also wrote a *Historia de la Antigua o Baja California,* which was published for the first time in Italian in 1789, after Clavijero's death.

Bibliography

Despite the fact that literary production, from the Conquest on, was abundant, no one wrote biographies or published bibliographic material on the writers of Mexico until Juan José de Eguiara y Eguren. Born towards the end of the seventeenth century, he was a doctor and president and professor at the University and had a reputation for being an expert in letters, law, philosophy, mathematics, and oratory. Although he wrote much on religion and philosophy, the only work we have left is the *Biblioteca Mexicana,* of which the first volume was published in 1755. This was the only volume published since the author died in 1763. It covers authors alphabetically through "C," and has a prologue explaining the plan for the complete work and sketching Mexican culture from its beginnings. The entire volume is written in Latin, including the titles of the works. The writers are listed by first names, the bibliography lacks critical sense, and, at times, has a high panegyrical tone. In spite of its shortcomings and incompleteness, however, this first work of bibliography represents a noble attempt to refute ignorance in Spain with regard to intellectual development in New Spain.

The efforts of Eguiara inspired José Mariano Beristáin y Souza to take up bibliographic work. He was born in Puebla in 1756 and went to Valencia, Spain, where he received the degree of Doctor of Theology. He fought Independence from the pulpit and with his pen; and had a stroke while preaching in the Cathedral of Mexico City and died shortly afterwards, in 1817. His bibliography is entitled *Biblioteca hispanoamericana septentrional.* He described it as a "catalogue and notices of the literary men who either born or educated, or flourishing in Spanish Southern America, have given to light some writing, or have left it for the press." The three volumes were published in 1816, 1819, and 1821. The author spanned some twenty years, giving information about some four thousand writers. Although somewhat inaccurate, it is a useful tool for research since its wealth of material makes it the only bibliographical and biographical dictionary of the period, giving authors and titles that otherwise would have been lost.

Scientific Writing

The expulsion of the Jesuits did not stop the cultural development of Mexico. In 1784, the first formal newspaper appeared, *La Gaceta de México.* Father José Antonio Alzate (1729–1790) had been publishing newspapers containing articles on geography, natural history, geology, medicine, etc. By 1792, the College of Mines was founded with such famed authorities as Fausto Elhúyar and Andrés del Río, the latter the author of the best work on mineralogy written in Spanish. The fine arts also progressed with the creation in 1783 of the Academy of St. Charles. Architecture was flourishing also with the works of the Spaniard Tolsá and the Mexican Tresguerras. The physical sciences were cultivated by Alzate; Francisco Javier Gamboa, a lawyer and a geologist; Joaquín Velázquez de León, a geodesist and astronomer; Antonio León Gama, an astronomer, geographer, and archaeologist; José Ignacio Bertolache, mathematician; and a botanist José Ignacio Mociño.

Philosophy

A noted philosopher, Juan Benito Díaz de Gamarra y Dávalos, flourished at this time. He was born in 1745 in Zamora, Michoacán. After graduating with a degree of Bachelor of Canon Law, he entered the Oratory of San Miguel el Grande in 1764. During 1767–1770 he travelled in Spain, Rome, Portugal, Italy, and received the degree of Doctor of Canon Law from the University of Pisa, Italy. In 1774 he published his *Antigüedades de Xochicalco* and his *Elementa Recentioris Philosophiae,* and in 1775 he was denounced before the Inquisition because of one of his conclusions on physics in the *Elementa.* He was absolved after giving complete and satisfactory explanations. In 1781 he published in Puebla his *Errores de la mente humana,* and several of his other works were published after his death in 1783. His *Elementa Recentioris Philosophiae* is his capital work, introducing modern philosophy through discussion of eclecticism, scepticism, anti-peripateticism, religiousness, tolerance, modernity, Copernicism, and Newtonism. His *Errors of the Human Mind* deals with misconceptions about health, human knowledge, and morals.

Drama

About the theatre in the eighteenth century, we know little. However, we find that Manuel Zumaya wrote a drama, *El Rodrigo* in 1708 and an opera, *Parténope* in 1711, both performed at the palace of the viceroy. Cayetano Cabrera Quintero was the author of the plays, *La esperanza malograda* and *El Iris de Salamanca.* Francisco Soria is the author of three dramatic works: *Guillermo Duque de Aquitania, Mágica mexicana,* and *La Genoveva.*

Anastasio Mariá de Ochoa (1783–1833) studied philosophy and canon law at the University and devoted himself entirely to letters. He translated Ovid, Racine, Boileau, Fenelon, and Beaumarchais from the French, and from the Italian, Alfieri. He was well versed in the literature of the Spanish Golden Age and wrote plays and one tragedy, *Don Alfonso,* for the theatre. His poems, published under the title *Poesías de un mexicano,* in New York, in 1828, portray the social life of Mexico at the end of the colonial period. Ochoa was a poet of transition between the last years of the eighteenth century and the Independence period. He was outstanding in comic or festive poetry, following in the footsteps of Alcázar, Lope, and Quevedo.

The Novel

The novel as a genre, for reasons previously discussed, was not to appear until the movement for independence exploded at the beginning of the nineteenth century. In the 1700's, Marcos Reynal Hernández and José González de Sancha came close to being novelists. Hernández, a professor of theology at the Seminario Tridentino in Mexico City, wrote a mystical work with novelistic pretensions called the *El peregrino con guía y medicina universal de la alma,* in 1750. González de Sancha, a clergyman, wrote in gongoristic style, and with mystical tendencies, a novel entitled *Fabiano y Aurelia* (1760).

NINETEENTH CENTURY AND THE WAR OF INDEPENDENCE

The *mestizo,* a new social class, was formed by the time of the War of Independence (1810–21). Together with the *criollos,* they formed a group apart in society — a group with aspirations toward constituting itself as a nationality. These tendencies, noticeable before, increased during the Age of Enlightenment of the Bourbon kings. The expulsion of the Jesuits had already brought to the surface the discontent and desire to change the *status quo.* During the reign of Charles III, the colonial army was created, putting into the hands of the Mexicans the arms necessary for freedom. The increase in royal income resulting from the financial and administrative reorganization brought about by Visitor General Gálvez accentuated the Mexican feeling of protest. Through its foreign policy — mostly one of opposition to England — the Spanish government aided in the emancipation of the English colonies, thus making the Mexicans see that emancipation in itself was legitimate and plausible. Two excellent viceroys, Bucareli and Revillagigedo, prevented the inevitable for a time. The Indians, who during the sixteenth century received the benefits of culture through the efforts of the missionaries, were now left outside the mainstream of culture. The same was true of peninsular Spaniards who were, for the most part, government officials. Thus it was up to the *criollos* and the *mestizos* to develop culture, and indeed, out of this group came the salient figures of Mexican letters during colonial times, from Alarcón and Sor Juana to the humanists, historians, philologists, and poets.

Intellectual innovation had come in the eighteenth century; in letters through the advent of neoclassicism, in philosophy through an initial opposition to scholasticism, in science through the introduction of experimental studies and the creation of the College of Mines, in plastic arts through the founding of the Academy of St. Charles, and in architecture through the works of Tolsá and Tresguerras. The Inquisition was a watchdog that tried to curtail thought and limit the movement for intellectual expansion, but by now its main function had almost been reduced to book prohibition — an attempt to keep New Spain in spiritual isolation. In spite of the Inquisition, the forbidden books continued entering the viceroyalty and disseminating the doctrines of Rousseau, Montesquieu, Diderot, and other Encyclopedists of eighteenth-century France, powerful instruments for the diffusion of the ideas of the French Revolution. Culture was actually hindered by the expulsion of the Jesuits, especially since the University of Mexico could not be looked to for cultural renovation and was in fact a deterring element, an institution engaged mostly in scholastic dialectics. Gongorism and conceptism persisted in literature and oratory, together with prosaism. The doctrines of the eighteenth-century Jesuits had not borne fruit yet. Navarette did not publish his verses until 1806.

The *Diario de México* was published in twenty-five volumes between 1805 and 1817 and counted in its columns one hundred and twenty poets, mostly neoclassical, and probably as many prose writers. The poetry was still neoclassical, although this current was beginning to decline in Spain. In 1808 was founded the Arcadia, a literary society similar to those in Europe and an institution destined to stimulate pastoral poetry. Literature, like the social structure of the colony, was on the eve of transformation.

Political Prose

The period of the War of Independence from 1810 to 1821 was to bring about great changes in Mexican society; literature could not remain idle. It took on a new aspect, the political aspect. It was literature of action, of dynamism, very similar to the type of literature written in the early part of the sixteenth century. It was natural that a literature of propaganda would develop during the struggle; many pamphlets were published, some aimed at the educated and some at the masses. The high point of pamphleteering came between 1811 and 1812. The royalists, of course, also used this means to persuade the social classes to remain loyal to the king. Among various pamphlets, we have "Patriotic letters of a father to his son, about the conduct that he must observe against the insurgent seductors," "Christian and political memoirs on how much New Spain must fear the disunion into parties," "Disillusionment of the Indians, making them see how much they owe the Spaniards," etc. Most of the pamphlets were published by the royalists, as the insurgents did not have readily available means of printing and disseminating material. But in 1811, the most capable of all insurgent pamphleteers appeared — Fernández de Lizardi. Freedom of the press under the new Spanish Constitution of 1812 allowed the partisans of independence to express themselves more readily, but between 1813 and 1819, the activity of the pamphleteers declined. Freedom of the press again in 1819 meant that 500 pamphlets would come from the presses in 1820, discussing the constitutional regime, freedom of thought, social or humoristic questions, theatrical criticism or complaints to authorities.

The establishment of Parliament or the *Cortes* in Cádiz, Spain, with Mexico represented for the first time, allowed the colonists to express themselves through political orators, and to fight for the defense of their rights and the interests of their country. Miguel Ramos Arizpe, 1775–1843, wrote the first Mexican Constitution and distinguished himself at the *Cortes* through his political speeches. Among the clerical orators, Beristáin, the bibliographer, stood out for his hatred towards the insurgents. In his sermon on Palm Sunday, preached in Mexico in 1815, he mingled Jesus Christ, Barabbas, Hidalgo, and Ferdinand VII.

Literature could not stand aloof from the revolution which was to leave indelible and deep marks upon it. Whereas literature had been isolated from the popular pulse and almost the prerogative of clergymen during colonial times, political literature was now born, and Mexican letters began to show the awakening of national feeling. National sentiment, which was to affect lyric poetry and the theatre and to reach its peak with the appearance of the first Mexican novel, was to become, after the War of Independence, a spiritual force giving literature in Mexico an unmistakable character. Poetry kept on struggling with the last cries of *gongorismo* and the new prosaic manner, but with the War of Independence it took a different path: glorification of the heroes of Independence. At first, war silenced the poets. The pseudo-classical love poetry disappeared, the religious poets kept almost complete silence, and satrical poetry, with Ochoa as example, remained. Then poetry ceased to be static and became dynamic. Its main purpose seems to be the dissemination of ideas, eluding, when possible, the censorship of both church and government. Fables and epigrams appeared. Even as late as 1816, Beristáin called for a poetry contest to celebrate the return of the Jesuits, an anomaly at such a time.

Poetry had prevailed up to the period of Independence, but now prose writings were to come to the fore — a natural corollary to a struggle for independence where the propagation of ideas on either side is a factor in the struggle. The prose at this time seemed to get away from gongoristic experiment, to escape the academic neoclassicism, and to become an instrument in the hands of new political writers who used it to get closer to the people. Everyday language, less artificial, more pliable and with greater plasticity, was used by many of these writers to communicate with the general public. This prose can be classified generally as literature of propaganda. The writers were essentially political and used their pens as weapons from either side.

Among the writers favoring the royalists was Dr. Agustín Pomposo Fernández de San Salvador (1756–1842). Descendant of a noble family, he was a lawyer for the royal *Audiencia* and one of the foremost lawyers in the viceroyalty. He also became president of the University three times. When the War for Independence broke out, Pomposo bitterly fought against the insurgents and supported the Spanish government; he did this in spite of the tragedies that were occurring in his own family. His son Manuel died in 1813 fighting for independence; his niece, Leona Vicario, was put in jail by the royalist government for having aided independence; but escaping from jail, fled to the battle field to marry Pomposo's former law clerk, Quintana Roo. Although Pomposo wrote some poetry, he is better known for his political prose with its rather extravagant titles. In 1810 he published the *Las hazañas de Hidalgo Quixote de nuevo cuño, facedor de tuertos,* etc. In 1813 he was to write *Desengaños que a los insurgentes de Nueva España seducidos por fracmasones agentes de Napoleón dirige la verdad de la religión Catolica y la experiencia.* In 1814 appeared his *El Modelo de los Cristianos pretsentado a los insurgentes de América.*

Born in the last third of the eighteenth century, Francisco Severo Maldonado died in 1832 with the distinction of having been perhaps the only writer on both the royalist and the insurgent sides. He seemed to be the initiator of political irresponsibility when he affiliated himself to the winning side and against the royalists. He was an arrogant and vain man. In 1810, while a priest in a small parish, he founded the first insurgent newspaper *El Despertador Americano.* After the decline of Hidalgo's star, Maldonado founded a royalist newspaper *El Telégrafo de Guadalajara.* It is obvious that Maldonado lacked the courage of his convictions when he called Hidalgo a New Washington, "a great soul full of wisdom and kindness," later on to accuse him of being a "Sardanapalus without honor and without shame." "Our liberating brothers" in November became "gangs of bandits" next February.

Of a different moral mettle was José María Cos who received his doctor's degree in 1805 from the University and was professor of grammar, rhetoric, philosophy, theology, and Latin at the Seminario Tridentino of Guadalajara. He was priest of a small parish when he joined the movement for Independence in 1811 and was responsible for founding the second newspaper among the insurgents, *El Ilustrador Nacional.* He made his own type from wood and used anil and oil for ink, after having built his own printing press. This newspaper was to be followed by *El Ilustrador Americano* in which he collaborated with Quintana Roo. Although he belongs more to political than to literary history, his newspaper articles, manifestoes, and proclamations show him to have been a man full of ardor, and impulsive.

Miguel Guridi y Alcocer was born in Tlaxcala in 1763 and died in Mexico City in 1828. He was a professor in Puebla, a doctor in theology and canon law, and a lawyer of the Royal College of Mexico. He was a representative to the Parliament or Cortes in Spain in 1810, having stayed in Spain for two years and at one time having been president of Parliament. After the war, he was a member of the Provisional Government Junta as well as a signer of the Declaration of Independence, and a representative to the first two Congresses. He was a fine religious and political orator as shown by his activities in the Spanish *Cortes* and in the Mexican Congress. He is supposed to have written a *Curso de filosofía moderna* and published an *Arte de la lengua latina* in 1805. He also appears with an ode and a sonnet in the compilation by Beristáin in honor of the statue of Charles IV in 1804. His *Apuntes de su vida* were compiled by him towards the end of 1801 and the early part of 1802, but were not published until 1806. These notes are very interesting for the history of customs and, of course, for an analysis of his personality.

One of the most interesting authors of the period of Independence was Father Servando Teresa de Mier, born of noble family in Monterrey in 1765. At sixteen he became a Dominican, and by the time he was twenty-seven was already a doctor in theology enjoying a prominent reputation as a preacher. On the twelfth of December, 1794, before the main dignitaries of the court, mainly, the viceroy, the Archbishop, and the *Audiencia,* he gave his famous sermon on the Virgin of Guadalupe. Since the bishop considered some of his statements daring, and even unorthodox, referring to the miracle of the apparition of the Virgin of Guadalupe, Mier was tried and condemned to ten years of exile in Spain, at the Monastery of Caldas. He was also to be prohibited from having a professorship, a pulpit, or a confessional, and had to give up his title of doctor. This exile gave him the first chance to practice what was to be a common occurrence in his life: escape from prison. He landed in Spain in 1795 and was locked up in the Monastery of Caldas. He escaped, was captured, and locked up in the Monastery of San Pablos in Burgos where he remained until the end of 1796. He asked to appear before the Council of the Indies and was ordered to go to a monastery in Salamanca; he disobeyed, was captured, and confined in the Franciscan monastery of Burgos. He escaped again, to the French border, and found refuge in Bayonne in 1801. He went next to Paris and opened an academy to teach Spanish, but he left for Rome in 1802 where he became secularized, and was given some honors by the Pope. Because of a satire defending Mexico, he was recaptured upon return to Spain, sent to Seville in 1804, and escaped for the third time. Captured again and returned to prison, he naturally escaped for the fourth time. He then lived for three years in Portugal, but when the war between Napoleon and Spain broke out, he joined the insurgents as a priest and chaplain, took part in several battles, and became a prisoner of the French but escaped. Meanwhile, the War of Independence had begun in Mexico, and Mier decided to go to London to work for Independence through his writings. There he met a young Spaniard, Francisco Javier Mina (who had taken part in the war against Napoleon in Spain).

They organized the famous expedition of 1817, and Mier accompanied Mina when he landed in Mexico. Captured by the Spanish government, he was sent to Mexico City and locked up in the dungeons of the Inquisition. With the dissolving of the Inquisition in 1820, Mier was sent to Spain; he escaped in Havana and made his way to the United States. He tried to return to Mexico in 1822 after Independence, but arriving in Veracruz, was locked up at the Fort of San Juan de Ulúa which was still in the hands of the Spaniards. Mier, as an ardent republican, was not in favor of Iturbide becoming an emperor. Hence again, he had to go to prison as an enemy of the Empire; but with the republican revolution in 1823, he was freed and declared himself in favor of a centralist rather than a federalist government. More a man of action than of contemplation, Father Mier was typical of his time. His chief work, the *Apología y relaciones de mi vida,* has been published in a modern edition under the title *Memoirs.* The *Apology* refers to the events following his sermon about the apparition of the Virgin of Guadalupe, while the narrative refers to details of his life from arrival in Spain in 1795 until the escape to Portugal. Restless as the spirit of the author, it is a travel book which reads like a novel, now serious, now comical, always pleasant. He also published in London in 1813, his two-volume *Historia de la revolución de la Nueva España* under the pseudonym of José Guerra. The Mexican Congress published a new edition in 1922. Although highly disorganized and confused (it seems to be a political discussion in which the spirit of the French Encyclopedists is apparent), this history can lay claim to being the first one written on the Wars of Independence. The book provides a portrait of Father Mier as a fighting spirit rather than as a disciplined historian.

Miguel Ramos Arizpe, born in 1775, was a descendant of pioneers in the northern part of Mexico. He spent his early youth in the north and in the country. Experiencing crude winters, irregular rains, and the constant hostility of savage Indians, he seemed to be an example of the frontier type described by Frederic Jackson Turner, a type which the Baron von Humboldt had already described in referring to New Biscay. Arizpe studied Latin, philosophy, and theology in Monterrey and later went to Guadalajara to continue his studies and to receive the degree of Bachelor of Philosophy. In 1803 he went to Mexico City to receive sacred orders. He was to receive a position in the Cathedral of Monterrey, but the bishop vetoed his appointment probably because of Arizpe's *criollo* leanings. Instead, he was sent to a small parish in what is now the state of Tamaulipas. Here he became a great benefactor, founding schools, teaching in them and demonstrating the use of the plow to the Indians. He received the degree of Doctor of Canon Law in 1808; again he was denied a higher position, and again he was sent to a small parish. For the third time he won a contest for a position in the Cathedral of Monterrey, and for the third time he was sent back

to the small parish. He continued his studies and in 1810 received the degree of Doctor of Laws. In the meantime, while Spain was being invaded by Napoleon, the Central Junta had appointed a Regency Council which requested twenty-six representatives from the American colonies to the future Parliament. Arizpe was elected representative for Coahuila to the Cádiz Parliament in 1810; he left for Mexico City and arrived in Spain in 1811. He distinguished himself in Parliament by supporting the independence of the colonies and showed his republican mettle by refusing to accept a monarchy. When some of his colleagues, because of death, absence or illness, could not participate in the *Cortes,* he was appointed to represent Puerto Rico, Caracas, the Internal Provinces of the West, and the Californias. He suffered persecutions for his brilliant defense of the rights of the colonies and was arrested in 1814, together with other representatives with whom he underwent imprisonment for twenty months. Although condemned to four years in prison, he was freed by the Spanish Revolution of 1820 and after eleven years' absence, he returned to Mexico in 1821. He was against the government of Iturbide. He also introduced the first printing press in Coahuila, and as a champion of federalism, was elected to the second Constitutional Congress, and drafted the Mexican Constitution of 1824 and was president of the new Congress on the same day that the Constitution was approved. He became a cabinet minister and later Dean of the Cathedral in Puebla before his death in 1843. Arizpe has often been called the Father of the Federation. He is typical of the generation of leaders of the Independence who with pen rather than sword won life for the new nations. He belonged to the group of intellectuals who drew up plans for the new government and who, with a vision of the political future of the Americas, were able to develop their political philosophies. His works include a *Memorial of the Natural, Political and Civil State of the Province of Coahuila, one of the Natural Provinces of the East in the Kingdom of Mexico and those of the New Kingdoms of Leon, New Santander, and Texas with an Exposition of the Defects of the General System; and particularly of its government, and of the Reforms and New Establishments which are necessary for its Prosperity,* published in 1812. By 1814 a translation into English had been printed in Philadelphia.

Juan Wenceslao Barquera was also a journalist and political writer, born in 1779 and died in 1840. He studied Latin, philosophy and law, receiving a license to practice in 1809. He participated in the neoclassical movement of the beginning of the nineteenth century and was an enthusiastic collaborator in the *Diario de México.* Through its columns he campaigned in favor of Independence while forming part of a secret society called Los Guadalupes which cost him imprisonment by the Inquisition. He wrote poetry after the fashion of Manuel de Navarrete, but is more famous for his writings on law, politics, and agriculture from 1805 to 1816.

Poetry

The Spaniards were going through their own War of Independence, started in 1808 when the troops of Napoleon invaded Spain. Neoclassical poets such as Manuel José Quintana, Nicasio Alvarez de Cienfuegos and Juan Nicasio Gallego were patriots who sang of the glories of the Spanish heroes of independence while condemning the French. Mexican poets of the period of independence imitated all three of these men, most particularly Quintana.

Joaquín María del Castillo y Lanzas (1781–1878) distinguished himself in several diplomatic and political positions as well as in poetry. A volume of his *Ocios Juveniles* was published in Philadelphia in 1835. His fame is probably greater than that of other members of the neoclassical group of the Independence, because of his poem "A la victoria de Tamaulipas." An imitation of Olmedo's ode on Bolivar, "To the victory of Junín," this poem is devoted to the victory of the Mexicans, Santa Anna and Mier y Terán, when they repelled the Spanish invader Barradas in his attempt to reconquer Mexico in 1826.

The literary career of Francisco Manuel Sánchez de Tagle (1782–1847), encompassed the end of the neoclassical period, the beginning of the heroic period of Independence, and the romantic period. Heir of a prominent family, Sánchez was a brilliant student, at nineteen appointed professor by the viceroy. A man of extreme prudence and fine character, he was able to occupy various posts under the colonial government, the Independence government, and the other governments that struggled for power after the period of Independence up to the Mexican War. His poetry naturally reflected the literary tendencies of the times, and he was neoclassical, heroic, and almost romantic. His *Obras Poéticas* (very much abridged by the author, who destroyed several of the poems himself), were published in Mexico after his death in 1852. Most representative of his heroic period is "Al Primer Jefe del Ejército Trigarante," an ode praising Agustín de Iturbide, the general responsible for ending the War of Independence on September 27, 1821.

Andrés Quintana Roo was born in Yucatán in 1787 and died in 1851. One of the two territories in Mexico now bears his name, honoring thus his service to the cause of Independence. In 1808 he received the degree of Bachelor of Arts in canon law from the University of Mexico. He became a lawyer after serving in the law office of Dr. Agustín Pomposo Fernández de San Salvador, and it was in the home of this well-known lawyer that he met Leona Vicario. Their romantic love affair and his participation in the War of Independence are joined together in the early life of Quintana Roo. He fought with his pen, establishing two famous newspapers: *Seminario Patriótico Americano* and *El Ilustrador Americano*. He was a representative to the Congress of Chilpancingo established by Morelos, and suffered persecution because of this political post. He presided over the National Constitutional Assembly that declared Independence and wrote the manifesto to the nation to that effect. His wife Leona accompanied him, after having been imprisoned and having escaped to marry him. Hunted down like beasts, the members of the Congress had to flee from one area to another, often seeking refuge in the roughest mountains of Mexico. It was in a mountain cave, in fact, that Leona gave birth to her first daughter. In 1818, although he had a chance to escape, he preferred to accept amnesty to save his wife from possible execution. After Mexico became independent, he devoted himself to politics and occupied several important positions in the government. Better known as a statesman, he wrote poetry that shows frequently the influence of Cicero and Horace. A critic has said that literary erudition in Quintana Roo often stifled spontaneity. The characteristic work that marked him as a heroic poet of the times is the "Diez y Seis de Septiembre." As most of its kind, this poem saluted with Pindaric enthusiasm the new era of freedom which presaged so much happiness.

At the same time, the heroic poets cast anathema against the mother country, Spain, under whose tutelage they had been born and New Spain had grown. Spain was to them the representative of an absolutism, a born enemy of the great reforms constituting the modern ideal. Born in 1793, Francisco Ortega died in 1849. The descendant of a noble family, he was left an orphan at a very tender age. He studied Latin and philosophy in Puebla where he also studied law and, at the same time, worked and wrote. Although he went later to Mexico City to study law, he never received a degree because he could not afford it. In 1816, he won a prize in the contest promoted by Beristáin to celebrate the return of the Jesuits and also was able to obtain an appointment at the Mint, thus being the first to establish the pattern to become so characteristic of literary men in Mexico: that of holding a position in the government for financial support while writing. Ortega was elected representative in 1822 to the First National Congress where as an ardent republican he fought against Iturbide when the latter wanted to become emperor. Later he occupied various positions in Congress and the administration. He was said to be the most correct and the purest versifier of his time. We can classify him essentially as an academic poet and a good neoclassicist in whom reason overpowered fantasy. His best poem is considered to be "La venida del Espíritu Santo," a religious poem influenced by Spanish eighteenth-century poetry. Also outstanding is his love poetry in pastoral style. As a heroic poet, his ode, "A Iturbide en su Coronación," is an invective, warning Iturbide of the possible consequences of becoming emperor. He urges him to listen to patriotism, to be faithful to history and to back away from the deep abyss that will open for him after his coronation. He praises him for his previous services to Mexico, but also warns him of the loss of love and gratitude of the Mexicans while revealing to him the future and fatal fate of tyrants.

José Clemente Orozco, with Diego Rivera a leading artist of Mexico's Revolution, included in one of his famous murals at Guadalajara the figure of Father Hidalgo, fiery priest and early instigator of rebellion against Spain.

The Novel

Although there had been only the scantiest signs of the novel in colonial times, suddenly a novel appeared in 1816 that was profoundly Mexican. It was *El Periquillo Sarniento,* written by José Joaquín Fernández de Lizardi. Undoubtedly the most important literary figure of the first quarter of the nineteenth century, Lizardi is more commonly known by the pseudonym, "El Pensador Mexicano." He was born in Mexico City in 1776 of a low middle-class family and died in 1827. He spent his early years in Tepozotlán, where his father was a doctor for the Jesuit seminary. He was sent to study at the University of Mexico but had to drop out for lack of funds. His earliest work (1808) is a hymn to Ferdinand VII entitled "Polaca en honor de Nuestro Católico Monarca el señor don Fernando Séptimo." Lizardi was in Taxco in 1812 when Morelos entered the town; and was imprisoned in Mexico City for having turned over arms and ammunition to Morelos, but was freed soon. Lizardi was a selfmade man who read the French Encyclopedists widely. Before 1811 he had already written his first pamphlets, and when freedom of the press came with the 1812 constitution of Cádiz, he founded his famous newspaper, *El Pensador Mexicano.* He was constantly in and out of jail for his articles. In 1814 *El Pensador Mexicano* closed down, but Lizardi soon published other periodicals, *Alacena de*

Frioleras in 1815, *Los Ratos Entretenidos* in 1819, *El Conductor Eléctrico* in 1820, *El Hermano del Perico* in 1824, *Las Conversaciones del Payo y el Sacristán* in 1824, and *El Correo Semanario de México* in 1826. In 1821 he declared himself for Iturbide, joined the insurgents and wrote from Tepozotlán. He arrived in Mexico City on the twenty-first of September, 1821, but was soon disillusioned by the turn of political events. In November, 1821, he wrote "Fifty questions against whoever wants to answer them" which gained him the hatred of the conservatives and the church. In 1822, he defended the Masons and as a result was excommunicated — a serious matter at the time — and in vain did he appeal four times to have the ban lifted. After the fall of Iturbide, the struggle between federalists and centralists began. Lizardi was a federalist and found himself once more in jail for having criticized Congress in 1823. In December, 1823, he made a speech on the church. He expected the Constitution of 1824 to curtail the power of the church, but again was disappointed. On April 27, 1827, he published his *Testamento y Despedida de El Pensador Mexicano,* dying shortly afterward on June 27. Lizardi was essentially a journalist, not concerned with style, beauty of form, or aesthetic feeling; he always went straight to the point. His object in life was to reform society and government, and this he expressed in both newspaper articles and novels. Besides founding many newspapers, Lizardi is supposed to have written nearly two hundred pamphlets on varied subjects. The bravest of propagandists for Independence, he was also a political writer and a moralist. He seems to have considered that literature should be both didactic and entertaining. Most of the time the didactic tendency predominated in Lizardi as a novelist. He wrote four novels. *El Periquillo Sarniento,* published in 1816 without the fourth volume dealing with slavery, was suppressed on November 29, 1816. *Noches tristes y día alegre* appeared in 1818, as well as the first volume of *La Quijotita y su prima.* By 1819, the second volume of *La Quijotita* had appeared. By the twenty-second of February, 1820 he had already finished his last novel, *Don Catrín de la Fachenda.* When constitutional government was established again in Mexico in 1820, Lizardi turned away from the novel and published *El Conductor Eléctrico.* He also published a pamphlet in which he wanted Independence to be granted by the *Cortes,* but a week later his pamphlet was prohibited and the next day he found himself in jail.

Lizardi's masterpiece is *El Periquillo Sarniento* which has been published in part in English under the title *The Itching Parrot.* It is an excellent picture of life in Mexico towards the closing of the colonial period. Yáñez sees Periquillo as a national type comparable to Babbitt in the United States and to Martín Fierro and Don Segundo Sombra in Argentina. Periquillo is the balanced expression of man and his local environment as well as of the surrounding nature. He seems to be ready for everything, for whatever may come. In telling us the story of his life, he runs into persons representing different aspects of the life of Mexico of the times. We find the scribe, the lawyer, the doctor, the military man, and their adventures all told in a logical, natural, and true-to-life fashion. Although often characterized as a picaresque novel, this book has one essential difference which should be pointed out. Whereas the heroes of the Spanish picaresque undertake their adventures in an unreal, at times artificial, and often exotic environment, Periquillo, with the exception of his adventures in Manila, always acted within the framework of Mexican reality and the colony established by Spain. This is probably why the Spanish picaresque heroes degenerate often into caricatures, and their adventures frequently lack continuity. As a typical product of the eighteenth century, Lizardi was progressive, a spokesman for reason and science, while at the same time being rebellious, sentimental, and Christian. He had faith in progress and in education and through his belief in Providence was free of the skepticism so prevalent in the eighteenth century. His humor was often used to prevent or to attack social ills as well as to mitigate the evils of censorship against free expression. His humor did not suffer from the rather cold, and at times virulent satire of the Encyclopedists, nor did it have the sombre aspect of romantic humor, but its moralizing purpose gave him special characteristics together with a certain melancholy often found in real humor. His tendency to moralize and to propagandize has been characterized as typically Mexican. He seemed possessed of the almost mystical or religious zeal to transform ideas and institutions which was to be typical of the nineteenth-century liberal party with its impulsiveness, tenacity, and almost intolerant attitude toward the church. Lizardi's goal in life seemed to be to give new orientation to the life of Mexico, sometimes portraying poverty and misery, other times depicting utopian situations which bring happiness to virtuous men. Essentially two currents affected his realism: the current of Spanish realism and that of enlightened realism. Lizardi was often accused of poor taste in choice of characters and type of language but he pictured the lower classes simply because he saw in them the reality of Mexico. The language he used gave his novels verisimilitude rather than the vulgarity with which he has often been charged, and of course today it is an accepted technique to have all characters speak the language of their milieu. The environment in which Lizardi's characters developed accentuated the realism that was an integral part of the essence of his work.

La Quijotita y su prima is a moral novel in which Lizardi's theories of education owe a great deal to Rousseau. Here he presented two women: one with a moral education and one without, but the main value of the novel is its description of customs. *Noches tristes y día alegre* was inspired by the *Noches lúgubres* of Cadalso, the first example of pre-romanticism in Mexican letters. Lizardi's last novel was *Vida y hechos del famoso caballero D. Catrín de la Fachenda,* published in 1832 after his death. Here he shifted from a lower-class hero to another social type — the *Catrín* or dandy of colonial times. The novel in style and flavor is similar to *Periquillo,* but lacks the realistic touch that Lizardi achieved in his first novel. He appeared to be trying to establish a moral parallel between Don Catrín and Periquillo, the latter having a sense of morality when he is doing wrong and trying to make amends; Don Catrín, however, not being willing to listen to his conscience and showing his cynicism, which is reminiscent of *El Buscón* of Quevedo. Lizardi also wrote poetry frequently, using as subjects the life of the lower classes which characterized him as a precursor of Guillermo Prieto. He is at his best in didactic poetry: his fables were printed in 1817. Lizardi also attempted the theatre and wrote the second part of a very popular melodrama of the times, *El Negro Sensible* (1825). The Coliseo would not perform his play because of the issue of slavery. Lizardi also wrote other plays, but they are not well known now. *The Testament and Farewell,* written just before his death, is very significant in the development of his ideology. Therein he declared himself a Catholic and confessed that he believed in the Holy Mother Church. However, he reiterated that although he accepted Catholic dogma, he did not believe in some of the superstitions, declaring also that he did not believe in the infallibility of the Pope. Later he went on to explain that he did not think that witches, vampires, and spirits existed even though the church had conjurations against them, nor did he believe in saints, dead souls, or devils that come back to earth. He also attacked the custom of attributing to saints certain properties to cure physical ills. With his dying breath he could not help attacking social ills such as the inefficiency of the police and the miserable condition of the Indians.

Drama

Manuel Eduardo de Gorostiza belonged to both Spain and Mexico and was a playwright, statesman, diplomat, soldier, and philanthropist. His chief role was probably that of impresario to restore the theatre to Mexico in the first half of the nineteenth century. His father was a general related to the Count of Revillagigedo, a famous Mexican viceroy; his mother was a descendant of Saint Teresa de Jesús. His father was also governor of Veracruz and brought about many improvements during his administration. After the father's death in 1794, the family moved to Spain, and two of the three sons became pages at the Court. Gorostiza started to study for the church but shifted to the military and at eighteen he had begun to stand out in politics. He was a captain of grenadiers in 1808 when Napoleon invaded Spain, and by 1814 he was already a colonel, whereupon he left the army and devoted himself to politics and letters. Together with other famous Spanish literati of Spain, he was exiled when Ferdinand VII came to power. In 1821 he left Spain for exile in London and when the Mexican representative came to Great Britain in 1824, Gorostiza offered his services to the new republic, after which he was accepted and entrusted with various diplomatic missions, which he carried out with great efficiency and patriotism. It was Gorostiza who first negotiated almost all of Mexico's first treaties with foreign powers, and, for that reason, he is frequently considered the founder of Mexican diplomacy. He returned to Mexico in 1833 and occupied various positions in the government. In 1836 he was minister plenipotentiary and extraordinary envoy to the United States at the time when the question of Texas was vitally discussed. He defended the right of Mexico but when American forces entered Mexican territory, he requested his passport. Later he became minister of the treasury and of foreign relations. As a philanthropist, he founded the "House of correction for young delinquents" in 1841. During the Mexican War he organized a battalion of artisans, and at sixty took part in the defense of the Monastery of Churubusco. He died in 1851. His plays, which are neoclassical, are *Indulgencia para todos, Las costumbres de antaño, Tal para cual o las mujeres y los hombres, Don Dieguito, Contigo pan y cebolla,* and *Don Bonifacio.* Others were arrangements of plays from Spain, France, and Germany. Gorostiza's *Teatro original* was published in Paris in 1822, his *Teatro escogido* in Brussels in 1824, and the *Apéndice al Teatro Escogido* in 1826. He is considered to be a continuator of Moratín and a precursor of Bretón de los

Herreros, and the most important figure in the theatre of his time. He is known for his easy dialogue, the diversity of his human types, and his accuracy in reproducing the customs of the times. He seems to have abandoned the theatre in 1820, although he wrote his *Contigo pan y cebolla* which was published in London in 1833. After going to live in Mexico, he published his *Don Bonifacio* and settled down to his main role of impresario.

Historians

Needless to say, historians were also affected by contemporary events. They seemed to be more interested in Mexico's present than her past. They all took part in political struggles, and they commented on events of their lifetime. Among the writers who favored the cause of liberalism were Bustamante, Zavala, and Mora. The outstanding conservative historian of the time was Alamán. Carlos María de Bustamante was an indefatigable worker. A native of Oaxaca, he was a journalist, and also studied Latin grammar, philosophy and theology. Later, in Mexico City, he received the degree of Bachelor of Arts, and became a lawyer in Guadalajara in 1801. When the War of Independence started, he refused to take part in it, but afterwards, when freedom of the press was suspended in 1812, he was afraid of being jailed, and joined up with Morelos. A member of the Congress of Chilpancingo founded by Morelos, he was persecuted for these activities, until he finally obtained a pardon in 1817. After Independence, he took an active part in politics, holding among other positions, that of representative in congress. Deeply affected by the Mexican War, he died in 1848. As well as being a writer, he was an editor and commentator. His original works include *Cuadro histórico de la Revolución Mexicana, Historia del Enperador Don Agustín de Iturbide, El Gabinete Mexicano durante el segundo período de la administración del Presidente Bustamante, Apuntes para la historia del General Santa Anna, Galería de Príncipes Antiguos Mexicanos, Campañas del General Félix María Calleja, Mañanas de la Alameda de Mexico* and *El Nuevo Bernal Díaz del Castillo o sea historia de la invasión de los Anglo-Americanos en México,* his last, and not completed book. He edited or commented upon the histories of López de Gómara, Father Bernardino de Sahagún, Father Francisco Javier Alegre, and Father Andrés Cavo, and he also penned numerous pamphlets and newspaper articles. A passionate writer, he had a style which was not beyond criticism, for he was picturesque and imaginative but at times degenerated into triviality. He often contradicted himself and seemed disorganized, illogical, partial, and inaccurate. In editing, frequently he altered the works of others, eliminated passages, expressed his own opinions as if they were the author's, and added useless footnotes. In spite of all these defects, he merits consideration as a historian because he compiled material relating to the political life in which he was often directly involved, and there are many books, which in spite of their faults, would now be forgotten or lost if it had not been for his editing.

Lorenzo de Zavala was born in Mérida in 1788 and studied theology there. He gave extremist speeches, founded newspapers, held perhaps the first professorship of constitutional law in the country, and carried on an insistent revolutionary campaign among the Indians, which many consider to be the origin of the Indian Wars in Yucatán. By 1814, he was imprisoned and deported to the castle of San Juan de Ulúa, where he remained until 1817, and studied medicine and English. He became the representative to the Spanish Parliament in 1820 and took part in the First National Congress in Mexico. Earlier siding with Iturbide, he later turned against him very bitterly and became a federalist, working for the establishment of the York Masonic Lodges which were to contribute so much to the struggles between federalism and centralism. He became governor of the State of Mexico, Minister of the Treasury, and later on had to escape to the United States. He travelled through Europe, and in Paris in 1831, wrote his famous historical work, *Ensayo histórico de las revoluciones de México*. In 1834 he represented Mexico in France. Despite the services that he had rendered Mexico, and probably because of ambition for wealth, Zavala, who had been a Jacobin and a champion of freedom, joined the Texas rebels and signed the Declaration of Independence of Texas as a representative for Harrisburg. He was elected vice-president of the Republic of Texas and died in 1863. A brilliant man, well-cultivated, he was frequently overpowered by passion and hence could not be serene and methodical, lacked historical perspective, and often omitted such details as dates and names. Nevertheless, he outlined the major problems in Mexico's history with sensibility and perspicacity. The first volume of his historical essay was printed in Paris in 1831 and the second in New York in 1832. His *Viaje a los Estados Unidos,* showing a talent for observation about people and nations, was published in 1834.

José María Luis Mora was born in 1794, became a priest and later received the degree of Doctor of Theology. He directed the *Semanario Político Literario* in 1821, opposed Iturbide, and was appointed to several posts in the government and the legislature. He favored confiscating the property of the church, abolishing the privileges of the church and of the military, and disseminating public education among the lower classes without interference from the clergy. He advocated freedom of speech, equality of foreigners with Mexicans in civil rights, and the establishment of trial by jury in criminal cases. He had to flee to Europe and lived in Paris for a while, then in 1847 went to England as minister plenipotentiary of Mexico and died in Paris in 1850. Mora believed in progress. He was a liberal who oscillated between the doctrines of Adam Smith and Jeremiah Bentham. Realizing that Mexico was impoverished by the accumulation of land and real estate in the hands of the few, he advised that land be divided into small portions, but he also was conscious of the dangers of a free distribution for as he said, "When the lands are given to people who have not acquired them by their labor or industry but by a free concession of the law, they never know how to appreciate them nor to get the best out of them as those whose habits of work have given them the necessary funds to buy them and to consider them their own." Mora was a keen social critic with definite bias. A strong individualist, he did not believe in the importance of the masses. Realizing the unstable social balance of Mexico, he did not believe that the ills of society could be remedied by violence. He had a natural aversion to the military; for he realized that the ambition of the military, their desire to make fortunes and their insubordinate habits and lack of respect for law were principal obstacles to progress in Mexico. He wrote, "Laws, magistrates, government, people, public and private funds all have been more or less under the military power." His federalism showed his hostility to the caudillos also. He pointed out not only the evils of the military but also those of the church. He had been a clergyman, and he knew the habits of the church with its wealth that had been accumulated during colonial times. He realized its influence, not only in spiritual but economical and political matters, feeling that in Mexico it was almost impossible to establish a foundation for public morals because of the continual confusion between social and religious duties. Mora had little sympathy for the Indians because he belonged to an earlier generation that had to show *limpieza de sangre* (pure blood) to enter schools of higher studies; he had had to demonstrate that he was Spanish and the descendant of old Christians without any admixture of Jewish, Moorish or Mulatto.

Mora published two books in Paris. His *México y sus Revoluciones* appeared in 1836. He had been gathering materials for this work since 1828 and began to write it in 1830. He had planned to include in the first part statistics relative to the general state of the Republic and to each one of the states and territories. A second part was to include history from the Spanish Conquest to the administration of Santa Anna. Three volumes were published, the first dealing with the situation and extension, physical structure and natural resources of the country, mining, industry, and commerce, administration of Mexico and Spanish domination, political and social organization, foreign affairs and income of the republic to the time of his writing. The second volume was never published, but the third covered the Conquest and various attempts to establish independence. The fourth volume dealt with the period from the beginnings of Independence to the death of Morelos. As a historian, he was noted for fairness, impartiality, sincerity, and serenity. His other book was called *Obras Sueltas,* in two volumes, and was published in 1837 in Paris. Here he unveiled his political personality, thoughts, desires, and principles of conduct. He wrote a political history of the different administrations in Mexico to 1837, and, in the second volume, he gathered his articles published in the *Semanario Político y Literario* and the *Observador de la República Mexicana.*

The conservative historian Lucas Alamán was born in 1792 and died in 1853. He was, so to speak, the other side of the Bustamante coin — methodical, logical, and well read. He witnessed the entrance of Hidalgo into Guanajuato which probably made quite an impression on him. He studied chemistry and mining at the College of Mines as well as botany and modern languages. From 1814 to 1820 he traveled through Europe and took courses in science at the Collège de France. He was well versed in classical languages and languages and literature of England, France, Italy, and Germany. Back in Mexico in 1820, he sailed for Spain as representative to the *Cortes* for his native province. After Independence, he again travelled through France and England, returning in 1823. He was Minister of Foreign Affairs and a member of the Conservative Party. As almost all the historians of his times, he was partisan, and political passion influenced his writings. He authored *Disertaciones sobre la historia de México* from 1844 to 1852, and *Historia de México,* 1849 to 1852. In the first work, he wrote about the Conquest and the making of the Spanish government into a viceroyalty. Alamán is frequently considered the best prose writer of his times. He planned his works well, was penetrating in his analyses and exact in his facts. For his opinions, he has been discussed, opposed, condemned, and praised. For some he was a wise man with great respect for human rights and who always praised virtue; for others he symbolized an enemy of Independence, a monarchist, a man who praised faithfulness of the colonies to Spain, who pointed out the kindness of the colonial government, and defended all the ideas and traditions of the Spanish monarchy.

Although not a historian *per se,* the Count de la Cortina y de Castro was a polygraph, a diplomat, and a noble gentleman as well as one of the outstanding figures of nineteenth-century Mexico. José Justo Gómez de la Cortina y Gómez de la Cortina was born in 1799. He ranked very high in Mexican society in Mexico and figures often in the book *Life in Mexico* by the Marquesa de Calderón de la Barca. At fifteen he was sent to Madrid where he studied logic, rhetoric, and humanities. He attended a military academy and became a professor of military geography, later leaving the military for the diplomatic service. He served in various legations and embassies of Spain in the Low Countries, Austria, England, and France, but by 1827 left diplomacy for letters and sciences. Appointed by Ferdinand VII Introductor of Ambassadors, colonel of the army, and gentleman of his service, the house of the Count in Madrid became a gathering place for famous literati. In 1832 we find him back in Mexico. There he wrote his *Cartilla social sobre los derechos y obligaciones del hombre en la sociedad civil.* In 1828 he had written the *Cartilla historial o Método para estudiar la historia.* He was a representative to Congress in 1834, later governor of the Federal District. He also occupied the post of Minister of the Treasury, general, senator, Inspector General of Highways, governor of the Department of Mexico and of the Federal District for a second time. He died in 1860. Cortina's literary work is scattered in pamphlets, newspaper and magazine articles, and monographs as well as scientific works on astronomy, meteorology, mathematics, physics, and geography. He founded *E Zurriago Literario* in 1839, and the *Ateneo de México* a literary society with a library and public lectures. Probably his most important work is the *Diccionario de sinónimos castellanos* in 1845. In 1843 his *Nociones elementales de numismática* appeared. He also wrote a moral and military primer in 1854, and a *Manual de voces técnicas castellanas de Bellas Artes.* He wrote the Legend of "Don Juan Manuel," "Eliezer y Nephtalí' and "Euclea, o la Griega de Trieste," and left unpublished a series of essays and notes on history, biography, genealogy, science, art, and poetry.

ROMANTICISM

Mexico did not have the literary struggle between classicism and romanticism that occurred in other countries, for very frequently the two tendencies lived happily together in Mexican literature. Romanticism came to Mexico about 1830 through French influence and later, through such Spanish romantics as Espronceda, the Duque de Rivas, and García Gutiérrez. The period from the 1830's to the collapse of Díaz's regime in 1910 can be considered one of the most brilliant periods of Mexican letters, and this through the efforts of both conservative and liberal writers. It was a period of continual search for national expression — the kind of search which is often hampered by academic tradition as well as political events. In Mexico the pure romanticist, all passion and exaltation, soon turned by functional adaptation into teacher and guide. Ignacio Ramírez and Ignacio Manuel Altamirano were the guides for the youth of their times. This period of nineteenth-century literature did not have the decisive aridity of the eighteenth century, and Mexico became romantic without having to struggle against neoclassicism. It was romantic because of the exaggeration of sensibility into sentimentalism and melancholy. It acquired political independence, and that was romantic. The internal struggles that take place up to 1867 were a propitious field for the rebellion required of romantics. As independent Mexico turned its back on the Spanish spirit, it realized its despair and its anguish, and poetry then turned towards France. Romanticism seemed an expression of a disillusioned soul, with a sense of total negation of Mexican life. Navarrete, Lizardi, and the Cuban poet, José María Heredia, were the writers preparing the way for romanticism. Rodríguez Galván and Fernando Calderón, taking advantage of the melancholy and disillusionment, took steps forward towards romanticism. From 1836–1856, the Academia de San Juan de Letrán was the gathering place for young poets: there romanticists and classicists met; there the first efforts were made toward the establishment of literature in Mexico. The Academia was to be succeeded by the Liceo Hidalgo which served the same purpose in the second half of the nineteenth century.

Romanticists discussed the romantic ego and its conditions, being conscious of its solitude, its sentimentality and its desire for glory. They had a feeling for landscape, night, the sepulchral themes, evaluations of the past — the Middle Ages, the Baroque, the Pastoral, and the Neoclassical. The romantic ideals were women, politics, and progress. The ego was their most radical characteristic. Mexican poets have been essentially poets of sentiment, inner poets, or poets of internal landscape. The natural courtesy of the Mexican has served to counteract the excessive personal exaltation of some romanticists. Traditionally, the Mexican had kept his eyes closed to the outer landscape, and landscape as such was frequently absent as a primordial theme of Mexican romanticism. Night, however, played an important part in romanticism as a result of the introspection of many Mexican poets. At any rate, the romantic ideals listed — women, politics, and progress — were commonly found among Mexican romantics because of the political and social events during the past century. Mexican romanticism was subdued, never reaching extremes, and never being able to add a theme of its own. It was a literary school without violence and without a complete break from the past; it was an importation treated placidly in Mexico in the course of its adaptation.

Poetry

The earliest romanticist was Fernando Calderón of Guadalajara (1809). He wrote verse in his adolescence and belonged to a political literary society called "La Estrella Polar." His first dramatic works, performed in Guadalajara and Zacatecas, had been written while he was a student. A liberal who fought against Santa Anna in 1835 and was seriously wounded and captured, he was exiled from Zacatecas in 1837 by the government and went to live in Mexico City under impoverished circumstances. He became a colonel in the national militia and was a state representative besides occupying other government positions. He died in 1845 without finishing his last drama and a long poem. His poetical works were published in 1844 and reprinted in 1850. His son gathered together all of the father's works and published them in two volumes with the title *Obras Completas* in Zacatecas in 1882. Although he had written lyric verse at an early age, his poetry is not abundant. Among his famous love poems were "A una rosa marchita" and "Los Recuerdos." More typically romantic are his "El Soldado de la Libertad" and "El Sueño del Tirano." Calderón was influenced by the romanticism of the Spanish as well as the French, Lamartine especially.

Ignacio Rodríguez Galván, born in 1816, was closer than Calderón to being a romanticist, since he could not find in himself the ideal that he pursued. He was dissatisfied and sought escape in time and in space. Like the European romantics, he seemed to seek happiness by breaking all barriers opposed to him. He was closer also to the Spanish tradition of the drama than Calderón. Working in the bookstore of his uncle, Mariano Galván Rivera, Galván began to read the books on the shelves and thus was awakened his desire to try writing. Towards the end of 1835 he began translating poetry and drama from the French, showing lyric inspiration and freshness along with the defects and qualities of romanticism: tears, melancholy, preoccupation with death, ruins, and the creation of environment. By 1840 he had abandoned the bookstore to attempt literature. Rodríguez Galván was a self-made man who learned Latin, French and Italian on his own. He led a miserable and unhappy life; and if one were to judge by his verses, poverty, sorrow and despair were his constant companions. He suffered also from a mysterious love affair as well as from the misfortunes of his country. At last he began to reap the harvest of his literary reputation and his situation was lightened by appointment to a lesser diplomatic post. He sailed from Veracruz towards South America, but even at this moment of modest triumph, fate was against him. Passing through Havana in 1842 he contracted yellow fever and died. Not a theorist of romanticism, he was a living romantic. He sang of love, glory, country and faith; his love poetry lamented inconstancy, treachery and disappointment; his love for country showed forth in historical or legendary evocations and in the description of types and landscapes of Mexico. He often warned about the misfortune that threatened his country; only his religious faith glowed in a faint ray amidst all darkness and despair. Galván's "Profecía de Guatimoc," a patriotic poem, is often considered the masterpiece of Mexican romanticism.

Guillermo Prieto's life spanned the total age of romanticism in Mexican literature. He was born in 1818 and died in 1897, after a full life in literature, teaching, politics, and public administration. His life paralleled the history of Mexico: placid in the early years, restless in youth and the middle years, tranquil in old age. He occupied several small bureaucratic posts and became eventually a congressman and Minister of the Treasury. He was often persecuted and exiled. After the empire of Maximilian collapsed, he continued in Congress, in journalism, and as a professor of political economics and history. A spiritual descendant of Lizardi — the poet of the people, his festive humor, his lack of artistic sensibility and his limited literary background made the similarity even more striking. Prieto was one of the founders of the Academia de San Juan de Letrán. During the War of Reform from 1857 to 1860, the French invasion from 1862 to 1864, and the empire of Maximilian from 1864 to 1867, Guillermo Prieto was the equivalent of the national poet. He satirized his enemies, praised his party, and some of his couplets became famous as battle cries. Because of his picturesque and folkloric qualities, Prieto is the most Mexican of lyric poets as Lizardi was the most Mexican of novelists. His *Romancero Nacional* of 1885 is almost a national epic covering the period from 1808 to 1821. However, his most typical poetic work is *Musa Callejera,* 1883, in which the essence of Mexico is manifested through the tenderness and the fantasy of the poet. He also published *Poesías escogidas* in 1877 and *Versos inéditos* in 1879. His prose works were represented by *Memorias de mis tiempos* (1828–1853), in which he describes the social, political, and literary life of Mexico. An incomplete work called *Viajes de orden suprema* was dated 1857, *Viaje a los Estados Unidos* was published in three volumes in 1877–1878; and a selection was made of his journalistic articles called *Los San Lunes de Fidel* (1923). Although he also authored a treatise on economics and another on history, over and above his political interests, Prieto had a great ambition — one which he came close to realizing — to become the national poet. He was extremely popular, less for his patriotic poetry than for his theatrical and dramatic behavior. He was a kind of Mexican Victor Hugo, attending literary gatherings, mixing with the people, using the familiar form "tú" with strangers who greeted him and being satirical with those whom he knew better. His "Los Cangrejos" became a hymn to the liberals against Emperor Maximilian. Writing in the popular vein did not come early in his career; but when he finally found his true medium, he visited tenements, squares and markets, fiestas, dances, banquets, and weddings. At times he went to the country to sing of the "charros," other times he visited hospitals and jails. He portrayed himself as an enemy of the police and the lawyers, and a friend of good judges. In a sense he was as Spanish as he was Mexican because his ballads or "romances" were descendants of the great stream of ballads of Spain. The octo-syllable line, the verse form used in the "romances," was the favorite of the Spanish romantics and also Prieto's favorite. He was related also to the satirists and fable writers of the eighteenth century, seeming to have inherited their prosaism. Prieto's nationalism was heightened when he saw his country threatened by the French and by the empire of Maximilian; and since it was inspired by Mexico, his poetry was more local than universal. His heroes were often sly, cruel, jealous, and tenacious; his heroines, self-sacrificing, brave, and quick. As a satirical and "costumbrista" poet, he was possessed of an almost classical humor reminiscent of Quevedo, Lope, and Góngora.

Although appearing somewhat later, Juan Valle must also be included among the romanticists. Considered the civic poet of the Reform Movement, he was born in 1838, and at the age of four or five became blind. His brother read him the Bible, Greek and Roman classics, Spanish poets of the sixteenth century and Mexican poets of his own time. His first poems appeared in newspapers in 1854. At sixteen he devoted himself to literary life completely. In 1855 he presented a play, *Misterios sociales,* which was to be published together with his poetry in 1862. A liberal, he was cruelly persecuted by the conservatives, and in 1857 was imprisoned and later exiled. He returned to Guanajuato only to be cast away again during the French invasion. He died in Guadalajara in 1864 or 1865. At first he seemed to come under the influence of Carpio and Pesado, classical poets, but later he turned to romanticism. His best poem, "La Guerra Civil," classified him as one of the major civic poets of his time.

Critics exaggerated the importance of Isabel Prieto de Landázuri when they compared her to Sor Juana Inés de la Cruz. Born in Spain in 1833, at the age of five she was brought to Mexico and spent her early years in Guadalajara, leaving when her husband was made Mexican Consul in Hamburg in 1876. She had studied the Spanish writers of the Golden Age as well as foreign literatures of the nineteenth century. She was a poet as well as a dramatist. Her first works appeared in 1851, with maternal love as the outstanding note. Her poems and translations of Hugo, Lamartine, and Chenier were published in Mexico in 1883.

Classicism

The period of Mexican history from the consummation of Independence to the end of the Second Empire was characterized by stormy struggles between the liberals and the conservatives, and these tendencies were also reflected in poetry. The revolutionary tendency was romanticism; the traditionalist or the conservative tendency was represented by the so-called classic poets of the nineteenth century. These were usually men of strongly humanistic education, very refined, objective, and somewhat cold. They not only followed the artificial neo-classicism of the end of the eighteenth century and the beginning of the nineteenth but tended to regress to the best earlier Spanish models and the classical writers of Greece and Rome. They did not improvise as the romantics did, but relied on their excellent literary preparation, which naturally lacked the spontaneity and rebellious spirit of the romantics. The outstanding figure among them was José Joaquín Pesado, born in Puebla in 1801, of a well-to-do family. He received an excellent education and was a scholar and possessed of a deep religious faith. At the age of twenty he had already studied Latin, Italian, French and English and had some knowledge of Greek, theology, political science, natural science and mathematics. At first a liberal, he took part in the politics of Veracruz in 1833 and 1834, and was Minister of the Interior in 1838 and of Foreign Affairs, 1845–46. His political and social ideology changed, and he joined the conservative party, becoming one of its most distinguished writers. In 1851 he went to Mexico City and when the University was reopened in 1854, he was appointed Doctor of Philosophy and placed in charge of a chair of literature. He died in 1860. His poetry is outstanding for its deep Christian feeling and its classical tie with the Italian and Spanish authors of the sixteenth century. A Spanish critic has called Pesado's elegy, "Al Angel de la Guarda de Elisa," "worthy of any Spanish poet of the Golden Age." As a descriptive poet, Pesado shows his nationalism by portraying scenes from the country and the villages in Mexico and depicting processions, bullfights, cockfights, markets, serenades, fireworks, banquets, etc. For the first time, he introduces Indian themes in Mexican poetry with the collection entitled, *Los Aztecas: translations* or *glosses*. Since Pesado did not know Indian languages, these must be original poems of Pesado's with an archeological background. The poet tried to penetrate the Indian soul, having them sing in Spanish as he felt they would have done in their own language. Among these poems are those attributed to Netzahualcóyotl, the only known Aztec poet. Pesado's sacred poetry is probably his best and is characterized by high inspiration and lofty tones. He also wrote two incomplete epics, and translations and imitations of other poets such as Theocritus, Sinesius, Manzoni, Lamartine,

Horace, Tasso, etc. Printed in 1839, his poems had a second edition in 1840 and a third, the most complete, in 1886.

Manuel Carpio was born in 1791, studied Latin, philosophy and theology in Puebla, and laid the foundation for his literary career by reading books on ancient religion and history and Greek and Latin classics. He received the degree of Doctor of Medicine in 1832 and at an early age translated the aphorisms and prognostics of Hippocrates and devoted himself to the medical profession as professor, writer, and doctor. Unlike many of his literary contemporaries, he usually abstained from politics. He died in 1860. It was not until the age of forty that Carpio began writing his first poetry which was to be collected by Pesado in 1849. Religious inspiration as well as classical taste dominated his work: the Bible, Greece, Rome, the Middle East as represented by Niniveh, Babylon, Syria, and Egypt, were his themes and lent an epic tone to his poetry, which was clear but at times prosaic, although plainly showing the descriptive bent of the author. His ode, "The Turk," the lament of a lover for the absence of his beloved one, shows romantic sensibility and melancholy, but most of Carpio's poetry is sacred or historical. Among his best biblical and Near-Eastern poems, we can point out "La Cena de

The monumentality of the head being modelled by the noted sculptor, Armando Quezada, not only looks to the Indian past, but is typical of many of the sculptured figures commissioned in modern times by the Mexican Government. Since the early days of the Revolution, the government has been one of the major patrons of the arts.

— Courtesy American Airlines of Mexico

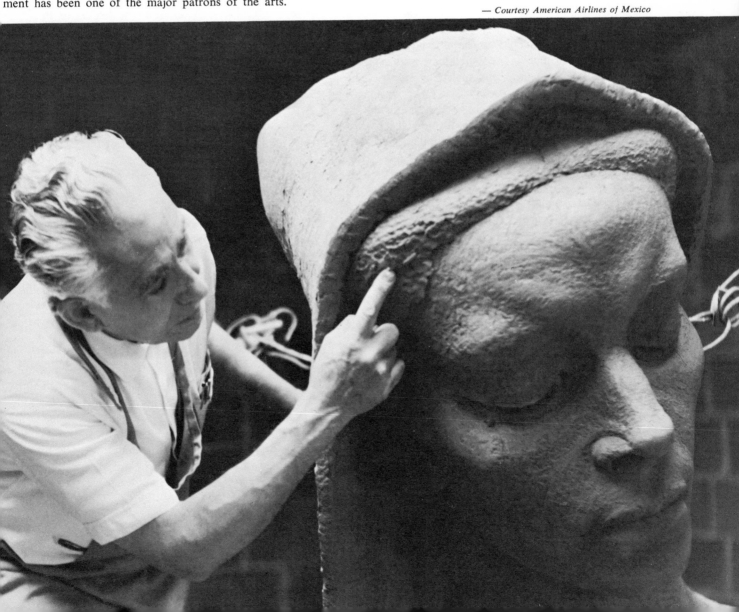

Baltasar"; and one of the best liked of his poems in his lifetime was the historical poem, "Napoleón en el Mar Rojo."

An exception to the association of classicists with conservatism and romantics with liberalism was Ignacio Ramírez (1818-1879), better known as "El Nigromante," in politics an enemy of the traditionalists and in poetry a classicist. As a student he appeared at the Academia de San Juan de Letrán to read an essay beginning, "There is no God." In the face of conservative protest he was painted in retrospect by Diego Rivera early in the twentieth century with his revolutionary essay in his hand. He wanted to sweep away wholly the altars, religion, Spanish tradition, political and social organization. As early as 1846, he was expressing the ideas that were to become the program of liberals in the War of Reform. A government employee in several different states, and a cabinet minister for Juárez, he was in and out of jail, persecuted, and exiled, but throughout the War of Reform, the French Intervention, and the Second Empire, continued to write controversial articles for provincial newspapers. When the republic was reestablished, he became a Supreme Court justice. His work, published in two volumes in 1889, includes poetry, speeches, historical, literary, economic, and social articles.

Another poet who encompassed the foremost epochs of the nineteenth century was José María Roa Bárcena (1827–1908). He began writing early in local newspapers, and in the midst of the struggles between liberals and the conservatives, he arrived in Mexico City in 1853. A man of deep religious and political convictions whose life was punctuated by sincerity, he immediately joined the conservatives. He wrote for their newspapers, supported the French Intervention and was a member of the Junta de Notables. Afterwards, he supported the empire of Maximilian; but when he saw that Maximilian was straying away from conservative principles, he prophesied his fall, and refused to take part in the administration. All this he did through the columns of the most influential conservative newspaper in Mexico City, *La Sociedad,* of which he was editor. After Maximilian was captured and executed, Roa Bárcena was imprisoned for a few months, but defended by the liberal press, he was freed and returned to private life never again to mix in politics. He began his poetic career with *Diana,* 1857; *Poesías líricas,* 1859; *Leyendas mexicanas, Cuentos y baladas del Norte de Europa y algunos otros ensayos poéticos,* 1862; *Últimas poesías líricas,* 1888; and *Últimas poesías líricas,* 1895. Roa Bárcena cannot be considered to be a great poet. His main characteristics are discretion and decorum. His *Diana* and his 1859 volume of lyric poetry as well as his Mexican legends of 1862 show romantic influence. He also translated Horace and Virgil from the classics, Schiller from a French edition, and Byron and Tennyson from English. His translation of "Mazzepa" by Byron is considered to be the best interpretation in Spanish. As a critic, his biographies of Gorostiza, Pesado, and Carpio are a contribution to Mexican literary history. He was also a historian who wrote *Catecismo de historia de México* in 1863, the *Ensayo de una historia anecdótica de México* and the *Recuerdos de la Invasión Norteamericana,* 1883.

Drama

Two outstanding romantic lyric poets happened also to be the best-known romantic dramatists: Calderón and Rodríguez Galván. Fernando Calderón's merit was greater as a dramatic poet than as a lyric poet. He started writing for the theatre very early, having presented his first play, "Reinaldo y Elina," in Guadalajara in 1827. Between 1827 and 1836 he had the following plays performed either in Guadalajara or in Zacatecas: "Zadig;" "Zeila o la esclava indiana;" "Armandina;" "Los políticos del día;" "Ramiro Conde de Lucena;" "Ifigenia;" and "Hersila y Virginia;" however, these works seem to have been lost. We only have four plays of his extant: *El torneo,* 1839, *Hermán o la vuelta del cruzado,* 1842, *Ana Bolena,* 1842, and *A ninguna de las tres.* It is very possible that up to the year 1835, he wrote and actually performed in the provinces many other plays that were never published, and about which we know little or nothing. *El torneo* was presented in Zacatecas in 1839. It is very likely that his historical play *Ana Bolena* and the comedy *A ninguna de las tres* were also performed for the first time in Zacatecas. After 1840 he begins to have his plays performed in Mexico City. *El torneo* served to inaugurate a new theatre there in 1841. By 1842, *Ana Bolena* was presented in Mexico City also. *A ninguna de las tres* was also performed in the same theatre, the same year, as was *Hermán o la vuelta del cruzado.* After the death of the author, his plays were performed in Mexico and outside of Mexico. It is a surprising thing that in the southwestern part of the United States some of his plays were performed towards the end of the nineteenth century and the beginning of the twentieth. Two other plays can be added to the author's dramatic baggage: *Andarse a las escondidas* and *Muerte de Virginia por la libertad de Roma.* Calderón was the first of the romantics in Mexico to succeed in the theatre. In his dramas he escaped from Mexican reality because his readings and preferences led him to other countries and other epochs; because the political situation of Mexico did not allow him to deal with contemporary topics; and because the Spanish companies that were touring Latin America, as well as the theatre public, preferred medieval subjects so characteristic of European romanticism. He thus could present lofty thoughts and feelings, which he considered inadequate for his own time, by seeking refuge in the past. Calderón knew the theatre and knew his public. Some of his plays have enjoyed a long life as witness the fact that some forty years ago his *La vuelta del cruzado* was performed in several places in New Mexico, and some thirty years ago Tucson was advertising the performance of one of his plays. Some critics consider his comedy, *A ninguna de las tres,* superior to Bretón de los Herreros' *Marcela, o ¿ a cuál de los tres?* which had suggested the play to Calderón. Rather than an imitation, it seems to be a reply to the work of the Spanish playwright; whereas in the case of Bretón, the question is which one of the three men Marcela should marry. Calderón answers none of the three girls is to be chosen by the hero. Here a young man refuses to select for his wife one of the three ladies, and he does it without appearing ridiculous or being discourteous. Calderón was criticizing the education given to girls, the provincial attitude, and imported fads, by satirizing the French leanings of Carlos, the sentimentalism of Leonor, the frivolity of María, and the pseudo-erudition of Clara. Calderón, like Lizardi, was not against women acquiring a real education, but he showed the absurdities of false knowledge. He was opposed to affectation and artificiality as specified by the three girls in their melancholy, vanity, and false culture. Here we find a definitely anti-romantic attitude in a romantic playwright; yet we must remember that Calderón was criticizing romanticism through his nationalism and that romanticism in Mexico never became a fighting banner against neoclassicism. The literary polemics that took place between romanticists and neoclassicists in other countries did not occur in Mexico; rather, romantics and classicists collaborated at the Academia de San Juan Letrán. Many classicists translated romantic poets from French, English, and Italian to Spanish.

Although a greater lyric poet than Calderón, Ignacio Rodríguez Galván was not as successful as a dramatist. His dramatic production is limited to a sketch, "La Capilla," 1837, and two dramas, *Muñoz, Visitador de México,* 1838, and *El privado del virrey,* 1842. His play, *Muñoz, Visitador de México* was performed in 1838. He had another distinction: unlike Calderón who was interested in European medieval themes, he brought Mexican themes to the stage. "La Capilla" was based on the famous conspirator Alonso de Avila who was executed for his part in the conspiracy to set Martín, the son of Cortés, on the throne of Mexico. *Muñoz, Visitador de México* has very little to do with the actual life of the famous Visitor, Alonso de Muñoz, sent to Mexico in August of 1567 to investigate the conspiracy of Martín Cortés. Of course, it must be said in defense of Rodríguez Galván that he probably did not know the famous chronicle of Juan Suárez de Peralta dealing with the conspiracy of the *criollos* and Martín Cortés, nor did he possibly know the *Noticia historica de la conjuración del Marqués del Valle,* published by the historian Manuel Orozco y Berra. However, Galván was proud of the fact that he was the first Mexican author to bring to the stage what he called Mexican drama. He showed a clear intuition of dramatic resources, a sense of action, and a lyric quality that moved the spectators of his times. His other drama, *El privado del virrey,* is the dramatization of the well-known Mexican legend of Don Juan Manuel, a better developed and more mature work although lacking the organic unity of the other drama. His dramatic characters are often more typically romantic than those of Calderón though possessed at times by an exaggerated frenzy. At no time did he achieve in the theatre the somberness, despair, and lyricism of his poetry.

Other dramatic poets of the times were Carlos Hipólito Serán, who left us, among other items, a satirical comedy of manners, *Ceros Sociales* in 1852; Pantaleón Tovar, a prolific writer of such plays as: *Misterios del corazón, Una deshonra sublime, La gloria del dolor, Justicia del cielo,* etc.; and Isabel Prieto de Landázuri, author of some fifteen plays, who had five performed and left only two in print, *Las dos flores* and *Las dos son peores.*

The Romantic Novel

After Lizardi, the novel began to develop and become more popular. The historical novel and the novel of adventure were preeminent, but at times the novel of customs was found. This *genre* has been discussed thoroughly by John Brushwood in his book, *The Romantic Novel in Mexico.* Justo Sierra, Sr., was a lawyer, a journalist, an historian and a man of letters in Yucatán. His son by the same name was to become more famous than the father in Mexican letters. Justo Sierra, Sr., was born in 1814 and died in 1861. He was the author of two novels, *La hija del judío* and *Un año en el Hospital de San Lázaro,* romantic works in the manner of Alexander Dumas and Eugene Sué.

Fernando Orozco y Berra, brother of the historian Manuel, was born in 1822 and died in 1851. He received a degree in medicine in Puebla in 1845 and practiced his profession; he was also a journalist in the liberal newspapers of the times and the author of several plays and unpublished verse. We know only his novel, *La guerra de treinta años,* 1850. It is not a war novel, and is actually nothing more than a portrayal of the hero's love affairs (supposedly the author), during his first thirty years. A veritable Don Juan, the hero began his romantic career at the age of seven. The action is located in Burgos and in Madrid, but dealt with real people in Puebla and Mexico City. Many of the ladies referred to in the book were said to have bought up copies of the novel, and it is now very rare.

Florencio M. del Castillo (1828–1863), began the study of medicine but soon turned to journalism and letters. He was a liberal congressman, fought against the French, was captured and confined to the prison of San Juan de Ulúa where he contracted fatal yellow fever. He wrote short novels and short stories, which were a novelty at the time. His theme was love, but he attempted psychological analysis of his characters. His longest novel is *La Hermana de los Ángeles,* study of a woman's self-sacrifice. His lamentations, over-idealizations, and his pedantic digressions tend to obscure his dramatic instinct. His collected novels, articles, and short stories were published in 1850.

Eligio Ancona (1836–1893), wrote historical novels, such as *La Cruz y la Espada* and *El Conde de Peñalva.*

The most outstanding romantic novelist was Juan Díaz Covarrubias, whose works sometimes seem more like novelistic attempts. He was born in 1837 and studied medicine in Mexico City, but while still a student, gained a reputation as a poet and novelist. The death of his mother and an unfortunate love affair lent a sombre tone to his poetry. A liberal, he went as a medical intern to lend his services on the battlefield at Tacubaya in 1859. He and other young doctors were captured by Márquez, the conservative general, and shot.

Díaz Covarrubias showed his strong nationalism in portraying Mexican types and scenes. His novels included *La sensitiva*, 1859; *Gil Gómez el Insurgente o La hija del médico*, 1859; *La clase media*, 1859; and *El diablo en México*, 1860. Love was a predominant theme in the novels of Díaz Covarrubias, and his presentation of that theme was thoroughly romantic. In *La sensitiva*, the heroine died of love for the hero, who arrived just in time to be present at her agony and to receive her last kiss. The theme of *La clase media* was the rehabilitation of the fallen woman — the heroine entered a convent rather than accept the hand of the hero. The author was influenced by Lamartine and Georges Sand in his social outlook. He was adept at writing dialogue, his narrative was interesting, and his descriptions vivid. Maturity would probably have yielded great fruits for this young novelist who was killed at twenty-one.

The outstanding nationalistic novelist of the period was Luis Gonzaga Inclán born in 1816 of a mulatto mother and a *criollo* father who was the overseer of a hacienda in the outskirts of Mexico City. At twelve he was studying Latin, but left his studies to return to the country where his father put him to work as a *peon* in the hacienda, an incident reproduced in his novel, *Astucia*. Later he was sent by his father to the state of Michoacán to work at the hacienda of Púcuaro, where he remained for seven years; afterwards he was to be administrator of some five other haciendas. During the Mexican War, he moved to Mexico City, where he acquired a lithography shop and a printing press and entered somewhat the field of popular literature, including novenas, verse narratives of catastrophes and sensational events, miraculous legends, *corridos*, and popular songs. A spontaneous writer, he began composing poems for his friends and collaborated in political newspapers of the times. In 1860 he wrote *Reglas con que un colegial puede colear y lazar*. In 1860, and possibly in 1867, appeared his *Recuerdos de "El Chamberín," o sea breve relación de los hechos más públicos y memorables de este noble caballo*, referring to a horse owned by Inclán which had learned many tricks and was the favorite of ranchers and city people. *Regalo delicioso para el que fuere asqueroso*, containing verse of a scatological nature, was another of his works.

His best novel, *Astucia, el Jefe de los Hermanos de la Hoja o Los charros contrabandistas de la Rama*, had the subtitle, "Historical novel of Mexican customs," and was published in two volumes in 1865 and 1866 respectively — a rare edition printed by Inclán himself. Another work published in verse in 1872 was *El Capadero de la Hacienda de Ayala*. Two other novels, *Los tres Pepes* and *Pepita la Planchadora*, have remained unpublished. *Los tres Pepes* was a novel of city customs dealing with the life and adventures of three students; while *Pepita la Planchadora* gives us a picture of the middle classes of Mexico, the tribulations of a working woman of that time, her way of living, her friends, etc. He also left unpublished a "Diccionario de mexicanismos o Gramática mexicana." When his son was making a trip in 1884, a fire broke out on board ship and all the manuscripts were burned. Unfortunately a wealth of historical documentation, if not artistic material, was lost. Inclán died in 1875. His novel, *Astucia*, was reprinted by the newspaper, *El Imparcial*, and a third edition appeared in 1908 in two volumes in which the illustrations of the first edition were reproduced. *Astucia* has vivid vernacular, strong characters and narrative, vivid descriptions, dramatic impact and a thoroughly Mexican environment. The author's observation of daily life in the country inspired his characterizations. Inclán himself traveled with the tobacco smugglers and knew them well. He was also familiar with the problems of the alcohol smuggler, for he himself sold alcohol. Long, at times tiresome, and often diffuse, the novel is more Mexican and nationalistic than Lizardi's *El Periquillo*, for Inclán was inspired by Mexican motifs and literally saturated with local color. Through its pages appear the master and the *peon*, the *charros*, the smugglers, the customs and the vicissitudes of the Mexican people in general, all portrayed with great realism. *Astucia* is a veritable dictionary of Mexicanisms: the linguistic adulterations and the corruptions that Spanish had suffered among the Mexican lower classes. Popular speech, whether urban or rural, is heard through characteristic expressions, Aztec words, and proverbs and maxims depicting regional idiosyncrasies. Inclán deliberately uses augmentatives and diminutives for effect, as well as the similes inspired by country life, especially those concerning animals. He had known the head of the smuggling *charros* in Púcuaro where both had worked until 1838. They met again in 1863, and Inclán said in his prologue that as soon as they recognized each other, their old friendship was renewed. As they exchanged experiences, Inclán persuaded his friend that the story must be written. The smuggler provided the plot, but Inclán wrote the novel. As a result, *Astucia* is both realistic and romantic.

Inclán seemed to have had a better conception of the art of novelistic composition, a more fertile imagination, greater dramatic interest, and more command of detail than any of his contemporaries. An instinctive and facile story-teller, he introduced impersonalism in the novel, a characteristic that was beginning to appear in the French novel of that epoch as a literary novelty. Inclán — a horseman, a man of the people — lacked culture and meditative grace, but he had the gift for writing even though he lacked the form. Not a craftsman, he was an instinctive novelist, undisciplined, but simple and natural in expression.

LITERATURE FROM 1867 TO 1910

The chief literary manifestations from 1867 to 1910 were post- or neo-romanticism, post-classicism, realism, and modernism. Mexico had just gone through the War of Reform, the French Intervention and the Empire of Maximilian. The minds of the intellectuals were more preoccupied with political problems than with literature. Poetry, literature in general, and research could not flourish under such tempestuous circumstances. After the collapse of the Second Empire, amnesty had been granted to the conservatives who, little by little, began returning to Mexico or to their previous occupations.

Ignacio Manuel Altamirano tried to reconcile the two factions in literature in 1869 by founding the magazine, *El Renacimiento*. This was the literary periodical that brought real intellectual amnesty to men of letters: conservatives and liberals came together through its columns as brothers, to work for a new Mexican literature; literary gatherings were common among the intellectual fraternity. *El Renacimiento* was a true spiritual weather vane of the times; Altamirano gathered about him old and young writers, Jacobins, imperialists, and moderate liberals; all lovers of the *belles lettres* invited to communicate intellectually through the magazine. All ideas, literary genres — the novel, poetry, short story, criticism, and history, translations of foreign writers both old and new — were given sanctuary in *El Renacimiento*.

The Academia de San Juan de Letrán which had functioned from 1836 to 1856 was succeeded by the Liceo Hidalgo and later by the Liceo Mexicano. The Mexican Academy had been founded in 1875, as an institution to promote literature and conserve the language. From the start the Academy contributed materials to the *Dictionary of the Spanish Language* as well as promoting critical studies which have appeared in the Academy proceedings. The flowering of literature which had begun shortly after 1867 continued throughout this period. All genres developed and prospered. During the last forty years of this epoch, poetry was the outstanding contribution from Mexican literature; Altamirano had already aspired to the creation of national poetry and the national novel. Romanticism dropped artificiality and sought reality for sincere and truthful expression of feeling. The influence of Spanish literature which had been predominant throughout the centuries continued, but French literature also became well known, and English and Italian literatures were beginning to be initiated in the new republic. Classicism, mainly in poetry, became less popular and was to decline even further through the efforts of Gabino Barreda who, placed in charge of higher education, believed in the philosophy of positivism and relegated humanism and classical culture to an inferior place.

Post-Romantic Poetry

The post-romantics continued their influence to the end of the century when modernism prevailed. We have already mentioned Ignacio Manuel Altamirano, who was born in 1834 and died in 1893. Of a humble family, he was an Indian who could not speak Spanish until after he was fourteen. In 1849 he was in Toluca studying Spanish, Latin, French, and philosophy, reading widely in his position as librarian and writing his first poetry and articles. Later he was a teacher, dramatist, and prompter with a theatrical company. In 1854 he took part in the revolution, entered politics, and began writing for the press. He joined the liberals when the War of Reform broke out and in 1861 was a representative. During the French Intervention and Empire of Maximilian, he fought against the conservatives and the invaders, but after 1867 he decided to bring the liberals and conservatives together in the magazine, *El Renacimiento*. He continued writing, distinguished himself in literary criticism, stimulated young writers, taught, and occupied several government positions. He left Mexico in 1889 to become Consul General in Spain, from there went to Paris and later to Italy where he died. Many consider him the greatest writer of his times.

Altamirano was a romantic by temperament, although he appeared to be a classicist in his manner of expression. He aspired to bring together the classicist and the romanticist and to form a nationalistic literature. A poet, he published his *Rimas* in 1880, with a predominantly descriptive tone. He believed that the best way to give Mexican poetry a national feeling, fusing into it the spirit of the race, was through description of the landscape.

José Rosas Moreno (1838–1883), was a liberal who suffered imprisonment and persecution. He was also a congressman and at times occupied different bureaucratic posts. Essentially the poet of children, as a rule, he is considered to be the best fable writer of Mexico. His romanticism was tempered by his tranquility and his placidity; he was not an original poet, nor a poet of lofty tones, but rather a man who sings in a minor key. His best collection of poetry is *Ramo de violetas,* 1891.

Manuel M. Flores was the poet of sensual passion. Born in 1840, he died in poverty, blind and forgotten, in 1885. In 1857 he was studying philosophy at the Colegio de San Juan de Letrán in Mexico City. He studied little, was misanthropic and wrote melancholy and passionate love poetry. By 1859 he had left school for bohemian life. Later he became a member of the liberal party, fighting and writing against the French. Captured and imprisoned in the castle of Perote, when Maximilian collapsed, Flores was a congressman several times, but later disappeared into obscurity. His poems, *Pasionarias,* were published in 1882. Although he is essentially considered an erotic poet, he also translated or imitated Bryon, Hugo, Lamartine, Shakespeare, Dante, Schiller, Lessing, and Heine. His main thought in life was woman, and his eroticism was not rhetorical, nor was it artificial as that of the neoclassicist or some of the romantics. It was real, for Flores was the poet of desire.

Justo Sierra, a disciple of Altamirano, inherited his mantle and became the master of the younger generations. He was a poet and orator, a short-story writer and a historian. Born in 1848, he inherited his literary inclinations from his father. In 1871 he became a lawyer. "Playeras" was an early poem that won him a reputation in literary circles. He was a radical and a Jacobin like his master, Altamirano, and collaborated in *El Renacimiento.* Like Zorrilla at the funeral of Larra in Spain, Sierra sang an elegy at the funeral of Acuña and became famous also. The death of his brother Santiago affected him deeply and made him turn from an impetuous lyric poet and a romantic short-story teller to a historian, a sociologist, and educator. He served in several political posts and eventually became Minister of Public Instruction and Fine Arts from 1905 to 1911 carrying on vast cultural innovations and crowning his career with the founding of the National University in 1910. After the Mexican Revolution broke out, he was sent to Spain in 1912 by President Madero as Minister. He died in Spain the same year. Although he was first a poet, he is considered a prose writer. His *Cuentos románticos* were published in 1896; however, they had appeared previously in magazines and newspapers of the times.

Post-romanticism culminated in Manuel Acuña, who not only wrote romantic poetry but lived a romantic life. He was born in 1849 and committed suicide in 1873. In 1865 he left his native city, Saltillo, to study medicine in Mexico City. Acuña is one of the great poets of Mexico. Even though he did not completely dominate poetic form, Acuña's personality, his imagery, and his poetic potentiality show him as a poet of genius. By temperament, he was a sentimentalist, and through his medical studies he became a materialist and a skeptic. Living in a world in which science was being elevated to the position of dogma, he was shipwrecked in a sea of doubts. Fortunately, his effusive sentiment was never completely stifled by his materialism and skepticism. His "Nocturno a Rosario" is one of the most beautiful love songs in Mexican poetry. It has been often quoted and has become popular throughout the Latin American world. "Ante un cadáver" shows his dogmatic materialism tempered by a mortal harmony. His poems were collected in 1874 together with his only romantic play, *El Pasado,* which had been performed in 1872.

Like Sierra, a disciple of Altamirano, Agustín F. Cuenca has been categorized as a romantic by some and a classicist by others. Born in 1850, he died at thirty-four. His poetic production was short but had a certain degree of exquisiteness. He was a descriptive as well as a love poet, a poet of hues and shades of meaning that often lead to subtleness somewhat reminiscent of the gongorists and the conceptists. His love poems, sometimes considered romantic, possess melan-choly, elegance and softness; his descriptive poems show sincere emotion. Some critics have seen Parnassian influence from French poets in his work, while others see him as a precursor of modernism for his elegance, his musicality, his refinement, and his technique. Cuenca is still not well known even to the specialist, and it was not until 1920 that a collection of his *Poemas selectos* was published. His classicism is free of academism and his tempered romanticism places him above pseudo-dramatism because of his humanistic education and his instinct as a true artist. His descriptions of the landscape follow the classical style, but through romantic influence, he adds subjective interpretation. His love poetry was reminiscent of the Epicureanism of ancient Greece and Rome and of the Spanish sixteenth-century tradition.

Juan de Dios Peza falls strictly within the Spanish tradition. He was neither a subtle nor an obscure poet. He was influenced by Campoamor, Núñez de Arce, and Bécquer. He was born in 1852 and died in 1910. His father was a prominent member of the conservative party and an official in the Second Empire. He began studying medicine, but shortly before graduating devoted himself to literature and journalism; he also served in the diplomatic service in Spain where he made Mexican poetry known through his anthology, *La lira mexicana.* Returning to Mexico, a tragedy in his family turned him into the poet of home and children; *Cantos del hogar* is one of his best-known collections. He was an effusive and tender poet when he sang of home and children. His popularity declined when he failed to adapt himself to modernism. His numerous volumes of poetry were published from 1873 to 1910; and he also wrote a comedy and two dramas as well as two books of criticism: *Poetas y escritores mexicanos,* 1877, and *Memorias, reliquias y retratos,* 1900.

Post-Classicist Poetry

Just as we had the post-romantics following the romantics, we also have the post-classicists following the classicists of the first half of the nineteenth century. Although he cannot be counted as one of the best post-classicist poets, we must include José María Vigil among them. He was born in 1829 and died in 1909. He studied Latin, philosophy, and law in Guadalajara, but left the university to fight for liberalism. He was a founder of the liberal newspaper, *La Revolución,* in Guadalajara; and he founded other magazines and literary societies. After the Second Empire had collapsed, he became a representative to Congress, justice of the Supreme Court and director of the National Library until his death. His work encompasses the fields of poetry, drama, criticism, and history. He was a poet in his youth, having published *Realidades y quimeras* in 1857 and *Flores de Anáhuac* in 1886, a volume of dramatic works. Although he follows the classical rules in his poetry, he often degenerates into prosaism; and he is better known for his translations into Spanish verse of the satires of Persius, 1879, and the epigrams of Martial, 1899. He was also a translator of Petrarch, Schiller, and Ronsard.

Monsignor Joaquín Arcadio Pagaza was probably the poet of the greatest sensibility among the post-classical poets. He was born in 1839 and died as Bishop of Veracruz in 1918. He received the priestly orders in 1862 and served for some twenty years in small parishes until 1895 when he was appointed Bishop of Veracruz. He often used the classical pen name of Clearco Meonio. He was a translator and paraphraser of Horace and Virgil; and in his original poetry, he follows their example by becoming the first of the Mexican bucolic poets. In 1887 he published his first volume of poetry, *Murmurios de la selva*. By 1890 he had already published his *María: Fragmentos de un poema descriptivo de la tierra caliente,* and *Algunas trovas íntimas* in 1893. His Latin translations and paraphrases of Horace and Virgil were published in 1905 and 1907 under the title, *Horacio y Virgilio*. Pagaza was attempting to translate the complete works of Virgil into Spanish, but published only a first volume in 1913. His bucolic poetry described the countryside, the natural landscape, arriving finally at the expression of all sentiment. He was not interested in narrating the life of shepherds of that mythical Arcadia, which was the inspiration of the pastoral or bucolic poets of the sixteenth century, and specifically of Navarrete at the beginning of the nineteenth century in Mexico. His bucolic poetry was not, thus, an academic device, but real coexistence with nature by a man who had experienced life in the country in Mexico. Surprisingly enough, Pagaza did not compose but a few religious poems. Religiousness in his poems seemed to be merely a theme, an excuse, or an occasion. He was the poet of bucolic peace who preferred a tame and contemplative landscape of native plateau and pueblos to the ardent, tumultuous, and passionate landscape of the subtropical Xalapa where he spent his last years. He was a poet of tenderness and peacefulness, of contemplation rather than reason, whose poetry showed a soft sadness and whose landscapes seemed to be seen through light tears.

Born in 1840, Ignacio Montes de Oca y Obregón had an excellent education in England and Rome. He spoke seven languages at seventeen and could write in prose and verse in four of them. He became a priest in 1863 and, upon returning to Mexico in 1865, he was Chaplain of Honor for Maximilian until the Empire fell. Tamaulipas called him to become its bishop in 1871, Linares later, and finally San Luis Potosí, dying in 1921 as he was about to return to Mexico after a long absence. He seemed to have had the grandeur and the presence of a Renaissance bishop, and he enjoyed an excellent reputation in his country and in Europe for his clear intelligence, his humanism, and his literary works. He became a member of the Arcadia under the name of Ipandro Acaico. In 1905 he received the honor of giving the funeral oration for Miguel de Cervantes when the celebration of the Third Centennial of *Don Quixote* was organized by the Royal Spanish Academy. He was the first complete translator into Spanish of Pindarus and of Theocrates, the bucolic poet. In his original poetry, he was elegant and vibrant with sensitivity. Between 1883 and 1913, he published eight volumes of his *Obras pastorales y oratorias* which included funeral orations, religious orations, and literary speeches. In 1877 he published his *Poetas bucólicos griegos,* the *Odas de Píndaro,* and *Ocios poéticos* in 1878. It was in this last book where we find all of his original poetry. He continued writing, and in 1914 appeared *A orillas de los ríos; Cien sonetos* in 1916; *El rapto de Elena,* translation from the Greek in 1917; *Otros cien sonetos de Ipandro Acaico,* 1918; *La Argonáutica* in two volumes in 1919–1920; and in 1921, *Nuevo centenar de sonetos* and *Sonetos jubilares.* In quantity and in quality he is considered the most outstanding of the Mexican Hellenists. The original poet was outdistanced by the translator and the humanist. Often the orator and the humanist were seen in his poetry, but unable to generate poetic emotion. A cold platonic asceticism, elegant and external, frequently weakens his poems. Pagaza, although frequently following the example of Montes de Oca, shows greater depth because he is a greater poet, and at the same time more human.

We can consider Manuel José Othón a post-classicist although he is a complex writer. Born in 1858, he died in 1906. He spent his life as a lawyer in small towns and villages of northern Mexico and was essentially a poet of the provinces. He wrote poetry from adolescence. In his first volume entitled *Poesías* (1880), we find many traces of romanticism. Sincerity was the keynote of his *Poemas rústicos* of 1902, which he called his first book. He declared that "we should express nothing that we have not seen, nothing that we have not felt or thought through somebody else's temperament because our spirit will no longer be speaking and will be lying to others, deceiving ourselves at the same time." Othón studied both Latin and Spanish classics in the seminary and became an authority on Cervantes. From the faraway north, he witnessed the beginnings of the *modernista* movement in Mexico. His poetry, full of life, was not to be curtailed by the formality of classicism, and he searched for wider environment and horizons. He remained aloof from modernism, but the *Revista Azul* started the new century by placing one of his poems on the first page. The feeling of loneliness, the aliveness of the landscape, and the communion with nature, were all romantic traits found in his poetry. But he did not use historical themes, and he escaped from the theme of death, from political ideals, from the idea of progress, and from heroic will. His post-classical inclinations carried him back to traditional Spanish meters and a certain poetic dignity; but he did not idealize the bucolic note, or insist on mythological motifs; instead, his nationalism caused him to depict the landscape of Mexico with great poetic sincerity. Instead of being thoroughly romantic, neoclassic or modern, this poet took refuge in his environments, the desertic landscape of northern Mexico, where conflicting literary schools could not affect him. Not ideal nature, not bucolic nature in the classical sense, but rustic nature became an integral part of his poetic experience. He preferred the countryside without human beings, merely with animals and the infinite presence of God; and thus there was a profoundly religious tone to his poetry. Othón felt at ease in his great loneliness, with himself and with the desert. This loneliness was a forerunner of that labyrinth of which Octavio Paz speaks in our times. Although Othón seemed to have been influenced by Pagaza, he, unlike Pagaza, did not pluck the monocord of his bucolic lyre, but was infused with a deep and universal sense of life and the world. Whereas the nature described by Pagaza invites to peace and rest, Othón's nature is rough, hostile, and inexorable.

The Novel and the Short Story

The novel and the short story from 1867 to 1910 continued for a while along the romantic path. A romantic writer who lived through early romanticism

and outlived most of the post-romantics was Manuel Payno. A short-story writer and novelist, he was born in 1810. After being sent to work in the customs offices in Matamoros, he later returned to Mexico City as a lieutenant colonel. In 1842 we find him as legation secretary in South America, also making his first trip to France and England. In 1844, he was sent to New York and Philadelphia to study the penitentiary system. He was a guerrilla fighter during the Mexican War and by 1850 was already Secretary of of the Treasury but had to go into exile when Santa Anna returned to power. He returned as Minister of the Treasury, and was persecuted. Together with other writers, he was captured in 1863 and sent to San Juan de Úlua, but he was set free when Maximilian arrived in Mexico. When the Republic came, he was a representative to Congress and a history professor. As a senator in 1882, he was sent to Paris as a colonization agent. Beginning in 1886, he was Consul in Spain for five years, during which time he traveled through Europe. He went back to the Senate upon his return and died in 1894. Payno wrote on historical, philo-

Frequent street exhibits of art in Mexico City point to the current public interest in painting. Although Mexican art of the past focused on architecture and sculpture, recent and contemporary Mexican painters such as Orozco, Rivera, Siqueiros, Tamayo, and others, have aroused critical and popular acclaim.

— *Courtesy Mexican Government Tourism Department*

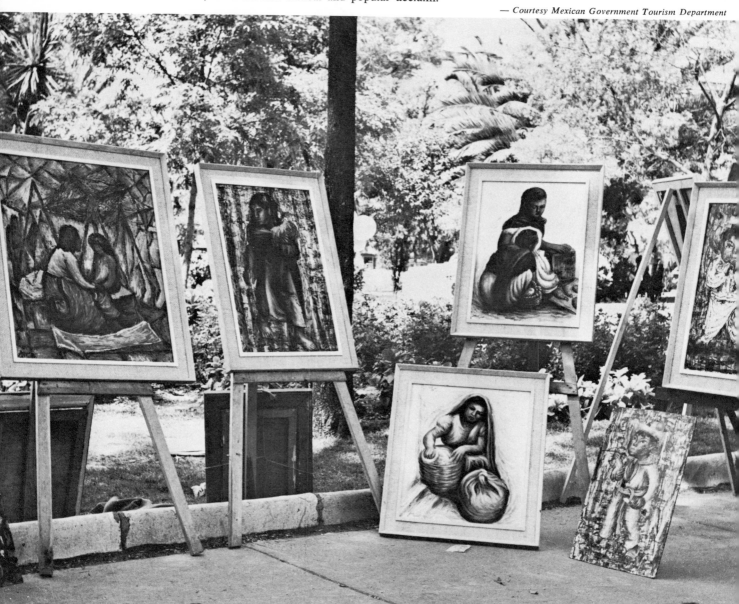

logical, political, and economic subjects in the newspapers of his times. His short stories and tales appear between 1839 and 1845. In that same year *El fistol del diablo* appeared, Payno being the first author to write long novels after Lizardi. He followed in Lizardi's footsteps in his descriptions of customs, language, proverbs, dress, etc. Payno was not a moralizer, but a capable weaver of plots, and he introduced the fantastic element in Mexican literature. *El fistol del diablo* was the first serial novel in the country, a genre which later would achieve great popularity. A second augmented edition appeared in 1859, and the third edition of 1887 changed the ending of the novel completely. *El hombre de la situación* was his second novel, printed in 1861.

By 1871 he had compiled in one volume, *Tardes nubladas,* his short stories and novelettes. Probably his most representative novel is *Los bandidos de Río Frío,* published in two thick volumes between 1889 and 1891, and conceived in Spain while he was serving Mexico in his diplomatic post. Payno called it "a naturalistic, humoristic novel of customs, crimes, and horror." The plot was based on a trial in real life, but the author incorporated episode after episode incessantly. Direct observation of types and their environment, the local color in some descriptions, and faithfulness in reproducing the speech of the people are the salient points of this novel, which, for the most part, neglects style and proportion.

Ignacio Manuel Altamirano is the first author to be concerned with the structure of the novel. Unlike those of previous writers, his novels seem to have an artistic structure: he attempts to give proportion and unity to his plots. To enhance his plot in emotional intensity and interest, he was concerned with harmonizing and distributing his episodes. He was not conscious only of plot, but also of characters and environment. Many of his personages, even the minor ones, seem to have been portrayals of people whom the author had known or heard about. In spite of all these qualities and his great desire to create the true Mexican novel, however, Altamirano lacked sufficient depth, force, and inspiration to succeed in his attempt. He wrote two novels and a novelette which were popular in his time and continue to be so. They are *Clemencia,* published in his newspaper *El Renacimiento* in 1869, and *El Zarco* written in 1888, but published posthumously in 1901. His novelette is *La Navidad en la montañas,* 1870. He was also the author of *La novia,* 1867, (the title was changed to *Las tres flores* when it appeared in *El Renacimiento*), *Una noche de julio* (title was later changed to *Julia*), and *Antonia.* He left two unpublished novels with the titles *Antonia y Beatriz* and *Atenea.*

Vicente Riva Palacio (1832–1896) was a well-known serial novelist. Born of a well-to-do family, he studied law but left the profession to take up arms against the French and the Empire. He became a general and was the one who received the sword of surrender from Maximilian at Querétaro, and his father was the lawyer who undertook the defense of Maximilian. Riva Palacio was essentially a journalist and a politician, becoming Minister for Development, Governor of the states of Mexico and Michoacán, Supreme Court Justice and finally Plenipotentiary Minister to Spain where he died. He also wrote poetry, plays, histories, and criticism. Notwithstanding, his popularity is based on his novels and he is frequently called the creator of the historical novel of Mexico. He consulted archives and penned the remembrance of his own experiences in the war against the French and against Maximilian as plots and details for his novels. Dumas seems to have been his model, although he owed a lot to the lesser French novelist, Eugene Sué, and the Spanish romantic writer, Fernández y González. The main function of the novel for Riva Palacio was to entertain. He amused his public with unusual adventures and details, dramatic and often horrifying. He was not concerned with direct observation from life nor with psychological analysis of his characters; but his plots often accumulated episode after episode and event after event. He was a master of the nineteenth-century serial technique, for he constantly kept his readers in suspense. Nevertheless he attempted to keep within the framework of history. From 1868 to 1870 he wrote six novels: *Calvario y Tabor,* dealing with the war against the French, and his colonial novels, *Martín Garatuza, Monja y casada, Virgen y mártir, Las dos emparedadas, Los piratas del Golfo,* and *La vuelta de los muertos.* By 1872 he had already published *Memorias de un impostor, Guillén de Lampart, Rey de México.* Printed in Madrid in the year of his death, *Cuentos del General* appeared posthumously. He also wrote a volume of criticism of contemporary authors with the title *Los Ceros,* 1882.

A lesser-known novelist who gained some distinction through the sentimental novel was Pedro Castera (1838–1906). Imitating Isaacs, the Colombian romantic, Castera wrote *Carmen* which has become better known in our times in a modern edition.

The originator of the short story proper was José María Roa Bárcena, the classical poet. In 1870 he published his short stories and a short novel under the title *Novelas.* In this volume he included "Noche al raso," a collection of realistic stories; "Una flor en su sepulcro," "Aminta Rovero," and "Buondelmonti," romantic narratives; and *La Quinta Modelo,* a short novel attacking the Utopian ideas of the liberals. He later wrote *Lanchitas,* one of the best of the suspense and mystery stories of Mexico; "El Rey y el bufón;" and "Combates en el aire." He also made some translations of short stories by Hoffman and Dickens. His own short stories show his ability to narrate, his natural style, his humor, and his mastery of the Spanish language. He was nationalistic also when he created animated pictures of Mexico, familiar scenes, landscapes, all saturated with genuine realism. All his personages developed in a thoroughly Mexican atmosphere reflecting the traditional customs of nineteenth-century Mexico. The imagination of the author and his artistic ability gave an appearance of verisimilitude and even of reality to *Lanchitas,* which as late as the 1940's was adapted for a mystery program in Chicago. Bárcena was skilful in the development of narrative and in interesting characters. Both his descriptive humor and his depiction of middle-class environment were reminiscent of Dickens.

The novel of manners or customs was cultivated especially by José Tomás de Cuéllar, better known by his pseudonym *Facundo.* Cuéllar was born in 1830, and participated in the defense of the castle of Chapultepec during the Mexican War in 1847. He later tried his hand at painting. By 1848 he was devoting himself to literature, had become a journalist, and tried the theatre. As a diplomat, he went to Washington and later became Under-Secretary of Foreign Affairs. Blind, he died in 1894. Although he was a dramatist and a poet, Cuéllar's fame rested on his novels and his writing about Mexican customs. An historical novel, his first work, *El pecado del siglo,* set in the eighteenth century in Mexico, was published in 1869. His complete works were published in twenty-four volumes between 1889 and 1892 under the title *La Linterna Mágica.* Included were his novels and sketches with such picturesque names as *Ensalada de pollos, Historia de Chucho el Ninfo, Baile y cochino, Los mariditos, Las jamonas, Gabriel el cerrajero o las hijas de mi papá,* etc. As a moralist, he did not quite succeed in suppressing the keen observer and the satirical humorist. In a sense he continued the work of Lizardi, but devoid of the moralistic aspect of the novels of "El Pensador Mexicano." His usually short novels show the hand of the painter who sketched quickly and who concealed didactic intention within the events of the narrative. He, like Roa Bárcena, studied the middle class. He emphasized their ridiculous aspects rather than their vices; and, frequently, their portrayal led to caricature. He was more interested in depicting distinctive types of the middle class than in complex characters. He was a faithful observer of environment and types, and a master of lively dialogue.

A direct descendant of Lizardi, Prieto, and Cuéllar among the "costumbristas," was Angel del Campo. Born in 1868, he led a rather uneventful life until his death in 1908. He attempted the study of medicine, and left it to become a journalist and writer. As a bureaucrat in a minor position in the Treasury, he wrote novels and humorous articles on current topics. The pseudonym *Tick-Tack* was used by Campo, the humorist, and *Micrós* was his pen name for short stories. These appeared in three volumes, *Ocios y apuntes,* 1890, *Cosas vistas,* 1894, and *Cartones* in 1897. His novel *La rumba* appeared in serial form in the newspaper *El Nacional.* His tenderness and human compassion seemed to echo Dickens and Daudet, whom he probably never read. Campo appears to have been a rather improvised and spontaneous development of his environment. A better artist than Lizardi, Campo had better taste than Prieto and was a better humorist than Cuéllar, since his narratives did not degenerate into caricatures. Micrós was a tender poet

who favored the underdog. Suffering and the animals frequently were the subject of his narratives. A better psychologist than his predecessors, he was able to convey his emotions and tenderness through details. His pictures of the lower and middle classes ring true.

Among later historical novelists of the period was Victoriano Salado Alvarez (1867–1931). He was not only a writer but also a lawyer, professor, journalist, politician, and diplomat. He attempted philology, history, literary criticism, and the novel. His first book, *De mi cosecha,* printed in 1899, is a collection of critical essays about contemporary Mexican authors which shows him as an opponent of the modernist movement in poetry. His short stories, *De autos,* were published in 1901, and his two historical novels, *De Santa Anna a la Reforma,* in three volumes in 1902, and *La Intervención y el Imperio* in four volumes in 1903. When he was initiated into the Mexican Academy, he read an interesting essay on "Mexicanisms surviving in North American English." *La vida azarosa y romántica de Don Carlos María de Bustamente* was published in 1933 after his death. His two novels are a picturesque history of Mexican life in the period from 1851 to 1867. They differ from all the romantic novels previously printed, and are perhaps comparable to the *Episodios Nacionales* of Benito Pérez Galdós. Alvarez, unlike Riva Palacio, was not interested in accumulating dramatic and startling incidents; but rather in reviving the historical past by portraying its highlights, its environment and customs, and delineating character so realistically one could believe the author had been there.

There were many other historical novelists. One more deserving mention is Heriberto Frías (1870–1928). His *Tomóchic* has a historical and autobiographical background dealing with the revolt of the Indians in the northern part of Mexico against the government of Díaz. Frías as an army officer took part in the campaign and could speak with authority as well as compassion of the deeds of the Indians and the cruelty of the government army officers in putting down the rebellion.

Drama

The theatre, unlike the other literary genres, did not reach a complete development. After the fall of the Second Empire, many plays and comedies of different types were performed. There was quantity but little quality. In 1876 for example, one Spanish actor gave forty performances of works of Mexican authors. Frequently, the plays were not rooted in a national environment, had little to do with the temperament and customs of the Mexicans, and more often than not belonged to the theatre of imitation. By 1890, very few Mexican authors were having their plays performed on the stage; one author of the time translated over two hundred works from the French, English, and Italian. The short plays or the "Género chico" of Spain was being imitated, for the most part with little success.

José Rosas Moreno, the poet of children, wrote one of the better plays about Sor Juana Inés de la Cruz in 1876. He also penned a satirical comedy in prose, *Los parientes,* and a comedy of manners and verse, *El pan de cada día.* Rosas Moreno was the first to write plays for children in his "El Año Nuevo," in 1874.

Born in 1841, Alfredo Chavero lived until 1906. He was a lawyer and a successful politician, an archeologist, historian, poet, novelist, and playwright. Even though his dramatic poetry was at times prosaic, he knew the technique of the theatre and theatrical effects. He was an indefatigable playwright whose works are extremely numerous. Inspired by the Indian past, he wrote a play in verse *Xóchitl* in 1877, and *Quetzalcóatl* in 1878. He passed on to colonial history with *La hermana de los Avilas* and in 1879, *Los amores de Alarcón,* considered his best work. From 1877 to 1881 he wrote *Bienaventurados los que esperan, La Ermita de Santa Fe,* and then *El valle de lágrimas, Sin esperanza, El sombrero, El autor de su desdicha, El huracán de un beso, El mundo de ahora,* and comic operas. Except for the earliest attempts, the plays of Chavero are laid in Paris, Madrid, Rome, or other foreign cities.

In spite of the fact that his work is uneven, the outstanding playwright of this period was José Peón y Contreras. He was born in Yucatán in 1843 and died in 1907. Coming from a distinguished family, he showed a disposition towards scientific as well as literary studies. He was a doctor of medicine at nineteen and, while still an adolescent, wrote *La cruz del paredón,* a fantastic legend, and three plays, *María la Loca, El castigo de Dios,* and *El Conde de Santiesteban.* By 1863 he was in Mexico City practicing medicine and holding the positions of representative and senator. His first poetry book called *Poesías* was published in 1868. His *Romances históricos mexicanos* (1871), imitating the romantic ballads of the Duque de Rivas, follow the example of Pesado and Roa Bárcena in attempting to depict Indian poetry. His *Romances dramáticos,* on the other hand, are inspired by Spanish themes as are the *Pequeños dramas,* a collection of twenty ballads. The life of Columbus is depicted in *Trovas Colombinas,* and the influence of Bécquer is seen in his *Ecos.* He was the author of two novels, *Taide,* 1885 and *Veleidosa,* 1891. In 1876 he had his first play performed, *¡Hasta el cielo!* In the same year *La hija del Rey,* his masterpiece and possibly the best of the Mexican romantic plays, was hailed with ceremony by many writers of Mexico who considered him the "Restorer of the Theatre." From 1876 to 1879 he wrote *El sacrificio de la vida, Gil González de Avila, Un amor de Hernán Cortés, Juan de Villalpando, Antón de Alaminos, Lucha de honra y amor, Esperanza, Impulsos del corazón, El Conde de Peñalva, Por el joyel del sombrero, El Capitán Pedreñales, Entre mi tío y mi tía, Doña Leonor de Sarabia, Vivo o muerto* as well as *El Conde Uconor, Por la Patria, El Padre José,* and *La eternidad de un minuto,* which probably came later. It was not until 1890 that Peón Contreras wrote another play, *Gabriela,* followed by *Soledad* in 1892, *Una tormenta en el mar* in 1893, *Laureana* in 1893, and *En el umbral de la dicha* in 1895. Among the many manuscript

plays that he left are *Margarita, Pablo y Virginia,* and *Gertrudis.* Peón Contreras stands out among the romantic dramatists with his colonial plays: *La hija del Rey,* by far his best work, *Gil González de Avila, Antón de Alaminos* and *Por el joyel del sombrero.* However, he was not so successful when he wrote of contemporary manners. He was a better dramatist in prose than in verse, and he had no peer in the colonial theatre. But as a post-romantic, he arrived too late. If he had been writing at the time of Calderón or Rodríguez Galván, he might have had more followers and greater importance in the development of the theatre in Mexico. Even in the publication of his works, Peón y Contreras was not highly successful — only eleven of his plays have been published.

The novelist Juan A. Mateos wrote for the theatre as early as 1864 and had his plays performed for several years. *Odio hereditario, La politicomanía, La hija del cantero, La Catarata del Niágara, Martín el Demente,* and *Borrascas de un sobretodo* all came before 1867. *La muerte de Lincoln* was published in 1867. Between the latter year and 1881, he had the following plays performed: *El novio oficial, El plagio, El otro, Los grandes tahures, La Monja Alférez, La rubia y la morena,* and *El ave negra.*

Literary Criticism

Mexican literary criticism came to life as a result of the extensive publication of newspapers and literary reviews and the importance gained by the artistic and scientific societies. The first to attempt literary criticism was, of course, Altamirano, whose criticism was aimed not so much at intrinsic evaluation as at stimulating young writers. Another critic of the time was Manuel Puga y Acal who wrote, in 1888, under the pseudonym of "Brummel," a book entitled *Los poetas mexicanos contemporáneos.* He was born in 1860 and died in 1930. Francisco A. de Icaza (1863–1925) discharged several diplomatic missions in Europe, but spent most of his life in Madrid. His critical work was concerned principally with Cervantes, Gutierre de Cetina, Juan de la Cueva, Mateo Alemán, and Lope de Vega, but in 1923 he also published a *Diccionario autobiográfico de conquistadores y pobladores de Nueva España.* He intended to do historical and literary research on the Mexican Colonial Period, but died before he could accomplish his purpose. Among other critics we can cite Olavarría y Ferrari, Francisco Sosa, Francisco Pimentel, José María Vigil, Manuel G. Revilla, and Victoriano Agüeros who edited the *Library of Mexican Authors* in seventy-eight volumes from 1896 to 1911.

History

Mexican history took on a new orientation during this period. There was no longer the historian whose writing was colored by political beliefs; but, instead, the dedicated men who did painstaking research to verify or to rectify episodes in Mexican history. Manuel

Orozco y Berra is one of the first names in historical and archeological research. Born in 1816, he constantly had to seek bureaucratic posts that would allow him to continue his research. After having obtained his engineering degree, he went on to study law. Among the many official government posts that he occupied was that of Director of the General Archives of the Nation, Minister of Development, and Justice of the Supreme Court. He opposed the French Intervention and refused to be a member of the Junta de Notables. Because of his financial difficulties, he took several posts during the Second Empire, finally becoming a Councillor of State. He was imprisoned after Maximilian's execution, but after two months, he was set free and was welcomed back to the Society of Geography and Statistics and to the Academy of Literature and Sciences from which he had been expelled for having served the Empire. His masterpiece, *Historia antigua y de la Conquista de México,* was started at this time: it was to be printed by order of the government at government expense when he died in 1881. He specialized in the early history of Mexico and did research in archeology attempting to decipher hieroglyphics and old Indian documents with the help of the works of the chroniclers, missionaries, and linguists. He is considered to be the best authority on the Aztecs and a historian of wide scholarship, analytical faculties, and clear and impartial judgment. His writings have not been collected as yet, but we know that he collaborated in the *Diccionario universal de historia y geografía,* having written the three-volume *Appendix.* By 1853, he had written *Noticia histórica de la Conjuración del Marqués del Valle,* and by 1857 the *Geografía de las lenguas y carta etnográfica de México,* an attempt to classify Indian languages and a study of the migration of Indian tribes in Mexico. His *Memoria para el plano de la ciudad de México* was printed in 1867 and the *Materiales para una cartografía mexicana* in 1871. After studying the different chronological systems, he attempted to solve the question of Mexican chronology in *Estudio de cronología mexicana.* The four volumes of *Historia antigua y de la Conquista de México* were published in 1880–1881. The first part deals with civilization; the second with prehistoric man in Mexico; the third with ancient history; and the fourth with the Conquest of Mexico. He also wrote a history of Spanish domination in Mexico.

Very similar to Orozco y Berra in his devotion to Mexican history was Joaquín García Icazbalceta (1825–1894). He has been called the great master of all Mexican scholarship, for he devoted his whole life to research and study. Coming from a wealthy family, he went to Spain in 1829 to flee political disturbances. He returned by 1836, and, under the influence of Alamán, he devoted himself to history. In 1849–1850 he published his translation of Prescott's *History of the Conquest of Peru* with some additions. Between 1852 and 1856, his first original works appeared in the *Diccionario universal de historia y geografía.* After setting up a small printing press in his home, he dedicated

himself to collecting an excellent library. He specialized in rare and valuable manuscripts and documents which many considered lost until that time. He collected, edited, and printed his first *Colección de documentos para la historia de México,* in two volumes between 1858 and 1866. The second collection was called *Nueva colección de documentos para la historia de México,* in five volumes and printed between 1886 and 1892. Not only did he reproduce reports, letters, narratives, itineraries, regulations, and decrees, etc., but for every volume there are introductions which are models of scholarship as well as style. His greatest work was in *Bibliografía Mexicana del Siglo XVI,* appearing in 1886. He spent some forty years in compilation of this listing of all books printed in Mexico between 1539 and 1600, as well as biographies, reproductions of title pages, bibliographical notes, etc., and finally the completeness and thoroughness of his scholarship were recognized. The sixteenth century was his field of specialization, and he disinterred material that genuinely advanced knowledge of customs, and culture, and gave us a complete picture of the formative process of a nation. He left other original works, among them a "Vocabulario de Mexicanismos."

Justo Sierra was a man who combined the gifts of a historian with the talents of a teacher. His main contribution was the attempt to make a synthesis of history whether he was dealing with world history as in his *Manual escolar de historia general* in 1891, or with Mexican history in *México: Su evolución social,* in 1900–01. With the collaboration of Pereyra, he wrote *Juárez, su obra y su tiempo* in 1905, as a supreme lesson in civic morality.

A follower of García Icazbalceta was Luis González Obregón, born in 1865. He was one of Altamirano's favorite pupils, and it was his teacher who convinced him to devote himself to letters. In 1888 he published biographical and bibliographical notes on Lizardi. In 1889 he started an annual publication on national bibliography which, unfortunately, appeared only that year. His work, *México Viejo* (1891–95), contains a series of articles on picturesque aspects of the history of the City of Mexico. Many other books were to be published between 1894 and 1923 dealing with Conquistadores, historians, precursors of Independence, the Inquisition, writers, the National Library, and the streets of Mexico. Just as García Icazbalceta, González Obregón concentrates on the colonial period, digging up customs and attempting a picture of culture during the Spanish domination. His historical writings are not cold and monotonous as are some scholarly books, for he often includes minute and charming details which help to popularize history. The historical writers of this period were legion. Here, because of their importance to literature, will be mentioned only Father Vicente de Paula Andrade for his *Ensayo bibliográfico mexicano del Siglo XVII,* from 1899, and Doctor Nicolas León for his *Bibliografía mexicana del Siglo XVIII,* printed in five volumes between 1902 and 1906.

MODERNISM

Toward the end of the nineteenth century, there was a certain restlessness in the world which was reflected in letters — it was a demolishing reaction or literary change similar to that brought about by romanticism. Increased study of literatures from other countries was a contributing factor to bring about this literary movement called modernism. It was not an isolated phenomenon in Spanish-American poetry, but had counterparts in France, Italy, Spain, England, Germany, and the United States. It is well expressed by an American critic in describing modernism as "the literary expression of that mood of unrest and of dissatisfaction with the prevailing worship and material success that marked the last few years of the nineteenth century." Mexico had been at peace for many years under the dictatorship of Porfirio Díaz. The "Científicos" were developing the country economically with the help of foreign concessions. The intellectual of the time, feeling stifled by the emphasis on positivism in philosophy and on economic aggrandizement in everyday life, felt that his ideas and his artistic sensibilities were beyond the comprehension of the average man. This "intellectual aristocrat" found an unsympathetic democracy that could not vibrate to his feelings, sentiments, and sensibilities. Thus the *modernista* turned away from the social, economic, and even political problems of his period to seek refuge in the world of his imagination, in the intellectual ivory tower. Mexican reality seemed to disappear for the *modernista* poet who was pursuing a fleeting and formless spiritual idea of Absolute Beauty. Absolute Beauty was to be found only in an imaginary world of his own creation, completely divorced from the world of reality. He felt that his manner of expression must be new, his metaphors and imagery unfamiliar. Considering Verlaine and his line, "Music above all things," as the principle of the new orientation, the poets sought to obtain the emotional effect of refined music through new rhymes, rhythms, invented words, and skilful alliteration. The Mexican *modernistas* belonged to the same family, but they cannot be said to belong to the same school as those of Europe. It must be noted that Mexico gave to the world at least two of the so-called precursors of modernism (Gutiérrez Nájera and Díaz Mirón), one of the foremost representatives of modernism in full bloom (Nervo), and one of the poets who changed the intellectual orientation of modernism from search for Beauty to search for Truth (González Martínez). Mexico also published the *Revista Azul* from 1894 to 1896, the foremost literary magazine in the first phase of modernism, and the *Revista Moderna* from 1898 to 1911, during the high point of modernism. Some of the *modernistas* retained romantic characteristics: individualism, disregard for the masses, obsession with death, skepticism, and rebelliousness.

Of course, the influence of the Parnassian and symbolist poets of France is always pointed out in connection with the modernists. Where romanticism had attempted a renovation in existing literature, modernism had succeeded in realizing it. In some Mexican poets, the romantic influence was more noticeable, while the symbolist influence appeared much more prevalent in others. In general, one might say that Parnassian influence was rather limited. Like any other movement, modernism became artificial and excessive in some poets, but there is no doubt that after modernism was incorporated into Mexican poetry, it added a beautiful and original touch. Some of the poets of the *Revista Azul* together with Gutiérrez Nájera were under the direct and belated influence of French romanticism and Parnassianism. With the *Revista Moderna* and under the influence of French symbolism, we reach a high point of the movement as represented by Nervo and the poets writing in that literary review.

Poetry

Manuel Gutiérrez Nájera was born in 1859, and died in 1895. He introduced a new period in Mexican letters by cultivating melody in the structure of the language. He has been considered both as a precursor and as a reformer. From his mother, he inherited sensibility and tenderness, and from his father, his fondness for letters. He read the Spanish mystics at an early age and later studied French and Latin. At the age of thirteen, he wrote his first article for a newspaper, an occupation which he was to follow for the rest of his life. He went from one newspaper to the other, writing many types of articles under different pseudonyms. He seemed to be the first Mexican writer to attempt to make a living by his pen. The magazine, *Revista Azul,* which he had founded with Díaz Dufoo, apparently had as great an influence as Altamirano's *El Renacimiento.* Overworked and exhausted by his alcoholic excesses, Nájera died at thirty-five. He wrote his first poetry under a religious influence — probably that of his mother. Soon, however, the love note and the French influence appear. Nájera's love poetry was not the classical form but rather a real and voluptuous medium. Through the French, he came in contact with other literatures, assimilating these varying influences to refine his verse, to give it fresh nuances, yet at the same time putting on a personal stamp. Bécquer and Campoamor as well as Hugo, Lamartine and Musset influenced him; Gauthier, Baudelaire and Verlaine were also to be found in his poetry. He succeeded in incorporating the French spirit into the Spanish form of expression. His poetry often has a light and airy rhythm. His aristocratic taste, the grace of his style, his inner delicacy and tender feeling, and his skeptical but elegant humor, all combine to temper his sensibilities. His best poems were probably written from 1880 to 1895. A year after his death, his poetry was collected in one volume, and between 1898 and 1903, his prose was compiled in two volumes which included light dramatic reviews, literary criticism, social notes, travel reports, "crónicas," fantasies, and short stories. To the short story he gave a new form (probably through French influence) in which the humorist and the poet walk together, now in reality, now in fantasy.

The complete poems of Salvador Díaz Mirón were published in 1941, including poetry written between 1876 and 1928. He was born in Veracruz and died in 1928. He devoted himself to politics and to journalism, and as a politician experienced jail and exile, but was essentially a man of letters. Mirón was a haughty aristocrat who held himself aloof from the conflicts and battles of literary schools and literary societies. As a modernist he seems to have lived in his own tower away from the masses, absorbed in the contemplation of vast horizons. In his first manner he had an influence on Darío and Chocano, but later his desire for renovation led him to a search for a new technique, which culminated in *Lascas* (1901), which he baptized as his only book. He left another unpublished volume of a similar nature entitled "Astillas y triunfos," which was never published. His early verses have the intensity of burning lava, but later, seeking perfection, he chiseled marble statues, always searching for perfect expression. Every syllable and every letter occupied its harmonious place to bring about a rhythmical ideal. His new manner had made him lose his spontaneity and the direct emotion to communicate to the reader, but it had gained him plastic and rhythmic riches. There is a parallel with Góngora in Mirón's search for perfection which was often to render him obscure. As he climbed higher toward perfection of form, he lost early readers who had been impressed first by his tenderness, love affairs, and sadness, and later by his arrogance, haughtiness, and heroic strength.

Some critics classify Luis G. Urbina as a direct successor of Gutiérrez Nájera. Urbina was born in 1868 and died in 1934. Like Rodríguez Galván, Urbina was a selfmade man. While he was still in his teens, his name had already appeared in the newspaper as the author of light "crónicas" and poems. He was poet, chronicler, reviewer, critic and historian of literature, and journalist. He occupied a position in the Ministry of Public Instruction and Fine Arts and was professor of literature. Together with Pedro Henríquez Ureña and Nicolás Rangel, he carried on literary research that resulted in the *Antología del Centenario* in 1910. Later he was director of the National Library and traveled through South America and Spain. His *Versos* of 1890 are the poems of early youth. In 1902, he published *Ingenuas*, also poems of his youth. It has been pointed out that the fundamental characteristic of his poetical work was its homogeneousness. His ideas and his feelings changed according to the times, but his aesthetic quality was always the same. From the very first poem he revealed himself completely, and his later work served simply to intensify his poetic sensibility and to correct his form of expression. He was not a sensational poet nor was he deeply esoteric. He lacked artificial subtlety but concentrated on the emotional traditions of love, sorrow, life, and death. The musical tone of his verses, his humor, the sadness

of his poems are reminiscent of Nájera, but unlike the latter, he was not much influenced by foreign poets, but possessed his own deeper melancholy and musicality. A better example of his later poetry is *Puestas de sol*, 1910. He also wrote *Lámparas en agonía* in 1914, *El glosario de la vida vulgar,* 1916, *El corazón juglar,* 1920, *Los últimos pájaros,* 1924, and in 1941, *El cancionero de la noche serena* was printed posthumously. He also wrote some seven books of prose including *La vida literaria de México,* (1917).

Born in the town of Tepic, Amado Nervo died in 1919. He spent his childhood in his native city and soon showed a precocious aptitude for letters. His mother gathered together some of the verses that he wrote and read them to the whole family. In 1884 he was sent to Jacona in the state of Michoacán to study at the famous school there. In addition to Spanish, he studied Latin, English, and French. He went on to the seminary in Zamora, studying science and philosophy from 1886 to 1888 and law in 1889. Returning to his first love, he attempted writing prose and verse. In 1891 he returned to the seminary and began his study of theology. He read religious books, was fascinated by religious life, and was studying to be a priest, but because of financial difficulties in his family, he left the seminary and started to earn a living with his pen. After returning briefly to Tepic, he began his career as a journalist in Mazatlán. Later, in Mexico City (between 1894 and 1898), he published his first literary works as well as many articles and translations in the newspapers. A daring novel, *El bachiller,* printed in 1895, was a subject of controversy, but at the same time made a name for Nervo. Upon the first anniversary of the death of Gutiérrez Nájera, he recited a poem which won him immediate popularity. When his *Místicas* was published in 1898, he won his accolade as a poet. Together with Jesús Valenzuela, Nervo was the founder of the *Revista Moderna,* the organ for the new poetry. In 1900, he traveled through Europe and in 1905 became a diplomat and was sent to Madrid. He remained in the Spanish capital until 1918, later to be appointed Plenipotentiary Minister to Argentina and Uruguay. Shortly after having given a recital in the capital of Uruguay, he died. When his body was brought back to Mexico, his funeral was an enormous popular gathering beyond that of any poet in the Americas.

Alfonso Reyes published Nervo's *Obras Completas* in twenty-nine volumes in Madrid between 1920 and 1928. *Mañana del Poeta,* 1938, includes an excellent introduction by Alfonso Méndez Plancarte as well as autobiographical pages, short stories, and poetry by Nervo. His poetry achieved three levels of development. The first level was Nervo, the symbolist. Under the aegis of the French symbolists, he suffered from préciosité, deliberately broke grammatical rules, rejoiced in subtlety, and discovered strange words and rhythms. He seemed to be engulfed in a literary and somewhat external mysticism and delighted in the exterior aspects of religion such as candles, missals, altars, domes, etc. *Perlas negras,* 1898; *Poemas,* 1901; *El éxodo y las flores del camino, Lira heroica,* 1902; and in 1905, *Los jardines interiores,* are typical of this first stage. In his second stage, Nervo withdrew from the external and began to explore his innermost thoughts. He found love, and this emotion lent serenity and tranquility to his life, while his poetry tended toward simplicity. His lyre pulsated to discretion and to his mastery of words. This was the period of *En voz baja,* (1909) and *Serenidad* (1914). Tragedy was to bring his poetic style to still a third stage. His beloved died; he saw death close at hand and suffered the pains of a loss against which he was powerless. These emotions led him to asceticism, and he attempts to elevate his spirit to complete renunciation. *Elevación,* 1917, in verse, and *Plenitud,* 1918, in prose, are typical of this period as well as *El estanque de los lotos.* After his death, *La amada inmóvil* and *El arquero divino* were published in 1922.

Amado Nervo's prose shows the many facets of his personality. He wrote essays, "crónicas," articles, novels, short stories and in 1910 a book on Juana de Asbaje. His novels include, besides *El bachiller; Pascual Aguilera* and *El domador de almas.* Among his short stories are the collection *Almas que pasan,* in 1906; *El diablo desinteresado, El diamante de la inquietud, Una mentira, Un sueño, El sexto sentido, Amnesia,* and *Cuentos misteriosos.* He showed himself to be an original teller of tales in his novels and short stories, but his later novelistic production passed from a strong nationalism to a cosmopolitan outlook. In his short stories and novels can be noted most clearly the evolution toward simplicity.

Enrique González Martínez completed the cycle of the great modernist poets in Mexico. Born in 1871, he died in 1952. He studied medicine in Guadalajara and practiced in Mazatlán. By 1911, he was in Mexico City working for a newspaper and teaching, filling certain government positions, and finally becoming a diplomat. He falls somewhere between the typically modernist group and the generation that followed, and his poetic trajectory can be described as an ascending line toward serenity and sincerity, seeking a more severe and deeper concept of life. His first volumes of poetry appeared in the provinces — *Preludios,* 1903; *Lirismos,* 1907; *Silénter,* 1909; and *Los senderos ocultos,* 1911. By the time he appeared on the scene in Mexico City, he was already recognized as a master among poets. It was then that he published *La muerte del cisne* in 1915; *La hora inútil* in 1916; *El libro de la fuerza, de la bondad y del ensueño* in 1917; *Parábolas y otros poemas* in 1918; *La palabra del viento,* 1921; *El romero alucinado,* 1923; *Las señales furtivas,* 1925; *Poemas de ayer y de hoy,* 1926; *Poesía, 1909–1929,* printed in 1930; *Poemas truncos,* 1935; *Ausencia y canto,* 1937; *El diluvio de fuego,* 1938; *Poemas,* 1940; *Bajo el signo mortal,* 1943; *Poesía (1898–1938),* in three volumes in 1940; *Poesías completas* in 1944; *Segundo despertar y otros poemas,* 1945; *Vilano al viento,* 1948; and *Babel,* 1949. He also translated some

French poets in 1915 and Belgian poets in 1918. Often his poetry was characterized as pantheistic, but in his case this simply meant adoring even the most humble thing in nature. He was an optimist with a large degree of melancholy; feeling the ephemeral nature of sorrow and considering it as transitory as pleasure, he sang about both of them with an undefinable melancholic tenderness after both had passed. A critic has said that for González Martínez "sorrow is not a tremendous guest, but a traveler who stops in his home and that tomorrow at dawn, shaking his sandals, will leave anew." His autobiography, *El hombre del buho,* printed in 1944, has the subtitle "Misterio de una vocación," and is an excellent description of himself and his poetical works from his earliest attempts to his lyric maturity.

The Realistic Novel

Shortly before the appearance of modernism in Mexico, the realistic novel developed. Usually credited with the introduction of realism in the novel is Emilio Rabasa, better known by his pseudonym *Sancho Polo.* Rabasa went beyond Cuéllar, for in his portrayal of environment and customs he did not neglect a study of characters and this gave the novel greater social importance. Rabasa was a social scientist who finally stifled the novelist in himself. Born in 1856, he became a lawyer in Oaxaca and went into politics and teaching. In 1891, he became governor of his native state of Chiapas and later a senator. As a lawyer and a sociologist, he published specialized books on constitutional trials, the political organization and the historical evolution of Mexico. His novels came early in his life and included *La bola, La gran ciencia, El cuarto poder,* and *Moneda falsa.* The first two were published in 1887 and the second two the following year. After his death in 1930, *La Guerra de Tres Años* which had been published in 1891 in the newspaper was printed. *La bola,* a word later to be used more frequently in Mexico to describe a revolution, showed how these revolts are started, how they develop, and how they triumph under the direction of rustics and small-time politicians. For Rabasa, *La gran ciencia* was politics. The novels *El cuarto poder* and *Moneda falsa* tell the story of the adventures of the revolutionaries in politics and in journalism in Mexico City. The author was a follower of Perez Galdós, but he also had a satirical side. Probably *La bola* is the best of his novels.

The first novelist of the rural environment was José López Portillo y Rojas. He was born in 1850 in a prominent family and became a lawyer. A long trip through England, France, Italy, and the Orient allowed him to become acquainted with French and English literatures. He was also a professor and a politician — a congressman, governor of Jalisco, and Minister of Foreign Affairs. He died in 1923. He wrote poetry, drama, travel books, history, and criticism. The first book he had published (1873) was his *Impresiones de viaje.* His poetry was gathered under the title *Armonías fugitivas* in 1892, and typical of his critical works is *Rosario la de Acuña* (1920). His history, *Elevación y caída de Porfirio Díaz,* appeared in 1921. In spite of these varied literary activities, he is to be considered essentially a novelist. He wrote both short stories and novels. His short story collections include *Seis leyendas,* 1883; *Novelas cortas,* 1900; *Sucesos y novelas cortas,* 1903; *Historias, historietas y cuentecillos,* 1918. *La parcela,* 1898; *Los precursores,* 1909; and *Fuertes y débiles,* 1919, are the titles of his three novels. He attempted the short story first, and apparently felt most capable in that genre. *La parcela* was the best rural novel of the nineteenth century as well as his best novel. The plot was very simple: an argument over a piece of land, by two neighboring ranchers, reminiscent of *The Mill on the Floss.* López Portillo's observation of reality was very strong, as demonstrated by the pictures he portrayed of the main characters, as well as the minor ones. He remained close to the truth in depicting the customs of the country and the regional speech of the characters. Pereda, the Spanish novelist, seemed to be his model in *La parcela.* He was opposed to French literary currents of the time and insisted upon underlining Mexican nationalism. He pointed out, "The only thing that we need to exploit the rich elements that surround us is to withdraw within ourselves and to diffuse ourselves less in foreign things."

Rafael Delgado completes the trio of Mexican novelists who follow the example of Spanish realism. He was as Mexican as Rabasa and López Portillo y Rojas but had a poetic note because of his delicate sensibility. He was more realistic than the previous two novelists and accentuated more the picturesqueness in his novels. He excelled beyond his two predecessors in his description of nature. Born in 1853, he had a deeply religious feeling which was reflected in his works. Most of his life was spent in his home state of Veracruz and he died in 1914. He attempted poetry, criticism, and the theatre, but his reputation was based on his novels. His four novels, *La calandria, Angelina, Los parientes ricos,* and *Historia vulgar* were published in 1891, 1895, 1903, and 1904, respectively. His short stories were collected in 1902 under the title, *Cuentos y notas.* Unlike López Portillo y Rojas, Delgado was not at his best in the short story. As a rule, his novels possessed a harmonious unity without ups or downs, and this was not true of his short stories. Probably his most significant novel was his first, *La calandria.* The plot of this story, as most of his plots, was simple: a poor girl deciding between a man of her class and a libertine dandy selects the latter to her sorrow. *Angelina* describes a student who returns to his small town and whose two loves conflict. He is left at the end without any. *Los parientos ricos* portrays the adventures and misadventures of a family who break away from the province, trusting the protection that wealthy relatives will provide. His narratives were simple, almost commonplace, and very true to life, but the importance of the novels lay in the incidents and details that appeared in them. Pluviosilla, (Orizaba) and Villaverde (Córdoba) were the two provincial cities whose environment he succeeded in reproducing faithfully.

The Naturalistic Novel

French influence which was felt among the *modernista* poets was also present in the novel, reaching its culmination with Federico Gamboa. Born in 1864, his early years were spent in constant financial struggles which tempered the youthful spirit. At twenty-four he embarked upon a diplomatic career and devoted most of his life to it, rising little by little to minister, ambassador, and Minister of Foreign Affairs. His literary work comprised the novel, autobiography, and the drama, but it was as a novelist that he excelled. His first book, *Del natural,* was published in 1888 in Guatemala, and was a series of short stories in which his powers of observation about contemporary life begin to appear. *Apariencias,* published in Buenos Aires in 1892, was his first long novel, although still a rather unsuccessful attempt. It is not until *Suprema ley* in 1896 that the real novelist appeared. The plot dealt with the infatuation of an insignificant court clerk for a woman accused of murder. The love affair makes the poor clerk destroy his home and leads him eventually to death. Zola and the Goncourt brothers are present here in their naturalism, and the naturalism of the Mexican writer shows through his insistence on detail, the abundance of descriptions, the exact reproduction of the environment, whether in the sinister prison or in the unhappy home of the clerk. *Metamorfosis* appeared in Guatemala in 1899, and dealt with the daring theme of the nun that became a woman in the arms of the man who took her away from the convent. By far the most popular book of Gamboa is *Santa,* first printed in Barcelona in 1902, with subsequent editions in 1905, 1910, 1915, 1919, 1925, 1927, 1929, 1935, 1938, etc. From the number of editions, it is evident that here we are concerned with the all-time best-seller of Mexican novels; thousands and thousands of copies have been printed and the movies and the theatre have made versions of it. Its popularity is due, no doubt, to its theme: the life of a prostitute, and here one sees the influence of Zola's novel, *Nana.* It is Gamboa's masterpiece. In spite of the theme and the naturalistic passages, the book seems to have a didactic purpose insisting on the horror of guilt. *Reconquista* appeared in Madrid in 1908 and narrated the return of the indifferent believer to religious faith. *La llaga* also came out in Madrid in 1913. It was the story of a prisoner in the Castle of San Juan de Ulúa, who attempted to start life over again through love. In this book is probably the most naturalistic passage of the novel as the hero watches a rat give birth to its young. Another novel *El evangelista,* was printed in New York in 1922. Gamboa's books of memoirs comprise a large part of his work and show his close

The forward strides of a modern people are suggested by this sculpture in relief on the Medical Center at the University City in Mexico, D.F. The figures are the work of Siqueiros, a controversial giant among contemporary Mexican artists.

relationship to the French naturalists. *Impresiones y recuerdos* is the first memoir, published in Buenos Aires in 1893. Here Gamboa related his memories of childhood and adolescence, the beginnings of his literary career, his journalistic career, his friends, and the impressions of his travels. Later came *Mi diario* which first came to life in Guadalajara in 1907, another volume in 1910, more in 1920, another in 1934, and still another in 1938. His diary was reminiscent of the journals of the Goncourt brothers, and — a commentary on events, people, and things from 1892 to 1911. He died in 1939, while he was director of the Mexican Academy.

CONTEMPORARY LITERATURE

The next major period of Mexican literature dates from the beginning of the so-called Mexican Revolution or the great Social Revolution of 1910, to the present time. An intellectual revolution in the year 1908 antedated the social revolution of 1910. Positivism, based on the doctrines of Auguste Comte, endured in Mexico longer than in France, thanks to its relationship to political domination. Gabino Barreda was placed in charge of organizing higher education in Mexico, and he revolutionized the schools by introducing and emphasizing positivistic ideas, neglecting, thus, the traditional classical education that had been heretofore imparted in Mexico. But in 1908 came a reaction against the official doctrine of positivism, primarily through the young intellectuals who composed the "Ateneo de la Juventud." The limitations imposed on the development of the human personality and the restrictions on education inspired the group to intellectual rebellion.

Philosophy

Although the work of the "Ateneo" lasted only until 1914, the effects of this cultural revolution had great impact on Mexican culture. Their main aspiration was a more idealistic philosophy and a criticism and revision of intellectual values. If the group failed to achieve many of its goals, it was because of the 1910 armed revolt which dispersed the intellectuals over many sections of Mexico. There were more than thirty members of the "Ateneo." The oustanding figures were Antonio Caso, Pedro Henríquez Ureña, José Vasconcelos, and Alfonso Reyes in prose, and Urbina and González Martínez in poetry. Born in 1883, Antonio Caso died in 1946. He was the chief philosopher of the group conducting a campaign against positivism and introducing modern philosophy in Mexico, thus promoting the exchange of ideas. He was responsible for starting the courses in philosophy at the College of Higher Studies of the National University, and he became the master of his generation. He was one of the great thinkers and writers of his nation who discussed many problems and analyzed the best representatives of human thought. He also tried his hand at poetry with *Crisopeya* in 1931 and *El político de los días del mar* in 1935. His philosophy is enclosed in his main work, *La existencia como economía, como desinterés y como caridad*, 1919, with a second edition in 1943.

He also wrote, among other works, *Problemas filosóficos*, 1915; *Filósofos y doctrinas morales*, 1915; *Discursos a la Nación Mexicana*, 1922; *Ensayos críticos y polémicos*, 1922; *El concepto de la historia universal*, 1922; *Doctrinas e ideas*, 1924; *El problema de México y la ideología nacional*, 1924; *Principios estéticos*, 1925; *Historia y antología del pensamiento filosófico*, 1926; *La filosofía de Husserl*, 1934; *Nuevos Discursos a la Nación Mexicana*, 1934; *La filosofía de la cultura y el materialismo histórico*, 1936; *La persona humana y el estado totalitario*, 1941; *El peligro del hombre*, 1942; and *México, Apuntamientos de cultura patria*, 1943. He opposed historic materialism and became the defender of freedom of thought and academic freedom.

Pedro Henríquez Ureña was born in 1884 and died in 1946. A Dominican, he arrived in Mexico for the first time in 1906. He was essentially an essayist and a critic. By example, he inspired his generation to be disciplined instead of improvised, and in a lecture "La influencia de la Revolución en la vida intelectual de México," he discussed the activities of the "Ateneo" and gave a bird's eye view of culture in Mexico at that time.

José Vasconcelos was born in 1881 and died in 1959. He was a thinker as well as a man of action, original in his thought and impetuous and stormy in his expression. A restless spirit, he undertook to reform Mexican education after becoming Minister of Public Education in 1921. He participated in the Revolution and lectured in 1910 on "Don Gabino Barreda y las ideas contemporáneas." Among his many books are *Divagaciones literarias*, 1919; *Pesimismo alegre*, 1931; *¿Qué es la Revolución?*, 1937. His autobiography is included in *Ulises Criollo*, 1936; *La Tormenta*, 1936; *El Desastre*, 1938; and *El Proconsulado*, 1939. His philosophical studies included *Pitágoras, una teoría del ritmo*, published in Havana in 1916; *Estudios indostánicos*, appearing in Madrid in 1920; *Tratado de metafísica*, 1929; *Etica*, 1932; *Estética*, 1935; *Historia del pensamiento filosófico*, 1937; *Manual de filosofía*, 1940; *Lógica orgánica*, 1945. His ideas on sociology and pedagogy were expounded in *La raza cósmica*, printed in Barcelona in 1925; *Indología*, also from Barcelona, 1927; *Bolivarismo y Monroísmo*, published in Santiago de Chile, 1935; and *De Robinsón a Odiseo*, Madrid, 1935. His historical works included *Los últimos cincuenta años*, 1924; *Breve historia de México*, 1936; *Hernán Cortés, creador de la nacionalidad*, 1941; and *Simón Bolívar*, 1939. He attempted the theatre with *Prometeo vencedor* in 1920 and *Los robachicos*, 1946; and the short story with *La cita*, 1945. His thought on the Americas was found essentially in *La raza cósmica*, *Bolivarismo y Monroísmo*, culminating in *Indología*. In this latter book is one of the few attempts by a Mexican to formulate a New World philosophy. Since the spiritual was of prime importance to Vasconcelos, the individual would prevail over society. To him, man was the measure of everything, his goal, the infinite, God. Therefore, between the soul and its end there can be intermediaries and auxiliaries, but none of them must constitute the end in itself. In order to obtain his ultimate end, man can desocialize himself, that is, isolate himself from society without this action being considered a sin. In other words, he summarized: society must serve the individual and not the individual society. Thus, he condemned all the systems that instituted a supreme human society or a state demanding regimentation of its component parts. Using these principles as his main goals, he went on to study a bigger America. Through its geography, he demonstrated its possibilities: the great American rivers, the tropical zones, the population mixture everywhere of Spanish and Indian elements. Democracy was the only form that he could see in considering the political institutions of the Americas, and socialism in the economic aspect. As for culture, which was a collective flourishing, he preferred Hispanic culture; he was a main exponent of "Latinidad." He opposed culture to civilization which he said is only technique. His message to Latin America was to recognize and magnify such a Hispanic ideal of culture. "Bolivarismo" was what he called the idea of creating a federation made up of all the American nations of Spanish culture in opposition to "Monroísmo" — the Anglo-Saxon idea of incorporating the twenty Hispanic nations into the nordic empire through the policy of Pan-Americanism. His ideas are reminiscent of Bolívar, and in Mexico, Lucas Alamán, who once proposed a customs union from the Rio Grande to Cape Horn. In *Indología*, he deals with the idea of American race. He employs "indología" in the sense of science of the Indies, science of the universe, not of the old Indies, nor the modern Indies, nor the geographical Indies, but the Indies in the sense of the Columbian dream of the roundness of the earth, the unity of the species and the concert of cultures.

Alfonso Reyes (1889–1959) studied at the Centro de Estudios Históricos in Madrid where he learned discipline and critical technique. He was the humanist of the "Ateneo de la Juventud" and possessed a tremendous culture and immense intellectual curiosity. He was critic, short story writer, poet, and scholar. He became an expert on Spanish literature through long residence and study in Spain. He travelled through Europe and Latin America on diplomatic missions. His work was so vast that it would take pages to list; suffice it to say that he wrote some seventeen volumes of poetry, three books of short stories, and many critical essays, prologues, and annotated editions, besides his translations from English and French, and his non-literary works. Several times his name was presented, unsuccessfully, as a candidate for the Nobel Prize for Literature.

The Novel

The novelist of the "Ateneo" was Carlos González Peña, 1885–1955. His novels include *De noche,* 1905; *La chiquilla,* published in Valencia in 1907–08; *La musa bohemia,* also printed in Valencia in 1909; and *La fuga de la quimera,* 1919. He also wrote essays, books on travel, and a history of Mexican literature, which was first published in 1928 and considered the best for its completeness and its literary judgments.

Drama

Three names stand out in drama during this period: Federico Gamboa, Marcelino Dávalos, and José Joaquín Gamboa. All three attempted to bring a nationalistic touch to the theatre. Federico Gamboa wrote *La ultima campaña* as early as 1894, and *Divertirse* in the same year; *La venganza de la gleba,* published in Guatemala in 1907; *A buena cuenta,* also 1907; and *Entre hermanos,* 1928; and *El perdón de los hijos.* His best play is *La venganza de la gleba.* It was the first serious attempt to have a rural drama performed on the Mexican stage, and its characters and the intention of the author seem to forecast the personages found in the novel of the Revolution.

Born in 1871, Marcelino Dávalos died in 1923. He was a lawyer and a politician who devoted himself completely to the theatre. His first play, *El último cuadro,* was performed in 1900 and is reminiscent of the post-romantic dramas of Echegaray. *Guadalupe,* 1903, deals with heredity and alcoholism in a regional environment. *Mascarada* was published in 1904. *Así pasan . . .* was performed in 1908 and dealt with the difficulties of an aging actress. *Nupcial* appeared in 1909 and in 1915 his *Teatro* was published in Veracruz. *El crimen de Marciano* is called a dramatic narrative dealing with a popular legend. *Jardines trágicos* was also performed in 1909. He reproduced the popular speech of the country in *¡Viva el amo!,* 1910. *Lo viejo,* 1911, and *Indisoluble,* performed in 1909, discuss social themes. His last play was *Aguilas y*

estrellas, appearing in 1916. He also compiled a *Monografía del teatro* in 1918. His plays were not in verse and his themes were invariably Mexican, two aspects which made him original in the history of the theatre in Mexico. He lacked artistic sensibility and literary taste, but his theatrical ability and his nationalistic topics made his plays outstanding in Mexico.

The third dramatist, José Joaquín Gamboa, was born in 1878 and, after devoting himself completely to the theatre, died in 1931. His first play, *La carne* or *Teresa,* 1903, presented the struggles of the heroine between mystical desires and spiritual love. *La muerte,* 1904, portrayed adultery among the upper classes. *El hogar,* 1905, showed the young man from the provinces who comes to Mexico City and, trying to find himself, returns to his home town. *El día del juicio,* 1908, presents Gamboa as a psychologist trying to analyze his characters. It was not until 1923 that he returned to the theatre with *El diablo tiene frío, Los Revillagigedo,* 1925; *Via Crucis,* 1925; *Cuento viejo,* 1925; *Si la juventud supiera,* 1927; *Espíritus,* 1927; *Las islas del amor,* 1928; *El mismo caso,* 1929; *Ella,* 1930; and his best and final play, *El caballero, la muerte y el diablo,* 1931. His collected plays appeared in 1938 under the title *Teatro.* From the beginning of his career, this playwright reproduced a Mexican environment and had good psychological command of his characters whom he was able to paint with a few strokes. Ironic humor and poetic tenderness seemed to be balanced in his work. At times he portrayed the lower classes of Mexico, and at other times he studied the upper classes, always keeping in mind the transformations through which Mexico was passing, making him a kind of theatrical historian of his times. In his later plays, he attempted new techniques.

The Colonialist Novel

The colonialist novel followed the novel of the Ateneo group, attempting to recreate a colonial atmosphere without being historically precise. This vogue lasted approximately from 1916 to 1926. Artemio de Valle Arizpe was the oldest of the group, born in 1888 and dying in 1961. He wrote novels and short stories, traditions and legends, as well as history. He became known in his later years as the "Chronicler of the City of Mexico." Among his novels and short stories are *Ejemplo,* 1919; *Vidas milagrosas,* 1921; *Doña Leonor de Cáceres y Acevedo y Cosas tenedes,* 1922; *Tres nichos de un retablo,* 1936; *Cuentos del México antiguo,* 1939; *El Canillitas,* 1942; *Amor que cayó en castigo,* 1945; and *La movible inquietud,* 1945. Valle Arizpe remained a colonial writer until the end while the rest of his group changed their orientation. The colonialist novel was an evasion from and a reaction to the preference for revolutionary themes. For political reasons, the colony had not been exploited for some time as a literary topic: the group contributed to intensifying and disseminating the knowledge of Mexico's colonial past.

Julio Jiménez Rueda, author of novels, plays, and critical studies such as *Historia de la literatura mexicana* (1928), was also a colonialist novelist during this period of his life. His novels include *Sor Adoración del Divino Verbo,* 1923; *Moisén,* 1924. As late as 1924, he published *Novelas coloniales* and *Vidas reales que parecen imaginarias,* 1947. In his plays he also joined the current of colonialism by writing *Camino de perfección,* 1908, dealing with the life of Sor Juana Inés de la Cruz. Likewise, Francisco Monterde was a colonialist in his *El madrigal de Cetina y el secreto de la escala* in 1918. Monterde attempted poetry, the novel, the theatre, and literary criticism, and was the author of an excellent bibliography of the theatre in Mexico (1933). He succeeded Jiménez Rueda at his death as director of the Mexican Academy. Ermilo Abreu Gómez has also tried his hand at the colonialist novel with *El corcovado,* 1924, and *La vida del Venerable Siervo de Dios Gregorio López,* in 1925. Besides a novelist, he wrote plays, literary criticism and bibliography. Genaro Estrada, born in 1887, died in 1937. In 1926 he published his *Pero Galín,* one of the best of the colonialist novels, involving a criticism of this type of novel. He had already published his *Visionario de la Nueva España* in 1921. He left a bibliography of Amado Nervo, and through his position in the Foreign Ministry was able to encourage the publication of many excellent bibliographies in the collection *Monografías bibliográficas mexicanas.* Manuel Horta was a short-story writer of the colonialists with his *Vitrales de capilla,* 1917, and *Estampas de antaño,* printed in 1919. He also published a biography of José de la Borda in 1928, a miner and philanthropist whose donations built the famous church of Santa Prisca in Taxco.

Poetry

Poetry was given new orientation by Ramón López Velarde, born in 1888 and dying while in his prime in 1921. His prose has been collected in *El minutero,* printed two years after his death. Although he only wrote three books of poetry, his influence on succeeding poets was almost as great as that of modernism on the poets of the last ten years of the nineteenth century and the first ten years of the twentieth century. *La sangre devota* appeared in 1916; *Zozobra* was published in 1919. *El son del corazón* did not appear until 1932.

The volume of *Obras completas* was published in 1945. A lyric poet who wrote of his province, to Mexican poetry he brought the sensation of smell and color, rhythm, complaint in a veiled tone, the melancholy of his region, and an almost religious feeling. Whereas in his first book he was objective, afterward he became subjective and almost introspective, using the external merely as a symbol. He unveiled his feelings with resignation. As he related his inner drama, he embellished it with the insignificant, the trivial, even when describing love. At times his verse was dissonant, but he could obtain marvelous effects from this new

rhythm. Often he seemed almost gongoristic in describing inner feelings in an ambiguous and obscure manner. He broke away from tradition, and even though he died too early to achieve a definitive poetic manner, he did influence poets that were to follow. Mexico, land of lyric poets, has no doubt had better poets than López Velarde but none as intimate, as mysterious, and as secret. His voice had accents of intimacy, his mystery was chiaroscuro, but his secret manner prevented the popularity of his works. The provincial aspect, the local color of his familiar themes, and his opaque and slow voice expressed the complex nature of the spirit of the poet.

The Bible and the catechism seemed to be his readings; Fuensanta, his only romantic love. The poet seemed to have been conscious of the two personalities that he enclosed within himself and was able to make them co-exist and express themselves, not one at a time, but simultaneously. Heaven and earth, virtue and sin, angel and devil, fought within him. López Velarde himself confessed the change that came over him after reading Baudelaire, but in his poetry, he is influenced not by the form, but rather by the spirit of the French poet.

Although we cannot establish direct imitation on the part of López Velarde of Baudelaire, we can note the similarity in themes such as agony, emptiness, horror, and sterility. Whereas in López Velarde, religiousness frequently turns into eroticism, in Baudelaire, eroticism sometimes turns into prayer. The presence of the Bible is felt in López Velarde's poetry as needed nourishment for his spirit and for the expression of his personality. His intimate and secret intuitions were often expressed through the mysteries of the Catholic religion and the practices, symbols, and objects of the Catholic church. He often saturated religion with an erotic feeling, as when he says that God gave him a feminine angel for his guardian. He himself said, "I cannot understand anything nor feel anything except through women. That is why I come with an erotic temperament to abstract questions." In his poetry, López Velarde made a daring attempt to unfold the hidden soul of a man, to bring out submerged anguish, and to express the tortures and restlessness of the spirit before eroticism, religiousness, and death.

As a result of the First World War, there were in Europe intellectuals who were looking for new norms and orientations, who broke with the past, and who no longer accepted traditional precepts. The same thing happened in Mexico when some of the vanguard movements in poetry appeared. One of the first to appear in a noisy manner, seeming like a revolution but ending like a spent fire-cracker was the *Estridentismo,* developed under the direction of Manuel Maples Arce. Born in 1898, he published poetry under such titles as *Rag, Tintas de abanico,* 1920; *Andamios interiores,* 1922; *Urbe,* 1924; *Poemas interdictos,* 1927; and *Incitaciones y valoraciones,* 1956. Belonging to the group were also Germán List Arzubide (1898) with *Esquina,* 1924; *El viajero en el vértice,* 1926, and *Plebe,* with the subtitle "Rebellion Poems," 1926; Salvador Gallardo with *El pentagrama eléctrico*, 1925; Luis Quintanilla (1900) with *Avión*, 1923; *Poemas, 1917–1923, Radio, Poema inalámbrico* and *Trece mensajes*, 1924; and Arquelas Vela (1899) with *El sendero gris y otros poemas, 1919–1920*, 1920. Among the novelists and short story writers of the group, we can name List Arzubide with *Mueran los gachupines*, historical tales of contemporary life; *Troka, el poderoso*, 1940; Arqueles Vela who wrote *La señorita*, etc., 1921; *El café de nadie*, 1926; and much later *Cuentos del día y de la noche*, 1945; as well as Xavier Icaza, (1902), *Dilema*, 1921; *Gente mexicana*, 1927; *La hacienda*, 1928; and *Panchito Chapopote*, 1928. Icaza also tried the theatre with *Magnavoz*, 1926; *Discurso mexicano*, 1926; and afterwards, *Coloquio Guadalupano*, 1931; *Retablo de Nuestra Señora de Guadalupe*, 1931; and *Trayectoria*, 1936. List Arzubide also penned *El movimento estridentista* in Jalapa in 1926. The group issued manifestoes, had its own magazine, *Irradiador*, and had a *Mecenas* when Maples Arce was secretary of the government in the state of Veracruz. Another magazine, *Horizonte*, was published between 1926 and 1927. The movement seemed to be opposed to literature and to reason, and showed a scorn for the older aesthetic principles and for the bourgeoisie. It was essentially a negative and destructive movement similar to Dadaism, offering no constructive substitutes. Rather than a genuine attempt to found a new aesthetics, the movement was an active mischief on the part of young men. The theoretical aspiration of the group was "a vital, fecund, and strong form of poetry" which could never be carried into practice. They kept the traditional structure of poetry simply as a point of departure for their strident and sensational images and metaphors.

Ateneo de la Juventud

In 1919, a group of poets founded a new Ateneo de la Juventud, poets who fell heir to the generation of the first Ateneo, many of whom had written under the influence of González Martínez — among them Pellicer, Ortiz de Montellano, González Rojo, José Gorostiza, and Torres Bodet. Little by little, the Ateneo dissolved, and some of its members gathered around *La Falange* (1922–1923) by Ortiz de Montellano and Torres Bodet, and later around *Ulises* (1927–1928) under the direction of Salvador Novo and Xavier Villaurrutia. To offer resistance to *Estridentismo*, and to set a more dignified example for literature, they came together in the magazine *Contemporáneos*, published between June 1928 and December 1931. Like the poets of the *Revista Moderna* in the previous century, the intellectuals of *Contemporáneos* were conscious of their art, capable in their technique, and aware of the best European models of their time. Bernardo Ortiz de Montellano was born in 1899 and died in 1949. His volumes of poetry include *Avidez*, 1921; *El trompo de siete colores*, 1925; *Red*, 1928; *Primero sueño*, 1931; *Sueños*, 1933; and *Muerte de cielo azul*, 1937. He

began with poems of a childish flavor but finally achieved a personal and serious intonation and such perfect composition that his later poems belong with the best of the group. His book, *Red*, is probably the culmination of his poetic expression. In *Los sueños*, he attempted surrealistic techniques. His *Muerte de cielo azul* rotates around the topic of dreams, anesthesia, and death. A posthumous volume was published in 1952 with the title *Sueño y poesía*. He also wrote short stories in *Cinco horas sin corazón*, 1940, and *El caso de mi amigo Azafeta*, 1946. He authored one play, *El sombrerón*, 1946. His other works include a *Sketch of modern Mexican literature*, 1931; *Indian Poetry of Mexico*, 1935; *Mexican Indian and Colonial Literature*, 1946; a *Biography of Amado Nervo*, 1943; and translations of T. S. Eliot, Rainer Maria Rilke, etc.

Carlos Pellicer was born in 1899. In 1921 he published *Colores en el mar y otros poemas*; *Piedra de sacrificos*, in 1924; *Seis y siete poemas* in 1924; *Hora y 20*, printed in Paris in 1927; *Camino*, also from Paris in 1929; *5 Poemas*, 1931; *Esquemas para una oda tropical*, 1933; *Hora de junio*, 1937; *Recinto*, 1941; *Exágonos*, 1941; *Discursos por las flores*, 1946; *Subordinaciones*, 1948; etc. He seems to have had an essential predilection for the palpitating forms of poetry such as the taste of words and the music of verse, thus defending one of poetry's eternal values. He was the poet of color, and his high tone and sonorous words as well as his admiration for heroism, lead him to produce civil poetry with such heroes as Bolívar, and a poetry of communion with nature as expressed by the waterfalls of Iguazú. He was the poet of air, fire, earth, water, death. He sang also of the tropics, his birthplace, with their exuberant fruits, flowers, and exotic animals, rivers and mountains, murmurs and silence. His love poetry is represented by *Horas de junio*, and his religious poetry by *Prácticas de duelo*. José Gorostiza, like Pellicer, also comes from tropical Tabasco. A diplomat, born in 1901, he wrote *Canciones para cantar en las barcas*, 1925, and *Muerte sin fin*, in 1939. Like other literary men of his generation, Gorostiza felt isolated, and submerged himself in his personal consciousness: he fled from solidarity towards solitude, from communion towards loneliness. He had a negative attitude reminiscent of Jorge Guillén in *Cántico*, and almost felt a moral duty to refuse collaboration. In his *Muerte sin fin*, a second edition of which has appeared in 1952 (and considered by many the best Mexican poem of the twentieth century) the poet is left in a world of images that are exact, pure, almost mathematical, symbols of a non-existent world. Joy is fleeting, just as time is fleeting. A man finds himself before nothingness or as the poet himself says, "Endless death of an obstinate death." With a deep philosophical content, *Muerte sin fin* is unquestionably one of the masterpieces of Mexican poetry, similar to *Primero sueño* by Sor Juana Inés de la Cruz.

Jaime Torres Bodet, born in 1902, has achieved a great reputation outside of Mexico, not only as Minister of Education and Minister of Foreign Affairs in

several administrations but also as first president of
UNESCO. His first book of poetry, *Fervor*, appeared
in 1918. Later came *El corazón delirante*, 1922; *Canciones*, 1922; *Nuevas canciones* in Madrid in 1923;
La casa, 1923; *Los días*, 1923; *Poemas*, 1924; *Biombo*,
1925; *Poesías* in Madrid in 1926; *Destierro*, also in
Madrid in 1930; *Cripta*, 1937; *Sonetos*, 1949; *Fronteras*,
1954; *Sin tregua*, 1957; and *Poesías escogidas*, 1957.
Torres Bodet has also written such novels and short
stories as *Margarita de Niebla*, 1927; *La educación sentimental*, Madrid, 1929; *Proserpina rescatada*, Madrid,
1931; *Estrella de día*, Madrid, 1933; *Primero de enero*,
Madrid, 1934; *Sombras*, 1937; *Nacimiento de Venus y
otros relatos*, 1941. His autobiography, *Tiempo de arena*,
appeared in 1955; and among his books of criticism are
Contemporáneos, 1928; *Perspectiva de la literatura mexicana actual*, 1928; and *Tres inventores de la realidad:
Stendhal, Dostoyevski, Pérez Galdós* in 1955. Endowed
with a wide culture and intellectual curiosity, this poet
attempts to interpret the great conflicts of human beings.

Xavier Villaurrutia, born in 1903, died at the age
of forty-seven. Certain critics consider that his loss to
poetry was the greatest since the early death of López
Velarde. An extremely sensitive writer, his poetry is
rich with symbols which express profound lyric anguish. In poetry he wrote *Reflejos* in 1926; *Nocturnos*,
in 1933; *Nostalgia de la muerte* in Buenos Aires in
1938; *Décima muerte y otros poemas*, 1941; *Canto a
la primavera otros poemas*, 1948. Appearing in 1928,
his only novel bears the title, *Dama de corazones*. He
has also made translations of Gide, Blake, Nerval,
Morand, Pirandello, and others. His preoccupations in
poetry are death, night, and love. There are surrealistic
touches in *Reflejos* and *Nostalgia de la muerte*. A perfectionist, he showed an intimate solitude and originality reminiscent of López Velarde. His criticism includes *La poesía de los jóvenes en México*, and *Textos
y pretextos*, 1941.

Enrique González Rojo (1899–1939), was the
son of Enrique González Martínez. He wrote free verse
and the *romance* or ballad. His work included *El puerto y otros poemas*, 1924; *Espacio*, Madrid, 1926; *Romance de José Conde*, 1939; and *Elegías romanas y
otros poemas*.

The co-founder of *Ulises*, Salvador Novo, was
born in 1904. He has published *XX Poemas*, 1925,
which shows a similarity to the French ultraists, from
which he withdraws in his later books *Espejo*, 1933;
Nuevo Amor, 1933; *Seamen rhymes*, Buenos Aires,
1934; *Romance de Angelillo y Adela*, 1934; *Décimas
en el mar*, 1934; *Poesías escogidas*, 1938; *Florido
laude*, 1945, and the short stories he had written, *El
joven*, 1928; *Return Ticket*, 1928; and *Jalisco-Michoacán*, 1933. Some critics consider him the best Mexican
poet because of his expression of deep solitude and
love emotion, and his skill in masking emotion by
a counter-characteristic of sharp irony. In 1924 was
published his critical work on modern American poetry
and another on modern French poetry. He inclines
toward English and American literatures and culture.

The Taller Group

Between 1938 and 1941, the magazine *Taller* was
founded by Rafael Solana and became the voice of a
contemporary group. Octavio Paz and Efraín Huerta
are the outstanding representatives of this group. In
opposition to the aestheticism of the "Contemporáneos," they turned their interest toward the problems of their times and are preoccupied with justice,
both in society and in international affairs. For
example, they sang of republican Spain during the
Spanish Civil War, from 1936 to 1939. Paz, however,
has apparently lessened his interest in the regeneration and redemption of man and nations as a poetic
theme, and seems to have been influenced by the surrealists during a stay in Paris. Huerta, after visiting
eastern Europe, has become interested in the Soviet
bloc, their organization and life. Octavio Paz has
written, among other works, *Luna silvestre*, 1933; *No
pasarán*, 1936; *Raíz del hombre*, 1937; *Bajo tu clara
sombra*, published in Valencia in 1937; *Entre la piedra
y la flor*, 1941; *A la orilla del mundo*, 1942; *Libertad
bajo palabra*, 1949, including his poetical work from
1935 to 1948; *Semillas para un himno*, 1954; *El arco
y la lira . . .*, 1956; *Piedra de sol*, 1957; etc. The most
prominent poet of the group, the main characteristic
of Paz is to transfer individual poetic experiences into
the total experience of the world. He is regarded as the
most significant poet because of his variety of themes,
originality, and lyric depth. In his *A la orilla del mundo*, Paz already showed his ability to capture the
essential destiny of lyric poetry. Love, solitude, pleasure, death face the world in his poems and sense its
burden and its blind feudalism. Paz became conscious
of the dangers of complete loneliness and unconditional
and nameless solidarity; he traveled dextrously between
these two extremes and, just as Guillén found a balance in contemplation, Octavio Paz found it in action.
His poetry is always tense: loneliness struggles against
solidarity, life against death, silence against words. He
himself stated his position very clearly in *Las peras
del olmo* (1957) when he argued that all poets of all
ages have affirmed the same thing, namely: "Desire
is a testimony of our withdrawn condition also, it is
an attempt to regain the half we have lost. And love,
like a poetic image, is the instant in which opposites
are reconciled." In his essays as in his poetry, Octavio
Paz tried to reconcile a restless solitude with an emotional communion with the world; witness his *El laberinto de la soledad*, (1950 with a second revised edition in 1959), a fundamental book for the study of
the Mexican.

The Tierra Nueva Group

From 1940 to 1942, the "Tierra Nueva" generation appeared with a magazine by the same title. To
this group belong Leopoldo Zea (1912), philosopher,
José Luis Martínez (1918), a literary critic, and Alí
Chumacero (1918), a poet. Chumacero made his

The Palacio de Bellas Artes in Mexico City is a center of performing arts as well as a museum of the artistic treasures of past and present. The National Symphony Orchestra of Mexico is shown here in the theatre under a majestic proscenium arch which supports a mosaic mural.

— Courtesy American Airlines of Mexico

name with *Páramo de sueños,* 1940, and *Imágenes desterradas,* 1948. A restrained romanticist, he has insisted on saying only what needs to be said. In 1957 he published his *Palabras en reposo.* His search for abstract tension is expressed with a depth of imagery and a difficult style which gives the appearance of coldness but reveals great internal conflict.

Poetesses

In 1941, the magazine *Rueca* gathered together a group of young women writers including Carmen Toscano who wrote *Trazo incompleto* in 1934 and *Inalcanzable y mío* in 1936. She is also author of a biography of Rosario de la Peña and several plays. Her main characteristics are subtle tenderness, and a discrete simplicity. Guadalupe Amor (1920) is the poet of this group who uses traditional meters and yet manages to achieve freshness in her verses. Deep religiousness and skepticism combine in her books, *Yo soy mi casa,* 1946, and *Polvo,* 1949. She presents the dramatic problems of life and death with bravery and daring; and she has also published *Puerta obstinada* in

1947; *Círculo de angustia,* 1948; *Poesía,* 1948; *Décimas a Dios,* 1953; *Otro libro de amor,* 1955; *Antología poética,* 1956; and *Sirviéndole a Dios de hoguera,* 1958. Borrowing the title of one of her previous books of poems, she published an autobiographical novel, *Yo soy mi casa* in 1957. In the mid-1930's, women poets in Mexico became more numerous as well as better known. Among the religious poets was Concha Urquiza (1910–1945) whose desire for divine love subdued the tempest of her passions. Her work in prose and in poetry is compiled in *Obras,* 1946. Emma Godoy, born in 1918, is one of the most brilliant poetesses of her generation. Her work includes religious as well as love poems and is represented by her *Pausas y arena,* 1948. Among the youngest of the religious poetesses is Gloria Riestra, born in 1929. Her religious verse shows her musicality as well as her lyricism. She has published two books of poetry, *La soledad sonora* in 1950, and *Celeste anhelo,* 1952. Margarita Michelena, born in 1917, possesses a fine sensibility and lyric purity. Her poetical work is represented by *Paraíso y nostalgia,* 1945, and *Laurel del ángel,* 1948. Margarita Paz Paredes, born in 1922, received a prize in 1947 for her poem "Canción de América." One of the most popular poetesses of Mexico, her main interests are the redemption of man, children, and the oppressed as well as the destiny and the rights of her race in international affairs. Her poetic works include *Sonaja*, 1942; *Voz de la tierra*, 1946; *El anhelo plural*, 1948; *Génesis transido*, 1948; *Andamios de sombra*, 1950; *Canto a México*, 1952; *Dimensión del silencio*, 1953; *Presagio en el viento*, 1955; *Casa en la niebla*, 1956; etc. Born in 1925, Rosario Castellanos studied aesthetics at the University of Madrid. She traveled through Europe and in her verse attempts to solve the enigmas of the Indian race of Mexico, and particularly those of Chiapas. Her poetical works are included in *Trayectoria del polvo*, 1948; *Apuntes para una declaración de fe*, 1949; *De la vigilia estéril*, 1950; *El rescate del mundo*, 1952; etc.

Poets of the Fifties

Among the poets of the fifties, there were those who concerned themselves mostly with structure or form and others who searched for a freer expression of exterior life. Rubén Bonifaz Nuño, born in 1923, is a classical scholar who uses a combination of Latin and Spanish meters in *Imágenes*, 1951, 1953; and who also has *Los demonios y los días*, 1956; and *El manto y la corona*, 1958, to his credit. One of the finest poets of his generation, he is an artificer of technique giving new melodic terms to traditional forms. His poetic work also includes *La muerte del angel*, 1945; *Poética*, 1951; and *Ofrecimiento romántico*, 1951. Jaime García Terrés, born in 1924, has been called by some critics a poet of ideas, and by others a poet of sentiment. By some he has been compared to Chumacero, though with more imagination than the latter, less abstraction, and less sensuality. He published *El hombre menor* in 1953 and *Las provincias del aire* in 1956, after having published his *Panorama de critica literaria en México* in 1941 and *Sobre la responsabilidad del escritor* in 1949. Marco Antonio Montes de Oca, with a great wealth of imagination, brought out *Contrapunto de la fe* in 1955, and *Pliego de testimonios* in 1956.

Provincial Poets

The cultivators of poetry are not restricted to the capital city. Guadalajara, for example, has had groups of poets publishing such literary magazines as *Bandera de provincias* (1929–1930); *Indice* (1936–1937); *Prisma* (1940–1941); *Ariel* (1949–) and *EtCetera* (1950) with the works of such poets as Gutiérrez Hermosillo, Elías Nandino, Adalberto Navarro Sánchez, María Luisa Hidalgo, and Emmanuel Carballo. San Luis Potosí has had *Letras Potosinas* (1943); *Estilo* (1945); and *Cuadrante* (1952). In Coahuila we find *Cauce* (1949) and *Papel de poesía* (1940). Veracruz has *La Palabra y el hombre* (1957).

To date, another poet of the stature of José Gorostiza or Octavio Paz has not appeared; but it must be remembered that Gorostiza was fifty-one when "Muerte sin fin" appeared, and Paz is still writing vigorously. The next decade will tell whether a poet will appear with the maturity and depth to take his place beside the contemporary great.

The Novel of the Revolution

Just as in the sixteenth century when epic literature took refuge in the narratives of the chronicles, the aftermath of the Revolution produced a literature that reflects the bitter reality developed between 1910 and 1920. Its main expression is the novel. These novels, frequently fragmentary, have been labeled the "Novel of the Mexican Revolution." For the most part these novels present the historical and political phase of the Revolution with great wealth of autobiographical detail. We cannot expect the novel of the Mexican Revolution to be revolutionary in form or literary technique. Nevertheless, it is different from the Mexican novel of the nineteenth century. A novelist of the Revolution needs no artificiality to show the moving realities that have had a strong and frequently direct effect on him. As a rule, the style of such novels is fast-flowing and somewhat journalistic, and the book has been structured through episodes or tableaux that have literary and often historical value as testimonies of truth. The epic struggle of the Revolution is going to be another expression of an original nationalism and the novel representing it, in its later phases, will be confronted by national problems, uncovering ills and social injustices. Its very marked sociological tendency at times makes it more of a document than a work of art. Through such novels, Mexico tries to find its self-definition; tries to clarify its personality; seeks its genuine and autochthonous expression much as it has done through its modern painters. The novelists of this group no longer turn away from Mexican reality. They study and probe the telluric depth of Mexico; they analyze seriously the traditions, customs, folklore, in short, the vernacular of each region, and even of each culturally indigenous group. However, they do not neglect urban life. Their novels may be divided as follows: 1) novel of the Revolution (the social revolution of 1910–1920) as such; 2) novel of the Cristero revolt; 3) novel of social contents (here we might have to make a new subdivision in order to sift out those concerning social injustices, exploitation or oppression, the city slums, urban lower classes, the proletarian, the political, etc.); 4) Indian or *indigenista* novel; and 5) the novel of provincial inspiration, which does not necessarily imply the novel with simply a rural setting.

The patriarch and high priest of the Novel of the Revolution was Mariano Azuela, born in 1873 and died in 1952. González has rightly said that Azuela was the novelist who gave responsibility to the Mexican, demanding of him honesty, sincerity and decorum. He demanded justice from the powerful, honesty from the intellectual, sincerity, purity of soul and rectitude from the clergy, integrity from the politician, generosity and kindness from the rich, and human dignity and decorum from the humble. Azuela became the liberator of the novel and its best Mexicanizer. Full justice has not yet been done to him. Usually the three principal stages of his novelistic work are categorized as the novel of the revolution, the vanguard novel, and the novel of social content. With the exception of his three vanguard novels (which Azuela wrote to prove to critics that he knew how), *La malhora* (1923), *El desquite* (1925), and *La luciérnaga* (1932), all his work falls in the category of realism. Important among his novels of the Revolution are *Los fracasados* (1908); *Mala yerba* (1909); *Andrés Pérez, maderista* (1911); *Los de abajo* (1915); *Los caciques* (1917); *Domitilo quiere ser diputado* (1918); *Las moscas* (1918); and *Las tribulaciones de una familia decente* (1918). By 1928 when the first of the so-called novels of the Revolution appeared, Azuela had stopped writing such novels ten years before. The last stage of his novelistic work — social content — studies the effects of the revolution on man and his environment. *El camarada Pantoja* is the best of this type (for the post-revolutionary novel what *Los de abajo* had been for the novel of the Revolution) and *Regina Landa* (1939); *Avanzada* (1940); *Nueva burguesía* (1941); *La marchanta* (1944); *La mujer domada* (1946); and *Sendas perdidas* (1949), the last published during his lifetime. In 1955, *La maldición* appeared, and a year later, *Esa sangre* as well as a translation of *The Flies* and *The Bosses*. *Esa sangre* deals with the return of Julián, the villain of *Mala Yerba*, to Mexico after being in Argentina and other places for many years. The changes that had been brought about by the Revolution are noted in the novel, and Julián soon realizes that the underdog is now in command. Azuela expressed his views on the Mexican novel in *Cien años de novela mexicana*, 1947, a series of lectures given at the Colegio Nacional.

Critics have said that the Novel of the Revolution reached its peak between 1928 and 1941. In retrospect, this year of 1928 seems to have been elected to launch the novelistic wave of the Revolution, a wave which changed almost completely the orientation of the Mexican novel as well as its technique. Azuela's *Los de abajo*, known largely through the efforts of Francisco Monterde, was published twice in Spain and once in Buenos Aires, besides being translated into French and English at this time. Also in 1928 and 1929 appeared *El águila y la serpiente* and *La sombra del caudillo* by Martín Luis Guzmán, the other great novelist of the Revolution. At this same time the mural painting of Diego Rivera and José Clemente Orozco had become established as a modern school in the world of art.

Morton has said that no matter what the values of the Novel of the Revolution may be, the genre is important for having set two precedents in Mexican literature: more than one example of the Novel of the Revolution holds a place of prominence in world literature and thus has brought needed recognition to Mexico. In addition, the Novel of the Revolution gave impetus to the creation of a Mexican novel *per se*, and points to the full realization of a national novelistic literature. Morton referred also to such values as the human sense of Mexican life, the concept of the Mexican spirit, the portrait of the Mexican himself, and the particular feelings of the various writers toward the revolution of social and psychological values of that novel. In spite of lack of inventiveness, absence of creative imagination and adaptation to historic reality, the revolutionary novelists, somewhat lacking in historical perspective, (either because of having taken part in the revolutionary movement, or because of having suffered its consequences), had nothing more to do than to copy that reality in order to write a novel. Manuel Pedro González has already pointed out that the dynamics of the Revolution, its redeeming aspirations, the vigorous personality of its leaders, the truculence and horror of its internal conflicts and its military actions, all were such that the novelist had no need of great inventive capabilities in order to write an entertaining work.

Martín Luis Guzmán was a member of the "Ateneo de la Juventud." Born in 1887, he left the country in 1913 for political reasons and later joined the revolutionary group of Pancho Villa. Again because of political difficulties he had to leave for Spain where he stayed from 1925 to 1936. It was in Spain that his two famous works, *El águila y la serpiente* and *La sombra del caudillo* were published. After he returned to Mexico, he became the editor of *Tiempo*, a news magazine similar to *Time*. In 1951 he began to release the memoirs of Pancho Villa.

While Azuela was interested in the problems of the underdog, Guzmán is searching for the origin of the Revolution to explain the mechanism of circumstances among the "upper dogs." A book of reminiscences and memoirs, *El águila y la serpiente* portrays young Guzmán as he left the university to fight in the revolution. *La sombra del caudillo* analyzes carefully and deeply the political intrigue that occurs at the end of a presidential period when the president is supporting his successor. There is still a question as to whether the caudillo represents Calles or Obregón, but there is no question that this is the best political novel of Mexico.

Rafael F. Muñoz was born in 1899 and met Pancho Villa at the impressionable age of sixteen. From then on, Villa was to be the inspiration for his literary work. In 1916, he left Mexico for the United States for political reasons. On his return in 1920, he began writing short stories which were published in newspapers and magazines. His first collection was *El feroz cabecilla* in 1928. In 1930 was published *El hombre malo y otros relatos*. Two more short-story collections, *Si me han de matar mañana*, 1934, and *Fuego en el norte*, 1960, have appeared. In 1931 in Madrid, he had published his first novel, *Vámonos con Pancho Villa*. Another novel, *Se llevaron el cañón para Bachimba* appeared in Buenos Aires in 1941.

José Rubén Romero (1890–1952) spent his early life until young manhood in the state of Michoacán.

He took part in the Revolution and had several official positions in the diplomatic service. He was consul, plenipotentiary minister, and ambassador. Romero published some poetry which is now almost impossible to get.

In the field of the short story and the novel, he published *Cuentos rurales,* 1915; *Mis amigos, mis enemigos,* 1921; *Apuntes de un lugareño,* Barcelona, 1932; *Desbandada,* 1934; *El pueblo inocente,* 1934; *Mi caballo, mi perro y mi rifle,* Barcelona, 1936; *La vida inútil de Pito Pérez,* 1938; *Anticipación a la muerte,* 1939; *Semblanza de una mujer,* 1941; *Una vez fui rico,* 1942; *Algunas cosillas de Pito Pérez que se me quedaron en el tintero,* 1945; and *Rosenda,* 1946. His *Apuntes de un lugareño* includes mostly reminiscences and incidents from his childhood and youth. He was disappointed and bitter about the Revolution in his first novel proper, *Mi caballo, mi perro y mi rifle.* His most famous novel is *La vida inútil de Pito Pérez* in which he creates a modern picaresque character. The episodes of his life, his satirical humor, his language, and his bitterness reflect his times.

Among other cultivators of the Novel of the Revolution are Agustín Vera with *La revancha,* 1930; Nellie Campobello with *Cartucho,* 1931; Gregorio López y Fuentes in *Campamento* (1931) made, from the technical point of view, one of the boldest experiments that have ever been made in the Mexican novel. He also wrote *Tierra,* 1932, and *Mi general,* 1934, within a revolutionary framework. José Mancisidor has written *Frontera junto al mar* and General Francisco Urquizo, *Recuerdo que . . .,* 1934, and his best novel *Tropa vieja,* 1943. Teodoro Torres (1891–1944) presented the conservative side of the revolution in two novels which have been unjustly forgotten: *La patria perdida,* 1935, and *Golondrina,* 1944, dealing with the depopulation of small towns brought about by the Revolution. Bernandino Mena Brito describes the revolution in the jungles in *Paludismo,* 1940, and Francisco Rojas González wrote *La Negra Angustias,* 1944, in which he created one of the best women characters of the Novel of the Revolution and for which he was given the national prize in literature. Miguel N. Lira, a popular poet and writer in the García Lorca vein, received the 1947 Lanz Duret Prize for *La escondida.*

The Cristero Novel

From 1927 to 1930, a revolt in Mexico consequent upon differences between the church and the state, was the inspiration for the novel of the Cristero Revolt. In 1930 in Marfa, Texas (although in reality it was in Mexico City), a priest, David G. Ramírez, published a novel *Héctor* with the pseudonym Jorge Gram which was the first of this type. The novel had very little circulation in Mexico where it was practically unknown until later editions were published. Fernando Robles in 1934 wrote *La Virgen de los cristeros,* and in 1936 *El santo que asesinó* about José de Léon Toral who shot President Obregón. Gram and Robles pre-

sented the point of view of the church. In 1937, José Guadalupe de Anda published *Los cristeros* which gives the opposite point of view; a most interesting and valuable novel for the background and social environment of the conflict. In 1942, Anda brought out *Los bragados* which showed what happened to some of the characters of *Los cristeros* after the Cristero Revolt. Aurelio Robles Castillo with *Ay Jalisco . . . no te rajes,* 1938, Ciro César Gallardo with *El maestro rural,* Jesús Goytortúa y Santos with his Lanz Duret Prize novel, *Pensativa,* 1945, and Alberto Quiroz with *Cristo Rey,* 1952, complete the cycle.

The Novel of Social Content

The novel of social content whose most vigorous writer is perhaps Azuela, may be subdivided, as we have observed elsewhere, into the novel of social injustice, the novel of exploitation or oppression, the novel of the slums and the proletarian novel. Of course, these categories are arbitrary — established here simply to facilitate classification of novels according to their themes or intentions. One of the youngest novelists who has devoted himself to painting the outer as well as the inner life of contemporary Mexico is José Revueltas. In 1941, was published his first novel, *Los muros de agua,* dealing with political exiles to the Pacific penal colony of Islas Marías. In 1943 he brought out his most important novel to date, *El luto humano* (1943), which appeared in English in 1947 as *The Stone Knife.* Because of the desperate and dramatic quality of his work, because of the vigor expressed in this epic of hunger and poverty, this novel of Revueltas, in spite of certain limitations, is one of the most outstanding works of protest in present-day Mexican literature. It was awarded first prize for Mexico in the Latin American novel contest conducted by Farrar and Rinehart in the year 1942 and the national prize in literature for the same year. Because of the tone, the treatment of themes, and the passionate and torrential sweep of his novels, Revueltas might be compared to William Faulkner. Revueltas, who had been an extreme leftist, seemed to deviate from the party line in *Los días terrenales,* 1949, and this novel was then withdrawn from the market. It is unfortunate indeed that he now seems to devote all his time to writing movie scenarios.

The Proletarian Novel

The proletarian novel is represented by José Mancisidor with *La ciudad roja,* 1932, of socialistic inspiration, and *La rosa de los vientos,* 1941, awarded a prize in the 1940 Latin American novel contest. Also *Mezclilla,* 1933, by Francisco Sarquis, *Chimeneas,* 1937, by Gustavo Ortiz Hernán, and *El doble nueve,* 1949, by José Guadalupe de Anda can be included in this classification.

The novel of the slums or of the urban lower classes is now being exemplified in novels such as *Yo, como pobre . . . ,* 1944, and *Más allá existe la tierra,* 1947, by Magdalena Mondragón; *Los olvidados,* 1944, by Jesús R. Guerrero; *Río humano,* 1949, a Lanz Duret Prize novel, by Rogelio Barriga Rivas.

The Indianist Novel

The Indian novel has been referred to as the "indigenista" novel because not only does it deal with Indian life, but it also attempts to describe the reactions, penetrate the soul, explain the way of thinking of the different Indian groups. It began with *Los hombres que dispersó la danza,* 1929, by Andrés Henestrosa and reached its high point with *El indio,* 1935, of Gregorio López y Fuentes and his *Los peregrinos inmóviles,* 1944. *El indio* represents the tragedy of the Indian community. López y Fuentes also wrote novels of the Revolution, political novels, etc. Mauricio Magdaleno with *El resplandor,* 1937, wrote one of the best novels of this type. He discusses the economic problems of the Otomí Indians. As far as the construction of the novel goes, *El resplandor* has the solid structure, human characters, and nervous and deliberate style that fits in very well with the development of the plot. *Nayar,* 1941, by Miguel A. Menéndez, deals with the jungle, the customs, the music of the Indians of Nayarit, the Coras. Miguel N. Lira published in 1947 *Donde crecen los tepozanes,* his first novel and one of the best of the "indigenista" novels. Ramon Rubín describes very well the Indians of Chiapas in *El callado dolor de los tzotziles* (1949), and in 1954 *La bruma se vuelve azul* portraying life among the Huichole Indians with a simple and dramatic approach.

The Provincialist Novel

The novel designated as of provincial inspiration seeks its motifs in the life of the provincial cities or towns and is to Mexican prose what the work of López Velarde is to poetry. José Luis Martínez, a subtle critic, has already mentioned that when the novelist has exhausted other themes, when he finally begins to probe the inner thoughts of men whom he has only seen at normal surfaces, he will discover the wealth of novelistic material in the provinces. Behind the monotonous life led by most of the inhabitants of the small provincial towns lies the unique core of Mexico, at the singular root of Mexican nationality. Poverty and religion are, above all, the two factors that move life in these towns, lacking in communication and exhausted by many depredations; material progress, confined to a handful of cities, is unknown here.

José Rubén Romero had already discovered and explored this new novelistic vein in his earlier books but most essentially in *Rosenda,* 1946, one of the most lyrical novels of its type. The principal protagonist of *Rosenda* will remain in the Mexican novel as the supreme example of the kindness and sweetness of the small-town women of Mexico. But this provincial novel culminates with *Al filo del agua,* published by Agustín

Yáñez in 1947, with a second edition in 1955, and a recent English translation. Sex and religion motivate the action of the novel. Even though the author needs more objectivity to make his characters talk, and in spite of Yáñez's omnipresence and a certain baroque quality of his style, this novel is one of the masterpieces to come out of Mexico and of Latin America in general.

There is a very clear and deep portrayal of characters and a complexity of vital problems both in the life of the protagonist and the social life of the town. Martínez has judged it thus: "It does not have the linear, superficial, or episodic design of almost all our narrative works; its structure, on the other hand, has an organic complexity; its characters are rich and with many shades; its stylistic resources do not omit any of the important conquests of the contemporary novel; the whole book, in short, gives us a living world in place of the fragmentary sketches that are common in our novels." Following the tradition of Altamirano in the nineteenth century, Yáñez in the twentieth tries to fuse the two currents, the classical or conventional which makes use of all the technical resources of the contemporary novel, and the nationalistic which is inspired by a purely Mexican milieu. The Mexican novelists of the future should heed, if not actually follow, the artistic trajectory of Yáñez if they are to achieve a truly Mexican novel.

In 1956 Juan Rulfo wrote his novel *Pedro Páramo,* which had a second edition in 1959, and a translation into English simultaneously. The author's imagination wanders from realism to fantasy, from narrative to evocation. The main character, giving the novel its title, moves in and out of death in the village of Comala which has disappeared but still keeps within its walls the gossip and everyday preoccupations of its former inhabitants.

The greatest novelistic success of the year 1957 was the publication of Rosario Castellanos, *Balún Canán,* a poetic narrative laid in her native state of Chiapas and showing her anthropological inclinations. In 1958 it was Carlos Fuentes who stands out with *La region más transparente* which went through two editions in that same year. This was essentially the novel of Mexico City portraying its society from the upper bourgeoisie and the aristocracy of the Díaz dictatorship to the proletariat. Although the action took place in 1951, it developed along several planes and times. Swaying between memories and contemporary reality, Fuentes paints a picture of a Mexican society that is still searching for its true expression. In 1959, Fuentes triumphed again with *Las buenas conciencias.* Where in his first novel Fuentes depicts anarchy and the disoriented senselessness of Mexican society, in his second he attempts to understand it. Here we have a novel of victims and accomplices, not a novel of the innocent and the guilty. His last novel, *The Death of Artemio Cruz* appeared in 1962. In 1959 Agustín Yáñez's *La creación* appeared. Structured like a symphony, the four movements go from the "andante" through the "creciente" and from the "galopante" to the "vehemente." Yáñez concerns himself with the artistic freedom and the struggle for creation regardless of tendencies and political programs. He mixes fiction with reality; and, thus, we find Orozco, Rivera, López Velarde, Revueltas, Dr. Atl, and others parading through the pages of this novel.

Considering the abundant production of novels in present-day Mexico, one realizes that the novelists are trying in many ways to find the most propitious way of creating the national novel of Mexico. There is no question that much progress has been made, but much more remains to be achieved.

Contemporary Drama

Without the social revolution of 1910 to 1920, the cultural beachhead which now has been opened, might still, perhaps, be hermetically sealed. Today, intellectuals in Mexico explore and exalt all the aesthetic values and possibilities hidden within Mexico's infinite variety of components. In the twentieth-century theatre, Monterde, making a classification of the first third of the century, signals four stages in the development of the theatre. The first one starts ot the beginning of the century and ends in 1909, a pre-revolutionary period. The second stage from 1910–1918 includes the beginning of the Revolution and comes to a halt with the end of the First World War. The third stage, 1919–1924, is a period of post-war and reconstruction in Mexico as well as in Europe. In the last stage, beginning in 1925, was first planted the seed of the theatre which was to bear fruit during the second third of the century. From 1900 to 1909, the tendencies of the nineteenth century still are prevalent. The second stage, 1910–1918, although a period of action in Mexico, is a period of revolutionary action hardly reflected in the theatre. From 1919 to 1924, playwrights attempted to do away with European influences. The period after 1925 set the foundation for a future national theatre of Mexico.

The Teatro de Ulises was started in 1928. The nationalistic movement of the seven authors — Gamboa, Diez Barroso, Noriega Hope, Monterde, Parada León, and the Lozano Garcías is initiated with the Pro Arte Nacional season in 1925, later to go into the *La Comedia Mexicana* in 1929. Yet these authors appeared to be following the example of Spanish dramatists of the end of the nineteenth and beginning of the twentieth century. With the Teatro de Ulises, nationalistic themes now seem to give conceptual sense of the theatre. The effort now is to create a universal theatre compatible with man and life in our times. Among these playwrights, we find then Villaurrutia, Novo, Gorostiza, etc. It is an experimental theatre called vanguard drama by the group, an exotic experiment which is to present new plays by new non-professional actors. The movement for the renovation of dramatic art in Mexico is to be found with this group and away from the commercial theatres.

The next group of playwrights is Escolares del Teatro with Celestino Gorostiza and Julio Bracho. Bracho is the director who organized groups of actors, introduced the teaching of the theatre, and later went on to be the founder of the Teatro de la Universidad. In 1931, Bracho had his group perform at a small theatre of the Ministry of Public Education, the Teatro de Orientación where *Proteo* by Monterde was presented. While Monterde got away from the nationalistic themes to adopt a classical theme, other writers like Magdaleno, Juan Bustillo Oro and Azuela remain firmly rooted in their nationalism. The Teatro de Orientación (in 1932) under the guidance of Celestino Gorostiza, struggled through the hardest and longest period of the renovation of the theatre; foreign and Mexican writers are represented in their performances. Villaurrutia attempts some of his plays after having tried a translation of foreign playwrights. Usigli appears in the last season, 1938, of the Teatro de Orientación. After this theatre declines, the newly born movie industry in Mexico attracts most of the actors, and many of the authors turn to literature or to journalism.

In 1943, a new effort at renovation was made through El Teatro de México — the culmination of all the efforts of the Mexican theatre to survive during a quarter of a century. In 1934, the Palace of Fine Arts was inaugurated; however, it did not promote the creation of a Mexican theatre that will define a Mexican spirit until the old Department of Fine Arts was transformed into the National Institute of Fine Arts. The Proa group of 1942 unveils new authors and encourages the old ones; later "La Linterna Mágica," 1926, the "Teatro de Arte Moderno," the "Teatro Estudiantil Autónomo," (1947) all contribute to the development of the Mexican theatre. It is in the drama then that Mexican literature has really progressed in the decade from 1950 to 1960: one might even call it a true flowering of dramatic writing. The large number of plays, the mushrooming of theatres in Mexico City, and the renewed interest on the part of the public in the works by Mexican writers, all have also inspired critical and scholarly studies about Mexican drama of the present century and of older days.

Mariano Azuela, our master novelist, also tried his hand at the drama. The third volume of his *Obras completas* (1960) contains his plays, among them his dramatic version of the world famous novel, *Los de abajo*. Among the playwrights who distinguished themselves before the 1950–1960 decade can be named Francisco Monterde, Salvador Novo, Luis G. Basurto, Celestino Gorostiza, Miguel N. Lira and, especially, the master of them all, Rodolfo Usigli, by far the best Latin-American playwright of the century. In the decade from 1950 to 1960 Monterde published *Presente involuntario* in 1957 and *Dos comedias mexicanas* in 1958. Novo brought out his sensational *La culta dama* in 1951 and *A ocho columnas* in 1956. Luis G. Basurto, although only in his forties, had already written for the theatre before 1950, and since then has published *Frente a la muerte*, 1952; *Todo una dama,* 1954; *Cada quien su vida,* his most successful work still playing in Mexico City, 1955; *Miércoles de ceniza,* 1956; and *Los reyes del mundo,* 1959. Celestino Gorostiza, a brother of the poet José, dared put on the stage *El color de nuestra piel* in 1953 and later had published *Columna social* in 1956. Lira, who published his play, *Vuelta a la Tierra* in 1938, presented *Tres mujeres y un sueño* in 1955. Rodolfo Usigli, who studied drama at Yale University, has inspired the new generation of dramatists while still being the lone wolf of the Mexican theatre. Though many of his plays were written long before, they were performed and published during the decade 1950–1960. His *Corona de sombra,* for instance, was written in 1943, performed in 1947, published in 1951 and reprinted in 1960. *Los fugitivos* appeared in 1950; *El niño y la niebla* was conceived in 1936 and performed and printed in 1951; *Aguas estancadas,* written in 1939, was put on the stage in 1952; *Jano es una muchacha,* one of his biggest box-office successes, was published in 1952; *La función de despedida* was written in 1949 and published in 1952; *Un día de éstos,* written in 1953, was performed in 1954; *Mientras amemos* came out in 1956. Although born in 1910, Federico S. Inclán did not begin writing plays until 1948. He first became known with *Luces de carburo,* performed in 1950. His *Espaldas mojadas cruzan el Bravo* was put on the stage in 1951, the same year that *El duelo* was performed. *Hidalgo* was staged in 1953 and printed in the same year. *Hoy invita la güera* was published in 1956, having made its appearance on the stage a year before. *Una mujer para los sábados* was staged in 1956. Juan José Arreola, better known as a writer of Kafka-esque stories, did publish a play, *La hora de todos* in 1954 which won a prize. Rosario Castellanos published a play in 1952 entitled *Tablero de damas.* In the same year, Magdalena Mondragón brought out *Dos obras de teatro* including "La sirena que llevaba el mar," written in 1945, and "El mundo perdido," 1946. In 1953 she had published *Porque me da la gana.* Emilio Carballido, one of the most promising of the new dramatists, staged *La zona intermedia* in 1953; *Rosalba y los llaveros,* also in 1950; *El lugar y la hora* in 1951; *La danza que sueña la tortuga* and *Felicidad* in 1955; *La veleta oxidada* in 1956; *La hebra de oro* in 1957; and *Teatro* (containing four plays) in 1960. Sergio Magaña wrote his best play, *Los signos del Zodíaco* in 1951 and published it in 1953 and 1956. His *Moctezuma II* was first staged in 1954, and that was also the year when he published his novel, *El molino del aire.* Luisa Josefina Hernández has contributed a great deal to the development of the drama in Mexico through her courses in the theatre at the University, in which she succeeded Usigli. She wrote *Aguardiente de caña* in 1951; *Botica modelo* which was given El Nacional Prize in 1953; *Los frutos caídos,* considered the best play of 1957; and *Los huéspedes reales* in 1958. Héctor Mendoza, born in 1932, had *Ahogados* performed in 1952 and *Las cosas simples* in 1953. Thus we see that there were among young writers

many promising dramatists whose development seemed to occur sometime in the decade between 1950 and 1960. Inclán, Carballido, Magaña, Mendoza, and Luisa Josefina Hernández will continue producing plays that will bring credit to the Mexican theatre.

Essay and Criticism

In the last decade literature in Mexico has also developed in the field of the essay and literary criticism. It was just before 1950 that Gabriel Méndez Plancarte, one of the great humanists of Mexico and the editor of *ábside* magazine, died in 1949. He was to be followed by Bernardo Ortiz de Montellano, a member of the "Contemporáneos" group. In 1955, Gabriel's brother, Alfonso Méndez Plancarte, who had succeeded him as editor of *ábside,* and who was likewise a capable humanist, also died, as did the literary historian and novelist Carlos González Peña. The great philosopher and educator José Vasconcelos also died. Julio Jiménez Rueda, the author of another one of the standard literary histories of Mexico as well as plays and novels, died in the year of 1959, but the greatest loss was the demise of Alfonso Reyes that same year. His reputation extended into the European world of letters. Poetry was one of his loves, but his fame was achieved through his essays and works of criticism: his *El deslinde,* 1944, stands as Mexico's major contribution to the study of the theory of literature.

Among the critics and essayists who made their reputation before the decade of 1950–1960, we can point out José Luis Martínez, José Rojas Garcidueñas, José María González de Mendoza, Andrés Henestrosa, etc. José Luis Martínez had already written his *Literatura mexicana Siglo XX* and *Problemas literarios,* waiting until 1958 to publish the two volumes of his anthology *El ensayo mexicano moderno.* Rojas Garcidueñas has continued his interest in colonial literature with the publication of *Bernardo de Balbuena, la vida y la obra* in 1958. Among the newer essayists and critics we can number Pablo Henrique González Casanova, Antonio Alatorre, Emmanuel Carballo, Abelardo Villegas and Leopoldo Zea. Antonio Caso with his *Discursos a la nación mexicana,* Vasconcelos with his *La raza cósmica* and *Indología,* Samuel Ramos with his *El perfil del hombre y la cultura en México,* and Leopoldo Zea with his collection *México y lo mexicano,* all have contributed to focus the attention of the people of Mexico on themselves and on their problems. Even though he made his start with the generation of the 40's with *El positivismo en México* in 1943, and with *Dos etapas del pensamiento hispanoamericano* in 1949, Leopoldo Zea became the teacher of the generation of the 50's, guiding them along philosophical paths. In 1952, he inspired the collection, *México y lo mexicano* and urged Mexican intellectuals to analyze themselves, their reactions, attitudes, aspirations, likes and dislikes. In 1953 he brought out *América como conciencia* and *La conciencia del hombre en la filosofía. La filosofía en México* appeared in 1955; *Del liberalismo a la*

revolución en la educación mexicana and *Esquema para una historia de las ideas en Iberoamérica* in 1956 and *América en la historia* in 1957. His style, facile and fluid, has brought to the philosophical essay many readers in intellectual circles.

The decade from 1950 to 1960 has assured the reputation of Octavio Paz and José Gorostiza in poetry without producing other poets to surpass them. While the interest in poetry is still strong, Mexican literature has found more fertile fields in these years. With Azuela dead and Yáñez returning to literature following his term of office as governor of the state of Jalisco, there are other writers who have made their mark in the last fifteen years. Juan Rulfo, Rosario Castellanos, and Carlos Fuentes seem to dominate the scene and to hold the key to the future of the Mexican novel. After the death of Alfonso Reyes, no critic of his calibre and his humanistic scholarship has appeared. Although not strictly a literary critic, Leopoldo Zea has guided the newer writers and provided the inspiration for self-analysis. His contribution to the studies of Mexican thought will prove invaluable. The decade from 1950 to 1960 seems to have contributed the most in the field of dramatic literature. With Usigli still writing, and with the collaboration of the newer set of playwrights (Inclán, Carballido, Magaña, Hernández, and others), we can truthfully say that the decade of the fifties has been the most promising for the Mexican theatre.

There seems to be little doubt that Mexican literature in the mid-twentieth century is in an active and promising state, although history's evaluation of major themes and figures will not be complete for

High-arched for dignity and grace, modern but not "ultra," the welcoming portals of the University Library at Hermosillo, Sonora, suggest the availability of literature and the other liberal arts to young Mexicans being educated today in the capital city of the nation's most progressive state.

many years to come. Nevertheless, interest is running high in several contemporary authors whose complete works either have recently been published or are being assembled and will soon be published for the first time. Among the modern writers of whom this is true are the novelists, Federico Gamboa and Mariano Azuela, the poet and novelist, José Rubén Romero, the dramatist Rudolfo Usigli, and the critic, Alfonso Reyes.

SUGGESTED READING

ALTAMIRANO, IGNACIO MANUEL. Translated by Harvey L. Johnson. *Christmas in the Mountains.* Gainesville: University of Florida Press, 1961.

ANNALS OF THE CAKCHIQUELS, THE. *The Original Text, with a Translation, Notes, and Introduction.* Translated by D. G. Brinton. Philadelphia: Brinton's Library of Aboriginal American Literature, No. 6.

ANNALS OF THE CAKCHIQUELS, THE. Translated by Adrián Recinos and Delia Goetz. Norman: University of Oklahoma Press, 1953.

ARCINIEGAS, GERMAN. *The Green Continent.* New York: Knopf, 1944.

ARREOLA, JUAN JOSE. Translated by George D. Schade. *Confabulario and other inventions.* Austin: University of Texas Press, 1964.

AZUELA, MARIANO. Translated by Anita Brenner. *Marcela (Mala Yerba)*. New York: Farrar and Rinehart, 1932.

_____. Translated by Enrique Mungía. *The Underdogs*. New York: Brentano's, 1929.

_____. Translated by Enrique Mungía. *The Underdogs*. New York: Signet Classics, 1963 (paperback); with a foreword by Harriet de Onís.

_____. Translated by Frances Kellam Hendricks and Beatrice Berler. *The Trials of a Respectable Family and The Underdogs*. San Antonio, Texas: Principia Press of Trinity University, 1963; prologue by Salvador Azuela, biographical sketch by Luis Leal.

_____. Translated by Lesley Byrd Simpson. *Two Novels of Mexico, The Flies, The Bosses*. Berkeley and Los Angeles: University of California Press, 1964.

BENITEZ, FERNANDO. *In the Footsteps of Cortés*. New York: Pantheon, 1952.

BLACKWELL, ALICE STONE. *Some Spanish-American Poets*. New York: 1929.

_____. *Some Spanish-American Poets*. 2nd edition, Philadelphia: University of Pennsylvania Press, 1937.

BRUSHWOOD, JOHN S. *The Romantic Novel in Mexico*. Columbia: University of Missouri Press, 1954.

CHILAM BALAM DE CHUMAYEL. Translated by Ralph L. Roys. Washington, D. C.: Carnegie Institution, No. 483, 1933.

CHILAM BALAM OF TIZIMIN. *The Book of, with Commentary. The Book of the Jaguar Priest*. Translated by Maud W. Makemson. New York: Henry Schuman, 1951.

COESTER, ALFRED. *A Literary History of Spanish America*. 2nd edition, New York: Macmillan, 1928.

COLFORD, WILLIAM E. *Classic Tales from Spanish America*. Great Neck, New York: Barron's Educational Series, 1962.

CORNYN, J. H. *Living Literary Men of Mexico*. Mexico: 1916.

CORTES, HERNANDO. Translated and edited by J. Bayard Morris. *Five Letters*. New York: Robert M. McBride and Company, 1929.

CORTES, LETTERS OF. Edited by Francis A. MacNutt., 2 vols. New York: Putnam, 1908; English translation with notes and biographical introduction.

CRAIG, G. DUNDAS. *The Modernist Trend in Spanish-American Poetry*. Berkeley: University of California Press, 1934.

CRANFILL, THOMAS MABRY. Edited by Thomas Mabry Cranfill. Translated and edited by George D. Schade. *The Muse in Mexico, A Mid-Century Miscellany*. Austin: University of Texas Press, 1959.

CRAWFORD, WILLIAM REX. *A Century of Latin American Thought*. Cambridge: Harvard University Press, 1945. Rev. ed., 1961.

CRUZ, SOR JUANA INES DE LA. Translated by Pauline Cook. *The Pathless Grove. A Collection of 17th Century Mexican Sonnets*. Prairie City, Illinois: Decher Press, 1950.

DIAZ DEL CASTILLO, BERNAL. Edited and translated by Albert Idell. *The Bernal Díaz Chronicles*. New York: Doubleday and Company, Inc., 1956.

_____. Edited and translated by Albert Idell. *The Bernal Díaz Chronicles*. Garden City, New York: Doubleday, 1957. (paperback).

_____. Translated by A. P. Maudslay. *The Discovery and Conquest of Mexico*. London: G. Routledge and Sons, Ltd., 1928.

_____. *The Discovery and Conquest of Mexico*. New York: Farrar, Strauss and Cudahy, 1956.

_____. Translated by Maurice Keatinge. *The True History of the Conquest of Mexico*. New York: Robert M. McBride and Company, 1938.

_____. Translated by Alfred P. Maudslay. *The True History of the Conquest of New Spain*. 5 vols., London: Hakluyt Society Publications, 1908–1916.

DURAN, FRAY DIEGO. *The History of the Indians of New Spain*. Davis Heyden and Fernando Horcasitas. New York: Orion Press, 1962.

ENGLEKIRK, JOHN E. "Notes on Whitman in Spanish America," *Hispanic Review*, VI (1938), 133-138.

_____. *Edgar Allan Poe in Hispanic Literature*. New York: Instituto de las Españas, 1934.

EYE OF MEXICO, THE. *Evergreen Review*, vol. 2, number 7 (Winter, 1959), 22-167.

FERNANDEZ DE LIZARDI, JOSE JOAQUIN. Translated and introduced by Katherine Anne Porter. *The Itching Parrot*. Garden City, New York: Doubleday-Doran, 1942.

FITTS, DUDLEY. *Anthology of Contemporary Latin American Poetry*, rev. ed. New York: New Directions, 1947.

FLAKOLL, DARWIN J. and ALEGRIA, CLARIBEL. *New Voices of Hispanic America*. Boston: Beacon, 1962.

FLORES, ANGEL. *An Anthology of Spanish Poetry*. New York: Doubleday, 1961. (paperback).

_____. *Spanish Drama*. Edited and with an introduction by Angel Flores. Queens College, New York: Bantam Books, New York, 1962. (paperback).

FLORES, ANGEL, and POORE, DUDLEY. *Fiesta in November. Stories from Latin America*, with an introduction by Katherine Anne Porter. Boston: Houghton Mifflin, 1942.

GAMBOA DE CAMINO, BERTA. "The Novel of the Mexican Revolution" in *Renascent Mexico*. New York: Covici-Friede, 1935, pp. 258-274.

GOLDBERG, ISAAC. *Studies in Spanish American Literature*. New York: Brentano's, 1920.

GONZALEZ PENA, CARLOS. Translated by Gusta Barfield Nance and Florence Johnson Dunstan. *History of Mexican Literature*. Dallas: Southern Methodist University, 1943. 2nd ed., 1945. Rev. ed., 1945.

GONZALEZ MARTINEZ, ENRIQUE. Translated by Alice Stone Blackwell. *Three Poems*. Washington, D. C.: Pan American Union, March 1927.

GONZALEZ OBREGON, LUIS. Translated by Thomas A. Janvier. *Legends of the City of Mexico*. New York: Harper and Brothers, 1910.

_____. Translated by Blanche C. Wagner. *The Streets of Mexico*. San Francisco:

GREEN, ERNEST S. and VON LOWENFELS, H. *Mexican and South American Poems*, San Diego, California: Dodge and Burbeck, 1892.

GUZMAN, MARTIN LUIS. Translated by Harriet de Onís. *The Eagle and the Serpent*. New York: Knopf, 1930.

HAYS, H. R. Edited and translated by. *12 Spanish American Poets — An Anthology*. English translations, notes, and Introduction by the Editor. New Haven: Yale University Press, 1943.

HENRIQUEZ URENA, PEDRO. *Literary Currents in Hispanic America*. Cambridge: Harvard University Press, 1945.

HERRING, HUBERT and WEINSTOCK, HERBERT, editors. *Renascent Mexico*. Introduction by Ernest Gruening. New York: Covici-Friede, 1935.

JOHNSON, MILDRED E. *Swan, Cygnets, and Owl: An Anthology of Modernist Poetry in Spanish America: Translations*. Columbia: University of Missouri, 1956.

JONES, WILLIS KNAPP, editor. *Spanish American Literature in Translation: A Selection of Poetry, Fiction and Drama Since 1888*. New York: Frederick Ungar, 1963.

LAS CASAS, BARTOLOME DE. Translated by John Phillips. *The Tears of the Indian* (Brevísima relación de la destrución de las Indias). Stanford, California: Academic Reprints, n.d. (1953?).

LEON-PORTILLA, MIGUEL. Translated by Jack Emory Davis. *Aztec Thought and Culture, A Study of the Ancient Nahuatl Mind.* Norman: University of Oklahoma Press, 1963.

LEONARD, IRVING A. *Baroque Times in Old Mexico.* Ann Arbor: The University of Michigan Press, 1959.

————. *Books of the Brave.* Cambridge: Harvard University Press, 1949.

LOPEZ DE GOMARA, FRANCISCO. *The Conquest of the West Indies (1578).* Introduction by H. I. Priestley. New York: Scholars' Facsimiles and Reprints, 1940.

LOPEZ Y FUENTES, GREGORIO. Translated by Anita Brenner. *El indio.* Indianapolis: Bobbs-Merrill, 1937. New York: Frederick Ungar, 1961. (paperback).

LUTRELL, ESTELLE. *Mexican Writers. A Catalogue of Books in the University of Arizona with Synopses and Bibliographical Notes.* Tucson: University of Arizona, 1920.

MAGDALENO, MAURICIO. Translated by Anita Brenner. *Sunburst.*

MENENDEZ, MIGUEL ANGEL. Translated by Angel Flores. *Nayar.* New York-Toronto: Farrar and Rinehart, Inc., 1942.

NERVO, AMADO. Dorothy Kress, *Confessions of a Modern Poet.* Boston: Bruce Humphries, 1935.

————. Translated by Alfonso Teja Zabre. *Plenitude.* Mexico: 1938.

————. Translated by William F. Rice. *Plenitude.* Los Angeles: J. R. Miller, 1928.

ONIS, HARRIET DE. *The Golden Land.* An Anthology of Latin American Folklore in Literature. New York: Alfred A. Knopf, 1948.

PAZ, OCTAVIO. (preface by C. M. Bowra; translated by Samuel Beckett). *Anthology of Mexican Poetry.* Bloomington: Indiana University Press, 1958.

————. Translated by Muriel Rukeyser. *Selected Poems of Octavio Paz.* Bloomington: Indiana University Press, 1963; a bilingual edition of 49 poems.

————. Translated with foreword by Muriel Rukeyser. *Sun Stone.* New York: New Directions, 1963.

————. Translated by Lysander Kemp. *The Labyrinth of Solitude; Life and Thought in Mexico.* New York: Grove Press, 1961. (paperback, 1963).

PELLICER, CARLOS. Translated by Lloyd Mallam, Mary and C. V. Wicker and Joseph L. Grucci. *Three Spanish American Poets: Pellicer, Neruda, Andrade.* Albuquerque: Swallow and Critchlow, 1942.

POPOL VUH. *The Sacred Book of the Ancient Quiché Maya.* Adrián Recinos (Spanish trans.), Sylvanus G. Morley and Delia Goetz (English trans.). Norman: University of Oklahoma Press, 1950.

RAMOS, SAMUEL. Translated by Peter G. Earle. *Profile of Man and Culture in Mexico.* Austin: University of Texas Press, 1962; introduction by Thomas B. Irving.

READ, J. LLOYD. *The Mexican Historical Novel, 1826–1910.* New York: Instituto de las Españas, 1939.

REYES, ALFONSO. Translated by Charles Ramsdell; foreword by Arturo Torres-Ríoseco. *Mexico in a Nutshell and Other Essays.* Berkeley and Los Angeles: University of California Press, 1964.

————. Translated by Charles Ramsdell. *Selected Essays of Alfonso Reyes.* Berkeley and Los Angeles: University of California Press, 1964; foreword by Arturo Torres-Ríoseco.

————. *The Position of America, and Other Essays.* New York: Knopf, 1950.

RULFO, JUAN. Translated by Lysander Kemp. *Pedro Páramo.* New York: Grove Press, Inc., London: John Calder Ltd., 1959.

SIGUENZA Y GONGORA, CARLOS DE. Edited and translated by Irving A. Leonard. *The Mercurio Volante de don Carlos de Sigüenza y Góngora: An Account of the First Expedition of Don Diego de Vargas into New Mexico in 1692.* Los Angeles: The Quivira Society, 1932.

————. *The Misfortunes of Alonso Ramírez.* Mexico: Imp. Mexicana, 1962.

SOLIS Y RIVADENEYRA, ANTONIO DE. Translated by Thomas Townsend. *The History of the Conquest of Mexico by the Spaniards.* 2 vols., Rev. and corr. by Nathaniel Hook. London: J. Osborn, 1738.

SPELL, JEFFERSON REA. *Contemporary Spanish-American Fiction.* Chapel Hill: The University of North Carolina Press, 1944.

————. *Rousseau in the Spanish World before 1833.* Austin: University of Texas Press, 1938.

STARR, FREDERICK. *Readings from Modern Mexican Authors.* Chicago: Open Court Publishing Company, 1904.

TORRES BODET, JAIME. Translated by Abel Plenn. *Death of Proserpina.* (Serially in *Mexican Life.* January-April, 1931).

————. Translated by Abel Plenn. *Margaret.* (Serially in *Mexican Life,* January-April, 1930).

————. Translated by Sonja P. Karsen. *Selected Poems of Jaime Torres Bodet.* Bloomington: Indiana University Press, 1964. A bilingual edition of 44 poems.

TORRES-RIOSECO, ARTURO. *Aspects of Spanish American Literature.* Seattle: University of Washington Press, 1964.

————. *New World Literature.* Berkeley and Los Angeles: University of California Press, 1949.

————. *The Epic of Latin American Literature.* Berkeley and Los Angeles: University of California Press, 1959. (paperback).

————, editor. Zoila Nelken and Rosalie Torres-Ríoseco, translators. *Short Stories of Latin America.* New York: Las Américas, 1963.

Translations from Hispanic Poets. New York: The Hispanic Society of America, 1938.

UNDERWOOD, E. W. *Anthology of Mexican Poets.* Portland, Maine: The Mosher Press, 1932.

USIGLI, RODOLFO. Translated by Wayne Wolfe. *Another Springtime.* New York: Samuel French, 1961.

————. Translated by William F. Sterling. *Crown of Shadows.* London: Allan Wingate, 1947.

VASCONCELOS, JOSE. Translated by W. Rex Crawford. *A Mexican Ulysses: The Autobiography of José Vasconcelos.* Bloomington: Indiana University Press, 1963. (paperback).

WALLACE, ELIZABETH. "Some Modern Mexican Poets," in *Renascent Mexico.* New York: Covici-Friede, 1935, pp. 275-291.

WALSH, THOMAS. *Hispanic Anthology:* Poems Translated from the Spanish by English and North American Poets. New York and London: Putnam, 1920.

————. *The Catholic Anthology.* New York: Macmillan, 1928.

YANEZ, AGUSTIN. Translated by Ethel Brinton. *The Edge of the Storm.* Austin: University of Texas Press, 1963.

ZEA, LEOPOLDO. Translated by James Abbot and Lowell Dunham. *The Latin American Mind.* Norman: University of Oklahoma Press, 1963.

Six Faces of Mexico | INDEX

Six Faces of Mexico | INDEX